HAND-BOOK
OF
THE INDIAN FLORA

HAND-BOOK

OF

THE INDIAN FLORA;

BEING A GUIDE TO ALL THE
FLOWERING PLANTS
HITHERTO DESCRIBED AS INDIGENOUS TO THE
CONTINENT OF INDIA.

By

Lieut. Colonel Heber Drury

IN THREE VOLUMES

VOL. III

GYAN

Published by

GYAN

Gyan Publishing House
5, Ansari Road
Daryaganj, New Delhi-110002
Phone: 011-47034999, 9811692060
E-mail: books@gyanbooks.com

Distribution Network
gyanbooks.com
India, USA, Canada, UK, Australia, France

ISBN: 978-81-212-8329-8 (Set)
978-81-212-8326-7 (PB)
First Published, 1869

2nd Impression 2023

Printed at: Gyan Press, Delhi.

HAND-BOOK OF THE INDIAN FLORA (Vol. III)
Author: HEBER DRURY

HAND-BOOK

OF

THE INDIAN FLORA;

BEING A GUIDE TO ALL THE

FLOWERING PLANTS

HITHERTO DESCRIBED AS INDIGENOUS TO THE

CONTINENT OF INDIA.

BY

Colonel Heber Drury,

AUTHOR OF THE

USEFUL PLANTS OF INDIA.

VOL. III.

London:

RICHARDSON & Co., 23, CORNHILL.

1869.

PREFACE.

THE present volume completes the enumeration of the Phanerogamic Flora of India. The Author would have felt more satisfied if some Orders, especially the Grasses, had been less incomplete; but these have unfortunately not received hitherto that attention which their importance deserves. With such materials, however, as are available the best compilation has been made, and if this work should prove useful, in however slight a degree, in aiding the future researches of the Indian Botanist, the Author will feel that the labour of seven years has not been entirely thrown away.

March 4th, 1869.

ORDER CXXV. PHYTOLACCACEÆ.

Calyx 4—5 sepaled: sepals more or less cohering at the base, equal or unequal, imbricated in æstivation: corolla very often wanting, petals inserted at the base of the calyx, equal to, or alternate with, or fewer than the sepals, free, minute, narrowly clawed: stamens hypogynous or nearly so, inserted at the base of the disc, equal to or alternating with the sepals, or more, outer alternate, inner opposite, seldom indefinite or arranged without order: filaments filiform, or tubulate from an ovate base, free, or combined below into a fimbriated or entire cup: anthers 2-celled, erect or incumbent, ovate, ovate-sagittate or oblong-linear, introrse, dehiscing lengthways, fixed by the back or base: cells opposite, connate: ovary simple or compound, consisting of many distinct or more or less connate verticilled carpels, sometimes compound and 1-celled: ovule 1, fixed by the base: styles introrsely lateral, running from the apex to the central angle of the carpels, distinct, uncinately recurved: stigma the inner surface of the styles: fruit surrounded by the calyx or by the base, many or 2-seeded: carpels free or connate, sometimes separating, 1-seeded, or monocarpous and 1-seeded, usually indehiscent: pericarp baccate, utricular, shell-shaped, nut-like, or samaroid: seed erect: albumen mealy: embryo annular: radicle inferior.—Herbs or undershrubs, erect or prostrate: leaves alternate, simple, sessile or petioled, membranaceous or slightly fleshy, usually quite entire, exstipulate, or with 2 free, tubulate and deciduous, or prickly and persistent stipules at the base of the petioles: flowers regular or irregular, hermaphrodite, seldom diœcious, pedicelled, seldom sessile, spiked, racemose or corymbosely glomerate, axillary, terminal and leaf-opposed: bracts or bracteoles 3, very seldom 2, persistent or deciduous, lower one usually larger.

GENUS I. GIESEKIA.

Pentandria Pentagynia. *Sex: Syst:*

Deriv. Named after Paul Dietrich Gieseke, a physician and professor of Hamburg.

GEN. CHAR. Flowers hermaphrodite, 1-bracteate: calyx 5-parted, segments herbaceous, sometimes coloured, whitish within, equal: corolla none: stamens 5—15, sub-hypogynous, free, singly or by twos or threes inserted at the bottom of the calyx, and alternate with its segments: filaments subulate from a broad ovate base: anthers elliptic, versatile: ovaries five (4—3 by abortion), sessile, verticilled, distinct, 1-ovuled: styles 5, short, adnate to the central angle of the ovaries, with a recurved apex, at length hooked: stigmas none: fruit wrapped in the calyx: carpels 3—5, free, subrotund, warty, 1-seeded, indehiscent: seed vertical, subovate, rostellate: testa crustaceous, fragile: albumen farinaceous: embryo annular: cotyledons linear.—Herbs, rarely frutescent: leaves alternate or somewhat opposite, quite entire, fleshy, densely granulated beneath with small subcutaneous glands: flowers small, pedicelled, greenish, afterwards very often purplish, arranged in leaf-opposed, simple, glomerate or umbellate cymelets: bracts at the base of the pedicel.

(1) G. PHARNACEOIDES. (*Linn.*)

Ident. Dec. prod. XIII. s. 2. p. 27.

Syn. Koelreuteria molluginoides, *Murray Comm. Goett.* 3. *p.* 67.—Pharnaceum occultum, *Forsk.*—G. occulta, *Roem. and Schult. Syst.* VI. *p.* 735.

Engrav. Wight's Icon. IV. t. 1167.—Roxb. Cor. II. t. 183.—Murray l. c. t. 2. fig. 1.

SPEC. CHAR. Herbaceous: leaves short-petioled, elliptic or elliptic-lanceolate, very obtuse, scarcely mucronulate, pale green above, glaucous white beneath: cymes subsessile, shorter than the leaf, ball-shaped, simple, 5—10-flowered, somewhat loose: flowers nearly equalling the pedicel, pale green: segments of the calyx nerveless.

A common weed in pasture grounds, flowering at all seasons, especially during the rains.

(2) G. MOLLUGONOIDES. (*R. W.*)

Ident. Wight's Icon. vol. IV. t. 1168.

SPEC. CHAR. Erect or ascending: leaves linear-lanceolate: corymb axillary: peduncles about the length of the leaves: flowers largish-pedicelled: leaves clothed beneath with short hairs; sepals membranous on the margin: corolla none.

Deesa, Bombay.

GENUS II. SURIANA.

Pentandria Pentagynia. *Sex: Syst:*

Gen. Char. Calyx 5-parted: petals 5, hypogynous, or inserted at the bottom of the calyx: stamens 5—10, some often abortive: carpels 5, bearing laterally within a filiform style, ending in a coriaceous, valveless, indehiscent nut: seed single from the base, obovately kidney-shaped, without albumen.

(1) S. maritima. (*Linn.*)

Ident. Linn. spec. 284.—Dec. prod. II. p. 91.—W. & A. prod. (*Sub verbo.*)

Engrav. Lam. Ill. t. 389.—Plum. gen. ed. Burm. 249, t. 1.

Spec. Char. Shrub: leaves simple, oblong-spathulate, thickish, somewhat velvety, without stipules, aggregated at the tops of the branches: flowers yellow, bracteate, almost terminal.

Maritime parts of the Peninsula.

ORDER CXXVI. SALSOLACEÆ.

Calyx 5, seldom 4, 3—2-sepaled: sepals more or less combined below, usually equal, glabrous or villous, herbaceous, greenish, juiceless or fleshy after flowering, capsular or baccate, furnished with small wings or spinelets, or else inappendiculate, keeled or unchanged, imbricated in æstivation: corolla none: stamens usually inserted on a receptacle or at the bottom of the calyx, 5, all fertile, opposite the sepals: filaments filiform or subulate, seldom longer than the calyx, sometimes combined into a very short cup: anthers 2-celled, erect, ovate or oblong, introrse, dehiscing lengthways, affixed by the back: cells opposite, connate, sometimes separated at the base: connecticum narrow, sometimes expanded into a terminal, erect, more or less dilated, petaloid, flat, hooded or vesicular appendage: ovary 1, ovate-oblong or depresso-globose, usually free, 1-celled: ovule 1, sometimes sessile and inserted at the bottom of the cell, sometimes horizontally affixed by a short cord or pendulous, amphitropal: styles 2, seldom 3, terminal, either long or short, subulate-filiform, more or less coalescing below, diverging at the apex: stigmas the extreme surface of the styles: in some genera the style is single, with 2—3 lanceolate or subulate, compressed or half-cylindric stigmas: fruit 1-seeded, involved by the calyx, indehiscent: pericarp membranaceous, articular, sometimes a caryopsis, very rarely a berry: seed horizontal or vertical, erect or inverted, lenticular or reniform: albumen copious, sparing or none, mealy, very rarely somewhat fleshy: embryo homotropal, curved or annular, peripherical, flat-spiral, or conical-spiral without albumen: cotyledons plano-convex, narrow.—Herbs or undershrubs, glabrous, pubescent or woolly: stems terete or angular, erect or ascending, continuous and leafy or jointed and leafless: leaves alternate, seldom opposite, simple, sessile or petioled, either membranaceous, dilated, quite entire, toothed, sinuate or cut, veined, or fleshy, succulent, semiterete or cylindric and almost veinless: stipules none: flowers very minute, regular, hermaphrodite, sessile or pedicelled, solitary or glomerulate, axillary, or panicled, spiked or subcymose: bracts or bracteoles 2, seldom contiguous, sometimes none, often keeled, concave, usually leafy, seldom deciduous with the fruit.

GENUS I. CHENOPODIUM.

Pentandria Digynia. *Sex: Syst:*

Deriv. From *Chen*, a goose, and *Pous*, a foot, in allusion to a fancied resemblance in the leaves.

Gen. Char. Flowers hermaphrodite, ebracteate: calyx 5-cleft or parted, sometimes by abortion 4—3-parted, segments concave, often keeled lengthways, never appendiculate: stamens 5, rarely less, inserted at the bottom of the calyx: anthers ovate: filaments filiform: ovary depressed and globose: styles 2, rarely 3, connected below, sometimes free: stigmas, the internal surface of the styles: utricle depressed, wrapped in the closed calyx: pericarp distinct, membranaceous, very thin: seed horizontal, lenticular.—Herbs, very seldom undershrubs, sprinkled with mealy dust: leaves alternate, quite entire, dentate or pinnatifid-sinuate: flowers in axillary or terminal spikes: glomerules rarely axillary, not spiked.

(1) C. AMBROSIOIDES. (*Linn.*)

Ident. Dec. prod. XIII. s. 2. p. 72.—Linn. spec. p. 320.

Syn. Atriplex ambrosiodes, *Crantz inst.* I. *p.* 207.—C. suffruticosum, *Willd.*—Ambrina ambrosioides, *Spach. veg. phan.* V. *p.* 297.

Engrav. Wight's Icon. t. 1786.

SPEC. CHAR. Stem 3—4-feet, herbaceous, erect, furrowed, branched: leaves petioled, ascending, oblong, attenuated at both ends, remotely sinuately toothed or nearly entire, glandulosely puberulous beneath, the upper ones linear-lanceolate, entire: racemes glomerato-spicate, compact, leafy: fructiferous calyx closed, not keeled: seeds obtuse on the margin, smooth, shining.

Waste grounds near Coimbatore, flowering during the rainy and cool season. Bombay. This plant exhales a peculiar aromatic odour. It is called in France 'Thé du Mexique.'

(2) C. LACINIATUM. (*Roxb.*)

Ident. Dec. l. c. p. 77.—Roxb. flor. Ind. II. p. 59.

SPEC. CHAR. Stem herbaceous, erect: leaves long-petioled, multifid, farinaceous: racemes panicled, contracted.

Near Calcutta.

(3) C. ALBUM. (*Moq.*)

Ident. Dec. l. c. p. 70.

1. *var. commune.*—C. album, *Linn.*—*Roxb. flor. Ind.* II. *p.* 58. —Atriplex alba, *Crantz.*—*E. B.* 24. *t.* 1723.

SPEC. CHAR. Stem herbaceous, erect, furrowed, striated: leaves petioled, rhomb-ovate, sinuately toothed, somewhat powdery, ashy green above, whitish below: racemes somewhat dense: flowers small, green.

Bengal, flowering in the cold season.

2. *var. viride.*—C. viride, *Willd.*—*Dec. l. c. p.* 71.—*Roxb. l. c.*

Leaves lanceolate, almost entire, scarcely mealy, green on both sides: racemes loose, concatenate.

Bengal. There is another variety, of which the angles of the stems and branches are of a fine purple colour, and the leaves and mealy panicles somewhat reddish.

GENUS II. ATRIPLEX.

Polygamia Monœcia. *Sex: Syst:*

Deriv. The Latin name for the Orache.

Gen. Char. Flowers mono-diœcious, males ebracteate: calyx 3—5-sepaled, inappendiculate: stamens 3—5, inserted on the receptacle: filaments filiform: anthers subrotund: female flowers sometimes bibracteate: calyx none: styles 2, filiform: stigmas the internal surface of the styles: fruit compressed, enclosed in the bracts: pericarp very thin, membranaceous, distinct, sometimes slightly adhering to the seed: seed vertical, sublenticular. —Herbs, sometimes shrubs: leaves alternate, rarely opposite, often hastate or triangular, angled, sinuately toothed or quite entire: flowers glomerulate, spiked, collected together.

(1) A. heterantha. (*R. W.*)

Ident. Wight's Icon. vol. V. t. 1787.

Spec. Char. Polygamo-diœcious: herbaceous, erect, glabrous: leaves petioled, ovate, pointed, membranous: male spikes axillary, sometimes racemose, some fertile flowers mixed with the sterile ones: calyx 4—5-sepals, or deeply 4—5-parted: stamens shorter than the lobes: female spikes long, slender, interrupted, glomerules 4—5, females with one or two male flowers in the centre: bracts of the females cohering near the base, ovate, blunt, enlarging with the fruit, at length suborbicular, glabrous.

Coimbatore, in salt clay soil, and among rubbish.

GENUS III. OBIONE.

Polygamia Monœcia. *Sex: Syst:*

Gen. Char. Flowers monœcious or diœcious: males ebracteate: calyx 4—5-sepaled, inappendiculate: stamens 4—5, inserted on the receptacle: filaments filiform: anthers ovate: females bibracteate: bracts more or less connected, at last inflated, hardened or corky: calyx none: styles 2, bristly filiform, combining below: fruit compressed, enclosed in the subcapsular muricated bracts: pericarp very thin, membranaceous: seed vertical, ovate, beaked.—Herbs or undershrubs, scurfy or mealy, pale or whitish: leaves alternate or opposite, ovate or ovate-rhomboid, quite entire or sinuately toothed: flowers collected together, glomerulate: fructiferous bracts more or less closed, often forming a 2-lipped theca at the top.

(1) O. Koenigii. (*Moq.*)

Ident. Dec. prod. XIII. s. 2. p. 109.

Syn. Atriplex cristata, *Koen.*—A. Kœnigii, *Wall.*—O. nummularia, *Moq.*

Engrav. Wight's Icon. t. 1790.

Spec. Char. Stem shrubby, procumbent, striated, sparingly branched, unarmed: leaves alternate, petioled, small, divaricate, obovate-orbicular, very obtuse, entire: scaly-white theca of the bracts subsessile, obovate, the apex very obtuse, margin somewhat sinuate, disc muricate, somewhat coriaceous.

Sea-coast near Tuticorin, Guzerat.

GENUS IV. SALICORNIA.

Monandria Digynia. *Sex: Syst:*

Deriv. From *Sal,* salt, and *Cornu,* a horn.

Gen. Char. Flowers hermaphrodite without scales, articulated: calyx toothed on the margin, surrounded towards the apex with a very small angular wing: stamens 1—2: filaments short, thickish: anthers ovate: ovary ovate: styles 2, subulate, connected below: utricle compressed, enclosed in the winged calyx: pericarp thin, membranaceous, and somewhat adhering to the seed: seed vertical, ovate-oblong, with a membranaceous integument.—Herbs or undershrubs, indigenous to the shores of seas and salt lakes, articulate, with or without leaves: flowers sessile, very minute, ternate, spicately approximated, lateral ones often barren and small: spikes terminal and lateral, opposite, elongated, straight: wing thickish, somewhat 3—5 angular: rhachis after the falling of the fruit excavated with regular scrobicles.

(1) S. brachiata. (*Roxb.*)

Ident. Dec. prod. XIII. s. 2. p. 145.—Roxb. fl. Ind. I. p. 84.

Engrav. Wight's Icon. t. 738.

Spec. Char. Stem erect: branches numerous, decussate, brachiate, opposite: joints cylindric, scarcely thickened at the apex: spikes pedunculate, thick, cylindric: wing subpentagonous-ovate, thickish: flowers very small, greenish.

Coromandel, on the sea-shores. Sunderbunds. Flowering in the cold season.

(2) S. herbacea. (*Linn.*)

Ident. Linn. spec. p. 5. No. 1.—Dec. l. c. p. 144.

Spec. Char. Stem herbaceous, somewhat erect: branches succulent, somewhat spreading: joints long, cylindric, thick-compressed at the top, emarginate, 2-cleft: spikes short-peduncled, thickish, cylindric, somewhat attenuated at the top: wing obovate, thickish.

Sea-shores of the Peninsula.

GENUS V. ARTHROCNEMUM.

Monandria Digynia. *Sex: Syst:*

Deriv. From *Arthron*, a joint, and *Knemos*, a limb, alluding to the articulated stem.

GEN. CHAR. Flowers hermaphrodite, without scales, hidden in the joints of the branches: calyx ventricose, 3—4-cornered, truncated at the apex, or 3—5-toothed, never appendiculate: stamens 1—2: anthers ovate: ovary ovate: styles 2, subulate: utricle compressed, wrapped in the inflated fleshy calyx: pericarp membranaceous, distinct: seed vertical, ovate, or lenticular, sub-rostellate with a double integument.—Herbs, shrubs, or under-shrubs, without leaves: flowers small, often ternate, lateral ones often sterile or male.

(1) A. INDICUM. (*Moq.*)

Ident. Dec. prod. XIII. s. 2. p. 151.—Roxb. fl. Ind. I. p. 85.

Engrav. Wight's Icon. t. 737.

SPEC. CHAR. Stem suffruticose, glaucous green, procumbent, jointed: branches herbaceous, alternate, twisted: joints very short, clavate, very thick, spongy, truncated at the apex, subbifid: spikes lateral, alternate, or opposite: flowers greenish.

Coromandel. Bombay. Sunderbunds. Flowering in the cold season.

GENUS VI. SUÆDA.

Pentandria Digynia. *Sex: Syst:*

GEN. CHAR. Flowers hermaphrodite, bracteolate: calyx urceolate, 5-parted, divisions equal, fleshy, at last inflated, not winged: anthers rotund-ovate: nectary annular, fleshy, or none: ovary superior, cylindric-ovate, truncated at the apex: style none: stigmas 3, rarely 4 or 5: utricle compressed: seed vertical, lenticular, with a double integument.—Herbs or undershrubs inhabiting sea-shores and salt deserts: leaves alternate, sessile, fleshy: flowers axillary: sessile or very short, pedicelled, sometimes adnate to the base of the leaves, often glomerulate: bracteoles very minute, scales transparent whitish.

(1) S. MONOICA. (*Forsk.*)

Ident. Dec. prod. XIII. s. 2. p. 156.

Syn. Salsola monoica, *Poir.*—Schoberia monoica, *Stend.*

Engrav. Wight's Icon. t. 1792.

SPEC. CHAR. Stem shrubby, diffuse, branchy: branches erect, spreading, glabrous: leaves long, terete, alternate at the base, stiff, glabrous; flowers, male and female mixed: seed lenticular or somewhat oblong, prominent at the point of the radicle, smooth, shining, black.

Sea-coast at Tuticorin.

(2) S. INDICA. (*Moq.*)

Ident. Dec. l. c. p. 156.—Roxb. fl. Ind. II. p. 62.

Syn. Salsola Indica, *Willd.*

Engrav. Wight's Icon. t. 1796.

SPEC. CHAR. Stem shrubby, very diffuse, branched: branches ascending, glabrous: leaves half round, attenuated below, obtuse, rigid, a little mealy: upper ones minute, oblong: flowers axillary, sessile, 3—5-clustered; seed obtuse-beaked, shining.

Sea-coast, Tuticorin, and other shores of the Peninsula.

(3) S. NUDIFLORA. (*Moq.*)

Ident. Dec. l. c. p. 155.

Syn. Salsola nudiflora, *Willd. spec.* II. p. 2323.

SPEC. CHAR. Stem shrubby, ascending, branched: branches erect, spreading, puberulous: leaves rather short, oblong-ovate, attenuated at the base, very obtuse, rigid, glabrous: flowers axillary, sessile, 5—10, densely clustered, hermaphrodite, upper clusters at length naked and spiked: seed beaked, shining.

Shores at Salsette, Sunderbunds, and eastern coast of the Peninsula.

GENUS VII. CHENOPODINA.

Pentandria Digynia. *Sex: Syst:*

Deriv. From *Chen*, a goose, and *Pous*, a foot, in allusion to some similarity in the leaves.

GEN. CHAR. Flowers hermaphrodite, bracteolate: calyx urceolate, 5-partite: sepals equal, fleshy, afterwards inflated, not winged: anthers round-ovate: staminodes none: nectary annular, fleshy, or none: ovary superior, slightly truncated at the apex:

style none: stigmas 2—3: utricle depressed, enclosed in the calyx: pericarp with a very thin pellicle, not adherent: seed horizontal, lenticular, with a double integument.—Herbs or undershrubs indigenous to sea-shores: leaves alternate, sessile, fleshy: flowers axillary, sometimes adnate at the base of the leaves, sessile, or very shortly pedicelled: bracteoles whitish, transparent.

(1) C. Indica. (*R. W.*)

Ident. Wight's Icon. vol. V. & t. 1793.

Spec. Char. Shrubby, diffuse, procumbent, very branchy, glabrous: leaves succulent, small oblong, somewhat clavate: flowers glomerulate, fructiferous: calyx globose, not inflated, green: seed depressed, glabrous, shining, brown.

Sea-coast in Tinnevelly.

GENUS VIII. CAROXYLON.

Pentandria Digynia. *Sex: Syst:*

Gen. Char. Flowers hermaphrodite, bibracteate: calyx 5-sepaled: sepals finally transversely winged at the back, erect, or rarely reflexed in fruit: filaments often distinct: anthers oblong, often appendiculate: staminodes none: nectary cup-shaped, obtusely 5—10-angled at the margin: style elongate or shortish: stigmas 2, subulate or ovate, smooth at the back, diverging: fruit depressed, clothed with the capsule, and 5-winged calyx: seed horizontal, with a simple membranaceous integument.—Herbs or undershrubs, with alternate or opposite, sessile, fleshy leaves, and axillary, sessile, solitary flowers: wings often dilated, very obtuse, membranaceous, scariose, unequal or nearly equal.

(1) C. Indicum. (*R. W.*)

Ident. Wight's Icon. V. & t. 1794.

Spec. Char. Fruticose, erect, very branchy: branches opposite, spreading: leaves fleshy, oval, sessile, glabrous: floriferous leaves exceeding the flowers: sepals ovate, bidentate at the apex: wing at first small, afterwards enlarging: filaments adhering at the base to the 5-toothed cup: anthers cuspidate: wings of the fruit orbicular, spreading, scariose.

Coimbatore, flowering in January. This genus is very nearly allied to Salsola, from which it principally differs in the cup-shaped nectary enclosing the base of the ovary.

GENUS IX. KOCHIA.

Pentandria Digynia. *Sex: Syst:*

Deriv. In honour of Herr Koch, a German botanist.

Gen. Char. Flowers hermaphrodite, ebracteate: calyx urceolate, 5-cleft, the divisions finally growing at the back into membranaceous wings: stamens often exserted, inserted at the bottom of the calyx: ovary depressed, globose: styles 2, divaricate, cohering at the base: utricle depressed, somewhat membranaceous, covered by the winged calyx: pericarp membranaceous: seed horizontal, somewhat umbilicate, with a membranaceous covering.—Herbs or undershrubs, villous or pubescent: leaves alternate, sessile, flat, narrow: flowers axillary, solitary or glomerulate, females winged, hermaphrodites sometimes wingless: wings often striated, sometimes coloured.

K. Indica. (*R. W.*)

Ident. Wight's Icon. V. & t. 1791.

Spec. Char. Herbaceous or suffruticose, erect, branched: branches ascending, and, like the branchlets, more or less woolly: leaves linear, lanceolate, sessile, villous on both sides: flowers 1—2 together in each axil: calyx very woolly: wing exceeding the calyx, scariose, nearly glabrous: seeds black.

Coimbatore, in salt soils, flowering in October.

ORDER CXXVII. BASELLACEÆ.

Calyx double, fleshy or membranaceous, often coloured, corolline, persistent: outer more or less combined with the inner, 2-cleft, 2-parted or 2-sepaled: segments subopposite, equal, erect or spreading, at length dry or baccate, expanded at the back into a vertical wing or keeled and ribbed below, often without wings or ribs, inner one 5-cleft or parted, segments equal or unequal, erect, seldom spreading: œstivation imbricated: corolla none: stamens perigynous, or rather hypogynous and combined below into a short urceolus, opposite the sepals, enclosed or slightly exserted: free portion of the filaments subulate, dilated below: anthers 2-celled, ovate or sagittate, introrse, dehiscing lengthways, fixed by the middle of the back: ovary 1, ovate or somewhat 3-cornered, free, 1-celled, 1-ovuled: style terminal, simple, short: stigmas 3, somewhat divaricated, thickened towards the apex, obtuse or 2-cleft, the stigma sometimes 3-lobed, seldom simple: fruit 1-seeded, wrapped by the calyx, dry, 2-winged or wingless, or baccate: pericarp crustaceous or membranaceous, without valves: seed vertical, ovate or subglobose: embryo spiral, with sparing albumen, or annular thickish, and with more or less copious mealy albumen: radicle descending: cotyledons plano-convex, somewhat leafy.—Herbs, seldom undershrubs, often scandent, stems somewhat angled: leaves alternate, very rarely opposite, petioled, simple, quite entire or obsoletely sinuate, exstipulate, subarticulate, fleshy, often succulent: flowers small, regular, hermaphrodite, often scarcely open in flower, pedicelled or sessile, solitary, arranged on axillary, simple or branched, narrow and somewhat lax spikes: bracts 3, remote or approximate, fleshy or membranaceous, deciduous or persistent: in pedicelled flowers lower one at the base, lateral ones at the apex of the pedicel.

GENUS I. BASELLA.

Pentandria Triandria. *Sex: Syst:*

Deriv. The Malabar name Latinised.

GEN. CHAR. Flowers succulent: outer calyx half closed, connected into a tube with the interior one beyond the middle, which is a little shorter, 2-cleft: sepals concave, ecarinate, not winged, inner one 5-cleft; stamens enclosed, connected below into a fleshy urceolus adnate to the calyx: anthers cordate-ovate: style short, tapering: stigmas 3, thickened towards the apex, entire: fruit depressed, globose, clothed with the calyx: pericarp cartilaginous: seed vertical, somewhat beaked.—Herbs, often climbing: leaves rarely opposite, fleshy: flowers sessile, arranged in simple or branched spikes.

(1) B. RUBRA. (*Linn.*)

Ident. Dec. prod. XIII. s. 2. p. 222.—Linn. spec. p. 390.

Syn. Gandola rubra, *Ramph.*

Engrav. Ramph. Amb. V. t. 154, fig. 2.—Lam. Ill. t. 215, fig. 1.—Wight Icon. t. 896.

SPEC. CHAR. Stem scandent, 3—4-feet, angular, brownish-purple: leaves ovate, acuminate, purplish: spikes nearly equalling the leaves, long-peduncled: flowers purple: outer divisions of the calyx oblong-elliptic: berries dark purple, obsoletely 4-lobed, greenish and purple at the apex before ripening: seeds pale brown.

Malabar. Bengal. The *B. alba* is a mere variety of the above.

(2) B. CORDIFOLIA. (*Lam.*)

Ident. Dec. l. c. p. 223.—Roxb. flor. Ind. II. p. 105.

Syn. B. crassifolia, *Wight.*

Engrav. Rheede Mal. VII. t. 24.

SPEC. CHAR. Climbing, stem variegated green and purple: leaves cordate, entire, undulated: spikes much shorter than the leaves, long-peduncled: flowers purplish without, whitish-green within: berries dark purple.

Malabar, flowering in the cool season.

(3) B. LUCIDA. (*Linn.*)

Ident. Dec. l. c. p. 224.—Linn. spec. p. 391.

SPEC. CHAR. Stems erect, purplish: leaves opposite, subsessile, orbicular-ovate, subcordate, greenish-purple: racemes shorter than the leaf, densely branched: flowers purple: berries red.

Most parts of the country.

ORDER CXXVIII. AMARANTACEÆ.

Calyx 3—5-sepaled, sepals free, or sometimes more or less combined at the base, equal or nearly so, subscariose, glabrous or afterwards pubescent, greenish or coloured, usually corolline, persistent, unchanged after flowering: æstivation imbricated: corolla none: stamens hypogynous, 5 fertile, opposite the sepals, 5 sterile, alternate with the fertile ones, or none: all free, or connate below into a cup or tube: fertile filaments filiform or subulate or dilated, sometimes 3-cleft, sterile ones quite entire or fimbriated, flat, sometimes very minute and unguiform or tooth-shaped: anthers 2 or 1-celled, erect, ovate or linear, introrse, dehiscing lengthways, affixed by the back: ovary 1, ovate, compressed, free,

1-celled, 1—many-ovuled: ovules attached to the bottom of the cell or appended by free erect cords, amphitropal: style terminal, simple, rather long, or short, sometimes scarcely any: stigma capitate or emarginately 2-lobed, or stigmas 2—3, subcylindric or filiform: fruit 1 or many-seeded, enclosed by the calyx, seldom naked: pericarp membranaceous, utricular or subcapsular, without valves or cut round and dehiscing, sometimes a caryopsis, very rarely a berry: seed slightly compressed, lenticular-reniform: albumen copious, central, mealy: embryo arched or circular, peripherical.—Herbs or undershrubs or small trees, glabrous, pubescent or woolly: stems erect or ascending, continuous or jointed: leaves opposite or alternate, simple, sessile or short-petioled, usually quite entire: stipules none: flowers minute, regular, hermaphrodite, monœcious or diœcious by abortion, sessile, glomerate or solitary, capitate or spiked, lateral ones sometimes abortive and changed into a crest, awn or glochis: bracts 3, usually contiguous: lower one larger, usually persistent, very rarely deficient, and then the axillary flowers are protected by a floral leaf: lateral ones usually keeled, concave, never leafy, more or less scariose, deciduous with the flower.

GENUS I. DEERINGIA.

Pentandria Monogynia. *Sex: Syst:*

Deriv. In memory of Dr. Charles Deering, an English botanical author.

Gen. Char. Flowers hermaphrodite, tribracteate: calyx 5-sepaled, sepals equal, spreading, reflex or erect: stamens combined below into a cup: anthers 2-celled: ovary 1-celled, many-ovuled: style almost none: stigmas 3—4, semicylindric, revolute: fruit a berry, inflated, subglobose, many-seeded: seeds vertical, lenticular-reniform.—Shrubs with alternate, quite entire leaves: flowers very shortly pedicelled, arranged in spikes, terminal, axillary, and from the highest wings, branched or simple, slender and leafless: bracts concave, coloured, persistent, lower one at the base, lateral ones at the apex of the pedicel.

(1) D. BACCATA. (*Wall.*)

Ident. Dec. prod. XIII. s. 2. p. 236.—Roxb. fl. Ind. I. p. 682.

Syn. Celosia baccata, *Retz obs.* v. p. 23.—D. celosioides, *R. Br. prod.* I. p. 413.—D. Indica, *Blume. bijdr.* p. 542.—*Spreng. syst.* I. p. 816.

Engrav. Wight's Icon. t. 728.—Rumph. Amb. V. t. 83. fig. 2. —Bot. Mag. t. 2717.

SPEC. CHAR. Stem suffruticose, angled, decumbent: leaves ovate or cordate-ovate, acute: spikes elongated, lax, branched: flowers shortly pedicelled, solitary, greenish: sepals afterwards reflexed.

Peninsula. Bengal. Silhet. Flowering in the cold season.

GENUS II. CELOSIA.

Pentandria Monogynia. *Sex: Syst:*

Deriv. From *Kelos*, burnt, the flowers of some species appear singed.

GEN. CHAR. Flowers hermaphrodite, tribracteate: calyx 5-sepaled, sepals equal, erect, spreading: stamens connate below into a small cup: anthers 2-celled, oblong: ovary 1-celled, many-ovuled: style short or elongated: stigmas 2—3, small, recurved: utricle subovate, transversely cut round, many-seeded, more or less wrapped by the calyx: seeds lenticular-reniform. —Herbs or undershrubs, erect, glabrous: leaves alternate, often running into the petiole: flowers showy and elegantly scariose, heaped together in spikes or terminal and axillary panicles: bracts concave, coloured, persistent.

(1) C. ARGENTEA. (*Moq.*)

Ident. Dec. prod. XIII. s. 2. p. 242.—Roxb. fl. Ind. I. p. 678.

Engrav. Wight's Icon. t. 1767.—Burm. Ind. t. 25.—Rheede Mal. X. t. 38.

SPEC. CHAR. Herbaceous, branched, glabrous: leaves sub-petioled, linear-lanceolate or nearly linear-acute: spikes terminal, long-peduncled, ovate-cylindrical or cylindrical, cuspidate: sepals 3 times longer than the bracts, erect, narrow, oblong-lanceolate, slightly keeled, somewhat 3-nerved: utricle ovate, pear-shaped: flowers small, white.

Peninsula. Malabar. Bengal. Flowering in the cold season.

(2) C. PULCHELLA. (*Moq.*)

Ident. Dec. prod. l. c. p. 238.

Syn. Celosia polygonoides, *Wall* (not *Retz*).

Engrav. Wight's Icon. t. 1768.

SPEC. CHAR. Stem herbaceous, branchy, glabrous: leaves ovate-lanceolate, ovate or rhombeo-ovate, acute, glabrous: spikes simple, interrupted, somewhat flexuose: flowers sessile, solitary: sepals longer than the bracts, acute, slightly keeled, 1-nerved: utricles pear-shaped.

Courtallum. Neilgherries. In moist soil and the vicinity of tanks and wet cultivation.

(3) C. POLYGONOIDES. (*Retz.*)

Ident. Retz. obs. II. p. 12. No. 85.—Dec. l. c. p. 238.

Syn. Achyranthes corymbosa, *Heyne herb.*—A. polygonoides, *Heyne* (not *Retz* or *Lam.*)

SPEC. CHAR. Stem herbaceous, erect, somewhat hispid, branched: leaves round or cordate-ovate, obtuse, ciliolate, puberulous: spikes somewhat long, rigid: flowers sessile, 2—3-glomerate: sepals acute, scarcely three times as long as the bracts, keeled, 1-nerved: utricles bottle-shaped, green: flowers whitish.

Malabar coast. Madras.

GENUS III. CHAMISSOA.

Pentandria Monogynia. *Sex: Syst:*

Deriv. In honour of M. Chamisso, the companion of Kotzebue.

GEN. CHAR. Flowers hermaphrodite, tribacteate: calyx 5-sepaled, sepals nearly equal, glabrous or puberulous: stamens connate below into a cup: anthers 2-celled, ovate: ovary 1-celled, 1-ovuled: style shortish or elongated: stigmas 2, subulate or very short: utricle subovate or subglobose, 1-seeded, transversely cut round the sides: seed lenticular-reniform.—Herbs or shrubs, erect or decumbent, glabrous or pubescent: leaves alternate: flowers in globose beads or slender spikes, axillary or terminal: bracts concave, coloured, persistent.

(1) C. ALBIDA. (*Moq.*)

Ident. Dec. prod. XIII. s. 2. p. 248.

Syn. Allmannia albida, *R. Br.*

Engrav. Wight's Icon. t. 1769.

SPEC. CHAR. Stem herbaceous, branchy, ascending, glabrous: leaves petioled, long-obovate, somewhat cuneiform, blunt or sub-emarginate, terminating in a minute point: heads of flowers lateral or terminal, peduncled, somewhat globose, compact: flowers short-pedicelled: sepals scarcely exceeding the bracts, very acute, slightly keeled, 1-nerved: utricle ovate.

In sandy soils near the sea-coast, flowering during the rains and cold season.

(2) C. NODIFLORA. (*Mart.*)

Ident. Dec. l. c. p. 249.—Roxb. fl. Ind. I. p. 678.

Syn. Celosia nodiflora, *Linn.*—Achyranthes nodiflora, *Roxb.* —Allmannia nodiflora, *R. Br.*

Engrav. Wight's Icon. t. 1770.—Burm. Zeyl. t. 5, fig. 2.

SPEC. CHAR. Herbaceous, ascending, branchy, glabrescent: leaves spathulate or wedge-shaped or oblong, obtuse, with a short point, glabrous or more or less pubescent: heads of flowers globose, lateral, and subsessile, or terminal and short-peduncled: flowers whitish-green, shortly pedicelled: sepals somewhat longer than the bracts, acuminated, keeled, 1-nerved: utricle globose.

Coromandel coast, in sandy soils.

(3) C. DICHOTOMA. (*Moq.*)

Ident. Dec. l. c. p. 249.

Syn. Celosia dichotoma, *Heyne in Roth.*

Engrav. Wight's Icon. t. 1771.

SPEC. CHAR. Suffruticose or herbaceous, dichotomously branched: leaves ovate-oblong, obtuse, short-pointed, pubescent, finely ciliate: heads of flowers lateral, subsessile, globose, dense: flowers greenish-yellow, short-pedicelled: sepals equalling the bracts, keeled; keel rough: utricle globose: seed smooth.

Courtallum.

(4) C. ASPERA. (*R. W.*)

Ident. Roth. nov. spec. p. 173 No. 3.

Engrav. Wight's Icon. t. 1772.

SPEC. CHAR. Stems herbaceous, branchy, ascending or more or less diffuse, rough with bristly hairs, or in old plants innocuous prickles: leaves hispid, subsessile, from linear blunt to oblong-lanceolate pointed: heads of flowers subsessile, globose, dense: bracts as long as the sepals, aristate, pilosē: sepals keeled, hairy on the keel: utricle ovoid.

Coimbatore. Mysore.

(5) C. PYRAMIDALIS. (*Moq.*)

Ident. Dec. l. c. p. 248.

Syn. Celosia pyramidalis, *Burm.*—C. albida, *Willd.*—Chamissoa albida, *Mart.*

Engrav. Burm. Ind. t. 25. fig. 1.

SPEC. CHAR. Stem herbaceous, erect or ascending, somewhat branched: leaves subpetioled, lanceolate, attenuated towards the base: heads of flowers dense, terminal and lateral, long-peduncled, oblong-conical: flowers subsessile: sepals somewhat exceeding the bracts, acute, keeled, 1-nerved: utricles oblong.

Coromandel coast.

GENUS IV. AMARANTHUS.

Monoecia Pentandria. *Sex: Syst:*

Deriv. From A, derivative, and *Maraino*, to wither, referring to the length of time the flowers retain their bright colours.

GEN. CHAR. Flowers monœcious, tribracteate: sepals 5, equal: stamens free: anthers 2-celled: ovary 1-celled, 1-ovuled: style none: stigmas 2—3, spreading: fruit a utricle, ovate, 2—3-beaked at the apex, 1-seeded, imperfectly enclosed in the calyx: pericarp often membranaceous, capsular: seed kidney-shaped: aril none.—Erect or diffuse herbs: leaves alternate, decurrent into the petiole, apiculated with a small incurved or straight point: flowers minute, purplish, reddish-brown, or green, collected in terminal panicled spikes or axillary clusters: bracts keeled, concave, persistent.

(1) A. SPINOSUS. (*Linn.*)

Ident. Dec. l. c. p. 260.—Roxb. Flor. Ind. III. p. 611.

Engrav. Wight's Icon. t. 513.—Rumph. Amb. V. t. 83. fig. 1.

SPEC. CHAR. Erect, 1—3 feet, somewhat striated, very glabrous, reddish: leaves long-petioled, rhomb-ovate or lanceolate-oblong, obtuse, with 2 spines in the axils: panicles sparingly branched: spikes erect, cylindric, acute, terminal ones long, stiffish, lateral ones middle-sized, somewhat distant: flowers dense, green: calyx nearly equalling the bracts: utricles 2—3-cleft at the top, somewhat wrinkled: bracts unequal, bearded: seed lenticular, polished, black.

Peninsula. Bengal. Malabar coast. Flowering in the cool and rainy season.

(2) A. Gangeticus. (*Linn.*)

Ident. Dec. l. c. p. 261.—Roxb. l. c. p. 606.

Spec. Char. Stem erect, furrowed and striated, glabrous, dark red, or greenish: leaves long-petioled, ovate or lanceolate-ovate, somewhat obtuse, dark green, sometimes purple below: spike terminal, very short, ovate, stiff: glomerules axillary, ovate: flowers thick, reddish-green: calyx shorter than the bracts: utricles enclosed in the calyx, 2—3-toothed at the apex, smooth.

Bengal, flowering in the rains.

(3) A. atropurpureus. (*Roxb.*)

Ident. Dec. l. c. p. 264.—Roxb. l. c. p. 608.

Spec. Char. Erect: leaves lanceolate, reddish-purple above, dark purple beneath: sepals 4—5, cuspidate: stamens 8: spike terminal: glomerules axillary: utricles shorter than the calyx, wrinkled.

Bengal.

(4) A. fasciatus. (*Roxb.*)

Ident. Dec. l. c. p. 265.—Roxb. l. c. p. 600.

Engrav. Wight's Icon. t. 717.

Spec. Char. Erect: leaves petioled, rhomb-ovate, acute: panicle terminal, sparingly branched: sepals 3, lanceolate-acuminate: stamens 3: spikes cylindric: bracts small, obtuse: utricles longer than the calyx, wrinkled: flowers greenish.

Peninsula. Bengal. Flowering in the rains.

(5) A. frumentaceus. (*Buch.*)

Ident. Dec. l. c. p. 265.—Roxb. l. c. p. 699.

Engrav. Wight's Icon. t. 720.

Spec. Char. Stem herbaceous, erect: leaves long-petioled, broad-lanceolate, acute: panicles terminal, erect: sepals subulate, acute: stamens 5: stigmas 3: seed subcompressed, smooth: utricles wrinkled.

Mysore. Coimbatore.

GENUS V. AMBLOGYNA.

Monœcia Triandria. *Sex: Syst:*

Deriv. From *Ambloma*, abortion, and *Gyne*, female, alluding to its reputed medical properties.

Gen. Char. Flowers monœcious, tribracteate. Male: calyx 3-sepaled: sepals equal, glabrous, erect: stamens 3, free: staminodes none: anthers 2-celled, ovate. FEMALE: calyx subglobose, infundibuliform, 5-cleft: segments equal, patent, scariose: ovary 1-celled, 1-ovuled: style very short, thickish: stigmas 2—3: fruit a utricle, ovate, 1-seeded, enclosed in the calyx: aril none: seed vertical, ovate-lenticular.—Herb, puberulous, glaucescent: leaves alternate, entire: flowers disposed in axillary glomerules: bracts keeled, concave, persistent.

A. POLYGYNOIDES. (*Rafin.*)

Ident. Dec. prod. XIII. sec. II. p. 270.—Roxb. fl. Ind. II. p. 602.

Syn. Amaranthus polygynoides, *Linn.*—Rœmeria polygynoides, *Mœnch.*—Albersia polygynoides, *Kunth.*—A. venticillatus, *Pavon.*

Engrav. Wight's Icon. t. 512.

SPEC. CHAR. Stem decumbent or ascending, angulate-striated, glabrous, red or green: branches diffuse, somewhat hairy: leaves obovate, cuneate at the base, very obtuse, glaucous below, sometimes white-spotted: glomerules much shorter than the petiole: 6—8-flowered: bracts subulate, white with a green nerve: flowers somewhat dense, white: sepals of the males as long as the bracts, of the females thrice as long: utricle narrow-ovate, smooth below, wrinkled and tubercled above, 3-cleft at the apex, indehiscent: seed acute at the margin, smooth, black.

Bengal, flowering in the cold season.

GENUS VI. MENGEA.

Monœcia Diandria. *Sex: Syst:*

GEN. CHAR. Monœcious, unibracteate: calyx 1-sepaled, lateral, erect, glabrous. MALE: stamens 1 or 2, free: staminodes none: anthers 2-celled. FEMALE: ovary 1-celled, 1-ovuled: style very short: stigmas 2—3, filiform, divaricate: utricle subovate, 1-seeded, naked: seed lenticular-reniform: aril none.—Herbs, much branched: leaves alternate: flowers collected in axillary and sessile glomerules, males terminal, somewhat solitary: bracts scaliform, keeled, membranaceous, persistent.

(1) M. TENUIFOLIA. *Dec.*

Ident. Dec. prod. XIII. s. II. p. 271.

Syn. Amaranthus tenuifolius, *Willd.*—A. angustifolius, *Roxb.*

Engrav. Wight's Icon. t. 718.

SPEC. CHAR. Herbaceous: stem erect, angled, striated, green: leaves lanceolate-linear or linear, much attenuated at the base, glabrous, glaucous-green: nerves prominent below; glomerules shorter than the petiole, subternate, few-flowered, rather lax: bracts lanceolate, green, nerved: sepal lanceolate, pale-greenish: stamens 1, rarely 2; ovary obovate: utricle 5-ribbed, smooth, green: seed lenticular, polished, black: flowers green.

Peninsula. Bengal. Flowering in the rainy season.

GENUS VII. EUXOLUS.

Triandria Monogynia. *Sex: Syst:*

Deriv. A word used by Theophrastus.

GEN. CHAR. Flowers monœcious, rarely hermaphrodite, tribracteate: calyx 3, rarely 5-sepaled: stamens 3, rarely 5 or 2, free: anthers 2-celled: ovary 1-celled, 1-ovuled: style very short: stigmas 3, filiform: fruit a utricle, 1-seeded: seed vertical, kidney-shaped: aril none.—Erect or diffuse herbs: leaves alternate or scattered, decurrent into the petiole, apiculated with a very small, straight, or slightly curved point: flowers heaped together in axillary heads, or axillary and terminal spikes, sometimes panicled: bracts keeled, conclave, persistent.

(I) E. CAUDATUS. (*Moq.*)

Ident. Dec. prod. XIII. s. 2. p. 274.

Syn. Chenopodium caudatum, *Jacq. Coll.*—Amarantus oleraceus, *Lam.*—A. gracilis, *Desf.*

Engrav. Wight's Icon. t. 1773.

SPEC. CHAR. Stem erect, angularly striated, glabrous, green: leaves long petioled, ovate or rhombovate, narrowing at both ends, bluntish, emarginate, glabrous, green: spikes ascending, somewhat interrupted below, more compact and subcylindrical above: flowers sessile, aggregated in dense glomerules, green: bracts longer than the sepals; utricle globose, pointed very rough: sepals 3.

Coimbatore, in waste ground. The species of Euxolus and Amarantus are most difficult to discriminate. In this the seed is enclosed in the thickened persistent indehiscent case or utricle, while in Amarantus the case splits all round, permitting the seed to drop out. In all other respects they are the same.

(2) E. POLYGAMUS. (*Willd.*)

Ident. Dec. l. c. p. 272.

Syn. Amarantus polygamus, *Linn.*—*Roxb. flor. Ind.* III. *p.* 603.

Engrav. Wight's Icon. t. 713-4.—Rumph. Amb. V. t. 82. fig. 1.

SPEC. CHAR. Stem erect, obsoletely angled, striated, pale green: leaves lanceolate or ovate-lanceolate, short-petioled, mucronate, petioles somewhat tumid at the base: bracts acute: sepals 3, narrow-lanceolate, slightly keeled: stamens 2: stigmas 3: glomerules shorter than the petiole, twin or solitary: flowers dense, green: calyx twice as long as the bracts: utricles ovate, wrinkled, 2—3-teethed at the apex, bursting irregularly: seed lenticular, somewhat inflated, shining, black.

Peninsula, flowering in the rainy season.

(3) E. OLERACEUS. (*Moq.*)

Ident. Dec. l. c. p. 273.

Syn. Amarantus oleraceus, *Linn.* — Pyxidium oleraceum, *Mœnch.*—Pentrius oleraceus, *Rafin.*—Albersia oleracea, *Kunth.*

Engrav. Wight's Icon. t. 715.—Willd. Am. t. 5. fig. 9.

SPEC. CHAR. Stem erect or ascending, striated, glabrous, whitish: leaves petioled, ovate, very obtuse, emarginate, rather wrinkled, pale green: spikelets axillary, shorter than the petiole, a little branched: spikes terminal, erect, abbreviated, thickish, rather obtuse, dense, rigid: flowers closely clustered, pale green: calyx twice the length of the bracts: utricles ovate, rather acute, smooth.

Peninsula. Malabar coast.

GENUS VIII. BANALIA.

Pentandria Monogynia. *Sex: Syst:*

Deriv. Called after Antonio Banal, a celebrated gardener, author of the 'Florula Monspeliensis.'

GEN. CHAR. Flowers hermaphrodite, 2—3-bracteate: calyx 5-sepaled, sepals equal, erect, glabrous: stamens 5, connate below into a cupula: staminodes none: anthers 2-celled, ovate: ovary 1-celled, 1-ovuled: style tapering: stigmas 2: utricle 1-seeded, enclosed in the calyx: seed lenticular: aril none.—Erect or ascending, glabrous herbs: leaves alternate or opposite, petioled or sessile, mucronulate: flowers terminal, panicled, glomerulate or solitary: bracts keeled, concave, persistent.

(1) B. THYRSIFLORA. (*Moq.*)

Ident. Dec. l. c. p. 278.

Syn. Achyranthes thyrsiflora, A. polygonata, *Wall.*—Celosia thyrsiflora, *Wall.*

Engrav. Wight's Icon. t. 1774.

SPEC. CHAR. Herbaceous, erect, branched, glabrous: leaves

rhomb-ovate or ovate-lanceolate, acuminate: spikes terminal, thyrsoid: bracts unequal, triangular-ovate, very acute, keeled, very concave: flowers sessile, solitary or 3—4-glomerulate, straw-coloured: sepals three times longer than the bracts, narrow-lanceolate, slightly keeled, 3-nerved: cupula angled at the margin: stamens shorter than the calyx: stigmas longish, revolute: utricle ovate, greenish: seed obsoletely beaked, black, slightly wrinkled.

Neilgherries.

GENUS IX. PSILOTRICHUM.

Pentandria Monogynia. *Sex: Syst:*

Deriv. From *Psilos*, naked, and *Thrix*, hair, destitute of hairs.

GEN. CHAR. Flowers hermaphrodite, tribracteate: calyx 5-sepaled, sepals equal, glabrous, or slightly villous: stamens connected below into a short cup: staminodes none: anthers 2-celled: ovary 1-celled, 1-ovuled: style elongated: stigma simple, capitate: utricle 1-seeded, perfectly enclosed in the connivent sepals: seed ovate, lenticular.—Herbs or undershrubs, branched, subtrichotomous, pubescent or glabrous: leaves opposite, petioled, entire: flowers heaped together in terminal or axillary spikelets: bracts keeled, concave, lower one persistent, lateral ones deciduous.

(1) P. NUDUM. (*Moq.*)

Ident. Dec. prod. XIII. s. 2. p. 279.

Syn. Achyranthes nuda, *Roxb.*—A. montana, *Klein.*—A. polygonoides, *Heyne.*

Engrav. Wight's Icon. t. 1775.

SPEC. CHAR. Stem suffruticose, erect or sometimes climbing among bushes: leaves short petioled, ovate-lanceolate or ovate-acute, glabrous: spikes axillary, short: rachis flexuose: flowers dense, very hairy: sepals much longer than the interior, short, very broad, oblique acuminated bracts.

In subalpine jungles of the Peninsula, sometimes climbing to the extent of several feet among bushes or other supports.

(2) P. FERRUGINEUM. (*Moq.*)

Ident. Dec. l. c. p. 279.

Syn. Achyranthes ferruginea, *Roxb.*—Leiospermum ferrugineum, *Wall.*

Engrav. Wight's Icon. t. 721.

SPEC. CHAR. Stem herbaceous, ascending, striated, ferruginous: leaves short-petioled, or rotund-obovate, very obtuse, glabrous, reddish: spikelets sessile, or peduncled, very acute: peduncles quadrangular: flowers dense, glabrous, pale red: calyx 2—3 times longer than the bracts: sepals 5-nerved, equal, lanceolate, acuminate: bracts narrow-lanceolate, acute: pistil nearly equalling the stamens: utricle ovate: seed ovate, smooth, black.

Peninsula.

(3) P. SERICEUM. (*Dalz.*)

Ident. Dalz. Bomb. flor. p. 216.

Syn. Achyranthes sericea, *Koen. in Roxb. flor. Ind.*

Engrav. Wight's Icon. t. 726.

SPEC. CHAR. Stem erect, tomentose: leaves petioled, broad-ovate, acuminate, silky: peduncles axillary, longer than the leaf, round, 2—3-cleft, stiff, tomentose: spikes flexuose.

Kattywar. Peninsula.

GENUS X. PTILOTUS.

Pentandria Monogynia. *Sex: Syst.*

Deriv. From *Ptilotus*, feathered, in allusion to the ciliated sepals.

GEN. CHAR. Flowers hermaphrodite, tribracteate: sepals 5, equal, erect, inner ones 3, with longish flexuose hairs at the margin: stamens connate at the base: staminodes none: anthers 2-celled, ovate or elliptic: ovary 1-celled, 1-ovuled: style elongated: stigma simple, capitate: utricle oblong, 1-seeded: inner sepals cohering below with wool, open at the apex: seed vertical, lenticular-reniform.—Herbs: leaves alternate, often narrow: flowers terminal, seldom axillary, enclosed below in stiff hairs, arranged in long or contracted spikes, or in small heads: bracts keeled, scariose, shining, persistent.

(1) P. OVATUS. (*Moq.*)

Ident. Dec. prod. XIII. s. 2. p. 281.

Syn. Psilotrichum ovatum, *Moq.*

SPEC. CHAR. Herbaceous: stem 2-feet, erect, tapering: branches striated, pubescent in the axils of the leaves: leaves short-petioled, ovate, glabrous above, pubescent below: spikelets solitary, 3—6-flowered, terminal ones very long-peduncled: flowers somewhat thick, reddish-hoary: calyx 3 times as long as the bracts.

Madras.

GENUS XI. ÆRUA.

Pentandria Monogynia. *Sex: Syst:*

Deriv. From *Eroua*, its Arabic name.

Gen. Char. Flowers hermaphrodite, tribracteate: sepals 5, equal, erect, woolly: stamens adhering at the base: staminodes dentate: anthers 2-celled: ovary 1-celled, 1-ovuled: style very short: stigmas 2, very small: utricle 1-seeded, enclosed in the calyx: aril none.—Herbs or undershrubs, more or less white, tomentose: leaves alternate, sometimes opposite, rarely verticelled: flowers densely heaped together in terminal or axillary spikes: bracts concave, persistent.

(1) Æ. floribunda. (*Wight.*)

Ident. Wight's Icon. V. t. 1776.

Spec. Char. Herbaceous, diffuse, procumbent, pubescent: leaves alternate, short-petioled, elliptic or obovate, obtuse, pubescent above, villous beneath: spikes axillary, solitary or 2—3-together, very woolly: bracts broad-ovate, mucronate, pubescent on the nerve: sepals very woolly on the back: staminodes equalling the filaments: stigma deeply 3-cleft, lobes reflexed.

Courtallum. Mysore. Coimbatore.

(2) Æ. Javanica. (*Juss.*)

Ident. Dec. prod. XIII. s. 2. p. 299.—Roxb. flor. Ind. II. p. 495.

Syn. Iresine Javanica, *Burm.*—Celosia lanata, *Linn.*—Illecebrum Javanicum, *Aiton.*—Ærua tomentosa, *Forsk.*—Achyranthes alopecuroides, *Lam.*—A. Egyptiaca, *Gmel.*—A. Javanica, *Pers.*—A. cana, *Roxb.*

Engrav. Wight's Icon. t. 876.—Burm. Ind. t. 60. fig. 2.

Spec. Char. Herbaceous: stem rigid, 1 cubit, erect or ascending, tomentose, hoary: leaves short-petioled, obovate-lanceolate, tomentose: spikes alternate, very flexuose, solitary, sessile, woolly, upper ones 15—20, arranged as a large lax panicle: flowers white: bracts glabrous, whitish: utricle oblong, green.

Malabar. Peninsula. Oude. Flowering all the year.

(3) Æ. scandens. (*Wall.*)

Ident. Dec. l. c. p. 302.

Syn. Achyranthes scandens, *Roxb.*

Engrav. Wight's Icon. t. 724.

Spec. Char. Suffruticose, scandent, pubescent, green: leaves alternate, short-petioled, elliptic or oblong, acuminated at both ends, very acute, mucronulate, pubescent: spikes alternate, sometimes opposite, solitary or twin, sessile or short-peduncled, somewhat woolly: 2 outer sepals elliptic, 3 inner ones narrow-lanceolate: bracts somewhat equal, ovate, whitish, lower one villous, lateral ones glabrous: style short: stigmas very minute: utricle orbicular, slightly compressed, glabrous: seed ovate-lenticular, obsoletely 2-beaked, shining, black.

Bengal. Bombay. Flowering from August to October.

(4) Æ. LANATA. (*Juss.*)

Ident. Dec. l. c. p. 303.—Roxb. l. c. p. 676.

Syn. Achyranthes lanata, *Linn.*—Illecebrum lanatum, *Linn.*—A. villosa, *Forsk.*

Engrav. Wight's Icon. t. 723.—Rheede Mal. X. t. 29.

SPEC. CHAR. Stem herbaceous, suffruticose below, ascending, much branched, somewhat tomentose: leaves alternate, short-petioled, obovate, mucronulate, pubescent on both sides: spikes solitary or biternate, sessile, ovate, woolly: flowers hoary white: calyx twice as long as the apiculated bracts: sepals keeled, 2 outer ones lanceolate with whitish nerves, inner ones sub-spathulate, greenish-nerved: utricles roundish, compressed, green: seed reniform, shining, black.

Peninsula. Malabar.

(5) Æ. BRACHIATA. (*Mart.*)

Ident. Dec. l. c. p. 304.

Syn. Achyranthes brachiata, *Linn.*—Illecebrum brachiatum, *do.*

SPEC. CHAR. Stems herbaceous, ascending, much branched, glabrous, green: branches sometimes opposite and brachiate: leaves oblong-ovate or obovate-oblong: spikes 3—4, subsessile, oblong-linear or linear, villous, sessile in all the axils: bracts ovate, whitish: flowers whitish: calyx thrice the length of the bracts, sometimes 4—3-sepaled by abortion: staminodes a little shorter than the filaments, very minute, somewhat triangular: utricle orbicular, glabrous, green: seed very small, lenticular, brownish-black.

Bombay. Madras.

(6) Æ. MONSONIA. (*Mart.*)

Ident. Dec. l. c. p. 305.

Syn. Celosia Monsonia, *Retz.*—Illecebrum Monsoniæ, *Linn.*—Achyranthes pungens, *Lam.*

Engrav. Wight's Icon. t. 725.

SPEC. CHAR. Stems suffruticose, sometimes procumbent, very flexuose, sometimes twisted, wrinkled, tomentose: leaves verticillate or opposite, sessile, subulate-linear, hairy, very numerous, sometimes recurved; spikes solitary, erect, short-peduncled, ovate-cylindric, woolly: calyx twice the length of the bracts: staminodes the length of the filaments: anthers ovate, yellow: utricle oblong, very slender, whitish: seed somewhat oblong, brownish-black: flowers rose-coloured.

Peninsula. Tranquebar. Neilgherries. Flowering in the cold season.

GENUS XII. ACHYRANTHES.

Pentandria Monogynia. *Sex: Syst:*

Deriv. From *Achuron*, chaff. alluding to the nature of the floral leaves.

Gen. Char. Flowers hermaphrodite, tribracteate: sepals 4—5, somewhat unequal: stamens 5, rarely 4, connected at the base: staminodes 5, smooth, or somewhat scaled, toothed at the apex, seldom entire, sometimes on the back towards the apex produced into an erect appendage either toothed or fimbriate: anthers 2-celled: ovary 1-celled, 1-ovuled: stigma simple, capitate: utricle, ovate-oblong, 1-seeded, enclosed in the calyx: seed vertical, sub-cylindric, oblong: aril none.—Herbs or undershrubs, erect or procumbent, rarely climbing: stem articulate: branches opposite, subtrichotomous: leaves opposite: flowers arranged on narrow spikes, rarely in hemispherical heads: bracts subulate, very acute, lower one persistent, lateral ones generally longer and spinescent.

(1) A. aspera. (*Linn.*)

Var. Indica.

Ident. Dec. prod. XIII. s. 2. p. 315.—Roxb. flor. Ind. I. p. 672.

Syn. Amarantus spicatus, *Pluk.*—A. obtusifolia, *Lam.*

Engrav. Wight's Icon. t. 1777.—Rheede Mal. X. t. 78.

Spec. Char. Stem suffruticose, erect, striated, pubescent: branches spreading, somewhat 4-sided, pubescent: leaves short-petioled, obovate-rotund, abruptly attenuated at the base, very obtuse, shortly acuminate, pubescent: spikes slenderly virgate, acute: flowers purplish-green, shining, awn of the lateral bracts about as long as the limb: calyx about twice as long as the bract: sepals obsoletely glabrous.

Common everywhere.

(2) A. RUBROFUSCA. (*R. W.*)

Ident. Wight's Icon. V. t. 1778.

SPEC. CHAR. Herbaceous: stems erect, branched, round, pubescent, branches ascending: leaves ovate-acuminate, short-petioled, finely pubescent on both sides: spikes virgate, compact: flowers pale greenish: awn of the bract as long as the limb: calyx longer than the bracts: sepals 3-nerved: staminodes truncated, fimbriated on the margin, about half the length of the filaments: style equalling the stamens.

Neilgherries, on moist soil.

(3) A. BIDENTATA. (*Blume.*)

Ident. Dec. l. c. p. 312.

Syn. A. aspera, *Zolling* (not *Linn.*).—A. hispida, *Moq.*

Engrav. Wight's Icon. t. 1799.

SPEC. CHAR. Herbaceous, erect, branched: stems obsoletely ascending: leaves short-petioled, oval, acuminate, slightly pubescent on both sides: spikes long, cylindric, loosely flowered: flowers horizontal, greenish-brown: lateral bracts very minute, 2-lobed, with a long stiff awn: lower one ovate, naviculate, pointed: calyx longer than the bracts, 1-nerved: staminodes minute, truncated, almost entire at the margin: filaments about the length of the style.

Neilgherries.

(4) A. BENGHALENSIS. (*Dec.*)

Ident. Dec. l. c. p. 317.

Syn. Illecebrum Bengalense, *Linn. Mant. p.* 213.—A. Bengalense, *Lam.* — Paronychia Benghalensis, *Roem. and Schult. Syst.* V. *p.* 521 (*not Juss.*).

SPEC. CHAR. Stem herbaceous, erect: leaves sessile, lanceolate, acuminate, pubescent, green on both sides: spikes small: flowers white.

Bengal.

GENUS XIII. CENTROSTACHYS.

Pentandria Monogynia. *Sex: Syst:*

Deriv. From *Kentron*, a sharp point, and *Stachys*, a spike.

GEN. CHAR. Flowers hermaphrodite, tribracteate: calyx 5-sepaled: sepals very unequal: stamens 2 or 5, connate at the base: staminodes 2—5, with scales bifid at the apex at the back towards the middle, produced into a narrow appendage, deeply fimbriate at the apex: anthers 2-celled, elliptic: ovary 1-celled, 1-ovuled: style filiform: stigma capitate: fruit a utricle, 1-seeded, enclosed in the calyx: seed ovate: aril none.—Aquatic herbs trichotomous; stem fistular: leaves opposite: flowers narrowly spiked, much opening after flowering, at last reflexed.

(1) C. AQUATICA. (*Wall.*)

Ident. Dec. prod. XIII. s. 2. p. 321.

Syn. Achyranthes aquatica, *R. Br.*—A. natans, *Hamilt.*—Celosia spinescens, *Koen.*—A. trichotoma, *Perottet.*

Engrav. Wight's Icon. t. 1780.

SPEC. CHAR. Stem erect, furrowed: branches angled, pubescent: leaves attenuated at both ends, wrinkled: bracts nearly equal, small, somewhat pubescent at the apex: sepals 5—6 times longer than the bracts, narrow-lanceolate, acute, 5-nerved: utricle minute, glabrous, brown: flowers greenish.

Northern Circars.

GENUS XIV. DIGERA.

Pentandria Monogynia. *Sex: Syst:*

Deriv. From the Arabic word *Didjar.*

GEN. CHAR. Flowers hermaphrodite, tribracteate, ternate, middle one fertile, lateral ones sterile, and fiually changing into a horizontal 4-branched crest: sepals 5, somewhat unequal: stamens free: staminodes none: anthers 2-celled: ovary 1-celled, 1-ovuled: style filiform: stigmas 2, very short, somewhat recurved; fruit a woody capsule, subglobose, 1-seeded, enclosed in the calyx: seed sublenticular.

(1) D. ARVENSIS. (*Forsk.*)

Var. perennans.

Ident. Dec. prod. XIII. s. 2. p. 324.—Roxb. flor. Ind. I. p. 694.

Syn. Achyranthes polygonides, *Retz.*—A. digera, *Poir.*—Chamissoa commutata, *Spreng.*—Desmochæta muricata, *R. W.*

Engrav. Wight's Icon. t. 732.

SPEC. CHAR. Stem perennial, irregularly tetragonal, glabrous: leaves alternate, ovate, roundish, often lanceolate, acute, sometimes rufescent at the margin: spikes erect, stiff: bracts ovate, whitish, lower one very concave: sepals twice as long as the bracts, sometimes 4 by abortion, ovate-lanceolate, exterior ones acute, 3-nerved, inner ones shorter, narrower, 1-nerved: anthers exserted, red: pistils reddish: capsule hard, 2-toothed at the apex, keeled, tubercled, greenish: crests shorter than the fruit, green: lower branches recurved, upper ones incurved, subtrilobate: seed not shining, brown: flowers small, red.

Peninsula.

GENUS XV. CYATHULA.

Pentandria Monogynia. *Sex : Syst :*

Deriv. The diminutive of *Cyathus*, a cup.

GEN. CHAR. Flowers hermaphrodite, tribracteate, slightly ternate, intermediate one fertile, lateral ones sterile, at last changed into hooked awns: sepals 5, hispid; stamens connate into a cupula at the base: staminodes denticulate at the apex, simple, or produced at the back into an erect, slender, biligulate appendage: anthers 2-celled: ovary 1-celled, 1-ovuled: styles filiform: stigma capitate: utricle oblong, 1-seeded, enclosed in the calyx: seed oblong-ovate.

(1) C. PROSTRATA. (*Blume.*)

Ident. Dec. prod. XIII. s. 2. p. 326.—Roxb. flor. Ind. I. p. 674.

Syn. Achyranthes prostrata, *Linn.*—C. geniculata, *Lour.*—Desmochæta prostrata, *R. W.*—Pupalia prostrata, *Mart.*

Engrav. Wight's Icon. t. 733.—Rheede Mal. X. t. 79.

SPEC. CHAR. Stem herbaceous, perennial, prostrate, or ascending: branches subtetragonal, slightly hairy: leaves opposite, obovate, pubescent, glaucous below: spikes virgate, slender, lax: sepals lanceolate, hairy, interior ones narrower, 3-nerved, hispid: staminodes minute, bifid at the apex: glochides 15—20, unequal, hooked at the apex, hairy below, yellowish: utricle glabrous, greenish: seed ovate-oblong, shining, pale chestnut: flowers greenish-red or purple or whitish-violet.

Peninsula, flowering in the cold season.

GENUS XVI. PUPALIA.

Pentandria Monogynia. *Sex : Syst :*

GEN. CHAR. Flowers hermaphrodite, tribracteate, ternate, middle one fertile, lateral ones sterile, changing into hooked awns or acute spines: sepals 5: stamens connate at the base: anthers 2-celled: ovary 1-celled, 1-ovuled: style elongated, filiform; stigma capitate: fruit a utricle, oblong, 1-seeded, enclosed in the calyx: seed subreniform.—Undershrubs, rarely herbs: branches and leaves opposite, very seldom alternate: flowers glomerulate, erect.

(1) P. ORBICULATA. (*R. W.*)

Ident. Dec. prod. XIII. s. 2. p. 330.—Wall. in Roxb. flor. Ind. ed. Car. II. p. 507.

Syn. Cyathula orbiculata, *Moq.*—Achyranthes orbiculata, *Roxb.*—A. rotundifolia, *Klein.*—Desmochæta orbiculata, *Wall.*

Engrav. Wight's Icon. t. 1783.

SPEC. CHAR. Stem prostrate: leaves orbicular, retuse, acute at the base, short-petioled, densely villous when young: fascicles densely tomentose, many flowered, globular, remote, with long brown bristles.

Sandy soils near Madras.

(2) P. ATROPURPUREA. (*Dec.*)

Ident. Dec. l. c. p. 331.

Syn. Achyranthes lappacea, *Linn.*—A. atropurpurea, *Lam.* —Celosia lappacea, *Medic. Bot. p.* 160.—Desmochæta atropurpurea, *R. W.*

Engrav. Wight's Icon. t. 731.—Rheede Mal. X. t. 359.—Burm. Zeyl. t. 18, fig. 1.

SPEC. CHAR. Stem suffruticose, subangled, striated: branches purplish, hispid, pubescent: leaves opposite, ovate, hispidly rough, dark green: calyx nearly twice as long as the bracts: sepals lanceolate, lower ones a little shorter: glomerules 8—20: bracts long, acuminate, hispid, lateral ones broadly ovate: glochides 15—20, long, dark purple, somewhat hispid below: seed elliptic, compressed, somewhat shining, black: flowers small, dark purple.

Courtallum, Malabar, and Coromandel coasts. Flowering in the cold and rainy seasons.

GENUS XVII. ALTERNANTHERA.

Pentandria Monogynia. *Sex: Syst:*

Deriv. The name refers to the stamens being alternately fertile and barren.

GEN. CHAR. Flowers hermaphrodite, tribracteate: calyx 5-sepaled, sepals equal or unequal, glabrous or villous: stamens connate in a cupula at the base; staminodes very small, dentiform or unguiform, entire: anthers 1-celled, ovary 1-celled, 1-ovuled: style short: stigma simple or capitate, 2-lobed or double: utricle ovate, 1-seeded, more or less enclosed in the calyx; seed vertical, sublenticular.—Herbs, rarely undershrubs, much branched: stems often articulated: leaves opposite: flowers arranged in terminal or axillary heads: bracts concave, lower one persistent: staminodes shorter than the filaments, more frequently entire, rarely eroded or denticulate.

(1) A. sessilis. (*R. Br.*)

Ident. Dec. prod. XIII. s. 2. p. 357.—Roxb. flor. Ind. I. p. 678.

Syn. Gomphrena sessilis, *Linn.*—Achyranthes ficoidia, *Lam.*—A. triandra, *Lam.*—Paronychia tetragona, *Moench.*—P. sessilis, *Desf.*—Achyranthes triandra, *Roxb.*

Engrav. Wight's Icon. t. 627.—Rheede Mal. X. t. 11.—Rumph. Amb. VI. t. 15. fig. 1.—Burm. Zeyl. t. 4, fig. 2.

Spec. Char. Stem herbaceous, suddenly branched, articulate, bifarious, pubescent: leaves ovate-lanceolate, opposite, attenuated below, entire at the margin, glabrous: heads of flowers much shorter than the leaves, 2—4 together: sepals ovate: staminodes as long as the filaments, longish, very acute, entire: calyx 2—3 times longer than the lateral bracts: utricle a little longer than the calyx, obcordate, compressed, acute lengthways on the margin, somewhat wrinkled: seed ovate, much compressed, scarcely shining, yellowish: flowers small, white.

Peninsula. Malabar. Flowering in the rainy and cold season.

GENUS XVIII. GOMPHRENA.

Pentandria Monogynia. *Sex: Syst:*

Deriv. From *Gomphos*, a club, alluding to the globose head of flowers.

Gen. Char. Flowers hermaphrodite or polygamous by abortion, tribracteate; calyx 5-sepaled, rarely 5-cleft, sepals equal or unequal, villous or glabrous: stamens connate into a tube or cupula, 3-cleft at the apex, the intermediate lobe antheriferous, lateral ones shorter or larger, fimbriated or entire: staminodes none: anthers 1-celled; ovary 1-celled, 1-ovuled: style none or elongated: stigma capitate, undivided or slightly 2-lobed, or 2 stigmas shortened or long-linear: utricle 1-seeded, enclosed in the calyx.

(1) G. hispida. (*Linn.*)

Ident. Dec. prod. XIII. s. 2. p. 411.

Engrav. Rheede Mal. IX. t. 72.

Spec. Char. Stem geniculate, fruticose, tetragonous, branched, hispid: leaves oblong, opposite, narrow, acute, eroso-crenate, with a few slight hairs: peduncles simple, rarely 3-cleft: heads of flowers terminal, erect, solitary, diphyllous: flowers white, afterwards bluish: sepals cuspidate.

Malabar.

ORDER CXXIX. NYCTAGINACEÆ.

Calyx corolline, tubular, variously coloured, often constricted in the middle: lower part harder and sometimes ribbed or striated, always persistent and enclosing the fruit: upper part bearing the corolla, seldom withering, usually deciduous: flowers hermaphrodite or diœcious (in Pisonia) by abortion: stamens definite, hypogynous, often connate at the base, and closely withering round the ovary, sometimes adherent to the base of the ovary, seldom free, exserted, unequal: filaments thin, elongated, sterile oncs shortened: anthers 2-celled, cells round, large, often separated, and as if bound by a connectivum: bracts at the base of the flowers, sometimes ovate or lanceolate, free or connate, forming a calyx-shaped involucre round the flowers, sometimes ovate-dilated, larger than the flower, coloured, sometimes very minute, 1—3 to each flower, deciduous or persistent: involucre sometimes gamophyllous, 3—5-teethed, 1—5-flowered, often spreading after flowering, sometimes polyphyllous, many-flowered, the number of leaves definite or indefinite: bracts dilated-coloured, usually threefold, surrounding sometimes a single flower in the middle, sometimes 3 flowers, namely, one seated on each bract, the peduncle co-adunate to the bract: ovary free, single, elongated, 1-ovuled: style simple, terminal or lateral: stigma simple, acute or globose, straight or revolute, branched or even pencil-shaped: fruit surrounded by the base of the perianth, hardened and increased, smooth or ribbed, striated, filling it or leaving an empty space: achenium simple, testa membranaceous: embryo incurved, in Pisonia straight: radicle inferior: albumen white, mealy, copious.—Trees, undershrubs, or herbs: branchlets axillary, sometimes abortive, and then forming spines: leaves seldom alternate or scattered, the leaf belonging to the spine or branchlet or axillary peduncle abbreviated, petioled, entire or waved: flowers glomerate, seldom on a spike or umbel, usually forming a branched panicle or brachiate cyme on numerous capitules: special pedicels short or scarcely any.

GENUS I. BOERHAAVIA.

Diandria Monogynia. *Sex: Syst:*

Deriv. Named after the celebrated Leyden physician Boerhaave.

GEN. CHAR. Bractéoles usually deciduous: perianth 2-parted in the middle, lower portion cylindric or obconical, dark, persistent, upper funnel-shaped or campanulate, coloured, deciduous, 5-lobed at the apex: stamens 1, 2, 3, seldom 4, springing from the base below the ovary, combining into a ring, often a little exceeding the perianth: anthers minute, round, 2-celled: ovary small, acute, surrounded and enclosed by the base of the perianth and stamens: style equalling the stamens: stigma obtuse: fruit surrounded by the hardened, often 5-ribbed base of the perianth, cylindric-obconical, truncated at the apex, rounded or acute, closed: seed 1: albumen mealy.—Herbs, annual or fruticose at the root: stems scandent, diffuse or creeping: leaves opposite, usually petioled: flowers arranged in irregular glomerules, sometimes ending in single axillary peduncles or diffused in extended panicles, more rarely forming a regular umbel, or verticels or spikes, small: perianth or fruit often clammy-glutinous.

(1) B. DIFFUSA. (*Linn.*)

Ident. Linn. sp. 4.—Dec. prod. XIII. s. 2. p. 452.—Roxb. flor. Ind. I. 148.

Syn. B. procumbens, *Roxb.*—B. erecta et diandra, *Burm.*

Engrav. Wight's Icon. t. 874.—Burm. Ind. t. 3. figs. 1—2.—Rheede Mal. VII. t. 56.

SPEC. CHAR. Glabrous or seldom pubescent: leaves entire or waved, lanceolate or ovate, acute or obtuse: peduncles or flower-bearing branchlets very slender, younger ones solitary, bearing a capitule at the apex, afterwards expanded and luxuriantly panicled: fruit slender, acute, striated, subclavate: flowers pale rose.

Coromandel. Travancore. Flowering nearly all the year.

(2) B. REPANDA. (*Willd.*)

Ident. Dec. l. c. p. 455.—Willd. spec. I. p. 22.

Syn. Valeriana Chinensis, *Burm.*—B. umbellata, *R. W.*

Engrav. Wight's Icon. t. 1766.—Burm. Ind. t. 6. fig. 3.

SPEC. CHAR. Stems diffuse, climbing, glabrous: leaves cordate-ovate, acuminate, sinuately repand: peduncles axillary, solitary, usually longer than the leaves; terminal umbels 3—6-flowered: flowers conspicuous, funnel-shaped, each supported on a longish pedicel: stamens 3 or 4, exserted: fruit clavate, glandulose, rough: flowers pink or rose colour.

Southern India, climbing among hedges and bushes.

(3) B. STELLATA. (*R. W.*)

Ident. Dalz. Bomb. flor. p. 213.

Engrav. Wight's Icon. t. 875.

SPEC. CHAR. Decumbent: leaves succulent, ovate-cordate, obtuse-mucronate: racemes long-peduncled: flowers verticelled, subsessile, interruptedly subspicate: ovary club-shaped, elongated, furrowed, with 5 elongated viscid glands at the apex: flowers white or pink.

Kattywar.

(4) B. REPENS. (*Linn.*)

Ident. Dec. l. c. p. 453.—Dalz. l. c. p. 213.

SPEC. CHAR. Herbaceous, creeping, diffuse: leaves ovate, obtuse, sinuate repand, pubescent, white beneath: peduncles axillary, short, bearing short umbels: fruit ovate-elliptic, ribbed, viscous: flowers small, deep pink.

Plains of the Deccan.

(5) B. FRUTICOSA. *Dalz.*

Ident. Dalz. l. c. p. 213.

SPEC. CHAR. Shrubby, erect, viscid and tomentose: leaves small, ovate, with a truncate base, sometimes triangular, much wrinkled on the other side: peduncle axillary, as long as the leaf, pedicels as long as the peduncle: fruit linear-oblong, sulcated, pubescent, tuberculated along the ribs: flowers umbellate, small, pink.

Sewnere fort. Ghauts east of Bombay. Flowering in September.

GENUS II. PISONIA.

Heptandria Monogynia. *Sex: Syst:*

Deriv. In honour of Piso, formerly a physician of Amsterdam.

GEN. CHAR. Bracteoles 1—3, minute, seldom persistent: perianth small, campanulate or cylindric, limb shortly 5-toothed: flowers seldom hermaphrodite, usually diœcious by abortion.

MALE: perianth campanulate: stamens 6—8, seldom 8—10, exserted, unequal: anthers 2-celled, cells ovate, separate. FEMALE: perianth cylindric: rudiments of short stamens round the ovary: ovary elongated: style usually lateral, more or less exserted: stigma divided, usually pencil-fimbriated in many acumens: fruit surrounded by the hardened perianth, cylindric-elongated with the apex spreading, or ovate elliptic with the apex closed, entire or ribbed, smooth or serrate-glandular and clammy, dry or somewhat fleshy.—Trees or shrubs: leaves scattered or opposite: flowers usually rose, cymose-corymbose, seldom umbelled.

(1) P. ACULEATA. (*Linn.*)

Ident. Linn. sp. 1511.—Dec. prod. XIII. s. 2. p. 440.—Roxb. flor. Ind. II. p. 217.

Syn. Tragularia horrida, *Koen. in Roxb. l. c.*—Pallavia aculeata, *Vell. fl. flum.* IV. *t.* 12.—P. loranthoides, *Kunth. in H. et B. nov. gen. et sp. suppl.* VII. *p.* 197.

Engrav. Lam. Ill. t. 861.—Wight's Icon. t. 1763-4.—Sloane Jam. II. t. 167. fig. 3—4.—Plum. Ic. ed. Burm. t. 227. fig. 1.

SPEC. CHAR. Fruticose, spinous, glabrous: spines hooked, axillary: leaves ovate, attenuated at both ends, petioled: flowers diœcious: fruit 5-ribbed: rib delicately serrated, clammy: flowers small, greenish-white.

Peninsula. South Concan. Bengal. Travancore. Flowering in March and April.

ORDER CXXX. POLYGONACEÆ.

Flowers hermaphrodite, polygamo-monœcious, or diœcious: calyx 3—6-sepaled or partite, persistent: segments either 3 in one row or 5 imbricated, or 4 or 6 imbricated in two rows, equal or unequal, outer ones sometimes winged or armed with spines, inner ones entire or toothed, fimbriated or spinulose: stamens perigynous, definite, 1—15, very often 6—8—9: filaments capillary or subulate, persistent, free, or very shortly connate: anthers 2-celled, dehiscing lengthways, oval or oblong, usually attached by the back: ovary free, ovate, or elliptic, compressed or 3-cornered, 1-celled: ovule 1, basilar, sessile or attached by a short cord: styles 2—4, free or more or less connate: stigmas capillate or discoid, or reniform, quite entire, smooth: achenium 1-celled, 1-seeded, indehiscent, closely covered by the increased dry or seldom baccate, sometimes winged calyx, enclosed or rarely exserted, 2—3—4-cornered, angles sometimes winged-like, entire, toothed or echinate: pericarp thin, crustaceous or membranaceous, very smooth, shining, or minutely dotted or grained and striated: seed erect, 2—3-cornered or terete, sometimes furrowed with 3—6 lobes: albumen copious, mealy: embryo antitropal: radicle superior.—Herbs, rarely shrubs: leaves alternate with thin scariose stipules, forming a sheath round the stem within the leaf-stalk: flowers small, sometimes coloured, clustered in the axils of the leaves or on spikes or racemes forming terminal panicles.

GENUS I. POLYGONUM.

Octandria Trigynia. *Sex: Syst:*

Deriv. From *Polys*, many, and *Gonu*, a knee, alluding to the jointed stems.

Gen. Char. Flowers hermaphrodite: calyx 5- (rarely 4—8-) parted, lobes entire, with quincuncial æstivation, all of the same shape, outer ones 2—3-keeled, concave or winged at the back: stamens 8, rarely 7—4, free, inserted at the bottom of the calyx and alternating with its lobes: filaments subulate, persistent: ovary free, compressed, or 3-cornered: styles 2—3, filiform, more or less connate, often very short: stigmas capitate, rarely mushroom-shaped, entire: achenium enclosed in the dry calyx, lenticular or pyramidately 3-cornered, very often acuminated with the base of the styles, angles acute or obtuse, entire, wingless: seed sessile.—Herbaceous or perennial, rarely suffruticose plants without tendrils: stems usually knotty or fistular: ochreæ uncoloured or more rarely herbaceous, ciliated or naked, or 2-parted or torn and many-cleft: floral bracts usually without leaves: leaves scattered, feather-nerved, cordate or sagittate, very rarely pinnatisect, often dotted with glands, and sometimes spotted: flowers axillary, solitary or aggregate, or racemose, spiked, capitate or panicled, small, white or red: pedicels jointed, usually fascicled.

(1) P. Barbatum. (*Willd.*)

Ident. Dec. prod. XIV. p. 104.—Roxb. flor. Ind. II. p. 289.

Engrav. Wight's Icon. t. 1798.

Spec. Char. Spikes twiggy, sometimes paired, often panicled, continuous, compact-flowered: bracts turbinate, imbricating, brown, fringed with white hairs, 1—2-flowered, about as long as the pedicels: flowers 6—8-androus: ochreæ loose, crowned with long bristling hairs: leaves oblong-lanceolate, rough: stem thick, erect, branched, rooting at the base.

Common on the banks of streams and watercourses in most parts of the country, flowering all the year.

(2) P. GLABRUM. (*Willd.*)

Ident. Willd. sp. II. p. 447.—Dec. l. c. p. 114.—Roxb. l. c. p. 287.

Engrav. Rheede Mal. XII. t. 77.—Wight's Icon. t. 1799.

SPEC. CHAR. Quite glabrous: ochreæ long, leaf-bearing below the middle, and with the bracts ciliated: leaves elongate-lanceolate, acuminate, attenuately petioled, glandular-dotted: spikes twin or panicled, narrow-cylindric: bracts somewhat imbricated, shortly turbinate, obliquely truncated, subacute, 2—4-flowered: calyx eglandular, fructiferous, ovate: stamens 6 (seldom 7—8), enclosed: style half-2-cleft, subexserted: achenium biconvex, shining.

Very common in similar places as the preceding.

(3) P. MINUS. (*Huds.*)

Ident. Huds. flor. Angl. I. p. 148.—Dec. l. c. p. 111.

Syn. P. strictum, *Allioni flor. Pedem. N.* 2051.—P. angustifolium, *Roth tent. flor. Germ.* II. 1. *p.* 453 (not *Poir*).—P. pusillum, *Lam. flor. Fr.* 3. *p.* 235.—P. subcontinuum, P. interruptum, *Meissn. in Wall. pl. As. rar.* III. *p.* 57.

Engrav. Wight's Icon. t. 1800.—Engl. Bot. t. 1043.

SPEC. CHAR. Stem procumbent or erect, slender, glabrous: ochreæ a little hairy, densely ciliated with longish thin bristles, leaf-bearing near the base: leaves linear or lanceolate, rounded at the base or seldom shortly attenuated, glabrous, slightly scabrous at the margin and nerve: spikes subracemose, erect, a little loose: bracts shortly turbinate, truncated, densely hairy-ciliated, exceeding the pedicels: stamens 5, seldom 8, and with the 2—3-parted style enclosed: achenium small, biconvex, much shining, smooth.

Neilgherries, in low wet ground.

(4) P. DONII. (*Meissn.*)

Ident. Dec. l. c. p. 105.—Meissn. in Wall. pl. As. rar.

Engrav. Wight's Icon. t. 1801.

SPEC. CHAR. Stem slender: ochreæ narrow, slightly hairy, densely ciliated with strong bristles, leaf-bearing above the base: leaves lanceolate, equally attenuated at both ends, puberulous or glabrate above, somewhat pellucid-dotted: spikes racemose, filiform, continuous, dense-flowered: bracts contiguous, narrow, densely and long bristly ciliated, 1—2-flowered, exceeding the pedicels: calyx somewhat eglandular, enclosing the organs.

Neilgherries, on wet grounds in woods.

(5) P. PEDUNCULARE. (*Wall.*)

Ident. Dec. l. c. p. 133.

Syn. P. dichotomum, *Blume bijdr. p.* 529 ?

Engrav. Wight's Icon. t. 1802.

SPEC. CHAR. Stem erect (?), somewhat unarmed or roughish or retrorsely strigose in the angles and below the knees: ochreæ somewhat beardless, thinly strigose at the base or naked: leaves lanceolate, attenuated at both ends, margin not scariose, cilioles antrorse, slightly scabrous: petiole almost equalling the ochrea: peduncles dichotomous, smooth or glandularly hispidulous: spikes short-oblong or subglobose: bracts somewhat beardless, furrowed, striated: stamens 5: achenium biconvex-subglobose, slightly impressed and dotted, shining.

Silhet. Peninsula. Neilgherries.

(6) P. HORRIDUM. (*Ham.*)

Ident. Dec. l. c. p. 133.—Roxb. l. c. p. 291.—Wall. l. c. p. 58.

Syn. P. sagittatum, *Don Nep. p.* 73.

Engrav. Wight's Icon. t. 1803.

SPEC. CHAR. Stem branched, 4-cornered, densely retrorsely aculeate, with the short petioles and rib of the leaves, dichotomous above: ochreæ narrow bristly-ciliate, retrorsely strigose at the base: leaves cordate or sagittate-lanceolate, margin scariose, spinulose-ciliated: spikes twin or dichotomously panicled, short-oblong or ovate, dense-flowered: peduncles glandulose-scabrous: bracts ovate, acuminate, ciliolate, obsoletely striated: stamens 6—8: style half-2—3-cleft: achenium granular-dotted, biconvex or obsoletely 3-cornered.

Bengal. Silhet. Assam. Peninsula. Flowering all the year.

(7) P. NEPALENSE. (*Meissn.*)

Ident. Dec. l. c. p. 128.—Meissn. ap. Wall. l. c. p. 59.

Engrav. Wight's Icon. t. 1804.

SPEC. CHAR. Stem erect or ascending, branched: ochreæ glabrous: upper leaves sessile, cordate-oblong, lower ones ovate, acuminate, prolonged from a subcordate base into a cuneate-winged petiole, which is auriculately stem-clasping at the base, beneath sparingly dotted with subpellucid immersed glands: capitules twin or (seldom) solitary, largish, supported by a leaf: peduncles glandulose-hispidulous at the apex: bracts scariose, acuminately acute: flowers urceolate, shortly 4—5-cleft, 6—8-androus, half digynous: achenium scrobiculate-reticulate.

Var a. GLABRUM (*Meissn. ap. Wall. l. c.*).—Leaves glabrous on both sides: capitules distinctly peduncled: calyx compressed, 4-cleft: achenium biconvex.

Assam. Canara. Neilgherries. Peninsula.

Var. b. SCABRIDUM (*Meissn. l. c.*).—Leaves subciliate, nerves hairyish: capitules sessile or short-peduncled: calyx compressed, 4-cleft: achenium biconvex.

Neilgherries.

(8) P. WALLICHII. (*Meissn.*)

Ident. Dec. l. c. p. 129.—Meissn. mon. p. 83.—Wall. l. c. p. 60.

Engrav. Wight's Icon. t. 1805.

SPEC. CHAR. Stem branched, glabrous, rooting at the base: ochreæ short-ciliated: leaves ovate, acuminate, eglandular, glabrous, ciliolate, shortly prolonged into a wingless leafy auricled petiole from a subcordate base, upper ones cordate-lanceolate, stem-clasping: capitules twin, middle-sized: peduncles glabrous: bracts scariose, ovate, obtuse, eciliate: flowers 5-cleft, 8- or rarely 6-androus, half-trigynous: achenium trigonal, obtuse-angled, granular-striated.

Neilgherries.

(9) P. CHINENSE. (*Linn.*)

Ident. Dec. l. c. p. 130.—Wall. l. c. p. 60.—Roxb. l. c. p. 289.

Syn. R. brachiatum, *Poir.*—P. corymbosum, *Willd.*—P. cymosum, *Roxb.*—Ampelygonum Chinense, *Lindl. in Bot. Reg.* 1838. *Misc.* 113.

Engrav. Wight's Icon. t. 1806.

SPEC. CHAR. Stem erect, branched: leaves ovate or oblong: auricles leafy, reniform at the base of the petiole, deciduous: corymb simple or panicled: peduncles hairy or scabrous, dichotomous or 3-cleft, supported by leafy cordate bracts: flowers 5-cleft, 8-androus, half-trigynous: achenium triquetrous: flowers white.

Courtallum. Peninsula. Bengal.

Var. a. THUNBERGIANUM (*Meissn. ap. Wall. l. c.*).—Leaves ovate or deltoid, subtruncate at the base, or rarely subcordate, more or less prolonged into the petiole, and with the branches glabrous or hispidulous on the nerves beneath: auricles of the petiole caducous: corymbs somewhat simple, contracted, eglandulose, hispidulous or glabrous: capitules small.

Assam. Neilgherries.—P. corymbosum, *Willd.*—P. dentiflorum, *Blume.*—Rumex umbellatus, *Houttyn.*—Coccoloba crispata, *Roxb.*

Var. b. OVALIFOLIUM (*Meissn. l. c.* 60).—Leaves ovate or oval, acuminated at both ends: auricles of the petiole large, often confluent with the petiole: corymbs somewhat panicled, dichotomous, hispidulous: capitules largish: bracts acuminate, almost equalling the flowers.

Peninsula. Canara. Neilgherries.

Var. c. BRACHIATUM (*Meissn. l. c. p.* 61).—Leaves ovate or oblong, cordate at the base or seldom subtruncated, roughish beneath on the nerves and veins: corymbs loosely panicled: peduncles slender, spreading somewhat eglandulose scabrous: capitules small: bracts shorter than the flower, often obtuse.

Khasia. Assam.

Var. d. SUBHASTATUM (*Meissn. l. c. p.* 61).—Leaves oblong and lanceolate, truncate at the base, subhastate or subcordate, glabrous, quite entire, flat: corymbs panicled, sparingly eglandular and scabrous: capitules small.

Assam.

Var. e. CORYMBOSUM (*Meissn. l. c. p.* 61).—Leaves oblong and lanceolate, suddenly attenuated at the base, quite entire, puberulous beneath on the nerve: corymbs simple, contracted (usually 3-headed), hispidulous, eglandulose: capitules largish.

Peninsula.

(10) P. MIQUELIANUM. (*Meissn.*)

Ident. Dec. l. c. p. 92.

Syn. P. elegans, *Roxb. var.?*

SPEC. CHAR. Stems many, glabrous, prostrate, elongated, few-branched, terete, striated: ochreæ short, somewhat hyaline, 6-nerved, cut and fimbriated, deciduous: leaves somewhat fleshy (?), spathulate-linear, obtuse, revolute at the edges, veinless, beneath 1-nerved, axils 1—3-flowered: pedicels thin, exserted, articulated at the base, somewhat longer than the closed, keeled and trigonal, base-attenuated calyx: stigmas exserted: achenium largish, equalling the calyx, faces ovate, smoothish, shining.

Fields near Mangalore. Canara.

(11) P. Roxburghii. (*Meissn.*)

Ident. Dec. l. c. p. 93.

Syn. P. Dryandri, *Spreng.*—P. Meyeni, *C. Koch in Linnæa* 22. *p.* 205.—P. hernarioides, *Benth. in Hook. Journ.* 1853. *p.* 194. —P. elegans, *Roxb. l. c. p.* 291.

Spec. Char. Many-stemmed, prostrate: branches very thinly striated: ochreæ hyaline, ciliated and torn, 1-nerved near the margin: leaves longer than the internode, spreading, linear, acute or linear-oblong, apiculated, slightly scabrous at the edge: axils 3—5-flowered: pedicels articulated below the middle, short: calyx keeled and trigonal, attenuated at the base: achenium shining, faces ovate-rhomb, obsoletely dotted at the apex and margin.

Common everywhere.

Var. a. longifolium (*Dec. l. c.*).—Leaves much longer than the internode, linear, acute, flat: ochreæ largish: pedicels shorter than the calyx or almost none.—P. Indicum, *Meisn. ap. Wall. l. c.*

Canara.

(12) P. flaccidum. (*Roxb.*)

Ident. Roxb. l. c. p. 291.—Dec. l. c. p. 107.

Syn. P. hydropiper, *Lour.*—P. glabrum, *Roxb. Don. Nep.* 71 (not *Willd.*).

Spec. Char. Everywhere scattered more or less with brown, sessile, pellucid glands: ochreæ narrow, bristly-ciliate: leaves lanceolate, acuminate, ciliolate, glabrous: spikes 1—3, erect, interrupted at the base: bracts somewhat contiguous, narrow, horizontally truncated, ciliated: pedicels at length exserted, organs enclosed: achenium granular, striated, somewhat shining.

In moist places. Ditches near Calcutta. Flowering in the rains.

Var. a. Ochreæ and nerves of the leaves slightly hairy: bracts ciliated or upper ones somewhat beardless.

Khasia.

(13) P. Hornimanni. (*Meissn.*)

Ident. Dec. l. c. p. 107.

Spec. Char. Everywhere glandulosely dotted: ochreæ slightly glabrous, moderately pilose-ciliated, leaf-bearing below the middle: leaves lanceolate, attenuated at both ends, glabrous, obsoletely ciliolate: spikes twin or racemose, long-filiform, interrupted at the base: bracts narrowly turbinate, 3—6-flowered, somewhat beardless: pedicels long-exserted, longer than the calyx, which is much attenuated at the base: achenium shining, obsoletely dotted, apex exserted.

Around Calcutta.

(14) P. LANIGERUM. (*R. Br.*)

Ident. R. B. prod. p. 419.—Dec. l. c. p. 117.

SPEC. CHAR. Whole plant hoary: ochreæ long, short-ciliated, or at length beardless: leaves lanceolate, acuminate, beneath more densely covered with white wool: spikes twin or racemose, linear: bracts somewhat imbricated, ovate, ciliate, or naked, almost equalling the pedicels: stamens 6 (seldom 7—8), and with the half-2—3-cleft style somewhat exserted: achenium somewhat round-lenticular (seldom 3-cornered), faces convex.

Var. INDICUM.—Stems slender, branched: ochreæ much shorter than the internode: leaves digital: spikes panicled, slender: bracts more or less canescent, beardless or the lowest ones ciliolate: calyx smaller: fructiferous one more ovate.—P. lanatum, *Roxb.*—P. lanigerum, *Meissn. in Wall. l. c. p.* 55.

Bengal. Peninsula.

(15) P. ORIENTALE. (*Linn.*)

Ident. Linn. sp. I. p. 519.—Dec. l. c. p. 123.

SPEC. CHAR. Whole plant softly hairy: stem tall, branched: ochreæ hypocrateriform: limb leafy, patent, ciliolate, deciduous: leaves ovate and oblong, acuminate, decurrent into the petiole: spikes panicle oblong, nodding: bracts ovate, acute, pubescent, 3—5-flowered: flowers largish, patent: stigmas hat-shaped: achenium obtuse at the base, faces depressed: flowers rose or white.

Var. PILOSUM (*Meissn. ap. Wall. l. c. p.* 54).—Spikes sometimes erect, straightish: flowers middle-sized: line in the angle of the achenium obsolete or none: pubescence of all the parts more copious, longer, often almost golden-silky.—*Roxb. l. c. p.* 286.—P. amœnum, *Blume.*—P. Cochinchinense, *Meissn. mon. p.* 55.—Lagunea Cochinchinensis, *Lour. Coch.* I. *p.* 271.

Calcutta, in wet places, flowering in the rainy season.

(16) P. TOMENTOSUM. (*Willd.*)

Ident. Dec. l. c. p. 124.—Willd. sp. II. p. 447.—Roxb. l. c. p. 287.

Syn. P. pulchrum, *Blume bijdr. p.* 530.

SPEC. CHAR. Whole plant covered with adpressed hairs: stem erect, furrowed, thick, glabrescent below: ochreæ long, limb membranaceous, erect, long-bristly-ciliate: leaves oblong-lanceolate, attenuated at both ends: spikes panicled, linear, straight, dense-flowered: bracts obtuse: ciliated angles of the achenium not lineate, faces convex: flowers white.

Ditches and rivulets in Calcutta and Bengal, flowering in the rainy season.

(17) P. EFFUSUM. (*Meissn.*)

Ident. Dec. l. c. p. 93.

Syn. P. hernarioides, *a. Meissn. in Wall. pl. As. rar.* III. *p.* 62.—P. Indicum, *Roth nov. sp. p.* 208 ?

SPEC. CHAR. Procumbent, glabrous: stems many, branched, elongated, filiform, thinly striated, smooth: ochreæ small, hyaline, nerveless, toothed and lacerated, and with the leaves shorter than the elongated internodes: leaves narrow-linear, veinless: axils 3—5-flowered: pedicels at length almost equalling the flower, articulated in the middle or above: achenium equalling the small calyx, faces ovate, shining, obsoletely striated at the apex.

Oude.

(18) P. ILLECEBROIDES. (*Meissn.*)

Ident. Dec. l. c. p. 94.

Syn. P. hernarioides, *b. Meissner in Wall. l. c. p.* 62.

SPEC. CHAR. Procumbent: stems many, filiform, branched, striato-angled, smooth: ochreæ very short, white, somewhat nerveless, densely lacerate-ciliate: leaves linear, obtuse or sub-mucronulate, somewhat equalling the short internodes, upper ones dwarf revolute at the margin: flowers in the upper axils 1—2, subsessile, very small: achenium enclosed, sharp-angled, smooth, shining.

Bengal.

(19) P. CILIOSUM. (*Meissn.*)

Ident. Dec. l. c. p. 95.

Syn. P. exiguum, *Meissn. in Wall. l. c. p.* 62.

SPEC. CHAR. Stem low, erect, branched from the base, decumbent, striated, slightly scabrous: ochreæ hyaline, tawny, somewhat nerveless, densely ciliated: leaves longer than the internode, narrow-linear, acute, 1-nerved, veinless, slightly scabrous: axils 1—2-flowered: pedicels shorter than the ochreæ and calyx, jointed at the base: calyx very small, keeled and trigonal: achenium enclosed, minute, smooth, shining.

Silhet. Upper Assam.

(20) P. Bishiræ. (*Hamilt.*)

Ident. Ham. MSS.—Dec. l. c. p. 102.—Meissn. in Wall. l. c. p. 56.

Spec. Char. Eglandulose: stem glabrous below, branches, peduncles and ochreæ densely covered with adpressed hairs, spike-bearing, twice dichotomous: ochreæ longish, narrow, short-ciliated, leaf-bearing below the middle: leaves subsessile, oblong-lanceolate, acuminate, acute at the base, slightly hairy: spikes linear-oblong, continuous, straight, dense-flowered: bracts imbricated, pubescent, ciliolate: pedicels exserted: stamens 8, and with the style exserted: achenium smooth, shining, faces broad-elliptic, angles slightly obtuse.

Sukanaghur. Peninsula?

(21) P. viscosum. (*Hamilt.*)

Ident. Ham. MSS.—Don prod. flor. Nep. p. 71.—Dec. l. c. p. 102.

Spec. Char. Stem branched, glandulose, hirsute: ochreæ short, lax, hirsute, ciliated: leaves ovate or lanceolate, hirsute or glabrate: spikes short, oblong, continuous: peduncles densely glandulose, hirsute, or slightly glabrous: bracts somewhat imbricated, hirsute, ciliated, nearly equalling the pedicels: calyx eglandulose: stamens 8, and with the style enclosed: achenium ovate-trigonal, obsoletely dotted: flowers purple.

Silhet. Upper Assam.

(22) P. stagninum. (*Hamilt.*)

Ident. Ham. MSS.—Dec. l. c. p. 104.—Meissn. in Wall. l. c. p. 56.

Spec. Char. Stem glabrous: ochreæ long, densely hairy, bristle-ciliated: leaves oblong-lanceolate, attenuated at both ends, densely villous, younger ones silky: spikes twin or somewhat panicled, oblong, dense-flowered: bracts imbricated, long-ciliated, exceeding the pedicels, and with the peduncles hairy: calyx somewhat eglandulose, externally pubescent: stamens 8, and with the style exserted.

Bengal.

(23) P. rivulare. (*Roth.*)

Ident. Roth nov. pl. sp. p. 206.—Dec. l. c. p. 104.—Roxb. l. c. p. 290.

Spec. Char. Ochreæ lax, adpressed, strigose, stiffly bristle-ciliate: leaves oblong-lanceolate: spikes oblong, flowers 6-androus.

Bengal. Circar mountains. Western Ghauts.

(24) P. MACRANTHUM. (*Meissn.*)

Ident. Dec. l. c. p. 107.

SPEC. CHAR. Ochreæ short, slightly bristly hairy, nerves running out into strong bristles: leaves oblong-lanceolate, long-acuminate, obtuse at the base, ciliated, slightly hairy or glabrescent above: pedicels at length short-exserted: calyx large, and minutely dotted: style at length exserted: achenium obtuse-angled, faces broadly ovate, smooth, very shining.

Marshes in the Khasia hills.

(25) P. ASSAMICUM. (*Meissn.*)

Ident. Dec. l. c. p. 111.

SPEC. CHAR. Stem erect, glabrous: ochreæ short, narrow, slightly bristly, bristles thin, longish, densely ciliated, leaf-bearing below the middle: leaves oblong-lanceolate, attenuated at both ends, ciliolate, glabrous, nerves and veins beneath densely hairy: spikes twin or subracemose, filiform, erect, straight, interrupted at the base: bracts contiguous, turbinate, obliquely truncated, glabrous, densely bristly-ciliate or upper ones somewhat naked, 1—2-flowered, equalling the pedicels: calyx small, eglandulose: stamens 5—6, and with the semibifid style enclosed: achenium elliptic-lenticular, biconvex, smooth, and very shining.

Assam.

(26) P. SCABRINERVIUM, *var.* CILIOLATUM. (*Royle.*)

Ident. Royle MSS.—Dec. l. c. p. 121.

SPEC. CHAR. Stem covered with subsessile glands: younger ochreæ exceeding the internodes, and with the lower bracts very shortly ciliolate: peduncles sparingly glandular or somewhat naked: spikes straight, linear, continuous, dense-flowered: bracts somewhat imbricated, eglandulose: stamens 6, enclosed: style semibifid.

Assam.

(27) P. SPHÆROSTACHYUM. (*Meissn.*)

Ident. Meissn. mon. p. 53. et ap. Wall. l. c. p. 52.—Dec. l. c. p. 125.

Syn. P. macrophyllum, *Don flor. Nep. p.* 70.—P tenue, *Don l. c.*—P. gracillimum, *Spreng. syst. c. p. p.* 154.

SPEC. CHAR. Leaves costate-crenulate at the margin, glabrous or puberulous beneath, lower ones lanceolate, obtuse, attenuated at the base, petiole wingless, upper ones sessile, linear: spike compact, short, oblong, or subglobose, truncated at the base:

bracts ovate, exceeding the very short pedicels: stamens exserted or enclosed.

Assam. Pundua.

(28) P. MICROCEPHALUM. (*Don.*)

Ident. Don l. c. p. 72.—Dec. l. c. p. 129.—Meissn. mon. p. 82. ap. Wall. l. c. p. 59.

SPEC. CHAR. Stem tall, slender, somewhat branched: ochreæ short-ciliate: leaves oblong, acuminate, cuneate-narrowed into the petiole, ciliated, eglandulose: petiole winged, half stem-clasping or wingless, leaflet at the base, reniform, ciliated, auricled on both sides: capitules twin, middle-sized, leafless: peduncles hispidulous or glabrous: bracts subscariose, opaque, oval, obtuse, eglandulose, ciliolate: flowers 5-cleft, octandrous: achenium trigonal, obtuse-angled, granular.

Silhet. Assam.

(29) P. CAPITATUM. (*Hamilt. MSS.*)

Ident. Dec. l. c. p. 129.—Don l. c. p. 73.—Meissn. l. c. p. 82.

Syn. P. repens, *Meissn. in Wall. l. c.* III. *p.* 60.

SPEC. CHAR. Stem rooting, branched, together with the ochreæ and leaves hispidulous with purplish pubescence: leaves ovate or elliptic, subacute: petiole very short, leafy-auricled on both sides: capitules twin or solitary, largish, dense-flowered: peduncles unequal, hispidulous at the apex: bracts paleaceous, ovate, acute, naked: flowers 5-cleft, octandrous: achenium obtusely trigonal, obsoletely granular.

Pundua.

Var. a. PINGUE (*Meissn. ap. Wall. l. c.*).—Branches elongated, lax: leaves thickish, often glabrescent: auricles of the petiole large, persistent: capitules size of a cherry.

Khasia.

Var. b. MACILENTUM (*Meiss. l. c.*).—Branches abbreviated: internodes contracted: leaves smaller: auricles of the petiole small, very fugacious: capitules size of a large pea.

Khasia.

(30) P. PERFOLIATUM. (*Linn.*)

Ident. Linn. sp. I. p. 521.—Dec. l. c. p. 132.—Roxb. l. c. p. 288.

Engrav. Burm. flor. Ind. t. 31. fig. 2.—Pluk. Alm. t. 398. fig. I.—Lam. Ill. t. 315. fig. 3.

SPEC. CHAR. Ochreæ leafy, pierced through by the stem, spreading: leaves peltate-triangular, obtuse on the nerve beneath, together with the petiole and angular-branched stem and peduncles retrorsely aculeate: spikes solitary, short, dense-flowered: stamens 8: style half-3-cleft.

Silhet.

(31) P. MURICATUM. (*Meissn.*)

Ident. Meissn. l. c. p. 74. et ap. Wall. l. c. p. 58.—Dec. l. c. p. 133.

SPEC. CHAR. Stem rooting at the base, branched, angular, and with the petioles sparingly asperulous or aculeate: ochreæ bristly-ciliate: leaves ovate or oblong, acuminate, obtuse, truncated at the base, cordate or subhastate, glabrous, slightly scabrous at the margin and nerves beneath: peduncles subdichotomous, asperulous or smooth: spikes short, filiform, lax: bracts ovate, acute, subciliolate, 1-flowered: stamens 6: achenium largish, acute-angled, smooth, shining, faces ovate, flat.

Assam.

(32) P. MOLLE. (*Don.*)

Ident. Don l. c. p. 72.—Dec. l. c. p. 136.—Meissn. l. c. p. 56. et ap. Wall. l. c. p. 61.

Engrav. Wight's Icon. t. 1807.

SPEC. CHAR. Fruticose, branched, everywhere softly pubescent: ochreæ long, equalling the petiole: leaves oblong, attenuated at both ends, silky-woolly beneath, rarely hispidulous, above at length glabrate: panicle leafless: racemes filiform, lax: bracts 3—5-flowered, equalling the short pedicels and the short glabrous calyx: lobes of the calyx equal, oval, faces of the shining achenium ovate-rhomboid, very minutely dotted.

Pundua.

(33) P. RUDE. (*Meissn.*)

Ident. Dec. l. c. p. 137.

SPEC. CHAR. Fruticose; branches flexuose, furrowed, and with the petioles hirsute, at length glabrous: ochreæ large, sparingly bristly, base persistent, truncated, nearly equalling the petiole: leaves elliptic-oblong, acuminated, attenuated at the base, slightly hairy, somewhat scabrous above, nerve beneath densely hirsute: panicles nearly equalling the leaves, the branches and bracts hispidulous, lower ones branched: bracts small, 1—3-flowered, nearly equalling the pedicels: calycine lobes equal, oval, faces of the enclosed achenium ovate-rhomboid, very minutely dotted.

Pundua.

GENUS II. RUMEX.

Hexandria Trigynia. *Sex: Syst:*

Deriv. A name applied by Pliny to the Sorrel-plant.

GEN. CHAR. Herbs or shrubs, with a thick root-stock and erect furrowed annual stems, the thin sheathing stipules never fringed on the edge, but soon becoming lacerated or jagged: lower leaves stalked, largish: flowers small, numerous, often red, usually pedicelled in whorl-like clusters, axillary or in terminal racemes, often branching into panicles: perianth deeply 6-cleft, when in fruit the 3 inner segments become enlarged and close over the triangular nut: styles very short, with fringed stigmas.

(1) R. WALLICHII. (*Meissn.*)

Ident. Dec. prod. XIV. p. 48.

Syn. R. acutus, *Roxb.*—R. Wallichianus, *Meissn. in Wall. pl. As. rar.* III. *p.* 64.

SPEC. CHAR. Stem thick, flexuose, divaricately branched, furrowed: leaves acute, lower ones oblong, subundulate, subcordate, upper ones flat, narrowed at both ends, uppermost ones linear, spreading: panicle simple: verticils supported by a leaf, dense-flowered, upper ones confluent: pedicels smaller than the small fructiferous calyx, turbinately thickened at the apex: valves ovate, lanceolate-acuminate, acute, all equally calliferous.

Bengal. Silhet. Oude.

(2) R. NEPALENSIS. (*Spreng.*)

Ident. Spreng. syst. II. p. 159.—Dec. l. c. p. 55.

Engrav. Wight's Icon. t. 1810.

SPEC. CHAR. Divaricately branched: leaves petioled, acute, radical ones oblong, subcordate, with a narrow base, cauline ones ovate-oblong, round and subcordate at the base, uppermost ones lanceolate: verticils remote, dense-flowered, uppermost ones somewhat leafless: pedicels somewhat longer than the largest fructiferous calyx, deflexed: valves ovate-oblong, obtuse, reticulated, subulate-fimbriate, one obsoletely calliferous: awls uncinate, scarcely longer than half the length of the valve.

Neilgherries. Pulney mountains.

(3) R. DENTATUS. (*Campd.*)

Ident. Campd. Rum. pp. 64 and 81.—Dec. l. c. p. 56.

SPEC. CHAR. Leaves petioled, somewhat obtuse, lower ones

oblong, subcordate, upper ones lanceolate or sublinear, suddenly cuneate at the base: verticils distinct, dense-flowered, all supported by a leaf: pedicels nearly equalling the fructiferous calyx: valves ovate-lanceolate, acuminated, acute, coarsely calliferous, 1—3-toothed, or here and there unarmed: teeth subulate, straight, spreading, nearly equalling the length of the valve.

Peninsula. Khasia.

(4) R. CHINENSIS. (*Campd.*)

Ident. Campd. l. c. pp. 63 and 76.—Dec. l. c. p. 60.

Syn. R. setaceus, *Ham. MSS. Meissn. in Wall. pl. As. rar.* III. *p.* 64.—R. persicaroides, *Thunb. flor. Jap. p.* 148 ?—R. crispus, *Lour.* (not *Linn.*)—R. Loureirii, *Campd. l. c.* ?—R. Loureirianus, *Schult.*—R. denticulatus, *Campd. l. c.* ?

SPEC. CHAR. Leaves petioled, lanceolate, acute, attenuated at both ends, radical ones elongated, subundulate: verticils dense-flowered, distinct, all supported by a linear leaf, lower ones remote: pedicels equalling the fructiferous calyx: valves ovate, acuminate, all coarsely calliferous: teeth 1—2, subulate on both sides below the middle, straight, very patent, somewhat longer than the valve.

Bengal. Silhet. Assam.

(5) R. VESICARIUS. (*Linn.*)

Ident. Linn. sp. I. p. 479.—Dec. l. c. p. 70.

Engrav. Barrel Icon. 1112.—Campd. Rum. t. 3, figs. 1 and 8.

SPEC. CHAR. Stem low, branched: leaves somewhat fleshy, petioled, ovate or deltoid, obtuse or acutish, usually cuneate-attenuate from a cordate or subhastate base, uppermost ones narrower: racemes simple or panicled, leafless: fascicles 2—5-flowered, remote: pedicels 1-flowered or generally bearing 2 flowers at the top, connate at the back: valves very large, entire, very unequal, calliferous or almost naked.

Peninsula.

GENUS III. FAGOPYRUM.

Octandria Trigynia. *Sex: Syst:*

Deriv. From *Phago*, to eat, and *Pyros*, wheat or grain. The fruit is eatable.

GEN. CHAR. Flowers hermaphrodite: calyx corolline, equally 5-parted, spreading, fructiferous, 1 not increased: stamens 8, filaments subulate, anthers oval, versatile: glands 8, nectariferous, hemispherical, seated at the bottom of the calyx, between the stamens: styles 3, free, filiform, deciduous: stigmas obtuse, scarcely thickened: achenium triquetrous, largish, far exceeding the calyx, angles acute or obtuse, sometimes toothed or expanded into a coriaceous wing, pericarp crustaceous, thin: embryo axile, straight, albumen mealy.—Herbs: stem branched, erect: ochreæ and bracts thinly membranaceous, obliquely truncated, beardless: leaves cordate-triangular or hastate, palminerved, petioled, or upper ones subsessile, stem-clasping: racemes subdichotomously cymose or panicled: pedicels fascicled, thin, jointed: flowers white or rose.

(1) F. TRIANGULARE. (*Meissn.*)

Ident. Meissn. ap. Wall. pl. As. rar. III. p. 63.—Dec. l. c. p. 144.

Syn. P. dibotrys, *Don prod. flor. Nep. p.* 73 ?

SPEC. CHAR. Leaves cordate-triangular or hastate, obtuse-angled, upper ones less elongated, nerves beneath and petioles at the apex puberulous: panicles long-peduncled, dichotomous: racemes conjugate, separate, divaricated, recurved: angles of the half-exserted achenium entire, very obtuse, thickened, faces ovate.

Assam.

ORDER CXXXI. LAURACEÆ.

Flowers hermaphrodite or diœcious by abortion, sometimes polygamous or monœcious, regular: calyx gamosepalous, free, herbaceous or corolline, rotate or infundibular or urceolate, 6—4—9-cleft, lobes imbricated in two rows equal, or outer ones smaller, deciduous or seldom persistent, tube generally persistent, usually more or less increased, and changed into a small cup surrounding the base of the fruit: stamens inserted at the base or throat of the calyx, definite, 3—4-seriate, in the female flowers changed into glands or scales or petaloid straps, in male or hermaphrodite ones partly barren or seldom all fertile: filaments free or very rarely monadelphous, filiform, usually shorter than the anthers, sometimes confluent with the latter: anthers ovoid or oblong, sometimes acuminated by a connectivum produced beyond the cells, 2-celled or 4-locellate, valves dehiscing from base to apex: stamens of the fourth series usually sterile, sometimes more perfect, stalked, capitate, glanduliform, sometimes imperfect or obsoletely sessile, scali- or dentiform, sometimes deficient: glands globose or ovoid or compressed, stalked or sessile, affixed to the third row of stamens, sometimes free between the stamens: pistils 2—3, connate into 1: ovary free, 1-celled, 1-ovuled: style filiform: stigma obtuse or discoid, often obsoletely 2—3-lobed: fruit fleshy, globose or ellipsoid, naked: seed exalbuminous.—Trees or shrubs, unarmed, very rarely climbing: leaves scattered, or seldom opposite, or subverticilled by intervals, exstipulate, simple, undivided or very rarely lobed, always quite entire: cymes racemose or panicled, often dichotomous, and with the shortened pedicels forming a capitulum or false umbel, supported at the base by a bract, or more rarely a 4—6-leaved involucre: flowers usually small, white, yellow, or greenish, usually fragrant: bark aromatic: leafy parts more or less dotted with bladders filled with ethereal oil.

GENUS I. CINNAMOMUM.

Enneandria Monogynia. *Sex: Syst:*

Deriv. From the Arabic word *Kinamon.*

Gen. Char. Flowers hermaphrodite or polygamous, panicled, naked: calyx funnel-shaped, 6-cleft, coriaceous, lobes breaking transversely at or near the base and deciduous from a cup-shaped tube, seldom persistent: stamens perfect, outer 6 eglandulose, inner 3 furnished above the base with 2 stalked or sessile glands: anthers with a slender filament of nearly equal length, ovate or oblong, superposedly 4-celled, upper cells smaller: staminodes 3, ovate or oblong, stalk short, naked or rarely bearing 2 glands: style equalling the ovary, slender: stigma obtuse or discoid, sometimes slightly 3-toothed: berry supported by the thickened base of the calyx.—Evergreen trees or shrubs: leaves opposite or nearly so, or here and there alternate, 3- or 3-fold-nerved: panicles axillary, usually collected into a terminal corymb, the branches cymosely 3—many-flowered: flowers white or yellow, bisexual.

(1) C. Wightii. (*Meissn.*)

Ident. Dec. prod. XV. s. 1. p. 11.

Spec. Char. Small tree: branchlets acutely tetragonal at the top: leaves stiffish-coriaceous, ovate, oval or oblong-elliptic, obtuse, tri- and triplinerved, beneath or on both sides densely and prominently reticulated, afterwards smooth, shining and glabrous above, beneath glaucous whitish, minutely and sparingly puberulous: panicles corymbosely branched above the middle, branches short, 3-cleft, branchlets 3-flowered: flowers subsessile, hoary or somewhat brownish, slightly tomentose.

Peninsula. Neilgherries. Probably identical with *C. Zeylanicum*.

(2) C. OBTUSIFOLIUM. (*Nees.*)

Ident. Nees in Wall. pl. As. rar. II. p. 73.—Dec. l. c. p. 12.

Syn. Laurus obtusifolia, ***Roxb. H. B.***

SPEC. CHAR. Large tree: leaves stiffly coriaceous, oval or ovate-oblong, acuminated, rounded or attenuated at the base, 3- or triplinerved, glabrous, shining above, somewhat deeply or obsoletely reticulated, beneath glaucous and densely and prominently reticulated: panicle terminal, hoary-tomentose, branches cymosely 2—7-cleft, 7—12-flowered.

Bengal. Silhet. Assam.

(3) C. ZEYLANICUM. (*Breyn.*)

a. var. COMMUNE.

Ident. Dec. l. c. p. 13.

Syn. Laurus Cinnamomum, *Linn.*—L. cassia, *Bot. Mag.*—C. Zeylanicum, *Blume.*—Persea Cinnamomum, *Spreng.*

Engrav. Burm. Zeyl. t. 27.—Bot. Mag. t. 1636.—Wight's Icon. t. 123.

SPEC. CHAR. Tree: leaves coriaceous, ovate or ovate-oblong from a very shortly narrowed or rounded base, obtuse or acutish, short-acuminated, 3—5-nerved: panicle terminal, large, somewhat silky hoary, pedicels equalling the flowers: capsule truncated, 6-cleft.

Peninsula.

b. var. INODORUM.—Dec. l. c.

Bark inodorous or slightly aromatic: leaves ovate or ovate-oblong, often equalling the panicle.

Peninsula. Neilgherries.

c. var. MICROPHYLLUM.—Dec. l. c. p. 14.—Burm. thes. Zeyl. p. 63.—Wight's Icon. t. 141?

Leaves small, ovate or lanceolate-oblong, from a rounded or acute base, obtuse, 3-nerved, with a pleasant odour of cinnamon.

Neilgherries.

d. var. CASSIA.—Dec. l. c. p. 14.—Laurus Cassia, *Burm.*—L. Cinn. *Roxb. H. B.*—Wight's Icon. t. 128.—Rheede Mal. I. t. 57.

Leaves elliptic or lanceolate-oblong from a narrow acute base, perceptibly attenuated towards the apex, 3- or triplenerved, rarely 5-nerved.

Peninsula. Chittagong. Silhet.

(4) C. PAUCIFLORUM. (*Nees.*)

Ident. Nees l. c.—Dec. l. c. p. 17.

Syn. C. recurvatum, *Wight's Icon. t.* 133?

SPEC. CHAR. Shrub (?): leaves opposite and alternate, stiffly coriaceous, ovate or ovate-oblong, rounded or shortly acute at the base, narrow acuminated, 3 or very shortly triplinerved: corymbs axillary, short, hoary puberulous, 5—3-flowered at the top.

Silhet. Assam. Khasia.

(5) C. TAMALA. (*Fr. Nees.*)

Ident. Dec. l. c. p. 17.—Nees l. c.

Syn. Persea Tamala, *Spreng.*

Engrav. Blume's Rumphia, t. 14. figs. 3, 4.

SPEC. CHAR. Small tree: leaves opposite and alternate, chartaceous, ovate or elliptic, or lanceolate-oblong, attenuately acuminate, shortly triplinerved, and with the branchlets glabrous: panicles axillary and terminal, many-flowered, minutely puberulous, branches cymosely 3—5-flowered: calyx somewhat silky, nearly equalling the pedicel, lobes ovate, obtuse, glabrescent, deciduous.

Silhet. Khasia..

(6) C. INERS, *var.* TRINERVE. (*Reinw.*)

Ident. Dec. l. c. p. 20.

Syn. C. nitidum, *Hook. Exot. Flor.*—C. eucalyptoides, *Nees in Wall. pl. As. rar.*—C. Rauwolfii, *Blume.*—C. ochraceum, *do.*—Laurus Malabathrica, *Roxb. H. B.*

SPEC. CHAR.—Small tree: leaves coriaceous, oval or oblong, nearly equally attenuated at both ends, usually 3-nerved, almost veinless, lateral nerves nearly reaching the apex, shining and glabrous above, glaucous beneath: panicles equalling or exceeding the leaves, slender, peduncled, lax, branchlets 3-flowered and with the flowers equalling the pedicel: lobes of the calyx falling off at the middle.

Peninsula. Concans. Malabar. Flowering in the cold season.

(7) C. Perothetii. (*Meissn.*)

Ident. Dec. l. c. p. 22.

Spec. Char. Tree: leaves opposite, long-petioled, stiffly coriaceous, elliptic-oblong or lanceolate, attenuated at both ends, triplinerved, veinless, golden tomentose, above soon glabrate, shining, a little tumid at the axils of the nerves: panicles short, cymosely 5—15-flowered: flowers subsessile, brown tomentose.

Neilgherries.

(8) C. Cecidodaphne. (*Meissn.*)

Ident. Dec. l. c. p. 25.

Syn. Tetranthera glaucescens, *Wall.*—C. glaucescens, *Nees.*

Spec. Char. Tree (?): leaves alternate, coriaceous, moderately petioled, oval-oblong, penninerved, glabrous, beneath or on both sides obsoletely veined and minutely reticulated: panicles short, collected into a terminal corymb, tawny or hoary tomentose.

Silhet. Malabar.

GENUS II. ALSEODAPHNE.

Enneandria Monogynia. *Sex: Syst:*

Deriv. From *Alsos*, a grove, and *Daphne*, a laurel.

Gen. Char. Flowers hermaphrodite, panicled, naked: calyx deeply 6-parted, lobes nearly equal: deciduous: filaments filiform or dilated, innermost 3 near the base increased by 2 subsessile glands: anthers ovate-oblong, 4-celled, innermost 3 extrorse: staminodes 3, stalked, without glands: capitulum cordate or sagittate: style filiform: stigma discoid or obtusely 3-cornered: berry lying at the base of a small, flat, quite entire calyx, supported by the thickened pedicel.—Trees: leaves alternate: panicles lateral or springing from the axils of the scales of the bud: flowers sometimes subumbellate.

(1) A. semecarpifolia. (*Nees.*)

Ident. Dec. prod. XV. s. 1. p. 28.

Syn. Laurus semecarpifolia, *Wall.*

Engrav. Wight's Icon. t. 1826-7.

Spec. Char. Small tree: leaves obovate, oval or ovate, obtuse, narrow at the base, minutely reticulated on both sides, shining and glabrous above, glaucous beneath: branchlets puberulous at the apex: panicles long, lax, cymosely umbelled at the ends of the branches.

Peninsula. Neilgherries. Canara.

GENUS III. PHŒBE.

Enneandria Monogynia. *Sex: Syst:*

Gen. Char. Flowers hermaphrodite, panicled, naked: calyx funnel-shaped, 6-cleft, lobes nearly equal, persistent with the indurated tube: filaments filiform, innermost 3 biglandulose at the base: anthers ovate, 4-celled, innermost 3 extrorse: staminodes 3, stalked, eglandulose, capitulum cordate, anther-shaped: style filiform: stigma angular discoid: berry supported by the indurated 6-cleft cupula, which is attenuated into a more or less thickened pedicel.—Trees: leaves alternate or somewhat verticillate, approximate, either tripli- or penninerved, buds small, leafily few-scaled: panicles axillary or terminal: flowers subcymose.

(1) P. Wightii. (*Meissn.*)

Ident. Dec. prod. XV. s. 1. p. 38.

Syn. P. paniculata, *R. W.*

Engrav. Wight's Icon. t. 1820.

Spec. Char. Leaves oblong-obovate or elliptic, glabrous and shining above, beneath with the branchlets and peduncles tawny pubescent: panicles axillary, racemiform, shorter than the leaf: flowers hoary tomentose.

Neilgherries.

(2) P. lanceolata. (*Nees.*)

Ident. Nees Syst. p. 109.—Dec. l. c. p. 34.

Syn. Laurus lanceolaria, *Roxb. H. C.*—Ocotea lanceolata, *Wall. pl. As. rar.* II. *p.* 71.

Engrav. Wight's Icon. t. 1821.

Spec. Char. Small tree: leaves chartaceous, lanceolate or oblong-lanceolate, acuminated, somewhat veinless or obsoletely reticulated, glabrous above or on both sides: panicle equalling the leaves, collected into a terminal corymb, long-peduncled.

Silhet. Assam. Khasia.

(3) P. angustifolia. (*Meissn.*)

Ident. Dec. l. c. p. 34.

Spec. Char. Small tree (?): leaves chartaceous, lanceolate, long-attenuated at both ends: panicles corymbiform, long-peduncled.

Khasia.

(4) P. GLAUCESCENS. (*Nees.*)

Ident. Dec. l. c. p. 36.

Syn. Ocotea glaucescens, *Wall. l. c.*

SPEC. CHAR. Small tree: leaves coriaceous, elliptic or oblong, obtusely acuminated, somewhat glaucous, glabrous, shining above, prominently veined beneath: panicles collected into a terminal corymb, branched from the middle or below: peduncles covered with loose tawny villous hairs: flowers slightly tomentose.

Var. a. FULVESCENS.—Panicles longer, tawny or somewhat rusty-coloured.—Laurus glaucescens, *Roxb. H. B.*

Silhet. Assam.

Var. b. CANESCENS.—Panicles shorter, whitish or whitish-hoary.

Chittagong.

(5) P. ATTENUATA. (*Nees.*)

Ident. Dec. l. c. p. 38.

Syn. Ocotea attenuata, *Wall. l. c. p.* 71.

SPEC. CHAR. Small tree: leaves coriaceous, oblong, ribbed, glabrous above, tawny puberulous beneath: ribs and veins thin, immersed above, prominent beneath: panicle equalling the leaf, collected into a terminal corymb, long-peduncled, hoary-tomentose.

Silhet.

GENUS IV. MACHILUS.

Enneandria Monogynia. *Sex: Syst:*

GEN. CHAR. Flowers hermaphrodite, panicled, naked: calyx chartaceous, deeply 6-parted, all persistent, unchanged, lobes equal, or outer ones a little shorter: filaments filiform, inner 3 furnished above the base with a stipitate gland on either side: anthers oblong, 4-celled, inner 3 extrorse: staminodes 3, without glands, capitulum cordate: style filiform: stigma discoid: berry sessile, globose, supported by the calyx.—Trees: leaf-bearing buds imbricately scaled: leaves alternate, penninerved: panicles subcorymbose, springing from the base of a terminal or axillary leaf-bud: bracteal scales deciduous: flowers usually large for the order.

(1) M. MACRANTHA. (*Nees.*)

Ident. Dec. prod. XV. s. 1. p. 40.

Engrav. Wight's Icon. t. 1824.

SPEC. CHAR. Small tree: leaves elliptic, membranaceous, deeply ribbed, obsoletely reticulated, glabrous, glaucous beneath: panicle canescent, exceeding the leaves: berry middle-sized.

Neilgherries.

(2) M. GLAUCESCENS. (*R. W.*)

Ident. Dec. l. c. p. 40.

Engrav. Wight's Icon. t. 1825.

SPEC. CHAR. Small tree: leaves coriaceous, oval and oblong, acuminulate or acute, densely, somewhat prominently, reticulated, and with the branchlets glabrous, glaucescent beneath: panicles collected into a terminal corymb equalling the leaves, covered with slight hoary tomentum: berry largish.

Western slopes of the Neilgherries. Canara. Concans.

(3) M. ODORATISSIMA. (*Nees.*)

Ident. Dec. l. c. p. 40.—Wall. l. c. p. 70.

Syn. Laurus Indica, *Lour.*

Engrav. Rumph. Amb. III. t. 42.

SPEC. CHAR. Small tree: leaves chartaceous or coriaceous, sharply oblong-lanceolate, acuminate, shining above, glaucous beneath: panicles collected into a terminal corymb, shorter than the leaf, silky canescent.

Silhet. Assam.

(4) M. KHASIANA. (*Meissn.*)

Ident. Dec. l. c. p. 42.

SPEC. CHAR. Small tree: leaves chartaceous, elongated-oblong, sharply acuminate, adult ones glabrous, glaucous beneath: panicles racemiform, shorter than the leaf, and with the younger branches minutely downy.

Khasia.

GENUS V. HAASIA.

Enneandria Monogynia. *Sex: Syst:*

GEN. CHAR. Flowers hermaphrodite or monœcious by abortion, panicled, naked: calyx a little fleshy, 6-cleft, deciduous, lobes unequal, outer 3 usually dwarf: filaments short, broadish, innermost 3 furnished with 2 subsessile glands at the base:

anthers subrotund, 2-celled, cells somewhat lateral, innermost 3 extrorse: staminodes triangular, subsessile or generally none: ovary 1-celled: style filiform: stigma discoid, triangular: berry oval, naked, placed on a thick fleshy pedicel.—Trees, with scattered leaves often collected at the ends of the branches, feather-nerved, leaf-buds small, scales few, leafy: panicles subterminal, often few-flowered: flowers small.

(1) H. Wightii. (*Nees.*)

Ident. Dec. prod. XV. s. 1. p. 61.

Engrav. Wight's Icon. t. 1831.

Spec. Char. Leaves elliptic, acute at both ends, finely reticulated, of the same colour on both sides: panicles shorter than the leaves: lobes of the calyx deciduous: fructiferous pedicels straight, slightly thickening upwards, shorter than the peduncle of the panicle: staminodes present in the male flowers.

Courtallum, flowering in August and September.

GENUS VI. BEILSCHMIEDIA.

Enneandria Monogynia. *Sex: Syst:*

Gen. Char. Flowers hermaphrodite or polygamous, racemose: racemes imbricated with deciduous scales: calyx 6-parted, lobes deciduous: anthers ovate-oblong, 2-celled, cells of the innermost ones lateral: glands 3- or 6-stalked, placed between the third or second row of stamens: staminodes 3, ovoid or subsagittate, very shortly stalked: ovary incompletely 2-celled, 3-ovuled: style filiform: stigma discoid: berry juiceless, naked, oblong, placed on the persistent base of the calyx, 1-celled.—Trees, nearly opposite or scattered, feather-nerved: racemes springing from the axillary leaf-bud: scales 1—few-flowered, afterwards deciduous: flowers yellowish.

(1) B. Roxburghiana. (*Nees.*)

Ident. Dec. prod. XV. s. 1. p. 63.

Syn. Laurus bilocularis, *Roxb. flor. Ind.* II. *p.* 311.

Engrav. Wight's Icon. t. 1828.

Spec. Char. Branches wide spreading: leaves opposite and alternate, broad lanceolar, shining, veined: racemes solitary under the leaves or axillary: filaments without glands: berries oblong, glaucous.

Common on the Western Ghauts.

(2) B. fagifolia. (*Nees.*)

Ident. Dec. l. c. p. 64.

Spec. Char. Leaves scattered, elliptic, shortly acuminated,

shining above: racemes equalling the petiole, subsessile, scaled at the base: lobes of the calyx lanceolate-linear.

Concans. Canara. Assam.

(3) B. Assamica. (*Meissn.*)

Ident. Dec. l. c. p. 64.

Spec. Char. Leaves opposite and sub-opposite: elliptic-oblong, obtusely acuminated, and with the branches glabrous: network of the veins rather prominent above and loose, very dense beneath.

Assam.

GENUS VII. APOLLONIAS.

Enneandria Monogynia. *Sex: Syst:*

Gen. Char. Flowers hermaphrodite, panicled, naked: calyx funnel-shaped, 6-cleft, persistent, lobes nearly equal: filaments filiform, innermost 3 furnished with 2 stipitate glands at the base: anthers oblong, 2-celled, innermost 3 extrorse: staminodes 3: style short: stigma depresso-capitate: berry oval, surrounded at the base by the hardened calyx.—Trees: leaf-buds naked: leaves scattered, feather-nerved: panicles axillary and sub-terminal: flowers small.

(1) A. Arnottii. (*Nees.*)

Ident. Dec. prod. XV. s. 1. p. 65.

Engrav. Wight's Icon. t. 1819.

Spec. Char. Leaves chartaceous, lanceolate, or oblong-lanceolate, attenuated at both ends, slightly reticulated and somewhat prominently ribbed, shining and glabrous above, younger ones beneath with the branchlets and short panicles sparingly puberulous.

Courtallum, flowering in July and August.

GENUS VIII. CRYPTOCARYA.

Enneandria Monogynia. *Sex: Syst:*

Deriv. From *Kryptos*, concealed, and *Karyon*, a nut, alluding to the seed.

Gen. Char. Flowers hermaphrodite, panicled, bracteate: calyx funnel-shaped, 6-cleft, tube urceolate, persistent, increasing, throat a little narrowed, lobes equal, afterwards deciduous: stamens inserted on the throat: filaments short, flat, innermost 3 bearing a sessile gland on both sides: anthers ovate-oblong, 2-celled, innermost 3 extrorse: staminodes 3, shortly stalked, ovate-oblong, acute, without glands: style filiform, short: stigma subcapitate: ovary entirely immersed in the calyx-tube: caryopsis free, enclosed.—Trees: leaves alternate, feather-nerved or rarely somewhat triplinerved: scales of the leaf-buds few, leafy: panicles axillary or terminal, short.

(1) C. Wightiana. (*Thwaites.*)

Ident. Thwaites en. Zeyl. I. p. 254.—Dec. prod. XV. s. 1. p. 70.

Engrav. Wight's Icon. t. 1829.

Spec. Char. Leaves stiffly coriaceous, elliptic and oblong, acuminated, glabrous above, glaucous beneath, minutely and sparingly puberulous, prominently ribbed and veined, and densely and obsoletely reticulated: panicles and branchlets tawny or rufous-tomentose.

Bombay.

Var. Griffithii (Dec. l. c.).—Leaves oblong, acuminulate, attenuated acute at the base, distinctly deep reticulated above: branchlets often glabrous, sparingly hoary tomentose at the apex only: flowers canescent, yellowish.

Canara.

(2) C. Stocksii. (*Meissn.*)

Ident. Dec. l. c. p. 71.

Spec. Char. Leaves chartaceous coriaceous, obovate and orbicular, very obtusely rounded or retusely emarginate, above glabrous, almost veinless, very densely dotted, beneath glaucine in the nerves, sparingly puberulous and minutely areolate between the transverse prominent veins: panicles short, tawny-tomentose: flowers yellowish.

Canara.

(3) C. Neilgherrensis. (*Meissn.*)

Ident. Dec. l. c. p. 71.

Spec. Char. Branchlets densely tawny-tomentose: leaves coriaceous, oval and oblong, obtusely subacuminate or obtuse, glabrous above, ribbed, veinless, glaucous beneatb, tawny-tomentose between the ribs, sparingly puberulous: panicles dense-flowered: peduncle tawny-tomentose: flowers yellowish, tomentose.

Neilgherries.

(4) C. FLORIBUNDA. (*Nees.*)

Ident. Dec. l. c. p. 71.—Wall. pl. As. rar. II. p. 69.

Syn. Laurus floribunda, *Wall. Cat.*

SPEC. CHAR. Leaves coriaceous, oval and oblong, acuminate or obtuse, glabrous on both sides, transversely veined: glaucine below, obsoletely areolate: panicles lax, hoary-tomentose.

Assam. Silhet.

(5) C. AMYGDALINA. (*Nees.*)

Ident. Dec. l. c. p. 72.—Wall. l. c. p. 69.

Syn. Laurus amygdalina, *Ham. in Wall. Cat.*

SPEC. CHAR. Leaves subherbaceous, elliptic, short-cuspidate, glabrous on both sides, thinly and densely reticulated: panicles axillary, nearly equalling the leaf, dichotomous: fruit without ribs.

Bengal, near Patgong.

GENUS IX. TETRANTHERA.

Diœcia Enneandria. *Sex: Syst:*

GEN. CHAR. Flowers diœcious, umbelled, involucred: calyx 6-cleft or parted, lobes deciduous, sometimes varying in number or none. MALE: stamens 9—12, inserted on the throat, filaments conspicuous, inner ones 3—6, with 2—1 sessile or stalked glands: all anthers introrse, oval or quadrangular-oblong, muticous, 4-celled, cells superposed, straight or oblique, lower ones often slightly lateral: staminodes none or rarely obsolete: rudiment of a pistil scarcely any.—FEMALE: stamens strap-shaped, glandulose: style filiform: stigma dilated, sublobate: berry placed at the top of the calyx, naked.—Trees and shrubs: leaves scattered, feather-nerved, undivided, perennial or seldom deciduous: leaf-buds incomplete: umbels 4—many-flowered, surrounded by a 4—6-leaved involucre, peduncled, springing from the axillary leaf-bud, solitary or fascicled, or corymbose or racemose on a very short or long common peduncle.

(1) T. TOMENTOSA. (*Roxb.*)

Ident. Dec. prod. XV. s. 1. p. 177.—Nees Syst. Laur. p. 511.

Engrav. Wight's Icon. t. 1834.

SPEC. CHAR. Tree: leaves ovate or elliptic-oblong or obovate, above glabrous deeply ribbed, very minutely scrobiculato-reticulate, beneath prominently veined, loosely or obsoletely reticulated, and with the petiole, branchlets, and involucres densely hoary-tomentose: umbels solitary, simple, scarcely exceeding the petiole, many-flowered.

Peninsula. Hills near Coimbatore.

Var. GLABRESCENS.—Leaves elliptic-oblong, attenuated at both ends, acuminated, glabrous above, beneath sparingly puberulous, loosely reticulated, and with the branchlets covered with villous hairs: umbels short-peduncled, often approximated.

Canara.

(2) T. LIGUSTRINA. (*Nees.*)

Ident. Dec. l. c. p. 180.—Nees in Wall. l. c. p. 65.

Engrav. Wight's Icon. t. 1835.

SPEC. CHAR. Small tree: leaves subcoriaceous, subcuneate at the base, oblong-lanceolate or obovate, obtuse, densely reticulated on both sides, glabrous: umbels simple, solitary, longish-peduncled, many-flowered, glabrous.

Peninsula.

Var. CELASTROIDES.—Leaves stiffer, reticulation thicker above, at least more prominent: petioles and peduncles longer.

Neilgherries.

(3) T. PANAMONJA. (*Hamilt.*)

Ident. Dec. l. c. p. 197.—Herb. Ham. in Wall. Cat. No. 2553. —Nees in Wall. l. c. p. 67.

Engrav. Wight's Icon. t. 1836.

SPEC. CHAR. Large tree: leaves coriaceous, elongated-oblong, shortly attenuated and acute at both ends, veinless between the deep ribs, glabrous, or beneath obsoletely veined and pale: racemes exceeding the petiole, slender, loose, tawny-tomentose.

Goalpara. Silhet. Assam. Courtallum.

(4) T. LAURIFOLIA. (*Jacq.*)

Ident. Dec. l. c. p. 178.—Nees in Wall. l. c. p. 66. 3. p. 30.

Syn. Glabraria tersa, *Linn. Mant. p.* 276.—Sebifera glutinosa, *Lour.*—Tomex sebifera, *Willd.*—Litsæa sebifera, *Pers.*—L. Chinensis, *Lam.*

SPEC. CHAR.—Tree: leaves elliptic or cuneate-oblong, and obovate, glabrous, or pubescent beneath: umbels fascicled or umbellate on the common peduncle, corymbosely racemose, many-flowered.

Var. a. ROXBURGHII (*Blume*).—Dec. l. c. p. 179.—T. apetala, *Roxb. Cor.* II. *t.* 147.—T. sebifera, *Spreng.*—Laurus involucrata, *Retz.*—Litsæa sebifera, *Juss.*—Tomex sebifera, *Willd.* (partly).—Umbels composite: rays nearly equal to the peduncle or longer:

lesser leaves oblong, obtuse or rounded or subacute, pubescent beneath, especially on the nerves.

Bengal. Peninsula.

Var. b. CITRIFOLIA (*Blume*).—Dec. l. c. p. 179.—T. citrifolia et tersa, *Spreng.*—T. apetala, *R. Br. prod.*—T. glabraria, *Nees.*—Glabraria tersa, *Linn. Mant.*—Umbels composite: rays usually shorter than the peduncle: leaves larger, short attenuated or acute, or rarely obtuse at the base, oval, ovate or oblong, slightly glabrous, puberulous on the nerves beneath.

Peninsula.

Var. c. PLATYPHYLLA (*Blume*).—Dec. l. c. p. 179.—T. geminata et platyphylla, *Nees.*—Litsæa platyphylla, *Pers. Poir. suppl.*—L. geminata, *Bl. Bidjr.*—Umbels composite: rays few, shorter than the peduncle, involucres longish, silky hoary: leaves larger, elliptic or oval-oblong, acute, or obtuse or rounded, puberulous or glabrous beneath.

Bengal. Silhet. Canara. Chittagong.

Var. d. RACEMOSO-UMBELLATA (*Blume*).—Dec. l. c. p. 180.—Umbels common at the top of the peduncle, corymbosely umbellate or shortly racemose: leaves oblong, obtuse at both ends, puberulous.

Silhet. Bengal.

(5) T. POLYANTHA. (*Wall.*)

Ident. Dec. l. c. p. 182.—Nees in Wall. l. c. p. 67.

SPEC. CHAR.—Tree: leaves herbaceous, lanceolate, attenuately acute at both ends, ribbed, densely pellucid-dotted, glaucous beneath: umbels fascicled or subcorymbose on a very short common peduncle.

Silhet. Assam.

(6) T. ANGUSTIFOLIA. (*Wall.*)

Ident. Dec. l. c. p. 183.

Syn. T. saligna, *Nees in Wall. l. c. p.* 67.

SPEC. CHAR. Tree: branchlets glabrous, and with the young leaves hoary silky at the apex: leaves chartaceous, acute at the base, lanceolate, acute, glabrous above, minutely or obsoletely reticulated, beneath very minutely puberulous: umbels almost solitary, short-peduncled, glabrous.

Silhet. Bengal.

(7) T. THOMSONI. (*Meissn.*)

Ident. Dec. l. c. p. 183.

SPEC. CHAR. Tree (?): quite glabrous: leaves coriaceous, obtuse or acutish at the base, elongated-oblong, nearly equally attenuated at both ends, above ribbed and veinless, beneath paler, obsoletely reticulated between slightly prominent veins: umbels thickly corymbose on a short solitary peduncle.

Silhet.

(8) T. MICRANTHA. (*Meissn.*)

Ident. Dec. l. c. p. 183.

SPEC. CHAR. Tree (?): leaves chartaceous, acute at the base, elliptic and oblong, acuminulate or obtuse, above ribbed, almost veinless, and with the branchlets glabrous, beneath paler, obsoletely veined, minutely puberulous: umbels sessile, 3—5 glomerate, very small, hoary-tomentose.

Peninsula?

(9) T. GLAUCA. (*Wall.*)

Ident. Dec. l. c. p. 185.

SPEC. CHAR. Tree: leaves chartaceo-coriaceous, equally attenuated at both ends, acutish or shortly acuminate, above ribbed obsoletely venulose or minutely reticulated, shining glabrous, beneath glaucous, the younger ones with the petiole and branchlets hoary-tomentose: umbels glomerate or fascicled, thickly or occasionally subcorymbose.

Var. a. ELLIPSOIDEA.—Dec. l. c.—T. glauca, *Wall. Nees in Wall. l. c. p.* 66.—Leaves obtuse or slightly attenuated at the base, oval and oblong, acutish or rarely obtuse, beneath for a long time hoary-tomentose: network scarcely prominent above.

Silhet. Assam.

Var. b. ELONGATA.—Leaves perceptibly attenuated, acute or rarely obtuse at the base, lanceolate-oblong, acute or acuminate, beneath very minutely hoary-tomentose or glabrous: network small, obsolete, or slightly prominent above.

Peninsula? Assam. Khasia.

Var. c. LÆVIGATA.—Leaves glabrous on both sides, very smooth above: involucre and flowers silky shining.

Courtallum.

(10) T. Khasyana. (*Meissn.*)

Ident. Dec. prod. l. c. p. 185.

SPEC. CHAR. Tree: branchlets covered with dirty white or hoary down: leaves chartaceous, obtuse at the base, elongated oblong, attenuated acute, very densely reticulated on both sides, glabrous, beneath glaucous, very minutely puberulous or glabrous:

nerve and ribs impressed above: umbels fascicled or densely corymbose on a thick common peduncle, tawny-tomentose.

Khasia hills.

(11) T. LÆTA. (*Wall.*)

Ident. Dec. l. c. p. 186.—Nees in Wall. l. c. p. 67.

SPEC. CHAR. Tree: leaves chartaceo-coriaceous, oblong or lanceolate-oblong, equally acute at both ends, densely or obsoletely reticulated, beneath glaucous: ribs thin, scarcely prominent: umbels fascicled on a very short common peduncle, tawny-tomentose.

Silhet. Assam.

(12) T. VENULOSA. (*Meissn.*)

Ident. Dec. l. c. p. 187.

SPEC. CHAR. Small tree: quite glabrous: leaves chartaceous, elliptic-oblong, narrowly and acutely acuminate, glaucous beneath: umbels fasicled.

Peninsula?

(13) T. WIGHTII. (*Nees.*)

Ident. Dec. l. c. p. 187.—Nees Syst. Laur. p. 823.

SPEC. CHAR. Small tree (?): leaves stiffly chartaceous, oblong-elliptic, attenuated at the base, obtusely apiculate or rounded, glabrous, dotted-reticulate and veined beneath: umbels agglomerated, subsessile.

Peninsula.

(14) T. MONOPETALA. (*Roxb.*)

Ident. Dec. l. c. p. 189.—Nees in Wall. l. c. p. 66.

Syn. T. macrophylla, *Wall.*—Litsæa monopetala, *Pers.*—L. polyantha, *Juss.*

Engrav. Roxb. Cor. II. t. 148.

SPEC. CHAR. Small tree: leaves long-petioled, herbaceous or chartaceous, oblong, oval, ovate or obovate, obtuse or rounded at both ends, glabrous above, beneath minutely puberulous: umbels fascicled or subcorymbose, shorter than the petiole, tawny- or hoary-tomentose: fructiferous pedicels scarcely thickened.

Var. a. SUBGLOMERATA.—Umbels very shortly peduncled, contiguous, collected into a glomerule: leaves chartaceous, acutish at the base, puberulous beneath.

Bengal. Oude. Assam.

Var. b. MINOR (*Blume Mus. p.* 378).—Umbels fewer, often less, fascicled or subcorymbose: leaves thin, often acutish at the base, beneath puberulous.

Silhet. Assam.

Var. c. ALNIFOLIA (*Blume, l. c.*).—Umbels fascicled, larger: leaves chartaceous or herbaceous, sometimes apiculate or acutish at the apex, puberulous beneath.

Chittagong. Silhet.

(15) T. LANCIFOLIA. (*Roxb.*)

Ident. Dec. l. c. p. 194.—Wall. pl. As. rar. II. p. 65.

SPEC. CHAR. Shrub (?): leaves chartaceous, obtuse at the base, elliptic or oblong-elliptic, obtusely acuminate, ribbed above, almost veinless, ashy or rufescent beneath: umbels glomerately fascicled, and with the petioles and branches brown-tomentose.

Silhet. Assam. Khasia.

(16) T. OLEOIDES. (*Meissn.*)

Ident. Dec. l. c. p. 195.

SPEC. CHAR. Small tree: leaves stiffly coriaceous, obtuse or acute at the base, oblong or lanceolate, glabrous, almost veinless above: racemes short, hoary-tomentose, somewhat silky.

Peninsula?

(17) T. CORDIFOLIA. (*Meissn.*)

Ident. Dec. l. c. p. 196.

SPEC. CHAR. Small tree: leaves coriaceous, cordate at the base, oval, ovate or obovate, shortly and sharply acuminated, beneath minutely reticulated, tawny-tomentose; racemes many times longer than the petiole, slender, lax, minutely tomentose.

Peninsula?

(18) T. GLABRATA. (*Wall.*)

Ident. Dec. l. c. p. 197.—Wall. l. c. p. 67.

Syn. Laurus salicifolia, *Wight ex Wall. l. c.*

SPEC. CHAR. Shrub (?): branchlets angled at the apex: leaves coriaceous, cuneato-attenuate at the base, oblong and lanceolate, acute, almost veinless, glabrous, glaucous-green above, tawny below: racemes longer than the petiole, tomentose, glabrescent.

Dindigul hills.

GENUS X. CYLICODAPHNE.

Diœcia Dodecandria. *Sex : Syst :*

Deriv. From *Kulix*, a cup, alluding to the cup-shaped calyx.

GEN. CHAR. Flowers diœcious, involucrate : calyx 6-, or rarely 4- or 8-cleft : lobes deciduous. MALE : stamens 6—18, inner 3 or 6 furnished at the base with 2 compressed sessile glands adnate to the filament : anthers 4-celled, all introrse : pistil scarcely any. FEMALE : stamens sterile, strap-shaped, furnished with stalked or adnate glands : style short or rarely filiform : stigma peltate : ovary enclosed by the tube of the calyx : berry surrounded by or half immersed in the tube of the calyx, which is converted into a more or less and increased truncated cup.—Trees and shrubs, with the habits of Tetranthera, nor to be distinguished from that genus by any essential and certain character, except by the cup-shaped calyx.

(1) C. WIGHTIANA. (*Nees.*)

Ident. Dec. prod. XV. s. 1. p. 200.—Nees in Wall. pl. As. rar. II. p. 68.

Syn. Tetranthera Wightiana, *Wall.*

Engrav. Wight's Icon. t. 1833.

SPEC. CHAR. Small tree : leaves stiffly coriaceous, acute at the base, elliptic or oval, or obovate-oblong, obtuse or acute, green above, almost veinless, glaucine or tawny beneath, and with the branchlets tomentose or glabrate : racemes hoary or brown-tomentose : inner leaflets of the involucre and calyx silky : stamens slightly hairy at the base.

Neilgherries. Courtallum. Assam.

(2) C. SEBIFERA. (*Blume.*)

Ident. Dec. l. c. p. 202.

Syn. Litsæa sebifera, *Bl. Bidjr.*—Tetranthera macrantha, *Wall.*—T. Roxburghii, *Haask pl. Jav.*—Lepidadenia Wightiana, *Nees Syst.* p. 583.

Engrav. Wight's Icon. t. 1837.

SPEC. CHAR. Shrub : branchlets angled : leaves coriaceous, unequal at the base, long-oblong, attenuately obtuse or acuminate, glabrous above, beneath with yellowish silky pubescence : racemes short, hoary-tomentose.

Neilgherries.

(3) C. NITIDA. (*Meissn.*)

Ident. Dec. l. c. p. 203.

Syn. Tetranthera nitida, *Roxb.*

SPEC. CHAR. Shrub: branchlets sharply angular at the apex: leaves coriaceous, attenuated at the base, oblong, obtuse, shining above: racemes slender, lax.

Silhet.

(4) C. OBLONGA. (*Meissn.*)

Ident. Dec. l. c. p. 205.

Syn. Tetranthera Doskia, *Don. prod. flor. Nep.*—T. oblonga, *Nees in Wall. l. c. p.* 67.

SPEC. CHAR. Shrub: leaves scattered, subcoriaceous, long-oblong, equally attenuated at both ends, acute, glabrous, glaucescent beneath, obsoletely veined: umbels shortly corymbose. hoary-tomentose.

Assam. Khasia.

Var. STOCKSII.—Leaves a shining green above: umbels subsessile, glomerate, fructiferous ones fascicled: cupula obovate-hemispherical.

Canara.

GENUS XI. ACTINODAPHNE.

Diœcia Enneandria. *Sex: Syst:*

Deriv. From *Aktin*, a ray.

GEN. CHAR. Flowers diœcious, several from an imbricately scaled bud, proper involucre none: calyx 6-cleft, lobes deciduous. MALE: stamens 9, outer 6 eglandulose, inner ones with a sessile or stalked gland on both sides: anthers oblong, 4-celled, all introrse: staminodes none. FEMALE: stamens sterile, strap-shaped, inner 3 biglandulose above the base: style filiform: stigma discoid, sublobed: berry placed on the persistent cup-shaped base of the truncated calyx.—Trees or shrubs: leaves scattered usually at intervals or at the apex of the branchlets, penni- or rarely triplinerved: flower-buds perulate, imbricately scaled: flowers axillary, glomerate, or fascicled, or racemose, or very rarely solitary, wrapped in the scales of the bud before flowering.

(1) A. RETICULATA. (*Meissn.*)

Ident. Dec. prod. XV. p. 212.

SPEC. CHAR. Small tree (?): leaves chartaceous-herbaceous, acute at the base, lanceolate-acuminate, acute, prominently reticulated on both sides; glabrous and shining above, paler below, and with the branchlets puberulous: flower-buds hoary-tomentose.

Khasia.

(2) A. ANGUSTIFOLIA. (*Nees.*)

Ident. Dec. l. c. p. 214.—Nees in Wall. pl. As. rar. III. p. 31.

Syn. Tetranthera angustifolia, *Wall.*

Engrav. Wight's Icon. t. 1841.

SPEC. CHAR. Tree: leaves coriaceous, acute at the base, elongated-oblong, obtusely acuminated, glabrous, shining above, glaucous beneath: umbels fascicled, very shortly peduncled, hoary- or tawny-silky.

Silhet.

(3) A. HOOKERI. (*Meissn.*)

Ident. Dec. l. c. p. 218.

SPEC. CHAR. Small tree: leaves chartaceous or coriaceous, acute at the base, elliptic, oblong, or lanceolate, acuminate, promiscuously penni- and triplinerved, glabrous above, beneath glaucous and tawny-tomentose or glabrate: flowers fascicled, tawny-villous, silky.

Peninsula.

Var. a. DASYPODA.—Leaves ovate or elliptic, or rarely lanceolate-oblong, usually triplinerved, new ones covered, together with the petiole and branchlets, with yellow villi.

Near Bombay. Concans.

Var. b. GLABRATA.—Glabrous, covered with dingy tomentum on the petioles and top of the branchlets: leaves acute or rounded at the base, elliptic and oblong, almost veinless above, beneath obsoletely transversely veined, often feather-nerved.

Concans.

Var. c. LONGIFOLIA.—Branchlets and petioles powdery-tomentose: leaves elongated-oblong and lanceolate, attenuated and acutish at both ends, glabrous, usually triplinerved.

Peninsula.

(4) A. LANATA. (*Meissn.*)

Ident. Dec. l. c. p. 219.

SPEC. CHAR. Small tree: leaves chartaceo-coriaceous, lanceolate, attenuately acute at both ends or acuminate, promiscuously feather-nerved or pseudo-triplinerved, and with the branchlets densely rufous-tomentose, marginate, afterwards glabrate, shining, dotted, beneath glaucous, minutely areolate: flowers fascicled, rufous-silky.

Neilgherries.

(5) A. OBOVATA. (*Blume.*)

Ident. Dec. l. c. p. 219.

Syn. Tetranthera obovata, *Ham. ex Wall.*—Tedradenia obovata, *Nees in Wall. l. c. p.* 64.—Litsæa obovata, *Nees Syst. Laur.*

SPEC. CHAR. Tree: leaves chartaceous, large, acute at the base, elliptic or obovate-oblong, acuminate, triplinerved, shining and glabrous above, beneath glaucous, veined, puberulous or glabrous: racemes longer than the petiole, tawny-villous.

Silhet. Assam.

GENUS XII. LITSÆA.

Diœcia Hexandria. *Sex: Syst:*

GEN. CHAR. Flowers diœcious: buds covered with scales: calyx 4—6-parted, lobes deciduous. MALE: stamens 6, inner 4 or 2 with 2 glands at the base: anthers introrse, 4-celled. FEMALE: stamens sterile, 4 or 6, strap-shaped or spathulate, innermost 2 or 3 furnished with a free or adnate gland on both sides: style filiform: stigma discoid: fruit a berry: pedicel thickened or obconical.—Trees or shrubs: leaves scattered: flower-bearing buds axillary, sessile, or very shortly peduncled: scales imbricated, deciduous: flowers fascicled or glomerate.

(1) L. ZEYLANICA. (*Nees.*)

Ident. Dec. prod. XV. p. 226.

Syn. Cassia Cinnamomea, *Pluk.*—Laurus Cassia, *Linn.*—L. involucrata, *Vahl.*—L. Ceylania, *Nees.*—Tetradenia Zeylanica, *do. in Wall. pl. As. rar.* II. *p.* 64.

SPEC. CHAR. Small tree or shrub: leaves chartaceous, lanceolate or oblong, attenuately subacute or acuminate, triplinerved, few-ribbed, above glabrous, beneath glaucous, and with the younger branchlets minutely silky-puberulous, afterwards glabrate: glomerules solitary or aggregate: yellowish-tomentose, silky.

Peninsula. Malabar. Travancore. Western slopes of the Neilgherries.

Var. a. CONCOLOR.—Leaves lanceolate, more deeply triplinerved, dotted or scrobiculately areolate on both sides: nearly of the same colour, beneath paler, scarcely glaucescent.—L. oblonga, *Nees Syst.*—Wight's Icon. t. 1844.

Neilgherries.

Var. b. RIGESCENS.—Leaves stiffly coriaceous, attenuate or acute at the base, elliptic or oblong or lanceolate, tri- or tripliserved, few ribbed, veinless, beneath glaucous or at last of the name colour.

Neilgherries.

Var. c. RUBRINERVIA.—Leaves coriaceous, shortly acute at the base, ovate or elliptic-oblong, acuminate, somewhat 3-nerved, obsoletely ribbed, minutely reticulated on both sides, at last veinless, beneath paler, scarcely glaucescent.

Neilgherries.

(2) L. LANUGINOSA. (*Nees.*)

Ident. Dec. l. c. p. 221.—Nees Syst. p. 634.

Syn. Tetranthera lanuginosa, *Wall.*—Tetradenia lanuginosa. —*Nees in Wall. pl. As. rar.* II. p. 64.

SPEC. CHAR. Tree: leaves interruptedly subverticillate and scattered, elliptic or lanceolate-oblong, attenuated or acuminated at both ends, triplinerved, glabrous and shining above, beneath glaucine, and with the petiole and branchlets afterwards glabrate: flowers densely glomerate, tawny-villous, silky.

Khasia.

(3) L. FOLIOSA. (*Nees.*)

Var. PUNCTICULATA.

Ident. Dec. l. c. p. 222.

Syn. Tetradenia foliosa, *Nees in Wall. l. c. p.* 64.

SPEC. CHAR. Small tree: leaves scattered or the upper ones nearly opposite, long-petioled, coriaceous, acute at the base, oval or oblong, obtusely acuminate, triplinerved, above or on both sides, distinctly dotted or at last smooth, beneath moderately glaucous: flower-bearing buds subsessile or aggregate, sparingly silky-puberulous or glabrous.

Silhet.

Var. a. IMPUNCTATA.—Leaves very smooth, beneath moderately glaucous, dots none or beneath here and there scarcely conspicuous.

Khasia.

Var. b. CÆSIA.—Leaves dotted or smooth, beneath grey or whitish-glaucous: branchlets at the apex sparingly and minutely tomentose.—L. furfuracea, *Nees Syst.*—Tetradenia furfuracea, *Nees ap Wall. l. c. p.* 64.

Chittagong. Canara.

(4) L. STRIOLATA. (*Blume.*)

Ident. Dec. l. c. p. 223.

SPEC. CHAR. Small tree: upper leaves nearly opposite, longish-petioled, coriaceous, acute at the base, oval and oblong, caudate-acuminate, triplinerved, veins thin, densely transversely striolate, not dotted, glabrous, beneath lavender-glaucous, afterwards of the same colour: glomerules silky, soon glabrate.

Silhet. Khasia.

(5) L. SCROBICULATA. (*Meissn.*)

Ident. Dec. l. c. p. 223.

SPEC. CHAR. Tree: leaves stiffly coriaceous, long-petioled, acute at the base, ovate-elliptic or oblong, acuminate, triplinerved, above or on both sides scrobiculately areolate, glabrous, beneath glaucous or afterwards of the same colour: glomerules subsessile, sparingly silky, puberulous or glabrate.

Neilgherries.

(6) L. UMBROSA. (*Nees.*)

Ident. Dec. l. c. p. 223.—Nees Syst. p. 623.

Syn Tetranthera umbrosa, *Wall.*—Laurus umbrosa, *Nees ap Wall. l. c. p.* 64.

SPEC. CHAR. Small tree: leaves short-petioled, coriaceous, acute at the base, elliptic and oblong, acuminate, triplinerved, smooth, glabrous, beneath glaucous: glomerules almost solitary, tawny-tomentose, silky.

Silhet.

Var. a. KHASYANA.—Leaves above or on both sides dotted-areolate, often transversely veined, beneath glaucous.

Assam. Khasia.

GENUS XIII. DAPHNIDIUM.

Diœcia Enneandria. *Sex: Syst:*

Deriv. A diminutive of Daphne.

GEN. CHAR. Flowers diœcious: scales of the flower-bud covered or involucrate: calyx 6—9-parted, lobes deciduous. MALE: stamens 9 or very rarely more, innermost 3 furnished with a sessile or stalked gland on each side of the base: anthers introrse, 2-celled: staminodes none. FEMALE: stamens sterile, innermost 3 biglandulose at the base: style filiform, thickish: stigma dilated, somewhat 2-lobed: berry placed at the base of the calyx.—Trees or shrubs: leaves scattered, palmate, or rarely feather-nerved:

flower-bearing buds axillary, subsessile: flowers fascicled or glomerate or rarely solitary, covered or umbellate, and supported by their own 4-leaved involucre.

(1) D. MELOSTAMACEUM. (*Nees.*)

Ident. Nees in Wall. pl. As. rar. II. p. 63.—Dec. prod. XV. p. 228.

SPEC. CHAR. Small tree: leaves coriaceous, acute at the base, oval and oblong, obtusely acuminated, prominently 3-nerved on both sides, transversely veined, lateral nerves disappearing towards the apex: flower-buds subaggregate, sessile, few-flowered.

Silhet. Assam. Khasia.

(2) D. PULCHERRIMUM. (*Nees.*)

Ident. Nees l. c. p. 63.—Dec. l. c. p. 229.

SPEC. CHAR. Small tree: leaves chartaceo-coriaceous, acute at the base, oblong or lanceolate, narrowly and acutely caudate-acuminate, tri- or rarely triplinerved, transversely veined, glabrous above, beneath lavender-coloured or whitish, sparingly puberulous or glabrate: flower-buds glomerately fascicled on a short peduncle, silky.

Khasia. Assam.

(3) D. CAUDATUM. (*Nees.*)

Ident. Nees l. c.—Dec. l. c. p. 230.

SPEC. CHAR. Shrub: leaves chartaceous, acute or obtuse at the base, oblong-lanceolate, attenuate, acuminate, 3-nerved at the top, glabrous above, beneath veined, tawny-tomentose together with the branchlets and flower-buds, nerves very prominent above and strongly veined beneath.

Silhet. Assam. Khasia.

(4) D. BIFARIUM. (*Nees.*)

Ident. Nees l. c.—Dec. l. c. p. 231.

Syn. Laurus nacusua, *Don. prod. flor. Nep. p.* 64.

SPEC. CHAR. Small tree: leaves chartaceous, acute or obtuse at the base, oblong or lanceolate, acuminate, of the same colour, glabrous, shining or obsoletely dotted above, beneath finely veined or reticulated, and with the branchlets tawny-tomentose: leaf-buds many-flowered, scales deciduous: pedicels hoary-tomentose.

Assam. Khasia.

(5) D. ELONGATUM. (*Nees.*)

Ident. Nees l. c.—Dec. l. c. p. 231.

SPEC. CHAR. Small tree: leaves lanceolate, attenuated at both ends, glabrous and almost veinless above, densely transversely veined beneath: female buds solitary, short-peduncled, hoary-tomentose.

Khasia.

GENUS XIV. POLYADENIA.

Diœcia Enneandria. *Sex: Syst:*

Deriv. From *Polys*, many, and *Aden*, a gland.

GEN. CHAR. Flowers diœcious, umbellulate, involucred: calyx 6-parted, lobes equal, deciduous. MALE: stamens 6—9, all the filaments bearing a stalked gland at the base: anthers 2-celled, introrse. FEMALE: stamens sterile, inner ones 1—2-glandular at the base: style middle-sized: stigma dilated, 2—3-lobed: berry ellipsoid, placed at the bottom of the calyx.

(1) P. RETICULATA. (*Nees.*)

Ident. Nees in Wall. pl. As. rar. II. p. 61.—Dec. prod. XV. p. 232.

SPEC. CHAR. Tree: leaves scattered, coriaceous, feather-nerved, elliptic, or long-oblong, acute or acuminate, glabrous or shining above, beneath tomentose or puberulous: umbels axillary, fasciculate-agglomerate, each furnished with a 4-leaved involucre.

Goalpara. Silhet.

GENUS XV. APERULA.

Diœcia Enneandria. *Sex: Syst:*

GEN. CHAR. Flowers diœcious, involucred: calyx 4—6-parted, lobes unequal, deciduous. MALE: stamens 6—9, inner 2—6 biglandular at the base: anthers introrse, 2-celled. FEMALE: stamens 9, rarely 6, spathulate, inner ones or all gland-bearing: style short: stigma peltate, 2—3-lobed: berry placed at the disc-shaped base of the calyx.

A. ASSAMICA. (*Meissn.*)

Ident. Dec. prod. XV. p. 240.

SPEC. CHAR. Small tree; leaves chartaceous, elongated-oblong and lanceolate, attenuated at both ends, above or on both sides minutely reticulated, beneath glabrescent: umbels subumbellate on a very short common peduncle, long-peduncled, pedicels longer than the flower, silky-hoary.

Assam.

GENUS XVI. GYROCARPUS.

Polygamia Diœcia. *Sex: Syst:*

Deriv. From *Gyros,* a circle or ring, and *Karpos,* fruit. The seed is winged, and turns round in falling.

GEN. CHAR. Flowers polygamous: limb of the cályx superior, 4—6—8-parted, lobes in the male flowers equal, small, in the hermaphrodite ones persistent, two opposite ones larger, growing out into an erect membranaceous spathúlate wing: stamens 4, filaments alternating with the free clavate glands, or with the same adnate to the base: anthers ovate: style short: stigma capitate: drupe coriaceous, long 2-winged at the top.—Trees: leaves simple, undivided, or here and there 2—3- (rarely 5-) lobed: panicles appearing early: flowers dichotomously cymose, axillary ones solitary hermaphrodite, rest male small: stamens exserted.

(1) G. ASIATICUS. (*Willd.*)

Ident. Willd. sp. IV. p. 982.—Dec. prod. XV. p. 248.

Engrav. Roxb. Cor. II. t. 1.

SPEC. CHAR. Tree: leaves ovate-triangular, subcordate, shortly 3—5-lobed and entire, above glabrous, beneath canescently pubescent: common peduncle shorter than the petioles, filaments puberulous: wings of the drupe narrow-cuneate, lanceolate, obtuse: flowers very small, greenish-yellow.

Mountains of Coromandel and other hilly parts of the Peninsula. Banks of the Kistna. Flowering in the cold season.

GENUS XVII. ILLIGERA.

Pentandria Monogynia. *Sex: Syst:*

GEN. CHAR. Flowers hermaphrodite: calyx 1—3-bracteolate at the base, tube short, narrow, adnate to the ovary, constricted at the top, lobes of the 10-parted biseriate limb equal, somewhat inflexedly valvate in æstivation, deciduous, inner ones or all petaloid: stamens inserted on an epigynous, 5-glandular ring, enclosed, alternating with the inner lobes of the calyx: filaments filiform, furnished at the base outside with two twin, approximate, small membranaceous hoods, extrorsely foveate, or opening by a pore at the oblique apex: anthers adnate, oblong: connectivum thickish, truncated: style filiform: stigma membranaceous, peltate, repand: drupe inferior, wingless, 1-seeded.—Climbing shrubs: leaves scattered, exstipulate, palmately trifoliolate, leaflets coriaceous, feather-nerved, quite entire: panicles axillary: flowers cymose.

(1) I. OBTUSA. (*Meissn.*)

Ident. Dec. prod. XV. p. 251.

SPEC. CHAR. Climbing: leaflets acute at the base, oval, rounded, very obtuse, deeply ribbed, almost veinless, and with the branches glabrous: drupes globose-oval, tawny-tomentose.

Peninsula.

GENUS XVIII. CASSYTHA.

Enneandria Monogynia. *Sex: Syst:*

Deriv. The Greek name of the Cuscuta, which this resembles.

GEN. CHAR. Flowers hermaphrodite: calyx urceolate, 6-cleft, persistent, outer lobes smaller, often dwarf, tube at last subglobose, fleshy: stamens 9, in 3 rows, inserted on the throat: uniform: filament short, broad: anther ovate, 2-celled: outer 6 stamens introrse, without glands at the base, inner 3 extrorse, with twin sessile glands at the base, adnate to the filament, alternating with 3 triangular or glanduliform, stalked, or rarely sessile, staminodes: ovary enclosed in the tube of the calyx, free: style short: stigma small, depressed: caryopsis somewhat fleshy.—Leafless, parasitic herbs, twining round other plants: leaves abortive, dwarf, scale-shaped: flowers glomerate, or spiked, or capitate, seldom fascicled or racemose, sometimes panicled, each with 3 bracts, small.

(1) C. FILIFORMIS. (*Linn.*)

Ident. Linn. sp. ed. I. p. 35.—Dec. prod. XV. p. 255.

Engrav. Wight's Icon. t. 1847.—Rheede Mal. VII. t. 44.—Hook. Ex. flor. t. 167.

SPEC. CHAR. Parasitic, herbaceous, leafless; stems long, twining, from a papilliform root: flowers small, in simple or compound spikes: fruit 1-seeded.

Common everywhere in hedges.

ORDER CXXXII. MYRISTICACEÆ.

Flowers diœcious: calyx 3-lobed, sometimes 2—4 lobed in the same plant, lobes valvate in æstivation: stamens 3—18, often 6—12, monadelphous, filaments connate, anthers alternating with the lobes of the calyx, linear or oval, 2-celled, dehiscing lengthwise, adnate at the back or base of the stem of the filaments, often connate, sometimes free from the middle or the base: connectivum perspicuous, often ending in a very short tooth proper to each anther or common to all: ovary superior: stigma subsessile, scarcely 2-lobed or depresso-capitate: ovule 1 from the base of the ovary: fruit fleshy, slowly dehiscing by 2, rarely 4, valves: seed sessile, often wrapped round by a sweet-smelling false aril, which is often lobed, and as if torn from the middle, red or orange, fleshy or thin: albumen ruminate: embryo small: cotyledons diverging, ovate, flat, or undulate: radicle short, inferior, conical.—Trees, often aromatic and abounding in acrid juice: leaves alternate, distichous, quite entire, often pellucid-dotted, feather-nerved: stipules none: racemes or panicles axillary, sometimes supra-axillary: flowers usually pedicelled, small, externally stellately tomentose: albumen often sebaceous or oily.

GENUS I. MYRISTICA.

Diœcia Monadelphia. *Sex: Syst:*

Deriv. From *Myrrha*, myrrh, alluding to the fragrant odour of the fruit.

GEN. CHAR. Same as that of the order.

(1) M. MALABARICA. (*Lam.*)

Ident. Dec. prod. XIV. p. 194.—Hook. and Thoms. flor. Ind. I. p. 163.

Engrav. Rheede Mal. VI. t. v.

SPEC. CHAR. Leaves narrow-oblong or elliptic-lanceolate, acute at both ends or obtuse, quite glabrous, glaucous beneath: male inflorescence axillary, dichotomously cymose, many-flowered, longer than the petiole, female few-flowered, alabastrum globose, pubescent externally, bract very broad, embracing the base: fruit oblong, tawny-hoary: aril lacunose, lobes twisted and folded into a cone at the top.

Forests of Malabar. Concans. The aril is not very fragrant, the nut scarcely aromatic.

(2) M. FARQUHARIANA. (*Wall.*)

Ident. Dec. l. c. p. 200.—Hook. and Thoms. l. c. p. 161 (partly).

SPEC. CHAR. Leaves lanceolate-acuminate, acute at the base, glabrous, stiffly coriaceous: nerves lateral, 12—15 on each side: male panicles axillary, composite, diffuse, 2—4 times shorter than the leaf, and with the flowers externally rusty-pulverulent: flowers at the apex umbellulate or nearly solitary, somewhat longer than the pedicel, ebracteate: calyx obovoid, subtrifid, lobes ovate, erect: anthers much longer than the stem, free at the top.

Mercara in Coorg.

(3) M. GLABRA. (*Blume.*)

Ident. Blume, bidjr. p. 576.—Dec. l. c. p. 202.—Hook. and Thoms. l. c. p. 161.

Engrav. Blume's Rumphia I. t. 64. fig. 1.

SPEC. CHAR. Leaves lanceolate or ovate-oblong, acute, long-narrowed at the base, glabrous: nerves on both sides 14—15: panicles axillary, branched, longer than the petiole: male flowers globose, nearly equalling the pedicel.

Silhet.

(4) M. LONGIFOLIA. (*Wall.*)

Ident. Dec. l. c. p. 204.—Hook. and Thoms. l. c. p. 156.

Syn. M. linifolia, *Roxb.*

SPEC. CHAR. Branchlets furfuraceous: leaves large, oblong-lanceolate, cordate at the base, rarely rounded, narrowed at the apex, obtuse, glabrous: nerves strong, 25—30 on each side: fascicles of flowers axillary, shorter than the petiole: peduncle and pedicels very short, velvety: anthers 12—18, around a concave disc: fruit oblong, tomentose.

Khasia hills. Chittagong.

(5) M. ERRATICA. (*Hook. and Thoms.*)

Ident. Hook. and Thoms. l. c. p. 156.—Dec. l. c. p. 205.

SPEC. CHAR. Branchlets mealy: leaves narrow-lanceolate or broad-linear, acute, attenuated at the apex, acute at the base, glabrous above, beneath together with the midrib and nerves ashy-mealy, nerves lateral, 23—26: flowers few, at the apex of an axillary peduncle: anthers 12, around a flat disc: fruit broad, oval or subglobose: tomentum very short, hoary: aril thickly fleshy, top lacerated.

Khasia hills.

(6) M. ATTENUATA. (*Wall.*)

Ident. Dec. l. c. p. 205.—Hook. and Thoms. l. c. p. 157.

SPEC. CHAR. Branchlets furfuraceous: leaves oblong-lanceolate, long-narrowed, acute or rounded at the base, glabrescent: nerves lateral, 15—20 on each side: peduncles axillary, few-flowered, pedicels longer than the peduncle, equal to or longer than the petiole: calyx subglobose, loosely tomentose: anthers 12, around a flat disc: fruit oval or oblong, tawny-tomentose: aril very thin, lobed at the apex.

Concan hills.

(7) M. GIBBOSA. (*Hook. and Thoms.*)

Ident. Dec. l. c. p. 205.—Hook. and Thoms. l. c. p. 158.

SPEC. CHAR. Small tree: branchlets glabrous: leaves narrow-lanceolate, acuminate, acute at the base, glabrous above, beneath somewhat mealy, glabrescent: nerves lateral, 19—20 on each side: fruit oblong, tomentose, oblique, occasionally gibbous: aril thin, somewhat lacerated at the top only.

Khasia hills.

ORDER CXXXIII. PROTEACEÆ.

Flowers hermaphrodite: calyx 4-cleft, regular or irregular: sepals 4, linear or spathulate, valvate in æstivation: stamens 4, opposite the segments of the calyx, inserted on them: filaments filiform, usually very short, free: anthers affixed by the back or base, 2-celled, linear oblong, ovate or cordate: ovary sessile or stalked, 1-celled: ovule 1, or 2 collateral, or several in 2 rows: style terminal, filiform, rarely very short, persistent or deciduous, equalling the calyx, or often long exserted, arched and recurved in the flower-bud: stigma undivided: fruit often compressed, or ventricose or gibbous, smooth or wrinkled, warty or echinate, sometimes indehiscent, 1-celled, 1—2-seeded: seed without albumen, sessile, ovoid or globose: embryo straight, with 2 cotyledons, sometimes more: radicle inferior.—Trees or shrubs.

GENUS I. HELICIA.

Tetrandria Monogynia. *Sex: Syst:*

Deriv. From *Helix*, a screw, alluding to the twisting of the petals.

GEN. CHAR. Flowers regular, racemose: calyx clavate-cylindric, straight, sepals 4, subspathulate, antheriferous below the apex, afterwards free, revolute, deciduous: anthers subsessile, linear or oval, apiculate or muticous: glands hypogynous, 4, free or connate: ovary short-stalked or sessile, 1-celled, ovules 2, ascending: style filiform: stigma vertical, clavate: follicle woody, indehiscent, 1-seeded by abortion: seed subglobose, wingless: leaves scattered, or here and there opposite, simple, dentate or entire: racemes axillary or terminal, simple: pedicels twin, 1-bracteate, free or half connate.

(1) H. ROBUSTA. (*Wall.*)

Ident. Dec. prod. XIV. p. 440.—Horsf. pl. Jav. p. 83.

Syn. Rhopala robusta, *Roxb. flor. Ind.* I. *p*. 363.

Engrav. Wight's Icon. t. 191.

SPEC. CHAR. Tree: leaves obovate-oblong, obtuse or acuminate, acutely serrated, almost quite entire below the middle, subcuneate-attenuate into a very short petiole, veins thin, densely reticulated, a little prominent beneath: racemes shorter than the leaf: pedicels short: glands hypogynous, connate into a 4-crenated small cup.

Silhet.

(2) H. EXCELSA. (*Blume*).

Ident. Dec. l. c. p. 441.—Horsf. l. c. p. 84.

Syn. Rhopala excelsa, *Roxb. l. c. p*. 365.

Engrav. Wight's Icon. t. 190.

SPEC. CHAR. Tree: leaves obovate or cuneate-oblong, obtuse or acuminate towards the apex, coarsely and obtusely serrated, lightly and loosely reticulated on both sides: racemes dense-flowered, and with the younger branchlets rusty-pubescent: pedicels short: ovary rufous-hirsute: scales hypogynous, free, round, glabrous.

Forests near Chittagong.

(3) H. NILAGIRICA. (*Bedd.*)

Ident. Beddome in Madr. Journ. July 1864 (cum fig.).

SPEC. CHAR. Glabrous: leaves broad-ovate, acute, attenuated at the base, coarsely and sharply dentate with large sinuses, except near the base, prominently reticulated: racemes densely flowered, much shorter than the leaves: pedicels generally 2-flowered, with a minute bract at the base of the pedicel: hypogynous glands connate into a 4-crenated cup.

Western slopes of the Neilgherries.

6

(4) H. Cochinchinensis. (*Lour.*)

Ident. Lour. flor. Coch. p. 83.—Dec. l. c. p. 442.

Syn. Rhopala Cochinchinensis, *R. Br. in Linn. Trans.* 10. *p.* 192.—R. robusta, *Spreng. syst.* I. *p.* 482 (partly, not Roxb.).

Spec. Char. Middling-sized tree: leaves petioled, ovate-elliptic, short acuminate, minutely serrated or here and there quite entire: racemes axillary, nearly equalling the leaves, dense-flowered: hypogynous scales half connate.

Assam.

ORDER CXXXIV. THYMELÆACEÆ.

Flowers hermaphrodite: calyx inferior, coloured, tubular, infundibuliform, campanulate or urceolate, tube continuous or articulately breaking above the base: limb 4—5 lobed, lobes connivent or spreading, imbricated in æstivation: scales hypogynous, 4—8, small, membranaceous, fleshy or filiform, placed round the ovary, free or concrete into a ring or cup, or adnate to the calyx: stamens 2 or 4—5, or 8, or 10, inserted on the throat or tube: filaments filiform, adnate to the calyx even to the middle of the tube or throat or base of the lobes, sometimes long and exserted: anthers 2-celled, oval, oblong, or linear, affixed by the base or back, erect or versatile, dehiscing by two longitudinal clefts: ovary free, 1—2-celled, ovule 1, solitary pendulous: style simple: stigma capitate, entire, papillose, rarely smooth: fruit indehiscent, nut-like, drupaceous, or baccate, 1-, seldom 2-celled, cells 1-, rarely 2—3-seeded: albumen none, or thin, or fleshy: embryo straight: radicle superior, short, straight.—Shrubs, seldom trees or herbs: hairs, when present, simple: leaves exstipulate, scattered or opposite, simple, undivided, quite entire, articulate at the base: inflorescence terminal or rarely axillary: flowers capitate, fascicled, umbellate, racemose or spiked, rarely solitary, usually without bracteoles, articulated with the pedicel or receptacle, often surrounded by a common (sometimes coloured) involucre, purple, white, yellow, or greenish, very rarely blue, often beautiful and fragrant, usually silky-pubescent outside.

GENUS I. CANSJERA.

Tetrandria Monogynia. *Sex: Syst:*

Deriv. The Malabar name Latinised.

Gen. Char. Calyx coloured, campanulate-urceolate, deciduous, throat without scales, limb 4-toothed, reflexed: small hypogynous scales 4, free, alternate with the stamens, denticulate: stamens inserted at the bottom of the calyx and opposite its lobes, filaments capillary, free, enclosed: anthers fixed at the base, short exserted: ovary sessile, fleshy, cell very small near the middle, ovule at first erect, afterwards reflexed: style terminal, filiform: stigma exserted, capitate, slightly 4-furrowed: fruit naked, ovoid: seed erect.—Climbing shrubs: leaves scattered, somewhat fleshy, quite entire, glabrous: spikes axillary, simple, solitary or aggregate: flowers small, yellow, stalked, with a small bract at the base.

(1) C. Rheedii. (*Gmel.*)

Ident. Dec. prod. XIV. p. 519.—Gmel. syst. I. p. 280.

Syn. C. Malabarica, *Lam.*—C. scandens, *Roxb.*—Daphne monostachya, *Willd.*

Engrav. Wight's Icon. t. 1861.—Roxb. Cor. II. t. 103.—Rheede, Mal. VII. t. 2—4.

Spec. Char. Branchlets minutely puberulous: leaves ovate or elliptic-oblong, acuminate, glabrous: spikes fascicled or solitary, thickish: calyx middle-sized, and with the rachis minutely puberulous.

Malabar. Coromandel.

GENUS II. DAPHNE.

Octandria Monogynia. *Sex: Syst:*

Deriv. The Greek term for the Laurel.

Gen. Char. Calyx coloured, rarely green, tubular or funnel-shaped, deciduous, rarely persistent, limb regular, 4-parted, spreading, throat without scales: anthers 8, in a double row, inserted on the throat, subsessile, oblong: style terminal, very short or none: stigma capitate: berry fleshy or coriaceous, naked, a long time enclosed by the calyx: seed nut-like.—Shrubs: leaves scattered or rarely opposite, coriaceous, evergreen: fascicles or heads of flowers 2—8-flowered, terminal, rarely lateral, sessile or peduncled, sometimes involucrate, very rarely panicled, axillary, racemose: calyx white or rose-coloured, yellow, or greenish, often very fragrant.

(1) D. Wallichii. (*Meissn.*)

Ident. Dec. prod. XIV. p. 540.

Syn. D. involucrata, *Wall. in As. res.* XIII. t. 6.—Eriosolena Wallichii, *Meissn. Gen.* II. *p.* 242.

Spec. Char. Leaves oblong-lanceolate, acuminate, veined, and with the branches glabrous: peduncles short: involucre 2-leaved, somewhat tomentose, caducous: leaflets obtuse: calyx silky-villous, lobes oblong, acute, many times shorter than the tube, inner ones smaller: ovary bearded at the top.

Khasia hills. Pundua.

(2) D. longifolia. (*Meissn.*)

Ident. Dec. l. c. p. 540.

Spec. Char. Leaves long-lanceolate, attenuated at both ends: peduncles somewhat tomentose, many times longer than the petiole: involucre 4-leaved, leaflets acuminate, pubescent, caducous: calyx downy, lobes oblong, acute, nearly equalling the narrow tube, inner ones shorter: ovary glabrous.

Pundua. Silhet.

(3) D. papyracea. (*Wall.*)

Ident. Wall. ap. Steud. Nom. ed. 2. p. 483.—Dec. l. c. p. 537.

Syn. D. odora, *Don. flor. Nep. p.* 68.—D. cannabina, *Wall. in As. res.* XIII. p. 315. and t. 7—8.—D. papyrifera, *Ham. MSS.*

Spec. Char. Tree: leaves lanceolate or oblong, veined, glabrous: fascicles terminal and lateral, sessile, bracteated: calyx funnel-shaped, pubescent, lobes ovate-oblong, shorter than the tube: ovary glabrous.

Khasia.

Var. a. latifolia.—Leaves lanceolate or elliptic-oblong: lobes of the calyx acuminate.

Pundua. Silhet.

Var. b. parvifolia.—Leaves smaller, oval-oblong.

Khasia.

GENUS III. LASIOSIPHON.

Decandria Monogynia. *Sex: Syst:*

Deriv. From *Lasios*, woolly, alluding to the tomentose capitules.

GEN. CHAR. Flowers pentamerous: calyx coloured, pubescent outside, tube slender, deciduous above the long hairy base, limb 5-parted, regular: scales 5, petaloid, alternate to the upper anthers, exserted, entire or 2-cleft: anthers 10, inserted at the throat in 2 rows, subsessile, attached by the back near the base, linear or oblong: ring hypogynous, membranaceous, surrounding the base of the ovary, very small.—Shrubs: leaves scattered or opposite, herbaceous: capitules terminal, often peduncled, usually many-flowered, surrounded by a many-leaved involucre: receptacle hemispherical, villous.

(1) L. ERIOCEPHALUS. (*Decaisne.*)

Ident. Dec. prod. XIV. p. 597.—Decaisne in Jacq. voy. p. 148.

Syn. Lachnæa eriocephala, *Heyne.*—Daphne eriocephala, *Wall.*—Gnidia eriocephala, *Meissn.*

Engrav. Wight's Icon. t. 1859.

SPEC. CHAR. Leaves scattered, lanceolate, acute, glabrous, involucral ones small, slightly shorter than the short peduncled capitulum, imbricated, oval-oblong, acute, hoary-tomentose, outer ones deciduous: calyx white-villous, with long hairs below, lobes oblong, obtuse: scales 5, minute, somewhat fleshy, obovate, emarginate.

Neilgherries.

(2) L. SISPARENSIS. (*Meissn.*)

Ident. Dec. l. c. p. 598.

Syn. Gnidia Sisparensis, *Gardn. Contrib. to Flora Ceyl. p.* 15.

Engrav. Wight's Icon. t. 1860.

SPEC. CHAR. Leaves oblong, veined, glabrous; floral ones ovate-oblong, silky-villous on both sides, a little shorter than the subsessile capitule: calyx brown-villous, hairy at the base, lobes ovate, obtuse: scales obcordate.

Western slopes of the Neilgherries, near Sispara.

(3) L. SPECIOSUS. (*Decaisne.*)

Ident. Dec. l. c. p. 598.—Decaisne l. c. t. 150.

Syn. Gnidia eriocephala, *Ralph. enum.* p. 113.

Spec. Char. Leaves scattered, very short-petioled, lanceolate, and oblong, prominently reticulated beneath, quite glabrous, involucral ones nearly equalling the short peduncled capitule, oblong, hoary, exterior ones slightly glabrous: calyx hoary, lobes ovate, obtuse, exceeding by half the 5 linear 2-cleft scales.

Mountains of India. Poonah, in the Deccan.

(4) L. Metzianus. (*Miq.*)

Ident. Miquel Anal. Bot. II. p. 3. t. 1.—Dec. l. c. p. 598.

Syn. Gnidia monticola, *Miq. in Sched. pl. Metz. Flora p.* 557.

Spec. Char. Leaves scattered, sessile, coriaceous, lanceolate, attenuated at both ends, acute, veined, and with the branchlets glabrous, involucral ones smaller, shorter than the subsessile capitule, oval-lanceolate, acute, hoary, outer ones slightly glabrous: calyx hirsute, a little swollen below the middle, long-bearded: lobes oblong-obtuse: scalelets 5, short, linear, entire: capitules globose, dense-flowered.

Western Ghauts. Canara. South Mahratta country.

GENUS IV. WIKSTRŒMIA.

Octandria Monogynia. *Sex: Syst:*

Gen. Char. Flowers tetramerous: calyx coloured, deciduous, tube cylindric or funnel-shaped, limb 4-cleft, equal, throat naked: perigynous scales none, hypogynous ones 4, very small, linear, free or connate below: anthers 8, in two rows at the top of the tube, subsessile, enclosed: ovary 1-celled, ovule pendulous: style terminal: stigma capitate: berry drupaceous, sometimes dry: seed inverse.—Trees or shrubs: leaves opposite, veined, deciduous: peduncles terminal and axillary, simple or rarely corymbosely branched, many-flowered at the top: flowers sessile or very shortly pedicelled, subcapitate or afterwards spiked or racemose from an excrescent axis.

(1) W. canescens. (*Meissn.*)

Ident. Dec. prod. XIV. p. 547.

Syn. Daphne canescens, *Wall.*—D. sericea, *Don. prod. flor. Nep. p.* 69 (not Vahl).

Spec. Char. Shrub branches twiggy, tomentose at the top: leaves scattered, herbaceous, short-petioled, lanceolate or oblong, acute, hoary-pubescent: peduncles terminal and in the uppermost axils thin, undivided: spikes few-flowered, capituliform: calyx slender, hoary-tomentose, lobes much shorter than the tube: ovary pubescent.

Khasia. Assam.

GENUS V. LINOSTOMA.

Decandria Monogynia. *Sex: Syst:*

GEN. CHAR. Flowers pentamerous: calyx coloured, half-5-cleft, deciduous, tube campanulate, lobes equal, spreading: scales 10, inserted on the throat, alternating with and shorter than the stamens, petaloid, oblong-linear, exserted: stamens inserted on the throat, nearly on one row, shorter than the lobes: filaments subulate, exserted, alternate, shorter: anthers adnate by the back, oblong, obtuse: ovary sessile, ovoid, hirsute, ovule pendulous: style terminal, capillary, exserted: stigma capitate, papillose: drupe (?) naked or a dry berry.—Shrubs: leaves opposite: floral ones membranaceous, of different shapes: umbels terminal.

(1) L. DECANDRUM. (*Wall.*)

Ident. Dec. prod. XIV. p. 599.

Syn. Nectandra decandra, *Roxb. flor. Ind.* II. *p.* 425.

SPEC. CHAR. Leaves opposite: lower ones coriaceous, lanceolate, acuminate, veins thin, parallel, densely transversely lineate, floral ones cordate-oblong, rather obtuse, loosely veined: calyx externally glabrous, tube hairy within: ovary villous.

Silhet mountains, near Chittagong.

GENUS VI. AQUILARIA.

Decandria Monogynia. *Sex: Syst:*

Deriv. The wood is called *Bois d'Aigle,* from the Latin *Aquila,* perhaps from its strength.

GEN. CHAR. Calyx campanulate, 5-cleft: scales of the throat 10, exserted, pilose, connate at the base into a crown: stamens 10: filaments adnate to the tube of the calyx, shortly free at the top, somewhat exserted: anthers fixed by the base: ovary sessile, 1-celled, ovule 1, pendulous from near the apex: style none, or exceeding the stamens: stigma convex or 2-cleft, papillose: capsule woody, obovate, compressed, 2-valved: seeds 2, or solitary by abortion, flat-convex.—Trees: leaves scattered: flowers axillary and terminal, umbellate or subsolitary.

(1) A. AGALLOCHA. (*Roxb.*)

Ident Dec. prod. XIV. p. 601. II. p. 59.—Roxb. fl. Ind. II. p. 422.

Engrav. Royle Ill. t. 36. fig. 1.

SPEC. CHAR. Large tree: leaves short-petioled, elliptic or lanceolate-oblong, acuminate, attenuated at the base, glabrous: umbels subsessile.

Silhet. Assam. Eastern Bengal, near Goalpara.

ORDER CXXXV. ELÆAGNACEÆ.

Flowers hermaphrodite, regular: calyx inferior, simple, tubular, limb 2—4-parted, usually coloured inside: stamens seldom free, usually connate with the calyx, and equal in number to and alternate with its segments: free portion of the filaments very short: anthers 2-celled, dehiscing by a double cleft, affixed by the back: pistil simple, free: ovary enclosed by the increased tube of the calyx: style erect, simple, stigmatose above: fruit 1-celled, 1-seeded, pericarp membranaceous: seed erect: embryo straight, surrounded by narrow albumen: radicle inferior: cotyledons narrow.—Trees and shrubs: branchlets often spinescent: leaves alternate, rarely opposite, simple, feather-nerved, quite entire, short-petioled: stipules none: leaf-buds naked: flowers solitary or aggregated in the lower axils of the branchlets, sessile or pedicelled, hence sometimes collected in spikes or axillary racemules, seldom arranged in axillary dichotomous cymes, yellow or seldom whitish, often fragrant: fruit acid or tasteless, yellowish or red, partly eatable.

GENUS I. ELÆAGNUS.

Tetrandria Monogynia. *Sex: Syst:*

Deriv. From *Elaia*, an olive, and *Agnos*, the chaste tree, from the resemblance the tree bears.

GEN. CHAR. Flowers hermaphrodite or male by the abortion of the pistil: limb of the calyx cylindric-campanulate below, 4-lobed, valvate in æstivation: fruit pseudo-drupaceous, limb afterwards deciduous.—Trees or shrubs: leaves alternate, petioled, quite entire: flowers pedicelled, axillary, solitary or aggregate, or forming short axillary leafed racemes, yellow or white within: fruit fleshy or dry.

(1) E. KOLOGA. (*Schlecht.*)

Ident. Dec. prod. XIV. p. 611.

Syn. E. latifolia, *Wight, Icon. t.* 1856.

SPEC. CHAR. Small tree: branchlets unarmed, densely rusty scurfy: leaves elliptic, obtuse at the apex, more or less acute at the base, above green, smooth, beneath with the flowers from silver and rusty scaly: flowers pedicelled, deflexed, afterwards growing out into short leafy axillary branchlets: tube of the calyx subcylindric, attenuated below, limb broader, urceolate-tubular, lobes broad ovate, acute, with short stellate hairs within, limb slightly constricted: style densely hairly: fruit ellipsoid, a little narrowed at both ends.

Neilgherries.

(2) E. CONFERTA. (*Roxb.*)

Ident. Roxb. flor. Ind. ed. Car. I. p. 460.—Dec. l. c. p. 612.

SPEC. CHAR. Shrubby: branches covered with rusty scurf: leaves elliptic or oblong-elliptic, glabrous, green above, beneath densely covered with silvery and rusty scurf: flowers arranged in very short many-flowered axillary racemes, scurfy as the leaves: tube of the calyx cylindric, limb 4-angular, broader, campanulated, slightly constricted below the triangular lobes: style densely hairy at the base: fruit oblong, succulent, red: flowers straw-coloured.

Western Ghauts. Silhet. Cochin. Flowering in January and February.

ORDER CXXXVI. SANTALACEÆ.

Flowers hermaphrodite or polygamo-diœcious: tube of the calyx not distinct from the pedicel, more or less connate with the ovary, usually bearing at the apex a single verticil, seldom two verticils of lobes: lobes of the single verticil or the inner one 5—4—3, often connate at the base, valvate in æstivation: stamens opposite the verticil lobes, inserted at their base or free part of the tube: filaments short: anthers erect at the apex of the filament, or usually inserted by the back and introrse, 2-celled, dehiscing lengthwise or upwards with a broad mouth: ovary inferior, either first free, afterwards connate, or adhering only by the base, 1-celled: style enclosed, entire or 2—3—4—5-lobed at the top: ovules pendulous, 2—3—5, simple: fruit nut-like or rarely baccate, indehiscent: seed 1 by abortion: albumen fleshy: embryo straight: radicle superior: cotyledons linear or oblong.—Herbs or shrubs, rarely trees, often parasitic: leaves without stipules, usually alternate, sometimes opposite, entire, feather-nerved or 3—5-nerved with oblique lateral nerves, usually narrow, seldom petioled: flowers white, greenish or dirty yellow or red, small: inflorescence terminal, when the leaves are opposite, usually indefinite with alternate leaves, flowers then spiked or capitate, or arranged in extra-axillary spikelets: peduncle connate with the floral leaf: bracteoles usually 2, lateral, accompanying a solitary flower or lateral flowers in a cymelet: pedicels none or short: fruit small and caducous.

GENUS I. PYRULARIA.

Polygamia Diœcia. *Sex: Syst:*

GEN. CHAR. Flowers hermaphrodite or unisexual, males subglobose below, females turbinate: calyx 5—4-cleft, valvate in æstivation: hairs long, entangled, or an ovate fimbriated scale stretching from the base of each lobe to the anther, and there adhering to the hairs: stamens opposite the lobes, inserted at their base: filament short, sometimes 2-forked at the apex: anther ellipsoid, 2-celled, cells very distinct, dehiscing, disc cup-shaped, 5-lobed at the margin, lobes ovate, obtuse, alternating with the tubes of the calyx: ovary half inferior in hermaphrodite, inferior in the female flowers: ovules 2—3, pendulous or divergent from the apex of the placenta: style enclosed, apex 2—3 lobed in hermaphrodite flowers, depresso-capitate in females: drupe inferior, pear-shaped, putamen thin, warty, 1-seeded: albumen fleshy, oily: embryo minute: radicle inferior.—Trees or shrubs: leaves alternate, entire: spikes or racemes long, pubescent: flowers sessile or pedicelled in the axil of a bract, externally pilose.

(1) P. WALLICHIANA. (*Alph. Dec.*)

Ident. Dec. prod. XIV. p. 629.—W. and A. in Ed. Journ. XV. p. 180.

Syn. Scleropyrum Wallichianum, *Arn.*—Sphærocarya Wallichiana, *R. W. Cat. No.* 948.—Idu Mulli, *Rheede.*

Engrav. Rheede Mal. IV. t. 18.—Wight's Icon. t. 241.

SPEC. CHAR. Large tree, here and there thorny: leaves ovate or ovate-lanceolate, acute or obtuse: male rachis dense-flowered: spikes axillary, solitary, twin or ternate, 2—3 times shorter than the leaf: bracts pubescent externally, lanceolate, under each male flower: tube of the male perianth turbinate, female obconical.

Malabar.

GENUS II. SPHÆROCARYA.

Pentandria Monogynia. *Sex: Syst:*

Deriv. From *Sphaira*, a globe, and *Karyon*, a nut, alluding to the seed.

GEN. CHAR. Calyx 5-parted: petals 5, minute, alternating with the stamens: scales 5, minute, fimbriated, inserted between the stamens and petals: ovary without a disc: style undivided: drupe inferior, smooth, globose, without a suture.

(1) S. LEPROSA. (*Dalz.*)

Ident. Dalz. Bomb. flor. p. 223.—Hook. Journ. Bot. III. p. 34.—Dec. prod. XIV. p. 629.

SPEC. CHAR. Tree: leaves oblong, coriaceous, glabrous, rounded at the base, acute at the apex: flowers subsessile, clustered on a scaly axillary tubercle: calyx with 5 very short orbicular divisions: petals linear-acute: filaments adnate to the petals: fruit spherical, covered with scurfy scales.

Warree country, in the Concan. Flowering in the cold season.

GENUS III. OSYRIS.

Diœcia Triandria. *Sex: Syst:*

Deriv. From *Ozos*, a branch, in allusion to the numerous pliant branches.

GEN. CHAR. Flowers diœcious or hermaphrodite: calyx slender in the male flowers, obconical in the others, deeply 3—4-lobed, lobes ovate-acute, one in the trimerous flowers opposite the bract, all in the tetramerous ones lateral towards the axis and bract, hairs in the middle few or none, distinct from the anther: stamens 3—4: filament short: anther 2-celled: disc concave, lobes round, clothing the upper and entire portion of the calyx: ovary fleshy, inferior: style short: stigmas 3—4: ovules usually 3, sometimes 2—4: drupe ovoid-globose, crowned with the remains of the lobes and disc: seed filling the drupe: albumen copious: embryo oblique: radicle superior: cotyledons lanceolate-terete, half-incurved, longer than the radicle.—Trees or shrubs: branches angled: leaves alternate or seldom opposite, flat, mucronate: male flowers heaped together at the apex of the peduncle, females solitary or few: bracts and bracteoles caducous.

(1) O. WIGHTIANA. (*Wall.*)

Ident. Dec. prod. XIV. p. 638.

Engrav. Wight's Icon. t. 1853.

Spec. Char. Shrubby, much branched, glabrous: young shoots 3-sided, with prominent, sharp angles: leaves from oblong-elliptic lanceolate to elliptic-obovate mucronate: male flowers umbellato-capitulate: peduncles axillary, 1—3-flowered, lengthening as the fruit advances: ovary conical: limb of the perianth 3-lobed: style short: stigma 3-lobed: fruit small, red when ripe.

Common on the Ghauts. Neilgherries. Pulney hills. Belgaum.

GENUS IV. THESIUM.

Pentandria Monogynia. *Sex: Syst:*

Deriv. From *Thes*, a labouring servant, alluding to the mean appearance of the plants.

Gen. Char. Flowers hermaphrodite: free part of the calyx sometimes hypocrateriform, usually funnel-shaped or campanulate, 5-, seldom 4-lobed, persistent: stamens from the base of each lobe: filament linear: anther oblong, 2-celled, cells dehiscing lengthwise: disc epigynous: ovary inferior: style reaching the stamens, or much shorter: stigma obtuse or capitate, sometimes obscurely 2—3-lobed: ovules 3, pendulous: nut ellipsoid, caducous, often crowned with the calyx: embryo in the axis of fleshy albumen: radicle superior, longer than the cotyledons.—Herbs or small shrubs: leaves alternate, 1—3-nerved: flowers axillary, solitary, or usually in 3—5-flowered cymes, sessile in the axil of a leaf or bract, or terminating the extra-axillary peduncles: solitary flowers usually bibracteolate, besides the bract, central ones of the cymes furnished only with the bract of the cyme, lateral ones then furnished with a bract and bracteole: cymes loose or approximate: calyx white, greenish, yellowish, or rarely purplish.

(1) T. Wightianum. (*Wall.*)

Ident. Dec. prod. XIV. p. 647.

Engrav. Wight's Icon. t. 1852.

Spec. Char. Suffruticose, diffuse, decumbent: leaves linear-lanceolate, acute: flowers solitary, or twin at the apex of the branches: bract linear-lanceolate, subulate, scarcely longer than the nut, bracteoles scarcely longer than the bract: nut ovoid, sessile.

Common in pastures on the Neilgherries.

GENUS V. SANTALUM.

Tetrandria Monogynia. *Sex : Syst :*

Deriv. From the Persian word *Sandal*, signifying useful.

GEN. CHAR. Calyx campanulate, 4-cleft, lobes ovate or triangular, base internally furnished with a small bundle of hairs stretching towards the anthers: stamens 4, rarely 5, opposite the lobes: filament ligulate or filiform: anther ovoid, 2-celled, cells deeply bilocellate, dehiscing lengthwise by a single cleft: disc concave: ovary inferior, 1-celled: style conical or cylindric: stigmas 2—3—4: placenta central, bearing pendulous ovules, the same number as the stigmas: drupe globose or obovoid, crowned with the cicatrix left by the fallen lobes of the calyx: seed inverted: embryo cylindric-fusiform: radicle superior, much longer than the cotyledons.—Trees or shrubs: leaves opposite, seldom alternate, entire: cymes when the leaves are opposite terminal and axillary: peduncles opposite or seldom alternate, when the leaves are alternate lateral peduncles alternate: bracts and bracteoles caducous.

(1) S. ALBUM. (*Linn.*)

Ident. Dec. prod. XIV. p. 683.—Roxb. flor. Ind. ed. Car. I. p. 462.

Engrav. Rumph. Amb. II. t. 2.

SPEC. CHAR. Tree: leaves ovate-elliptic, acute at the apex: panicles terminal and lateral, many-flowered: pedicels nearly equalling the tube of the calyx: drupe size of a large cherry, turning black.

Hilly tracts of the Peninsula. Mysore. There is a variety, *S. myrtifolium*, with lanceolate leaves, which grows in the Circar mountains. It is figured in 'Roxburgh's Coromandel Plants.'

ORDER CXXXVII. HERNANDIACEÆ.

Flowers monœcious, in threes in a leafy 4-leaved involucre, intermediate one female, sessile, with an areolar repand-truncate, persistent, calyculate 4-merous involucel, lateral ones male, pedicelled, 3-merous, not involucelled: calyx herbaceous, tube short, narrow, in the female jointed, upper part deciduous, limb in males 6-, in females 8—10-parted, regular, lobes in 2 rows, 1-nerved, puberulous, valvate in æstivation, inner ones a little narrower.—MALE: stamens 3, inserted at the throat of the calyx, placed before the outer lobes, and shorter than them, erect-connivent: filaments short, monadelphous at the base, each surrounded at the base by 2 collateral, subsessile, fleshy, subglobose glands, or one 2-lobed or undivided adnate to the base or margin of the filament, or free, seldom without glands: anthers oval, didymous, muticous, adnate to a broadish connectivum, erect, turgid in front, 2-celled, the wall at length free from the connectivum by the whole longitudinal cleft, and extrorsely revolute like a valvelet, deciduous, and leaving the connectivum naked: rudimentary pistil none.—FEMALE: glands of the throat 4, or seldom 5, undivided or 2-lobed, placed before the outer lobes: ovary enclosed in the tube of the calyx, free, sessile, 1-celled, ovule 1, pendulous from the apex, anatropal: style terminal, filiform, equalling the calyx, deciduous: stigma fleshy, dilated, irregularly 2—4-crenated or lobed: drupe dry, ovate, 8-furrowed or smooth, enclosed in the membranaceous, bladder-shaped, truncated pervious tube of the calyx, free, spongiose, 1-seeded: seed inverted, subglobose, testa crustaceous: albumen none: embryo orthotropal: cotyledons large, fleshy, lobed, torulose: radicle superior.—Trees: leaves exstipulate, scattered, coriaceous, petioled, ovate or peltate, quite entire: nerves palmate or pinnate: peduncles axillary or terminal, bearing a compound corymbiform cyme bracteate at the ramifications.

GENUS I. SARCOSTIGMA.

Diœcia Pentandria. *Sex: Syst:*

Deriv. From *Sarx*, *Sarcos*, flesh, and *Stigma*.

GEN. CHAR. Flowers diœcious: calyx cupular, 4—5-toothed: corolla 4—5-parted, tube adnate to a short torus, lobes recurved at the apex, æstivation valvate. MALE: stamens 5, inserted on the tube, alternate to the lobes: filaments free, filiform: anthers versatile, 2-cleft: rudimentary pistil small, pubescent: glands and staminodes none. FEMALE: sterile stamens 5, alternating with the sepals, linear: ovary pubescent, 1-celled, ovules 2, collateral, pendulous from the apex of the cavity: stigma sessile, thick, subcapitate, or obliquely reniform, deciduous: drupe oblong, seated on the hardened calyx, putamen wrinkled, 1-seeded: seed exalbuminous.—Twining shrubs: leaves scattered, exstipulate, coriaceous, quite entire, feather-nerved, reticulated, glabrous: spikes long, somewhat interrupted: flowers glomerate, small.

(1) S. KLEINII. (*W. and A.*)

Ident. Wight et Arn. in Ed. Phil. Journ. 14. p. 299.—Dec. prod. XV. s. 1. p. 265.

Engrav. Wight's Icon. t. 1854.

SPEC. CHAR. Leaves oblong-elliptic: spikes pubescent.

Malabar. Courtallum. Travancore.

ORDER CXXXVIII. BEGONIACEÆ.

Flowers unisexual, monœcious. MALES: sepals 2, opposite, valvate in æstivation: petals usually 2, alternate to the sepals, complicate in æstivation, sometimes none, or 3—7: stamens many, inserted on a more or less convex torus, free, or variously monadelphous: filaments extended above into the connectivum, cells 2, adnate to the connectivum, dehiscing lengthwise: pistil none. FEMALES: lobes usually 2—5, sometimes 6—8, when twin valvate in æstivation, opposite, when 3 or 4, inner 1—2 smaller, when 5 æstivation quincuncial, outer lobes then usually larger, when 6—8 imbricately arranged: styles usually 3, sometimes 2 or 4—5, more or less connate at the base: ovary inferior: ovules very numerous, anatropal: capsules usually 3-celled, the external membrane easily distinct from the ovary, wings when present springing from the external membrane, one wing usually larger than the rest, in 2-celled capsules alternating with the cells: dehiscence loculicidal, fissures at the back of the wings, or by clefts near the wings: seeds small, obovate, ellipsoid or subcylindric: albumen none: embryo ellipsoid or obovate, very obtuse at the hilum, the other extremity very shortly 2-lobed into 2 cotyledons.—Herbs or undershrubs, sometimes shrubs or small trees: leaves distichous or very rarely subverticillate, stipulate, petioled, unequal-sided, usually denticulate, teeth often bearing bristles, sometimes variously lobed, even many-cleft or partite, never composite, hairs simple, rarely stellate, scattered on the upper surface, on the lower particularly at the nerves: stipules free, often caducous: peduncles axillary, divided into bisexual cymes: bracts stipular, opposite: male flowers prior to the females, which are in the lower axils of the dichotomy: lobes, and often the ovary and whole cyme, coloured rose or white, seldom red or yellow.

GENUS I. CASPARYA.

Monœcia Polyandria. *Sex: Syst:*

Gen. Char. Male flowers: sepals 2: petals 2: stamens inserted on a pulvinated disc, free, anthers elongated, laterally dehiscing by 2 clefts. Female flowers: lobes 5—6: styles 3, 2-cleft: branches often divided: ovary 3-celled, placentæ bipartite from the inner angles of the cells: capsules 3-winged or horned, flat above or produced into a more or less elongated cone: style quickly orbate, wings or angles equal, afterwards cleft lengthwise from the base, dehiscent, and therefore truly loculicidal.—Herbs or shrubs: leaves penni-subpalmate, or palmatinerved: cymes frequently unisexual and few-flowered: flowers purple, rose, or whitish, female ones often bibracteolate at the base.

(1) C. oligocarpa. (*Alph. Dec.*)

Ident. Dec. prod. XV. p. 276.

Spec. Char. Perennial: stem herbaceous, simple: leaves obliquely ovate-acuminate, cordate, palmately 7—8-nerved, younger ones glandulosely puberulous, soon glabrate, undulate, denticulate, or subentire: stipules lanceolate, caducous: peduncles axillary, much shorter than the petiole, 1—6-flowered: bracts lanceolate, caducous: sepals and petals of the male flowers elliptic, nearly equal: fruit of the female flowers solitary, subglobose, somewhat fleshy, 4-corneredly-horned at the back of the cells.

Khasia. Chittagong.

(2) C. polycarpa. (*Alph. Dec.*)

Ident. Dec. l. c. p. 277.

Spec. Char. Perennial: stem herbaceous: leaves obliquely ovate-acuminate, subcordate, palmately 8-nerved, undulated, denticulate: stipules lanceolate, caducous: peduncles axillary, shorter than the flexuose petiole, many-flowered: bracts lanceolate, caducous: sepals and petals of male flowers elliptic: fruits from the same peduncle 2—8, subglobose, somewhat fleshy, 4-cornered, horny.

Assam.

(3) C. Silhetensis. (*Alph. Dec.*)

Ident. Dec. l. c. p. 277.

Spec. Char. Perennial, tuberous, stemless: petioles long, velvety: leaves obliquely ovate, acute, cordate, palmately 8-nerved, scattered with a few short hairs on both sides, slightly denticulate: stipules lanceolate, acuminate: peduncles many times shorter than the petiole, velvety: males many-flowered at the top, females few-flowered: sepals of males ovate, concave, velvety externally: petals 2, shorter, obovate: female flowers not bracteolate: lobes 4, oblong, outer ones larger: ovary ovoid, obtusely 4-lobed, subcordate at the base, velvety.

Silhet mountains.

GENUS II. BEGONIA.

Monœcia Polyandria. *Sex: Syst:*

Deriv. In honour of M. Michael Begon, a Frenchman and promoter of botany.

Gen. Char. Male flowers: sepals 2: petals usually 2, sometimes none, rarely 3—7: stamens sometimes more or less monadelphous by the concrete filaments: anthers usually elongated, laterally dehiscing in two divisions, sometimes shortened, or the cells dehiscing towards the top. Female flowers: lobes often 6, or 3—2, or 6—8, outer ones usually larger: styles 3, very rarely 5—4, more or less cohering at the base, caducous, 2-forked or auriculately 2-lobed: ovary externally 3-ribbed or winged, 3-celled: placentæ from the inner angles entire, or 2-parted: capsule usually unequally 3-winged, greater wing ascending, dehiscence lateral or stretching to the base.—Herbs or undershrubs, or shrubs, furnished with a tuber stalk or stem, sometimes subscandent: leaves penninerved or palminerved, dentate or undivided, occasionally lobed, teeth usually bristly, lower side of the leaf often pale-dotted: stipules and bracts nearly similar, persistent or caducous: cymes axillary, rarely lateral, often many times dichotomous, bisexual: flowers white, rose, more rarely red, very seldom yellow.

(1) B. minima. (*Bedd.*)

Ident. Beddome in Madras Journ. Lit. July 1864.

Spec. Char. Leaves radical, rhomboid-ovate to cordate-acuminate, bristly crenate, long-petioled, furnished above with a few weak hairs, beneath glabrous, pellucid-dotted: scapes longer than the leaves, with one leaf near the base: peduncles dichotomous or alternate, bracteated, several-flowered: male flowers 4-petaled, 2 inner petals narrower: females 5-petaled: capsule 3-winged.

Moist rocks at Devalicottah, in Wynaad.

(2) B. picta. (*Smith.*)

Ident. Dec. prod. XV. p. 312.

Syn. B. echinata, *Royle.*

Engrav. Smith ex. Bot. t. 101.—Hook. ex. flor. II. t. 89.—Lodd. Bot. Cab. t. 571.—Bot. Mag. t. 2962.—Royle Ill. t. 80. f. 1.

Spec. Char. Perennial: tubers twin, globose: stem erect, short, hispidulous: leaves ovate, cordate, 7-nerved, obtuse, acute or acuminate, irregularly crenato-dentate, above sparingly, beneath pubescent at the nerves and petiole: stipules lanceolate-acuminate: peduncles few-flowered: bracts ovate, or oblong-acuminate, hairy externally: sepals of male flowers broad-ovate crenulate, hairy outside: petals shorter, obovate: female flowers not bracteolate: lobes 5, outer ones ovate, hairy externally and at the margin, inner ones obovate: capsule pear-shaped, 3-winged, hoary-pubescent, wings ovate-acute, ascending, unequal: flowers pale rose.

Khasia.

(3) B. Josephi. (*Alph. Dec.*)

Ident. Dec. l. c. p. 313.

Spec. Char. Perennial, tuberous: stem herbaceous, simple: leaves peltate, with an excentric umbilicus, ovate, denticulate at the margin, besides variously lobed or lobate-dentate, above sparingly hairy or glabrous, beneath at the nerves pilose or glabrous: stipules ovate, caducous: peduncles and petioles elongated, many-flowered: bracts oblong, obtuse, caducous: sepals of male flowers broad, elliptic: petals obovate-oblong, shorter: female flowers not bracteolate, inner lobes smaller: capsule obtuse at the base, truncated above, the lateral wings triangular, small, the 3rd long extended, ovate-oblong.

Khasia hills.

(4) B. Concanensis. (*Alph. Dec.*)

Ident. Dec. l. c. p. 314.

Spec. Char. Perennial, tuberous: stem low, herbaceous, ascending, simple: leaves ovate-acute, cordate, palmately 7—9-nerved, undulately toothed at the margin, denticulate, above here and there pilose, beneath at the nerves especially slightly hairy: petiole long, glabrous: stipules ovate-lanceolate: peduncles long, branches dichotomous, erect: bracts lanceolate, acuminate, subciliate: sepals of male flowers broad-oval, petals obovate: female flowers not bracteolate: lobes five, outer ones ovate, much larger: capsule turbinate, 2 wings roundly ribbed, the 3rd large, ovate-triangular above, obtuse.

Concans. Mountains near Bombay.

(5) B. PEDUNCULOSA. (*Wall.*)

Ident. Dec. l. c. p. 314.

Engrav. Wall. pl. As. rar. I. t. 97.

SPEC. CHAR. Perennial, tuberous: stem slighty hairy: leaves ovate-oblong, acute or acuminate, unequally cordate, one lobe largely rounded, irregularly dentato-serrate, above sparingly hairy, beneath only at the nerves and on the petiole: stipules ovate-acuminate, ciliated: peduncles many-flowered: bracts ovate-oblong, acute or bristly acuminate, glabrous: sepals of male flowers ovate: petals 2, obovate-oblong, shorter: female flowers scarcely bracteolate: lobes 5, obovate, nearly equal: capsule broad-ovate, 3-winged, acutish at the base, above cordate, wings ascending unequal, ovate or subacute.

Silhet mountains. Khasia. Assam.

(6) B. ARNOTTIANA. (*Alph. Dec.*)

Ident. Dec. l. c. p. 322.

Syn. Diploclinium Arnottianum, *Wight's Icon. t.* 1815.

SPEC. CHAR. Perennial: caudex short, covered by stipules and roots: leaves ovate-rotund, palmately 7—8-nerved, cordate, membranaceous, crenulato-dentate, sparingly above and beneath hairy only on the nerves and on the petiole: stipules ovate-acuminate: scapes somewhat longer than the petiole: flowers few, approximate: bracts ovate-oblong, obtuse: sepals of male flowers round: petals obovate-oblong, somewhat shorter: outer lobes of the female flowers 2, broad-ovate, inner two narrower: capsule broad-oval, lateral wings rotund, nearly equal.

Dense forests at Courtallum.

(7) B. OVATIFOLIA. (*Alph. Dec.*)

Ident. Dec. l. c. p. 328.

SPEC. CHAR. Perennial, tuberous, somewhat stemless: leaves ovate-acute, subcordate, undulate, denticulate or entire: nerves 7—8-palmate, above here and there hairy or glabrous, beneath puberulous or glabrous on the nerves and petiole: stipules lanceolate, small: scapes or peduncles nearly equal to the petiole, 1—4-flowered at the top: bracts lanceolate, acuminate: sepals of male flowers ovate: petiole elliptic, shorter: female flowers not bracteolate: 2 lobes rotund, third inner one obovate, smaller: capsule broad, turbinate, wings triangular-ovate, truncated above, 1 larger.

Khasia.

(8) B. CORDIFOLIA. (*Alph. Dec.*)

Ident. Dec. l. c. p. 328.

Syn. Diploclinium cordifolium, *Wight's Icon. t.* 1816.

SPEC. CHAR. Perennial: caudex short, covered by the rootlets and stipules: leaves ovate-rotund, palmately 7—8-nerved, deeply cordate, crenulato-dentate, above sparingly, beneath hairy on the nerves and petiole: stipules ovate-acuminate: scapes longer than the petiole, many-flowered: bracts lanceolate, acuminate: sepals of the male flowers rotund, petals shorter, obovate-oblong: 2 lobes of the female flowers broad-obovate, 3rd obovate-oblong, equal in length: capsule nearly equally 3-winged.

Forests of Malabar.

(9) B. FALLAX. (*Alph. Dec.*)

Ident. Dec. l. c. p. 329.

Syn. Diploclinium Lindleyanum, *Wight's Icon. t.* 1817 (not Walp.).

SPEC. CHAR. Woody (?): branches glabrous: leaves obovate-oblong, acuminate, unequally cordate, short petioled, penninerved, irregularly undulato-angular, here and there denticulate, glabrous on both sides: stipules caducous, oblong: peduncles axillary, much shorter than the leaves, many times dichotomous: bracts ovate (?), small, caducous: sepals of male flowers broadly obovate: petals narrow obovate, shorter: 2 lobes of female flowers obovate, 3rd inner one obovate-oblong, smaller: capsule obovately 3-winged, abruptly narrowed and acute at the base, lateral wings slightly unequal, ovate-acute or rotund.

Courtallum. Malabar.

(10) B. RUBRO-VENIA. (*Hook.*)

Ident. Dec. l. c. p. 347.

Engrav. Hook. Bot. Mag. t. 4689.

SPEC. CHAR. Perennial: rhizome thick: branches tawny velvet: leaves ovate-acuminate, obtuse at the base or subcordate, penninerved, undulate, here and there denticulate, glabrous above, vaguely white-spotted, beneath tawny velvet and purplish, especially on the nerves: petioles velvety: stipules long-ovate-lanceolate, terminated by a bristle, hairyish at the back: peduncles erect, longer than the petiole, glabrous, 6—10-flowered at the apex: bracts nearly resembling the stipules: sepals of male flowers elliptic, striated with purple: petals 2, obovate-elliptic, equal: female flowers not bracteolate: lobes 5, ovate, exterior ones striated: capsule obtuse at the base, 2 lateral wings rib-shaped, 3rd ovate-oblong, obtuse.

Khasia. Assam.

(11) B. laciniata. (*Roxb.*)

Ident. Roxb. flor. Ind. III. p. 649.—Dec. l. c. p. 347.

Engrav. Bot. Mag. t. 5021.

Spec. Char. Stem herbaceous, tawny-tomentose, afterwards glabrous: leaves palmately 6—7-nerved, cordate, unequally ovate-rotund, variously and acutely lobed, irregularly toothed and denticulate, above sparingly hispidulous, ciliated at the margin, beneath especially at the nerves and petioles tawny-tomentose: stipules lanceolate-acuminate, tomentose externally: peduncles shorter than the leaf, tawny-tomentose, many times dichotomous at the top: lower bracts lanceolate acute, upper ones oblong, obtuse: sepals of male flowers broad-ovate, externally subpubescent: petals elliptic, shorter: female flowers not bracteolate, lobes oblong-elliptic: capsule nodding, body ellipsoid subpubescent, 2 lateral wings rib-shaped, 3rd larger, ovate, descending.

Garrow hills. Silhet. Assam. Khasia.

(12) B. barbata. (*Wall.*)

Ident. Dec. l. c. p. 348.

Spec. Char. Perennial: caudex and stem tawny-hispid: petioles elongated, tawny-tomentose: leaves obliquely ovate-acuminate, cordate, palmately 7-nerved, membranaceous, crenulato-dentate, scattered above with short hairs on the margin, and beneath at the nerves hispid with longer hairs: stipules lanceolate, long-acuminate, hairy: peduncles few-flowered at the top: bracts narrow-lanceolate, hairyish, caducous: sepals of male flowers 2, ovate, hairy outside: petals obovate, shorter, denticulate at the margin: capsule nodding, obovately 3-winged, here and there villous, deprived of the styles, 2 wings lateral, rib-shaped, 3rd larger, ovate, descending.

Silhet.

(13) B. Thomsoni. (*Alph. Dec.*)

Ident. Dec. l. c. p. 349.

Spec. Char. Rhizoma oblique, hairy: stem short and with the petioles woolly: leaves obliquely ovate, short acuminated, cordate, palmately 7—8-nerved, sinuate, remotely dentate, on both sides and at the margin covered with scattered hirsute hairs: stipules lanceolate, long acuminated with a bristle, hirsute externally: peduncles axillary, much shorter than the petiole, externally hispid: sepals of male flowers elliptic, hairy at the back: petals oblong, somewhat shorter, glabrous.

Khasia hills.

(14) B. Rex. (*Putzeys.*)

Ident. Putzeys in Fl. des serr. et jard. V. t. 2. 1255-6.—Dec. l. c. p. 350.

Engrav. Bot. Mag. t. 5101.

Spec. Char. Perennial, stemless: rhizome thick: leaves large, ovate, short acuminate, cordate, palmately feather-nerved, crenato-sinuate, variegated, and with the petiole sparingly hairy: stipules lanceolate, bristly acuminate, hispid at the back: scape longer than the petioles, many times dichotomous at the top: bracts ovate, acuminate, glabrous, caducous: sepals of male flowers broad ovate, glabrous: petals obovate, scarcely shorter: lobes of female flowers 5, elliptic, nearly equal: capsule nodding, glabrous, 2 wings rib-shaped, narrow, 3rd oblong-ovate, obtuse, lengthened out towards the base.

Assam.

(15) B. trichocarpa. (*Dalz.*)

Ident. Dalzell in Hook. Journ. 1851. p. 230.—Dec. l. c. p. 350.

Spec. Char. Perennial, tuberous: stem erect, herbaceous, simple: leaves ovate-acuminate, cordate, palmately 7—8-nerved, irregularly angled and sinuate, much toothed, sparingly above, beneath shortly pilose, especially at the nerves: stipules lanceolate, acuminate, hairyish: peduncles longer than the petiole: bracts ovate-acuminate, dentate, and with the pedicels pubescent: sepals of male flowers externally puberulous, broad-rotund: petals obovate-oblong, shorter: female flowers pubescent externally: 2 outer lobes round, 3 inner ones much shorter: capsule nodding, ellipsoidly 3-ribbed, glabrescent.

Foot of the Syhadree hill, in Western India.

(16) B. brevicaulis. (*Alph. Dec.*)

Ident. Dec. l. c. p. 350.

Spec. Char. Perennial, tuberous, somewhat stemless: leaves broad ovate, obtuse or shortly acute, unequally cordate, palmately 7-nerved, undulated, denticulate, younger ones toothless, bristly, above hairy at the nerves: stipules oblong or lanceolate: peduncles nearly equalling the petiole, few-flowered: bracts ovate-acute, subdentate, very small: sepals of male flowers broad-ovate: petals elliptic, shorter: capsule nodding, base obtuse, deprived of the styles, 2 wings rib-shaped, very small, 3rd much larger, ovate-oblong, lateral or tending towards the base.

Khasia.

(17) B. integrifolia. (*Dalz.*)

Ident. Dalz. in Hook. Journ. 1851. p. 230.—Dec. l. c. p. 351.

Spec. Char. Tuberous: stem low, herbaceous, simple and

with hairyish petioles: leaves obliquely ovate, obtuse or rarely subacute, cordate, palmately 7—8-nerved, entire, or here and there denticulate, beneath roughish at the nerves: stipules ovate or elliptic, obtuse: peduncles longer than the petioles, 2—3-dichotomous: bracts elliptic, ciliolate, caducous: sepals of male flowers round: petals obovate-oblong, shorter: bracteoles of female flowers distant, caducous: lobes obovate: capsule nodding, 3 wings lateral, 1 afterwards larger, descending, rounded.

Foot of the Syhadree hill, in Western India.

(18) B. crenata. (*Dryander.*)

Ident. Dryander in Trans. Linn. Soc. I. p. 162. t 14. fig. 3.—Dec. l. c. p. 356.

Spec. Char. Annual (?), subtuberose: stem low, slender, erect, glabrous: leaves ovate, obtuse or acute, lower ones cordate, upper ones obtuse at the base, palmately 7—8-nerved, irregularly crenato-denticulate, glabrous above, beneath together with the petioles here and there pilose, or glabrous: stipules ovate or oblong: peduncles slender, many-flowered: bracts lanceolate: sepals of male flowers 2, broad ovate: petals 2, obovate, shorter: female flowers not bracteolate: lobes 5, outer ones accrescent: capsule subglobosely 2—3-winged, not greater than the persistent lobes, wings expanded below, obtuse.

Salsette. Concans.

(19) B. Canarana. (*Miq.*)

Ident. Miq. Ann. Bot. III. p. 18.—Dec. l. c. p. 356.

Spec. Char. Root very small, tuberous and fibrillose: stem slender, erect, simple: leaves ovate-rotund, palmately 7-nerved, somewhat regular, cordate, sinuately angled, crenate and denticulate, above sparingly, beneath rarely pilose at the nerves: stipules and bracts ovate-lanceolate, acute: peduncles long, slender, 2—3 times dichotomous at the top: sepals of male flowers 2, ovate or obovate: petals 2, narrow-obovate, shorter: female flowers not bracteolate: lobes 4, outer 2—3 ovate, accrescent, coloured externally, inner 2—1 obovate, shorter: capsule turbinately globose, torose, 2—3 winged, not larger than the lobes, afterwards laterally expanding below, unequal, middle-sized.

Canara. Mangalore.

(20) B. subpeltata. (*R. W.*)

Ident. Dec. l. c. p. 386.

Engrav. Wight's Icon. t. 1812.

Spec. Char. Perennial, tuberous, stemless: petiole of a single leaf long, hairy, limb ovate-rotund, palmately-nerved, cordate, serrato-dentate, hairy, hairs of the petiole more frequent at the top: scapes nearly equalling the petiole, here and there hairy, few-flowered at the apex: bracts ovate-lanceolate, acute or obtuse: sepals of male flowers ovate-rotund: petals elliptic-oblong, acute, scarcely shorter: female flowers not bracteolate: lobes 5 (?), nearly equal in length, inner ones narrower: capsule pyriformly 3-ribbed, glabrous, acute at the base, wings nearly equal.

Malabar.

(21) B. ALBO-COCCINEA. (*Hook.*)

Ident. Dec. l. c. p. 389.

Syn. B. Grahamiana, *R. W.*—Mitscherlichia albo-coccinea, *Kl. Begon.* 73. *t.* 6. *fig. A.*

Engrav. Wight's Icon. t. 1811.—Hook. Bot. Mag. t. 4172. —Lindl. Bot. Reg. 1846. t. 39.

SPEC. CHAR. Stemless: leaves peltately 10—11-nerved, reniform-rotund, coriaceous, undulate at the margin, pubescent at the nerves beneath, margin and petiole, afterwards glabrous: stipule broadly oblong, acuminate: scapes twice as long as the petiole, and with the dichotomous peduncles pubescent, afterwards glabrate: bracts ovate, puberulous, caducous: sepals of male flowers broad-ovate, puberulous externally: petals obovate, shorter: bracteoles of female flowers lanceolate, puberulous, caducous: outer lobes 2, broad-ovate, puberulous externally, 3rd inner one obovate, somewhat shorter: capsule ovately 3-winged, obtuse at the base, mucronate above by the falling of the styles, wings nearly equal.

Woods at Courtallum.

(22) B. DIPETALA. (*Grah.*)

Ident. Dec. l. c. p. 391.

Syn. Haagea dipetala, *Kl. Begon. p.* 104.

Engrav. Bot. Mag. t. 2849.—Bot. Cab. t. 1730.—Lindl. and Paxt. fl. gard. I. t. 14.—Wight's Icon. t. 1813.

SPEC. CHAR. Fruticose, erect: leaves obliquely ovate-acute, palmi- penni- 7—9-nerved, semicordate, duplicato-dentate, ciliated with soft spines, hairy above, nearly smooth beneath, not spotted: stipules ovate-oblong, mucronate, membranaceous, caducous: peduncles shorter than the leaf, nodding, many times divided: bracts ovate-oblong, acute, caducous: sepals of male flowers large rotund: petals none: female flowers not bracteolate: lobes 2, large rotund: capsule elliptic 3-winged, obtuse at both ends, wings equal.

Rocky, shady places on the Neilgherries. The leaves of this species are not spotted as incorrectly represented in the Bot. Mag. quoted above.

(23) B. HYDROPHILA (*Miq.*)

Ident. Dec. l. c. p. 392.

SPEC. CHAR. Perennial, erect: leaves oblong, acuminate, very unequal at the base, cordate, palmi- penni- 6—8-nerved, here and there dentate, and frequently denticulate, hairs above few and scattered, beneath none: stipules ovate-oblong, bristly apiculate, caducous: cymes axillary, few-flowered, shorter than the petiole: bracts ovate-oblong, obtuse: sepals of the male flowers ovate-rotund: petals none: lobes of the female flowers 2: capsule obovate-rotund, base obtuse, styles falling off, above subacute, wings nearly equal.

In water near Mercara. Neilgherries and elsewhere in the Peninsula.

(24) B. MALABARICA. (*Lam.*)

Ident. Lam. dict. I. p. 393 (not Roxb. or Wall.).—Dec. l. c. p. 392.

Engrav. Rheede Mal. IX. t. 86.

SPEC. CHAR. Herbaceous, glabrous: leaves ovate-oblong, acuminate, unequally cordate: lower lobe larger, rounded, nearly equalling the petiole, penni- palmati-nerved, undulato-dentate: stipules oblong-acuminate, caducous: peduncles axillary, much shorter than the leaf, few-flowered: bracts ovate, caducous: sepals of the male flowers 2, rotund: petals none: lobes of the female flowers 2, large, obovate: capsule obovately 3-winged, truncated, wings equal, surrounding the cells on all sides.

Concans. Neilgherries. Courtallum and Malabar, in sandy and rocky places.

(25) B. ROXBURGHII. (*Alph. Dec.*)

Ident. Dec. l. c. p. 398.

Syn. Diploclinium Roxburghii, *Miq. flor. Ind. Bat.* I. *p.* 692.—B. Malabarica, *Roxb. flor. Ind.* III. *p.* 648.

SPEC. CHAR. Perennial, herbaceous: stems many, suberect, fleshy, younger ones having leaves ovate-acuminate, unequally half-cordate, hispid, irregularly and acutely serrato-dentate: stipules oblong: peduncles axillary, short, many-flowered: bracts minute: sepals of male flowers 2, rotund: petals 2, narrower: lobes of female flowers larger than the males: ovary 4-celled: placentæ in each cell twin, reniform.

Moist places in Chittagong.

ORDER CXXXIX. DATISCACEÆ.

Flowers usually diœcious, sometimes hermaphrodite or polygamous: calyx of male flowers 3—9-cleft, of hermaphrodite and female ones adnate to the ovary, and 3—8-toothed at the apex: corolla none, but small teeth sometimes in the first age of the flower alternate with the calycine lobes, interior to them, afterwards indistinguishable, or stamens alternate with the calycine lobes, sometimes holding the place of a corolla in male and hermaphrodite flowers: stamens 3—11, in male flowers inserted on the calyx, in hermaphrodite flowers 3 only, alternating with the calycine teeth, in females none: anthers 2-celled, erect, inserted on the filaments by a point at the back, cells dehiscing lengthwise extrorsely: ovary in male flowers, scarcely any in hermaphrodite, and female ones inferior, 1-celled, sometimes half-open by fissures at the apex: placentæ parietal, alternating with the calycine lobes: styles opposite the lobes of the calyx, papilliferous inside at the top, sometimes 2-parted, divisions linear, papillose: ovules many, anatropal, somewhat horizontal: capsule membranaceous, subdehiscent within the teeth of the calyx: seeds oblong, very numerous, small: testa striated lengthways, and impressed with dots: albumen sparing: embryo cylindric: radicle long: cotyledons very short.—Herbs or trees: leaves exstipulate, alternate, usually unequally pinnate, rarely palmatinerved, and somewhat unequal-sided: flowers smallish, arranged in the axils of the leaves, or together with the racemes, or unisexual indefinite spikes, fascicled, very shortly pedicelled, the central flower of each fascicle opening first.

GENUS I. TETRAMELES.

Diœcia Tetrandria. *Sex: Syst:*

Deriv. From *Tetras*, four, and *Melos*, a limb, alluding to the four divisions of the perianth.

GEN. CHAR. Flowers diœcious. MALE: calyx 4-cleft: stamens 4, opposite the calycine lobes, longer than them: anthers shorter than the filament: disc flattish, interior to the stamens, 4-lobed, lobes obtuse, alternating with the stamens. FEMALE: calyx oblong-quadrangular, 4-toothed at the apex, with occasionally the addition of 1—2 smaller teeth: stamens none: styles 4, opposite the teeth of the calyx, longer than them, entire, longitudinally furrowed within, bearing a papillose stigma at the top: capsule somewhat dehiscent above at the furrowed base of the styles.—Trees: leaves developing after the flowers, palmatinerved, somewhat unequal-sided; toothed or subentire, peticled: spikes unisexual, many from the apex of the branches: flowers fascicled or solitary in the axils of the bracteoles, sessile.

(1) T. NUDIFLORA. (*R. Br.*)

Ident. R. Br. in herb. Horsf.—Dec. prod. XV. p. 411.

Syn. T. Grahamiana, *R. W.*

Engrav. Horsf. pl. Jav. rar. t. 17.—Wight's Icon. t. 1956.

SPEC. CHAR. Large tree: leaves broad-oval, acute or acuminate, unequally toothed, here and there sublobate, polished above, beneath white-tomentose: styles shorter than the tube of the calyx: spikes of male flowers diffuse, branched, females pendent: flowers numerous, yellowish.

Western Ghauts. Trichore forests. Courtallum. There is probably no distinction between the Javan and Indian species.

ORDER CXL. ARISTOLOCHIACEÆ.

Flowers monochlamydeous and hermaphrodite, gynandrous: calyx sometimes regular 3-lobed, sometimes and usually irregular, and then various in shape, tube usually inflated above the apex of the ovary, enclosing the organs in a bladder, then more or less produced, and at length expanded into a 1- or 2-lipped or peripherous limb, persistent or withering and deciduous: stamens 6, seldom 5, or 12, very rarely 18—36: filaments short, free, or cohering below, or adhering to the style and stigmas: anthers 2-celled, extrorse, cells parallel, dehiscing lengthways: ovary inferior, 6-celled, ovules many, anatropal, marked with a thick raphe, inserted in two rows at the central angle of the cells, seldom 4-celled, and then inserted in one row in the middle breadth of the dissepiments: styles most usually 6, very rarely 3 or many, more or less connate at the base into a styline column, the stigma-bearing apex divided into lobes: fruit crowned with the persistent limb of the calyx, capsular, most usually 6-cornered, 4- or generally 6-lobed, most frequently 6—4-valved, dehiscence septicidal, or at the apex, or basilar, the peduncle itself partly dividing: seeds many, horizontal: albumen copious, fleshy or somewhat horny, enclosing the minute embryo: cotyledons equal, flat-convex, fleshy: radicle next the hilum.—Perennial herbs, often with a creeping or tuberous rhizome, or undershrubs or shrubs often twining: leaves alternate simple: petiole very often dilated at the base, cordate or cordate-reniform, edentate, exstipulate: flowers rarely terminal, almost always axillary, solitary or rarely spicately or racemosely cymose, sometimes bracteate, of various sizes, brown or dark lurid purple in colour, odour usually fetid.

GENUS I. BRAGANTIA.

Gynandria Hexandria. *Sex: Syst:*

Deriv. Named in memory of the Duke of Braganza.

Gen. Char. Limb of the calyx small, regular, more or less deeply tripartite, segments broad, erect or spreading, throat sometimes ringed: stamens 6—10 in one row: anthers 2-celled: filaments short or none, cohering in various ways: ovary inferior, elongated, narrow, narrower at the base and apex, roundly tetragonal and 1-furrowed on one side, 4-celled, many-ovuled, ovules in one row: styline column short, sometimes expanded at the top into a radiated disc, sometimes divided into 3—6 entire legs, stigmatose: capsule long, slender, tetragonal, valves keeled: seeds in one row, trigonal, transversely wrinkled, external covering crustaceous, inner membranaceous.

(1) B. Wallichii. (*R. Br.*)

Ident. Dec. prod. XV. p. 430.

Syn. Apama siliquosa, *Lam.*—Trimeriza piperina, *Lindl. Bot. Reg. Sub. t.* 1543.

Engrav. Rheede Mal. VI. t. 28.—Lam. Encyc. Ill. t. 640.—Wight's Icon. t. 520.

Spec. Char. Shrubby: branches hispid at the top, more or less geniculate: leaves oblong-lanceolate, acuminate, rounded at the base, or more frequently somewhat cuneately narrowed, upper surface deep shining green, glabrous, lower pale, shortly hispid, short-petioled: spikes axillary, short, solitary or twin or ternate, hirsute, 4—8 flowered: limb of the calyx campanulate, segments 3, broad-ovate, acutish, pubescently hispid externally: ovary hirsute: stamens 9, appendiculate: anthers incurved, inner surface long, hairy hispid: capsule erect, 4-angled, marked with a prominent middle nerve, slender, about 4 inches long.

South Concan. Canara. Malabar. Travancore.

GENUS II. ARISTOLOCHIA.

Gynandria Hexandria. *Sex: Syst:*

Deriv. From *Aristos*, best, and *Locheia*, parturition, from its reputed medical qualities.

GEN. CHAR. Calyx coloured, tubular, swelling above the ovary into a globose or ovoid bladder, narrowed beyond into a tube, either straight, arched, or refracted, at length expanded into a limb, which is very often irregular, sometimes peripherical, dentate or lobed, often 1—2-lipped, the lips varying in shape and size: anthers 6, rarely 5, extrorse, 2-celled, cells parallel, contiguous, dehiscing lengthwise: ovary inferior, 6-celled, ovules many, inserted in 2 rows at the central angle of the cell: styline column simple, cleft above, rarely parted in 3, usually 6 stigmatose lobes: capsule 6-celled, many-seeded, 6-valved: seeds many in one row, often boat-shaped with inflexed margins: albumen thickly fleshy.—Herbs, shrubs, or undershrubs, often twining: leaves alternate, rarely lobed, never toothed, exstipulate: flowers lurid, often large, unusually fetid.

(1) A. BRACTEATA. (*Retz.*)

Ident. Retz. obs. bot. fasc. 5. p. 29. No. 80.—Dec. prod. XV. p. 478.—Roxb. flor. Ind. III. p. 490.

Syn. A. bracteolata, *Lam.*—A. Mauritiana, *Pers. Ench.*

SPEC. CHAR. Stems and branches weak, trailing on the ground: leaves reniform, glaucous: flowers axillary, solitary, peduncled: peduncles furnished at the base with a kidney-shaped, curled, sessile bract: flowers dark purple, hairy inside.

Guzerat. Deccan. Coromandel. Banks of the Jumna. Flowering nearly all the year.

(2) A. INDICA. (*Linn.*)

Ident. Linn. sp. I. p. 360.—Dec. l. c. p. 479.

Engrav. Rheede. Mal. VIII. t. 25.

SPEC. CHAR. Shrubby, twining: leaves linear, wedge-shaped or obovate, 3-nerved, pointed, waved, smooth, 2—4 inches long:

racemes axillary, shorter than the leaves: capsules oblong, pendulous: flowers erect, dark coloured.

Concan hills. Coromandel. Deccan. Flowering in the rainy season.

(3) A. ACUMINATA. (*Lam.*)

Ident. Lam. Encyc. I. p. 254.—Dec. l. c. p. 479.

SPEC. CHAR. Perennial, twining, smooth: leaves cordate, entire, somewhat acuminate: racemes axillary, simple or compound, drooping, shorter than the leaves: petioles slightly channelled: corolla with a funnel-shaped tube: capsule pear-shaped, dehiscing, with 5 valves: flowers dark greenish-purple.

South Concan. Silhet. Chittagong. Flowering nearly all the year.

ORDER CXLI. EUPHORBIACEÆ.

Flowers unisexual: calyx free, gamosepalous, segments equal or unequal, entire or variously cut and toothed at the margin, glabrous or covered with hairs, sometimes coloured: corolla polypetalous or very rarely monopetalous, hypogynous or more or less distinctly perigynous or none, hairy or glabrous, coloured, but never blue: petals alternating with the calycine segments, usually imbricated at the margin, rarely twisted, and occasionally differing in æstivation from the calyx: stamens indefinite, in the male flowers central or inserted at the bottom or above the base of the calyx: filaments free, or 1—polyadelphous, erect or variously incurved: anthers free or cohering, opening in various ways: ovary superior, usually 3-celled: carpels connate round a central column, which remains after the fruit has fallen: cells 1—2 ovuled: style usually short, and divided in as many branches as there are cells in the ovary, branches again variously divided, more or less reflexed, papillose above: ovules pendulous from the upper internal angle of the cells, sessile, solitary or germinately collateral: fruit usually capsular, tricoccous, opening elastically: cocci usually 2-valved: cotyledons more or less flattened: albumen more or less copious.—Large or small trees, shrubs or undershrubs, perennial or annual herbs, often containing a poisonous juice, elastic resin, or watery juice: leaves alternate, rarely opposite or verticillate, petioled or sessile, usually bistipulate at the base, almost always simple, seldom trifoliolate: limb entire or toothed or lobed, penninerved or palmatinerved: inflorescence axillary or terminal, definite or indefinite, variously arranged.

GENUS I. EUPHORBIA.

Dodecandria Trigynia. *Sex: Syst:*

Deriv. Named after Euphorbus, physician to Juba, king of Mauritania, who is said to have first applied the plants medicinally.

Gen. Char. Involucre somewhat regular, campanulate, turbinate or hemispherical, 5 primary lobes membranaceous, 5 secondary ones alternating with the first and glanduliferous: male flowers pedicelled, ecalyculate, furnished at the base with ciliated-lacerated bracteoles, arranged in 5 rows opposite the primary lobes of the involucre: female flower central, pedicelled, supported by the 3—6-lobed calyx, usually ecalyculate: styles 3, distinct or more or less united, 2-cleft: lobes stigmatose at the apex or inner side: seeds pendulous, with or without a wart.—Monœcious, very rarely diœceous plants, consisting of herbs, shrubs and trees: leaves scattered and opposite, seldom verticillate, stipulate or exstipulate, floral ones opposite or ternate: inflorescence definite cymose, cymes axillary or terminal, 2—5-tomous, often arranged in a false umbel, sometimes unilateral by abortion, racemiform, spiciform, or reduced to a solitary involucre: leaves at the base of the umbel verticillate: involucres usually enclosing the males as well as the female flower: glands of the involucre somewhat stalked, thickish, fleshy, usually horizontal or inclining outwardly, commonly broader than long, flat or concave, rounded or truncated at the outer margin, semilunate, 2-horned, occasionally increased by a membranaceous appendage: male flowers varying in number, rows or fascicles radiately arranged, very often indistinguishable from the mutual compression of flowers and bracts: pedicel of the female flower exserted after fruiting, again erect after the ripening of the capsule: capsule smooth or warty, the two valvelets of the shell elastic: seeds crustaceous, variously tubercled, wrinkled or furrowed, clothed with a very thin aril, often expanded into a wart at the top of the seed: cotyledons linear, more or less ovate.

(1) E. HALOPHILA. (*Miq.*)

Ident. Miquel Anal. bot. Ind. III. p. 16.—Dec. prod. XV. s. 2. p. 13.

Syn. E. pallens, *Dillw. rev. Hort. Mal. p.* 55.—E. articulata, *Dennst. in Hort. Mal.*

Engrav. Rheede Mal. X. t. 58.

SPEC. CHAR. Undershrub, glabrous, glaucescent: stems procumbent, thickish, alternately branched: leaves somewhat cordate at the base, ovate, obtuse, entire: stipules interpetiolar, triangular, ciliated, often 2-cleft: cymes axillary, short peduncled, many times 2-cleft: floral leaves oblong, lobes of the turbinate involucre triangular, ciliated: glands very narrowly appendiculate: styles very short, 2-cleft: shells of the capsule obtusely keeled. seed globose, smooth.

Sea-shore at Mahè and Tellicherry, western coast.

(2) E. PYCNOSTEGIA. (*Boiss.*)

Ident. Boiss. Cent. Euph. p. 9.—Dec. l. c. p. 18.

SPEC. CHAR. Annual: stem erect, glabrous, dichotomous: leaves sparingly hairy, subsessile, cordate at the base, ovate, obtuse, or shortly acuminate, sharply serrulate, with a whitish margin, upper ones condensed into oblong spikes: stipules interpetiolar, ovate-triangular, fimbriated: involucre long, turbinate: lobes oblong, denticulate: glands transversely oblong, appendage white, much broader than them, obovate, obsoletely repand, two lower appendages of the glands larger, somewhat oblique: capsules hairy: shells obtusely keeled: styles short, 2-lobed, subcapitate at the apex: seed obtusely ovate-tetragonal, beset with large, irregular, depressed tubercles.

Neilgherries. Malabar. Concan.

(3) E. ZORNIOIDES. (*Boiss.*)

Ident. Dec. l. c. p. 19.

SPEC. CHAR. Annual: stem erect, glabrous, dichotomous: leaves subsessile, subcordate at the base, oblong or linear, obtuse, mucronulate, sharply serrulate, floral ones cordate-ovate, approximated into loose, oblong spikes: stipules interpetiolar, very short: involucre turbinate, hirsute within: lobes ovate, slightly fimbriated: glands transversely ovate, appendage rose-coloured, entire or repand: styles short, 2-cleft, thickened at the apex: seed ovate-tetragonal, smooth or thinly papillose.

Malabar. Concan. Near Bombay.

(4) E. ELEGANS. (*Spreng.*)

Ident. Spreng. Syst. III. p. 794.—Dec. l. c. p. 19.

Syn. E. variegata, *Roth.*—E. platylepis, *Decaisne in Jacq. voy. p.* 156 *and t.* 157.—E. strobilifera, *Dalz. in Hook. Journ. Bot.* 1851. III. *p.* 229.—E. dichotoma, *Roxb. flor. Ind.* II. *p.* 471.

SPEC. CHAR. Annual, softly hispid: stem erect, elongated, shortly branched and leafy towards the top: leaves subsessile, unequal at the cordate base, ovate, obtuse, serrulate towards the apex, upper ones densely imbricated into ovate spikes: stipules bristly, small: involucres shortly turbinate, laterally cleft, hairy on both sides, lobes obovate denticulate at the apex: glands transversely oblong, appendage large, rose-coloured, wedge-shaped, obsoletely repand: shells of the hairyish capsule rounded: styles united at the base, 2-cleft, oblong-clavate: seed ovate-tetragonal, transversely 4—5-furrowed, minutely tubercled.

Asserghur. Malabar and Concan. Deccan. Aurungabad. Flowering in February.

(5) E. FIMBRIATA. (*Boiss.*)

Ident. Dec. l. c. p. 19.

Syn. E. cristata, *var. major*, *Roth.*

Engrav. Boiss. Euph. Ic. t. 8.

SPEC. CHAR. Annual, softly hispid: stems erect, alternately or dichotomously branched: leaves subsessile, with an unequal cordate base, ovate, serrulate: upper ones densely imbricated into rounded capitula: stipules tubulate, short: involucres long turbinate, hairy, throat white-ciliate, lobes linear-lanceolate: glands wax-coloured transversely oblong, appendage reddish, broad, parted into 7—9 plumose bristly segments: styles deeply 2-cleft, capitate: shells of the hirsute capsule somewhat keeled: seed oblong-tetragonal, 4—5-furrowed, tuberculate.

Madras.

(6) E. PILULIFERA. (*Linn.*)

Ident. Linn. Am. ac. III. p. 114.—Dec. l. c. p. 21.

Syn. E. hirta, *Linn. l. c.*—E. capitata, *Lam.*—E. globulifera, *Kunth. in H. B. nov. gen.* II. *p.* 56.—E. verticillata, *Vell. fl. Flum.* V. *t.* 16.—E. nodiflora, *Steud. nom.*

Engrav. Burm. Zeyl. t. 104 and t. 105. fig. I.—Jacq. Ic. I. t. 478.—Jacq. Coll. V. t. XI. fig. I.

SPEC. CHAR. Annual, crisply pubescent: stems erect or ascending, simple or sparingly branched, above more or less slightly bristly: leaves short-petioled, with a very unequal, wedge-shaped or truncated base, ovate-rhomboid or oblong-lanceolate, acute, serrulate or dentate: stipules linear fimbriated: cymes axillary, sessile or short-peduncled, globosely capituliform, many-headed: involucres turbinate, hairy, glabrous within, lobes triangular: glands orbiculate, slightly concave, appendage obsolete or very narrow: styles very short, 2-lobed, capitate: shells of the yellowish hairy capsule keeled: seed reddish, sharply oblong-tetragonal, transversely wrinkled: flowers small, greenish.

A common weed everywhere, flowering all the year.

(7) E. BRACTEOLARIS. (*Boiss.*)

Ident. Boiss. Cent. Euph. p. 8.—Dec. l. c. p. 22.

SPEC. CHAR. Annual: branched from the neck: stems thinly filiform, erect-spreading, dichotomous, hairyish: leaves thin, short-petioled, beneath pale, slightly hairy, ovate, obtuse, repand at the top: stipules triangular-lanceolate, very short: cymes axillary and terminal, very shortly peduncled, few-headed, corymbosely capitate, floral leaves numerous, small: lobes of the turbinate involucre lanceolate: glands small, orbiculate, appendage white, roundish, equally broad or narrower: styles 2-cleft, short: shells of the hairy capsule round: seed oblong-tetragonal, partly wrinkled.

Neilgherries.

(8) E. INDICA. (*Lam.*)

Ident. Lam. dict. II. p. 423.—Dec. l. c. p. 22.

Syn. E. granulata, *var. decumbens*, *Forsk.*—E. decumbens, *Willd.*—E. androsæmoides, *Dennst.*—E. hypericifolia, *Hochst.*—E. cassioides, *Presl.*

Engrav. Rheede Mal. X. t. 51.

SPEC. CHAR. Annual, glaucescent: stems ascending or decumbent, puberulous, branchy: leaves sparingly puberulous, short-petioled, obovate, obtuse, paler beneath, remotely serrulate: stipules bristly ciliated, base dilated: cymes loosely capituliform, axillary, short peduncled, usually supported by a pair of leaves equalling them: involucres turbinate, lobes triangular, slightly fimbriated: glands ovate, appendage ovate-rotund, white, equally broad or narrower: styles short, 2-cleft: shells of the hairy capsule somewhat keeled: seed ovate-tetragonal, transversely wrinkled.

Peninsula and elsewhere?

(9) E. NOTOPTERA. (*Boiss.*)

Ident. Dec. l. c. p. 26.

SPEC. CHAR. Annual, glabrous: stem erect, dichotomous, internodes very long: leaves short-petioled, very unequal at the base, linear-oblong or linear, obtuse, mucronulate, subrevolute at the margin, remotely serrulate, often deflexed: stipules interpetiolar, broad, very short: involucres campanulate, terminal, solitary, or ternate, pedicellate, supported by linear acute floral leaves longer than them, lobes ovate, pectinately fimbriated: glands transversely oblong, appendage broader, somewhat repand at the margin: styles 2-cleft: shells of the globosely depressed capsule narrowly 2-winged at the back, wrinkled: seed ovate-quadrangular, densely tubercled.

Bombay. Canara. Mysore. Malabar.

(10) E. SERPENS. (*Kunth.*)

Var. INDICA.

Ident. Dec. l. c. p. 29—30.

Syn. E. microphylla, *Roth.*—E. Heyneana, *Spreng.*—E. orbiculata, *Miquel.*

SPEC. CHAR. Annual, glabrous: stems filiform, prostrate, branchy: leaves unequal at the base, retuse, often obscurely denticulate at the apex: stipules truncated, often 2-parted or deeply torn: involucres solitary in the uppermost axils, but approximated from the shortness of the internodes: appendages of the glands often very narrow: shells of the capsule sharply keeled: seed ovate-tetragonal, undulated with 2—3 very obscure wrinkles.

Bengal. Madras.

(11) E. CORRIGIOLOIDES. (*Boiss.*)

Ident. Boiss. Cent. Euph. p. 11.—Dec. l. c. p. 32.

SPEC. CHAR. Perennial, glaucescent: stems with a thickish rhizome, prostrate, elongated, sparingly branched, roughish or glabrate: leaves subsessile, remotish, very unequal at the base, subrotund or oblong, very obtuse, sharply serrulate, above often red-spotted, glabrous, or beneath rough with short hairs: stipules interpetiolar, short, triangular, fimbriated: cymes densely many-headed, subsessile, aggregate and terminal in the uppermost axils: leaflets minute, lanceolate, dentate, intermixed: involucres small, turbinate, glabrous or slightly hairy: lobes long, deeply palmatipartite: glands transversely ovate, appendage broader than them, obsoletely lobed: capsule slightly hairy: shells keeled; styles long, deeply 2-cleft, subclavate at the top: seed ovate-subtetragonal, smooth, strongly dotted.

Concan. Mysore and Carnatic. Madras.

(12) E. SANGUINEA. (*Hochst et Steud.*)

Var. NILAGHIRICA.

Ident. Hochst et Steud in Schimp. pl. Arab.—Dec. l. c. p. 35.

Syn. E. Nilaghirica, *Miq. Anal. Bot.* III. *p.* 17.

SPEC. CHAR. Annual, glabrous, glaucescent: stems ascending, elongated, branched: leaves very unequal at the base, elliptic-rhomboid, somewhat incurved, very obtuse, remotely serrulate: stipules long, subulate from a 2—3-cleft broader base: involucres solitary, approximated in the uppermost axils: floral leaves linear-spathulate, intermixed: lobes linear-lanceolate, entire: glands margined with an irregularly and deeply 3—5-parted rose-coloured appendage: styles 2-cleft, divaricate: shells of the glabrous capsule keeled: seed ovate-tetragonal, covered with a few irregular wrinkles.

Neilgherries.

(13) E. COCCINEA. (*Roth.*)

Ident. Roth. pl. Ind. p. 228.—Dec. l. c. p. 37.

SPEC. CHAR. Perennial: stems filiform, fragile, procumbent, dichotomously branched, densely covered with white wool: lower internodes elongated: leaves entire, very unequal at the base, obovate, obtuse, hairy above or glabrate, beneath densely covered with white hairs: stipules linear-lanceolate, villous: involucres 3—4-glomerulate in the upper axils, short pedicelled, intermixed with lesser orbiculate leaves, turbinate, covered with white wool externally, hairy at the throat: lobes oblong, ciliated: glands transversely oblong, appendage purple denticulate: styles erect, longish, 2-cleft: capsule covered with white wool, depressed, deeply 3-furrowed: shells keeled: seed-oblong-tetragonal, minutely pitted.

Near Ahmednugger, in the Deccan.

(14) E. THYMIFOLIA. (*Burm.*)

Ident. Burm. flor. Ind. p. 8.—Dec. l. c. p. 47.

Syn. E. thymifolia, *var. b. Linn.*—Do. *Lam. dict. Roxb. flor. Ind.* II. *p.* 473.

SPEC. CHAR. Annual: stems filiform, prostrate, much branched, crisply hairy: leaves petioled, somewhat unequal at the base, oblong, obtuse, serrulate-crenulate, glabrous or usually hairy beneath: stipules long lanceolate, fimbriately toothed: involucres axillary, heaped together into very short axillary leafy racemes from the shortness of the internodes, turbinate, deeply cleft: glands stipitate, ovate-rotund, appendage 2—3-lobed: styles 2-cleft: capsules very shortly stalked, erect, hairy, obtusely keeled:

seed reddish, oblong-tetragonal, transversely 4—5-furrowed: flowers-greenish.

Peninsula, flowering all the year.

(15) E. ROSEA. (*Retz.*)

Ident. Retz. obs. IV. p. 26.—Dec. l. c. p. 50.

Syn. E. parviflora, *Lam. dict.*—E. satureioides, *do.*

Engrav. Boiss. Cent. Euph. t. 21.

SPEC. CHAR. Perennial: stems prostrate, geniculate, dichotomously branched, hairy: internodes long, of the floral branchlets very short: leaves glaucescent, thickish, very unequal at the base, obovate, obtuse, minutely crenulate at the top, rameous ones heaped together, somewhat distichous, linear-spathulate, entire or 3—5-denticulate, with a somewhat truncated apex: stipules triangular, fimbriated: involucres terminal, 1—2, usually 3—7, corymbulose, campanulately turbinate, lobes ovate, 3—5-cleft; glands suborbiculate, appendage 6 times larger, semi-ovate rhomboid: styles long, united at the middle, 2-cleft, somewhat thickened at the top: capsule minutely tubercled: shells somewhat keeled: seed ovate-tetragonal, acute, irregularly and coarsely pitted and wrinkled.

Tranquebar. Carnatic. Near Madras.

(16) E. ERYTHROCLADA. (*Boiss.*)

Ident. Dec. l. c. p. 25.

SPEC. CHAR. Annual, glabrous: stem erect, alternately and dichotomously much branched, straight, red; internodes long; leaves very shortly petioled, oblong or oblong-spathulate from a very unequal rounded base, very obtuse, serrulate: stipules scarcely perspicuous; involucres axillary, supported by a pedicel, solitary, turbinate, reddish, white-velvety within: lobes very short, triangular, ciliated: glands transversely ovate, appendage somewhat narrower, rose coloured, slightly eroded; styles very short, 2-cleft: shells of the depressed capsule sharply keeled: seed ovate-tetragonal, obsoletely beset with 2—3 transverse wrinkles.

Deccan.

(17) E. NERIIFOLIA. (*Linn.*)

Ident. Linn. Hort. Cliff. p. 196.—Dec. l. c. p. 79.

Syn. E. ligularia, *Roxb. flor. Ind.* II. *p.* 465.

SPEC. CHAR. Small tree: branches obsoletely pentagonal, prickles stipular, short, diverging, black: leaves obovate-oblong, obtuse, mucronulate, attenuated into a short petiole: cymes sessile or subsessile in the upper axils, 1—3-headed, rarely dichotomously several-headed: leaflets under the involucre ovate, membranaceous: involucre hemispherical: lobes large, ovate, erect, fimbriated at the margin: glands transversely ovate: styles, united at the middle, undivided, capitate at the apex: capsule acutely 3-cornered.

Bombay. Concan. Deccan. In woods and near temples.

(18) E. Nivulia.

Ident. Ham. in Linn. Trans. XVI. p. 886.—Dec. l. c. p. 79.

Syn. E. nereifolia, *Roxb. flor. Ind.* II. 467.

Engrav. Wight's Icon. t. 1862.—Rheede Mal. II. t. 83.

Spec. Char. Shrubby, somewhat verticillately branched: podaria shortly conical, truncated, very much scattered, spirally arranged in 2 rows: prickles stipular, short, divaricate: leaves obovate-lingulate, obtuse, attenuated at the base, short-petioled, middle nerve somewhat keeled beneath: cymes axillary, short-peduncled, 3-headed: lobes of the hemispherical involucre broad, truncated, denticulate: styles united at the middle, scarcely thickened at the top.

Guzerat. Chittagong. Coimbatore and other parts of the Peninsula.

(19) E. antiquorum. (*Linn.*)

Ident. Linn. Hort. Cliff. p. 196.—Dec. l. c. p. 81.

Engrav. Rheede Mal. II. t. 42.—Wight's Icon. t. 897.

Spec. Char. Shrubby, 3-cornered: branches spreading or decumbent, repandly toothed: prickles stipular, short, diverging: leaves obovate-spathulate, attenuated at the base: cymes solitary or twin from the upper lobes of the angles, 3—1-headed: floral leaves ovate, membranaceous and torn at the margin, shorter than the involucre: lobes of the involucre connivent, ovate, fimbriated: styles united at the base, undivided: capsule deeply 3-furrowed: shells compressed, keeled.

Common in most parts of the country, flowering in the cold season.

(20) E. tortilis. (*Rottl.*)

Ident. Rottler in Wight Icon. III. p. 898.—Dec. l. c. p. 81.

Engrav. Wight's Icon. t. 898.

Spec. Char. Shrubby, 3—4-cornered: branches spirally twisted, angles compressed, repandly toothed: prickles diverging: cymes, fascicled in the sinuses of the ribs, short-peduncled, 3-headed: floral leaves oblong, minute: involucres campanulate: styles very short, united at the base, dilated at the apex, 2-lobed.

Peninsula.

(21) E. TRIGONA. (*Haw.*)

Ident. Haw. pl. succ. p. 127.—Dec. l. c. p. 82.

Engrav. Wight's Icon. t. 1863.

SPEC. CHAR. Shrubby, 3-cornered, faces channelled; branches erect, strangulate, angles compressed, lobately toothed: leaves obovate, obtuse, mucronate, much attenuated at the base: prickles short and thick: cymes solitary in the sinuses of the angles, very shortly peduncled, 3-headed: leaves under the involucre ovate, minute: lobes of the hemispherical involucre broad-ovate, fimbriated: styles united, undivided, perceptibly thickened at the top.

Common in stony places at Coimbatore.

(22) E. CATTIMANDOO. (*W. Elliott.*)

Ident. Dec. l. c. p. 83.

Engrav. Wight's Icon. t. 1993.

SPEC. CHAR. Shrub or small tree, sharply pentagonal, deeply furrowed between the ribs, angles flattened, repandly toothed: prickles thin, divergent: leaves sessile, cuneate-obovate, cuspidate: cymes 3—7-headed, frequent: leaflets at the fork and under the involucres ovate-mucronate: lobes of the hemispherical involucre ovate, fimbriated; styles long-united, undivided, not thickened at the apex: capsule deeply 3-furrowed, calyculate, shells laterally somewhat compressed, keeled, leaves of the calyculus acute.

Near Vizagapatam, flowering after the fall of the leaf.

(23) E. ACAULIS. (*Roxb.*)

Ident. Roxb. flor. Ind. II. p. 472.—Dec. l. c. p. 93.

SPEC. CHAR. Perennial: rhizome tuberous, cylindric, frequently scarred at the apex: leaves sessile from the top of the fleshy rhizome, cuneiform, crenulate, dentate: peduncles terminal, 2—3 times dichotomous from the base: leaflets at the divisions white-membranaceous, ovate, truncated, mucronulate, uppermost ones remote from the involucre: involucres in the divisions and terminal, peduncles hemispherical, pedicelled, with spathulate, truncated, fimbriated pectinate lobes: glands transversely and narrow-oblong: capsule long-stalked, depressed, deeply 3-furrowed: shells laterally somewhat compressed, keeled: seed globose, smooth.

Bengal. Bababooden hills, in Malabar.

(24) E. Khasyana. (*Boiss.*)

Ident. Dec. l. c. p. 120.

Spec. Char. Perennial, glabrous: stem erect, striated, branching above: umbel 4—5-rayed, rays 3—5-cleft, bifid: leaves entire, sessile, and long-attenuated at the base, oblong-linear, acute, thickish, umbellary ones elliptic, floral ones ternate, narrowed at the base, ovate, mucronulate: involucres turbinate: lobes ovate, hairy: glands transversely oblong: styles obscurely 2-lobed: capsule globosely depressed, beset with hemispherical warts: seeds subglobose, obscurely raised and pointed: wart much depressed.

Khasya.

(25) E. peltata. (*Roxb.*)

Ident. Roxb. fl. Ind. II. p. 474.—Dec. l. c. p. 137.

Spec. Char. Annual, glabrous: stem erect, branched: rays of the umbel 5, long, 3—4-cleft, afterwards 2-cleft: leaves sessile, attenuated at the base, oblong-lanceolate, acute, serrulate, floral ones oblong: lobes of the campanulate involucre lanceolate, obtuse, exceeding the glands: glands stalked, transversely oblong: capsule somewhat spherical, 3-furrowed: shells rounded.

Coromandel.

(26) E. dracunculoides. (*Lam.*)

Ident. Lam. dict. II. p. 428.—Dec. l. c. p. 139.

Syn. E. lanceolata, *Rottl. in Spreng. syst.* III. *p.* 791.—*Roth. pl. Ind. p.* 229.

Engrav. Boiss. Ic. t. 91.

Spec. Char. Annual, usually many-stemmed: stems erect, leafy, from straightly branched axils: rays of the umbel 2—3, elongated, many times dichotomous: leaves narrowly linear-lanceolate, acutish, attenuated at the base, floral ones abbreviated, lanceolate from a broader base: lobes of the turbinate involucre ovate, denticulate-ciliate: glands semilunate, transversely broader, horns of equal length, or shorter than the breadth of the glands: styles free, short, 2-cleft: capsule depressed, deeply 3-furrowed: seed oblong, blackish, leprous with whitish tubercles, often meeting in lines at the base.

Bengal. Madras. Concan.

(27) E. Rothiana. (*Spreng.*)

Ident. Spreng. syst. III. p. 796.—Dec. l. c. p. 156.

Syn. E. glauca, *Roxb. flor. Ind.* II. *p.* 473.—E. læta, *Roth. pl. Ind. p.* 230.

Gen. Char. Annual, glabrous, glaucescent: stem erect, striated, branched: rays of the umbel in threes, twice 2-cleft: leaves entire, long, narrow, linear, acutish, scarcely attenuated at the base, of the umbel short, lanceolate, floral ones ovate-triangular, often sinuately trilobed, broad: involucre campanulate: lobes oblong, denticulately torn: glands transversely broader, often irregularly pectinately toothed between the short broad horns: filaments hairy: capsule ovate-depressed, 3-furrowed, sparingly hairy: seed lavender-colour, ovate.

Concan. Bombay. Bundelcund.

(28) E. oreophila. (*Miq.*)

Ident. Miq. Anal. Bot. III. p. 17.—Dec. l. c. p. 156.

Spec. Char. Annual or perennial: stem erect, striated, branched: branches twiggy, leafy, often exceeding the central umbel: rays of the umbel 5—8, long, twice or three times 2-cleft: leaves entire, alternate at the base, linear-lanceolate, obtuse, mucronulate, somewhat revolute at the margin, umbellary ones lanceolate, floral ones cordate at the base, triangular-ovate, acute: lobes of the involucre ovate, 2-lobed, ciliated: glands often increased between the horns with a small tooth: filaments hairy: capsule ovate, depressed: seed ovate, marbled: wart depressed and beaked.

Mountains of Southern India. Malabar. Concan. Mysore. Carnatia.

Var. a. pubescens.—Leaves and pedicels of the capsule pubescent.

Canara.

Var b. Wightiana.—Taller: stems thicker, angled: leaves firmer, broader.—E. Rothiana, *Wight Icon. t.* 1864 (not Spreng.). —E. Wightiana, *Bois. Cent. Euph. p.* 37.

Neilgherry hills.

GENUS II. ACTEPHILA.

Monœcia Hexandria. *Sex: Syst:*

Deriv. From *Acte,* a height, and *Philos,* partial to.

Gen. Char. Segments of the male calyx imbricated: petals equal in number to the calycine segments, alternating: stamens inserted round the base of the rudiment of an ovary: anthers opening by two slits, cells adnate lengthwise: cells of the ovary

2-ovuled: stigmas free: capsules tricoccous, shells 2-valved: seeds destitute of aril and wart, exalbuminous: radicle of the embryo minute: cotyledons thick, unequal.—Trees or shrubs: leaves alternate, simple, feather-nerved, entire, glabrous, stipules soon deciduous: flowers diœcious or monœcious, produced from axillary buds, males 3—5-aggregated, females solitary and long-pedicelled or in monœcious species mixed with the males: segments of the calyx 5: male disc 5-lobed: filaments free at the base or connate below: ovary 3-celled: styles 3, connate below, the free portion 2-cleft: capsules 6-seeded: seeds obtusely 3-cornered, smooth.

(1) A. Thomsoni. (*Muller.*)

Ident. Mull. Arg. in. Linn. vol. 34. p. 65.—Dec. prod. XV. s. 2. p. 222.

Spec. Char. Small tree, diœcious: segments of the female calyx linear-lanceolate, acute, beset at the base within by a row of glands: petals linear-lanceolate, stiff, entire, about 3 times shorter than the calyx: leaves rhombo-obovate, obtusely cuspidate-acuminate, cuneate-narrowed at the base: peduncle of female flowers 3-flowered: pedicel elongated, many times equalling the calyx: glands short, truncated, crenulate.

Mysore. Carnatic.

(2) A. excelsa. (*Muller.*)

Ident. Mull. Arg. in Linn. vol. 32. p. 78.—Dec. l. c. p. 222.

Syn. Anomospermum excelsum, *Dalz. in Hook. Journ. Bot.* 1851, *p.* 228.—A. Neilgherrensis, *R. W.*

Engrav. Wight's Icon. t. 1910.

Spec. Char. Large tree, monœcious: calyx somewhat membranaceous, segments suborbicular, rounded, obtuse: petals of either sex oblong-ovate, somewhat entire: leaves elliptic or lanceolate, acute at both ends, smooth, shining: stipules scale-shaped: flowers fascicled, females long-pedicelled: capsule large, globose, smooth.

Conoor, in dense forests. Malabar and Concan. Silhet. Khasia. Flowering in April and May.

GENUS III. MOACURRA.

Diœcia Pentandria. *Sex: Syst:*

Deriv. The native name.

Gen. Char. Segments of the male calyx quincuncial: petals equal in number to the segments of the calyx, alternating, females none: stamens alternating with the petals: glands of the disc opposite the petals, alternating with the filaments, situated between the rudimentary ovary and the stamens: cells of the ovary 2-ovuled: fruit capsular: seeds with a red aril, albuminous.

(1) M. GELONOIDES. (*Roxb.*)

Ident. Roxb. fl. Ind. II. p. 70.—Dec. prod. XV. s. 2. p. 227.

Syn. Celastrus acuminatus, *Wall. cat. No.* 4342.

SPEC. CHAR. Small tree: leaves oblong-ovate or ovate, acute at the base, alternate, long cuspidate-acuminate at the apex, glabrous, entire: stipules subulate: male flowers more or less heaped together in pubescent panicles in the axils of the leaves, pedicelled: female ones with longer pedicels: male petals linear-spathulate, entire, coloured: filaments free: anthers ovoid, with 2 slits inwards: connectivum much thickened, stiff, scrobiculate: glands of the male disc linear-ellipsoid, fleshy: ovary 2-celled, depressed at the top: styles connate below, dilated, recurved.

Silhet.

GENUS IV. SAUROPUS.

Monœcia Decandria. *Sex: Syst:*

GEN. CHAR. Male calyx imbricated in æstivation: petals suppressed: disc extra-staminal or suppressed, 6-lobed round the staminal column, lobes opposite the sepals: stamens central: anthers with 2 slits, cells adnate lengthwise: cells of the ovary 2-ovuled: fruit fleshy, finally bursting.—Shrubs, rarely under-shrubs: flowers monœcious, axillary, very shortly racemulose: male calyx small, females growing larger, more deeply divided, 6-parted, 6-cleft or lobed: anthers situated at the top of the staminal column, distinct, clefts extrorse: ovary 3-celled: styles 3, more or less distinctly 2-parted or cleft: fruit soon dryish, almost corky, then slowly opening as a capsule.

(1) S. ALBICANS. (*Muller.*)

Ident. Dec. prod. XV. s. 2. p. 240.

SPEC. CHAR. Shrub: branchlets angular: male calyx 6-lobed or cleft, very small: ovary obtuse at the apex.

Var. a. GENUINUS.—Leaves oblong-ovate or ovate or ovate-lanceolate acuminate, acute at the base.—Clutia androgyna, *Linn. Mant. p.* 128.—S. albicans, *Blume.*—*Miq. flor. Ind. Bat. I.* 2. *p.* 366.—S. Indicus, *R. W.*—Agyneia ovata, *Miq.* l. c. p. 367.—Wight's Icon. t. 1952.

Courtallum. Khasia.

(2) S. TRINERVIUS. (*Muller.*)

Ident. Mull. Arg. in Linnæa, V. 32. p. 72.—Dec. l. c. p. 242.

Syn. Phyllanthus trinervius, *Wall. Cat. No.* 7922.

SPEC. CHAR. Shrub: branchlets slightly angled: leaves tripli—quintuplinerved: segments of the male calyx afterwards reflexed, linear-elliptic: ovary cylindric, truncated: stipules linear-lanceolate, long-acuminate: leaves ovate-lanceolate, abruptly narrowed at the base: flower-bearing branchlets elongated, bearing many bracts.

Silhet. Khasia hills.

(3) S. QUADRANGULARIS. (*Muller.*)

Ident. Mull. Arg. l. c.—Dec. l. c. p. 242.

Syn. Phyllanthus quadrangularis, *Willd.*

SPEC. CHAR. Undershrub: branches tetragonal, branchlets acutely tetragonal: stipules lanceolate-ovate or acuminate: male calyx 6-lobed, orbicular-depressed: lobes emarginately bilobulate: leaves broadly elliptic or obovate, membranaceous: flowers few.

Malabar. Concan.

(4) S. CERATOGYNUM. (*Baill.*)

Ident. Baill. Etud. gén. Euph. p. 635.—Dec. l. c. p. 243.

Syn. Ceratogynum rhamnoides, *R. W.*—Phyllanthus tenellus, *Wall.*—P. Leschenaultii (*var.* tenellus), *Müll. Arg. in Linnæa l. c. p.* 38.—P. rotundifolius, *Wall.*—P. bacciformis, *do.*—P. Myrtillus, *do.*

Engrav. Wight's Icon. t. 1900.

SPEC. CHAR. Undershrub: male calyx deeply 6-parted: segments linear-lanceolate, almost connivent into a sphere: glands membranaceous, separated from the staminal column and inserted at the base of the calycine segments, hooded: segments of the female calyx broad rhombeo-ovate, acute: leaves broad ovate, obtuse or subcordate at the base, shortly acute at the apex: pedicels all solitary, nearly twice equalling the calyx.

Peninsula.

GENUS V. ANTIDESMA.

Diœcia Pentandria. *Sex: Syst:*

Deriv. From *Anti*, instead of, and *Desmos*, a chain, the bark being used for ropes.

GEN. CHAR. Segments of the male calyx imbricated: petals suppressed: stamens opposite the segments, inserted round the rudiment of the ovary: anthers 2-cleft, cells pendulous from the top: glands of the disc situated between the rudimentary ovary and stamens, alternating with the filaments and calycine segments: ovary 1-celled, cell 2-ovuled: fruit drupaceous, indehiscent: seeds without aril or warts, albuminous: radicle long, thin: cotyledons broad-ovate, flattened.—Small trees, rarely shrubs: leaves alternate, simple, bistipulate, short-petioled, feather-nerved: flowers always diœcious, spiked, or racemose, numerous, small: rachis simple or branched: calyces of either sex 3—8-merous: segments free, small, more or less obscurely coloured: stamens equal in number to the calycine segments, or fewer or more numerous: filaments free, exceeding the calyx, often spirally twisting when dry: cells of the anthers opening outwards: ovary 3-celled: style usually terminal, divisions short, stiff, partly 2-lobed: drupe most frequently 1-seeded by abortion, somewhat fleshy.

(1) A. Ghæsembilla. (*Muller.*)

Ident. Dec. prod. XV. s. 2. p. 251.

Spec. Char. Spikes panicled, densely flowered: bracts small, oblong-obovate, acute, ciliated: male calyx sessile, deeply 5-(7-) parted: disc hairy: ovary ovoid, clothed with pale rusty hairs.

Var. a. paniculatum.—Tree: spikes very densely flowered, usually most thickly covered with woolly down: branchlets rusty or tawny-tomentose: stipules linear-lanceolate: leaves elliptic or obovate, obtuse or very shortly apiculate at the apex, often slightly cordate at the base, rusty-pubescent, especially at the ribs, afterwards glabrate above: spikes rusty-tomentose: fruit obovoid, very slightly compressed: pedicels 3—4 times shorter than the fruit.—A. paniculatum, *Roxb. flor. Ind.* III. *p.* 770. *Wight's Icon. t.* 820.

Concan. Bengal. Flowering in June.

Var. b. genuinum.—Spikes less dense flowered, and less composite, more thin, often longer, less densely covered with woolly down: fruit-bearing pedicels longer.—A. Ghæsembilla, *Gærtn. fr.* I. *p.* 189. *t.* 39.—A. pubescens, *Roxb. Cor.* II. *t.* 167. *Flor. Ind.* III. *p.* 770. *Wight's Icon. t.* 821.

Silhet. Vingorla. Circar mountains. Flowering in the hot season.

(2) A. oblongatum. (*Muller.*)

Ident. Dec. l. c. p. 254.

Spec. Char. Small tree: stipules lanceolate-subulate, nearly equalling the petiole: racemes with large bracts below, flower-bearing bracts linear-lanceolate: calyx small, 3—4-parted beyond the middle: segments orbicular-ovate, acute: disc thick, glabrous: leaves lanceolate, very sharply cuspidate-acuminate, glabrous, ashy brown: drupe ellipsoid, smoothish, undulate-foveate, obtuse at both ends.

Khasia.

(3) A. Menasu. (*Muller.*)

Ident. Dec. l. c. p. 257.

Syn. A. Bunias, *Wall. Cat. No.* 7882.—A. Alexiteria, *Gærtn.*

Spec. Char. Small tree: branchlets softly ashy-pubescent: leaves elliptic-lanceolate, shortly cuspidate, subacute at the base, pubescent at the ribs, afterwards glabrate: racemes simple or paniculately branched: bracts hairy, lanceolate, exceeding the pedicels; calyx hairy within, deeply 3—4-parted: segments ovate, acutish: disc urceolate, lobed, glabrous: drupes slightly compressed, ovoid.

Canara. Khasia. Flowering in March and April.

(4) A. nigricans. (*Tulasne.*)

Ident. Tul. in Annal. des Sc. Nat. 1851. p. 225.—Dec. l. c. p. 258.

Syn. A. Alexiteria, *Willd.* (*not Gærtn.*).

Spec. Char. Small tree: branchlets obscurely tawny-tomentose: leaves oblong-obovate, acuminate, subobtuse at the base: stipules subulate, exceeding the petioles: racemes 2—3-times shorter than the leaves, densely flowered, somewhat paniculately branched, pubescent, becoming black in drying: bracts hairy, ovate-lanceolate, equalling the pedicels: calyx very minute, 4—3-parted almost at the base: segments ovate, acute, afterwards reflexed: disc entire, thick, hemispherical, glabrous: rudiment of the ovary shortly obovoid, glabrous.

Silhet.

(5) A. simile. (*Muller.*)

Ident. Dec. l. c. p. 259.

Syn. A. Bunius, *Wall. Cat. No.* 7282 (*not Spreng.*).

Spec. Char. Shrub: branchlets densely ashy-pubescent: leaves elliptic-lanceolate, acuminate, obtuse at the base, younger ones hairy at the ribs: stipules pubescent, linear-lanceolate, exceeding the short petioles: younger spikes dense-flowered, exceeding the spreading flowers on account of the lanceolate bracts, somewhat squarrose; calyx sessile, 3-parted, triandrous: segments ovate, acute, denticulato-subciliate at the margin: disc glabrous: rudiment of the ovary obconical, glabrous.

Silhet.

(6.) A. Roxburghii. (*Tulasne.*)

Ident. Tul. in Annal. des. Sc. Nat. 1851. p. 234.—Dec. l. c. p. 261.

Syn. Stilago tomentosa, *Roxb. flor. Ind.* III. *p.* 757.—A. tomentosum, *R. W.*

Engrav. Wight's Icon. t. 767-8.

Spec. Char. Tree: branchlets rufescently pubescent, soft: leaves oblong-obovate or obovate-lanceolate, long-acuminate, narrowed towards the base, pubescent above: spikes often paniculately branched, slender, at length loose-flowered, spreading, pedicels of the flowers scarcely to be distinguished: bracts obovate, acute, spreading, hispidulous: calyx hairy, usually 3-lobed, rarely 4—5-lobed, subsessile: male disc glabrous, much evolved, female pubescent: ovary oblong-ovoid, densely hairy: flowers green.

Silhet. Flowering in May and June.

(7) A. comptum. (*Tulasne.*)

Ident. Tul. l. c. p. 190.—Dec. l. c. p. 262.

Spec. Char. Shrub: young branchlets obscurely tawny-pubescent: leaves lanceolate, long acuminate, attenuated at the base, glabrous: stipules narrow, shortish, not exceeding the petiole, tawny-pubescent: racemes spiciform, glabrous: spikes simple or paniculately few-branched, much shorter than the leaves, sparingly tawny or obscurely pubescent: bracts spreading, ovate, acute, small: calyx short-pedicelled, 3-toothed, very small, rusty-tomentose on both sides, especially at the margin inside: disc entire, glabrous: ovary ovoid, above glabrous, the rest tawny pubescent: drupe globose.

Courtallum hills.

(8) A. Bunius. (*Muller.*)

Ident. Dec. l. c. p. 262.

Spec. Char. Spikes strong: bracts ovate: female calyx shortly pedicelled with the male, shortly 3—4 cleft, triandrous: disc of male flowers thick, glabrous: ovary ovoid, glabrous.

Var. a. sylvestre.—Tree: younger branchlets rusty-tomentose: leaves lanceolate-elliptic, acute at the base: rudiment of the ovary trigonal-obovoid, rusty, with hairs at the base only.—A. sylvestre, *Lam. Dict.*—Stilago Bunius, *Roxb. flor. Ind.* III. *p.* 758.—A. glabrum, *Tul. l. c. p.* 188. *Rheede Mal.* V. *t.* 26.

Silhet. Concan?

Var. b. Wallichii.—Tree: branchlets rusty-pubescent: leaves acute at the base: rudiment of an ovary all glabrous or endowed with a very few hairs at the summit.

Madras.

(9) A. DIANDRUM. (*Tulasne.*)

Ident. Tul. l. c. p. 198.—Dec. l. c. p. 266.

SPEC. CHAR. Stipules linear-lanceolate, longish : bracts broad-ovate, rotund obtuse : calyx urceolar, shortly 4-toothed, diandrous : disc hairy : ovary obovoid, attenuated above, glabrous.

Var. a. OVATUM.—Tul. l. c. p. 198.—Shrub : branchlets tawny-tomentose : leaves broad ovate or obovate or elliptic, at both ends rotund-obtuse or shortly and obtusely acutate, often mucronulate : calyx glabrescent within.—A. sylvestre, *Wall. Cat. No.* 7281.

Mountainous districts.

Var. b. GENUINUM. — Shrub : branchlets tawny-tomentose : leaves elliptic, subacuminate, glabrous, pubescent or subciliated at the margin : petioles rusty-villous : racemes terminal, paniculately branched, rusty, somewhat glabrous : calyx glabrous outside, tawny-hairy within : drupe ellipsoid, shortly acuminate, putamen compressed, coarsely pitted.—A. diandrum, *Roth. Spreng.*—Stilago diandra, *Roxb. Cor.* II. *t.* 166. *Flor. Ind.* III. *p.* 759.

Circar Mountains. Neilgherries. Canara. Flowering in June.

Var. c. LANCEOLATUM.—Tul. l. c. p. 199.—Shrubby : branchlets and leaves afterwards glabrous : leaves lanceolate, narrowed at the base and apex, sharply acuminated at the apex : racemes at first spiciform, dense-flowered, slender, flowers at length slenderly pedicelled.—A. lanceolarium, *Wall. Cat. No.* 7284. *Wight's Icon. t.* 766.—Stilago lanceolaria, *Roxb. l. c. p.* 760.

Chittagong. Khasia.

Var. d. PARVIFOLIUM.—Tul. l. c. p. 198.—Small tree : branchlets soon glabrate : leaves obovate-lanceolate, acute at both ends, narrowed towards the base.—A. Wallichianum, *Presl. Epimel. p.* 235.

Silhet.

GENUS VI. PHYLLANTHUS.

Monœcia Decandria. *Sex : Syst :*

Deriv. From *Phyllon*, a leaf, and *Anthos*, a flower, the flowers being produced from the edges of the leaves.

GEN. CHAR. Segments of the male calyx imbricated : petals none : glands of the disc alternating with the calycine segments, or suppressed : stamens central : cells of the (2—15-celled) ovary 2-ovuled : fruit capsular, 2—polycoccous : seeds ecarunculate, without aril, albuminous : embryo straightish : cotyledons flattened.—Trees or usually shrubs, very often undershrubs, rarely herbs : flower-bearing branchlets very often distichous, sparingly leafy, or with the leaves reduced to scales: leaves distichous, various in form and size, most usually glabrous, never long-petioled, entire, feather-nerved, bistipulate: inflorescences axillary, monœcious or diœcious, or even in the same branchlet, the lower or intermediate ones unisexual, distinct from the rest by their sex, sometimes with the sexes mixed, some unisexual or all bisexual, sometimes reduced to a single flower: flowers fascicled or solitary: calyces small, even very minute, 9—4-parted or shorter divided, segments biverticillately imbricated, usually 6—5: stamens 15—2, very often 3, filaments free or variously even with the connectivum, connate, erect: clefts of the anthers extrorse: rudiments of the ovary none: ovaries 15—2-celled, most usually 3-celled: styles equal in number to the cells, usually slender, occasionally connate, commonly 2-cleft or parted, or 2-lobed, or slightly furrowed, obtuse or acute, usually smooth: fruit a dehiscent capsule, dry, in some at first fleshy, and afterwards capsular: shell sometimes somewhat bony: seeds smooth, or rough with warts, or variously ribbed.

(1) P. MULTILOCULARIS. (*Muller.*)

Ident. Mull. Arg. in Flora Ratisb. 1865. p. 370.—Dec. prod. XV. s. 2. p. 279.

Syn. Agyneia multilocularis, *Willd.*—Bradleia multilocularis *Spreng. Roxb. flor. Ind.* III. p. 696.—B. nitida, *Wall. Cat.* (*not Roxb.*).—B. pubera, *Wall. Cat.* (*not Roxb.*).—B. Phillipensis, *Wall. Cat.*—Agyneia pubera, *Wall. Cat.* (*not Linn.*).—Glochidion multiloculare, *Mull. Arg. in Linnæa* v. 32. *p.* 59.

SPEC. CHAR. Small tree: branchlets acutely angular, brown-purplish: stipules triangular-lanceolate: leaves ovate or obovate-lanceolate, acute at the base, narrowed rotund-obtuse at the apex, mucronulate, beneath densely reticulated, purplish-brown or glaucescent: segments of male calyx obovate, obtuse, of female 6—many-parted, segments ovate: flowers fascicled: ovary 10—15-celled, depresso-globose, glabrous: styles short, connate into a depressed thick cone: ovary 10—15-ribbed lengthwise, grey: capsules large, depressed, concave at both ends: flowers greenish cream-coloured.

Bengal. Silhet. Flowering nearly all the year.

(2) P. LITTORALIS. (*Muller.*)

Ident. Mull. Arg. l. c.—Dec. l. c. p. 280.

Syn. Glochidion littorale, *Bl. bidj. p.* 585.—Bradleia littorea, *Steudel.*—B. obtusa, *Wall. Cat.*—Agyneia impuber, *do.* (*not Linn.*).

SPEC. CHAR. Small tree: leaves orbicular or ovate-elliptic or broad-obovate, acutish at the base, beneath brown, glabrous: inner segments of the male calyx shorter than the rest, oblong-elliptic, obtuse, of the female broad-elliptic, obtuse, glabrous: anthers

5—6: male pedicels short, females flower-bearing, almost none: ovary 12—10-celled, very shortly silky-pubescent: styline column 10—12-furrowed, glabrous, base broad, shortly conical: stigmas emarginately retuse at the apex: capsules moderately depressed, lightly many-furrowed, puberulous at the apex.

Peninsula.

(3) P. ZEYLANICUS. (*Muller.*)

Ident. Dec. l. c. p. 281.

Syn. Bradleia Zeylanica, *Gærtn.*—Glochidion Zeylanicum, *Ad. Juss. Tent. Euph. p.* 107. *t.* 3.—Agyneia obliqua, *Willd.* Bradleia obliqua, *Spreng.*—Glochidion Bancanum, *Miq. flor. Ind. Bat. suppl.* 449.

SPEC. CHAR. Small tree: branchlets glabrous: stipules triangular-ovate, acuminated, stiff, recurved, persistent: leaves oblong-elliptic, obtuse or shortly acuminate, usually lightly cordate at the base, above more or less pale, shining, beneath purplish-brown, densely transversely ribbed: flowers somewhat numerous in the axils of the leaves: fascicles often shortly peduncled and supra-axillary: pedicels fascicled: segments of the male calyx broad-ovate, obtuse, often one or the other of the inner ones with 2 auricles at the base, of the female subrotund or broad-ovate: stamens 5—6: ovary 7—4-celled, globose, glabrous: styline column conical, 7—4-lobed at the apex, with emarginate lobes: capsule ovoid-globose, lightly depressed, scarcely furrowed, apiculated with the styline crown.

Canara.

(4) P. NITIDUS. (*Muller.*)

Ident. Mull. Arg. l. c. p. 370.—Dec. l. c. p. 282.

Syn. Bradleia nitida, *Roxb. fl. Ind.* III. *p.* 699.—Glochidion nitidum, *Dalz. Bomb. flor. p.* 235.

SPEC. CHAR. Small tree or shrub: leaves oblongate-ovate, acute, unequal-sided at the base, glabrous, shining, pale above: stipules minute, acute, inflorescences very shortly peduncled, somewhat supra-axillary: flowers of either sex mixed in each inflorescence, females, however, much more numerous, and many times shorter-pedicelled than the males: calycine segments ovate, acute: ovary 5—6-celled, glabrous: styline column conical, truncated, 5—6-cleft at the apex: lobes emarginately bilobulate: anthers 5—7: capsule depresso-globose, 10—12-furrowed.

Valleys of the Circar mountains. South Concan. Vingorla. Flowering in January.

(5) P. LANCEOLARIUS. (*Muller.*)

Ident. Mull. l. c.—Dec. l. c. p. 282.

Syn. Bradleia lanceolaria, *Roxb. fl. Ind.* III. *p.* 697.—Glochidion lanceolaria, *Dalz. l. c.*—B. acuminata, *Wall. Cat. No.* 7855.—Glochisandra acuminata, *R. W.*—B. Zeylanica, *Wall. l. c.*

Engrav. Wight's Icon. t. 1905.—Lodd. Bot. cab. t. 839.

SPEC. CHAR. Shrub: leaves elliptic-lanceolate, or oblongate-elliptic, acute, shining: segments of the female calyx oblong-ovate, of the male lanceolate, narrowed at both ends: male flowers fascicled, females glomerate: ovary 8—6-celled, sub-globose, pale silky: styline column cylindric-conical, longer than the ovary, hoary-silky, shortly 8—6-toothed at the apex: capsule subglobose, depressed at the apex, furrowed.

Common on the Ghauts. Silhet. Behar. Khasia. Chittagong.

(6) P. TOMENTOSUS. (*Muller.*)

Ident. Mull. Arg. l. c.—Dec. l. c. p. 283.

SPEC. CHAR. Shrub, sparingly branched towards the apex: leaves ovate or elliptic, acute, lightly cordate at the base, sparingly pubescent above, subtomentose beneath: flowers fascicled: calyces tomentose, female 4—6-parted, outer-segments broad-ovate, inner ones narrow-elliptic: stamens 5: ovary 4—5-celled, silky-tomentose, 6-angled at the base: styline column thick, conical, shortly 4—5-lobed, silky tomentose as far as the lobes.

Canara. Malabar. Concan.

(7) P. OBLIQUUS. (*Muller.*).

Ident. Mull. Arg. l. c.—Dec. l. c. p. 284.

SPEC. CHAR. Flowers of either sex fascicled: segments of the 6-parted male calyx broad-ovate, obtuse, of the female ovate: ovary 4—5-celled, sub-globose, pale silky: styline column conical, obtuse, 4—5-cleft: capsule depressed.

Var. GENUINUS.—Small tree: stipules broad triangular-ovate, acuminate, persistent: leaves elliptic or oblong-ovate, or ovate-lanceolate, acute, subobtuse, unequal-sided at the base, often lightly curved: female flower-bearing pedicels long: ovary silky as far as the base of the styline column, which is glabrous: capsules 4—5-coccous, 10—8-furrowed: seeds chestnut-brown.—Glochidion obliquum, *Decaisne Herb. Tim.* III. *p.* 481.—Agyneia obliqua, *Wall. Cat. No.* 7863.—A. flexuosa, *do.*

Peninsula?

(8) P. Canaranus. (*Muller.*)

Ident. Mull. Arg. l. c.—Dec. l. c. p. 284.

Spec. Char. Shrub: leaves oblong-obovate or oblong-elliptic, acute, obtuse or very shortly acutish at the base, pale above, purplish-brown beneath: flowers fascicled: segments of the 4—6-parted female calyx oblong-ovate, somewhat unequal: ovary 5—6-celled, glabrous: styles connate into a rather thin cylindric column, 6-cleft at the apex: capsules globose, slightly depressed at the base and apex, scarcely furrowed, beaked with the persistent styline column.

Canara. Mysore.

(9) P. Hohenhackeri. (*Muller.*)

Ident. Mull. Arg. l. c.—Dec. l. c. p. 288.

Spec. Char. Tree: leaves ovate-lanceolate, acuminate or subcuspidate, narrowed at the base, brown, more or less shining above: male flowers pedicelled, females sessile: female calyx 4-toothed: segments of the 6-parted male calyx oblong-elliptic: ovary 4-celled, glabrous: styline column much depressed, thick, a little shorter and broader than the ovary, deeply cruciately 4-cleft: capsule depressed, 4-coccous, 8-furrowed, crowned by the styline column.

Canara. Malabar. Concan.

(10) P. fagifolius. (*Muller.*)

Ident. Mull. Arg. l. c.—Dec. l. c. p. 288.

Spec. Char. Male flowers pedicelled, females sessile: segments of the 6-cleft female calyx triangular-ovate, of the male oblong-ovate: ovary globose, 4—6-celled, glabrous: styline column depressed, thick, radiately 4—6-cleft at the top.

Var. a. concolor.—Tree: branchlets of the same obscurely green colour: stipules oblongate-ovate, recurved at the margin: leaves oblong or lanceolate-ovate, acuminate, acute at the base, ashy-green above, purplish-brownish beneath, somewhat unequal-sided: male calyces obovate, females slightly puberulous externally, about 3—8-glomerate in the axils: styline column grey.

Chittagong. Neilgherries.

Var. b. cœsius.—Branchlets intensely grey above: styline column grey: leaves often narrower, paler above.

Neilgherries.

(11) P. Thomsoni. (*Muller.*)

Ident. Mull. Arg. l. c.—Dec. l. c. p. 293.

Spec. Char. Small tree: stipules subulate-acuminate, ovate-lanceolate at the base: leaves oblong-elliptic, shortly acute at both ends, intensely white-glaucous beneath, afterwards slightly rubescent and distinctly veined: pedicels of either sex elongated: calycine segments broad-elliptic, obtuse: ovary 3-celled, glabrous: styline column very short, 3-furrowed: capsule depressed, 3-coccous, deeply 3-furrowed.

Khasia hills.

(12) P. ASPERUS. (*Muller.*)

Ident. Mull. Arg. l. c.—Dec. l. c. p. 297.

SPEC. CHAR. Shrub: branchlets hispidulous, obscurely tawny-tomentose: stipules linear-lanceolate: leaves elliptic, ovate or obovate, minutely mucronulate, pubescent on both sides, rough with whitish tubercles: pedicels of either sex short, males densely pubescent, females tomentose: calyces subtomentose: segments of the females oblong-obovate, subacute: ovary globose, 4-celled, very slightly tomentose: styline column subcylindric, pubescent, twice or nearly 3 times equalling the ovary, and almost equally broad.

Malabar. Concan.

(13) P. SILHETICUS. (*Muller.*)

Ident. Mull. Arg. l. c. p. 378.—Dec. l. c. p. 297.

SPEC. CHAR. Small tree: branchlets tomentose, with short, dark, tawny, or rufescent hairs: petioles red-hairy: leaves oblong-elliptic, obtuse or slightly cordate at the base, above pubescent on the nerves, beneath at the margin and on the ribs densely pubescent and soft, marked everywhere with a yellowish line: pedicels short: ovary globose, 4-celled, obscurely tomentose: styline column conical, scarcely exceeding the ovary: capsule depressed, deeply 6-furrowed, pubescent, very small.

Silhet.

(14) P. ASSAMICUS. (*Muller.*)

Ident. Mull. Arg. l. c.—Dec. l. c. p. 297.

SPEC. CHAR. Small tree, quite glabrous, except the pedicels and ovaries: leaves ovate-lanceolate, cuspidate-acuminate, acute at the base, slightly unequal-sided, brown: male pedicels pubescent, fruit-bearing ones scarcely exceeding the diameter of the capsule, females scarcely any: segments of the male calyx oblong-elliptic: ovary 4—3-celled, depressed, globose, sparingly whitish-silky: styline column conical-cylindric, glabrous, a little exceeding the ovary in length, and much narrower, obsoletely 4—3-cleft at the apex: capsules numerous, small, depressed, smoothish, rufescent, 4-coccous, afterwards glabrate.

Upper Assam.

(15) P. DIVERSIFOLIUS. (*Muller.*)

Ident. Mull. Arg. l. c.—Dec. l. c. p. 297.

SPEC. CHAR. Male flowers fascicled, females glomerate: calyces small: segments elliptic, subacute at both ends: ovary globose, 2—4-celled, obscurely silky, ending in a 3—4-lobed, somewhat silky, conical styline column: capsule depressed, deeply 3—4-furrowed, very shortly pubescent.

Var. a. LONGIFOLIUS.—Shrub: branchlets glabrous, or younger ones puberulous and afterwards glabrate: leaves more elongated, lanceolate: capsules hoary-pubescent.—Glochidion ellipticum, *Wight's Icon. t.* 1606.

Malabar and Concan.

Var. b. WIGHTIANUS.—Undershrub (?): branchlets glabrous: leaves acute at the base, very unequal-sided, long cuspidate-acuminate.—Bradleia Wightiana, *Wall. Cat. No.* 7862.

Peninsula.

(16) P. NEILGHERRENSIS. (*Muller.*)

Ident. Mull. Arg. l. c.—Dec. l. c. p. 303.

Syn. Glochidion Neilgherrense, *Wight's Icon. ad. n.* 1907.

SPEC. CHAR. Small, low tree: leaves lanceolate-elliptic, obtuse or acute, slightly unequal-sided, and often curved inwards, glabrous, pale above, beneath rufescent-brown: male flowers short pedicelled, females sessile aggregate in trees: male calyx 6-parted, female 6-cleft: female segments often connate in pairs: concectivum very long: ovary depressed-globose, 5—6-celled, silky: styline column thick, truncated, 5—6-lobulate, 3—4 times longer than the ovary: capsule depressed-globose, very shortly and sparingly tawnyish-silky.

Ootacamund, Neilgherries.

(17) P. ARBOREUS. (*Muller.*)

Ident. Mull. Arg. l. c.—Dec. l. c. p. 303.

Syn. Glochidion arboreum, *R. Wight.*

Engrav. Wight's Icon. t. 1907.

SPEC. CHAR. Tree: branchlets pubescent: leaves oblong-ovate, acuminate, unequal-sided at the base, rounded on one side, acute on the other: pedicels of either sex mixed, males a little exceeding the petioles, gradually thickened, females scarcely any: male flowers fascicled, females glomerate: male calyx 6-parted, female somewhat 6-cleft: female segments broad, tri-angular-ovate, often partly connate in pairs and pubescent externally: connectivum elongated: ovary 5-celled, glabrous: styline column much exceeding the calyx and ovary, thick, subovoid, truncated, 5-toothed, at the base much broader than the ovary, and as if lengthened out backwards.

Shevagherry hills, near Courtallum.

(18) P. Malabaricus. (*Muller.*)

Ident. Mull. Arg. l. c. p. 69.—Dec. l. c. p. 305.

Spec. Char. Shrub: branchlets puberulous, more or less flexuose: stipules lanceolate-subulate, entire: leaves oblong- or lanceolate-elliptic, shortly and acutely cuspidate-acuminate, subacute at the base, brown and darkish: flowers numerous, males slenderly pedicelled, females subsessile, glomerate, sexes mixed; segments of the male calyx lanceolate, at length elongated: ovary 3—4-celled, globose, puberulous: styline column obconical-cylindric, not constricted at the base, nearly equalling the ovary in diameter, twice or a little beyond it in length, sharply erect at the apex, 6—8-lobulate, greyish puberulous.

Malabar and the adjacent districts.

(19) P. Perrotetianus. (*Muller.*)

Ident. Mull. Arg. l. c.—Dec. l. c. p. 307.

Spec. Char. Small tree: stipules ovate: leaves lanceolate-elliptic, acute at both ends, slightly unequal-sided, glabrous, olive-green, beneath rufescent-brownish: female flowers sessile, subsolitary: female calyx 5—6-toothed, obconical, rufous-puberulous: ovary 5—6-celled, globose, glabrous: styline column broadly obconical, truncated, slightly 5—6-cleft, a little exceeding the ovary in length, in breadth equalling it at the base and not constricted: lobes furrowed at the back: capsule 5—6-coccous, much depressed.

Neilgherries.

(20) P. velutinus. (*Muller.*)

Ident. Mull. Arg. in Flora Ratisb. l. c. p. 380.—Dec. l. c. p. 309.

Spec. Char. Shrub: leaves oblong-elliptic or oblong-obovate, pubescent, shortly acuminate, acute at the base: petioles densely tomentose: flowers pedicelled: ovary 4-celled, globose, silky-tomentose: styline column cylindric-obovoid, truncated at the apex, 4-cleft, somewhat twice exceeding the ovary, whitish-tomentose: lobes 4-furrowed at the middle: capsules subglobose, small, tomentose.

Neilgherries. Khasia.

(21) P. Heyneanus. (*Muller.*)

Ident. Mull. Arg. in Flora Ratisb. l. c.—Dec. l. c. p. 311.

Syn. Gynoon Heyneanum, *W. and A. ex. Dietr. Syn. pl.* 5. *p*. 388.—Giochidion Heyneanum, *R. Wight.*

Engrav. Wight's Icon. t. 1908.

Spec. Char. Small tree: leaves lanceolate, acuminate, acute at the base, usually slightly unequal-sided, rusty-pubescent beneath: male pedicels glabrous, females pubescent: segments of the male calyx ovate, acute, glabrous, female oblong-obovate, acuminate, pubescent; ovary 5-celled, silky, globose: styline column long-obconical, 3 times equalling the ovary in length, much narrower than the ovary at the base.

Peninsula.

(22) P. bicolor. (*Muller.*)

Ident. Mull. l. c.—Dec. l. c. p. 311.

Syn. Bridelia acuminata, *Wall. Cat. No.* 7885.—Phyllanthus acuminatus, *Vahl.*—Glochidion acuminatum, *Mull. Arg. in Linnæa* V. 32. *p*. 68.

Spec. Char. Small tree: branchlets pale tawny and silky pubescent at the apex: leaves lanceolate, long-acuminate, acute at the base, usually slightly unequal-sided, above pubescent on the ribs, the rest glabrous, beneath more or less silvery-pale or whitish, always beneath much paler, and very shortly pubescent: male flowers fascicled, females at first subglomerate: pedicels of either sex pubescent: calycine segments oblong-elliptic, obtuse, inner ones narrower and a little shorter: ovary 3—4-celled, globose, silky: styline column cylindric-obconical, above a little broader, shortly 3—5-cleft, 3 or 4 times equalling the ovary in length, thinner than it at the base, thicker at the apex, long exceeding the calyx: capsule small, depressed, deeply furrowed, umbilicately depressed at the base and apex.

Eastern Bengal.

(23) P. Khasicus. (*Muller.*)

Ident. Mull. l. c.—Dec. l. c. p. 311.

Spec. Char. Shrub: stipules ovate-lanceolate, acuminate: leaves elliptic or obovate-lanceolate, long cuspidate-acuminate, acute at the base, unequal-sided: male pedicels slender, females scarcely any: segments of the female calyx oblong-elliptic, glabrous, inner ones smaller: ovary 3-celled, glabrous, globose, passing gradually into the styline cylindrico-clavate column: styline column 4—5 times longer than the ovary, 3-toothed, all glabrous: capsule depressed, 3-furrowed.

Khasia hills.

(24) P. Wightianus. (*Muller.*)

Ident. Mull. Arg. in Linnæa V. 32. p. 6.—Dec. l. c. p. 334.

Syn. Chorisandra pinnata, *R. Wight.*

Engrav. Wight's Icon. t. 1994.

Spec. Char. Shrub: branchlets numerous, about 9—12-leaved, appearing like a pinnate leaf, glabrous: leaves elliptic or obovate, obtuse at both ends, membranaceous, pale: segments of the male calyx elliptic, obtuse, more or less undulated at the margin, of the female moderately unequal: glands of the male flowers free: disc hypogynous, 5—6-lobed.

Southern Peninsula. Pondicherry.

(25) P. longipes. (*Muller.*)

Ident. Mull. Arg. l. c. p. 11.—Dec. l. c. p. 341.

Syn. Peltandra longipes, *R. Wight.*—Croton pedunculatum, *Wall. Cat. No.* 7767.

Engrav. Wight's Icon. t. 1891.

Spec. Char. Tree: branchlets subflexuose, glabrous: leaves ovate-lanceolate, gradually acuminate towards the apex, obtuse at the base, repandly subdentate at the margin: female pedicels afterwards very long: calyx green-herbaceous: staminal column 5-lobed: capsule subglobose, depressed at the top.

Quilon.

(26) P. peltandra. (*Muller.*)

Ident. Mull. Arg. l. c.—Dec. l. c.

Syn. Peltandra parvifolia, *R. Wight.*

Engrav. Wight's Icon. t. 1892.

Spec. Char. Tree: leaves ovate, short-acuminate, obtuse at the base, entire: flower-bearing branchlets small, shorter than the petioles, densely bracteate: bracts broad-ovate, obtuse, fimbriately cut above: female pedicels about equalling the leaves: segments of both calyces obovate, obtuse: male disc subentire, female repandly 6-lobed.

Malabar.

(27) P. reticulatus. (*Muller.*)

Ident. Dec. l. c. p. 344.

Spec. Char. Flowers fascicled: ovary 12—6-celled, globose, glabrous: styles short, erect, 2-lobed: capsules subglobose, depresso-truncated at the apex.

Var. a. genuinus.—Shrub: branchlets softly grey or somewhat tawny, or pubescent with sordid hairs: branches sometimes partly scandent: leaves broad or narrow elliptic, ovate, or obovate, obtuse, acutish at the base, brownish-green above, beneath of the same colour or glaucescent: stipules triangular-linear, broadish at the base, lowest ones of the branchlets more or less distinctly spinescently hardened and recurved: female pedicels a little longer than the males: fruit at first somewhat berry-shaped, then more dry, depresso-globose, obtusely 6—12-ribbed.—P. reticulatus, *Poir.* — Anisonema reticulatum, *Adr. Juss. Euph. t.* 4. *fig.* xi.—Kirganelia reticulata, *Baill. Etud. p.* 613.—Phyllanthus multiflorus, *Willd. Roxb. flor. Ind.* III. *p.* 664 (*not Poir*).—A. multiflorum, *Wight's Icon. t.* 1899.—P. pentandrus, *Roxb. in Thwaites' Enum. pl. Zeyl.*—P. Wightianus, *Wall. Cat.*—P. Prieurianus, *Mull. Arg. in Linn.* V. 32. *p.* 12.—A. dubium, *Bl. bidjr.* —Kirganelia dubia, *Baill. Etud. Gen. Euph.*—K. puberula, *do.*

Common in all India.

Var. b. GLABER.—Mull. Arg. in Linnæa, V. 32, p. 12.—Glabrous: a common variety of the preceding —K. multiflora, *Thwaites l. c.* —K. Wightiana, *Baill. l. c. p.* 614.—P. Wightianus, *Wall.*— K. eglandulosa, *Baill. l. c.*—K. intermedia, *Baill. l. c.*—P. multiflorus, *Wall.* (*not Poir*).—P. Kirganelia, *Roxb. flor. Ind.* III. *p.* 668.—P. Jamaicensis, *Grisebach flora of West Indies*, p. 34.

(28) P. EMBLICA. (*Linn.*)

Ident. Linn. spec. p. 1393.—Dec. l. c. p. 352.—Roxb. flor. Ind. III p. 671.

Syn. Emblica officinalis, *Gærtn.* — Phyllanthus glomeratus, *Wall.*

Engrav. Lodd. Bot. Cab. t. 548.—Baill. Etud. p. 627. t. 24. fig. 20—24.—Adr. Juss. Tent. Euph. t. 5. fig. 15.—Wight's Icon. t. 1896.

SPEC. CHAR. Tree: leaves densely distichous, narrow linear-elliptic, obtuse at both ends, or a little acute at the apex, recurved at the margin, glabrous: petioles very short: flowers very numerous, fascicled, males pedicelled, females sessile: glands of the male flowers very often none: urceolus hypogynous, cylindric, with many small divisions at the apex: anthers shortly apiculated: ovary ovoid: styles large, compressed above, twice dichotomously divided, papillose, connate at the base into a column nearly equalling the ovary: fruit globose, large, subbaccate, fleshy, slowly opening as a capsule.

Common in most parts of India.

(29) P. POLYPHYLLUS. (*Willd.*)

Ident. Willd. sp. vol. IV. p. 586.—Dec. l. c. p. 352.

Syn. P. taxifolius, *Don. prod. Flor. Nep. p.* 63.—P. racemosus, *Wall. Cat. No.* 7902.

Engrav. Wight's Icon. t. 1895. fig. 2.

SPEC. CHAR. Shrub: leaves narrow or linear-oblongate-elliptic, obtuse at both ends, mucronulate at the apex, densely approximated, recurved at the margin, glabrous, equally broad for some distance: stipules triangular, ovate or lanceolate, denticulate, acuminated: flowers fascicled, very shortly pedicelled, rising from the very small densely bracteated branchlets, all very shortly pedicelled: glands of the male flowers distinct: disc hypogynous, dwarf, annular-crenulate: anthers shortly apiculated: ovary globose: styline column slender: styles thin, elongated, 2-cleft: capsules 3-furrowed: seeds pale, deeply pitted.

Mysore and Carnatic. Concans.

(30) P. LAWII. (*J. Grah.*)

Ident. Grah. Cat. of Bombay plants p. 181.—Dec. l. c. p. 353.

SPEC. CHAR. Shrub: branchlets fascicled: stipules triangular-lanceolate, hardened: leaves linear-elliptic, subacute, slightly cordate at the base, paler beneath: flowers axillary in the branchlets, densely bracteate, somewhat fascicled: pedicels short: calycine segments elliptic: glands of the male flowers free, of the females connate into an hexagonal urceolus: anthers shortly apiculate, straightly erect: ovary smooth: styles connate, nearly a third part of their length archedly recurved above and 2-lobed.

Near Bombay.

(31) P. STYLOSUS. (*Griff.*)

Ident. Griff. Posth. papers. II. p. 33.—Dec. l. c. p. 353.

SPEC. CHAR. Low undershrub: leaves half-spreading: monœcious flowers of either sex aggregated in the axils of the leaves, upper axils only bearing male flowers: calycine segments reflexed: glands of male flowers distinct: styles elongated, deeply 3-parted.

At the margins of torrents in Khasia.

(32) P. BŒOBOTRYOIDES. (*Muller.*)

Ident. Mull. Arg. in Linnæa V. 32. p. 15.—Dec. l. c. p. 354.

SPEC. CHAR. Shrub, glabrous: branchlets acutely quadrangular, above after the fall of the leaves somewhat paniculately floriferous: stipules lanceolate, recurved, stiff, paler and subscariose at the margin: leaves oblong-ovate or ovate-lanceolate, acute or acuminate, obtuse at the base, subcoriaceous, brown: racemes axillary: monœcious flowers racemosely situated in axillary branchlets, solitary or sometimes twin, females sessile, males shortly pedicelled: calycine segments coriaceous, oblong-ovate: glands of male flowers free, obovoid-trigonal, of females narrow, slightly free: anthers shortly apiculate: styline column equalling the ovary, free part of the styles bipartite, spreadingly recurved.

Silhet.

(33) P. JUNIPERINOIDES. (*Muller.*)

Ident. Mull. l. c. p. 18.—Dec. l. c. p. 358.

Syn. P. spinulosus, *Wall. Cat. No.* 7987.

SPEC. CHAR. Shrub, glabrous: stipules afterwards spinescent: leaves small, oblongate-ovate, shortly acuminated or obtuse, cordate at the base: styles erect, 2-cleft: flowers axillary, small, subsolitary, shortly pedicelled: calycine segments oblong-ovate, subacute: glands of either sex small, of male flowers free, of female connate into a 6-lobed urceolus: staminal column entire: anthers oblong, apiculated: ovary glabrous: capsule subglobose, acutish: seeds very lightly pitted.

Malabar. Concan.

(34) P. PENDULUS. (*Roxb.*)

Ident. Roxb. flor. Ind. III. p. 662.—Dec. l. c. p. 359.

SPEC. CHAR. Shrub, glabrous: branches flexuose, often somewhat pendulous: leaves lanceolate-elliptic, subacute, coloured at the margin, upper ones smaller: flowers monœcious: racemules situated in the lower part of the branchlets at length half-equalling the leaves, densely bracteated in 4 rows, pendulous: female flowers solitary in the upper axils: calycine segments orbicular-ovate, acute: disc of either sex urceolar: ovary globose: styles spreading divergingly, 2-cleft.

Peninsula, flowering in the rainy season.

(35) P. MADERASPATENSIS. (*Muller.*)

Ident. Mull. Arg. l. c. p. 19.—Dec. l. c. p. 362.

SPEC. CHAR. Branchlets tetragonal: flowers fascicled, females solitary, mixed with 1—5 males in each axil: pedicels short: calycine segments of either sex rhomb-obovate, narrowly white margined, at length larger, adpressed in fruit: filaments strong, very shortly free at the apex: styles short, thick, 2-cleft or lobed: seeds regularly rough-dotted.

Var. a. THONNINGII.—Mull. Arg. l. c.—Undershrub: leaves obovate-lanceolate, upper ones more or less linear: male flowers 1—3 in each axil.—*Wight's Icon. t.* 1895.

Mysore. Carnatic.

Var. b. GENUINUS.—Undershrub, perennial: leaves broader or narrower cuneate-obovate or lanceolate, abruptly acuminate at the apex: male flowers 2—4-nate: glands of either sex free, of the male flowers suborbicular, of the females oblong: capsules lightly trigonal: seeds a little rough.—*Roxb. flor. Ind.* III. 654. —P. andrachnoides, *Willd.*—P. obcordatus, *Roxb.*—P. Javanicus, *Poir ex Speeng. Syst.*—P. gracilis, *Roxb. flor. Ind.* III. 654.

Peninsula.

(36) P. Rheedii. (*R. W.*)

Ident. Wight's Icon. vol. V.—Dec. l. c. p. 363.

Syn. P. flaccidus, *Thwaites Enum. Pl. Zeyl. p.* 283.

Engrav. Wight l. c. t. 1895. fig. 1.—Rheede Mal. II. t. 27.

Spec. Char. Perennial: branchlets angular: stipules linear-lanceolate, long and sharply subulate-acuminate: leaves broad or narrow obovate, very shortly acute, subacute at the base, glaucescent beneath: flowers almost twin or solitary, females few, all shortly pedicelled: segments of the male calyx oblong-ovate, subacute: glands elegantly stellulately tubercled: staminal column shortly 3-cleft: styles reflexed, divergingly and sharply half-2-cleft: seeds very minutely 4—5-ribbed lengthways: capsules depresso-globose.

Peninsula.

(37) P. urinaria. (*Linn.*)

Ident. Linn. spec. pl. p. 1393.—Dec. l. c. p. 364.—Roxb. flor. Ind. III. p. 660.

Syn. Nymphanthus Niruri, *Lour.*—P. alatus, *Bl. bidjr.*—P. leprocarpus, *R. Wight.*

Engrav. Wight's Icon. t. 1894. fig. 4.

Spec. Char. Perennial undershrub: branchlets winged, angular: leaves narrow oblongate-elliptic, short or long acuminated, subacute at the base, sometimes lanceolate-obovate, always more or less scabrous or ciliolate-serrulate at the margin, commonly densely approximated, in the branchlets obliquely inserted: female flowers solitary, sessile, lower, males upper, somewhat twin, shortly pedicelled: segments of the female calyx ovate: ovary somewhat scaly papillose: styles flattened, recurved, 2-cleft, divisions hookedly recurved: capsules somewhat scaly warted: seeds transversely ribbed.

Peninsula, flowering nearly all the year.

(38) P. Hookeri. (*Muller.*)

Ident. Mull. Arg. l. c. p. 19.—Dec. l. c. p. 366.

Spec. Char. Undershrub: stipules linear-lanceolate, exceeding the very short petioles, denticulately scabrous at the margin: leaves oblongate-obovate, shortly mucronulate, a little oblique at the base: flowers fascicled: segments of the female calyx ovate.

obtuse: glands of male flowers free, subglobose, of the females connate into an entire urceolus: staminal column shortly 3-cleft, rather slender: styles short, 2-partite, recurved: seeds striolated lengthways in transversal ribs.

Khasia, at 3—4000 feet.

(39) P. Griffithii. (*Muller.*)

Ident. Mull. Arg. l. c.—Dec. l. c. p. 384.

Spec. Char. Shrub: flower-bearing branchlets lightly angled, striated, spreading, densely leafy: stipules scariose, lacerately toothed, triangular-ovate, auriculately lengthened at the base: leaves ovate-lanceolate, acute at both ends, paler below: flowers of either sex fascicled in the axils of the leaves, diœcious, pedicelled: calycine segments of both sexes oblong-ovate, soon narrowly reflexed: glands of the male flowers orbicular, of the females connate into a crenate urceolus: anthers very small: staminal column very slender, lightly 3-cleft: styles thread-like, deeply 2-parted: ovary smooth: capsules globose, 3-furrowed: seeds smooth.

Khasia.

(40) P. Rœperianus. (*Muller.*)

Ident. Dec. l. c. p. 385.

Spec. Char. Stipules at the base on one side auriculated, on the other long semihastate: glands of male flowers free, somewhat smooth: filaments partly connate.

Var. a. genuinus.—Undershrub: branchlets smooth: leaves narrow ovate-lanceolate, glaucous beneath, cuneately contracted at the base, recurved at the margin: staminal column 3-cleft to the middle: flowers densely bracteated, very small.

Silhet.

Var. b. parvifolius.—Branchlets papillosely scabrous in the angles: flowers smaller, linear-obovate, narrowed at the base, acute, or now and then subcordate, subglaucous beneath: staminal column partly 3-cleft.

Khasia hills.

(41) P. prætervisus. (*Muller.*)

Ident. Mull. Arg. l. c.—Dec. l. c. p. 385.

Spec. Char. Shrub: branchlets solitary or subfascicled: stipules acuminate, toothed: leaves obovate, rotund-obtuse, acute at the base, pale beneath: flowers monœcious, somewhat solitary: glands of male flowers free, subrotund, of females connate into a 6-crenated urceolus: segments of either calyx oblong-obovate, obtuse: filaments nearly entirely free: styles deeply 2-cleft, spreading: capsule small: ovary and seeds smooth.

Khasia hills.

(42) P. MIQUELIANUS. (*Muller.*)

Ident. Mull. Arg. l. c.—Dec. l. c. p. 391.

Syn. Macræa ovalifolia, *R. W.*

Engrav. Wight's Icon. t. 1902, fig. 4.

SPEC. CHAR. Shrub, diffusely branched: stipules triangular-ovate, acuminated or long-cuspidate, lacinulate, long semihastate at one side of the base: leaves oblong-ovate, subobtuse at both ends, glaucous beneath: pedicels fascicled, females at length nearly equalling the leaves: glands of the disc free, thick, smooth: filaments free: cells of the anthers divergent at the base: ovary papillosely scabrous: styles 2-parted, recurved, divisions hooked at the apex: seeds rough-dotted.

Neilgherries.

(43) P. SIMPLEX. (*Muller.*)

Ident. Dec. l. c. p. 391.

SPEC. CHAR. Male pedicels twin or in threes, females sub-solitary, exceeding the males: segments of the female calyx ovate, at length reflexed: glands of male flowers free: ovary papillose: styles deeply bipartite, slender: seeds rough-dotted.

Var. a. GENUINUS.—Undershrub: stems simple or sparingly branched, erect, or ascending, leaf-flower-bearing all or nearly all their length: leaves narrow linear-lanceolate, obtuse at both ends or acute, beneath glaucous: stipules ovate, very shortly acuminate, auriculately half-hastate at the base, brown: glands of the male flowers orbicular-reniform, of the females connate into a crenate-lobate undulated urceolus: ovary lightly papillose: capsules depresso-globose: seeds rather densely dotted with warts.—*Retz. obs.* 5. *p.* 29.—*Roxb. flor. Ind.* III. *p.* 654.—P. anceps, *Vahl.*

Peninsula.

Var. b. OBLONGIFOLIUS.—Mull. Arg. l. c. p. 32.—Leaves linear-elliptic, rather obtuse at both ends.—Macræa oblongifolia, *Wight's Icon. t.* 1902. *fig.* 1.—Melanthesa rupestris, *Miq. flor. Ind. Bat.* I. *part* 2. *p.* 371.

In various parts of the country.

(44) P. MACRÆI. (*Muller.*)

Ident. Mull. Arg. l. c. p. 29.—Dec. l. c. p. 393.

Syn. Macræa Rheedii, *R. W.*

Engrav. Wight's Icon. t. 1901.—Rheede Mal. V. t. 27.

Spec. Char. Undershrub: stipules broadly triangular-ovate, unequally half-cordate at the base, denticulate, lacerate, scariose: leaves ovate-elliptic, obtuse at both ends, very shortly acute at the apex: pedicels fascicled, females at length elongated: filaments free: glands of male flowers free, smooth, of females connate into a repandly lobed urceolus: ovary with very short hairs: styles short: seeds dotted with warts at the back.

Pulney hills.

(45) P. Leschenaultii. (*Muller.*)

Ident. Mull. l. c. p. 37.—Dec. l. c. p. 398.

Spec. Char. Shrub: stipules ovate-linear-lanceolate, crenate or inciso-denticulate, deciduous: leaves obovate or oblong-obovate, paler below: male pedicels capillaceous, fructiferous ones thickened above: segments of male calyx ovate, paler at the margin: urceolus hypogynous, sublobate: male flowers somewhat in threes, females solitary: glands of male flowers suborbiculate, papillose: filaments connate into a column for about half their length: styles bipartite, longish: seeds lightly costulate lengthwise, striated transversely in the ribs.

Neilgherries. Khasia hills.

(46) P. rotundifolius. (*Muller.*)

Ident. Dec. l. c. p. 405.

Spec. Char. Annual: flowers somewhat twin, shortly pedicelled: fructiferous calyx accrescent: segments obovate, broadly hyaline-margined: ovary smooth: styles 2-lobed: seeds ribbed lengthways at the back.

Var. a. genuinus.—Branchlets above sharply angled, slightly scabrous: fructiferous calyx open, larger than the capsule; leaves broad or narrow-obovate, obtuse or acutish: glands of female flowers almost altogether free: staminal column quite entire: styles spreading.—P. rotundifolius, *Willd.*

Pondicherry. Assam.

Var. b. striolatus.—Leaves orbicular-ovate, very shortly acute: calyx and stipules densely glandulosely striolate.—P. Urinaria, *Willd.*

Peninsula?

(47) P. Niruri. (*Muller*).

Ident. Dec. l. c. p. 406.

Spec. Char. Flowers twin or females solitary, all short-pedicelled: segments of the fructiferous calyx narrow-obovate, small, not accrescent: styles very short, revolutely 2-lobed at the apex: capsules depressed, very small: seeds ribbed lengthways: ribs transversely very minutely striolated.

Var. a. SCABRELLUS.—Mull. Arg. l. c.—Herbaceous or perennial: branchlets somewhat distinctly angular, slightly scabrous: leaves obtuse: female calyces open, equalling the capsule.

Bengal.

Var. b. GENUINUS.—Herbaceous: branchlets not angular, smooth: leaves oblong-elliptic, roundly obtuse at both ends: fructiferous calyx dilated, covered by the capsule: glands of female flowers almost free: staminal column entire: ovary smooth, glabrous: styles shortly 2-lobed.—*Linn. sp. p.* 1392. *Willd.*—Nymphanthus Niruri, *Lour.*

Common everywhere.

Var. c. DEBILIS.—Mull. Arg. l. c.—Herbaceous: branchlets somewhat angular: leaves linear-obovate or linear-lanceolate.—*Willd. sp.* 4. *p.* 382.—P. Niruri, *Thwaites Enum. pl. Zeyl. p.* 282.

Peninsula, in rice fields.

(48) P. DISTICHUS. (*Muller.*)

Ident. Dec. l. c. p. 413.

Syn. Cicca disticha, *Linn. Willd.*—P. Cheremila, *Roxb. H. B. p.* 104.—P. longifolius, *Roxb. flor. Ind.* III. *p.* 672.—P. Cicca, *Mull. Arg. in Linn.* V. 32, *p.* 50.

Engrav. Lam. Encycl. II. t. 757. fig. 1.—Rheede, Mal. III. t. 47-8.

SPEC. CHAR. Shrub: branchlets flower-bearing, but never leaves at the same time: leaves oblong-ovate, acute or acuminate, beneath more or less glaucescent: flower-bearing branchlets leafless, solitary or aggregated, filiform, interruptedly or rather densely fascicle-bearing: lower fascicles few, often bisexual, rest upper ones all male: pedicels capillaceous: calyx glabrous, the female longer: ovary tetramerous, glabrous: segments of male calyx suborbicular: glands of the disc of male flowers free, subglobose: capsules subglobose, 4-coccous, 4-furrowed: flowers small, reddish.

Native place uncertain. Common in gardens. Fruit subacid and wholesome; used for pickles and preserves. Flowering in the hot season.

(49) P. INDICUS. (*Muller.*)

Ident. Mull. Arg. l. c. p. 52.—Dec. l. c. p. 417.

Syn. Prosorus Indicus, *Dalz. in Hook. Journ. Bot.* 1852. *p.* 345.—*Thwaites Enum. pl. Zeyl. p.* 281.

Engrav. Thwaites in Hook. l. c. p. 299. t. x.

SPEC. CHAR. Small tree: flowers diœcious: leaves oblong-elliptic or elliptic-lanceolate, acute at both ends, membranaceous: female pedicels in threes: disc of male flowers flattish, thick, margin entire, free from the calyx: capsule of a bluish tinge.

Southern Ghauts of the Western Coast.

(50) P. Roxburghii. (*Muller.*)

Ident. Mull. Arg. l. c. p. 47.—Dec. l. c. p. 420.

Syn. P. tetrandrus, *Roxb. flor. Ind.* III. *p.* 674.

Spec. Char. Shrub: branchlets puberulous: stipules oblongate-triangular-ovate: leaves ovate-lanceolate, unequal at the base, acute, acuminate at the apex, sparingly rufous-pubescent beneath: fascicles many-flowered: calycine segments ovate, acuminate, laciniate-fimbriate: glands of the disc connate only below: ovary depresso-globose, 6-furrowed, glabrous.

Silhet.

(51) P. fimbriatus. (*Muller.*)

Ident. Mull. Arg. l. c. p. 47.—Dec. l. c. p. 422.

Syn. Reidia fimbriata, *R. Wight.*

Engrav. Wight's Icon. t. 1904. fig. 1.

Spec. Char. Shrub: stipules of the leaves of the branches triangular-ovate, of the branchlets triangular-lanceolate, long-acuminate: leaves oblong-ovate, obtuse at the base, gradually acuminated at the apex: segments of the calyx ovate, acutish, all lacerate-denticulate at the margin: glands of the male disc orbicular, smooth: urceolus hypogynous, entire: ovary smooth, glabrous: styles short, bipartite, erect.

Neilgherries.

(52) P. Baillonianus. (*Muller.*)

Ident. Mull. Arg. l. c. p. 47.—Dec. l. c. p. 422.

Syn. Reidia latifolia, *R. W.*—Epistilium latifolium, *Thwaites Enum. pl. Zeyl.*—E. cordifolium, *Baill. Euph. p.* 648.

Engrav. Wight's Icon. t. 1904. f. 2.

Spec. Char. Shrub: stipules triangular-ovate at the base, lanceolate-subulate: leaves rhombovate, unequal-sided at the base, one side obtuse or semicordate, the other subacute, gradually acuminated: segments of both calyces broadly elliptic-ovate, entire: urceolus of either sex somewhat adhering to the calyx, somewhat entire, whitish within, remarkably rough with tubercles: ovary glabrous.

Courtallum.

(53) P. macrocalyx. (*Muller.*)

Ident. Mull. Arg. l. c. p. 48.—Dec. l. c. p. 423.

Spec. Char. Shrub: leaves elliptic, obtuse or acutish at both ends, equal-sided at the base: stipules ovate-lanceolate, brown: calycine segments broad-ovate, females the largest: disc of male flowers urceolar, lobulate, of the female flowers broad, girting the glabrous ovary, somewhat torulose and densely rough with grains.

Malabar and Concan.

(54) P. Wightianus. (*Muller.*)

Ident. Mull. Arg. l. c. p. 47.—Dec. l. c. p. 425.

Syn. Reidia floribunda, *R. Wight Icon. t.* 1903.

Spec. Char. Shrub: leaves ovate, obtusely acuminate at the apex, more or less unequal-sided, pale reddish, densely pubescent beneath: male flowers numerous, females solitary, long-pedicelled: pedicels and calyces densely puberulous: calyces of either sex similar, purplish, pubescent externally: segments oblong-ovate, lanceolate, hairy ciliated at the margin: glands free, scabrous: ovary densely beset with long tubercles, torn at the apex: styles bipartite as far as the base.

Peninsula. Neilgherries.

GENUS VII. MELANTHESOPSIS.

Monœcia Triandria. *Sex: Syst:*

Deriv. From its resemblance to *Melanthesa*, so called from its dark flowers.

Gen. Char. Male calyx deeply gamosepalous, turbinate, 6-lobed in 2 rows, lobes imbricated, transversely sub-appendiculate at the back: petals none: stamens central: anthers 2-cleft: cells adnate lengthways: cells of the ovary 2-ovuled: fruit baccato-capsular, tricoccous: seeds arillate, albuminous, ecarunculate: cotyledons broad, equalling the radicle.—Trees or shrubs: flowering branchlets solitary or fascicled, at the base as if involucred with scales, distichously leafy: leaves shortly petioled, feather-nerved, entire, bistipulate, very often becoming brownish-black in drying: flowers monœcious, axillary, males lower in the flowering branchlets, very shortly racemulose or fascicled in the densely bracteated very short axillary smaller branches, females occupying the upper axils, usually solitary: female calyx usually turbinate, to the middle or even shorter, 6-cleft, rotately spreading above: stamens 3, monadelphous: clefts of the anthers extrorse: connectivum produced more or less above the cells: ovary 3-celled, round-obtuse, always smooth and unarmed, glabrous: styles

2-parted: seeds endowed with a hilar cavity · embryo lightly curved.

(1) M. PATENS. (*Muller.*)

Ident. Dec. prod. XV. s. 2. p. 437.

SPEC. CHAR. Leaves membranaceous: female flowers solitary, males proceeding from minute about 6—9-bracteolated racemules: calyx obconical, sharply lengthened out, and crenately 12-lobed round the base of the segments.

Var. a. OBLONGIFOLIA.—Shrub: leaves oblong-ovate or oblong-elliptic, obtuse or subacute at both ends, glaucous pale beneath: pedicels somewhat reflexed, subcapillaceous: fruit subglobose, obtusely 3-furrowed.—M. obliqua, *Wight's Icon. t.* 1898. *Rheede Mal.* V. *t.* 43.

Silhet.

Var. b. TURBINATA. —Leaves slightly approximate, ovate.—Phyllanthus turbinatus, *Roxb. flor. Ind.* III. *p.* 666.

Mountains of Orissa.

Var. c. VULGARIS.—Leaves slightly approximate, broadly elliptic, round obtuse at both ends, obscurely glaucescent beneath: male pedicels capillaceous, flexuose, females straight, stronger. —Melanthesa turbinata, *Wight's Icon. t.* 1897.

Khasia. Mysore. Concan. Malabar. Common on the Neilgherries.

Var. d. GENUINA.—Leaves small, more approximate, obovate or ovate or broad-elliptic: pedicels more slender, males aggregated: ovary shortly turbinate-ovoid, broadly truncated: styles 2-partite to the middle.—Phyllanthus patens, *Roxb. flor. Ind.* III. *p.* 667.

Near Chittagong.

GENUS VIII. BREYNIA.

Monœcia Triandria. *Sex: Syst:*

GEN. CHAR. Male calyx deeply gamosepalous, turbinate, 6-lobed in 2 rows, transversely sub-appendiculate at the back: petals none: stamens central: anthers 2-cleft: cells adnate lengthways: cells of the ovary 2-ovuled: fruit baccato-subcapsular, tricoccous: seed exarillate, ecarunculate, albuminous: radicle shorter than the broad cotyledons.—Shrubs, agreeing in habit and character with the preceding genus, but different in the structure of the seeds and absence of aril.

(1) B. RHAMNOIDES. (*Muller.*)

Ident. Dec. prod. XV. s. 2. p. 440.

SPEC. CHAR. Leaves membranaceous: male flowers proceeding from the densely 6—15-bracteated small branches, sharply trigonal-obconical, smooth: lobelets of the male truncated calyx inflexed: fructiferous calyx small, not accrescent: connectivum of the anthers not lengthened out: ovary contracted below the apex and with depressed top: capsule disciform and tumid at the top.

Var. GENUINA.—Shrub: leaves ovate or oblong-ovate, acutish, glabrous, somewhat of the same colour.—Phyllanthus rhamnoides, *Willd.*—Melanthesa rhamnoides, *Wight's Icon. t.* 1898.—P. vitis Idœa, *Roxb. flor. Ind.* III. *p.* 665.—P. tinctorius, *Vahl. sched. ex Baill. Euph. p.* 633.

Peninsula. Mysore. Bengal.

GENUS IX. PUTRANJIVA.

Diœcia Triandria. *Sex: Syst:*

Deriv. From *Putra*, a son, and *Juvvi*, a native term applied to various kinds of Ficus.

GEN. CHAR. Segments of the calyx lightly imbricated: petals and disc none: stamens central: anthers with 2 clefts: cells adnate lengthways: cells of the ovary 2-ovuled: fruit not opening as a capsule: endocarp bony: seed albuminous: cotyledons flat, ovate, palmiti-nerved.—Trees: leaves alternate, shortly petioled, bistipulate, thickly feather-nerved, more or less serrato-dentate: inflorescences situated in the axils of the leaves: flowers diœcious, males glomerate or fascicled, females longer pedicelled, few or solitary: male calyx 2—5-parted, female 4—6-parted: segments narrow: stamens 3—2: filaments monadelphous, diadelphous or free: anthers globosely ellipsoid, thickish, obtuse at both ends: ovary 3—2-celled: fruit 1-celled by abortion, 1-seeded.

(1) P. ROXBURGHII. (*Wall.*)

Ident. Wall. Tent. Flor. Nep. p. 61.—Dec. prod. XV. s. 2. p. 443.

Syn. Nageia Putranjiva, *Roxb. flor. Ind.* III. *p.* 766.

Engrav. Wight's Icon. t. 1876.

SPEC. CHAR. Branchlets and petioles pubescent: leaves elliptic, unequal-sided at the base, serrately denticulate: glomerules of male flowers numerous: segments of male calyx densely ciliate-pubescent, sparingly puberulous at the back: ovary tawny-silky: fruit oblong-ellipsoid, clothed with thick, pale, rusty hairs: flowers small, yellowish-white.

Coromandel mountains. Concans. Oude. Palghaut. Flowering in the hot weather.

GENUS X. SECURINEGA.

Diœcia Pentandria. *Sex: Syst:*

Deriv. From *Securis*, an axe, and *Nego*, to refuse, alluding to the hardness of the wood.

GEN. CHAR. Segments of both calyces quincuncial: petals none: male disc extrastaminal, glands alternating with the calycine segments and stamens: stamens inserted round the rudiment of an ovary: anthers 2-cleft, cells cohering lengthways: cells of the ovary 2-ovuled: fruit capsular, tricoccous: shells 2-valved: seeds ecarunculate, exarillate, albuminous: embryo almost straight: radicle nearly equalling the cotyledons: cotyledons fleshy, lightly curved.—Trees or shrubs: leaves minutely bistipulate, feather-nerved, reticulately veined, entire, membranaceous or chartaceous, very often brownish-green, beneath often glaucescent: flowers always axillary, males fascicled, short pedicelled, females less numerous than the males, or solitary and longer pedicelled: calyces 5-parted: segments persistent, ovate, outer 2 commonly a little smaller than the rest: glands of the male disc most usually free, ovoid or ellipsoid, longer than broad, often angular: disc hypogynous 5-lobed: stamens 5, opposite the segments: filaments free: anthers introrsely or laterally, or most frequently distinctly extrorsely 2-cleft, oblong-ellipsoid, emarginately obtuse at both ends: rudimentary ovary 2—3-partite; ovary 3-celled, smooth: styles 3, shortly connate at the base, 2-cleft or lobed at the apex: fruit more or less fleshy, opening as a capsule, tricoccous: shell 2-seeded: seeds obtusely 3-cornered, smooth: cotyledons narrow ovate, elliptic or obovate.

(1) S. OBOVATA. (*Muller.*)

Ident. Dec. prod. XV. s. 2. p. 449.

Syn. Xylophylla obovata, *Willd. Enum. pl. Hort. Berol.*—Drypetes Bengalensis, *Spreng. Syst.*—S. Abyssinica, *A. Rich. tent. flor. Abyss.*—Leptonema melanthesoides, *Muller in Hook. Journ. Bot.* 1857. *p.* 17.—Phyllanthus virosus, *Baill. Etud. gen. Euphorb.*—Fluggea microcarpa, *Blume Bijdr. p.* 580.—F. leucopyrus, *Dalz. Bomb. Flora p.* 236 (*non alior*).—F. Abyssinica, *Baill. l. c. p.* 593.—F. ovalis, *ejusd. l. c.*—F. virosa, *ejusd. l. c.* (*not Dalz.*).—F. Sinensis, *ejusd. l. c.*—F. arborescens, *Boj. Hort. Maurit. p.* 278.

Engrav. Baill. Etud. l. c. t. 26. fig. 39—43.

SPEC. CHAR.—Tree: branchlets more or less acutely 4-cornered, glabrous: leaves oblong-ovate or subelliptic, obtuse or retuse, sometimes acute, subcuneate at the base: male flowers fascicled, females subfascicled, fewer: calycine segments lacerate-denticulate, or outer ones more or less entire: filaments exserted: glands of male flowers almost 4-winged: younger styles narrowly recurved, divisions entire or irregularly 2-lobed: fruit capsular, lightly depresso-globose, pure white, succulent.

Widely distributed throughout the country.

(2) S. GRISEA. (*Muller.*)

Ident. Dec. l. c. p. 451.

SPEC. CHAR. Shrub: branchlets numerous, distichously leafy: leaves elliptic, shortly acute at both ends, brown, glaucescent beneath, glabrous: female flowers solitary: capsules globose: styles suberect, scarcely 2-lobed.

Khasia hills.

(3) S. LEUCOPYRUS. (*Muller.*)

Ident. Dec. l. c. p. 451.

Syn. Fluggea leucopyrus, *Willd.*—Xylophylla Lucena, *Roth.*—F. xerocarpa, *Ad. Juss.*—F. virosa, *Dalz. Bomb. flora.*—F. Wallichiana, *Baill. Etud. Euph. p.* 592.—Phyllanthus virosus, *Willd.*

Engrav. Wight's Icon. t. 1875.—Ad. Juss. Tent. Euph. t. 2. fig. 7.

SPEC. CHAR. Tree: branchlets spinescent at the apex, glabrous: leaves obovate, obtuse or retuse, acute or cuneate-narrowed at the base, paler below: calycine segments broadish hyaline at the margin, and usually deeply lacinulate: male flowers very numerous: capsule depresso-globose: branches of the styles narrow, entire.

Peninsula.

GENUS XI. BACCAUREA.

Diœcia Decandria. *Sex: Syst:*

Deriv. So named from the golden colour of the berries.

GEN. CHAR. Calyx imbricated in æstivation: petals none: disc suppressed or developed: stamens inserted round the base of the rudimentary ovary: anthers 2-cleft: cells connate lengthways: cells of the ovary 2-ovuled: fruit not opening as a capsule, central column, however, developed: seeds arillate, albuminous: cotyledons ovate, 3-nerved: radicle short.—Trees: leaves alternate, petioled, bistipulate, simple, feather-nerved, most frequently elliptic or obovate-lanceolate, acute at the base, obtusely cuspidate-acuminate at the apex, entire or somewhat toothed, distantly gland-bearing at the margin beneath: ribs beneath prominent, glabrous or clothed with simple hairs: inflorescences axillary, racemiform- or somewhat spiciform-panicled, unisexual: flowers diœcious or male in some branches, in others of the same tree female, bracteate, usually situated in threes or fives in the axil of each bract, pedicelled: bracts often for a long distance connate with the partial peduncle: calyces of either sex 4—5-parted: segments of the male calyx sometimes unequal: stamens 4—10: filaments free: rudimentary ovary lobed: ovary 2—5- or more frequently 3-celled: stigmas subsessile, broadish, 2—3-lobed or torn, more or less strongly papillose: fruit half-fleshy, thick-skinned, 5—2—1-celled, cells 2—1-seeded.

(1) B. SAPIDA. (*Muller.*)

Ident. Dec. prod. XV. s. 2. p. 459.

Syn. Pierardia sapida, *Roxb. flor. Ind.* II. *p.* 252.—P. microstachys, *W. & A.*

Engrav. Wight's Icon. t. 1912-13.

SPEC. CHAR. Tree: racemes aggregate, pendulous from the trunk and woody branches, rusty-puberulous: leaves lanceolate-obovate, acute at the base, repandly subdentate at the margin: male flowers ternate in the axil of the bracts, females solitary, all shortly pedicelled: bracts ovate or lanceolate: calycine segments lanceolate: ovary oblong-ellipsoid, rusty-silky: fruit globose-ellipsoid, lightly incurved, somewhat narrowed at both ends, rufescent-puberulous, pulpy-red when ripe: seeds covered with a fibrous blood-red aril.

Eastern Bengal. Malabar forests.

(2) B. COURTALLENSIS. (*Muller.*)

Ident. Dec. l. c. p. 459.

Syn. Pierardia Courtallensis, *R. Wight.*

Engrav. Wight's Icon. t. 1912.

SPEC. CHAR. Tree: racemes proceeding from the woody trunk, fascicled: leaves lanceolate-obovate, acute at the base, obtusely cuspidate-acuminate at the apex, stiffly membranaceous: stamens 4—6: segments of the male calyx orbicular-elliptic, obtuse, concave, females linear-lanceolate: ovary subglobose, rufous-silky.

Courtallum.

(3) B. PROPINQUA. (*Muller.*)

Ident. Dec. l. c. p. 463.

SPEC. CHAR. Tree: branchlets densely leafy above, rufescently pubescent: leaves elliptic or lanceolate-obovate, obtusely cuspidate-acuminate, acute at the base, glabrous above: panicles or racemes somewhat spiciform, not pendulous, 2—3 times shorter than the leaves, flexuose, tawny-pubescent: bracts ovate-lanceolate, exceeding the flowers, persistent, spreading, acuminate: male calyx 4—5-partite, segments broadly ovate, subrotund: middle flower of the glomerules of either bract longer pedicelled than the lateral ones: stamens 6—8: fruit ellipsoid, subacute at both ends, silky-pubescent.

Silhet.

GENUS XII. APOROSA.

Diœcia Pentandria. *Sex: Syst:*

GEN. CHAR. Segments of the male calyx imbricated: petals and disc none: stamens inserted round the rudimentary ovary: anthers 2-cleft, cells cohering lengthways: cells of the ovary 2-ovuled: embryo straight in copious albumen: radicle thin.—Trees: leaves alternate, petioled, bistipulate, usually lanceolate-ovate, entire or repand-dentate: petioles swollen at the base and apex, sometimes distinctly biglandulose at the apex: flowers diœcious, arranged in densely imbricato-bracteated spikes, very small: bracts broadly ovate, 3—1-flowered, increased by 2 bracteoles: male calyx 3—6-parted, female 5-parted, segments shorter and more obtuse than the males: stamens 2—5, usually 2: filaments free: anthers 2-cleft, subglobose, opening lengthways inwards, usually at length exserted: rudimentary ovary cylindric, minute or even almost obsolete: ovary 2—3-celled: stigmas 3—2, 2-lobed or cleft, strongly lacinulately papillose: fruit by abortion usually 1-seeded.

(1) A. DIOICA. (*Muller.*)

Ident. Dec. prod. XV. s. 2. p. 472.

Syn. Alnus dioica, *Roxb. flor. Ind.* III. *p.* 580.—Aporosa Roxburghii, *Baill. Etud.* p. 645.

SPEC. CHAR. Tree: leaves oblong- or lanceolate-elliptic, subacute at the base, acuminate at the apex, usually entire: male spikes 2—3-aggregate, females numerous, densely pubescent: male bracts densely imbricated, concave, hispidly ciliated, reaching the top of the flowers, females ovate: female flowers sessile: segments of the male calyx ovate-lanceolate, of the female ovate: ovary oblong-ovoid, pubescent: stigmas 2, minute, 2-lobed: fruit acutely subellipsoid.

Silhet. Assam.

(2) A. LINDLEYANA. (*Muller.*)

Ident. Dec. l. c. p. 473.

SPEC. CHAR. Female spikes subsolitary: male bracts broader than long, subfimbriate-denticulate at the margin, females broad ovate: female flowers shortly pedicelled: bracteoles ciliolate at the margin: segments of male calyx obovate: anthers 2—3: ovary ovoid, acuminate, silky-pubescent: stigmas deeply 2-partite, strongly long-papillose: fruit subglobose, very shortly conical-sharpened.

Var. GENUINA.—Tree: stipules ovate-lanceolate, obtuse, erect, caducous, tawny-pilose: leaves lanceolate-ovate, acute, obtuse or acute at the base, entire: male bracts minutely ciliate-denticulate at the margin, scarcely exceeding the calyx: male flowers subsessile, segments of the calyx entire: fruit pale or reddish.—Scepa Lindleyana, *Wight's Icon. t.* 361.—A. Lindleyana, *Baill. Etud.*—A. affinis, *do.*

Canara. Northern India.

(3) A. SPHÆROCARPA. (*Muller.*)

Ident. Mull. Arg. in Flora Ratisb. 1864. p. 519.—Dec. l. c. p. 473.

SPEC. CHAR. Tree: leaves elliptic-lanceolate or lanceolate-elliptic, acuminate, acute at the base, entire: female peduncles rusty-pubescent: bracts very broad, not exceeding the flowers: segments of the male calyx broadly orbicular-ovate: anthers 3: fruit regularly globose.

Near Mangalore, in Canara.

GENUS XIII. BISCHOFFIA.

Diœcia Pentandria. *Sex: Syst:*

GEN. CHAR. Segments of the male calyx quincuncially imbricated: petals none: stamens inserted round the rudimentary ovary, opposite the calycine segments: anthers 2-cleft, cells connate lengthways: cells of the ovary 2-ovuled: fruit sub-baccate: mesocarp fleshy: endocarp tricoccous, parchment-like: seeds without warts, sparingly albuminous: radicle three times shorter than the large, flat, cordate-ovate cotyledons.—Large trees: leaves alternate, trifoliolate, long-petioled, terminal leaflet longer than the rest: limb of the leaves ovate, crenato-dentate at the margin: inflorescences axillary, large, more or less panicled: flowers very numerous, small: calyx of both sexes deeply 5-parted, female one sometimes bearing 3 staminodes opposite the calycine segments: filaments 5, free: anthers broadly ovoid, emarginate at both ends, opening outwards, yellow: ovary 3-, rarely 4-celled, ovoid, terete: styles entire, stiff, sublinear, recurved, connate at the base.

(1) B. JAVANICA. (*Muller.*)

Ident. Dec. prod. XV. s. 2. p. 478.

SPEC. CHAR. Fructiferous pedicels thickened, long exceeding the fruit: fruit slightly wrinkled, very shortly contracted and angled at the base.

Var. a. GENUINA.—Leaves subelliptic, obtuse at the base, cuspidate-acuminate at the apex; male panicles almost equalling the leaves, large, females commonly reduced to a raceme, branched below: segments of the male calyx suborbicular, brown, densely glandular-striolate, at length reflexed.—B. Cumingiana, *Decaisne in Jacq. voy. p.* 153.—B. Rœperiana, *Baill. Etud. t.* 26. figs. 25—32.—Stylodiscus trifoliatus, *Benn. in Horsf. Plant. Jav. Rar. p.* 133. *t.* 29.—Microelus Rœperianus, *W. and A. in Edin. New Phil. Journ.* 14. *p.* 298.—*Wight's Icon. t.* 1880.—Andrachne trifoliata, *Roxb. flor. Ind.* III. *p.* 728.

Neilgherries. Chittagong. Hurdwar. Flowering in February.

Var. b. OBLONGIFOLIA.—Leaflets narrow-acute at the base, elliptic-obovate.

Malabar.

Var. c. LANCEOLATA.—Leaflets narrowed at the base, ovate-lanceolate.—B. trifoliata, *Hooker Icon. t.* 844.

Near Bombay.

GENUS XIV. CYCLOSTEMON.

Diœcia Polyandria. *Sex: Syst:*

Deriv. From *Kuklos*, a circle, and *Stemon*, a stamen.

GEN. CHAR. Segments of the calyx imbricated: petals none: stamens inserted round an intrastaminal disc: anthers 2-cleft: cells connate lengthways: cells of the ovary 2-ovuled: fruit indehiscent: seeds compressed, ecarunculate: radicle shorter than the cotyledons.—Trees: leaves alternate, simple, entire or toothed, stiffish or coriaceous, with two deciduous stipules: leaves unequal-sided at the base: flowers diœcious, more or less numerously fascicled: calyx of either sex 4—5-parted, two outer segments a little larger than the rest: disc concave, thin: stamens 4—40: filaments free, erect: anthers oblong-ovoid or ellipsoid: connectivum not lengthened out: ovary 4—2-celled, 4—2-furrowed: styles entire, connate at the base, containing broadly triangular-ovate subsessile stigmas, sometimes narrow, sublinear and elongated: fruit more or less fleshy, 4—2-coccous, somewhat crustaceous, by abortion 4—1-seeded.

(1) C. INDICUS. (*Muller.*)

Ident. Mull. Arg. in Linnæa v. 32. p. 81.—Dec. prod. XV. s. 2. p. 481.

SPEC. CHAR. Leaves ovate or elliptic-lanceolate, long cuspidate-acuminate, narrow acute at the base, glabrous: flowers longish-pedicelled: pedicels and male calyces glabrous, females silky-pubescent: segments of the male calyx ciliated at the margin: anthers 6—4: central disc thick, undulated, hypogynous, sub-lobate: ovary silky: styles slender, peltiform, dilated at the top.

Khasia. Malabar and Concan.

GENUS XV. HEMICYCLIA.

Diœcia Polyandria. *Sex: Syst:*

GEN. CHAR, Segments of the male calyx imbricated: petals none: stamens inserted round the margin of the central disc: anthers 2-cleft: ovary 1-celled, 2-ovuled: fruit not capsular: seed ecarunculate, copiously albuminous: cotyledons fleshy membranaceous, suborbicular, about three times equalling the thin radicle. —Trees, usually middle-sized: branches spreading: leaves alternate, shortly petioled, entire or toothed: stipules soon deciduous: flowers diœcious, fascicled: calyces of either sex deeply 4—5-parted, two segments altogether exterior: stamens 8—25: filaments free, erect, younger anthers distinctly outwardly 2-cleft, clefts soon lateral: disc hypogynous entire or crenated at the margin, intrastaminal, occupying the centre, concave: ovary subglobose: ovules collaterally pendulous at the apex of the placenta: style scarcely any: stigma first somewhat disc-shaped, reniformly cut as far as the middle in the side of the placenta, afterwards broadly reniform with more open lobes, deciduous: fruit 1-seeded by abortion: endocarp bony or coriaceous, globose or irregularly ovoid and angular, smooth: testa membranaceous, brown: cotyledons cordate at the base.

(1) H. SEPIARIA. (*W. and A.*)

Ident. Wight et Arn. in Edin. Phil. Journ. v. 14. p. 297 —Dec. prod. XV. s. 2. p. 487.

Engrav. Wight's Icon. t. 1872.—Baill. Etud. t. 27. fig. 7.

SPEC. CHAR. Small tree: leaves ovate or elliptic, obtuse or emarginate, lightly cordate at the base, entire or repand-denticulate, glabrous: flowers fascicled: stamens about 7—10: calycine segments suborbicular, concave, silky-pubescent outside; central disc not elevated in the middle: ovary and fruit globose.

Travancore. Peninsula.

(2) H. VENUSTA. (*Thwaites.*)

Ident. Thwaites in Hook. Journ. Bot. 1855. p. 272.—Dec. l. c. p. 488.

Engrav. Wight's Icon. t. 1992 (under Astylis).

SPEC. CHAR. Tree: leaves lanceolate, acuminate, narrowed at the base, entire, glabrous: stamens 5—8: central disc flat.

Western slopes of the Neilgherries.

GENUS XVI. BRIDELIA.

olygamia Monœcia. *Sex: Syst:*

Deriv. Named after the great muscologist, Professor Bridel.

GEN. CHAR. Segments of the male calyx valvate in æstivation, regular: petals as many as the segments, and alternating with them: disc developed: stamens verticillately inserted in a central column: anthers 2-cleft: cells of the ovary 2-ovuled: fruit stony, afterwards incompletely breaking as a capsule: seeds ecarunculate, the hilar side 1-furrowed, albuminous: radicle very short: cotyledons broad, flattened, hilar side concave.—Trees: leaves short-petioled or subsessile, usually broadly or narrowly obovate, elliptic or ovate, entire or toothed, often rufescently hairy: flowers rarely diœcious, spiked or glomerate, bracteate: bracts stipular, deeply bicuspidate, and when furnished with a limb tricuspidate: calyces of either sex regularly 5-parted, segments of the males persistent, of females afterwards often deciduous: petals 5, commonly much shorter than the sepals, of either sex spathulate at the base, males usually triangular-obovate above and variously 3—5-lobed, females narrower and more entire: disc double, adnate to the male calyx, outer side of the female similar to the male, inner ascending and more or less loosely girting the ovary, 5-lobed or toothed at the apex: anthers ovoid: styles 2, bipartite: fruit at length incompletely bicoccous, 2—1-seeded: mesocarp fleshy: endocarp bony: embryo straight or lightly curved.

(1) B. RETUSA. (*Muller.*)

Ident. Dec. prod. XV s. 2. p. 493.

SPEC. CHAR. Flowers diœcious, spiked: spikes axillary, somewhat leafless: petals of female flowers spathulate-lanceolate entire, of the males obovate, unguiculate, lobulate: berries globose, obtuse.

Var. a. GENUINA.—Branchlets pubescent: leaves oblong-elliptic or ovate, or obovate or lanceolate-obovate, subacute or obtuse, lightly cordate at the base or obtuse or more rarely narrowed, above glabrous, beneath minutely pubescent and rufescent at the ribs and veins or glaucous-rufescent: flowers spiked, rarely glomerate at the same time in the same specimens.—Cluytia retusa, *Linn.*—B. retusa, *Spreng. Syst. Baill. Etud. t.* 25. *figs.* 25—34.—C. spinosa, *Roxb. Cor. t.* 172.

Canara. Behar. Circars. Assam. Flowering in July and August.

Var. b. SQUAMOSA.—Leaves lanceolate-ovate, lightly cordate at the base, glabrous: flowers glomerate or shortly spiked in the axils of the leaves.—Cluytia squamosa, *Lam. Encycl.*—B. montana, *Wall. Cat. Baill. Etud.*

Malabar. Concan.

Var. c. ROXBURGHIANA.—Branchlets tawny-tomentose, at length glabrate: leaves narrowly oblong-elliptic or oblong-obovate, beneath softly tawny-pubescent or subtomentose, slightly shining on the yellowish margin, at length glabrescent: flowers glomerate. —B. crenulata, *Roxb. flor. Ind.* III. *p.* 734.

Banks of the Megna. Neilgherries. Flowering in May.

(2) B. STIPULARIS. (*Blume.*)

Ident. Bl. Bijdr. p. 597.—Dec. l. c. p. 499.

Syn. Cluytia stipularis, *Linn. Mant. p.* 127.—B. scandens, *Willd. Roxb. flor. Ind.* III. *p.* 736.—C. scandens, *Roxb. Cor. t.* 173.—B. retusa, *Ad. Juss. Tent. Euph. p.* 27. *t.* 7. *fig.* 22 (*not Spreng.*).—B. Zollingeri, *Miq. flor. Ind. Bat.* I. *p.* 364.

SPEC. CHAR. Leaves entire, elliptic or obovate or oblong-obovate, obtuse at the apex, obtuse or slightly cordate at the base, pubescent above, densely rufescent beneath: branchlets flexuose, tawny-tomentose or pubescent: stipules lanceolate: bracts leaf-shaped and stipulaceous: male flowers sessile, females shortly pedicelled, tawny-silky: calycine segments ovate-triangular, long-acuminate, at length spreading, accrescent: petals of female flowers stiffish, ovate: disc urceolar, deep: berry ellipsoid, when young acute: flowers yellowish-green.

Circars. Peninsula. Common on the banks of the Gutpurba, near Duddi. Hilly parts of the Concan. Flowering nearly all the year.

(3) B. MONTANA. (*Willd.*)

Ident. Willd. Spec. IV. p. 978.—Dec. l. c. p. 500.—Roxb. flor. Ind. III. p. 735.

Syn. Cluytia montana, *Roxb. Cor. t.* 171.

SPEC. CHAR. Middling-sized tree: branches spreading, glabrous: stipules very small: leaves oblong-obovate, slightly narrowed towards the base, obtuse at the apex, entire, glabrous: flowers mixed, glomerate in the axils: petals of female flowers suborbiculate-ovate, shortly unguiculate, nearly resembling those of the males, undulate: urceolus of female flowers lobulate, deeply surrounding the ovary: berries globose, obtuse.

Bengal. Hilly districts. Flowering in April.

(4) B. HAMILTONIANA. (*Muller.*)

Ident. Mull. Arg. in Linnæa v. 34. p. 77.—Dec. l. c. p. 500.

SPEC. CHAR. Leaves membranaceous: female flowers sessile: petals ovate, of males orbicular-rhomboid, angular, all shortly unguiculate: berry globose, ellipsoid.

Var. a. GENUINA. Branchlets glabrous: stipules lanceolate-linear, deflexed, spreading: leaves oblong-obovate, more or less cuneate-narrowed at the base, acutish at the apex, entire or subrepand-dentate, beneath sparingly pubescent: glomerules of leaves indistinctly stalked either with leaves or bracts.

Behar. Near Monghyr.

Var. b. GLABRA.—Mull. Arg. l. c.—Leaves even when young glabrous, adult ones a little firmer, and more distinctly reticulately veined.

Concan.

GENUS XVII. CLEISTANTHUS.

Polygamia Monœcia. *Sex: Syst:*

Deriv. From *Kleistos*, shut up, and *Anthos*, a flower.

GEN. CHAR. Segments of the calyx valvate: petals alternating: lobes of the disc alternate with the petals: stamens verticillately inserted on a central column: anthers 2-cleft: cells of the ovary 2-ovuled: fruit capsular: seeds ecarunculate, without aril, sparingly albuminous: cotyledons membranaceous, thin, variously folded.—Trees: flowers small, glomerated or spiked: leaves alternate, simple, entire, oblong-ovate or elliptic, glabrous, short-petioled, at the base often minutely auriculately bistipulate: flowers monœcious or diœcious: calyces of either sex 5-partite, segments at length deciduous: petals 5, males small, unguiculate, broadly spathulate, truncated, crenate above, females more developed and entire, commonly lanceolate-spathulate: extrastaminal disc long-urceolate, long adnate to the calyx, free crenulate or 5-lobed or 5-parted at the margin: hypogynous one broadly urceolate, loosely girting the stem or base of the ovary: filaments radiately ascending from the point of insertion, free: anthers 2-cleft inwards, ovoid: rudimentary ovary more or less 3-lobed at the top, nearly equalling the anthers: ovary always 3-celled, subglobose, more or less distinctly stipitate: styles 3, usually 2-cleft to the middle: capsules 3-coccous, shells 2-valved, 2—1-seeded: seeds often subconnate in pairs, usually broadly emarginate at the base, or entire: testa very thinly crustaceous.

(1) C. PATULUS. (*Muller.*)

Ident. Dec. prod. XV. s. 2. p. 505.

Syn. Cluytia patula, *Roxb. flor. Ind.* III. *p.* 733.—Bridelia patula, *Hook. et Arn. Bot. Beech. p.* 212.—Amanoa Indica, *R. Wight Icon.*—A. patula, *Thwaites Enum. pl. Zeyl. p.* 280.—Lebidiera patula, *Mull. Arg. in Linn.* v. 32. *p.* 81.

Engrav. Roxb. Cor. t. 170.—Wight's Icon. t. 1911.

SPEC. CHAR. Large tree: stipules small: leaves shortly petioled, ovate or oblong-ovate, acute or obtuse at the base, cuspidate-acuminate at the apex, entire, glabrous: flowers more or less sessile, axillary, subglomerate and arranged in short axillary interrupted spikes: calycine segments oblong-ovate: petals similar, shortly unguiculate, cuneate-obovate, acutish, hairy at the back: bracts ciliated: ovary hairy: capsules at length rough with tubercles: gynophore dilated, hairy.

Circar mountains. Courtallum.

(2) C. OBLONGIFOLIUS. (*Muller.*)

Ident. Dec. l. c. p. 506.

SPEC. CHAR. Flowers glomerate and arranged in terminal spikes or usually small lateral ones: calyx glabrous: petals shorter, obcordate, tridentate: capsules smooth, glabrous.

Var. a. SCABER.—Leaves beneath very shortly pubescently scabrous.

Eastern Bengal.

Var. b. GENUINUS.—Branchlets slender, straight: leaves shortly petioled, oblong-ovate, acute, entire, subglaucous beneath: bracts hirsute: flowers numerous, small, pale: calycine segments ovate-lanceolate, acuminate: hypogynous urceolus 5-toothed: shell by abortion 1-seeded.—Cluytia oblongifolia, *Roxb. flor. Ind.* III. *p.* 731.—Bridelia oblongifolia, *Hook. et Arn. Bot. Beech. p.* 212.

Silhet. Khasia.

(3) C. CHARTACEUS. (*Muller.*)

Ident. Dec. l. c. p. 507.

Syn. Amanoa chartacea, *Baill. Etud. p.* 582.

SPEC. CHAR. Branchlets pubescent: leaves ovate-lanceolate, shorter at the base, longer acute at the apex, at first hairy and somewhat silvery shining above, afterwards glabrate, pale brownish: flowers glomerate, sessile, glabrous: calycine segments ovate: petals narrow, glabrous: bracts rusty-silky: capsules subglobose, glabrous: rudimentary ovary glabrous.

Silhet.

(4) C. MALABARICUS. (*Muller.*)

Ident. Dec. l. c. p. 508.

Syn. Lebidiera Malabarica, *Mull. Arg. in Linnæa, v.* 32. *p.* 81.

SPEC. CHAR. Branchlets rufous-villous: stipules long, narrow: petioles densely rufous-villous, at length glabrate: leaves obovate-lanceolate, shortly cuspidate-acuminate, narrowed at the base, beneath crisply rufescently pubescent: stipules exceeding the petioles, linear-lanceolate, subulate-acuminate: flowers glomerate, subsessile: calycine segments glabrous, narrow-lanceolate: petals obovate-spathulate, somewhat 3-lobed: ovary scattered with tawny hairs: fruit globose, 3-celled.

Malabar. Concan.

(5) C. STIPULARIS. (*Muller.*)

Ident. Dec. l. c. p. 509.

Syn. Bridelia stipularis, *Hook. et Arn. Bot. Beech. p.* 211 (*not Linn.*).—Lebidiera stipularis, *Mull. Arg. l. c. p.* 81.

SPEC. CHAR. Branchlets slightly tomentose: stipules lanceolate, long-acuminate, comose at the apex of the branchlets, yellowish, thin, tomentose: leaves ovate or ovate-elliptic, obtuse at both ends, glabrous above, grey-tomentose beneath: flowers short pedicelled: calycine segments triangular-ovate, subtomentose externally: petals of male flowers long-unguiculate triangular obovate, subentire, folded, puberulous at the back: disc above very shortly loosened from the calyx, crenated: rudimentary ovary 3-lobed.

Neilgherries.

GENUS XVIII. LEBIDIEROPSIS.

Polygamia Monœcia. *Sex: Syst:*

GEN. CHAR. Segments of the calyx valvate in æstivation, petals alternating with them: glands of the disc adnate to the calyx, perigynous, alternating with the petals: stamens verticillately inserted on a central column: anthers erect: rudiment of an ovary developed: cells of the ovary 2-ovuled: fruit capsular: seeds ecarunculate, exarillate, not furrowed at the hilum, sparingly albuminous: radicle of the straight embryo short: cotyledons flat, fleshy, suborbicular.

(1) L. ORBICULARIS. (*Muller.*)

Ident. Dec. prod. XV. s. 2. p. 509.

Var. a. COLLINA.—Tree: leaves elliptic or obovate, round-obtuse, obtuse or slightly cordate at the base, soon glabrate or beneath pubescent on the rib: flowers subsessile, softly grey-hairy white: calycine segments oblong-triangular-ovate: petals very minute, above irregularly rhomboid, glabrous: capsules glabrous: seeds globose.—Cluytia collina, *Roxb. flor. Ind.* III. *p.* 732. *Cor. t.* 169.—Bridelia collina, *Hook. et Arn. Bot. Beech. p.* 211.—C. patula et retusa, *Wall.*—L. collina, *Mull. Arg. in Linnæa v.* 32. *p.* 80.

Circars.

Var. b. GENUINA.—Leaves smaller, glabrous, beneath pale glaucous, often almost orbicular.—Andrachne orbicularis, *Roth. Nov. Plant. Ind. or. p.* 364.

Bengal.

Var. c. LAMBERTI.—Leaves same as in the preceding, but hairy beneath at the ribs and margin: petioles grey-villous: capsules smaller: bracts and calyx externally villous: calycine segments many times exceeding the petals: glands almost distinct from each other.

Bengal.

GENUS XIX. CROTON.

Monœcia Decandria. *Sex: Syst:*

Deriv. From *Kroton,* a tick; the seeds resemble that animal.

GEN. CHAR. Male calyx 5- (4—6-) parted, segments imbricated at the apex only: petals equal in number to the sepals: glands of the disc alternating with the petals: stamens central, usually 10—20: filaments inflexed with the anthers at the apex: anthers more or less fixed by the base, at length oscillating, erect, 2-cleft: cells of the ovary (2—4-, very often 3-) 1-ovuled: styles dichotomously divided: fruit capsular: shell 2-valved. seeds carunculate: embryo straight in albumen: cotyledons ovate, equalling the radicle.—Trees, or more frequently shrubs and perennial herbs, rarely annual: leaves alternate, petioled, bistipulate, toothed or entire, rarely lobed: flowers commonly monœcious, arranged in a raceme often spiciform, most frequently terminal, lower ones female: segments of the female calyx 4—6, commonly 5: male petals nearly always, females rarely developed: receptacle very frequently woolly-pubescent: anthers introrse in the open flowers: capsules most frequently tricoccous.

(1) C. JOUFRA. (*Roxb.*)

Ident. Roxb. flor. Ind. III. p. 685.—Dec. prod. XV. s. 2. p. 519.

SPEC. CHAR. Tree: young branchlets silvery scaly: leaves broad ovate-lanceolate, acuminate, serrated, glabrous, not silvery beneath, approximate at the apex of the branchlets, biglandulose at the base: racemes subterminal or axillary, many times exceeding the leaves: petals of either sex lanceolate, woolly: stamens 12: styles deeply 2-parted: lower flowers of mixed sexes, calyces externally scaly.

Silhet.

(2) C. OBLONGIFOLIUS. (*Roxb.*)

Ident. Roxb. flor. Ind. III. p. 685.—Dec. l. c. p. 573.

SPEC. CHAR. Tree: younger branches with the young leaves and inflorescences covered sparingly with yellowish scales:

stipules stiff, subulate: leaves more or less elliptic or ovate or obovate, toothed or entire, acute at both ends, below at the base biglandulose: racemes abounding in flowers: bracts 1—3-flowered: segments of the female calyx triangular-lanceolate, of the male pale at the margin and densely scurfy: stamens 10—12: filaments woolly near the base: styles once deeply bipartite: capsules subglobose, covered with scurfy scales: flowers small, green.

In woods near Calcutta. Malabar. Concan. Canara. Flowering in March.

(3) C. reticulatus. (*Muller.*)

Ident. Dec. l. c. p. 580.

Syn. C. hypoleucus, *Dalz. in Hook. Journ. Bot.* 1853. *v.* 3. *p.* 123.

Spec. Char. Shrub: branches, petiole, and rachis of the inflorescence covered with rusty hairs: leaves scattered, collected at the tops of the branchlets, lanceolate, cuspidate-acuminate, acute at the base, repand-denticulate, covered beneath with silvery hairs: stipules subulate: racemes many-flowered: female calyx accrescent: disc hypogynous, repand-crenate, at length 5-lobed: stamens 15—18: filaments glabrous: ovary covered with rufous hairs: styles twice deeply bipartite: segments stiff, furrowed at the back: capsules not muricated.

Malabar and Concan hills.

(4) C. aromaticus. (*Linn.*)

Ident. Linn. spec. pl. p. 1005.—Dec. l. c. p. 588.

Syn. C. tiliæfolius, *Lam. Encycl.*—C. lacciferus, *Gærtn. fruct.* II. *t.* 107.

Spec. Char. Tree: branches, petioles, and leaves roughish, with stellate hairs: leaves long-petioled, bearing stalked glands at the base, ovate, acute, cordate at the base, denticulate, glands yellowish: racemes lax, spiked: bracts broadly subulate, males 1-flowered, equalling the flowers: petals snowy-woolly at the margin: disc hypogynous, urceolar, subentire: filaments about 30, bearded near the base, glabrous, shining brown: ovary hispid with stellate hairs: styles once 2-cleft, divisions subspathulate entire or 2-lobed or cleft: capsules ellipsoid- or obovoid-subglobose, scabrous: seeds very minutely puberulous.

Neilgherries. Malabar and Concan.

(5) C. chlorocalyx. (*Muller.*)

Ident. Mull. Arg. in Linnæa. v. 34. p. 109.—Dec. l. c. p. 590.

Spec. Char. Shrub: leaves lanceolate, cuspidate-acuminate,

narrowed at the base, denticulate at the margin, heaped together at the apex of the branchlets, shortly petioled, stipitately biglandulose at the apex: younger ones tomentose with thin rusty stellate hairs, soon glabrate: stipules very small, somewhat gland-shaped: segments of the female calyx at length foliaceous, elliptic-lanceolate, acute at both ends, denticulate at the base, very green: stamens about 15: filaments glabrous: racemes terminal, with a single female flower at the base: female pedicels shorter than the calyx: male petals puberulous at the margin, females subulate: ovary glabrous, obovoid, deeply impressed at the summit: styles connate into a column, free part twice 2-parted.

Silhet.

(6) C. CAUDATUS. (*Muller.*)

Ident. Dec. l. c. p. 599.

SPEC. CHAR. Leaves longish petioled, bearing stalked glands at the base: flowers somewhat caudately racemose: male bracts 1—5-flowered: male flower-buds mutic: male petals snowy-woolly at the margin: stamens about 30: filaments bearing white wool towards the base: ovary hispid: styles 2-parted almost to the very base, filiform: capsules large, globose, ellipsoid, coriaceous, thick-skinned: seeds smooth, minutely puberulous.

Var. a. DENTICULATUS.—Shrub: leaves scabrous, puberulous above, beneath softly villous and whitish: disc hypogynous, abbreviated, somewhat entire.—Bl. bidjr. II. p. 603.

Bengal. Assam.

Var. b. GENUINUS.—Shrub: primary branches often very long, sometimes scandent: leaves oblong-ovate, acuminate, cordate or obtuse at the base, serrated, with stalked glands at the base and margin, scabrous puberulous on both sides: disc hypogynous, shortly lobed or entire.—C. drupaceus, *Roxb. flor. Ind.* III. *p.* 684.—C. aromaticus, *Gærtn. fr. v.* 2. *t*. 107 (*not Linn.*).—C. lacciferus, *Wight Icon. t.* 1915 (*not of others*).

Silhet. Khasia. Bengal. Assam.

(7) C. TIGLIUM. (*Linn.*)

Ident. Linn. Spec. pl. p. 1004.—Dec. l. c. p. 600.—Roxb. flor. Ind. III. p. 682.—Willd. Spec. pl. IV. p. 543.

Syn. C. acutus, *Thunb. flor. Japon. p.* 269.—C. Jamalgota, *Ham. in Trans. Linn. Soc.* 14. p. 258.—Tiglium officinale, *Klotsch.*

Engrav. Burm. Zeyl. t. 90.—Rumph. Amb. IV. t. 42.—Rheede Mal. II. t. 33.

SPEC. CHAR. Shrub or small tree: branchlets and petioles

glabrous, pale green: stipules somewhat recurved, and resembling bracts: leaves ovate, acute, obtuse at the base, more or less crenato-serrulate at the margin, sometimes almost entire, limb a little shorter than the petioles, firm, with 2 sessile glands at the base: racemes many-flowered, bracts lanceolate-subulate: male flower-buds mutic: segments of the male calyx ovate, whitish membranaceous at the margin: female petals subulate, capitately thickened at the apex: stamens 15—18, filaments glabrous: ovary hairyish: styles long, slender, 2-cleft beyond the middle, furrowed at the back, incurved like a hook at the apex: capsules large, ellipsoid, longer than broad, obtusely 3-cornered, pale: flowers greenish-yellow.

Neilgherries. Peninsula. Assam. Flowering in the hot season.

(8) C. PERSIMILIS. (*Muller.*)

Ident. Mull. Arg. l. c. p. 116.—Dec. l. c. p. 618.

SPEC. CHAR. Leaves very shortly petioled, biglandulose at the base: stipules subulate, very short: raceme long, many-flowered: bracts 1—5-flowered, very small: segments of the male calyx of the same colour: filaments bearded at the base: ovary clothed with hairs: styles 2-parted: capsules very large.

Var. GENUINUS.—Shrub: leaves lanceolate-elliptic, hairy, cuspidate-acuminate, acute at the base, entire or repand-toothed: calyx pubescent: ovary hairyish. — C. oblongifolius, *Thwaites Enum. pl. Zeyl. p.* 276 (*not Roxb.*).

Eastern Bengal. Khasia. Assam.

(9) C. LÆVIFOLIUS. (*Blume.*)

Ident. Bl. bidjr. p. 603.—Dec. l. c. p. 619.

Syn. C. tiglioides, *Bl. l. c.*—C. diadenus, *Miq. flor. Ind. Bat.*

SPEC. CHAR. Tree: leaves lanceolate-elliptic, acuminate, acute at the base, almost entire, biglandulose beneath at the base: stipules bristly-subulate, long: racemes many-flowered, terminal and axillary, often more or less numerous towards the apex of the branchlets, sometimes leafless, sometimes bearing one or more leaves at the base: bracts lanceolate-ovate, 1—5-flowered: female flowers lax: male flower-buds apiculate, subglobose, females oblong: disc 5-lobed: filaments glabrous: ovary slightly tomentose: styles 3—4, once bipartite, segments stiff: capsules depresso-globose.

Khasia. Silhet.

GENUS XX. AGROSTISTACHYS.

Diœcia Decandria. *Sex: Syst:*

Deriv. So called from the grass-like spikelets of flowers.

GEN. CHAR. Male calyx valvate, female quincuncial: male petals double the number of the segments of the calyx, females equal in number: stamens central: cells free almost as far as the apex, pendulous from the connectivum, unequally 2-valved: rudimentary ovary none: cells of the ovary 1-ovuled: capsules tricoccous.—Shrubs: leaves bistipulate, alternate, petioled, feather-nerved: flowers diœcious, arranged in supra-axillary spikes: spikes short, densely bracteated in 6, 3, or 2 rows: bracts 3—1-flowered, imbricated, scariose: terminal flower of each spike shortly pedicelled, lateral ones males, sessile or all pedicelled: lateral bracts of the female spikes sterile: male petals 6, females 5: stamens 10—12, biverticillate, upper verticil 4—6-androus: filaments connate at the base: anthers 2-cleft within: ovary 3-celled: styles 3, connate below, free portion 2-cleft, divisions divergent, papillose: seeds size of a pea, solitary.

(1) A. INDICA. (*Dalz.*)

Ident. Dalzell in Hook. Journ. Bot. (1850) p. 51.—Dec. prod. XV. s. 2. p. 726.—Thwaites Enum. pl. Zeyl. p. 279.

SPEC. CHAR. Shrub: stipules ovate-lanceolate, subulate-acuminate, striated lengthways, very quickly deciduous: leaves obovate-lanceolate, acute, cuneate-narrow at the base, repand-toothed: spikes of either sex aggregated in the axils of the leaves: bracts broadly triangular-ovate, acute, concave, somewhat silky: calycine segments lanceolate: petals lanceolate-obovate, equalling the calyx: anthers apiculate: ovary glabrous.

Malabar. Concan. Syhadree hills. Mysore.

GENUS XXI. SARCOCLINIUM.

Diœcia Decandria. *Sex: Syst:*

Deriv. From *Sarx, sarcos,* flesh, and *Kline,* a couch, alluding to the fleshy disc.

GEN. CHAR. Male calyx valvately parted, female quincuncial: petals of either sex alternating with the sepals: disc of both sexes developed: stamens central, outer ones opposite the petals: cells of the anthers pendulous from the apex of the filament: cells of the ovary 1-ovuled: capsules tricoccous: seeds ecarunculate.—Shrubs or middling-sized trees: branchlets densely leafy and clammy at the apex: leaves bistipulate, shortly petioled, entire or serrated, coriaceous, more or less rufescent: flowers diœcious, arranged in simple, long, axillary racemes, flower-bearing from the base: bracts of female racemes 1-flowered, males commonly 3-flowered: male calyx [5-parted, female 5—4-parted: petals shorter than the calyx: disc 5-glandular, glands alternating with the petals, females at length cohering at the base: stamens biverticillate, alternating: anthers 2-cleft within: ovary 3-celled: styles 3, connate at the base, 2—4-cleft.

(1) S. LONGIFOLIUM. (*R. Wight.*)

Ident. Dec. prod. XV. s. 2. p. 727.

Engrav. Wight's Icon. t. 1887-8.

SPEC. CHAR. Shrub: stipules broad-ovate, deciduous: leaves stiffly coriaceous, veinless, spathulate, entire, flat, shortly contracto-acuminate at the apex, rufescent on both sides: racemes erect, spreading, shorter than the leaves: female pedicels jointed a little above the middle: segments of the female calyx glandulously denticulate: ovary pubescent: styles connate at the base into a very short column, narrowly and horizontally spreading: capsules small: seeds smooth, blackish.

In Alpine forests on the northern slopes of the Neilgherries.

GENUS XXII. CROZOPHORA.

Monœcia Decandria. *Sex: Syst:*

GEN. CHAR. Male calyx valvate: calyx of both sexes alternating with the sepals, male calyx confounded with the base of the staminal column: anthers 2-cleft: cells of the ovary 1-ovuled: fruit a fleshy capsule, tricoccous: seeds ecarunculate: cotyledons broad, much longer than the radicle.—Small shrubs or perennial or annual herbs, usually filled with purple juice, beset with hairs: leaves alternate, stipulate, shortly or long petioled, ovate or lanceolate, usually repand-toothed, herbaceous, with two glands at the base: flowers monœcious: racemes axillary, bearing a few female flowers at the base: petals of the flowers of both sexes developed, or of the females only rudimentary, when developed, narrow, hairy at the back, and somewhat resembling the sepals, free among themselves, but alternately often slightly cohering: stamens 1-, 2-, 3-verticelled: filaments monadelphous: anthers erect, extrorsely 2-cleft: ovary 3-celled: styles 3, connate at the base, with 2 feet: capsules 3-seeded, 3-shelled: seeds spuriously arillate: testa smooth or rough with tubercles.

(1) C. PLICATA. (*Muller.*)

Ident. Dec. prod. XV. s. 2. p. 747.

SPEC. CHAR. Leaves long-petioled, repand-toothed or somewhat 3-lobed, or without lobes, plicato-undulate: male petals lanceolate-ovate entire, females somewhat linear: stamens 12—15:

cells somewhat oblique: ovary slightly tomentose: styles deeply 2-cleft: seeds rough.

Var. a. ROTTLERI.—Annual or perennial: leaves broadly triangular-ovate, somewhat 3-lobed or repand: bracts small: fructiferous pedicels a little exceeding the capsule.—Spreng. Syst. III. p. 850.—C. Moluccanus, *Willd.*—C. hastatus, *Burm. t.* 63. *fig.* I. —C. Burmanni, *Spreng. l. c.*

Peninsula.

Var. b. GENUINA.—Annual or perennial: whole plant clothed with a whitish or somewhat tawny thick hairy covering: leaves broadly ovate, somewhat 3-lobed, more or less woolly: bracts small: fructiferous pedicels a little exceeding the capsule.—Croton plicatus, *Vahl.*—C. plicata, *Adr. Juss. Euph. p.* 28.

Malabar. Carnatic. Mysore.

Var. c. PROSTRATA.—Procumbent: leaves ovate, oblique at the base, repand, scarcely 3-lobed: lowest bracts of the racemes leafy: fructiferous pedicels at length 2—3 times exceeding the capsules.—Croton plicatum, *Roxb.* (*not Vahl.*).—C. tinctorium, *Burm. flor. t.* 62. *fig.* 2.—C. asper, *Koen. ex Roxb. l. c.*—Crozophora prostrata, *Dalz. Bomb. flor. p.* 233.

Concans.

(2) C. OBLIQUA. (*Adr. Juss.*)

Ident. Adr. Juss. Tent. Euph. p. 28.—Dec. l. c. p. 749.
Syn. Croton obliquus, *Vahl.*—C. oblongifolius, *Delile Flore d'Egypte p.* 139. *t.* 51. *fig.* I.—Crozophora oblongifolia, *Adr. Juss. l. c.*

SPEC. CHAR. Shrub: all the parts densely covered with a flocculent, more or less rufescent hairy wool, except the ovary: male petals obovate-lanceolate, entire, females linear, equalling the calyx: leaves as in the preceding: ovary bearing scales: styles 2-cleft.

Northern India.

GENUS XXIII. SYMPHYLLIA.

Monœcia Pentandria. *Sex: Syst:*

Deriv. From *Syn*, together, and *Phyllon*, a leaf; the flowers are mixed with the leaves.

GEN. CHAR. Male calyx valvate, female imbricated: petals and disc of either sex none: stamens alternating with the sepals and equal in number: anthers 2-cleft, fixed by the base, cells below long free among themselves, equal: cells of the ovary 1-ovuled: fruit capsular.—Shrubs, subdichotomously branched: leaves collected at the tops of the branches, subverticelled or equally distant in the branchlets, minutely stipulate, almost sessile, minutely denticulate or entire, beneath not maculately glandular: flowers monœcious; inflorescences terminal, paniculately spiciform, short, bearing a few female flowers at the base or uppermost axils of the leaves: male calyx 3—6-parted, female 5—6-parted: filaments free: anthers erect, emarginate at both sides: rudimentary ovary columnar: ovary 3-celled: styles shortly connate into a column, then divaricately spreading above, densely fimbriately papillose within: young fruit fleshy, 1-seeded by abortion.

(1) S. MALLOTIFORMIS. (*Muller.*)

Ident. Mull. Arg. in Linnæa v. 34. p. 136.—Dec. prod. XV. s. 2. p. 764.

SPEC. CHAR. Shrubby: leaves alternate, oblong-elliptic, acute, entire, uppermost ones not collected together, slightly petioled, obtuse at the base: spikes a little shorter than the leaves: flowers rather densely arranged in glomerules: male flowers numerous, longer than the pedicels, shortly pubescent.

Southern slopes of the Neilgherries. Malabar. Concan.

(2) S. SILHETIANA. (*Baill.*)

Ident. Baill. Etud. gén. Euph. p. 474. t. XI. figs. 6—7.—Dec. prod. l. c. p. 764.

SPEC. CHAR. Shrubby: young branches tawny-pubescent, soon glabrate: stipules triangular-lanceolate, tawny-puberulous, soon deciduous: leaves spathulate-lanceolate, long cuspidate-acuminate, young ones hairy: inflorescences about twice as short as the leaves, often paniculately branched: male sepals puberulous: ovary slightly tomentose: common base of the styles columnar, scarcely equalling the ovary, tomentose: segments pubescent.

Silhet. Khasia.

GENUS XXIV. CLAOXYLON.

Diœcia Polyandria. *Sex: Syst:*

GEN. CHAR. Male calyx valvate: petals none: glands of the hypogynous disc developed, alternating with the sepals: stamens central, on an elevated receptacle: anthers 2-cleft: cells fixed by the base, erect: rudimentary ovary none: cells of the ovary 1-ovuled, opposite the sepals or fewer, one posterior: fruit capsular: seeds ecarunculate.—Shrubs and trees, rarely herbs: leaves alternate, stipulate, petioled, often purplish or violet-reddish, with 2—4 teeth-shaped stipels at the base above, never spotted glandular beneath: flowers diœcious, seldom monœcious, small, arranged in simple axillary racemes, bearing either fascicles or glomerules: male calyx 3- rarely 4-parted, female 3—2-parted: glands of the hypogynous disc usually free, of the male flowers various, sometimes covering the whole receptacle, scattered among the bases of the filaments, sometimes cohering into a disc around the receptacle, sometimes developed in both ways at the same time in the flowers: stamens numerous: filaments free, short: anthers opening either inwardly or outwardly: ovary 3—2-celled: styles simple, shortish, spreading, coarsely papillosely stigmatose within: capsules 3—2-coccous, 3—2-seeded: seeds coloured a lively red, globose: testa pitted, depressed, sometimes scrobiculate.

(1) C. Indicum. (*Muller.*)

Ident. Dec. prod. XV. s. 2. p. 782.

Spec. Char. Leaves membranaceous: racemes at length elongated, flower-bearing from the base, whitish tomentose: male bracts 7—3-flowered: hypogynous glands pale, elliptic, afterwards broader, somewhat confluent at the base: anthers 25—15: glands of the male receptacle snowy-penicillate at the apex: ovary pale-tomentose: stigmas lacerately papillose: shells whitish-silky on both sides.

Var. a. genuinum.—Shrub: branchlets pale tawny-pubescent above: leaves subrhomboid-elliptic, acutish at both ends: racemes very long: male pedicels a little exceeding the open calyx.—Erythrochilus Indicus, *Rein. ap. Bl. Bidjr. p.* 615.—C. Indicum, *Haask —Miq. flor. Ind. Bat.*—Croton Halecum, *Roxb. flor. Ind.* III. *p.* 683 (?).

Southern Peninsula.

(2) C. mercurialis. (*Thwaites.*)

Ident. Thwaites Enum. pl. Zeyl. p. 271.—Dec. l. c. p. 790.

Syn. Tragia mercurialis, *Linn.*—Mercurialis alternifolia, *Lam. Encyc.*—*Baill. Etud. p.* 490.—Micrococca mercurialis, *Benth. in Hooker's Niger Flora, p.* 503.

Spec. Char. Annual: stem erect, more or less purplish: leaves oblong-rhomboid or rhomb-lanceolate, acute at both ends, obtusely serrate: rhachis of the racemes filiform, bearing very minute, short-pedicelled, solitary, or 2—4-fascicled male flowers in the axils of the bracts, the females above: bracts ovate-lanceolate: ovary densely strigose-hirsute: styles very short: seeds very coarsely pitted.

Pondicherry. Malabar. Mysore. Carnatic.

GENUS XXV. ACALYPHA.

Monœcia Octandria. *Sex: Syst:*

Deriv. From *A, Kalos* and *Aphe*, not pleasant to the touch.

Gen. Char. Male calyx valvate, female imbricated, of this one of the segments is anticous: petals and disc none: stamens occupying the centre on an elevated receptacle: anthers 2-cleft: cells free, pendulous from the apex: rudimentary ovary none: cells of the ovary 1-ovuled, 2 anterior, 1 posterior: fruit capsular: seeds carunculate: embryo straight in albumen: radicle nearly equalling the ovate cotyledons.—Shrubs, undershrubs, perennial or annual herbs: leaves alternate, longish petioled, sometimes almost sessile, never quite entire: petioles bistipulate at the base: inflorescences uni- or bisexual, and then the male flowers uppermost: male flowers numerous in the axils of bracts, [arranged in a densely glomerate-flowered, often continuous spike, very small, at length articulately deciduous, females usually 1 or 2—3 in the axils of the bracts, sessile or rarely pedicelled: male calyx 4-parted: female 3—5-parted: stamens normally 8: filaments free: ovary 3-celled: styles 3, free or shortly connate at the base, simple, seldom altogether entire: capsules tricoccous, very often more or less concealed by variously developed female bracts: seeds smooth, pitted, or tubercled.

(1) A. PANICULATA. (*Miq.*)

Syn. Miq. Flor. Ind. Bat. vol. I. p. 2. p. 406.—Dec. prod. XV. s. 2. p. 803.

Syn. A. racemosa, *Baill. Etud. gén. Euphorb. p.* 443.—A. Wallichiana, *Thwaites Enum. pl. Zeyl. p.* 271.

SPEC. CHAR. Perennial or shrubby, pubescent: leaves ovate, acuminate, subobtuse at the base, flaccid, coarsely cut and serrated, long-petioled, palmatinerved, membranaceous: female bracts 3-flowered, fructigerous ones broadly ovate, obtuse, very small: segments of the female calyx glandular-ciliate: male spikes axillary, very thin, dense-flowered, almost equalling the petioles in length: female panicles usually a little exceeding the petioles, fructiferous ones terminal, minutely puberulous, loose-flowered, lower ones axillary: pedicels long exceeding the very small female bract: segments of the female calyx ovate-lanceolate, afterwards reflexed: ovary glandulosely submuricated: styles deeply palmately 3—7-parted, the basilar portion rough with glands: capsule deeply tridymous, long exceeding the fructigerous bracts: seeds scabrous.

Neilgherries.

(2) A. FRUTICOSA. (*Forsk.*)

Ident. Forsk. Descr. p. 161.—Dec. l. c. p. 822.

Syn. A. betulina, *Retz. obs.* 5. *p.* 30.—A. amentacea, *Roxb. flor. Ind.* III. *p.* 676.

SPEC. CHAR. Shrub, of heavy odour and pubescent with sessile waxy, golden-yellowish glands: leaves rhomb-ovate or rhomb-lanceolate, acute or acuminate at both ends, serrated, firmly membranaceous, beneath densely covered and shining with golden glands: spikes unisexual, very shortly peduncled, or androgynous and males, males commonly shorter than the leaves, erect or at length pendulous, hoary, androgynous ones increased at the base by 1—4 female bracts: female spikes lax flowered, 5—8-bracteate: female bracts 1-flowered, exceeding the capsule, reniform crenate-denticulate: male calyx pubescent externally: ovary densely hairy and scattered with waxy glands: styles pectinate with long slashes: capsules hoary tomentose: seeds smooth.

Peninsula, near Madras and Pondicherry. Mysore. Carnatic.

(3) A. CAPITATA. (*Willd.*)

Ident. Willd. Spec. pl. iv. p. 525.—Dec. l. c. p. 843.

SPEC. CHAR. Shrub: branchlets pubescent or hispidulous: leaves very shortly petioled, ovate, obtuse, very small, obtusely serrated: male spikes shortly pedicelled, axillary, females terminal, sessile, short, few-flowered: female bracts 1-flowered, fructigerous, exceeding the capsule by about one half, 7—9-lobed: male calyx pubescent externally: ovary silky-hairy: styles shortly fimbriated-lacinulate.

Mysore. Carnatic. Malabar.

(4) A. ALNIFOLIA. (*Willd.*)

Ident. Willd. Spec. l. c.—Dec. l. c. p. 843.

Engrav. Hook. Comp. II. t. 29.

SPEC. CHAR. Shrub: branchlets and petioles hispid, with long horizontal hairs: leaves longish-petioled, orbicular-ovate, obtuse or very shortly acute, slightly cut and serrated, membranaceous, hairy on the ribs and margin: spikes unisexual, axillary, males peduncled, females terminal, shortened, bearing about 4—7 bracts: female bracts 1-flowered, about 5-lobed to the middle, lobes ovate obtuse: male calyx papillose: ovary silky-hispid: styles very long, shortly fimbriate-lacinulate the whole length: capsule hispid: seeds largish, subglobose, smooth.

Golden Rock, near Trichinopoly, rare.

(5) A. INDICA. (*Linn.*)

Ident. Linn. Spec. pl. p. 1003.—Dec. l. c. p. 868.—Roxb. flor. Ind. III. p. 675.

Syn. A. spicata, *Forsk. Descr. p.* 160.

Engrav. Wight's Icon. t. 877.

SPEC. CHAR. Annual or perennial: glabrescent or pubescent: leaves rhomb-ovate, acute or obtuse at the apex, coarsely serrated, membranaceous, petioles longer than the limb: spikes sessile, loosely bract-bearing, males at the apex by a short space: female bracts 3—5-flowered, fructigerous, very broadly truncate-obovate, campanulate, far exceeding the capsules, at length coarsely repand-toothed, males very minute, ovate-lanceolate: segments of the female calyx oblong-ovate acuminate, sparingly ciliated at the margin: ovary hispidulous: styles about 3-cleft: seeds smooth, acutish.

A common weed, everywhere widely distributed.

(6) A. BRACHYSTACHYA. (*Hornemann.*)

Ident. Hornem. Hort. Hafn. p. 909.—Dec. l. c. p. 870.

Syn. A. conferta, *Roxb. flor. Ind.* III. *p.* 677.—A. elegantula, *Hochst. in Schimp. pl. Abyss. No.* 1708.

SPEC. CHAR. Annual: leaves long-petioled, broadly ovate, acute, slightly cordate at the base, serrated, membranaceous: spikes axillary, sessile, subaggregate, androgynous, 2—3 times shorter than the leaves: fructigerous bracts green, whitish at the base: segments spreading, two lowermost smaller, stipular, reflexed: female bracts about 3—5-, 2—5-flowered: ovary rough with tubercles and hairy above: styles somewhat pectinately 3—5-lacinulate: seeds smooth.

Neilgherries.

(7) A. MALABARICA. (*Muller.*)

Ident. Mull. Arg. in Linnæa vol. 34. p. 42.—Dec. l. c. p. 871.

SPEC. CHAR. Annual: stem tawny-hirsute: leaves ovate, acutish at both ends, serrate, stiffish: spikes sessile, somewhat solitary, shortish, male portion scarcely exceeding the upper female bract, peduncled, capituliform: female bracts 2—5-flowered, fructiferous, almost twice exceeding the capsules, furnished with stalked glands at the margin: male calyx glabrous: ovary hairy: seeds minute, scabrous.

Malabar. Concan.

(8) A. FALLAX. (*Muller.*)

Ident. Mull. l. c. p. 43.—Dec. l. c. p. 872.

Syn. A. corchorifolia, *Vahl. ex Baill. etud. Euph. p.* 443.

SPEC. CHAR. Annual: leaves longish petioled, broad-ovate, obtuse, very shortly subcuneate at the base, serrated: spikes long-peduncled, thin, androgynous, axillary: male portion of the spikes exceeding the ultimate female bract: female bracts 1-flowered, hairy, glandular-ciliated, broadly truncate-ovate, scarcely exceeding the capsule: slashes of the styles filiform, here and there connate in pairs: ovary hairy: seeds smooth.

Peninsula.

(9) A. CILIATA. (*Muller.*)

Ident. Mull. l. c. p. 44.—Dec. l. c. p. 873.—Roxb. flor. Ind. III. p. 676.

Syn. A. fimbriata, *Baill. Rec. d'Obs. bot.* I. *p*. 272.

Engrav. Wight & Arn. Ann. Nat. Hist. vol. II. p. 111. t. 5.

SPEC. CHAR. Annual: leaves ovate, long petioled, shortly cuspidate-acuminate, acutish at the base, coarsely serrated, membranaceous: spikes sessile, ovoid, much shorter than the petiole: female bracts 2-flowered, segments scattered with few long hairs, fruit-bearing ones broadly truncate-obovate, campanulate, prominently ribbed externally, almost twice equalling the capsule, divided for a third part or almost to the middle into about 17—21 suberect segments: divisions of the female calyx oblong-ovate, of the male densely papillose: ovary sparingly hairy above: seeds smooth, acutish at the apex.

Southern Peninsula.

GENUS XXVI. ALCHORNEA.

Diœcia Octandria. *Sex: Syst:*

GEN. CHAR. Male calyx valvate, female imbricate: petals of either sex none: male disc none, female developed or suppressed: stamens central, outer ones, if more numerous than the segments of the calyx, alternating: anthers 2-cleft: cells free among themselves for about half the lower part: rudimentary ovary none: cells of the ovary 1-ovuled: fruit capsular: seeds ecarunculate: cotyledons elliptic, usually scarcely equalling the radicle.—Trees or shrubs: leaves alternate, petioled, bistipulate, elliptic or ovate, commonly serrated, spotted glandular beneath: spots brown, sharply circumscribed: flowers diœcious or even monœcious, and then very often situated in branches, distinguished by the sex: males glomerate, very often arranged in more or less interrupted, simple, or paniculately branched spikes: females simply spiked or racemose, solitary or rarely in threes in the axil of the bracts: male calyx 4-, or rarely 2—3-parted: female 6—5-, or usually 4-parted or cleft: stamens somewhat numerous or 8—4, commonly alternating in 2 rows: filaments connate at the base into a dwarf urceolus: anthers introrse or extrorse: ovary 3—2-celled: styles as many as the cells of the ovary, connate or usually free at the base, entire or 2-parted, somewhat channelled: capsules usually opening distinctly from the base towards the apex, 3—1-coccous, 3—1-seeded: seeds more or less scabrous, with tubercles.

(1) A. TILIÆFOLIA. (*Muller.*)

Ident. Mull. Arg. in Linnæa vol. 34. p. 168.—Dec. prod. XV. s. 2. p. 903.

Syn. Stipellaria tiliæfolia, *Benth. in. Hook. Journ. Bot.* (1854) p. 4.

SPEC. CHAR. Shrub: leaves broad-ovate, cuspidate-acuminate, truncate at the base, 3-nerved, glandular-denticulate: male glomerules 2—5-flowered: male and female spikes simple, female many-flowered: segments of the female calyx linear-lanceolate: ovary slightly tomentose and muricately tubercled: styles puberulous at the back: capsule ellipsoid, muricated.

Silhet. Khasia. Goalpara.

GENUS XXVII. TRAGIA.

Monœcia Triandria. *Sex: Syst:*

Deriv. In honour of Jerome Bock, generally called Tragus, a German botanist.

GEN. CHAR. Male calyx valvate, female imbricated: petals none: stamens central, inserted round a very small rudimentary ovary: anthers 2-cleft, fixed by the back, cells adnate lengthways to the connectivum: cells of the ovary 1-ovuled: in the female calyx (if 6-parted) opposite the outer segments, 1 posterior, 2 anterior: styles connate below: seeds ecarunculate, exarillate.— Shrubs, undershrubs or perennial herbs, scandent or twining, rarely annual erect herbs, usually clothed, like nettles, with more or less stinging hairs: leaves alternate, bistipulate, long or short petioled, usually ovate, membranaceous: flowers monœcious, racemose: racemes terminal, male flowers above, females usually 1—3: male calyx 5—3-parted, female 8—3- or usually 6—5-parted, fructigerous one usually enlarged and stinging: disc hypogynous or none: stamens 40—1: filaments free or central, more or less connate at the base: anthers ovoid, dehiscing lengthwise, introrse or extrorse: clefts perpendicular or rarely subhorizontal: ovary 5-, or usually 3-celled: styles 5—2, simple, more or less papillose inside: capsules 5—2—1-coccous, 5—1-seeded: seeds globose.

(1) T. MIQUELIANA. (*Muller.*)

Ident. Dec. prod. XV. s. 2. p. 942.

SPEC. CHAR. Petioles much shorter than the limb: segments of the female calyx 10—12-lacinulate, enlarged and hardened when in fruit: ovary very shortly tomentose, and at the same time sparingly hairy or otherwise: styles connate for half their length and beyond into a slender cylindric column, free portion revolute.

Var. a. BICOLOR.—Undershrub: stems twining, hispid above

and tawny-tomentose: leaves lanceolate-ovate, acuminate, slightly cordate at the base, sharply serrulate, stiffish, lower side of the younger ones and apex of the branches rusty-tomentose, then pale, developed leaves firm, densely tomentose beneath, and then hairy-pubescent: male bracts sublinear, tawny-villous: ovary not hirsute: seeds scaly, tumidly bilabiate at the apex.

Neilgherries.

Var. b. UNICOLOR.—Younger parts not rusty, puberulous, and at the same time somewhat covered with snow-white hairs: leaves more membranaceous, subglabrous, and longer petioled.

Malabar. Concan.

(2) T. INVOLUCRATA. (*Muller.*)

Ident. Dec. l. c. p. 943.

SPEC. CHAR. Segments of the female calyx pinnately about 8—12-lacinulate, enlarged and hardened when in fruit: lacinulæ narrow, spreading, afterwards connivent by the dorsal side of the segments: ovary strigosely hispid: styles somewhat free, oblong-ovoid, obtuse: capsules large: seeds scaly, tumidly bilabiate at the apex.

Var. a. RHEEDIANA.—Undershrub, perennial or annual: stems hispid: stipules almost equalling the shorter petioles, lanceolate from a broad-ovate or cordate, equal or unequal, or somewhat hastately bilobed base: leaves ovate or oblong-ovate, serrated or toothed, entire at the apex, more or less hirsute, lower ones shorter acuminate or obtuse, upper ones long acuminate or cuspidate: male bracts narrowed at the base: segments of male calyx very hispid: capsules deeply tridymous, whitish-hispid.—T. involucrata, *Jacq. Icon. rar. t.* 190.—*Rheede Mal.* II. *t.* 39.

Peninsula. Malabar.

Var. b. CANNABINA.—Undershrub or perennial: all leaves palmately 3-parted, partitions linear-lanceolate, or lateral ones obliquely linear-elliptic, coarsely serrated.—T. Cannabina, *Linn. Suppl. p.* 415.—*Willd. Spec.* IV. *p.* 326. *Ad. Juss. Tent. Euph. t.* 15. *fig.* 49.—Croton hastatus, *Linn. Syst. Ed.* 13. *p.* 722.—C. urens, *Linn. l. c. Pluk. Alm. Phyt. t.* 120. *fig.* 6.

Malabar. Western Ghauts. Flowering nearly all the year.

GENUS XXVIII. TREWIA.

Monœcia Polyandria. *Sex: Syst:*

Deriv. In honour of C. J. Trew, of Nuremberg, a botanical author.

GEN. CHAR. Male calyx valvate, female imbricated: petals and disc none: stamens inserted on a hemispherical receptacle, central: anthers 2-cleft: rudimentary ovary none: cells of the ovary

1-ovuled: fruits suberose-fleshy, not opening as a capsule: seeds ecarunculate with copious albumen.—Tree: leaves opposite: flowers diœcious, racemose: male calyx 3—4-parted, female unequally 3—4-parted: stamens numerous, about 80: filaments free: anthers opening vertically lengthways, outer or lower ones distinctly introrse: ovary 3—4-celled, cells 2 (where the ovary is 4-celled,) anterior and 2 posterior, when the ovary is 3-celled cells sometimes anterior, sometimes the posterior ones reduced into 1: styles shortish: stigmas equal to the number of cells, elongated, simple, strongly papillose within: seeds exarillate.

(1) T. NUDIFLORA. (*Linn.*)

Ident. Linn. Spec. append. p. 1661.—Dec. prod. XV. s. 2. p. 953.—Roxb. flor. Ind. III. p. 837.

Syn. Tetragastris ossea, *Gærtn.*—Trewia macrophylla, *Roth.*—Rottlera Indica, *Willd.*—R. Hoperiana, *Bl. Sched. ex Baill. Etud. gén. Euph. p.* 423.

Engrav. Wight's Icon. t. 1870-71.—Baill. l. c. t. 18. figs. 18—23. —Gærtn. fruct. II. t. 109. fig. 5.—Ad. Juss. tent. Euph. t. 9. fig. 29.—Rheede Mal. I. t. 42.

SPEC. CHAR. Large tree: stipules linear-subulate, very caducous: leaves broad ovate, acute or acuminate, cordate or obtuse or subcuneate at the base, entire, 5-nerved, membranaceous, biglandular at the base, young ones villous or pubescent on both sides and below, especially in the lower part, sprinkled with gold-shining, very small, waxy glands, but soon altogether destitute of them: racemes axillary, males often exceeding the leaves, flower-bearing almost the whole length, females few-flowered: bracts very small: male calyx globose: segments of the female calyx long-acuminate, here and there cohering in pairs: anthers emarginate at the base and apex: ovary pale tawny, silky: fruit 4—3-coccous, subglobose, smooth, pendulous: seeds smooth.

In sandy places near the shore and elsewhere in the Peninsula. Flowering in February and March.

GENUS XXIX. MALLOTUS.

Diœcia Polyandria. *Sex: Syst:*

GEN. CHAR. Male calyx valvate: petals none: disc in the female flowers none, or very rarely developed in the males: stamens inserted on an elevated dilated centre: rudimentary ovary none: cells of the ovary 1-ovuled: fruit capsular: seeds ecarunculate: albumen copious: cotyledons broad, far exceeding the radicle.—Trees and shrubs: leaves alternate or opposite, bistipulate, sometimes peltate at the base, occasionally lobed, sprinkled beneath with shining or afterwards brown or rufescent disc-shaped glands: flowers diœcious or rarely monœcious, racemose or spiked: inflorescences terminal or spuriously axillary: male calyx 3—5-

parted, female 3—5-parted: stamens numerous: filaments free or cohering at the base: anthers dehiscing lengthways: ovary 2—5-celled, very often 3-celled: styles simple, as many as cells in the ovary, coarsely papillose within, connate at the base into a distinct styline column: capsules 2—5-coccous.

(1) M. BARBATUS. (*Muller.*)

Ident. Mull. Arg. in Linnæa vol. 34. p. 184.—Dec. prod. XV. s. 2. p. 957.

Syn. Rottlera barbata, *Wall. Baill. Etud. gén. Euphorb. p.* 423.

SPEC. CHAR. Small tree: leaves broadly round-obtuse at the base: lobes shortly triangular, acute, upper side pubescent, lower tomentose: prominently denticulate at the margin: female flowers simply racemose: racemes long, fructiferous ones rusty-floccose: female calyx 4-cleft: hypogynous disc dwarf with 1—8 stiff lacinulæ, thickened at the apex: capsules 3—4-coccous, subglobose.

Concan.

(2) M. ROXBURGHIANUS. (*Muller.*)

Ident. Mull. Arg. l. c. p. 186.—Dec. l. c. p. 962.

Syn. Rottlera peltata, *Roxb. flor. Ind.* III. *p.* 828.

Engrav. Wight's Icon. t. 1873.

SPEC. CHAR. Small tree: young branches petioles, and inflorescences tawny-pubescent: stipules linear-lanceolate, villous: leaves broadly triangular-ovate, acuminated, base round-obtuse and peltate, repand-denticulate, membranaceous: hypophyllous glands very small, somewhat golden: male racemes long: bracts linear, subulate-bistipulate, females 1-flowered, males 3—5-flowered: female flowers spiked: capsules very shortly echinate: prickles thick and densely hairy: flowers greenish-yellow.

Silhet. Khasia. Assam. Flowering in April and May.

(3) M. ALBUS. (*Muller.*)

Ident. Mull. Arg. l. c. p. 188.—Dec. l. c. p. 965.

Syn. Rottlera alba, *Roxb. flor. Ind.* III. *p.* 829.—R. tetracocca, *do. p.* 826.—R. mappoides, *Dalz. Bom. b. flor. p.* 230.

SPEC. CHAR. Tree: younger branchlets with the petioles, both sides of the leaves, and inflorescences very densely covered with short rusty stellate hairs, afterwards with the upper side of the leaves glabrate: leaves broadly triangular-ovate, shortly acuminate, very shortly acute at the base, slightly peltate or not peltate, biglandular above, subentire or repand-denticulate, rusty white above, opaque above: inflorescences terminal, paniculately spiciform, rusty-tomentose: bracts triangular-ovate: female calyx unequally 4—5-parted segments ovate and lanceolate, deeply connate at the base: stamens about 80: ovary 4-celled, rusty-tomentose, at length softly echinately tubercled: tubercles floccose: capsules echinate: seeds ellipsoid, very lightly tubercled.

Silhet. Assam. Mysore. Carnatic. Canara.

(4) M. MURICATUS. (*Muller.*)

Ident. Mull. Arg. l. c. p. 191.—Dec. l. c. p. 972.

Syn. Claoxylon muricatum, *R. Wight.*—Axenfeldia intermedia, *Bail. Etud. gén. Euph. p.* 419.—Rottlera muricata, *Thwaites Enum. pl. Zeyl. p.* 273.

Engrav. Wight's Icon. t. 1886.

SPEC. CHAR. Small tree: young parts densely covered with rusty, shining, resinous, small discs: leaves short-petioled, bimaculate at the base above, lanceolate-elliptic, acuminate, obtuse or subacute with a narrowed base, repand-toothed, stiffly membranaceous: flowers spicately racemose: female racemes long, terminal, soon made axillary by the development of the uppermost branches, males sometimes very large, and then pale and densely imbricated with bracts: bracts short, broad, concave: male calyx globose: segments 3, suborbiculate, segments of the female calyx narrow lanceolate, shortly connate at the base: stamens about 50: ovary globose, muricate-echinate: prickles soft, hairy: capsule echinate.

Courtallum. Belgaum.

(5) M. STENANTHUS. (*Muller.*)

Ident. Mull. Arg. l. c.—Dec. l. c.

SPEC. CHAR. Small tree: leaves opposite, unequally petioled, acuminate, acute at the base, repand-toothed or entire, stiffly membranaceous, above at the base many-spotted, beneath resinous-dotted: male racemes axillary: flowers almost sessile: bracts very small, ovate: segments of the male calyx elliptic: stamens 18—23.

Southern Peninsula.

(6) M. AUREO-PUNCTATUS. (*Muller.*)

Ident. Dec. l. c. p. 973.

Syn. Rottlera aureo-punctata, *Dalz. Bomb. Flora p.* 230.

SPEC. CHAR. Shrub: leaves opposite, not peltate, oblong-obovate, acuminate, attenuated towards the base, short-petioled, glabrous, shining, sprinkled beneath with few hairs and frequent golden-dotted glands: stipules linear, rusty, caducous: racemes shorter than the leaf, females about 4—5-flowered, axillary and terminal: male flowers fascicled in fives: segments of the female calyx cohering into a spathe cleft on one side: stamens numerous:

connectivum produced into a gland 2-lobed at the apex: style elongated: capsule large, armed with soft, hairy, subsetiform prickles.

Hilly parts of the Concan. Meera hills.

(7) M. Lawii. (*Muller.*)

Ident. Mull. Arg. l. c. p. 192.—Dec. l. c. p. 974.

Spec. Char. Small tree: leaves elliptic or obovate-lanceolate, often slightly subfalcately curved, narrowed at both ends, cuspidate at the apex, acute or obtuse at the base, repand-toothed, spotted at the base, golden-dotted beneath: flowers spicately racemose: female racemes few-flowered, axillary: male bracts 3—7-flowered: male pedicels fascicled, jointed at the apex: stamens about 50—60: connectivum obtuse or apiculate: male calyx pubescent, 3-parted, female spathaceous, soon deeply 1—2-parted: ovary densely and long echinate: prickles soft, thin, hairyish: styline column very short.

Malabar. Concan.

(8) M. distans. (*Muller.*)

Ident. Mull. Arg. l. c. p. 194.—Dec. l. c. p. 976.

Spec. Char. Undershrub: branchlets, petioles, and inflorescences clothed with dense tawny pubescence: leaves ovate, acute, or slightly obtuse, slightly peltate at the base, glabrous above, pubescent beneath, and sparingly golden-dotted: female racemes distantly few-flowered: calyx 3—4-parted, segments lanceolate-ovate, obtuse: female bracts 1-flowered, linear-lanceolate: ovary densely tawny-tomentose.

Carnatic.

(9) M. atrovirens. (*Muller.*)

Ident. Mull. l. c. p. 195.—Dec. l. c. p. 978.

Spec. Char. Undershrub: leaves lanceolate-obovate, acute at the base, not peltate, dotted thick with rusty glands beneath, darkish brown above and glandular-dotted: segments of the female calyx 5, linear-lanceolate, acute: racemes axillary: stamens about 40: anthers emarginate at both ends: connectivum narrow: ovary smooth, glabrous, densely covered with rusty glands: stigmas recurved, strongly papillose.

Courtallum.

(10) M. Philippensis. (*Muller.*)

Ident. Mull. Arg. l. c. p. 196.—Dec. l. c. p. 980.

Syn. Croton Philippensis, *Lam. Encycl.*—C. punctatus, *Retz. Willd.*—C. coccineus, *Vahl. Willd.*—C. montanus, *Willd.*—Rottlera tinctoria, *Roxb. flor. Ind.* III. *p.* 827.

Engrav. Roxb. Cor. II. t. 168.

Spec. Char. Small tree or undershrub: younger branchlets, petioles, and inflorescences rusty-tomentose: leaves rhomb-ovate or rhomb-lanceolate, acuminate, acute at the base, not peltate, biglandular above, entire or slightly toothed, clothed with scarlet tomentum beneath, glabrous above: spikes of either sex axillary and terminal, rusty-tomentose: male bracts 3-flowered, female 1-flowered: bracts triangular-ovate, acute: segments of the female calyx ovate-lanceolate: stamens 12—15: ovary densely scarlet or at length purple-glandular: capsules slightly trigonous globose, covered with scarlet dust.

Common in most parts of the country.

(11) M. repandus. (*Muller.*)

Ident. Mull. Arg. l. c. p. 197.—Dec. l. c. p. 981.

Syn. Croton rhombifolius, *Willd.*—Rottlera viscida, *Bl. bidjr. p.* 608.—R. dicocca, *Roxb. flor. Ind.* III. *p.* 829.—R. dioica, *Baill. Etud. gén. Euph. p.* 423.—R. rhombifolia, *Thwaites Enum. Zeyl. pl. p.* 272.

Spec. Char. Undershrub, subscandent: branchlets, petioles, and inflorescences tawny-tomentose: leaves triangular or rhomb-ovate, acute, obtuse at the base, repand-toothed, yellowish-green, glabrous above, slightly tomentose beneath, sprinkled with pale gold-shining waxy glands: spikes in the branchlets terminal or terminating the few-leaved axillary branchlets, paniculately branched, often longer than the leaves, tawny: male bracts 3-flowered, females commonly 1-flowered, thickened at the base: male calyces globose, shortly pedicelled, tawny, sprinkled within with large pale grains: stigmas branched, papillose: capsules glandulose: seeds globose, reticulated.

Chittagong. Malabar. Bengal.

GENUS XXX. CLEIDION.

Diœcia Polyandria. *Sex: Syst:*

Gen. Char. Male calyx valvate, female imbricated: petals none: disc suppressed or female developed: stamens inserted on a conical receptacle, verticils alternating accurately among themselves, whence the anthers are arranged in very distinct vertical rows: younger anthers inserted on the filament obliquely peltately at the back about the middle: cells 4, 2 on each side, distinct, opening somewhat crossways round the point opposite the insertion: rudimentary ovary none: cells of the ovary 2—3, 1-ovuled: fruit capsular: seeds ecarunculate: cotyledons large, much longer than the radicle.—Shrubs: leaves alternate, subulate-bistipulate, toothed, beneath near the base sub-urceolately 2—6-glandular: flowers diœcious: inflorescences axillary: female flowers loosely racemose or solitary, and long-pedicelled in the axils of the leaves: males interruptedly glomerato-spicate or fascicled racemose or paniculate: female calyx 3—4-parted: stamens numerous, arranged in about 6 verticils, and in 8—15 vertical rows: filaments free, dilated at the base: connectivum very often produced beyond the cells, and more darkly coloured than the anthers: styles 2—3, filiform, 2-cleft or parted, papillose within: capsules 2—3-coccous: seeds exarillate, subglobose: cotyledons cordate at the base.

(1) C. Javanicum. (*Blume.*)

Ident. Bl. bijdr. p. 613.—Dec. prod. XV. s. 2. p. 987.

Syn. Rottlera uranda, *Dalz. Bomb. flor. p.* 230.

Spec. Char. Tree: stipules long-acuminate, soon deciduous: leaves lanceolate or lanceolate-elliptic, acute at both ends or acuminate at the apex, repand-toothed: flowers racemose, fascicled: female pedicels thickened at the apex, thinly clavate: filaments not dilated at the base: segments of the female calyx triangular, acute, ciliated at the margin: vertical rows of anthers about 12—15: styles connate at the base into a longish column, free portion 2-cleft beyond the middle: ovary 2-celled, cells lateral: female flowers solitary in the axils of the leaves: capsule large, thick-skinned: seeds smooth, pale, globose.

Malabar. Concan. Bengal. Flowering in November.

GENUS XXXI. MACARANGA.

Diœcia Polyandria. *Sex: Syst:*

Gen. Char. Male calyx valvate, female imbricated: petals none: stamens central on a convex receptacle: anthers not arranged regularly in vertical rows, fixed by the back, 3—4-celled, connectivum incomplete, shorter than the cells: rudimentary ovary none: cells of the ovary 1-ovuled: fruit capsular: seeds not carunculate, albuminous: cotyledons broad, much longer than the radicle.—Trees: leaves alternate, often bistipulate, more or less peltate at the base, often sprinkled beneath with waxy glands: flowers diœcious, glomerate or fascicled, arranged in spikes or simple or paniculately branched axillary racemes: stamens below 15, in some species very few: younger fruit commonly a little fleshy, opening as a capsule when ripe, unarmed or variously armed.

(1) M. gummiflua. (*Muller.*)

Ident. Dec. prod. XV. s. 2. p. 1000.

Syn. Mappa gummiflua, *Miq. flor. Bat.*—M. truncata, *Mull. Arg. in Linnæa v.* 34. p. 198.—M. Wallichii, *Baill. Etud. gén. Euph. p.* 430.

Spec. Char. Tree: stipules narrow-lanceolate: leaves slightly peltate at the base, and at length broadly retuse, triangular-ovate, acute, entire, glaucescent beneath, sprinkled with waxy yellowish or rufescent glands: male panicles pyramidate abbreviated: lower male bracts petioled, rhomb-ovate, small, thick, entire: upper ones more membranaceous, sessile, triangular-ovate, acuminate: females very small, 3-flowered: stamens 14—9: ovary 2-celled, waxy glandulose, unarmed, glabrous: capsules small.

Khasia. Assam.

(2) M. digyna. (*Muller.*)

Ident. Dec. l. c. p. 1007.

Syn. Claoxylon digynum, *R. Wight.*—Rottlera digyna, *Thwaites Enum. pl. Zeyl. p.* 273.—Mappa digyna, *Mull. Arg. in Linnæa vol.* 34. *p.* 198.

Engrav. Wight's Icon. t. 1884.

Spec. Char. Small tree: leaves lanceolate, long-cuspidate-acuminate, obtuse or slightly cordate at the base, lightly repand-toothed, biglandular at the base above, the same colour on both sides, beneath densely glandular, with brown waxy dots: racemes spiciform, simple, very slender: female calyx 3—4-parted: anthers 10—15: stigmas very long: ovary puberulous, more or less obsoletely echinate: capsules dotted rough.

Neilgherries.

(3) M. Indica. (*R. Wight.*)

Ident. Wight's Icon. vol. 5. p. 2. p. 23.

Engrav. Wight l. c. t. 1883.

Spec. Char. Tree: stipules triangular-ovate, glabrous, glaucescent: leaves orbicular-ovate, acute or very shortly cuspidate-acuminate, rounded obtuse from a broad peltate base, not emarginate-retuse, entire, soon glabrate and glaucescent beneath, covered with waxy dotted glands, young ones densely rusty-tomentose: flowers of either sex panicled: male bracts petioled, elliptic, all occupied by a large elliptic disc-shaped gland: females linear-lanceolate, without glands: stigma ascending, sublinear, acute, flexuose.

Neilgherries. Travancore. Flowering in December and January.

(4) M. FLEXUOSA. (*R. Wight.*)

Ident. Wight Icon. vol. 5. p. 2. p. 23.—Dec. l. c. p. 1010.

Engrav. Wight Icon. t. 1949. fig. 3.

SPEC. CHAR. Tree: branches of the male inflorescence flexuose: bracts leafy at the axils of the panicles, rhomb-ovate, acuminate, coarsely cut and serrated, lanceolate-linear from the triangular base of the glomerules, ending in a thick gland: segments of the male calyx orbicular-elliptic, entire: stigma broad, torn, crenated: ovary adpressed.

Courtallum.

(5) M. TOMENTOSA. (*R. Wight.*)

Ident. Wight's Icon. vol. 5. p. 2. p. 23.—Dec. l. c. p. 1010.

Engrav. Wight's Icon. t. 1949. fig. 1.

SPEC. CHAR. Tree: young parts obscurely rusty-tomentose: stipules largish, triangular-ovate, acuminate, rusty-pubescent: leaves orbiculate-ovate, acute, broadly round from a peltate base, rusty-tomentose, afterwards puberulous, beneath sprinkled with brown, shining glands: inflorescences axillary, half equalling the leaves, straight, shortly branched, racemiform, interruptedly glomerule-flowered: bracts denticulate, males rhomb-ovate, many-flowered, females afterwards ovate, 1—2-flowered, cuneate at the base: segments of the male calyx cuneate-obovate: ovary much incurved: stigma subovoid, obtuse, deflexed: filaments 3, free: seeds globose, smooth.

Malabar and Travancore.

(6) M. PELTATA. (*Muller.*)

Ident. Dec. l. c. p. 1010.

Syn. Osyris peltata, *Roxb. flor. Ind.* III. *p.* 755.—M. Roxburghii, *R. Wight.*—M. Wightiana, *Baill. Etud. gén. Euph. p.* 432.—Mappa (?) peltata, *R. Wight.*

Engrav. Wight's Icon. t. 817 and 1949. fig. iv.

SPEC. CHAR.—Tree: leaves orbiculate-ovate, short acuminate, rounded at the base: stamens 3: bracts toothed, males ovate, acute, many-flowered, females elliptic-lanceolate, 1—2-flowered: segments of the male calyx ovate, acuminate: ovary incurved, dotted with glands.

Circar mountains.

(7) M. INVOLUCRATA. (*Muller.*)

Ident. Dec. l. c. p. 1011.

SPEC. CHAR. Female bracts 2—3-flowered, leafy, subpetioled,

ovate, long-acuminate, toothed, beset above close to the margin with patelliform glands, males small, triangular-ovate, acuminate: female calyx tubular-conical, soon separating at the base, mouth entire: ovary globose, incurved, softly echinate, prickles soft, hirsute: stigma very long, linear, recurved.

Var. GENUINA.—Tree: younger branchlets tawny-pubescent, afterwards puberulous: stipules subulate: leaves broadly triangular-ovate, acuminate, sometimes obsoletely 3-lobed, rounded at the narrow peltate or shortly inciso-cordate base, 3—7-nerved and 4—6-glandular at the base, softly puberulous above, beneath dotted with waxy glands, and densely villous: female inflorescence long-peduncled, all dense-flowered: stigmas hispid at the back: seeds globose, wrinkled.—Urtica involucrata, ***Roxb. ex Wall. Cat.***—M. involucrata, ***Baill. Etud. gén. Euph. p.*** 432.

Bengal.

GENUS XXXII. HOMONOYA.

Diœcia Polyandria. *Sex: Syst:*

GEN. CHAR. Male calyx valvate, female imbricated; petals and disc none: stamens central, polyadelphous: anthers 1-celled, adnate, opening by a short cleft, subglobose: rudimentary ovary none: cells of the ovary 1-ovuled, 2 anterior, 1 posterior: capsules 3-coccous: seeds ecarunculate.—Shrubs: leaves alternate, bistipulate, entire or toothed, subcoriaceous: stipules very caducous: inflorescences axillary, often unisexual, flower-bearing from the base: male flowers spiked, females spicately racemose: bracts commonly 1-flowered: male calyx 3-parted, female quincuncially 5-parted: stamens very numerous: bundles numerous, connate below, congested and polyandrous at the apex, central ones soon destitute of anthers: cells of the ovary 3—4: styles as many as the cells, simple, narrow, much and densely papillose, shortly connate at the base: capsules 3-seeded, often small: seeds smooth, with spurious membranaceous aril.

(1) H. RETUSA. (*Muller.*)

Ident. Mull. Arg. in Linnæa vol. 34. p. 200.—Dec. prod. XV. s. 2. p. 1022.

SPEC. CHAR. Leaves sessile, sparingly scurfy beneath: male inflorescences depauperated: segments of the female calyx ovate: stigmas twice shorter than the capsule, longish papillose: ovary and small capsule smooth.

Var. a. GENUINA.—Mull. Arg. l. c.—Leaves cuneate-obovate, retuse at the apex, about half longer than broad.—Adelia retusa, ***Wight's Icon. t.*** 1869.

Malabar. Concan. Deccan. Circars.

Var. b. CUNEATA.—Mull. Arg. l. c.—Leaves lanceolate-spathulate, round or subtruncated, obtuse at the apex, about three and a half times longer than broad, crenately toothed, rufescent beneath: connectiva reddish: ovaries pubescent.

Peninsula. Malabar. Concan.

(2) H. RIPARIA. (*Lour.*)

Ident. Lour. Flor. Cochinch. p. 637.—Dec. l. c. p. 1023.

Syn. Adelia neriifolia, *Roth. Roxb. flor. Ind.* III. *p.* 849.—Ricinus salicinus, *Haask.*; *Pl. Jav. Rar. p.* 264.—Hæmatospermum salicinum, *Baill. Etud. gén. Euph. p.* 293.

Engrav. Wight's Icon. t. 1868.

SPEC. CHAR. Leaves linear-lanceolate, acuminate, subacute at the base, very often entire, willow-like, beneath sparingly pubescent and scurfy: inflorescences long, many-flowered, erect, slender: segments of the female calyx persistent, ovate-lanceolate: stigmas longer than the capsule, shortish papillose: ovary and capsule here and there muricated, small, pubescent.

Khasia. Coromandel. Concan and Deccan rivers. Flowering in the hot season.

GENUS XXXIII. JATROPHA.

Monœcia Monadelphia. *Sex: Syst:*

Deriv. From *Iatron*, a remedy, and *Phagein*, to eat. Some species are used in medicine, others as food.

GEN. CHAR. Calyx of either sex imbricated: petals alternating with the sepals, developed or suppressed: glands of the disc opposite the sepals, alternating with the petals or their empty place: anthers 2-cleft: cells free below, inserted a little below the middle: cells of the ovary 1-ovuled, 1 behind: fruit capsular: seeds carunculate: cotyledons flattened, broad, palmately nerved: radicle short.—Frutescent, seldom arborescent plants: leaves alternate, bistipulate, commonly long-petioled, entire or lobed: flowers monœcious, commonly corymbosely panicled: panicles bisexual, dichotomously branched, bearing female flowers in the forks: calyces quincuncial: petals, when developed, free and slightly imbricated at the margin: stamens 6—2-verticillate: filaments connate below: anthers extrorsely or introrsely 2-cleft: staminodes 8—10, situated within the hypogynous disc: ovary 3-celled: styles equal in number to the cells of the ovary, connate below, free portion once or twice 2-cleft: capsules 4—2-coccous.

(1) J. WIGHTIANA. (*Muller.*)

Ident. Dec. prod. XV. s. 2. p. 1080.

Syn. J. villosa, *R. Wight.*

Engrav. Wight's Icon. t. 1169 (under J. peltata).

SPEC. CHAR. Shrub : leaves broadly peltate, long-petioled, orbicular-ovate, obtusely 3—5-lobed, pale velvety-tomentose on both sides, but thicker and softer beneath : inflorescence and calyx softly tomentose : petioles naked : bracts linear-lanceolate : calycine segments oblong-ovate, acute, entire : cymes corymbiform : petals slightly cohering a part of the way, males villous within : ovary and styles silky-pubescent : stigmas 2-parted : capsules globose, large.

Foot of the hills near Coimbatore.

(2) J. NANA. (*Dalz.*)

Ident. Dalzell Bomb. flor. p. 229.—Dec. l. c. p. 1083.

SPEC. CHAR. Shrub : leaves broadly triangular-ovate, 3-lobed almost to the middle or entire : lobes entire, intermediate lobe broadly ovate, abruptly acuminate, 2 lateral ones lanceolate-ovate, quite glabrous, paler beneath : cymes panicle-shaped, few-flowered : bracts linear-lanceolate, entire : segments of the female calyx linear-lanceolate, gradually acuminate : ovary oblong-ovoid, glabrous.

Stony places near Poonah.

GENUS XXXIV. TRIGONOSTEMON.

Monœcia Decandria. *Sex : Syst :*

Deriv. So called from the triangular stamens.

GEN. CHAR. Calyx of either sex imbricated : petals alternating with the sepals, developed or suppressed : stamens central on a receptacle : anthers 2-cleft : cells of the ovary 1-ovuled : fruit capsular : seeds ecarunculate.—Trees and shrubs : leaves bistipulate, alternate, oblong, feather-nerved, serrulate or entire, often congested at the ends of the branches, firm : flowers monœcious : inflorescences often unisexual, commonly axillary : calyces quincuncial : anthers various in number, extrorse or introrse : rudimentary ovary none : ovary 3-celled : styles 3, connate at the base, once or twice dichotomously divided : capsules 3-coccous, 3-seeded : seeds exarillate.

(1) T. Lawianus. (*Muller.*)

Ident. Mull. Arg. in Linnæa v. 34. p. 212.—Dec. prod. XV. s. 2. p. 1105.

Syn. Croton Laurianum, *Nimmo in Grah. Cat. Bomb. pl. p.* 251.—Dimorphocalyx glabellus, *Thwaites Enum. pl. Zeyl. p.* 278.

Spec. Char. Tree: stipules triangular: leaves elliptic or obovate-lanceolate, acutish at both ends, stiffly membranaceous: segments of the female calyx ovate-lanceolate or lanceolate-elliptic, at length becoming black: teeth of the male calyx very short, triangular or obliterated: disc rufous-pubescent, of the male 5 glands free, of the female connate into an urceolus: stamens in 2 verticils: cells of the anthers cohering, fixed at the middle of the back or below the middle: segments of the styles erect, subulate: ovary silky-puberulous: seeds smooth.

Malabar. Concan.

(2) T. Hookerianus. (*Muller.*)

Ident. Dec. l. c. p. 1109.

Syn. Silvæa Hookeriana, *Baill. Etud. gén. Euph. p.* 342.

Spec. Char. Shrub: younger branchlets, leaves, and inflorescences tawny-pubescent: leaves spathulate-lanceolate, cuspidate-acuminate, obtuse or subcordate at the narrowed base: male racemes abbreviated, subsessile: segments of the female calyx narrow-lanceolate, entire, nearly equal: male petals obovate, female oblong-ovate: disc of either sex 5-glandular: ovary whitish hispid.

Silhet.

(3) T. semperflorens. (*Muller.*)

Ident. Dec. l. c. p. 1110.

Syn. Cluytia semperflorens, *Roxb. flor. Ind.* III. *p.* 730.—Silvæa semperflorens, *Hook. and Arn. in Bot. Beech. p.* 211.

Spec. Char. Shrub: branchlets densely pubescent: stipules subulate: leaves subsessile, obovate-lanceolate, acuminate, minutely toothed, sprinkled with few hairs at the ribs: flowers axillary, subfascicled, females few; hypogynous disc 5-lobed: segments of the female calyx oblong-ovate: petals of male flowers broadly obovate: divisions of the styles subulate-acuminate: ovary hirsute: capsules tricoccous, villous, olivaceous: male flowers purple, females larger than the males, green.

Silhet, flowering all the year.

GENUS XXXV. GIVOTIA.

Diœcia Dodecandria. *Sex: Syst:*

Gen. Char. Male and female calyx imbricated: petals alternating with the sepals: disc situated between the petals: stamens central on a convex receptacle: anthers 2-cleft: cells adnate the whole length, fixed by the back: cells of the ovary 1-ovuled: fruit not opening as a capsule, destitute of a central column: endocarp indehiscent, bony: seeds ecarunculate: albumen copious.—Tree: leaves alternate, long-petioled, densely tomentose together with all the young parts: flowers diœcious, panicles terminal, many-flowered, peduncled: calyces quincuncial: stamens about 15: clefts of the anthers longitrorse: rudimentary ovary none: ovary 3—2-celled: styles 3—2, connate at the base, 2-cleft: fruit fleshy, by abortion 1-celled, 1-seeded: seeds not spuriously arillate: cotyledons cordate at the base.

(1) G. rottleriformis. (*Griff.*)

Ident. Griffith Plant. Hort. Calc.—Dec. prod. XV. s. 2. p. 1112.

Engrav. Wight's Icon. t. 1889.

Spec. Char. Small tree, much branched: leaves orbicular-ovate, acuminate, coarsely repand-toothed, membranaceous, stellately tomentose, above afterwards glabrescent, indumentum at first whitish, then tawnyish or somewhat rusty: petioles with few glands above the middle: panicles exceeding the leaves, alternately bearing branches: bracts long, linear: segments of the calyx obovate, glabrous within: petals obovate: hypogynous disc urceolar, lobed, pubescent: filaments hairy at the base, about twice as long as the anthers: ovary puberulous: styles stiff, spreading, 2-cleft to the middle: fruit oblong-ellipsoid, minutely ashy-tomentose: seeds globose-ellipsoid, smooth, pale.

Subalpine forests. Malabar. Southern Mahratta country. North Deccan, rare.

GENUS XXXVI. CODIÆUM.

Monœcia Polyandria. *Sex: Syst:*

Gen. Char. Calyx of both sexes imbricated: petals alternating with the sepals and glands of the extrastaminal disc: stamens central, inserted on an elevated receptacle: anthers 2-cleft: rudimentary ovary none: cells of the ovary 1-ovuled, alternating with the inner sepals: fruit capsular: seeds carunculate.—Trees or shrubs: leaves opposite, or more often alternate, penninerved, entire: flowers monœcious: inflorescences terminal or axillary, racemiform or rarely umbelliform, bisexual or rarely unisexal:

calyces 5-parted, quincuncial, seldom 3-parted: disc developed in both sexes: filaments free or connate into a column: cells of the anthers lateral or opening extrorsely: styles 3—4, simple, terete, thin, connate at the base, usually subulate-acuminate, or 2-cleft or 2-parted.

(1) C. UMBELLATUM. (*Muller.*)

Ident. Dec. prod. XV. s. 2. p. 1118.

Syn. Croton umbellatum, *Willd. Dalz. Bomb. flor.*—Blachia umbellata, *Baill. Etud. gén. Euph. p.* 387.

Engrav. Wight's Icon. t. 1874.—Baill. l. c. t. 19. fig. 18—20.

SPEC. CHAR. Shrub: branches somewhat dichotomously branched: leaves elliptic-lanceolate, obtusely cuspidate-acuminate, acute at the base, stiffly membranaceous, green, paler below: peduncles long, slender: flowers of both sexes umbellated: male petals truncate-obovate, 3 times shorter than the calyx: male disc 4—5-glandular, female urceolar: stamens 10—15: styles slender: ovary smooth, glabrous: seeds marbled.

Peninsula.

GENUS XXXVII. CHÆTOCARPUS.

Diœcia Dodecandria. *Sex: Syst:*

Deriv. From *Chaite*, hair, and *Karpos*, fruit.

GEN. CHAR. Calyx of both sexes imbricated: glands of the extrastaminal disc situated before the sepals: stamens inserted between the disc and rudimentary ovary, outer ones alternating with the glands and sepals: anthers 2-cleft, fixed by the base: rudimentary ovary developed: cells of the ovary 1-ovuled: fruit capsular: seeds carunculate: cotyledons broad: radicle very short.—Trees: leaves alternate, bistipulate, petioled, entire, eglandulose, coriaceous: stipules narrow, deciduous: flowers diœcious, densely fascicled on thick, scaly, bracteated, axillary cushions: males short-pedicelled: calyces decussately 4-parted: petals suppressed, their empty place alternating with that of the sepals and glands of the disc: disc many-lobed: stamens 8—16: filaments connate into a column below, all hairy or villous: cells of the anthers introrse lengthways: rudimentary ovary 2—3-cleft: ovary 3-celled: styles 3, connate at the base, deeply 2-parted, papillosely stigmatose: capsules 3-coccous, 3-seeded, armed with stiff, rough, glochidiate bristles or subconical tubercles: seeds smooth, shining, adorned at the apex with a large 2-lobed wart.

(1) C. castaneæcarpus. (*Thwaites.*)

Ident. Thwaites Enum. pl. Zeyl. p. 275.—Dec. prod. XV. s. 2. p. 1122.

Syn. Adelia castanicarpa, *Roxb. flor. Ind.* III. p. 848.—C. pungens, *Thwaites in Hook. Journ. Bot.* 1854. *p.* 301.

Spec. Char. Shrub or small tree : sometimes middle-sized or even large : leaves lanceolate-ovate, acuminate, acute at the base, coriaceous, shortly puberulous, soon glabrate : sepals more or less pubescent at the margin : capsules longer than the pedicels : seeds black, shining.

Silhet. Khasia. Chittagong.

GENUS XXXVIII. BALIOSPERMUM.

Monœcia Polyandria. *Sex : Syst :*

Deriv. From *Balios*, spotted, and *Sperma*, a seed.

Gen. Char. Calycine segments of both sexes imbricated : petals none : disc of male flowers extrastaminal : stamens central on an elevated receptacle : anthers 2-cleft, cells adnate the whole length : rudimentary ovary none : cells of the ovary 1-ovuled : fruit capsular : seeds carunculate : cotyledons broad : much exceeding the radicle.—Shrubs or perennial herbs, sprinkled with a few adpressed hairs : leaves alternate, glandulosely bistipulate, petioled, repand-toothed, biglandular at the lowest base of the limb : flowers monœcious, axillary, very small : inflorescences compactly paniculiform or racemiform, peduncled, above males or sexes mixed, females at the base : rachis commonly densely and minutely bracteate : fructigerous pedicels recurved : male calyx 5-parted : female disc urceolar : stamens 15—30, and more numerous : anthers 2-cleft lengthways : ovary 3—4-celled : styles 3—4, cohering at the base, spreading above, half 2-cleft : capsules 3- or rarely 4-coccous, 3—4-seeded : warts small : testa of the seeds smooth.

(1) B. sinuatum. (*Muller.*)

Ident. Mull. Arg. in Flora. Ratisb. (1864) p. 470.—Dec. prod. XV. s. 2. p. 1125.

Spec. Char. Shrub : leaves lanceolate or lanceolate-spathulate, sometimes simply acuminate, obtuse at the base, sometimes obconically dilated above and broadly sinuate-lobed : male panicles racemiform, very long, at least exceeding the leaves, narrow : branchlets distant, spreading horizontally : glands of the male disc free.

Near Mishnee, in Eastern Bengal.

(2) B. MONTANUM. (*Muller.*)

Ident. Dec. l. c. p. 1125.

Syn. Jatropha montana, *Willd.*—Croton polyandrum, *Roxb. flor. Ind.* III. *p.* 682.—B. baliospermum axillare, *Bl. bidjr. p.* 604.—B. polyandrum, *R. Wight.*—B. Indicum, *Decaisne in Jacq. voy. p.* 154.—B. Moritzianum, *Baill. Etud. gén. Euph. p.* 395.

Engrav. Wight's Icon. t. 1885.—Decaisne l. c. t. 155.—Bryn. Centur. p. 118. t. 54.

SPEC. CHAR. Undershrub or perennial: stems numerous, subherbaceous: upper leaves lanceolate, acute at the base, lower ones broader, ovate and often cordate at the base, sinuately toothed or deeply 3-lobed, marked with long scattered hairs: inflorescences commonly bisexual, sometimes unisexual in the branches: males more lax than the females, and longer peduncled, all shorter than the petioles: fructigerous pedicels deflexed: sterile bracteoles numerous: segments of male calyx orbicular-ovate, of female lanceolate-ovate or lanceolate: stigmas oblong-obovate: urceolus of either sex 5—6-lobed: ovary silky-hairy: capsules subglobose, tridymous, puberulous: seeds smooth, at length marbled.

Hills in Bengal. Northern parts of the Peninsula. Malabar.

(3) B. CALYCINUM. (*Muller.*)

Ident. Mull Arg. in Flora Ratisb. p. 470.—Dec. l. c. p. 1126.

SPEC. CHAR. Shrub: branchlets rusty-tomentose, afterwards powdery: leaves lanceolate, ovate or obovate, acuminate, subacute and bistipellate at the base, repand-serrated: inflorescences very long, males abounding in flowers, at length exceeding the leaves, branches ascending, branchlets subdivaricate: sterile bracteoles none: hypogynous disc urceolar, extrastaminal, 1—5-glandular: ovary pubescent: capsules globose, deeply tridymous: seeds smooth, marbled.

(4) B. MICRANTHUM. (*Muller.*)

Ident. Mull Arg. in Linnæa vol. 34. p. 215.—Dec. l. c. p. 1126.

SPEC. CHAR. Perennial: leaves elliptic or ovate-lanceolate, sharply acuminate, subacute at the base, repand-toothed or entire, membranaceous, pale: panicles slender and long-peduncled, long or very long, many-flowered: fructigerous pedicels erect: stigmas slender: glands of the male disc free: ovary minutely puberulous: capsules depresso-globose, deeply furrowed, tridymous, glabrate.

Khasia. Silhet.

GENUS XXXIX. GELONIUM.

Diœcia Polyandria. *Sex: Syst:*

Gen. Char. Calycine segments imbricated: petals none: male disc extrastaminal (often suppressed): stamens occupying the centre on an elevated receptacle: anthers 2-cleft: cells adnate nearly the whole length: rudimentary ovary none: cells of the ovary 1-ovuled: fruit at length capsular: seeds ecarunculate.—Small trees and shrubs: leaves bifariously alternate or rarely opposite, bistipulate, shortly petioled, feather-nerved, entire or toothed, thinly coriaceous, very often pale green: flowers diœcious, fascicled, commonly very numerous, fascicles leaf-opposed or axillary in the opposite-leaved species: segments of both calyces quincuncial, broadly imbricated, often unequal, very tenacious: disc of male flowers usually none, female urceolar, often associated with antheriferous staminodes: stamens more or less numerous, 6—60: filaments free, mixed with the glands of the receptacle: clefts of the anthers introrse: ovary 3—2-celled, seldom 4-celled: stigmas sessile, 3—2-cleft: fruit fleshy-capsular, 3—2-coccous, 3—2-seeded or by abortion 1-seeded: testa nearly always smooth.

(1) G. multiflorum. (*Adr. Juss.*)

Ident. Adr. Juss. Tent. Euph. p. 111.—Dec. prod. XV. s. 2. p. 1127.

Syn. G. fasciculatum, *Roxb. Flor. Ind.* III. *p.* 832.—Suregada multiflora, *Baill. Etud. gén. Euph. p.* 396.

Engrav. Bot. Mag. t. 3231.—Adr. Juss. l. c. t. 10. fig. 31 a.

Spec. Char. Small tree, glabrous: leaves lanceolate-elliptic, acute at both ends, entire or with few teeth below the apex, yellowish-green: flowers numerous, arranged in oblong subracemiform fascicles: stigmas flattish, 2-cleft, the segments obversely triangular, cut, and many-cleft or lobed: ovary 3-celled.

Coromandel. Near Pondicherry.

(2) G. lanceolatum. (*Willd.*)

Ident. Willd. spec. pl. IV. p. 832.—Dec. l. c. p. 1127.—Roxb. flor. Ind. III. p. 831.

Ident. Wight's Icon. t. 1867.

Spec. Char. Small tree, very much branched: leaves ovate-lanceolate, obtuse or subobtuse, acute at the base, entire, stiffish, glabrous: female flowers thickly pedicelled, younger ones resinous: stamens very numerous: ovary 3-celled: styles 2-cleft, thick, lobes spreading, crenately roughish or entire: ovary ovoid, glabrous: capsules warty.

Peninsula. Balaghaut mountains. Bengal. Flowering in the hot season.

(3) G. ANGUSTIFOLIUM. (*Muller.*)

Var. ELLIPTICUM.

Ident. Dec. l. c. p. 1128.

SPEC. CHAR. Undershrub: leaves lanceolate-elliptic, acute at both ends: flowers arranged in very short, few-flowered, aggregated racemules: stamens 25—35: ovary 3-celled: capsules depresso-globose, smooth.

Malabar. Travancore.

GENUS XL. SEBASTIANIA.

Monœcia Triandria. *Sex: Syst:*

GEN. CHAR. Calycine segments of either sex imbricated: petals none: male disc none: stamens central: anthers 2-cleft: cells adnate lengthways: rudimentary ovary none: cells of the ovary 1-ovuled: fruit capsular, endowed with a central developed columella: seeds caruneulate: chalaza situated at the base.—Undershrubs or shrubs, seldom trees: leaves alternate, bistipulate, very often feather-nerved, and often more or less glandularly toothed: herbaceous or seldom coriaceous: flowers very seldom diœcious, spicately racemose: inflorescences terminal or axillary, very often bisexual, females at the base, rest males: female bracts 1-flowered, males 1—3-flowered, loose or densely imbricated: segments of the female calyx 3, furnished at the base within with very small subulate-dentiform glands, or destitute of them: stamens 2—3: filaments almost free: anthers opening extrorsely, more or less emarginate at both ends: ovary 3-celled, smooth or tubercled or muricated: styles 3, simple, shortly connate or free below: capsules tricoccous, smooth or armed, dry, commonly tridymous: columella persistent: seeds smooth or rough: caruncula peltately sessile, equal at the base, more or less thin: cotyledons oblong-ovate or orbicular in copious albumen.

(1) S. CHAMÆLEA. (*Muller.*)

Ident. Dec. prod. XV. s. 2. p. 1175.

Syn. Tragia Chamælea, *Linn.*—Microstachys Chamælea, *Adr. Juss. Tent. Euph.* p. 49.—Cnemidostachys Chamælea, *Spreng. Syst.* iii. *p.* 835.—Elachocroton asperococcus, *F. Muell. in Hook. Journ. Bot.* 1857, p. 17.—Stillingia asperococca, *Baill. Etud. gén. Euph. p.* 517.—Stillingia Chamælea, *Baill. l. c. p.* 516.—C. linearifolia, *Mig. flor. Ind. Bat. suppl.* I. *Sumatra*, p. 460.

Engrav. Rheede Mal. II. t. 34.—Burm. Zeyl. t. 25.

Spec. Char. Perennial or herbaceous: stipules ovate, acute, ciliated: leaves petioled, linear-elliptic or lanceolate, obtuse, subacute at the base, minutely and sharply serrulate, pubescent or more often subglabrous, with the branchlets brownish or rufous-glaucescent: inflorescences shorter than the leaves, thin: bracts ovate, very short, increased on both sides by a cylindric, stipitiform gland truncated at the apex: female flowers 1—5, situated below the spike or at the base of the spike itself: female calyx much larger than the male: segments densely lacero-ciliated, biglandular within: segments of the male calyx ovate, ciliated: ovary armed, glabrous: seeds ellipsoid: flowers small, greenish.

Coromandel. South Concan. Flowering in the cold season.

GENUS XLI. EXCÆCARIA.

Monœcia Diadelphia. *Sex: Syst:*

Deriv. From *Excæcare*, to blind, alluding to the dangerous acrid juice of the plants.

Gen. Char. Calycine segments imbricated: petals and disc none: stamens central: anthers 2-cleft: cells adnate lengthways: rudimentary ovary none: cells of the ovary 1-ovuled: styles not blade-shaped, compressed: ripe fruit opening as a capsule (dry or fleshy), furnished with a developed central columella: seeds ecarunculate: chalaza basilar: embryo vertical: cotyledons broad. —Trees and shrubs: leaves most frequently alternate, bistipulate, petioled, feather-nerved or rarely palmatinerved, firm: flowers monœcious, rarely diœcious, arranged generally in bisexual spikes, bearing 1—2 female flowers at the base, the rest males, sometimes terminal, sometimes axillary: calyces 3—2-merous: segments long or short connate: sepals sometimes free, developed or very reduced in the male flowers: stamens 3—2: filaments free or shortly connate at the base, sometimes connate their whole length: anthers extrorse: ovary 3—2-celled: styles 3—2, simple, connate below, stigmatose within: fruit dry or fleshy, always furnished with a central columella: seeds coloured, white, red, or scarlet: testa smooth or rough with tubercles.

(1) E. baccata. (*Muller.*)

Ident. Dec. prod. XV. s. 2. p. 1211.

Syn. Sapium baccatum, *Roxb. flor. Ind.* III. *p.* 694.—Stillingia baccata, *Baill. Etud. gén. Euph. p.* 513.—S. paniculata, *Miq. flor. Ind. Bat. suppl.* I. *p.* 461.

Engrav. Wight's Icon. t. 1950.

Spec. Char. Tree: leaves long-petioled, ovate, entire, long cuspidate-acuminate, paler and subglaucous beneath, and glandular spotted next the margin near the base and below the apex: petioles not glandular: racemes spiciform, slender, terminal, and in the upper axils shorter than the leaves, some altogether males, some females below and then often increased above by more or less abortive flowers: bracts very broadly ovate, males many-flowered: male pedicels shortly exserted, jointed below: male calyx irregularly 2-cleft: segments lacerately toothed: styles almost free: capsules berry-shaped, thickly fleshy, subglobose, obtuse: seeds adhering and persistent long after the fall of the shells: flowers greenish.

Silhet. Khasia. Assam. Flowering in March and April.

(2) E. INSIGNIS. (*Muller.*)

Ident. Dec. l. c. p. 1212.

Syn. Falconeria insignis, *Royle Ill. Bot. Him. p.* 354.—F. Wallichiana, *do.*—F. Malabarica, *R. Wight.*

Engrav. Royle l. c. t. 84.—Wight's Icon. t. 1866.

SPEC. CHAR. Small tree: leaves elliptic, cuspidate-acuminate, acute at the base, membranaceous, clayey-green or green-brownish, densely reticulately veined beneath: petioles biglandular at the apex: spikes unisexual, dense-flowered: segments of the male calyx crenate-denticulate or entire: capsules dry, berry-shaped, ovoid, 2—3-furrowed.

Rajpore. Neilgherries. Vingorla hills. The milky juice is highly poisonous.

(3) E. COCHINCHINENSIS. (*Lour.*)

Ident. Lour. flor. Cochinch. 2. p. 750.—Dec. l. c. p. 1215.

Syn. E. crenulata, *R. Wight.*

Engrav. Wight's Icon. t. 1865.

SPEC. CHAR. Small tree or shrub: leaves opposite, obovate-lanceolate, long acuminate at both ends, crenate-serrate, petioles without glands: stipules narrow-lanceolate: bracts very broadly ovate, acuminate, all 1-flowered, short: male calyx subsessile, 3-parted: segments of both sexes laciniately toothed, oblong-ovate: stamens 3: branches some male, some female, or female flowers 1—2 sometimes situated at the base of the spikes: glands of the bracts small, wrinkled.

Hills of the Peninsula.

(4) E. INDICA. (*Muller.*)

Ident. Mull. Arg. in Linnæa vol. 32. p. 123.—Dec. l. c. p. 1216.

Syn. Sapium Indicum, *Willd. Roxb. flor. Ind.* III. *p.* 692.—S. Hurmais, *Ham. in Trans. Linn. Soc. vol.* 17. *p.* 229.—Sclerocloton ellipticus, *Hochst. in Flora Ratisb. p.* 85. *Baill. Etud.*—Stillingia Indica, *Baill. Etud. p.* 513.—S. bingyrica, *do.*

Engrav. Wight's Icon. t. 1950.—Baill. l. c. t. 8. fig. 17. and t. 6. figs. 11, 12.

Spec. Char. Small tree: leaves short-petioled, membranaceous, lanceolate, acuminate at the apex, acute at the base, serrate or serrulate, 2—4-glandular at the base: stipules ovate-lanceolate: bracts triangular-ovate, acute, puberulous: glands deeply undulately furrowed: styles slender: male flowers 3—5 in the axil of each bract, all pedicelled, exceeding the bract: pedicels slightly hairy: segments of both calyces lacero-denticulate: females with many glands inside at the base: stamens 3: ovary 3—2-celled: capsules globose, woody, scarcely tridymous: seeds smooth.

Coromandel. Concan. Assam. Bengal. Flowering nearly all the year.

(5) E. oppositifolia. (*Jack.*)

Ident. Jack in Calc. Journ. Nat. Hist. vol. 4. p. 386.—Dec. l. c. p. 1219.

Syn. Stillingia oppositifolia, *Baill. l. c. p.* 518.

Spec. Char. Small tree: stipulates subulate-acuminate, with a scariose brown, broad-ovate base: leaves elliptic-lanceolate, acuminate at the apex, acute at the base, crenate-dentate: male spikes shorter than the leaves, forming, on account of the many-rowed imbricated bracts, a cylindric catkin, densely floriferous from base to apex: bracts stiff, thick, brown, callosely mucronate, slightly exceeding the flowers: male calyx subsessile, bibracteolate: sepals free.

Mysore, Concan, and Malabar.

(6) E. Agallocha. (*Muller.*)

Ident. Dec. l. c. p. 1221.—Linn. Spec. p. 1451.—Roxb. flor. Ind. III. p. 756.

Syn. Commia Cochinchinensis, *Lour.*—Stillingia Agallocha, *Baill. Etud. l. c. p.* 518.

Engrav. Lam. Illustr. t. 805.—Bauer Illustr. pl. Norf. t. 182.—Rumph. Amb. vol. II. t. 79—80.

Spec. Char. Small tree or shrub: leaves ovate or elliptic, obtuse at the base, entire or crenate-serrulate: male spikes amentiform, dense-flowered, cylindric: female racemes shorter than the male spikes, and in separate branches, both axillary, solitary or rarely twin or ternate: bracts destitute of distinct glands, but everywhere glandulosely thickened: male calyx sessile, covered by the bract: female sepals ovate, acuminate, with one gland on both sides of the base inside: stamens 3: anthers long-exserted after flowering: styles shortly connate at the base: capsules sulcately 3-lobed: seeds subglobose: flowers greenish.

Salt marshes of the Sunderbunds and Bombay. Flowering in the hot season.

Var. CAMETTIA.—Dec. l. c. p. 1221.—Leaves ovate or elliptic: spikes as in the former: capsules and seeds nearly 3 times larger. —E. Camettia, *Willd.*—E. Agallocha, *Hook. Comp.* II. *t.* 30. *Wight's Icon. t.* 1865. *Rheede Mal.* V. *t.* 45.

Travancore backwaters and other salt marshes in the Peninsula. Flowering in the hot season. The juice is highly poisonous, and should be cautiously handled, as it produces serious inflammation and pain.

GENUS XLII. DALECHAMPIA.

Monœcia Icosandria. *Sex: Syst:*

Deriv. In honour of James Dalechamp, a French botanist of the sixteenth century.

GEN. CHAR. Flowers of either sex enclosed in a compressed, 2-leaved, bisexual involucre: segments of the male calyx valvate, of the female imbricated: petals none: male disc none, females seldom developed: stamens central on a convex receptacle: anthers 2-cleft: cells adnate lengthways: rudimentary ovary none: cells of the ovary 1-ovuled: fruit capsular: seeds ecarunculate; cotyledons flattened.—Shrubs, seldom erect, usually twining and scandent: leaves alternate, bistipulate, petioled, feather-nerved or palmati-nerved, undivided or divided into lobes or segments, or even in petioled leaflets, commonly membranaceous: flowers monœcious, axillary, peduncled: involucres commonly large, leafy, very often paler than the leaves or more brightly coloured and more membranaceous, strongly bistipulate, bearing at the same time in the inflorescence female flowers below, males above: female involucels 3-flowered, males many-flowered, increased on the upper side by pale, many-crested, waxy, sterile flowers: male calyx 4—5-parted, female 5—12-parted, the segments of this more or less pinnately laciniated, of that entire: stamens 60—5, commonly about 20: filaments connate into a longish column: anthers opening extrorsely: ovary 3—4-celled, 3—4-ovuled: styles connate into a cylindric or clavate column, which is obtuse or more or less dilated or lobed at the apex: capsules 3—4-coccous, 3—4-seeded: shells stiff, subglobose: seeds globose or ellipsoid or truncate: cotyledons ovate.

(1) D. INDICA. (*R. W.*)

Ident. Wight Icon. pl. Ind. and t. 1882. Dec. prod. XV. s. 2. p. 1241.

SPEC. CHAR. Scandent shrub : leaflets 3, distinctly petiolulate, ovate or obliquely lanceolate-ovate, acuminate, serrated, sparingly pubescent above, softly puberulous beneath : leaflets of the involucre 3-cleft and lobed, 5-nerved, serrate-denticulate : stipules and bracts linear-lanceolate, female bracts acute, 3-lobed : segments of the female calyx about 11, pinnately cut, smaller divisions on both sides about 10, subulate : ovary pubescent : styline column slender, equally urceolar-dilated at the apex.

Dindegul mountains.

(2) D. SCANDENS. (*Muller.*)

Var. VELUTINA.

Ident. Dec. l. c. p. 1244.

Engrav. Wight's Icon. t. 1881.

SPEC. CHAR. Scandent : leaves velvety beneath, sharply serrulate : involucres serrate-denticulate : segments of the female calyx very hispid : stipules and bracts of the involucre ovate or linear-lanceolate : female bracts entire : ovary tomentose : styline column cylindric, subtrilobulate at the apex, pubescent beneath : capsules middle-sized.

Neilgherries.

ORDER CXLII. URTICACEÆ.

Flowers polygamous, monœcious or diœcious, spiked, capitate or panicled, sometimes placed on a fleshy receptacle, usually surrounded by a common involucre, bracteolate or naked : male perianth 4—5-parted, imbricated in æstivation : stamens equal in number to and opposite the sepals : filaments free, filiform or subulate, inflexed in æstivation, elastically leaping up when in flower, more or less irritable : anthers introrse, 2-celled, attached by the back, cells opposite, contiguous, sometimes separated at the base and apex, dehiscing lengthways : rudimentary ovary sessile or stalked : female perianth 2—4-leaved, leaflets usually unequal or rudimentary, limb 2—4-toothed or parted : stamens none or scale-shaped rudiments: ovary sessile, free, 1-celled: ovule 1, basilar, sessile, orthotropal: style terminal, simple: stigma subcapitate or penicillate: fruit naked or closed by the persistent perianth, indehiscent: seed erect: testa membranaceous: albumen fleshy, copious: embryo antitropal in the axis of the albumen: cotyledons ovate, flat: radicle short, cylindric.—Herbs or shrubs, sometimes arborescent: leaves opposite or alternate, simple, petioled, feather-nerved, entire, toothed or serrated, seldom palmatinerved, lobed, usually with stinging hairs interspersed with down: stipules petiolar, free, entire or lobed, seldom deciduous, or altogether none.

GENUS I. FLEURYA.

Tetrandria Monogynia. *Sex: Syst:*

GEN. CHAR. Male perianth 4-parted: stamens 4: female perianth 2—4-parted: leaflets unequal: stigma long-filiform: achenium obliquely ovate, slightly compressed, margined with a narrow wing, naked.

(1) F. INTERRUPTA. (*R. W.*)

Ident. Wight's Icon. VI. t. 1975.—Dalz. Bomb. flor. p. 238.

Syn. Urtica interrupta (*var. laxiflora*), *Linn.*

SPEC. CHAR. Herbaceous, erect, bristly all over: young branches and under surface of the leaves pubescent: leaves long-petioled, cordate-ovate, acute or acuminate, coarsely serrated, triple-nerved: peduncles axillary, solitary, as long or longer than the leaves, bearing small lateral panicles at unequal distances: male calyx 4-parted: achenium tubercled on the discs.

Common weed in gardens and elsewhere.

GENUS II. GIRARDINA.

Tetrandria Monogynia. *Sex: Syst:*

GEN. CHAR. Perianth 4-parted: segments of the 4-parted female perianth unequal, 3 connate at the base, the fourth free: achenium obliquely ovate, lenticular compressed, smooth.

(1) G. HETEROPHYLLA. (*Dalz.*)

Ident. Dalz. Bomb. flor. p. 238.

Syn. Urtica heterophylla, *Willd.* — G. Leschenaultiana *Decaisne.*

Engrav. Wight's Icon. t. 1976.—Rheede Mal. II. t. 41.

SPEC. CHAR. Leaves broad-cordate, 7-lobed: lobes oblong, acute, coarsely serrated, clothed on both sides with fine whitish down, armed above with thin scattered prickles, thickly clothed beneath with the same: male and female flowers in distinct, glomerate, peduncled spikes: flowers small, green.

Common on the slopes of the Ghauts. Coromandel. Concans. Flowering in the rainy season. The least touch of any part of this plant produces intense pain.

GENUS III. SPLITGERBERA.

Tetrandria Monogynia. *Sex: Syst:*

GEN. CHAR. Flowers monœcious, arranged in fascicled spikes: common involucre 4-leaved, unequal: stamen-bearing flowers on the lower part of the stem: fascicles 4—6-flowered: perianth 4-parted: leaflets equal, valvate: stamens opposite the sepals: filaments petaloid, subulate, at first inflexed, afterwards spreading: anthers 2-celled: female flowers above the males: perianth ovate, almost adnate to the ovary: limb free, usually 3-toothed: ovary 1-celled: style cylindric, passing into a long, villous stigma.—Undershrub: leaves opposite or tern, oval, entire or 2-lobed, membranaceous, crenate at the margin: spikes axillary, shorter than the leaf.

(1) S. SCABRELLA. (*Dalz.*)

Ident. Dalz. Bomb. flor. p. 239.

Syn. Urtica scabrella, *Roxb. flor. Ind.* III. *p.* 581.

Engrav. Wight's Icon. t. 691.

SPEC. CHAR. Shrubby, spreading: leaves large, opposite, cordate, serrate, harsh, 3-nerved: spikes axillary, erect, cylindric: male flowers crowded, short and in the lower axils: females generally solitary: flowers small, greenish.

Concan hills. Chittagong. Silhet. Assam. Flowering in August and September.

(2) S. MACROSTACHYA. (*R. W.*)

Ident. Wight's Icon. VI. t. 1977.

SPEC. CHAR. Suffruticose, erect, hairy all over: leaves long-petioled, opposite, cordate-ovate, acute, 3-nerved, serrated: spikes axillary, filiform, interrupted, 3—4 times the length of the leaves: male fascicles 6—8-flowered, female 10—12 or more.

Coimbatore. Neilgherries. Courtallum, in moist shady woods.

GENUS IV. ELATOSTEMMA.

Tetrandria Monogynia. *Sex: Syst:*

GEN. CHAR. Flowers monœcious or diœcious, on heads distinguished by the sex, involucred, sessile or pedicelled on a flat, somewhat fleshy receptacle, 1—2—3-bracteolate: male perianth 4—5-parted, leaflets equal, concave: stamens 4—5: filaments filiform, at first inflexed: anthers introrse, 2-celled, attached by the back: cells opposite: female perianth 2—3—4-leaved, leaflets unequal, often very small or none: ovary free, ovate-elliptic, 1-celled: ovule 1, basilar, sessile, orthotropal: stigma sessile: segments many-parted: achenia elliptic, seated on a fleshy receptacle, wrapped in bracteoles: seed erect.—Herbs or undershrubs: leaves alternate, oblique, quite entire, coarsely toothed, tubercled, rough, stipulate: capitula axillary, sessile or shortly peduncled.

(1) E. SURCULOSUM. (*R. W.*)

Ident. Wight's Icon. VI. t. 2091.

SPEC. CHAR. Erect, spreading on all sides by means of suckers: leaves subsessile, ovate-acuminate, unequal-sided, coarsely-serrated except near the base, lineolate, glabrous: male receptacle peduncled, involucrate, male flowers pedicelled, 4-lobed: female receptacle and flowers sessile, flowers mixed with numerous pedicelled sterile ones: sterile ones simply capitate or 3—4-lobed: nut oval, ribbed.

Neilgherries, near the banks of streams or rills.

(2) E. CUSPIDATUM. (*R. W.*)

Ident. Wight's Icon. l. c. t. 1983.

SPEC. CHAR. Diœcious, herbaceous, erect, sparingly branched: leaves subsessile, alternate, very unequal-sided, cuspidately acuminate, coarsely serrated, sprinkled with a few bristly hairs, and closely lineolate above, pubescent on the nerves beneath: receptacles axillary, sessile, oval, peltate, furnished with tooth-like appendages on the margin, some males, mixed with the female flowers, longer pedicelled: ovary ovate, base embraced by the 3-lobed calyx.

Neilgherries, on the banks of streams and other moist ground.

(3) E. LINEOLATUM. (*R. W.*)

Ident. Wight's Icon. l. c. t. 1984.

SPEC. CHAR. Diœcious, herbaceous or suffruticose, erect, branched, glabrous: leaves sessile, unequal-sided, abruptly acuminate, with a few serratures on the convex edge, coriaceous, glabrous on both sides, marked above with numerous thick lineoles, pellucid-dotted: male receptacles deeply 2-lobed, membranous: flowers numerous, each at first embraced by a membranous involucre, afterwards by the elongation of the pedicel, exserted: calyx 4-parted: stamens 4, involute in æstivation.

Neilgherries. Malabar.

(4) E. OVATUM. (*R. W.*)

Ident. Wight's Icon. l. c. t. 1985.

SPEC. CHAR. Herbaceous, diœcious or polygamous, erect, sparingly branched: leaves opposite, unequal-sized, ovate, acute, serrated, short-petioled, pubescent, and sprinkled with stronger bristles above, glabrous, except on the veins beneath, 3-nerved, the lateral pair very slender: receptacles axillary, fleshy, pedicelled: fructiferous flowers short-pedicelled, mixed with numerous longer-pedicelled imperfect ones: calyx 4-cleft: male plant like the female, but longer: receptacle with total absence of female flowers.

Neilgherries, in wet soil.

(5) E. OPPOSITIFOLIUM. (*Dalz.*)

Ident. Dalz. in Hook. Journ. Bot. III. p. 179.—Bomb. flor. 239.

SPEC. CHAR. Herbaceous: stem simple, smooth, naked at the base: leaves rather long petioled, opposite, lanceolate-acuminate, coarsely dentate-serrate, 3-nerved, sparingly hairy above, quite smooth beneath, upper ones the largest: heads of flowers solitary, peduncled, in the alternate axils: peduncles shorter than the petiole: common receptacle flat, discoid, simple: male and female flowers mixed.

Western Ghauts, flowering in September.

(6) E. cuneatum. (*R. W.*)

Ident. Wight's Icon. l. c. t. 2091.—Dalz. Bomb. flor. p. 239.

Spec. Char. Erect, simple; leaves obovate-cuneate, unequal-sided, crenately serrated towards the apex, pilose on both sides, above mixed with scattered bristly hairs: receptacles sessile, unisexual: fertile flowers few, sessile, mixed with numerous pedicelled 3 to 4-lobed sterile ones: nuts oval-ribbed.

Mahim woods, Bombay. Belgaum.

GENUS V. CONOCEPHALUS.

Diœcia Tetrandria. *Sex: Syst:*

Deriv. From *Konos*, a cone, and *Kephale*, head, in allusion to the inflorescence.

Gen. Char. Flowers diœcious, capitately spiked. Male: perianth tubular, 3—4-cleft, segments erect, slightly fleshy, somewhat hooded: stamens 3—4: filaments fleshy, pyramidal: anthers introrse, exserted, 2-celled, cordate, cells divaricated at the base. Female: perianth tubular, 3—4-cleft, segments often unequal: ovary oblong, 1-celled: ovule 1: style simple: stigma oblong, lateral: achenia covered by the sub-baccate perianths, slightly compressed, densely congested: seed pendulous: albumen sparing, afterwards disappearing.—Climbing shrubs: leaves alternate, elliptic-oblong, repand: capitula subcorymbose, axillary, or lateral by the falling of the leaves.

(1) C. niveus. (*R. W.*)

Ident. Wight's Icon. VI. t. 1959.—Dalz. Bomb. flor. p. 239.

Spec. Char. Arboreous, erect-branched: leaves ovate-lanceolate, acute or acuminate, 5-nerved, acutely serrated, somewhat bullate above, prominently reticulated and white beneath, strigosely hispid on both sides: inflorescence cymose: fruit capitate, drupaceous: drupes small, yellow, globose.

Concan and Ghaut forests. Neilgherries.

(2) C. concolor. (*Dalz.*)

Ident. Dalz. l. c.

Spec. Char. Shrubby: leaves very large, irregularly scattered, 3-nerved, perfectly smooth, oblong-ovate, acute, green on both sides: female flower axillary.

Phoonda Ghaut.

(3) C. NAUCLEIFLORUS. (*Lindl.*)

Ident. Lindl. in Bot. Reg. 14.

Syn. Urtica naucleiflora, *Roxb.*—C. suaveolens, *Blume.*

Engrav. Wight's Icon. t. 684.—Blume pl. Jav. rar. I. t. 12. —Bot. Reg. t. 1203.

SPEC. CHAR. Diœcious, shrubby, twining: leaves alternate, cordate, entire: glomerules globular, compact, male ones panicled: flowers yellowish, fragrant.

Chittagong. Silhet. Flowering nearly all the year.

(4) C. GLOBULIFER. (*Roxb.*)

Ident. Roxb. l. c. p. 593.

SPEC. CHAR. Diœcious, shrubby, scandent: leaves alternate, long-petioled, oblong, entire, villous: panicles axillary: glomerules globular, compact, panicled.

Silhet, flowering in February and March.

GENUS VI. LAPORTEA.

Diœcia Pentandria. *Sex: Syst:*

GEN. CHAR. MALE: perianth 5-parted: stamens 5. FEMALE: inner leaflets of the perianth larger, leafy: stigma long-subulate: achenium obliquely ovate, slightly compressed, somewhat tubercled, enclosed by the inner unchanged leaflets of the perianth.

(1) L. TERMINALIS. (*R. W.*)

Ident. Wight's Icon. VI. t. 1972.

SPEC. CHAR. Herbaceous, diœcious, erect, all bristly: leaves alternate, long-petioled, ovate-acuminate, acutely mucronate, serrated, very rough above: male panicles in the lower axils, compact, about the length of the petioles: flowers subsessile: females 2—3 from the upper axils, long-peduncled, loose, pedicels at length winged: calyx 4-sepaled: style longish: stigma acute.

Neilgherries, flowering in October and November.

GENUS VII. PILEA.

Monœcia Tetrandria. *Sex: Syst:*

GEN. CHAR. Flowers monœcious, male and female on the same panicle, bracteate. MALE: perianth 4-parted, leaflets equal, concave: stamens 4, opposite the sepals: filaments filiform, at first inflexed, afterwards leaping up elastically: anthers introrse,

2-celled, attached by the back: cells opposite. FEMALE: perianth 3-lobed, 1 lobe larger, cucullate, muticous, 2 collateral ones less flat: stamens rudimentary 3, scale-shaped: ovary free, ovate-elliptic, 1-celled: ovule 1, sessile, orthotropal: stigma terminal, sessile, parted into several segments: achenium enclosed, smooth or tubercled: seed erect.—Herbs: leaves opposite, usually long-petioled, stipulate, quite entire or toothed, glabrous or beset with hairs: flowers glomerate in axillary panicles.

(1) P. TRINERVIA. (*R. W.*)

Ident. Wight's Icon. VI. t. 1973.

SPEC. CHAR. Herbaceous, erect.: glabrous, stems succulent and juicy: leaves opposite, longish petioled, ovate-elliptic, 3-nerved, acuminate, deeply and acutely mucronate-serrated, smooth, shining, deep green above, paler and dull below: panicles axillary, loose, shorter than the leaves.

Neilgherries, in damp woods, flowering in the rainy season.

(2) P. RADICANS. (*R. W.*)

Ident. Wight l. c. t. 1974.

SPEC. CHAR. Herbaceous, procumbent and rooting at the base, afterwards ascending: leaves opposite, short-petioled, cordate-ovate, acute, deeply serrated, 3-nerved, glabrous and smooth on both sides, deep green, membranous: panicles from the axils of the upper leaves, dichotomous, long-peduncled: male flowers tetrandrous: female 3-lobed, with 3 abortive stamens exceeding the lobes of the calyx: style none: achenium ovate, compressed, smooth.

Neilgherries.

GENUS VIII. CHAMABAINIA.

Monœcia Tetrandria. *Sex: Syst:*

Deriv. From *Chamai*, on the ground, and *Baino*, to go, alluding to the creeping habit of the plant.

GEN. CHAR. Monœcious: male calyx 4-cleft: lobes equal: stamens 4, inflexed in æstivation, rudimentary ovary clavate.—FEMALE: 2 or 3 sessile flowers aggregated on the axil or within a bract: sepals 2, minute: style very short: stigma somewhat capitate, penicillate: achenium ovate.

(1) C. CUSPIDATA. (*R. W.*)

Ident. Wight's Icon. VI. t. 1981.

SPEC. CHAR. Herbaceous, ramous, diffuse, creeping, rooting at the joints, branches ascending: stipules 4, large, scariose: leaves opposite, petioled, ovate, acute, serrated, 3-nerved, pilose on each side: flowers axillary, fascicled, mixed, males pedicelled: calyx deeply 4-cleft: lobes with a bristly tooth-like appendage at the apex: stamens twice exceeding the calyx: rudimentary pistil clavate: female flowers numerous, sessile, very minute, aggregated in fascicles of 2 or more flowers embraced by a bract.

Neilgherries.

GENUS IX. FORSKOLIA.

Monœcia Monandria. *Sex: Syst:*

GEN. CHAR. Flowers androgynous, sessile on a woolly receptacle, surrounded by a subcampanulate 5—6-cleft involucre: females in the centre. MALE: perianth 1-leaved, galeate at the apex: stamen 1: filament filiform: anther extrorse, 2-celled, attached by the back: cells opposite. FEMALE: perianth tubular-ventricose, woolly, limb quite entire: ovary elliptic, 1-celled, 1-ovuled: ovule sessile, orthotropal: style terminal, short: stigma linear, unilateral: utricle membranaceous, enclosed by the persistent perianth: seed erect from the base.—Herbs: leaves alternate, stipuled: involucres axillary, sessile, united.

(1) F. URTICOIDES. (*R. W.*)

Ident. Wight's Icon. VI. t. 1982.

SPEC. CHAR. Procumbent, ramous, rooting below: branches ascending, slender, diffuse: leaves opposite, petioled, ovate or subcordate, serrated, pilose on both sides: involucres axillary, campanulate, 5-toothed, 4-flowered, 3-pedicelled male, and 1-sessile female: male calyx 2-lobed with 1 stamen, female tubular, enclosing the ovary, 5-toothed: style long: stigma villous, pointed: achenium ovate, glabrous.

Neilgherries, in damp woods at Ootacamund.

GENUS X. URTICA.

Monœcia Tetrandria. *Sex: Syst:*

Deriv. From *Uro*, to burn, in reference to the stinging properties of most of the species.

GEN. CHAR. Flowers monœcious or diœcious, spiked or glomerate-capitate. MALE: perianth regular, 4—5-cleft: segments valvate: stamens 4—5, opposite the sepals: filaments filiform, at first inflexed: anthers 2-celled, elliptic, incumbent. FEMALE: perianth 4-leaved; leaflets erect, cruciately opposite, outer ones smaller, inner ones persistent, sometimes baccate: ovary free, 1-celled: ovule 1, erect, orthotropal: stigma sessile, subcapitate, villous, penicillate or long-filiform: achenium oblong, slightly compressed, smooth or tubercled, naked or enclosed: seed erect.

—Herbs, annual or sometimes suffrutescent: hairs stinging: leaves alternate or opposite, inciso-serrated: flowers in panicles or axillary racemes, very rarely capitate.

(1) U. CRENULATA. (*Roxb.*)

Ident. Roxb. flor. Ind. III. p. 591.

Engrav. Wight's Icon. t. 686.

SPEC. CHAR. Shrubby, diœcious, erect: leaves alternate, oblong, acute, crenated: spikes axillary, compound dichotomous: flowers greenish.

Khasia hills, flowering in the rains.

(2) U. PARVIFLORA. (*Roxb.*)

Ident. Roxb. l. c. p. 581.

Engrav. Wight l. c. t. 690.

SPEC. CHAR. Diœcious, herbaceous, erect, armed with numerous strong, harsh, stinging bristles: leaves opposite, ovate-lanceolate, serrated: stipules undivided: female spikes quatern, compound, glomerate.

Rohilcund.

(3) U. PULCHERRIMA. (*Roxb.*)

Ident. Roxb. l. c. p. 588.

Engrav. Wight's Icon. t. 683.

SPEC. CHAR. Diœcious, shrubby: leaves alternate, lanceolate, serrated, 3-nerved: veins reticulate, hoary and pitted beneath: spikes axillary, paired, compound, glomerate, recurved: male flowers pentandrous.

Chittagong.

(4) U. NIVEA. (*Linn.*)

Ident. Spreng. Syst. III. p. 843.

Syn. U. tenacissima, *Roxb. l. c. p.* 590.

SPEC. CHAR. Shrubby, erect, branched: leaves alternate, long-petioled, broad cordate, coarsely serrated, hoary beneath: panicles axillary: flowers in round fascicles, male ones on the lower panicles, females above.

Silhet. Assam.

(5) U. ACUMINATA. (*Roxb.*)

Ident. Roxb. l. c. p. 592.

SPEC. CHAR. Subarboreous, hairy: leaves petioled, broad-lanceolar, entire, acuminate: female glomerudes axillary, small, globular.

Chittagong, flowering in the cold season.

(6) U. BICOLOR. *(Roxb.)*

Ident. Roxb. l. c. p. 589.

SPEC. CHAR. Shrubby: leaves alternate, short petioled, lanceolate, serrate, 3-nerved, scabrous above, hoary underneath: glomerules axillary, sessile.

Mountains of Bareilly.

(7) U. TRINERVIA. *(Roxb.)*

Ident. Roxb. l. c. p. 582.

SPEC. CHAR. Shrubby: leaves opposite, broad-lanceolate, crenate, 3-nerved: panicles axillary, the length of the petioles.

Chittagong, flowering in April.

(8) U. INÆQUALIFOLIA. *(Roxb.)*

Ident. Roxb. l. c. p. 594.

SPEC CHAR. Shrubby, erect, hispid: leaves alternate, sessile, unequally falcate, lanceolate, entire, acuminate: glomerules axillary.

Chittagong, flowering in April.

GENUS XI. POUZOLZIA.

Monœcia Pentandria. *Sex: Syst:*

GEN. CHAR. Flowers monœcious, rarely diœcious. *Male.* Perianth 4—5, rarely 3-parted: stamens 4—5, rarely 3: rudimentary pistil minute or wanting. *Female.* Perianth tubular, contracted at the apex, persistent, enclosing the seed or nut, at maturity sulcately ribbed or 2—3—4-winged, bidentate at the apex: style short or none: stigma prolonged, filiform, glandulose on one side: nut ovate, crustaceous, fragile: seed erect, sparingly albuminous: embryo axile, inverse: radicle cylindric, remote from the hilum.—Herbaceous, suffruticose or shrubby plants, creeping, procumbent, ascending or erect: leaves ternately verticelled, opposite or alternate, entire or rarely serrated, 3-nerved, or triple or quintuple-nerved, variously pilose, very rarely glabrous: flowers axillary, glomerate, short-pedicelled: clusters at first nearly all males mixed with few sessile, ovate, ribbed wingless fruits, afterwards towards the end of the floriferous branches, the male flowers diminish in number and are replaced by female ones producing winged fruit.

(1) P. INDICA. *(R.W.)*

Ident. Wight's Icon. vi. t. 1980—81.—Dalz. Bomb. flor. p. 240.

Syn. Parietaria Indica *Linn.*

SPEC. CHAR. Ascending, lax: leaves tripled-nerved, alternate, short-petioled, uniform, reduced in size towards the ends of the branches, ovate-lanceolate, subacuminate, pilose: flowers few, axillary, glomerate, tetrandrous: fruit ovate, 8-ribbed, apiculate.

A common weed in gardens.

(2) P. PENTANDRA. *(R.W.)*

Ident. Wight l. c. t. 2096. No. 20.

Syn. Urtica pentandra, *Roxb.*

SPEC. CHAR. Stem branched, 4-sided towards the apex: leaves sessile, narrow-lanceolate, cordate, pilose on both sides, scabrous above: flowers pentandrous: fruit winged, cordate.

Island of Caranjah. Near Calcutta. Assam.

(3) P. INTEGRIFOLIA. *(Dalz.)*

Ident. Dalz. in Hook. Journ. Bot. III. p. 134.

Engrav. Wight l. c. t. 1979 fig. 1.

SPEC. CHAR. Suffruticose: stem compressed, with a line of hairs on each side: leaves opposite, sessile, with a cordate base, lanceolate-acuminate, 3-nerved, entire, pubescent: male and female flowers together, clustered in the axils of the leaves: male perianth 4-parted, filaments flattened: female fruit-bearing perianth 2—3-winged, with 8—10 ribs between the wings.

Poondah Ghaut, flowering in September.

(4) P. STOCKSII. *(R.W.)*

Ident. Wight l. c. t. No. 18. Dalz. Bomb. flor. p. 240.

Syn. P. ramosissima, *R.W. No.* 19.

SPEC. CHAR. Straggling, branched, seeking support and then ascending: stem and branches 4-angled, furrowed between, glabrous: petioles short, connected by a broad scarious stipule: leaves glabrous except the hispid margin, from oval-obtuse at both ends to cordate-ovate, obtuse, floral ones sessile, narrow ovate-lanceolate obtuse: flowers few, axillary, pentandrous: fruit ovate, ribbed, or broadly 2—3-winged.

Belgaum. Coimbatore. Annamullay forests.

(5) P. ACUTA. *(R.W.)*

Ident. Wight l. c. No. 3.

SPEC. CHAR. Erect, sparingly branched: leaves sessile, sub-cordate, lanceolate, acuminate, somewhat scabrous above, slightly hoary on the nerves beneath: stipules deciduous: flowers axillary, subsessile, tetrandrous: fruit winged and ribbed, winged ones broad cordate at the base, bicuspidate at the apex: ribbed ones simply ovate.

Courtallum, flowering in July and August.

(6) P. OVALIFOLIA. *(R.W.)*

Ident. Wight l. c. No. 4.

SPEC. CHAR. Somewhat diffuse, ascending or seeking support: leaves sub-sessile or very shortly petioled, oval, acutish at the base, sharply acuminate, pilose on both sides, scabrous above: stipules ovate, deciduous: flowers pentandrous: fruit ovate or slightly cordate at the base, ciliate at the apex.

Alpine Jungles.

(7) P. MYSORENSIS. *(R.W.)*

Ident. Wight l. c. No. 5.

SPEC. CHAR. Erect, glabrous: leaves short-petioled, oblong-lanceolate, obtuse or sub-cordate at the base, acuminate at the apex, smooth above, glabrous or slightly pilose on both sides, ciliate on the margin: flowers pentandrous: fruit ribbed.

Bababooden Hills, Mysore, flowering in December.

(8) P. TOMENTOSA. *(R.W.)*

Ident. Wight l. c. No. 8.

SPEC. CHAR. Stem and under surface of the leaves tomentose: leaves sessile, ternately verticelled, oblong, ovate-lanceolate, rounded or sub-cordate at the base, acute or sub-acuminate, scabrous above: stipules reflexed: flowers numerous, pentandrous, sub-sessile: fruit wingless, ribbed.

Neilgherries, flowering in August and September.

(9) P. HETEROCARPA. *(R.W.)*

Ident. Wight l. c. No. 9.

SPEC. CHAR. Erect, sparingly branched: stems terete glabrous: leaves ternately verticelled, triple-nerved, short petioled, narrow lanceolate, acuminate at both ends, smooth, downy above, hoary beneath: flowers numerous, sessile, pentandrous: fruit varying from slightly ribbed to broadly winged, the winged ones deeply cordate at the base.

Western slopes of Neilgherries, flowering in December.

(10) P. BENNETTIANA. *(R. W.)*

Ident. Wight l. c. t. 1978.

Syn. P. ternata, *Bennett.* Wight No. 11.

SPEC. CHAR. Erect, sparingly branched: stem and upper surface of the leaves scabrous: leaves ternate, short-petioled, ovate-lanceolate, slightly unequal-sided, obtuse or sub-cordate at the base, ending in a long tapering acumen, pilose above, especially on the nerves, beneath: flowers numerous, sub-sessile, pentandrous: fruit in the same fascicles ovate, simply ribbed, or broadly 2—3-winged, the two winged ones rather deeply cordate at the base.

Neilgherries. Courtallum.

(11) P. LONGIFOLIA. *(R. W.)*

Ident. Wight l. c. No. 12.

SPEC. CHAR. Erect: stem 4-angled, scarcely branched, clothed with rough hairs: leaves ternate, sub-sessile, linear-lanceolate, broadest and sub-cordate at the base, tapering, acuminate at the apex, pilose on both sides, scabrous above, the under surface netted with dark coloured veins: fascicles few-flowered: flowers tetrandrous: fruit broadly winged and deeply cordate.

Courtallum, flowering in September.

(12) P. WIGHTII. *(Bennett.)*

Ident. Wight l. c. No. 13.

SPEC. CHAR. Erect, scarcely branched, terete: leaves sessile, opposite or ternate, narrow linear-lanceolate, tomentose beneath, downy and slightly rough above, the extreme ones much smaller: flowers tetrandrous: fruit broadly winged, ciliated, cordate at the base, somewhat forked at the apex.

Pulney mountains, flowering in September.

(13) P. CONCINNA. *(R. W.)*

Ident. Wight l. c. No. 14.

SPEC. CHAR. Erect, terete, glabrous: leaves opposite and ternate, sessile, lanceolate, spreading, acuminate, the extreme ones much smaller and cordate, acute, all downy on the nerves beneath and scabrous above: flowers tetrandrous, axillary, sessile, few: calycine lobes lanceolate acute: fruit ovate and winged.

Courtallum.

(14) P. ASPERA. (R. W.)

Ident. Wight l. c. No. 15.

SPEC. CHAR. Erect, very ramous, terminal shoot long and slender: stem and branches terete, very rough: leaves ternate, rarely opposite, sessile, broad ovate-cordate, acute, 5-nerved at the base, rough on both sides, those on the flower-bearing branchlets much reduced, even to mere scales, cordate acute: flowers tetrandrous: fruit all ovate, ribbed not winged.

Annamullay hills, flowering in July.

(15) P. DALZELLII. (R. W.)

Ident. Wight l. c. No. 21.

SPEC. CHAR. Procumbent, glabrous: leaves subsessile, ovate or cordate-ovate, acute, glabrous except a line of prickly hairs on the margin: floral leaves small, sessile, broad cordate at the base, acute: flowers axillary, few, pentandrous: fruit ovate, broadly ribbed or winged, furnished between with a thick spongy protuberance.

Canara.

(16) P. SCABRA. (R. W.)

Ident. Wight l. c. No. 22.

SPEC. CHAR. Erect, scarcely branched: stems terete, glabrous: lower leaves short-petioled, ovate, obtuse at the base, pointed: scabrous above, roughly pilose beneath, flower-bearing portion long and slender with minute bract-like sessile cordate leaves: fascicles few-flowered: flowers tetrandrous: fruit winged, inconspicuously winged between.

Annamullay mountains, flowering in July and August.

(17) P. CAUDATA. (Bennett.)

Ident. Wight l. c. No. 22.

SEC. CHAR. Erect, branched: stems terete, glabrous: leaves sessile, sub-cordate, truncate at the base, lanceolate acute or acuminate, membranous, smooth and glabrous on both sides: flower-bearing shoots slender, with minute bract-like cordate acute leaves: flowers tetrandrous: fruit simply ovate, ribbed and winged in the same fascicles.

Courtallum. Annamullay mountains. Flowering in September.

(18) P. wallichiana. *(R. W.)*

Ident. Wight l. c. No. 24.

Spec. Char. Fruticose, erect, branches terete, pubescent: leaves short-petioled, lanceolate, obtuse at the base, tapering above to a slender point, hispid on the margin, otherwise glabrous above, velvetty beneath, flower-bearing ones narrow-lanceolate, much reduced in size: flowers tetrandrous: fruit ovate, ribbed, wingless.

Neilgherries. Iyamullay hills near Coimbatore. P. ovata *(R. W.)* is a variety with scabrous leaves and P. oblongifolia *(R. W.)* with longer leaves.

(19) P. neilgherrensis. *(R. W.)*

Ident. Wight l. c. No. 26.

Spec. Char. Erect, sparingly branched: stems terete, scabrous: leaves petioled, lanceolate, obtuse at the base, tapering to a point, acute, lower ones slightly foliate, softly pubescent beneath, scabrous above: flower-bearing ones alternate, reduced in size and becoming broadly ovate-cordate towards the ends of the spikes: flowers tetrandrous: fruit on the lower portions of the spikes all ovate, ribbed, towards the apex, winged and ovate, mixed.

Neilgherries. Kotergherry ghaut.

(20) P. trialata. *(R. W.)*

Ident. Wight l. c. No. 28.

Spec. Char. Erect, scarcely branched: stem terete, hispidly pubescent: leaves ovate-lanceolate, sub-acuminate, slightly unequal-sided, hispid towards the margin, smooth on the disk, pubescent or slightly hoary beneath: floral ones smaller: flowers tetrandrous: fruit simply ovate and winged in the same fascicles, the latter 3-winged.

Iyamullay, flowering in August.

(21) P. cymosa. *(R. W.)*

Ident. Wight l. c. No. 29. t. 1971—2.

Spec. Char. Shrubby: leaves sub-sessile, opposite, many-nerved, pubescent on both sides: male inflorescence cymose, cymes axillary, paired: flowers petrandrous: fruit sessile, one or two at the base of each peduncle, ribbed not winged.

Eastern slopes of the Neilgherries, flowering in August and September.

(22) P. ROTUNDIFOLIA. *(R. W.)*

Ident. Wight l. c. No. 31.

SPEC. CHAR. Erect, sparingly branched: stems pubescent, obscurely 4-sided, sides furrowed: leaves alternate, long-petioled, broadly ovate or sub-orbicular, pointed: flowers sessile, axillary, pentandrous: fruit few-ribbed.

Courtallum, flowering in August and September.

(23) P. ELLIPTICA. *(R. W.)*

Ident. Wight l. c. No. 32.

SPEC. CHAR. Erect, branched, pubescent: stems terete: leaves alternate, elliptic, acute at both ends, hoary beneath, roughish above: flowers axillary, sessile, pentandrous, female ones in the same fascicles: fruit ovate, even, or scarcely ribbed.

Malabar.

(24) P. BICUSPIDATA. *(R. W.)*

Ident. Wight l. c. No. 33.

SPEC. CHAR. Erect, sparingly branched: stems succulent: leaves alternate, long-petioled, ovate-lanceolate, acuminate, smooth above, pubescent beneath: flowers glomerate, axillary, sessile, pentandrous: fruit ovate, sub-compressed, bicuspidate at the apex, not ribbed.

Courtallum, flowering in August and September.

(25) P. ROSTRATA. *(R. W.)*

Ident. Wight l. c. No. 34.

SPEC. CHAR. Erect, branched: stems glabrous: leaves long-petioled, alternate, membranous, broad-ovate, acuminate, glabrous on both sides: flowers glomerate, sessile, pentandrous: fruit broadly 4-winged, beaked.

Malabar. Canara.

(26) P. AURICULATA. *(R. W.)*

Ident. Wight l. c. No. 36.

SPEC. CHAR. Erect, branched, branches hoary towards the extremities: leaves alternate, longish-petioled, lanceolate, acute at both ends, roughish above, pubescent beneath: flowers sessile, glomerate, pentandrous: fruit 4-winged, wings enlarging upwards, sub-orbicular above, auricle-like.

Neilgherries. Iyamullay hills. Flowering in August and September.

(27) P. RHEEDII. *(R. W.)*

Ident. Wight l. c. No. 37.

Engrav. Rheede Mal. xi. t. 30.

SPEC. CHAR. Erect, branched, branches glabrous: leaves alternate, petioled, broadly ovate or sub-cordate at the base, acuminate or simply acute, slightly pilose on both sides: flowers glomerate, pentandrous: fruit flattened, imperfectly 4-winged, beaked, wings abruptly truncated.

Malabar. Neilgherries.

(28) P. SCABRIDA. *(R. W.)*

Ident. Wight l. c. No. 38.

SPEC. CHAR. Erect, branched, branches somewhat strigose: leaves alternate, reduced in size towards the extremities, lanceolate, acute at both ends, at first nearly smooth, afterwards scabrous above, pubescent beneath: flowers pentandrous: fruit 4-angled or imperfectly winged, prominently ribbed between the wings.

Neilgherries, flowering in August and September.

(29) P. MINOR. *(R. W.)*

Ident. Wight l. c. No. 40.

SPEC. CHAR. Decumbent, diffuse, branches slender, filiform: leaves small, lower ones broadly ovate obtuse, pilose, upper ones smaller, ovate obtuse, all sub-sessile: flowers few, axillary, sessile, tetrandrous: fruit both simply ovate, somewhat 4-angled and 4-winged, apiculate.

Near Alleppy, Travancore.

(30) P. TUBEROSA. *(R. W.)*

Ident. Wight l. c. No. 44.

Syn. Urtica tuberosa, *Roxb. flor. Ind.* III. *p.* 587.

Engrav. Wight's Icon. t. 697.

SPEC. CHAR. Roots tuberous: stems annual, flaccid: leaves alternate, ovate, acute, hairy: flowers axillary, glomerate, tetrandrous, fruit ovate, not ribbed.

Circass, in moist soil.

(31) P. VESICARIA. *(R. W.)*

Ident. Wight l. c. No. 45.

Syn. Urtica vesicaria, *Roxb. l. c.*

Engrav. Wight l. c. t. 695.

SPEC. CHAR. Shrubby, erect: leaves broadish lanceolate, acute at both ends, petioled, downy on both sides: flowers axillar sessile, tetrandrous: fruit ovate, surrounded at the base by sever inflated permanent vesicles.

Circar mountains.

(32) P. PILOSA. *(R.W.)*

Ident. Wight l. c. No. 47.

SPEC. CHAR. Diffuse, branched, climbing or spreading on the ground: leaves ovate, sub-sessile, acute, pilose, those of the extremities alternate, near the base opposite: flowers glomerate, tetrandrous: fruit deeply furrowed or 4-winged with a 2-cleft apiculus.

Malabar?

(33) P. TETRAPTERA. *(R.W.)*

Ident. Wight l. c. No. 48.

SPEC. CHAR. Erect or ascending, branched: leaves membranous, pilose, nearly all alternate, a few of the lower pairs opposite, longish-petioled, elliptic-lanceolate, acute at both ends, or sometimes ovate-lanceolate, upper ones much smaller and narrower than the lower: flowers few, glomerate, axillary, sessile, tetrandrous: fruit in the lower axils prominently ribbed, in the upper ones usually broadly 4-winged.

Hills near Coimbatore, flowering in August and September.

(34) P. JOHNSONIANA. *(R.W.)*

Ident. Wight l. c. No. 49.

SPEC. CHAR. Decumbent: stems slender, filiform, somewhat strigose: leaves longish-petioled, pilose, alternate, from oval obtuse to ovate-lanceolate, sub-acute, floral ones reduced: flowers few, axillary, sessile, males tetrandrous, with a conspicuous rudimentary pistil woolly at the base: fruit ovate, compressed, furrowed or broadly 4-winged, beaked.

Cochin.

(35) P. PYRAMIDATA. *(R.W.)*

Ident. Wight l. c. No. 50.

SEC CHAR. Straggling, ascending or erect, branches slender, 4-angled, deeply furrowed between: leaves alternate or first few pairs opposite, lower ones short-petioled, ovate-lanceolate, upper ones sessile, linear acute all roughish above, pilose beneath: stipules broad-cordate, cuspidate: flowers few, axillary, sessile, tetrandrous: calyx fringed with long bristly hairs: fruit ovate, furrowed or broadly 4-winged.

Quilon in Travancore.

ORDER CXLIII. ULMACEÆ.

Trees or shrubs: leaves alternate, simple, serrate, slightly scabrous: flowers lateral in the branchlets, fascicled, sessile, hermaphrodite or seldom polygamous by abortion: perianth free, turbinate-campanulate, limb erect, 4-5—seldom 8—cleft, lobes imbricated in æstivation: stamens inserted at the base of the calyx, equal to the sepals in number and opposite, seldom more: filaments filiform, free: anthers introrse, 2-celled, affixed by the back: cells obliquely opposite, dehiscing lengthwise: ovary free, composed of 2 carpels, margins of the latter inflexed, constituting a 2-celled dissepiment: ovules solitary in the cells, attached near the apex, or in a 1-celled ovary hanging to the top of the cavity, anatropal: styles two, continuous to the carpels, divaricately spreading, stigmatose within nearly their whole length: fruit surrounded at the base by the persistent perianth, membranaceous, samaroid, or coriaceous, smooth or scaly, 1-celled by abortion, 1-seeded: seed pendulous: testa membranaceous: albumen none: embryo orthotropal: radicle short.

GENUS I. HOLOPETALA.

Polygamia Monœcia. *Sex: Syst:*

Deriv. From *Holos* all, entire, and *Petalon* a petal.

Gen. Char. Calyx 4—8-parted, hairy: stamens 7—9, scarcely longer than the calyx: ovary pedicelled, oval compressed: styles two, nearly as long as the ovary: fruit compressed, winged all round.

(1) H. integrifolia. *(Planch.)*

Ident. Planch. Ann. des Scien. Nat. T. III. v. 10.

Syn. Ulmus integrifolia, *Roxb. flor. Ind. II. p.* 68.

Engrav. Wight's Icon. t. 1968.—Roxb. Cor. I. t, 78.

Spec. Char. Large tree: leaves alternate, short-petioled, ovate, sometimes cordate, entire, smooth, shining: stipules lanceolate: flowers polygamous: male and bisexual mixed in cymes along the naked branches: capsule orbicular, leafy, compressed, emarginate, 1—2-celled, indehiscent.

Circar Mountains. Hurdwar Concans. Ghauts near Arcot. Flowering in the cold season.

(2) H. LANCIFOLIA. *(Roxb.)*

Ident. Roxb. l. c. p. 66 (under Ulmus.)

SPEC. CHAR. Large tree: leaves obliquely lanceolate, equally and obtusely serrulate, obtusely acuminate: flowers numerous, small, long-pedicelled, fascicled in the lower axils, hexandrous: capsules unequally obcordate, scariose, very thin, winged.

Chittagong Hills, flowering in March.

GENUS II. CELTIS.

Polygamia Monœcia. *Sex: Syst:*

Deriv. One of the ancient names given to the Lotus.

GEN. CHAR. Flowers polygamous, hermaphrodite or males by abortion of the ovary: perianth 5-leaved, persistent, leaflets equal, concave, imbricated in æstivation: stamens five: filaments incurved at the apex, at length straightish: anthers introrse, 2-celled, cordate-acuminate, fixed by the back: ovary ovate, 1-celled: ovule one, amphitropal: stigmas two, terminal, long acuminate, spreading or recurved, glandular pubescent: drupe fleshy, smooth: seed pendulous, arched.—Trees: leaves alternate, serrated: flowers axillary, solitary, pedicelled.

(1) C. ROXBURGHII. *(Planch.)*

Ident. Planch. Ann. soc. nat. S. III. p. 302—Dalz. Bomb. flor. p. 237.

Syn. C. trinervia, *Roxb. flor. Ind. II. p.* 65.

SPEC. CHAR. Small tree: leaves obliquely ovate-cordate, acuminate, glabrous, 3-nerved: flowers pentandrous: male ones from the base of the young shoots or solitary under the bisexual ones: bisexual flowers on slender, villous, axillary racemes.

Common on the Ghauts.

(2) C. WIGHTII. *(Planch.)*

Ident. Planch. l. c. p. 307.

Engrav. Wight's Icon. t. 1969.

SPEC. CHAR. Leaves oblong, abruptly acuminate, somewhat

acute at the base, quite entire, 3-nerved, lateral pair of nerves extending from the base to the apex: stipules somewhat peltate: cymes about the length of the petioles or sometimes twice as long: berry shortly rostrate, smooth: flowers pale bluish.

Neilgherries, flowering nearly all the year.

(3) C. SEROTINA. *(Planch.)*

Ident. Planch. l. c. p. 301.

Engrav. Wight l. c. t. 1970.

SPEC. CHAR. Leaves obliquely ovate, acuminate, acute at the base, serrated from the apex to below the middle, glabrous: inflorescence axillary or from the axils of fallen leaves: fructiferous pedicels usually 3 together, one free, the other two united at the base: berry nearly oval, glabrous.

Neilgherries.

(4) C. TOMENTOSA. *(Roxb.)*

Ident. Roxb. l. c. p. 66.

SPEC. CHAR. Shrubby: leaves long-cordate, acuminate, serrulate, 3-nerved, scabrous above, very downy underneath: thyrses axillary, short, dense.

Chittagong, flowering in April.

GENUS III. SPONIA.

Polygamia Monœcia. *Sex: Syst:*

GEN. CHAR. Flowers polygamous, hermaphrodite or male by abortion of the ovary: perianth 5-leaved, persistent, leaflets equal, concave, imbricated in æstivation: stamens five: anthers introrse, 2-celled, extrorsely refracted with a connectivum articulated with the filament: ovary ovate-cylindric, 1-celled: ovule one, amphitropal: stigma 2 cleft, curved inwards: drupe fleshy, unequal-sided: seed pendulous, arched.—Trees or shrubs: leaves alternate, somewhat 3-nerved, entire or serrated, glabrous or pubescently scabrous: flowers axillary, cymosely panicled.

(1) S. WIGHTII. *(Planch.)*

Ident. Planch, l. c. p. 264.

Syn. Celtis orientalis, *Roxb. flor. Ind. II. p.* 65.

Engrav. Wight's Icon. t. 1971.—Rheede Mal. iv. t. 40.

SPEC. CHAR. Small tree: leaves ovate-oblong: cuspidate, cordate and unequal at the base, younger ones white pubescent beneath:

cymes very shortly peduncled, as long as the petiole: male flowers dense, females more loose: stigmas covered with long threads: berry small: flowers minute, green.

Hilly parts of the Concan. Peninsula. Silhet. Assam. Flowering all the year.

(2) T. VELUTINA. *(Planch.)*

Ident. Planch. l. c.

Engrav. Wight l. c. t. 1990.

SPEC. CHAR. Branchlets and leaves softly velvetty: traves ovate-oblong, cuspidately acuminate, slightly unequal at the base, cordate or rounded, serrated, beset above with rough points: cymes short-peduncled or sub-sessile, equalling or twice as long as the petioles, many-flowered: male flowers exteriorly hairy: berries ovate, glabrous or slightly hairy.

Coimbatore. Neilgherries.

ORDER CXLIV. MORACEÆ.

Trees or shrubs, lactescent, usually scandent, leaves undivided or lobed, alternate, entire: stipules persistent or deciduous: flowers diœcious or monœcious. MALE. Perianth 3—4 parted, leaflets ovate, concave, imbricated in æstivation: stamens 3—4, inserted at the bottom of the calyx, and opposite its lobes: filaments filiform or subulate, smooth or transversely wrinkled, at first inflexed: anthers introrse, 2-celled, ovate or sub-globose, attached by the back, erect or incumbent, cells somewhat opposite, dehiscing lengthways. FEMALE. Perianth 4—5 parted, outer segments larger: ovary sessile, ovate, 1-celled: ovule one, inserted at the middle of the partition, amphitropal, incurved; style 2-cleft, segments usually unequal stigmatose within: achenia or utricles 1-seeded, enclosed by baccate perianths, free or coalescing into one, or contained within fleshy receptacles: seed single, uncinate: testa crustaceous, fragile: albumen fleshy, more or less copious: embryo homotropal, uncinate: cotyledons oblong, incumbent: radicle more or less long, looking towards the top of the fruit.

GENUS I. I. COVELLIA.

Monœcia Monandria. *Sex: Syst:*

Gen. Char. Receptacle without an involucre, villous, throat scaly, ebracteolate within, pilose: flowers on the same receptacle bearing stamens superior, few, stamen bearing ones sessile: perianth 3-leaved: stamen one, filament cylindric, anthers 2-celled, subrotund, cells contiguous at the base and apex, separated in the middle by a connectivum: pistil-bearing flowers pedicelled: perianth 3—5 parted, unequal, sometimes very small: ovary sessile, 1-celled: style lateral, bearded above the middle: stigma infundibuliform, somewhat oblique, 2-toothed.—Leaves opposite or alternate.

(1) C. guttata. *(R. W.)*

Ident. Wight's Icon. vi. t. 1966.

Spec. Char. Arboreous, scandent, the branches afterwards ascending: branches glabrous and smooth, younger ones pubescent: leaves ovate-cordate, acuminate, 3-nerved, entire, villous beneath: receptacles glomerate on the older branches, pubescent: perianth 6-lobed: stigma dilated, ciliate, umbilicate.

Orange Valley, near Kotergherry, Neilgherries, on the banks of the stream, flowering in August and September.

(2) C. macrocarpa. *(R. W.)*

Ident. Wight l. c. t. 1965.

Syn. Pogonotrophe macrocarpa, *Miquel.*

Spec. Char. Arboreous, climbing: young parts pubescent: leaves long-petioled, ovate, equal or somewhat unequal-sided, abruptly narrow acuminate, rounded at the base, 3—5-nerved, 2—3-costulate: receptacles glomerate, globose, pubescent, spotted: fruit green, white-spotted, size of an orange.

Pulney mountains, climbing on trees, in fruit during October.

(3) C. oppositifolia. *(Gasp.)*

Ident. Gasparini Ric. 85. t. 8. fig. 36—42.

Syn. Ficus oppositifolia, *Willd. Roxb. flor. Ind. III. p.* 561. Sycomorphe Roxburghii, *Miq. in Ann. sc. nat. III. s. I.* 35.

Engrav. Roxb. Cor. II. t. 124.—Wight l. c. t. 638.

Spec. Char. Small tree: trunk erect: young shoots scabrous, and covered with much short white hair, fistulous and interrupted at the insertion of the leaves, leaves opposite, short, round or oblong, slightly serrate, glandular in the axils of the veins beneath, shining above, downy beneath: fruit axillary and peduncled, racemed on the naked, woody branches, round, about the size of a large nutmeg, covered with short, white hair, with several equi-distant ridges.

Banks of rivulets in the Peninsula.

(4) C. GLOMERATA. *(Miq.)*

Ident. Miq. l. c.—Dalz. Bomb. flor. p. 243.

Syn. Ficus glomerata, *Roxb.*

SPEC. CHAR. Large tree: trunk crooked, thick and high, bark of a rusty-greenish colour and rough: leaves alternate, petioled, oblong or broad-lanceolate, tapering equally to each end, entire, very slightly 3-nerved, smooth on both sides: racemes compound or panicled, issuing immediately from the trunk or large branches: fruit pedicelled, nearly as large as the common figs, clothed with soft down.

Western Coast.

(5) C. DŒMONUM. *(Miq.)*

Ident. Miq. l. c. Dalz. l. c. p. 244.

Syn. Ficus Dœmona, *Koen. Roxb. flor. Ind. III. p.* 562.

Engrav. Wight l. c. t. 641.

SPEC. CHAR. Shrubby: leaves generally opposite, cuneate-oblong, pointed, serrate, scabrous above, downy beneath, with a green gland in the axils of the veins: fruit for the most part in pairs in radical withering racemes, often underground, of the size of a large nutmeg, obovate, very hairy, obscurely ridged.

Western Coast. Peninsula.

GENUS II. EPICARPURUS.

Diœcia Tetrandria. *Sex: Syst:*

GEN. CHAR. Flowers diœcious. *Male.* Spicate-amentaceous: perianth 4-leaved, bibracteolate: stamens four: filaments elongated. *Female.* Somewhat solitary: perianth 4-leaved, persistent, at length increasing: ovary stalked, 1-celled: ovule one, amphitropal: style lateral, deeply 2-cleft, segments filiform, stigmatose: berry stalked with the perianth: seed parietal, orbiculate, compressed. Lactescent, branched trees: trunk usually thorny: leaves alternate, shortly petioled, oblong, serrulate: stipules subulate, deciduous.

(1) E. ORIENTALIS. *(Blume.)*

Ident. Blume bidjr. p. 488.

Syn. Trophis aspera. *Willd.*

Engrav. Wight's Icon. t. 1961.

SPEC. CHAR. Arboreous: leaves alternate, short-petioled, obovate, cuspidate-acuminate, serrated towards the apex, very rough above: male flowers capitate, heads axillary, aggregated, short-peduncled: females axillary, 1—2-together, longish-pedicelled: fruit drupaceous, 1-seeded, testa crustaceous.

Common everywhere. The leaves are used in polishing wood.

(2) E. SPINOSA. *(R.W.)*

Ident. Wight l. c. vi. t. 1962.

Syn. Trophis spinosa *Roxb.* (not *Willd.*)

SPEC. CHAR. Arboreous, thorny: leaves oblong-lanceolate, coarsely serrated towards the apex, glabrous: male flowers aggregated in the axils of the leaves and thorns, axillary: calyx deeply 5-parted, lobes lanceolate, much longer than the fruit.

Courtallum.

GENUS III. DORSTENIA.

Monœcia Diandria. *Sex: Syst:*

GEN. CHAR. Receptacle fleshy, concave flat: flowers numerous, in the pits of the receptacle, males and females mixed. *Male.* Pits superficial: perianth none: stamens 2 or more: filaments filiform: anthers 2-celled, globose-didymous. *Females.* Solitary in the pits: perianth none: ovary shortly stalked, ovate, 1-celled: ovule one, amphitropal: style lateral, filiform, stigma 2-cleft: fructiferous receptacle sub-succulent, enclosing the utricles: seed parietal, uncinate.—Stemless herbs: leaves radical, palmati or pinnatifid: receptacle terminating the scape, quadrangular or subrotund, or sometimes linear.

(1) D. INDICA. *(R.W.)*

Ident. Wight's Icon. vi. t. 1964.

SPEC. CHAR. Herbaceous, at first procumbent and rooting, afterwards ascending and erect: stem and petioles pilose: leaves penninerved, elliptic or elliptic-lanceolate, unequally serrated towards the apex, sparingly hairy above, more thickly on the veins beneath: peduncles axillary, solitary, cernuous or drooping: receptacle peltate, variously lobed on the margin.

Pulney mountains. Neilgherries. Courtallum.

GENUS IV. STILPNOPHYLLUM.

Monœcia Monandria. *Sex: Syst:*

Deriv. From *Stilpnos* shining, and *Phyllon* a leaf.

GEN. CHAR. Receptacle involucrate, bracteolate within: flowers on the same receptacle staminigerous mixed with the pistil-bearing ones, sessile or peduncled, enclosed by imbricated bracteoles: perianth 3-leaved, leaflets valvate. *Male.* Stamen one, filament very short, anther 2-celled, cordate. *Female.* Ovary sessile, 1-celled: style lateral: stigma thick, short, papillose.

(1) S. ELASTICUM.

Ident. Endl. gen. suppl. iv. p. 35.

Syn. Ficus elastica, *Roxb.* Macrophthalma elastica *Gaspar.*

Engrav. Wight's Icon. t. 663.

SPEC. CHAR. Tree: leaves oval or oblong, pointed, thick, firm, glossy: fruit in axillary pairs, sessile, oval, smooth: stipules nearly as long as the leaves, smooth, rose-coloured.

Khasia hills.

GENUS V. UROSTIGMA.

Monœcia Monandria. *Sex: Syst:*

Deriv. From *Oura* a tail, and *Stigma*, alluding to the prolonged appendage of that organ.

GEN. CHAR. Receptacle involucrate, bracteolate on all sides within: flowers on the same receptacle pistil-bearing with the staminigerous ones mixed, or the former uppermost, all pedicelled, pedicels imbricately bracteolate: perianth 3-leaved, leaflets imbricated. *Male.* Stamen one, filament cylindric or compressed, anther 2-celled, sub-globose. *Female.* Ovary sessile, 1-celled: style lateral: stigma elongated, villous.

(1) U. BENGALENSE. *(Gaspar.)*

Ident. Gasparrini Ricerche 81 t. 7 fig. 1—5. Dalz. Bomb. flor. p. 240.

Syn. Ficus Bengalensis, *Linn.* F. Indica, *Roxb.*

Engrav. Wight's Icon. t. 1989. Rheede Mal. I. t. 28.

SPEC. CHAR. Branches drooping roots, which form stems: bark smooth and of a light ash-colour: leaves alternate, about the extremities of the branchlets, petioled, ovate-cordate, 3-nerved, entire, smooth and shining when old: fruit paired, axillary, sessile, of the size and colour of a cherry, downy, appearing in the hot season.

All over India.

(2) U. RELIGIOSUM. *(Gaspar.)*

Ident. Gaspar. l. c. Dalz. l. c. p. 241.

Syn. Ficus religiosa, *Roxb.*

Engrav. Rheede Mal. I. t. 27. Wight l. c. t. 1967.

SPEC CHAR. Large tree: leaves long-petioled, ovate-cordate, narrow-acuminate, entire or repandly undulate towards the apex, quite smooth: fruit paired, axillary, sessile, vertically compressed, when ripe, of the size and colour of a small black cherry, appearing in the hot season.

Common throughout the country.

(3) U. LAMBERTIANUM. *(Miq.)*

Ident. Miquel in Hook. Journ. Bot. vi. p. 565.

SPEC CHAR. Leaves long-petioled, ovate-oblong, margins obsoletely repand-undulate, abruptly and obtusely acuminate, truncate at the apex, between membranaceous and coriaceous, shining, 3-nerved: fruit axillary, twin, sessile, globose, glabrous, with 3-bracts at the base, puberulous on the back.

Bombay.

(4) U. INFECTORIUM. *(Miq.)*

Ident. Miq. l. c. Dalz. Bomb. flor. p. 241.

Syn. Ficus infectoria, *Roxb.*

Engrav. Wight l. c. t. 665.

SPEC. CHAR. Leaves rather long-petioled, membranaceous, oblong or sub-lanceolate-oblong, moderately and acutely acuminated, obtuse or rounded, or sub-cordate at the base, quite entire, or very slightly repand: fruit small, sessile, twin, globose, smooth, when ripe white.

The Concans.

(5) U. PSEUDOTJIELA. *(Miq.)*

Ident. Miq. l. c. Dalz. l. c.

Syn. Ficus tjiela, *Roxb.*

Engrav. Wight l. c. t. 668.

SPEC. CHAR. Large tree: leaves long-petioled, ovate-oblong, pointed, entire, firm, smooth on both sides, shining, particularly above, with numerous simple and parallel veins: fruit paired, axillary, sessile, a little turbinate, smooth, size of a cherry, when ripe purple.

On the Ghauts. Coromandel mountains and plains. Fruit ripening in the hot season.

(6) U. retusum. *(Miq.)*

Ident. Miq. l. c. p. 581.

Spec. Char. Leaves moderately petioled, broadly obovate or somewhat rounded, dilated at the apex, very shortly and obtusely apiculate or retuse, slightly emarginate, between membranaceous and coriaceous, veins half-spreading, about 10 on each side, rather distinct, the rest capillary, finely reticulated : petioles deeply furrowed on the upper-side : fruit axillary twin, sessile, bracts puberous.

Bombay.

(7) U. nitidum. *(Miq.)*

Ident. Miq. l. c. Dalz. l. c. p. 242.

Syn. Ficus nitida, *Roxb.* F. Benjaminea, *Roxb.*

Engrav. Wight l. c. t. 642.—Rheede Mal. III. t. 55.

Spec. Char. Branchlets somewhat 3-cornered, leaves with moderate or rather long petioles, elliptic or obovate or sub-rhombeo-elliptic, obtusely and shortly sub-apiculate, acute or sub-cuneate at the base, slightly 3-nerved, veins on each side several, sub-immersed or distinct beneath, confluent near the margin, but with no sub-marginal nerve, coriaceo-mambranaceous : stipules ovate-lanceolate, smooth or puberulous : fruit axillary, twin, sessile, globose, smooth, size of a pea, with 3 obtuse bracts : petioles with a narrow groove in front.

Peninsula. Khasia hills.

(8) U. Benjamineum. *(Miq.)*

Ident. Miq. l. c. Dalz. l. c.

Syn. Ficus striata, *Roth.*

Spec. Char. Branchlets slender, flexuose, weak, hanging : petioles round, rather short : leaves ovate or elliptic-ovate acuminate, coriaceous, like parchment, surrounded by a smooth margin, veins capillary, horizontal, united into an arched nerve : fruit axillary, sessile, like peas : bracts 3, ovate-obtuse, deciduous : fruit smooth, shining, greenish-yellow, with a dash of purple.

Southern Maratha Country.

(9) U. dasycarpum. *(Miq.)*

Ident. Miq. l. c. Dalz. l. c.

Spec. Char. Branchlets and fruit densely tomentose : leaves shortly-petioled, broadly ovate or elliptic, shortly or obtusely acuminate, rounded or slightly cordate at the base, repand-undulate, thickly coriaceous, smooth above, beneath with the petioles tomentose and pubescent: costal veins 3 to 10, spreading, confluent at the margin, much reticulated and very prominent beneath, fruit axillary, sessile, generally twin, ellipsoid obtuse at both ends, bracts 3, obtuse, membranaceous, pubescent.

Bombay.

(10) U. CORDIFOLIUM. *(Dalz.)*

Ident. Dalz. l. c. p. 242.

SPEC. CHAR. Tree: leaves on very long petioles, broad-cordate, with a short and sudden acumination, rather membranaceous with waved margins, finely reticulated beneath (lateral veins spreading and prominent), perfectly smooth: fruit paired, sessile, round, smooth, black, of the size and appearance of a black cherry.

Ghauts.

(11) U. VOLUBILE. *(Dalz.)*

Ident. Dalz. l. c.

Syn. U. Ampelos, *Koen.* *Dalz. l. c. p.* 315?

SPEC. CHAR. Climbing, shrubby, and often a tree with a stem as thick as a man's arm: leaves alternate, very shortly petioled, somewhat ovate, suddenly acuminated, very unequal-sided, cuneate towards the base: lateral nerves, 3 to 4 on each side, prominent spreading, uniting in arches, pale-green, hard and roughish to the touch, though smooth, 3 to 4 inches long, sometimes a little toothed on the margin: fruit small.

Rocky places on the Ghauts. Tanjore.

GENUS VI. FICUS.

Polygamia Diœcia. *Sex: Syst.*

GEN. CHAR. Receptacle fleshy, closed, globose or pear-shaped, scaly, bracteated at the base, throat closed by small scales: flowers numerous, very small, pedicelled on the inner surface of the receptacle, packed together, diœcious, or upper ones male, rest female. *Male.* Perianth 3-parted: stamens 3: filaments capillary: anthers introrse, 2-celled, incumbent. *Female.* Perianth 5-cleft, tube decurrent into the pedicel: ovary somewhat laterally placed on a short gynophore, 1-celled: ovule one, amphitropal: style lateral, continuous to the gynophore, filiform, stigma shortly 2-cleft: fructiferous receptacle succulent: seed parietal, uncinate: testa hard, fragile.—Lofty trees or climbing shrubs, lactescent: leaves alternate, entire or lobed, stipulate: stipules large, convolute, concealing the terminal buds, deciduous or persistent: receptacles axillary, solitary, or packed together, very rarely terminal and racemose.

(1) F. ACUTILOBA. *(Miq.)*

Ident. Miquel in Hook. Journ. Bot. VI.—Dalz. Bomb. flor. p. 243.

SPEC. CHAR. Branchlets puberulous, when old, smooth, shining, dark-coloured: leaves moderately petioled, ovate-oblong, 3 to 5-lobed, base obtuse, 3-nerved, lobes elliptic or lanceolate-acute, denticulate, middle one longer, sub-serrate or coarsely toothed on both sides, especially beneath, scabrous and harsh, fruit axillary, solitary peduncled, small, between pear-shaped and globose, with 3 bracts at the base.

Malabar Hill, Bombay. Ghauts.

(2) F. ASPERRIMA. *(Roxb.)*

Ident. Roxb. flor. Ind. III. p. 554.

Engrav. Wight's Icon. t. 633.

SPEC. CHAR. Branches at length smooth: leaves alternate or opposite, oblong-acuminate, obtuse at the base, remotely toothed upwards, rigid, very rough and harsh, 3-nerved and with 3 to 4 costal veins on each side: fruit axillary, peduncled, globose, hoary, pubescent and slabrous.

Bombay. Circars.

(3) F. HETEROPHYLLA. *(Linn.)*

Ident. Spreng. Syst. III. p. 785.—Dalz l. c.—Roxb. l. c. p. 532.

Syn. F. aquatica, *Koen.* F. rubescens, *Vahl.*

Engrav. Wight l. c. t. 659.—Rheede Mal. III. t. 62.

SPEC. CHAR. All rough and harsh: leaves alternate shortly-petioled, rigid, membranaceous, above roughish, and of a deep-green, below pale, oblong-acute, acute at the base, serrated, entire or 3-lobed or sub-pinnatifid, of all shapes: fruit axillary, solitary, rarely twin, between turbinate and globose.

Common in moist places.

(4) F. TRILOBA. *(Buch.)*

Ident. Buch. in. Voight Hort. Calc. p. 284.

Syn. F. hirsuta, *Roxb.*—F. hirta, *do.* III. *p.* 531 (not *Vahl.*)

Engrav. Wight l. c. t. 670.

SPEC. CHAR. Arboreous: young parts hirsute: leaves round cordate, 3—5-lobed, serrate-dentate, lobes acute: fruit receptacles in pairs, axillary, sessile, oval, very hairy, appearing in the hot season.

Silhet. Assam.

(5) F. CARICOIDES. *(Roxb.)*

Ident. Roxb. flor. Ind. III. p. 529.

SPEC. CHAR. Sub-arboreous: leaves cordate, crenate, villous: calyx 5—6-leaved: fruit receptacles axillary, solitary, long-peduncled, turbinate, umbilicate, wrinkled, appearing and ripening all the year.

Patna. Gya. Rohilcund. Lucknow.

(6) F. VIRGATA. *(Roxb.)*

Ident. Roxb. l. c. p. 530.

Engrav. Wight l. c. t. 649.

SPEC. CHAR. Shrubby: leaves broad-cordate, obtuse, serrate-crenate, 3-nerved, downy: fruit receptacles axillary, solitary, ovate, the size of a pea, longish-peduncled, appearing and ripening the whole year.

Rohilcund.

(7) F. REPENS. *(Roxb.)*

Ident. Roxb. l. c. p. 535.

Engrav. Wight l. c. t. 636.

SPEC. CHAR. Somewhat shrubby, creeping: leaves obliquely cordate, lobed, serrate-dentate: fruit-receptacles axillary, solitary, peduncled, obovate, roughish, appearing and ripening the whole year.

Bengal.

(8) F. RADICANS. *(Roxb.)*

Ident. Roxb. l. c. p. 536.

Engrav. Wight l. c. t. 671.

SPEC. CHAR. Shrubby, scandent, rooting: leaves oblong, entire, long-linear, acuminate: fruit-recepatcles axillary, solitary, or paired, long-peduncled, globular, size of a currant, appearing and ripening all the year.

Silhet.

(9) F. SCANDENS. *(Roxb.)*

Ident. Roxb. l. c. p. 536 (not *Lam.*)

Engrav. Wight l. c. t. 643.

SPEC. CHAR. Shrubby, scandent: leaves short petioled, ovate, entire: fruit receptacles axillary, paired, longish-peduncled, globular, rough, size of a black currant, appearing and ripening the whole year.

Silhet.

(10) F. GOOLEREEA. *(Roxb.)*

Ident. Roxb. l.c p. 538.

SPEC. CHAR. Leaves opposite, obovate, serrate, downy: fruit-receptacles paired, long-peduncled, nearly round, downy, with an elevated scaly margin round the umbilicus.

Hindosthan.

(11) F. LACCIFERA. *(Roxb.)*

Ident. Roxb. l. c. p. 545.

Engrav. Wight l. c. t. 656.

SPEC. CHAR. Arboreous: leaves long-petioled, from cordate to oval, obtuse, pointed, shining, 3-nerved: fruit-receptacles axillary, sessile, oval, smooth, size of a gooseberry, appearing in the hot season and ripening in the rains.

Silhet.

(12) F. RUMPHII. *(Blume.)*

Ident. Blume Rumphia, p. 437.—Roxb. l. c. p. 548.

Syn. F. cordifolia, *Roxb.*

Engrav. Rumph. Amb. III. t. 91, 92.—Wight l. c. t. 640.

SPEC. CHAR. Arboreous: leaves long, slender, petioled, ovate-cordate, acuminate, glossy: fruit-receptacles axillary, sessile, paired, globular, smooth, size of a cherry, appearing in the hot season.

Bengal.

(13) F. EXCELSA. *(Vahl.)*

Ident. Roxb. l. c. p. 552.

Engrav. Wight l. c. t. 650.—Rheede Mal. III. t. 58.

SPEC. CHAR. Arboreous, smooth: leaves short-petioled, bifarious, obliquely oblong, smooth: fruit-receptacles axillary, solitary or paired, peduncled, somewhat turbinate, smooth, size of a cherry, appearing in the hot season.

Peninsular. Malabar.

(14) F. VAGANS. *(Roxb.)*

Ident. Roxb. l. c. p. 537.

Engrav. Wight l. c. t. 655.

SPEC. CHAR. Shrubby, scandent, rooting to other trees: leaves long-petioled, cordate, villous beneath: fruit-receptacles axillary, paired or solitary, long-peduncled, nearly globular, size of a nutmeg.

Chittagong. Silhet.

(15) F. ROXBURGHII. *(Wall.)*

Ident. Wall. Cat.

Syn. F. macrophylla, *Roxb. l. c. p.* 556.

Engrav. Wight l. c. t. 673.

SPEC. CHAR. Arboreous: leaves round cordate, thin, nerved: fruit-receptacles collected in bundles near the root of the stem and on the lower parts of the branches, turnip-shaped, 8—12-ribbed, hairy, as large as the common fig, appearing and ripening all the year.

Chittagong. Silhet.

(16) F. LANCEOLATA. *(Roxb.)*

Ident. Roxb. l. c. p. 557.

Engrav. Wight l. c. t. 645.

SPEC. CHAR. Shrubby: leaves lanceolate, smooth, entire: fruit-receptacles in bundles near the root of the trunk and larger branches, peduncled, warty, compressedly turbinate, deeply umbilicate, size of a small common fig, appearing and ripening more or less throughout the year.

Chittagong.

(17) F. CUNIA. *(Buch.)*

Ident. Roxb. l. c. p. 561

Syn. F. conglomerata, *Roxb. l. c. p.* 559.

Engrav. Wight l. c. t. 669.—Rheede Mal. III. t. 61.

SPEC. CHAR. Arboreous: leaves alternate, semi-cordate, cuspidate, rough: fruit-receptacles turbinate, ribbed, pedicelled, hairy, umbilicated, in pairs or in threes on long procumbent radical and cauline compound leafless branches, appearing and ripening throughout the year.

Coromandel. Rajmahal. Oude.

(18) F. TOMENTOSA. *(Roxb.)*

Ident. Roxb. l. c. p. 550.

Engrav. Wight l. c. t. 647.

SPEC. CHAR. Branches dropping small roots: leaves oblong, cordate, pointed, very downy underneath: fruit axillary, paired, sessile, woolly.

Southern Peninsula.

(19) F. TUBERCULATA. *(Roxb.)*

Ident. Roxb. l. c. p. 554.

Engrav. Wight l. c. t. 651.

SPEC. CHAR. Small tree: leaves short-petioled, oblong, entire, acute, rough: fruit-receptacles paired, peduncled, roundish, size of a large pea, tubercled.

Coromandel mountains.

(20) F. HEDERACEA. *(Roxb.)*

Ident. Roxb. l. c. p. 538.

Engrav. Wight l. c. t. 653.

SPEC. CHAR. Shrubby, scandent, rooting: leaves ovate, smooth: fruit-receptacles axillary, paired or solitary, sub-sessile, round, scarlet.

Chittagong.

(21) F. FRUTICOSA. *(Roxb.)*

Ident. Roxb. l. c. p. 533.

Engrav. Wight l. c. t. 654.

SPEC. CHAR. Shrubby, spreading: leaves petioled, sub-ovate, entire, quite glabrous, harsh: fruit-receptacles in pairs, longish-peduncled, round.

Chittagong.

(22) F. RAMENTACEA. *(Roxb.)*

Ident. Roxb. l. c. p. 546.

Engrav. Wight l. c. t. 657.

SPEC. CHAR. Arboreous, branches rooting: leaves long, ovate-cordate, acute, entire, glabrous, strongly marked with parallel veins: petioles short, ramentaceous: fruit-receptacles axillary, paired, short-peduncled, smooth, red

Chittagong.

(23) F. comosa. *(Roxb.)*

Ident. Roxb. l. c. p. 552.

Engrav. Wight l. c. t. 658.

Spec. Char. Large tree: branchlets slender, pendulous: leaves oblong, ventricose, pointed, smooth: fruit-receptacles in pairs, usually terminal, turbinate, smooth, red.

Circar mountains.

(24) F. angustifolia. *(Roxb.)*

Ident. Roxb. l. c. p. 554.

Engrav. Wight l. c. t. 660.

Spec. Char. Large tree: leaves sub-opposite, lanceolate, smooth, acute: fruit-receptacles paired, long-peduncled, turbinate, smooth.

Circar mountains.

(25) F. scabrella. *(Roxb.)*

Ident. Roxb. l. c. p. 532.

Engrav. Wight l. c. t. 661.

Spec. Char. Shrubby, scandent: leaves alternate, short-petioled, oblong, remotely serrulate-dentate, scabrous: fruit-receptacles axillary, solitary, peduncled, turbinate, tubercled, size of an olive: scales of the umbilicus ciliate.

Chittagong.

(26) F. obtusifolia. *(Roxb.)*

Ident. Roxb. l. c. p. 546.

Engrav. Wight l. c. t. 662.

Spec. Char. Arboreous: leaves alternate, short-petioled, from cureiform to linear-oblong, thick, glossy: fruit-receptacles axillary, paired or solitary, sessile, round, smooth, yellow.

Chittagong.

(27) F. acuminata. *(Roxb.)*

Ident. Roxb. l. c. p. 538.

Spec. Char. Shrubby, scandent: leaves short petioled, lanceolar, entire, smooth, long-ensiform at the apex: fruit-receptacles twin, sub-sessile.

Chittagong.

(28) F. SQUAMOSA. *(Roxb.)*

Ident. Roxb. l. c. p. 531.

SPEC. CHAR. Shrubby: leaves alternate, short-petioled, turbinate, very scabrous: stipules permanent: fruit solitary or twin, short-peduncled, turbinate, very scabrous, scaly about the apex.

Rohilcund.

(29) F. HIRTA. *(Roxb.)*

Ident. Roxb. l. c. p. 531.

SPEC. CHAR. Arboreous: young parts very hairy: leaves long-petioled, cordate, ciliate, serrated, slightly hairy above, very downy beneath, petioles very shaggy: stipules lanceolate: fruit-receptacles paired, sessile, ovate, hirsute.

Silhet.

(30) F. SCLEROPHYLLA. *(Roxb.)*

Ident. Roxb. l. c. p. 546.

SPEC. CHAR. Large tree: leaves short-petioled, linear-oblong, hard and glossy: fruit-receptacles in pairs, short-peduncled, round, yellow.

Chittagong.

(31) F. URTICIFOLIA. *(Roxb.)*

Ident. Roxb. l. c. p. 553.

SPEC. CHAR. Leaves cordate, 3-nerved, serrate, hispid above, downy underneath: fruit-receptacles in pairs, long-peduncled, turbinate in a rather remote 3-leaved calyx, downy.

Mountains north of Bengal.

(32) F. ROTUNDIFOLIA. *(Roxb.)*

Ident. Roxb. l. c. p. 555.

SPEC. CHAR. Leaves round, scollop-serrate, downy beneath: fruit-receptacles peduncled, numerous about the base of the annual shoot, round, hairy.

Mountains north of Bengal.

ORDER CXLV. ARTOCARPACEÆ.

Milky trees or shrubs: leaves alternate, petioled, simple, entire, or serrate, or pinnately or palmately lobed: stipules free, caducous: flowers monœcious or diœcious, collected together on fleshy, naked or involucrated receptacles, seldom spiked: males rarely destitute of a perianth, stamens and scales densely packed above a globose receptacle, usually with a perianth placed upon a globose or club-shaped receptacle, or more or less densely capitate or spiked, naked or bracteolate, very often sessile on a flat or convex receptacle, surrounded by a many-leaved involucre: perianth 2—3—4-leaved, leaflets usually connate into a tube: stamens as many as the lobes of the perianth or fewer, inserted at the base and opposite them: filaments filiform or linear, free or combined: anthers 2-celled, dehiscing lengthwise: female flowers solitary within an involucre, with or without a perianth, densely capitate or collected on a globose receptacle: perianth limb 2—3—4-cleft or even entire: ovary one, sessile, free, 1-celled: ovule one, style terminal or lateral, often 2-cleft, lobes stigmatose, or undivided, terminated by the simple lateral or radiately many-cleft stigma: fruit various, surrounded by a baccate or dry involucre, or composed of fleshy consolidated calyxes, enclosing numerous nuts: seed erect, parietal or pendulous; embryo with more or less albumen, straight: cotyledons thick, fleshy, often very unequal: radicle short, straight or incurved, directed towards the vertex of the ovary.

GENUS I. ANTIARIS.

Monœcia Tetrandria. *Sex: Syst:*

GEN. CHAR. Flowers monœcious: male involucre many-flowered, many-leaved, leaflets imbricated, connate at the base, surrounding an orbicular, flat or convex receptacle: florets sessile, densely packed: perianth 3—4-leaved: stamens 3—4, filaments very short: anthers extrorse, 2-celled, cell opposite: female involucre 1-flowered, urceolate, many-cleft at the apex: perianth none: ovary 1-celled: ovule pendulous, anatropal: style terminal, 2-cleft, divisions filiform, stigmatose: drupe formed from the fleshy involucre: seed pendulous. —Trees or shrubs, milky: leaves alternate, very shortly petioled, stipulate, unequal-sided, sub-cordate oblong, quite entire, repand or denticulate, costately veined: peduncles axillary, sub-solitary, simple or somewhat branched.

(1) A. SACCIDORA. *(Dalz.)*

Ident. Dalzell in Hook. Journ. Bol. III. p. 232.

Syn. Lepurandra saccidora, *Nimmo in Grah. Cat. Bomb. pl. p.* 193.

Engrav. Wight's Icon. t. 1958.

SPEC. CHAR. Large tree: leaves stipulate, alternate, oblong-elliptic, dentate-serrulate, scabrous, short petioled: flowers on a convex, fleshy, pedicelled receptacle: fruit purple, size of a filbert, 1-seeded.

Concan hills. Khandalla Ghaut. Waree country. Coorg. Flowering in October.

GENUS II. ARTOCARPUS.

Monœcia Monandria. *Sex: Syst:*

Deriv. From *Artos,* bread, and *Karpos* fruit.

GEN. CHAR. Flowers monœcious: males densely clustered together on a club-shaped, ament-like receptacle, ebracteolate: perianth 2—3-leaved, leaflets erect, more or less cohering at the base: stamen one, filament linear, flattened: anther 2-celled, cells opposite: females densely capitately clustered on a globose receptacle, concrescent: ovary free, 1-celled: ovule one, parietal, amphitropal: style long filiform, exserted, lateral: stigma undivided or 2-cleft: syncarp baccate, muricated with utricles between fleshy-thickened densely glued together perianths (many barren ones intermixed), the apices of the perianths pyramidate, free: utricles membranaceous, marked with the remains of the style, dehiscing lengthways: seed ovate, parietal.—Milky trees: leaves alternate, short-petioled, obovate, entire, pinnatifid-lobed, scabrous beneath: stipules very large, coriaceous, hiding the buds: peduncles axillary, at first enclosed in spathiform stipules, soon deciduous, lateral by the fall of the leaf.

(1) A. HIRSUTA. *(Lam.)*

Ident. Lam. encycl. III. p. 201. Roxb. flor. Ind. III. p. 521.

Engrav. Wight's Icon. t. 1957. Rheede Mal. III. t. 32.

SPEC. CHAR. Leaves elliptic, obtuse, or rounded at both ends, glabrous above, hairy especially on the nerves, beneath: male catkins long cylindric, about the thickness of a quill, at first ascending or erect, afterwards pendulous: females oval, size of an egg: fruit globose, echinate.

Malabar. Travancore.

(2) A. Lakoocha. *(Roxb.)*

Ident. Roxb. flor. Ind. III. p. 524.

Engrav. Wight l. c. t. 681.

Spec. Char. Leaves oval, entire, pointed, smooth above, downy beneath: catkins axillary, male sub-sessile, female short-peduncled, globular: fruit with a smooth surface, of an irregular roundish form, yellow when ripe.

Caranjah Hill. Bassein. Bengal.

(3) A. integrifolia. *(Willd.)*

Ident. Willd. iv. p. 184. Roxb. l. c. p. 522.

Syn. A. heterophylla, *Lam.* Polyphema Jaca, *Lour.*

Engrav. Roxb. Cor. III. t. 250. Wight l. c. t. 678. Rheede Mal. III. t. 26, 27, 28. Bot. Mag. 55 t. 2833—4.

Spec. Char. Leaves petioled, oval, firm, deep shining green above: male ament about 2 inches, female oblong: fruit very large, oblong-muricated, growing from the trunk.

Peninsula. Bengal.

(4) A. Chaplasha. *(Roxb.)*

Ident. Roxb. l. c. p. 525.

Engrav. Wight l. c. t. 682.

Spec. Char. Leaves in the adult obovate, entire, in the young ones pinnatifid: aments axillary, long-peduncled, sub-rotund: fruit spherical.

Tipperah. Chittagong.

ORDER CXLVI. PODOSTEMACEÆ.

Flowers hermaphrodite or unisexual by abortion, axillary or terminal, solitary or aggregated, distichously spiked or sub-racemose, very small: spathe sessile, simple, tubulose, at length irregularly bursting, or 2—3-many-leaved, enclosing a solitary at first sessile flower, then very often the flower elevated on a more or less long stalk: perianth none or 2—3-many-leaved, leaflets free, sometimes unilateral: stamen one, two, or indefinite, hypogynous, surrounding and adpressed to the ovary: filaments free, or cohering at the base, or even combined into a tube, compressed, acute, sometimes 2-forked at the apex: anthers introrse, 2-celled, affixed at the back above the base, erect, ovate or oblong: cells opposite, dehiscing lengthways: ovary globose or elliptic, 2—3-celled, placentæ broadly swelling from the central angle of the cells, or 1-celled by abortion: ovules numerous ascending, amphitropal: styles the number of the cells, undivided or 2-cleft, persistent, stigmatose within: capsule ribbed, 2—3-celled, crowned by the persistent styles, opening by 2—3-valves, which fall off from the dissepiments: seeds very minute, imbricated: albumen none: embryo orthotropal: radicle inferior, very short.—Aquatic herbs, submersed, stems usually floating: leaves alternate, occasionally imbricated, laciniated or entire, laciniæ usually capillary, very tender, decurrent into the stem and branches, destitute of stomata.

GENUS I. DICRÆA.

Monadelphia Digynia. *Sex: Syst:*

Gen. Char. Staminodes two, equal, linear, the third usually aborting: stamens 2, monadelphous: anthers ovate: pollen didymous: stigmas short, subulate, short, entire: capsule many-nerved: flowers radical, solitary, terminal or racemose.

(1) D. longifolia. *(R. Wight.)*

Ident. Wight's Icon. v. t. 1916—4.

Spec. Char. Stems compressed, branched, alternately nodose, lower nodes leafy only, terminal ones flower-bearing: leaves of the lower nodes long-linear, strap-shaped, of the flower-bearings ones sheathing at the base, subulate above, 2—3-times the length of the 3-lobed spathe: capsule 3-ribbed.

Malabar.

(2) D. dichotoma. *(Tul.)*

Ident. Gardner in Calc. Journ. Nat. Hist. (under Podostemon.)

Engrav. Wight l. c. t. 1916—2.

Spec. Char. Stems long, naked, compressed, slender, flexible, sparingly and dichotomously branched: branches simple, long, nearly parallel, somewhat flexuose, sparingly floriferous towards the apex: leaves few, subulate, short, partly cohering: capsule 8-ribbed, ribs somewhat prominent.

Pycarrah river, Neilgherries.

(3) D. Wightii. *(Tul.)*

Ident. Gardn. l. c. (under Podostemon.)

Engrav. Wight l. c. t. 1916—3.

Spec. Char. Stems compressed, 2-edged, flexuose, bud-bearing at the angles : leaves narrow-linear, simple, sheathing at the base : capsule 8-striated.

Pycarrah river, Neilgherries.

(4) D. rigida. *(Tul.)*

Ident.. Gardn. l. c. (under Podostemon.)

Engrav. Wight l. c. t. 1916—5.

Spec. Char. Branches long, rigid, dichotomous, parallel, leafless: the flowering ones compressed: flowers secured with a double involucre.

Pycarrah river, Neilgherries.

(5) D. stylosa. *(R. Wight.)*

Ident. Wight l. c. 1917—2.

Spec. Char. Stems very long, branched, compressed, leafless: flowers distichous on the margin: involucre 4-leaved, imbricating, distichous, inner pair smaller, outer nearly equalling the spathe, obtuse, sheathing at the base, sub-cuspidate at the point: styles pubescent, equalling or exceeding the ovary: capsule 6-ribbed.

Mountain streams in Malabar.

(6) D. Wallichii. *(Tul.)*

Ident. Tulasne Ann. des Sc. (3rd Series) II. 1849.

Syn. Podostemon Wallichii, *R. Br.*

Engrav. Wight l. c. t. 1916—1.

Spec. Char. Frond greenish, middle-sized, lobately crisped on the margin, veined, free and fructiferous on the circumference: capsule 8-ribbed, obtuse: valves somewhat incurved at the apex.

Silhet.

GENUS II. HYDROBRYUM.

Monadelphia Digynia. *Sex: Syst:*

Deriv. From *Hydor*, water, and *Bryo*, to grow, alluding to the habitat of the plants.

Gen. Char. Involucre small, ellipsoid, bladder-shaped, splitting along one side only and then boat-shaped, 2-valved: staminodes 2, linear: stigmas 2, sometimes tooth-like, entire, sometimes dilated, membranous, wedge-shaped, toothed: capsule 8—12-ribbed.—Frondose herbs with scattered floriferous buds and few leaves.

(1) H. GRISEUM. *(Tul.)*

Ident. Tul. Ann. des Sciences.

Syn. Podostemon griseum, *Gardn. Calc. Journ. Nat. Hist.*

Engrav. Wight's Icon. t. 1918—3.

SPEC. CHAR. Rhizome unequal, repand, greyish: leafy buds numerous: fronds decumbent, sub-orbicular, lobes undulated, greyish: flowers springing from the upper part of the frond: scales 6, distichous: spathe somewhat 2-valved, rough: capsule 8-nerved.

Pycarrah river, Neilgherries.

GENUS III. MNIOPSIS.

Monadelphia Digynia. *Sex: Syst:*

Deriv. From *Mnion*, moss, and *Opsis*, appearance.

GEN. CHAR. Involucre utriform, obovate, somewhat tubular, mouth several-lobed or toothed: staminodes 2—3, linear, the middle one attached to the anther-bearing filament, or wanting: stigmas sometimes thick, several-lobed, sometimes slightly elongated, entire: capsule spherical, quite smooth, small.—Caulescent or frondose herbs: flowers terminal, or sub-racemose.

(1) M. HOOKERIANA. *(Tul.)*

Ident. Tulasne l. c. vol. II.

Engrav. Wight l. c. t. 1918—4.

SPEC. CHAR. Rhizome frond-like, thick, variously repand, bearing buds on the margin, buds 1-flowered: leaves few, short or scale-like, ovate-oblong, entire, distichously equitant: stigmas angular, elongated, entire, distinct.

Rivers near Bombay.

(2) M. JOHNSONII. *(R. Wight.)*

Ident. Wight l. c. t. 1918—5.

SPEC. CHAR. Rhizome decumbent, sub-orbicular, variously repand on the margin: flower-buds scattered over the surface, 1-flowered:

leaves 4—6, short-ovate, obtuse, imbricating: stigmas dentiform: capsule globose, not ribbed.

Rivers in Malabar.

GENUS IV. DALZELLIA.

Triandria Trigynia. *Sex: Syst:*

GEN. CHAR. Perianth calycine, 3-parted, veinless, lobes equal, imbricated in æstivation: stamens free, alternate with the lobes: stigmas sessile, linear, short, diverging: capsule 3-celled, longitudinally 9-ribbed.—Frondose plants broadly expanding on all sides, linearly branched: leaves entire: bud connate into an open tube: flowers scattered and terminal.

(1) D. FOLIOSA. *(R. Wight.)*

Ident. Wight's Icon. v. t. 1919—2.

SPEC. CHAR. Rhizome spreading, lichen-like, lobed and free on the margin, buds for the most part on the free margins: leaves numerous, fascicled round the base of the pedicel, linear, pointed: no sheath: pedicel 2—3-times the length of the leaves,

Rivers in Salsette, near Bombay.

(2) D. LAWII. *(R. Wight.)*

Ident. Wight l. c. t. 1919—3.

SPEC. CHAR. Rhizome spreading, margins free, gemmiferous: leaves surrounding the sheath few, short, broader than those within, somewhat lanceolate: those of the sheath very numerous, short, needle-shaped, recurved: capsule ovoid, scarcely angled.

Salsette, near Bombay.

(3) D. PEDUNCULOSA. *(R. Wight.)*

Ident. Wight l. c. t. 1919—4.

SPEC. CHAR. Rhizome spreading, margins free, lobed, gemmiferous: leaves all aggregated and united to form the sheath, short, bristle-like: peduncle 6—8-times the length of the sheath, very slender: capsule ovoid, round or scarcely angled.

Salsette, near Bombay.

(4) D. RAMOSISSIMA. *(R. Wight.)*

Ident. Wight l. c. t. 1920.

SPEC. CHAR. Rhizome very long, slender, much branched with numerous lateral floriferous branchlets, with one or several flowers aggregated towards the apex, each flower-bud usually accompanied with 2 slender filiform leafy branchlets: leaves subulate, imbricating, outer ones short, obtuse, middle ones longer, acute, inner ones forming the short sheath: filaments very short, afterwards elongated: anthers oblong, sagittate at the base, cells distinct: styles filiform, hispid, the length of the ovary.

Rivers in Malabar, near Cochin.

(5) D. PULCHELLA.

Ident. Tulasne Monogr. Podost. p. 189 (under Terniola).—Dalz. Bomb. flor. p. 245.

Syn. Lawia pulchella, *Tul.* Mnianthus pulchellus, *Walpers.*

SPEC. CHAR. Rhizome thin, linear, branched, short: flower-bearing here and there: leaves linear, marked with a whitish line in the middle, distichous, interior ones the flower-bearing bud, verticelled and united at the base: pedicel of middling length.

Concan rivers.

(6) D. LONGIPES.

Ident. Tul. l. c.—Dalz. l. c. (under Terniola.)

Syn. Mnianthus longipes, *Walp. Ann. III.* 443.

SPEC. CHAR. Rhizome thin, broadly linear, sparingly branched: leaves long-linear, acute, marked with a whitish line, near the flower inserted in a circle, and at the same time united downwards: flowers long-pedicelled.

Concan rivers.

ORDER CXLVII. CHLORANTHACEÆ.

Shrubs or small trees with aromatic taste and smell: branches nodosely articulated: leaves opposite, petioled, simple, penninerved, serrated or rarely quite entire, petioles connate at the base into a short stem-clasping sheath bistipulate on both sides: inflorescence spiked, terminal or rarely axillary: flowers small, hermaphrodite, densely spiked, or diclinous, males spiked, females sub-panicled, sessile, each somewhat immersed in a navicular bract or seldom naked: perianth none: stamens in the males solitary, few, and sustained by a small bract at the base, or packed and imbricated, naked: filament very short: anther 2-celled, cells linear, margining the connectivum, dehiscing lengthwise, in the hermaphrodites one stamen or three, conferruminate with the back of the ovary: filaments keeled, connate at the base: lateral ones smaller: anther 1-celled, furnished with a 1 celled anther, the intermediate longer anther 2-celled, cells opposite, open lengthways: ovary one, sessile, 1-celled: ovule one, orthotropal: stigma terminal, sessile, sulcate-emarginate or sub-bilobed, deciduous: drupe baccate, sub-globose or triquetrous, 1-seeded, putamen thin, fragile: seed pendulous: testa membranaceous: albumen copious, fleshy: embryo small, enclosed in the apex of the albumen: radicle inferior opposite the point of insertion of the seed from the diameter.

GENUS I. CHLORANTHUS.

Triandria Monogynia. *Sex: Syst:*

Deriv. From *Chloros*, green, and *Anthos*, flower.

Gen. Char. Flowers loosely spiked, each bracteated: stamens 3, inserted on the ovary above the base: filaments broadly dilated, 3-lobed, middle lobe bearing a perfect 2-celled anther, each of the lateral ones a 1-celled one: ovary ovate, 1-celled: ovule pendulous: stigma sub-capitate or depressed: drupe 1-seeded.—Annual herbs or under-shrubs: branches nodosely jointed: leaves opposite, petioled, entire or serrated, petioles dilated at the base, connate with intra-axillary stipules: spikes axillary or terminal, simple or branched.

(1) C. Indicus. *(R.W.)*

Ident. Wight's Icon. vi. t. 1945.

Spec. Char. Shrubby, branched: leaves short-petioled, broad oval, obtuse at both ends, crenately serrated, glabrous: peduncles terminal, spicately panicled: flowers numerous, sessile.

Station not given.

GENUS II. SARCANDRA.

Monandria Monogynia. *Sex: Syst:*

Deriv. From *Sarx* flesh, and *Aner*, *andros*, male, in allusion to the fleshy filament.

GEN. CHAR. Flowers sessile in a boat-shaped bract: perianth none: stamen one, inserted on the ovary: filament thick and fleshy: anther introrse, 2-celled: ovary 1-celled with a single pendulous ovule: stigma sessile, depressed: drupe 1-seeded: embryo enclosed in fleshy albumen: radicle inferior.

(1) S. CHLORANTHOIDES. *(Gardner.)*

Ident. Gardn. in Calc. Journ. vi. p. 348.

Engrav. Wight's Icon. t. 1946.

SPEC. CHAR. Shrubby: branches nodosely articulated: leaves opposite, petioled, penninerved, coarsely glanduloso-serrate: petioles uniting at the base into a short, stem-clasping sheath: inflorescence terminal, paniculately spiked.

Pulney mountains. Courtallum.

ORDER CXLVIII. PIPERACEÆ.

Perennial herbs, seldom annual, succulent, stem scarcely any or usually branched, erect or creeping, or shrubs very often scandent, seldom arborescent, nodosely branched: leaves alternate, opposite or verticelled, petioled or very seldom sessile, quite entire, fleshy, coriaceous or membranaceous: stipules in some plants none, in others petiolar, twin, free or adnate, deciduous or persistent: flowers arranged on peduncled, axillary, solitary, filiform, cylindric or globose aments, densely packed, lax, most frequently sessile, each supported by a bract, but destitute of a perianth, naked: stamens most frequently 2, situated at either side of the germen, seldom 3—5, sometimes 10: filaments deciduous or persistent, thin or thick, free or adnate to the base of the germen, sometimes very short: anthers extrorse, 2-celled, oblong, ovate or reniform, cells apposite or opposite, or adnate lengthways to the connectivum, dehiscing lengthways: germen one, 1-celled: style none or cylindric, simple: stigma one, sessile, simple, penicillate, or stigmas 2—6, thick, lanceolate or oblong: berries without juice or pulpy, distinct or cohering in masses, oblong, globose, 3—4-gonal, sometimes cuneiform: seed erect from the base, integument membranaceous, coriaceous or sub-crustaceous, smooth or areolate: albumen mealy, fleshy or sub-cartilaginous, solid or hollow in the centre: embryo minute, half-immersed at the apex of the albumen, antitropal: radicle short, superior: cotyledons two, very short, obtuse, hypogæous in germination.

GENUS I. PEPEROMIA.

Diandria Monogynia. *Sex: Syst:*

GEN. CHAR. Flowers perfect, densely or loosely amentaceous: bract petioled or sub-sessile, persistent or deciduous: stamens 2, lateral, free: germen ovate or oblong, sessile or sometimes half immersed on the rhaches, 1-celled: stigma undivided, sessile or on the styliform apex of the germen, sub-orbicular: berry sometimes sessile, sometimes pedicelled or stalked or contracted at the base, obliquely ovate or sub-globose: seed conformable, erect: albumen mealy.—Herbs, sometimes suffrutescent, erect or creeping, very often rooting, branched, succulent: branches and leaves alternate, opposite or verticelled, usually petioled, ribbed or many-nerved, sometimes coloured, glabrous, pubescent or tomentose: aments axillary, or spuriously terminal from the axils of the uppermost leaves, or leaf-opposed, pedicelled, rhachis smooth or pitted.

(1) P. DINDIGULENSIS. *(Miq.)*

Ident. Miquel syst. Piper. 63.

Engrav. Wight's Icon. t. 1921.

SPEC. CHAR. Erect, branches opposite: succulent, puberulous or rarely glabrous: leaves shortly petioled, opposite (lower ones sometimes alternate and the terminal ones ternate): elliptic, obovate, or the larger ones rhombeo-obovate, acute at the base, rounded, obtuse or shortly acuminate at the apex, 5-nerved, sparingly puberulous or sometimes glabrous: catkins terminal, short peduncled, filiform erect, flowers somewhat remote: stigma puberulous: berries globose.

Pulney Mountains. Anamally Hills. Neilgherries.

(2) P. HEYNEANA. *(Miq.)*

Ideut. Miq. l. c.

Engrav. Wight l. c. t, 1922—1.

SPEC. CHAR. Erect, decumbent, and rooting below, succulent, stem pilose or glabrous: leaves opposite, the upper ones in whorls of three and four, lanceolate-elliptic, obtuse or emarginate at the apex, acute or cuneate at the base, glabrous, brown spotted, sometimes slightly ciliate at the apex, 1-nerved with smaller vein-ribs, or somewhat 3-nerved from the 2 ribs rising at the base: catkins axillary and terminal, peduncled, filiform, erect: flowers somewhat remote: ovary ovate, bearing the stigma on the apex.

Alpine stations in woods or open rocky ground near springs.

(3) P. PORTULACOIDES. *(Dietr. Miq.)*

Ident. Dietr. Miq. in Wight l. c. t, 1922 Hook. Journ. Bot. v. p. 550.

SPEC. CHAR. Succulent, glabrous, sparingly branched, creeping, deeply rooting, leafless below: leaves opposite, upper ones ternate, short petioled, succulent, glanduloso-punctuate, obovate, oblong, or sub-spathulate, obsoletely 3, rarely 5-nerved: aments axillary and terminal, solitary, longish peduncled shorter than the peduncles, cylindrical, obtuse.

Common in Alpine localities.

(4) P. REFLEXA. *(Dietr. Miq.)*

Ident. Dietr. Miq. in Wight Icon. t, 1923—1.

SPEC. CHAR. Succulent, coriaceous, rooting at the base, ascending, erect, di-or-trichotomously branched, slightly puberulous or glabrous: leaves ternate or quaternate, (rarely six at the forks), petioled, pellucid-dotted, rhomb-elliptic, obtuse or roundish, contracting below into a short petiole, minutely puberulous, obsoletely 3-nerved below, speckled with depressed brown points: petioles united into a ring at the base: peduncles terminal, nearly as long as the catkins: catkins cylindric, deeply pitted, rough.

Neilgherries and other Alpine ranges.

(5) P. COURTALLENSIS. *(Miq.)*

Ident. Miq. in Hook. Journ. Bot. v. p. 549.

Engrav. Wight l. c. t, 1923—2.

SPEC. CHAR. Erect, succulent, glabrous, oppositely and alternately branched: leaves moderately petioled, opposite, or the upper ones verticelled, and usually larger, all varying in form and size, elliptic-oblong, or obovate, acute, or attenuated at the base, rounded or alternately obtuse and emarginate at the apex; and there the younger ones ciliolate, equal or unequal-sided, pellucid-punctuate, pale beneath, obsoletely 1 or 3-nerved: catkins axillary or terminal, solitary or aggregated, erect, straightish, longish peduncled, rather densely flowered: berries somewhat immersed, obliquely ovate.

Courtallum, forming patches on branches of trees or on moist rocks, flowering in August and September.

(6) P. Wightiana. (*Miq.*)

Ident. Miq. in Wight Icon. vi. t, 1924.

Spec. Char. Herbaceous, succulent, erect, rooting at the base, pubescent: leaves alternate, or the upper ones opposite, petioled, the lower ones smaller, roundish or obovate, the rest elliptic or obovate-elliptic obtuse, acute at the base, glabrous, the younger ones somewhat ciliate at the apex, obsoletely 3-nerved, pellucid pointed, pale beneath: aments longish peduncled, axillary, solitary, or the terminal ones aggregated, filiform, erect, remotely flowered: berries ovate, sub-oblique.

Malabar, in woods.

GENUS II. POTHOMORPHE.

Diandria Monogynia. *Sex: Syst.*

Deriv. Plants having the appearance of a *Pothos.*

Gen. Char. Flowers perfect, densely amentaceous on a filiform rhachis: bracts long-stalked, peltate, leaf triangular or oblong, glandulose, villous-fimbriate, persistent: stamens 2, lateral, free, filaments thin, anthers reniform, 2 celled: germen 3-cornered: stigmas 3, cylindric-filiform, recurved: berries obovate-turbinate, triangular by mutual pressure, truncate at the apex, glabrous pericarp very thin, loosening: seed smooth, integument crustaceous: albumen mealy, very white.—Under-shrubs, erect, beset with numerous pellucid glands: leaves large, cordate, sometimes peltate, many-nerved, glabrous, puberulous or seldom tomentose, petioles sheathing, winged: aments sub-umbellate on axillary branches, unequal, pedicelled, enclosed before flowering by the petiole and stipulaceous, afterwards deciduous, bracts: berries very minute, obovate-trigonal.

(1) P. subpeltata. (*Miq.*)

Ident. Miquel. Syst. Piper. 202.

Engrav. Wight's Icon. t, 1925.

Spec. Char. Leaves membranaceous, pellucid-dotted, roundish-reniform, cordate, acute, 11—13-nerved, middle nerve 3-cleft above the base: petioles partly winged, wing evanescent: peduncles paired, unequal, 2 or several-spiked: bracts triangular, ciliated: seed black, areolate, obovate, 3-sided.

Courtallum. Eastern slopes of the Neilgherries, and other sub-Alpine forests in moist localities.

GENUS III. CUBEBA.

Diœcia Pentandria. *Sex: Syst:*

GEN. CHAR. Flowers diœcious, amentaceous, sessile. MALES. Bracts oblong, sessile, imbricated: stamens 2—5: filaments tapering, anthers ovate or reniform. FEMALES. Bracts peltate, subsessile, persistent, oblong or orbiculate, often hairy beneath: germen sessile, ovate: stigmas 3—5, sessile, short, thick, hispidulous above: berries with a constricted base spuriously pedicelled, sub-globose, pericarp thin: seed roundish, integument coriaceo-membranaceous, or horny: albumen mealy.—Small trees or scandent shrubs: leaves petioled, 3-many-nerved or ribbed, glabrous or pubescent: aments leaf-opposed at the cauldine knots, males slender, females stronger, fructiferous ones simulating a raceme.

(1) C. WALLICHII *(Miq.)*

Ident. Miquel. Syst. Piper. 285.

Engrav. Wight's Icon. t, 1932.

SPEC. CHAR. Leaves not dotted, oblong, slightly unequal-sided, acute, deeply cordate, equal at the base, lobes rounded, 9 to 13-plinerved, the three middle nerves remote from the base: berry-bearing catkins spreading, thick, berries globose, a little produced at the apex by the remains of the stigma, pedicel thickened upwards.

Malabar.

GENUS IV. CHAVICA.

Diœcia Diandria. *Sex: Syst:*

Deriv. The Malabar name Latinised.

GEN. CHAR. Flowers diœcious, very densely amentaceous, aments leaf-opposed, those bearing pistils thicker: bracts stalked, peltate, persistent, leaf round or rhomboid, coriaceous. MALES. Bracts short, stamens 2 lateral, seldom 3—4: filaments short, anthers ovate sub-globose, connectivum thickish. FEMALES. Germen sessile, oval, angular: stigmas 3—6, sessile, cuspidate, short, thick, puberulous above: berries closely sessile on the tumid rhachis, polygonous, pulpy, umbonate with the rudiments of the stigmas: seed oblong or lenticular, integument crustaceous, very finely pitted, shining: albumen granular mealy, sometimes horny at the circumference.—Scandent shrubs: leaves alternate, petioled, cordate-rounded, ovate, oblong, lanceolate, equilateral or oblique, coriaceous or membranaceous, glabrous or pubescent, ribbed, multiple or digitinerved, often different on the same stem, stipuled: aments leaf-opposed, peduncled, diœcious, cylindric or very rarely globose, berry-bearing ones swollen: bracts coloured, berries horizontal.

(1) C. PEEPULOIDES. *(Miq.)*

Ident. Miq. l. c. t, 1927.

Syn. Piper peepuloides, *Roxb. flor. Ind.* I. 157.

SPEC. CHAR. Young parts puberulous: leaves membranaceous, pellucid-dotted, glabrous, lower ones ovate, equal-sided, rounded at the base, acuminate at the apex, septuple or 7-nerved, upper ones oblong-lanceolate or lanceolate, unequal-sided, slightly unequal at the base, acute or acuminate at the apex, quintuple-nerved: male catkins short-peduncled, straight or curved, much shorter than the leaves: bracts shortly pedicelled, peltate, orbicular.

Silhet. Khasia hills.

(2) C. SYLVATICA. *(Miq.)*

Ident. Miq. l. c. t, 1930

Syn. Piper sylvaticum, *Roxb. l. c. p.* 158.

SOEC. CHAR. Stem fruticose, scandent, glabrous, leaves petioled, equally cordate, obtuse, base of the lobes broad orbicular, 5—7-nerved, glabrous: male catkins shortly peduncled, slender, female, short, cylindrical: stamens four.

Assam. Khasia hills.

(3) C. SPHŒROSTACHYA. *(Miq.)*

Ident. Miq. l. c. t, 1931.

SPEC. CHAR. Glabrous: leaves somewhat coriaceous, scarcely pellucid-dotted, elliptic, unequal-sided, acute, or cuneate at the base, acuminate, acumen blunt, sometimes mucronate, septuple-nerved: male catkins filiform, female globose: bracts pedicelled, orbiculate: stigmas thin, short, recurved, connate at the base.

Neilgherries in flower and fruit all the year, climbing over trees.

GENUS V. MULDERA.

Diœcia Decandria. *Sex: Syst:*

GEN. CHAR. Flowers diœcious, amentaceous, each bursting from a fleshy, gibbous cup, at first closed and afterwards transvereley cleft and somewhat helmet-shaped 2-lobed. MALES. Stamens 5—10, in one or two rows, mixed with bristle-shaped hairs: filaments short, thick, anthers ovate, cells separated by a thick connectivum. FEMALES. Germen sub-globose: stigmas 3—4, linear, puberulous: berries sub-globose, supported by a fleshy cup: seed conformable, hilum broad: albumen radiate, horny at the circumference, mealy in the centre. — Shrubs, arborescent, erect or climbing: leaves alternate, petioled, coriaceous, glabrous, tripli-septupli-nerved: flowers on a rachis at first as if naked, with closed bracts, afterwards thickened: berries large, rather remote, red.

(1) M. Wightiana. *(Miq.)*

Ident. Miq. in Wight Icon. t, 1943.

Spec. Char. Leaves ovate or ovate-elliptic, obliquely and acutely acuminate, equal and roundish at the base, septuple-nerved, the three middle nerves continued to the apex, (reddish beneath), membranaceous coriaceous, pellucid-dotted: male catkins long-peduncled, filiform, longer than the leaves, many-flowered: cups reflexed, clavate, opening transversely near the apex, hairy within.

Courtallum in dense forests, flowering in July and August.

(2) M. galeata. *(Miq.)*

Ident. Miq. l. c.

Spec. Char. Leaves broad or lanceolate-elliptic, somewhat ovate and acuminate, slightly unequal-sided, obtuse or acutish at the base, septuple or quintuple-nerved, the middle nerves from a little above the base extending to the apex, somewhat stiffly coriaceous, pellucid-dotted, female catkins long-peduncled, shorter than the leaves, glabrous: flowers rather remote, cups obliquely clavate, the exterior lip galeate, interior smaller: ovary depressed, globose: stigmas 3—4, small.

Courtallum. Neilgherries. Probably the female plant of No. 1.

(3) M. trichostachya. *(Miq.)*

Ident. Miq. l. c. t, 1944.

Spec. Char. Upper leaves lanceolate, or oblong-lanceolate, equal-sided, acutely acuminate, base equal, obtuse or acute, quintuple-nerved, coriaceous, pellucid-dotted: peduncles glabrous, about the length of the petioles: male catkins elongated: cups obliquely sub-globose, constricted at the base, puberulous or hairy within.

Malabar, in forests climbing on trees.

GENUS VI. PIPER.

Diandria Trigynia. *Sex: Syst:*

Gen. Char. Flowers diclinous or perfect, amentaceous, rather remote: bracts coriaceous, oblong, linear, adnate, so approximated by the base apex and elevated margins, that each flower is enclosed by the apex of its own bract, the next resting on the base and margins of the two collateral ones, very rarely rounded and attached by the centre. Perfect flowers. Stamens 2, lateral, filaments very thick, often adhering to the base of the germen, a long time persistent, anthers cordate-reniform, cells separated: germen sessile, ovate: stigmas 3—4, very seldom 5, thickly lanceolate or oblong, puberulous, deflexed. STAMINIGEROUS FLOWERS. Stamens 2—3, more tender. PISTILLIGEROUS FLOWERS. Germen as in the perfect flowers, without the rudiments of stamens: berries sessile, oblong or globose, pulpy: seed conformable, integument membranaceous or thickly coriaceous: albumen horny-mealy, radiate. —Scandent shrubs, seldom small trees: leaves alternate, petioled, usually coriaceous, multipli or digitinerved, glabrous or pubescent, stipules petiolar adnate and leaf-opposed, deciduous: aments leaf-opposed, peduncled, most frequently pendulous, filiform: berries remote, sessile.

(1) P. SYLVESTRE. *(Lam.)*

Ident. Miquel in Hook Journ. Bot. v. p. 552.

Engrav. Wight's Icon. t, 1937.

SPEC. CHAR. Stem shrubby, scandent, rooting: leaves membranaceous, pellucid-dotted, glabrous, green above, glaucous beneath, ovate-acuminate, oblique at the base, or in the lower ones somewhat cordate and equal, 7-nerved, the three middle ones extending to the apex: male catkins peduncled, filiform, pendulous: bracts linear-oblong: female about the length of the leaves, bracts oblong, roughish beneath: stigmas 4, reflexed, deciduous.

Courtallum. Western Ghauts, climbing on trunks of trees.

(2) P. HOOKERI. *(Miq.)*

Ident. Miq. l. c. iv. p. 437.—Dalz. Bomb. flor. p. 315.

SPEC. CHAR. Branches, petioles, peduncles and nerves on the under side of the leaves hairy: leaves between coriaceous and membranaceous, thickly pellucid-dotted, smooth above, broadly ovate and equal-sided, shortly acuminate, the acumen obtuse, 5—7-nerved: peduncle longer than the petiole: bracts oblong, decurrent and adnate: ovary ovate: stigmas 4, short, thick, puberulous.

Mahableshwar hills.

(3) P. ATTENUATUM. *(Hamilt.)*

Ident. Hamilt. in Wight Icon. vi. t, 1933.

SPEC. CHAR. Scandent, rooting and giving off suckers, young shoots glabrous: leaves membranaceous, obsoletely pellucid-dotted, glabrous above, the petioles veins and nerves beneath roughish, the lower ones long-petioled, cordate, ovate-acuminate, 9-nerved, upper ones broadly ovate, truncated at the base, 7 or septuple-nerved: female catkins slender, filiform, short-peduncled, peduncle much shorter than the leaves: bracts adnate, oblong: ovary elliptic: stigmas 4, roundish, reflexed.

Eastern slopes of the Neilgherries.

(4) P. TRIOICUM. *(Roxb.)*

Ident. Roxb. flor. Ind. I. p. 157.

Engrav. Wight's Icon. t, 1935—6.

SPEC. CHAR. Shrubby, sarmentose, and creeping: leaves coriaceous, dark green above, light glaucous below, somewhat obliquely elliptic, acuminate, rounded or sub-acute at the base, the upper ones lanceolate-oblong, 5- 7- tuple-nerved: catkins trioicous: males filiform, females more rigid and shorter: bracts 3 series, of the hermaphrodite 4 series, the younger ones delicately ciliate, some glabrous: floriferous pit rough: ovary sub-globose, 3—4 stigmas: floriferous calycule of the hermaphrodite catkins 2-lobed.

Circars. Southern. Peninsula in forests.

(5) P. NIGRUM. *(Linn.)*

Ident. Roxb. flor. Ind. I. p. 150.

Engrav. Wight's Icon. t, 1934.—Rheede Mal. vii. t, 12.

SPEC. CHAR. Shrubby, climbing, rooting: leaves coriaceous, glabrous, pale glaucous beneath, lower ones roundish-ovate, about equal-sided, slightly cordate or truncated at the base, septuple or noveno-nerved, namely the three middle ones separating above the base and extending to the point, upper ones ovate-elliptic, usually unequal-sided, acutely acuminate, 7—5-nerved: catkins hermaphrodite or female, filiform, pendulous, shortly peduncled, shorter than the leaves: bracts linear-oblong, yellow on the margin: rachis between the bracts rough: stamens 2, thick, stigmas 3—4, rarely 5, thick, lanceolate: berries globose, red when ripe: floriferous calycule in the hermaphrodite catkins 4-lobed.

Malabar forests.

(6) P. NEPALENSE. *(Miq.)*

Ident. Miq. in Wight Icon. vi. t, 1938.

SPEC. CHAR. Younger leaves membranaceous, adult ones membranaceo-coriaceous, glabrous on both sides, pellucid-dotted, lower ones obliquely ovate or elliptic-ovate, nearly equal and rounded at the base, acuminate, and like those of the branches 7-tuple-nerved, those of the male plant narrower: female catkins erect, afterwards spreading about the length of the leaves: bracts oblong, beneath, and the rachis roughish: ovary acuminate: stigmas 3—4, lanceolate, deflexed, pubescent: berries ovate, acute.

Courtallum, in dense forests, climbing on trees.

(7) P. Wightii. *(Miq.)*

Ident. Miq. l. c. and t, 1939.

Spec. Char. Leaves coriaceous, membranaceous, finely pellucid-dotted, glabrous, smooth above, beneath on the younger ones sparingly hairy, ovate or elliptic-ovate, shortly acuminate, slightly unequal, rounded at the base, 7-nerved: female catkins afterwards elongating, equalling or exceeding the leaves, spreading: peduncles longer than the petioles: bracts oblong, linear, somewhat membranaceous: stigmas 3 or 4.

Pulney mountains. Courtallum.

(8) P. arborescens. *(Miq.)*

Ident. Miq. l. c. and t, 1940.

Spec. Char. Shrubby, scandent, younger leaves membranaceous, adult ones thick, coriaceous, shining above, glaucescent beneath, puberulous on the nerves, elliptic or ovate-elliptic, obliquely shortly acuminate, unequal at the base, 5 or somewhat 7-tuple-nerved: peduncles about the length of the petioles: male catkins short, somewhat curved: bracts orbicular, diandrous: females filiform, pendulous, at length very long: bracts linear-oblong, sessile: stigmas 3—4: berries oblong, red when ripe.

Neilgherries.

(9) P. argyrophyllum. *(Miq.)*

Ident. Miq. l. c. and t, 1941.

Spec. Char. Glabrous: upper leaves membranaceous, thickly white-spotted beneath, light opaque green above, obliquely elliptic-lanceolate, taperingly acuminate, nearly equal-sided, acute or cuneatly tapering at the base, the lower septuple, the upper ones quintuple-nerved, the lateral nerves not extending to the apex: female catkins peduncled: peduncles about the length of or exceeding the petioles: bracts oblong, glabrous above, sub-ciliate: ovary elliptic, glabrous: stigmas 3—4, broadly lanceolate from the base, revolutely recurved, pubescent: berries ovate, shortly beaked, black when dry: testa of the seed dark brown, shining, wrinkled.

Courtallum. The *P. hymenophyllum. (Miq.)* Wight Icon. t, 1942 appears to be the female plant of the preceding.

ORDER CXLIX. CUPULIFERÆ.

Flowers monœcious, spiked, spikes for the most part unisexual, sometimes females at the base, males above: male flowers solitary or glomerate on an amentum, with or without bracts: stamens 5—20 from the bottom of the perianth, free, filaments slender, anthers 2-celled: rudimentary ovary free or none: pollen globose, smooth, 3-lobed. Female flowers single or few immersed in a cupula, the cup bracteate at the base, furnished with scales, and even sometimes with prickles, or slowly growing segments: perianth regular, usually 6-lobed: ovary inferior, 1—3- (seldom 4—7-) celled: ovules twin in each cell, erect or pendulous, anatropal, furnished with a double integument: styles as many as the cells, superposed on them, undivided, stigmatose upwards: fruit consisting of a small cup and nut (called an acorn), cup sometimes cleft: seed one, with abortive ovules: albumen none: embryo with a small superior radicle and fleshy cotyledons.—Trees, rarely shrubs: leaves alternate, penninerved, with stipules: male spikes caducous: cotyledons mealy, sometimes edible.

GENUS I. QUERCUS.

Monœcia Enneandria. *Sex: Syst:*

Deriv. From the Celtic *Quer*, fine, and *Cuez* a tree.

Gen. Char. Male flowers solitary on a catkin: seldom ternate, usually surrounded by a caducous bract: perianth regularly or irregularly 4—7- (usually 5—6-) lobed: stamens varying in number: filaments exserted: anthers 2-celled, usually muticous: rudimentary pistil usually none, if present, globose, free, hirsute: female flowers solitary in a single cupula, sometimes approximated in connected cups: perianth 3—8-usually 6-lobed at the apex: ovary inferior, 1-celled above, 3-celled below, the placentæ scarcely cohering at the centre, cells 2-ovuled: ovules inserted at various points, hemianatropal upwards: styles 3, placed above the cells, one looking to the bract, usually ligulate spreading, sometimes linear, erect: fruit a scaly or zoned cup, the acorn more or less free, exserted or enclosed: seed one by abortion: testa membranaceous: cotyledons thick, usually flat-convex and entire: radicle superor.—Trees: stipules fugacious: leaf-buds stipulaceous, scaly: catkins pendulous or erect, usually males, seldom androgynous, springing from the lower axils or lateral buds: female peduncles from the following axils or terminal leaf-buds, few-flowered, terminated by a flower, the other flowers usually abortive, few coming to maturity, each flower involucrated by a cup.

(1) Q. Griffithii. *(Hook. & Thoms. ined.)*

Ident. Dec. prod. XVI. s. 2. p. 14.

Spec. Char. Younger branches and petioles slightly glabrous: leaves obovate or obovate-oblong, very shortly petioled, obtuse or acute at the base, acute at the apex, dentato-serrate, teeth muticous, adult ones slightly glabrous above, stellately pubescent beneath: stipules linear, hairy outside: fruit 2—3-sub-sessile at the top of the branch: scales of the hemispherical cup much adpressed somewhat silky, lower ones ovate obtuse, upper ones lanceolate obtuse or the uppermost ones acute: acorn glabrescent twice as long as the cup.

Khasia mountains.

(2) Q. serrata. *(Thunb.)*

Ident. Thunb. flor. jap. p. 176—Dec. l. c. p. 50—Roxb. flor. Ind. III. p. 641. *(var.)* Dec. l. c. p. 51.

Spec. Char. Younger branches silky pubescent: leaves oblong or lanceolate, acuminate or rarely obtuse, crenate-serrated, teeth long-bristly, younger ones above sparingly beneath, especially at the nerves and margin silky, adult ones glabrous: aments loose-flowered: bracts broadly ovate, puberulous externally: perianth 4-lobed, puberulous outside: anthers globose: female flowers very shortly peduncled, solitary or twin: cups hemispherical: scales ashy velvetty, lowest ones ovate-oblong, middle and upper ones gradually longer, lanceolate-linear, oblong, or all at last spreading.

Khasia. Silhet. The variety has broader stipules and larger male flowers.

(3) Q. fenestrata. *(Roxb.)*

Ident. Roxb. flor. Ind. III. p. 633.—Dec. l. c. p. 84.

Engrav. Wight's Icon. t. 219.

Spec. Char. Younger branches puberulous: leaves narrow at the base, elliptic-obovate or oblong-lanceolate, acuminate, quite entire, coriaceous, glabrous: spikes solitary or fascicled, simple, equalling the leaf or longer, hoary-velvetty: glomerules of male flowers usually 3-flowered, 3-bracteate: external bract ovate-acute: perianth 5—6-parted, velvetty externally: fruit fascicled or solitary up to the spike: cups sub-globose: scales ovate-acute: acorn globose scarcely exceeding the cup.

Silhet mountains.

(4) Q. DEALBATA. *(Hook. & Thoms.)*

Ident. Hook. & Thoms. in. herb. Boiss. (non. Wall. nec. Royle).—Dec. l. c. p. 85.

Syn. Q. dealbata, *Royle in icon.* (not the text.)

SPEC. CHAR. Younger branches thinly velvetty: leaves acute at the base, lanceolate, acuminate, entire, coriaceous, younger ones very thinly puberulous, adult ones glabrous, shining above, puberulous at the nerves beneath: parenchyma whitish, glabrate: aments somewhat branched, shorter than the leaf: fascicles of male flowers approximated: bracts puberulous at the back, outermost one larger, lateral ones ovate-obtuse: lobes of the 6-parted perianth elliptic, outwardly puberulous: female flowers connate at the base into a fascicle: younger fruits sub-globose: scales ovate-lanceolate, inflexed at the apex, velvetty.

Khasia hills. Eastern Bengal.

(5) Q. SPICATA. *(Smith.)*

Ident. Smith in Rees Cycl. 29. No. 12.—Dec. l. c. Don prod. flor. nep. p. 56.

Syn. Q. squamata, *Roxb. flor. Ind. III. p.* 638. Q. elegans, *Blume.*

Engrav. Wight's Icon. t. 213.—Wall. pl. as. rar. I. t. 46.

SPEC. CHAR. Sub-dioicous: leaves elliptic-oblong or oblong-lanceolate, acuminate, quite entire, coriaceous, glabrous: spikes solitary or fascicled, simple, hoary velvetty: male glomerules elongated, 3-bracteate, bracts acuminate, external one more or less exceeding the nearest flower: perianth 6-cleft, hairy externally: fruit densly fascicled as far as the spike: cups connate at the base, broadly cup-shaped: scales ovate-lanceolate, adpressed, convex, velvetty: acorn ovoid-globose many times exceeding the cup.

Silhet. Chittagong. Eastern Bengal.

Var.—brevipetiolata. Petiole shorter: outer bracts of the male flowers somewhat shorter, not exceeding the nearest flower.

Khasia.

(6) Q. LAPPACEA. *(Roxb.)*

Ident. Roxb. flor. Ind. III. p. 637.—Dec. l. c. p. 87.

Engrav. Wight's Icon. t. 220.—Hook. Icon. t. 224.

SPEC. CHAR. Younger branches tawny velvet: leaves lanceolate or oblong, acuminate, entire, short-petioled, younger ones on both sides, adult ones pubescent beneath: male and hermaphrodite spikes axillary, solitary, dense-flowered : bracts lanceolate, acuminated, shorter than the flower : flowers mostly fascicled : perianth 5—6-parted, hairy externally : fruit glomerate or solitary up to the spike : scales of the hemispherical cup lanceolate, acute, imbricated, diffusely spreading : acorn hairy, exceeding the cup by one half.

Silhet mountains. Assam. Eastern Bengal.

(7) Q. ACUMINATA. *(Roxb.)*

Ident. Roxb. l. c. p. 636.—Dec. l. c. p. 90.

Engrav. Wight's Icon. t. 221.

SPEC. CHAR. Younger branches pubescent : leaves oblong or broad-lanceolate, acuminate, entire, glabrous : female spikes axillary, shorter than the leaf, pubescent, many-flowered : fruit alternate, solitary, cup hemispherical, scales lanceolate sub-verticillate, acute, spreading : acorn ovoid, exceeding the cup three or four times in length.

Chittagong.

(8) Q. OXYODON. *(Miq.)*

Ident. Miq. Ann. Mus. Lugd. Bat. p. 114.—Dec. l. c. p. 98.

SPEC. CHAR. Branchlets and petioles glabrous : leaves slenderly petioled, lanceolate-oblong, narrowly and sharply acuminated, slightly unequal at the base, densly spinous-serrated except the base and upper part of the acumen, adult ones glabrous above, beneath cinerascent with a grey floccose stellate covering : cups scattered on the spike with 5—6-ovate bracts at the base.

Khasia hills.

(9) Q. SEMISERRATA. *(Roxb.)*

Ident. Roxb. l. c. p. 632.—Dec. l. c. p. 99.

Engrav. Wight's Icon. t. 211.

SPEC. CHAR. Younger branches rusty tomentose, leaves lanceolate, acute, serrated from the middle : fruit usually twin in the axils, sessile or shortly peduncled : cup shortened, broadly hemispherical, tomentose, furnished with 4—5-concentric entire blades.

Silhet.

(10) Q. LANCEÆFOLIA. *(Roxb.)*

Ident. Roxb. l. c. p. 634.—Dec. l. c. p. 102.

Syn. Q. lucida, *(Roxb. l. c.)*

Engrav. Wight's Icon. t. 212.

Spec. Char. Younger branches glabrous: leaves lanceolate or oblong, acuminate, entire, coriaceous, glabrous: aments erect, long, simple or branched: male flowers usually solitary: bracts 3, ovate, pubescent outside, lateral ones smaller: lobes of the 6-parted perianth ovate, puberulous outside: female flowers scattered, spiked: fruit alternate: cup ovoid, narrowed at the base, closed or irregularly cleft at the apex, slightly velvetty outside, zones 4—6-oblique and horizontal, linear, obscurely crenato-dentate: acorn ovoid, somewhat silky.

Silhet. Eastern Bengal

GENUS II. CASTANOPSIS.

Monœcia Enneandria. *Sex: Syst:*

Deriv. Plants resembling the Chestnut tree.

Gen. Char. Male flowers fascicled on an ament, surrounded by bracts: perianth regular, 5—6-lobed, stamens usually twice the number of the lobes: filaments slender, elongated: anthers very small, 2-celled: rudimentary pistil globose, free, hirsute: female flowers 3—1 within a scaly involucre: perianth 6-parted, lobes obtuse, in two rows: styles 3, linear, opposite the outer lobes of the perianth: ovary 3-celled, cells 2-ovuled: fruit consisting of an involucre and 3—1 enclosed nuts: involucre sub-globose, echinated on all sides with prickles slowly rising outside the scales, seldom crested with conical tubercles, at first closed, afterwards irregularly cleft or indehiscent: nuts cartilaginous, free: seed single by abortion: cotyledons thick, mealy, flat-convex: radicle superior—Trees with the habit and inflorescence of Oaks.

(1). C. Indica. *(Alph. Dec.)*

Ident. Dec. prod. xvi. S. II. p. 109.

Syn. Castanea Indica, *Roxb. flor. Ind. III. p.* 643.

Engrav. Wight's Icon. t. 417.

Spec. Char. Tree: younger branches and inflorescence tawny velvet: leaves elliptic or oblong, usually obtuse at the base, acute at the apex, remotely serrated, adult ones glabrate above, tawny pubescent beneath: male flowers usually ternate on a long erect ament, external bract of each fascicle ovate-acute, lateral ones shorter, oblong, sepals pubescent: female spikes nearly equalling the aments: female flowers usually solitary in the involucre: fruit scattered, echinate, prickles subulate, principal one diffuse or recurved hairy, lesser ones accessory, glabrous, straight.

Silhet. Chittagong. Khasia. Eastern Bengal.

(2) C. castanicarpa. *(Spach.)*

Ident. Spach. hist. Veg. phan. xi. p. 85.—Dec. l. c. p. iii.

Syn. Quercus castanicarpa, *Roxb. Cor. III. p.* 296. Castanea Roxburghii, *Lindl. in Wall. pl. as. rar. II. p.* 6.

Engrav. Wight's Icon. t. 769.

Spec. Char. Younger branches pubescent: leaves very large oblong or obovate-oblong, acuminate, entire: adult ones glabrous above, a little hairy on the nerve beneath: female spikes pubescent, flowers in three's or seldom solitary, alternate, scattered: lower bract lanceolate acuminate, equalling the perianth: ripe involucre globose, densely echinated, at length cleft.

Chittagong.

(3) C. Hystrix. *(Alph. Dec.)*

Ident. Dec. l. c. p. III.

Spec. Char. Younger branches hairy: leaves elliptic or oblong, acuminate, entire, sometimes undulate-dentate towards the apex, coriaceous, younger ones tawny tomentose beneath, adult ones sub-glabrate: fruit few at the apex of a stiff peduncle, globose, densely echinated with a spinous involucre, prickles ramous from the base, linear-acuminate, silky, except the point.

Khasia hills.

(4) C. tribuloides. *(Alph. Dec.)*

Ident. Dec. l. c. p. III.

Syn. Quercus tribuloides, *Sm. in Rees. Cycl.*—Castanea tribuloides, *Lindl. l. c.* Q. armata, *Roxb. Cor.* Q-ferox, *Roxb. flor. Ind. III. p.* 640. C. armata, *Spach. l. c. p.* 185. C. sphærocarpa, *Wall. pl. as. rar. II. p.* 5.

Engrav. Wight's Icon. t. 770—218.—Roxb. Cor. III. t. 296.

Spec. Char. Younger branches and inflorescence tawny velvet: leaves lanceolate or oblong-lanceolate, acuminated, hairy, adult ones glabrate: spikes elongated, erect, unisexual: male flowers entire, solitary or ternate: bracts of the fascicle ovate-acute, lower ones larger: female flowers ternate between very obtuse bracts: fruit ovate-globose echinated with a spinous involucre, prickles narrow from a broadish base, acute, straight or somewhat recurved, velvetty, except at the top, simple, or divided from the base, at length distant and often falling.

Khasia. Chittagong.

(5) C. ECHIDNOCARPA. *(Alph. Dec.)*

Ident.. Dec. l. c. p. 112.

SPEC. CHAR. Younger branches glabrous: leaves oblong-lanceolate, acuminate, entire, or 1—3 toothed towards the apex, younger ones finely puberulous beneath: female spikes equalling the leaf: flowers solitary: bracts round: fruit globose, ashy-velvet, 1-seeded: prickles conical, acute, somewhat scattered, short, simple, echinate.

Khasia mountains.

ORDER CL. JUGLANDACEÆ.

Flowers unisexual: males on axillary aments, females on terminal spikes, occasionally both mixed on a single panicle: male calyx 2—6-parted, adnate to a scale-liked bract: stamens 3-36: filaments free, very short: anthers erect, 2-celled, dehiscing lengthways: female flowers terminal, clustered and surrounded with small bracts, or in lax racemes enclosed in a 1-flowered involucre: calyx connate with the ovary, cup-shaped, 3-many toothed at the apex: corolla 4-toothed: ovary 2—4-celled at the base, 1-celled at the apex: style short: stigmas 2, seldom 4: drupe 1-stoned, fleshy or membranaceous, indehiscent or irregularly cleft or dehiscing by four valves: seed erect, without albumen, smooth or wrinkled, 2—4-lobed and divided by partial dissepiments cut into it: cotyledons fleshy, oily, sinuous: radicle superior, very short.—Trees with alternate pinnate leaves: stipules none: flowers inconspicuous.

GENUS I. ENGELHARDTIA.

Monœcia Pentandria. *Sex: Syst:*

GEN. CHAR. Inflorescence sometimes paniculately branched, lateral branches male amentiform, terminal one female, spiciform: sometimes the male part consisting of 2—4-axillary aments growing on a common rhachis, the female part spiciform, terminal or axillary: perianth of the male sessile flower adnate to a 3-toothed or lobed bract, usually 3—6-lobed, elongated, anterior lobe opposite the bract, 4 lateral, 1 posterior opposite the rhachis often abortive: stamens 5—13, filaments very short: female flowers very numerous, sessile or very shortly pedicelled: a bract forming the outer perianth, below cup-shaped connate at the base with the flower, above 4-lobed much longer than the flower, externally villous at the base, 3 anterior lobes linear-lanceolate, posterior lobe opposite the rhachis 2-many crenated, auricle-shaped: cotyledons contortuplicate.

(1) E. SPICATA. *(Blume.)*

Ident. Bl. bijdr. p. 528. flor. Jav. t. 1. et. 5.—Dec. prod. xvi. S. II. p. 140.

Syn. E. Roxburghiana. *Wall. in pl. as. rar. II. p.* 85 *t.* 199. Juglans pteracocca, *Roxb. H. B.*

SPEC. CHAR. Tree: leaves about 5-pairs usually abruptly pinnatisect: leaflets petioluled, stiff-coriaceous, ovate-lanceolate, unequally attenuated at the base, acuminated at the apex, acute, quite entire: aments inserted on a common rachis: male flowers puberulous outside: stamens 8—13: anthers pubescent: spikes growing from the prior young shoots: female flowers sessile, intermediate lobe of the outer perianth twice as long as the lateral ones.

Khasia. Chittagong.

ORDER CLI. SALICACEÆ.

Flowers diœcious arranged in catkins on terminal branchlets, sessile or shortly pedicelled, supported by a bract:—*Males.* Perianth none: torus swelling into a gland or obliquely truncated ring or urceolus: stamens exserted from the centre of the disk, 2 or more: filaments filiform, free or monadelphous: anthers 2-celled: cells parallel, dehiscing lengthways: rudimentary ovary none. *Females.* Perianth none: ovary free, sessile, margins of the 2 carpels connate, or more or less inflexed: ovules numerous, ascending, anatropal: styles two, more or less connate, each terminated by a 2—3-lobed stigma: capsule 1-celled, 2-valved, many-seeded, valves opening at the top, afterwards revolute: seeds erect, small: testa membranaceous: thread very short, thick: albumen none: embryo orthotropal: radicle looking towards the base of the fruit.

GENUS I. SALIX.

Diœcia Diandria. *Sex: Syst:*

Deriv. From *Sal*, near, and *Lis*, water, Celtic; in allusion to the place of growth.

GEN. CHAR. Bracts of the catkin undivided: stamens 2—5: filaments free or cohering at the base, seldom connate into a column: ovary 1-celled: ovules numerous, anatropal: style very short, stigmas 2, bilobed: capsule 1-celled, 2-valved: seeds comose.—Tall trees or shrubs growing in moist places near the banks of streams: leaves alternate, entire, serrate or quite entire, stipules leafy persistent, or scaly deciduous; buds covered with a simple scale: catkins sessile or peduncled.

(1) S. TETRASPERMA. (*Roxb.*)

Ident. Roxb. flor. Ind. III. p. 753.—Dec. prod. xvi. s. 2 p. 192.

Syn. S. ichnostachya, *R. W.*

Engrav. Wight's Icon. t. 1953.—4.—Roxb. Cor. I. t. 97.

SPEC. CHAR. Catkins lateral, peduncled, male long, lax and few-flowered: female cylindric, rather dense, elongated: peduncle 3—6-leaved: scales oblong, spathulate, puberulous: capsule long-pedicelled, ovoid, glabrous: leaves lanceolate, elongated, long-acuminate, glaucous beneath, quite entire or serrulated.

Rivulets on the Ghauts, and other similar places in the Peninsula, flowering in the hot and rainy season.

Neilgherries. Khasia hills. Oude.

(2) S. UROPHYLLA. (*Lindl.*)

Ident. Dec. prod. l. c. p. 194.—Anders. Mon. Sal. p. 5.

Syn. S. Zollingeriana, *Miq. flor. Ind. Bat. I.* 2. *p.* 462.

SPEC. CHAR. Tree: aments peduncled, supported by small leaves, erect, curved, at first dense-flowered: scales ovate-rotund, densely hoary-pilose: capsules ovate-lanceolate, quite glabrous, brownish: pedicel 2—3-times exceeding the nectary: style short: stigmas thick, curved outwards: leaves lanceolate, acuminate, quite entire, softly hirsute with a few hairs, above at least afterwards glabrate.

Oude.

ORDER CLII. MYRICACEÆ.

Shrubs or small trees: leaves alternate, simple, entire, serrated or cut, seldom quite entire, sprinkled with resinous dots: stipules none or fugacious: flowers sessile, in axillary or terminal, simple or paniculately racemose, monœcious or diœcious catkins, solitary between concave bracts: males in filiform catkins: bracteoles 2: stamens 2—8: filaments filiform, short, often unequal, free or connate at the base into a short stalk: anthers extrorse, 2-celled, fixed by the base, cells sub-opposite, dehiscent: female flowers in cylindric orovate catkins: hypogynous scales 2—6, peltate or increased within at the base by a fleshy gland: ovary 1, lenticular-compressed or sub-globose, connate at the base with the hypogynous scales, 1 celled: ovule 1, erect: style very short: stigmas 2, elongated, subulate or lanceolate, papillose, spreading: fruit dry, indehiscent, drupaceous, 1-seeded: seed erect, basilar: testa very thinly membranaceous: albumen none: cotyledons plano-convex, fleshy: radicle slightly tapering, short, superior.

GENUS. MYRICA.

Tetrandria Digynia. *Sex: Syst:*

Deriv. From *Myrio*, to flow: the plants are found near the banks of rivers.

Gen. Char. Flowers mono-diœcious. *Male.* Aments filiform: bracts 1-flowered, bibracteolate: stamens 2—8: filaments free, or connate at the base: anthers 2-celled: *Fem.* Aments ovate or cylindric: bracts 1-flowered, bibracteolate: hypogynous scales concrescent with the base of the ovary: ovary 1-celled, 1-ovuled, style very short with 2 elongated stigmas: drupe 1-seeded: seed erect.—Resinous shrubs or small trees: leaves alternate, entire, serrated or laciniated, or sometimes pinnatifid cut.

(1) M. integrifolia. (*Roxb.*)

Ident. Roxb. flor. Ind. III. p. 765.

Engrav. Wight's Icon. t. 764—5.

Spec. Char. Shrubby: leaves lanceolate, entire, smooth: male aments solitary, smaller ones densely approximated, very short, condensed, few flowered: bract of the male flower ciliated: scales of the female ament reniform-cordate, 1—2-flowered: drupe oval, granulated: stamens four, almost equalling the bract: bracteoles of female flower 2.

Khasia hills, flowering in December and January.

(2) M. sapida. (*Wall.*)

Ident. Wall. tent. flor. nep. p. 59. t. 45.

Spec. Char. Tree: leaves lanceolate, acuminate or obtuse at the apex, quite entire, glabrous, coriaceous or stiff: aments cylindric, alternate, remote with a pubescent rhachis: male flowers with an ovate puberulous bract: stamens 3—5, longer than the bract: anthers glabrous: female flowers with a pear-shaped granular fruit, nut very hard, attenuated at both ends.

Khasia hills.

ORDER CLIII. CASUARINACEÆ.

Trees: branches and branchlets verticillate, nodosely jointed: leaves none: sheaths short, many-toothed, striated: flowers monœcious or diœcious; males arranged in spikes, females in terminal capitula: male flowers bursting from within the uppermost sheaths of the branchlets, each furnished at the base with a small, persistent bract: perigonium 2-leaved, stiffly membranaceous: bracteoles, occupying the right and left side from the axis of the flower: leaflets less than the bracteoles, first enclosed by them and cohering like a cup at the apex, afterwards thrown off by the increasing stamen: stamen 1, central: filament at first very short, afterwards elongated, filiform, thickened at the base: anther 2-celled, incumbent: cells sub-opposite, dehiscing lengthways: female flowers capitate in the apex of the branchlets, each sessile in the axil of a persistent bract: bracteoles 2, navicular, at first spreading, afterwards growing together at the base, at first hiding the fruit: perigonium none: ovary sessile, lenticular-compressed, 1-celled, 1-ovuled: style very short, terminal: stigmas 2, filiform, elongated: fruit from the bracts and bracteoles connate in the form of a cone: caryopsis compressed, ending at the apex in a membranaceous wing: seed 1, appended to the apex of the cell: albumen none: embryo orthotropal: cotyledons oblong, flat: radicle very small.

GENUS I. CASUARINA.

Monœcia Monandria. *Sex: Syst:*

Gen. Char. Same as the Order.

(1) C. EQUISETIFOLIA. (*Forst.*)

Ident. Forst. Gen. pl. Austr. p. 103.—Dec. prod. xvi. s. 2. p. 338.

Syn. C. litorea, *Rumph.* C. africana. *Lour.* C. muricata, *Roxb.* C. lateriflora, *Poir.* C. litoralis, *Salisb.*

Engrav. Forst. l. c. fig. 52. Lam. Ill. t. 746. Miq. Rev. t. 5. Rumph. Amb. III. t. 57.

SPEC. CHAR. Large tree: leaves verticelled, furrowed, jointed: joints ending in a cup in which the next joint sits: male aments cylindric, terminating the leaves: scales 6-8 in a verticil, united at the base, pointed and woolly: flowers as many as desirous in the verticil: corolla consisting of two opposite boat-shaped ciliated scales: filaments single: female flowers on a different tree: aments oval, short-peduncled: scales 6-8 in a verticil, with a single flower between each: corolla none: cones oval, size of a nutmeg, armed with the sharp points of the 2-valved capsule: seeds small, with a large wedge-shaped membranaceous wing: flowers greenish.

Chittagong, and from thence spreading over the coasts of the Peninsula. Fowering in the hot season.

ORDER CLIV. GNETACEÆ.

Flowers monœcious or diœcious on cylindric capituliform catkins, bracts decussately opposite: *Male flowers.*—Perianth tubular, soon transversely 2-valved from the top: stamen erect from the centre, solitary, or more coalescing into an undivided column or branched from the apex: anthers 1—4-celled, cells contiguous or separated, adnate, and open from the apex towards the base. Female flowers naked or clothed with a 2-leaved involucre: ovary sessile, 1-celled: ovule one, erect: orthotropal: fruit sub-drupaceous, enclosed in the leaflets of the involucre, or naked: seed one: testa membranaceous: albumen copious, fleshy: embryo antitropal in the axis of the albumen: radicle superior, cylindric.

GENUS I. GNETUM.

Monœcia Monandria. *Sex: Syst:*

Deriv. From the word *Gnemon*, the name of the plant in the Island of Ternate.

GEN. CHAR. Flowers diœcious or monœcious in the same verticils: catkins cylindric, interruptedly verticilled, jointed, each verticil surrounded by cup-shaped involucre: flowers immersed in fascicled paleæ.—*Males*. Perianth 2-valved at the top: filament simple or 2-cleft: anther 2-celled, didymous, cells dehiscing at the apex by an oblong pore.—*Females*. Flowers naked, destitute of a proper involucre: ovary sessile: ovule solitary, erect: drupe baccate, 1-seeded.

(1) G. SCANDENS. *(Roxb.)*

Ident. Roxb. flor. Ind. III. 518. Dec. prod. xvi. s. 2. p. 351.

Syn. Thoa edulis, *Willd.*

Engrav. Wight's Icon. t. 1955.—Rheede Mal. vii. t. 22.

SPEC. CHAR. Shrubby; scandent: young shoots jointed and swollen at the insertion of the leaves: leaves opposite, oblong, glossy, entire: peduncles axillary and terminal with 1-2 opposite pair of cylindric catkins, and a terminal one: drupe oblong, reddish orange when ripe: flowers small, greenish.

Eastern slopes of the Neilgherries. Common in jungles on the Western Coast. Chittagong. Assam. Flowering in March and April.

ORDER CLV. CYCADACEÆ.

Trees or shrubs, resembling Palms: stem cylindric, simple, marked with the scars of fallen leaf-stalks: leaves pinnated, usually circinate when young; leaflets finely veined, somewhat obliquely inserted on the petiole: calyx and corolla none: male flowers collected in terminal cones, consisting of scales covered over their lower side with 1-celled anthers, often collected in two's or three's, splitting lengthways: female flowers consisting of naked ovules placed beneath peltate scales, at the base of flat ones, or on the margins of contracted leaves: seeds bony: albumen fleshy or mealy: cotyledons unequal, connate at the apex: radicle superior.

GENUS CYCAS.

Diœcia Icosandria. *Sex: Syst:*

Deriv. The Greek name of a Palm said to grow in Æthiopia.

GEN. CHAR. Same as in the Order.

(1) C. CIRCINALIS. (*Linn.*)

Ident. Roxb. flor. Ind. III. p. 744.—Spreng. syst. III. p. 907. Dec. prod. xvi. s. 2. p. 526.

Engrav. Rheede Mal. III. t. 13. 21. Rumph. Amb. t. 22. 23. Bot. Mag. 55. t. 2826-7.

SPEC. CHAR. Trunk cylindrical, unbranched, surmounted with a terminal bud, consisting of a male cone composed of peltate scales: leaves pinnated, thorny, springing from the apex of the trunk.

Malabar. South Concans. Forests near Trichore. Flowering in May.

ORDER CLVI. ROXBURGHIACEÆ.

Perianth 4-leaved, campanulate, persistent: leaflets cruciately opposite (two exterior, two interior) distinct, almost equal, ovate-lanceolate, narrow-acuminate, sub-caniculate, many-nerved, externally green, inwardly coloured, inner ones a little broader: stamens 4, inserted at the bottom of the perianth, opposite the leaflets and shorter than them, erect: filaments short, thick, connate at the base: anthers 2-celled, introrse, connectivum continuous with the filaments: cells narrow, bilocellate, adnate at either angle of the prominent dissepiment to the lower part of the connectivum, suddenly constricted above and there empty up to the apex: ovary free, sessile, obliquely ovate, obtuse, smooth, compressed, 1-celled: ovules numerous, seated at the bottom of the ovary, sessile, erect, anatropal: stigma sessile, capitate, entire: capsule follicular, 2-valved, compressed, 1-many seeded: seeds fixed at the bottom of the capsule, erect, ribbed, obliquely beaked at the apex: testa thick, coriaceous: albumen fleshy: embryo straight.

GENUS ROXBURGHIA.

Tetrandria Monogynia. *Sex: Syst:*

Deriv. Named in honour of Dr. James Roxburgh, the eminent Indian botanist.

GEN. CHAR. Same as the Order.

(1) R. GLORIOSOIDES. (*Jones.*)

Ident. Jones in Roxb. flor. Ind. II. 234. Kunth. Enum. pl. v. 287.

Syn. R. viridiflora, *Smith Ex. bot. I. p.* 111. R. gloriosa, *Pers. syn.* 412. Stemona tuberosa, *Lour. Coch.* II. 402.

Engrav. Wight's Icon. t. 2061. Roxb. Cor. I. t. 32.—Smith l. c. t. 57. Wall. pl. As. rar. III. t. 282.Bot. Mag. t. 1500.

SPEC. CHAR. Scandent: leaves scattered, ovate-oblong, slighty cordate, acuminate, sub-mucronate: peduncles axillary, solitary, racemosely 1—3-flowered: outer leaflets of the perigonium 13-, inner 15-nerved: flowers large, green, whitish within.

Silhet. Circar mountains. Chittagong. Pulicat hills (2,000 feet). Fowering in August and September.

ORDER CLVII. SMILACEÆ.

Flowers hermaphrodite or diœcious: perianth 6-very rarely 4, 8, or 10-leaved, regular, persistent or deciduous: leaflets distinct or more or less connate: æstivation imbricated: stamens as many as the leaflets, perigynous or hypogynous: filaments free: anthers 1—2-celled, introrsely dehiscing: ovary free, or half-adnate to the base of the perianth, 1—5-celled: ovules twin, collateral or many biseriate, very seldom solitary, pendulous and orthotropal: styline column terminal: stigma 3-cleft, 3-lobed or entire: berry 1—3, very rarely 2—4—5-celled, cells 1 or more seeded: seeds nestling in pulp, usually globose: testa thinly membranaceous: albumen fleshy or horny: embryo straight, usually minute.—Perennial herbs, stemless or caulescent, undershrubs or shrubs, often scandent, rooting or twining: leaves scattered, opposite or verticilled, in some reduced to scales: flowers solitary, fascicled, umbellate, racemose or panicled, axillary and terminal: pedicels very often jointed.

GENUS. I. SMILAX.

Diœcia Hexandria. *Sex: Syst:*

Deriv. From *Smile*, a scraper, the stems are rough from prickles.

GEN. CHAR. Flowers diœcious: leaflets of the perianth 6, distinct, unequal (outer ones broader), deciduous, very rarely connate:

stamens 6, inserted at the base of the leaflets, anther wanting in the female flowers: anthers 1-celled, biloculate, fixed by the base, introrse: ovary free, 3- very rarely 1 or 6-celled, obliterated in the male flowers: ovules solitary, seldom twin, pendulous, orthotropal: stigmas 3, sessile, distinct, very rarely connate: berry globose, 1—3-seeded: testa membranaceous, adnate to cartilaginous albumen: embryo very small.—Under-shrubs, seldom herbs, scandent, with tendrils: tendrils twin, petiolar: leaves scattered, petioled, reticulately digito-nerved: flowers umbellate, umbels axillary, solitary, sometimes racemose in leafless branchlets: pedicels not jointed.

(1) S. ovalifolia. *(Roxb.)*

Ident. Roxb. flor. Ind. III. p. 794.

Engrav. Wight's Icon. t. 809.—Rheede Mal. vii. t. 31.

Spec. Char. Stems climbing, cylindric, larger parts armed with sharp, incurved prickles: tendrils paired, simple: leaves alternate, short-petioled, oval, 5—7-nerved, smooth, entire: petioles short-winged, channelled: umbels axillary, compound: umbellets globular: flowers greenish: berries red, smooth, succulent, 2—3-seeded.

Common in jungles in Malabar and Travancore. Concans. Flowering in the hot season.

(2) S. macrophylla. *(Roxb.)*

Ident. Roxb. l. c. p. 793.—Dalz. Bomb. flora p. 246.

Spec. Char. Scandent: stem and branches cylindric and prickly: leaves short petioled, round, entire, 5-nerved, glossy: tendrils petiolar, undivided: female peduncles axillary, solitary, branched, each with a large globular umbellet of greenish-yellow pedicelled flowers: berries size of a pea, red, smooth, 1—2-seeded, round.

Southern Ghauts. Chorla.

(3) S. Zeylanica. *(Linn.)*

Ident. Linn. flor. Zeyl. p. 364.—Kunth. Enum. pl. v. p. 249.

Engrav. Wight's Icon. t. 2057—8.

Spec. Char. Stem scandent, obscurely 4-angled, beset, especially the male, with numerous small recurved prickles: leaves from cordate-ovate acuminate to sub-orbicular, abruptly retusely acuminate 5-nerved, the outer pair slender: peduncles axillary, usually two, sometimes 3-umbelled: flowers longish pedicelled, male 6-androus, without rudimentary pistil: females with 3 rudimentary stamens opposite the outer sepals: berry globose, 3-seeded.

Eastern slopes of the Neilgherries. Flowering from September to December.

(4) S. MACULA. *(Royle.)*

Ident. Roxb. l. c. p. 796.—Don. prod. flor. Nep. p. 49.

Engrav. Wight's Icon. t. 2059.—Royle Ill. I. t. 94 fig. 1.

SPEC. CHAR. Shrubby, scandent, angular, armed with numerous small prickles: leaves broad, sub-reniform-cordate at the base, tapering to a blunt point, 7-nerved: racemes, male and female, axillary, flexuose, with the flowers fascicled on the flexures, short-pedicelled: female with six rudimentary stamens: berries red when ripe.

Eastern slopes of the Neilgherries, climbing over trees to a great extent.

(5) S. RETUSA. *(Roxb.)*

Ident. Roxb. l. c. p. 793.

SPEC. CHAR. Scandent, terete, very prickly: leaves sub-ovate, cordate, retuse, with a triangular point, tripli-nerved: stipules amplexicaul: flowers greenish.

Bengal, flowering in the hot season.

(6) S. PROLIFERA. *(Roxb.)*

Ident. Roxb. l. c. p. 795.—Royle Ill. I. 381.

SPEC. CHAR. Branchlets prickly: leaves elliptic, abruptly cuspidate-acute, recurved at the apex, sub-rotund at the base, triplinerved, stiffly membranaceous: petioles keeled at the back, vaginate auriculate below: umbels 8—10, long peduncled, racemosely arranged on a common axillary peduncle: outer leaflets of the perianth oblong, slightly acute, inner ones narrow linear, sub-spathulate: anthers oblong, obtuse, a little shorter than the filament: flowers green.

Rajmahal. Chittagong. Silhet. Oude. Flowering in February and March.

(7) S. LANCEÆFOLIA. *(Roxb.)*

Ident. Roxb. l. c. p. 792.

SPEC. CHAR. Scandent: stem and branches unarmed, terete, smooth: leaves lanceolate, 3-nerved, smooth: umbels simple, axillary, solitary, peduncled: calycine segments linear-oblong: roots tuberous.

Silhet.

(8) S. GLABRA. *(Roxb.)*

Ident. Roxb. l. c. p. 792.

SPEC. CHAR. Scandent: stem and branches unarmed, terete, smooth: leaves lanceolate, acuminate, rotund at the base, 3-nerved, nerves smooth, glaucous beneath: umbels axillary, simple, sessile, solitary: calycine segments broad, obcordate: anthers sessile: roots tuberous.

Silhet.

(9) S. OXYPHYLLA. *(Wall.)*

Ident. Kunth. Enum. pl. v. p. 238.—Wall. Cat. No. 5128.

SPEC. CHAR. Glabrous, prickly: branches terete, obsoletely striated: leaves oblong, long acuminate, recurved at the point, decurrent at the back into the keeled petiole, 5-nerved, membranaceous: peduncles axillary, solitary, simple, bibracteated above the base, many-flowered, exceeding the petiole: outer leaflets of the perianth oblong, slightly acute, inner ones a little less: anthers sub-ovate-oblong, obtuse, 3-times shorter than the filament.

Silhet. Chittagong.

(10) S. HOHENHACKERI. *(Kunth.)*

Ident. Kunth l. c. p. 240.—Hohen. pl. Ind. or No. 122.

SPEC. CHAR. Glabrous, branchlets angled, prickles straight, scattered: leaves elliptic-oblong, acuminate, narrowed into the petiole, recurved, 5-nerved, membranaceous: petioles without tendrils: peduncles axillary, simple, bibracteate above the base, many flowered, exceeding the keeled petiole: outer leaflets of the perianth linear-oblong, slightly obtuse, inner ones linear, narrowed above: anthers linear-oblong, obtuse, 3-times shorter than the filaments.

Near Mangalore, in Canara.

(11) S. LAURINA. *(Kunth.)*

Ident. Kunth. l. c. p. 248.

Syn. S. laurifolia, *Roxb. fl. Ind. III. p.* 793.

SPEC. CHAR. Scandent, somewhat angled, prickly: leaves lanceolate and narrow-oblong, accuminate, tripli-nerved, glabrous: umbels composite: berries 3-lobed, 1—3-seeded: bases of the petioles persistent, furnished below the tendrils with two broad, semi-cordate stipules.

Garrow Hills.

(12) S. COLLINA. *(Kunth.)*

Ident. Kunth. l. c. p. 261.

Syn. S. pseudo-China, *Roxb.* (not *Linn.*)

SPEC. CHAR. Scandent: stem and branches unarmed, terete, glabrous: leaves cordate or cordate-oblong, acuminate, 5-nerved: petioles sub-cylindric, without stipules.

Garrow Hills.

ORDER CLVIII. DIOSCOREACEÆ.

Flowers diœcious, very rarely monœcious. *Males.* Perianth more or less deeply 6-parted, rotate, funnel-shaped, campanulate, urceolate, usually coloured, segments equal or unequal, æstivation imbricated: stamens 6, generally distinct, shorter than the perianth: anthers 2-celled, attached by the back, dehiscing lengthways, introrse: ovary inferior, rudimentary: obsoletely turbinate or none. *Females.* Perianth superior, more or less constricted above the ovary, limb 6-parted: segments spreading, or urceolately connivent: stamens 6, but sterile: styles 3, more or less connate, sometimes very short: stigmas 3, undivided or usually 2-cleft, recurved and plaited upwards: ovary inferior, triangular, 3-celled: ovules 2 in each cell, suspended from the inner angle at different heights, anatropal: fruit capsular, very rarely baccate, crowned by the persistent calyx, 3-celled, 3—6-seeded: seeds flat-compressed in the capsules, sometimes surrounded by a wing, sometimes only winged above and below, wingless in the berries: testa thin, adnate to the albumen, usually continued in a wing: albumen fleshy, cartilaginous, embryo minute, situated below the hilum: cotyledon flat.—Perennial herbs or undershrubs, twining, rarely procumbent: rhizome usually tuberous, fleshy, sometimes above ground, large: leaves petioled, scattered, sometimes opposite, reticulately digitate-nerved, entire, sometimes digitately lobed or dissected, usually cordate, glandular-dotted, more or less pellucid: petioles often geniculate above the base, sometimes with two glands or two spines at the base: inflorescence axillary, spiked or racemose, simple or branched: flowers solitary, glomerate or fascicled, bracteate at the base, small, inconspicuous.

GENUS I. DIOSCOREA.

Diœcia Hexandria. *Sex: Syst:*

Deriv. Named after Pedanius Dioscorides, a famous Greek author and physician.

Gen. Char. Flowers diœcious: capsule triquetrous, loculicidally 3-valved: seeds in the cells twin, surrounded by a membranaceous wing: herbs or shrubs usually twining to the left: the rest as in the order.

(1) D. sativa. *(Linn.)*

Ident. Linn. spec. 1463.—Kunth. Enum. pl. v. 341.

Engrav. Rheede Mal. viii. t. 51.—Lam. Ill. t. 818.

Spec. Char. Leaves alternate, sub-rotund-ovate, long-cuspidate, sinuate-cordate, glabrous, 9—13-nerved, outermost nerves 2-cleft, transverse veins almost simple: stem terete, smooth: male spikes fasciculately panicled, females aggregated, simple.

Malabar.

(2) D. glabra. *(Roxb.)*

Ident. Roxb. flor. Ind. III. 804.

Spec. Char. Twining, glabrous: branches terete, smooth: leaves opposite, ovate-oblong, truncated and rounded at the base or very slightly cordate, acuminate-cuspidate, 7-nerved, membranaceous, glaucescent beneath: male spikes axillary, in three's or four's, or all simple, longer than the petiole, or one in each axil simply branched and very long: branches 3—6, sub-flexuose: flowers solitary, sessile: segments of the perianth urceolately connivent, inner ones smaller, sub-obovate: stamens inserted at the bottom of the perianth, short.

Silhet. Lower Bengal. Peninsula west of the Ganges.

(3) D. alata. *(Linn.)*

Ident. Linn. spec. 1462.—Roxb. l. c. 797.

Engrav. Wight's Icon. t. 810.—Rheede Mal. vii. t. 38.

Spec. Char. Rhizome oblong: stems quadrangular, sometimes prickly below: leaves opposite, ovate-oblong, cuspidate, cordate-sagittate, glabrous, 5—7-nerved, outermost nerves 2-parted: male spikes verticillately spiked: flowers green.

Both Concans, flowering in the rainy season.

(4) D. ANGUINA. *(Roxb.)*

Ident. Roxb. l. c. p. 803.

SPEC. CHAR. Tubers cylindric: stems twining, terete, villous: leaves opposite and alternate, cordate, 5-nerved: male spikes dense, pendulous: females axillary, erect, long, simple or composite, villous: flowers small, remote, green, villous.

Near Calcutta, flowering in the rainy season.

(5) D. OPPOSITIFOLIA. *(Linn.)*

Ident. Linn. Spec. 1463.—Roxb. l. c. p. 804.

Engrav. Wight's Icon. t. 813.

SPEC. CHAR. Herbaceous: smooth: leaves opposite, cordate-ovate-lanceolate, acute, 3—7-nerved: male flowers panicled, females spiked.

Coromandel. Ghauts about Khandalla. Flowering in the rainy season.

(6) D. TOMENTOSA. *(Hohenhacker.)*

Ident. Hohenhacker pl. Ind. or. No. 286.—Kunth l. c. p. 391.

SPEC. CHAR. Branches tomentose, unarmed: leaves scattered, ternately trisected, segments cuspidate, membranaceous, glabrous above, hoary-tomentose beneath, terminal one elliptic-oblong: lateral ones half cordate-ovate: male racemes axillary and terminal, solitary, the one doubly, the other simply branched, exceeding the leaves: segments of the bibracteolate perianth ovate, nearly equal, urceolate-connivent: flowers pedicelled, solitary, minute.

Near Mangalore in Canara.

(7) D. TRIPHYLLA. *(Linn.)*

Ident. Linn. Spec. 1462.—Kunth l. c. p. 392.—Dalz. Bomb. flor. p. 247.

Engrav. Rheede Mal. vii. t. 33.—Jacq. Ic. t. 627.

SPEC. CHAR. Twining: branches furrowed, slightly hairy and prickly: leaves scattered, ternately 3-divided, membranaceous: segments cuspidate, terminal one elliptic-oblong, lateral obliquely ovate: male racemes axillary, in threes, generally all simple: rachis and pedicels clothed with whitish hairs: capsules obovate-oblong, pubescent.

Concan. Malabar.

(8) D. PENTAPHYLLA. *(Willd.)*

Ident. Willd. Spec. iv. 789.—Roxb. l. c. p. 806.

Engrav. Wight's Icon. t. 814.—Rheede Mal. vii. t. 35.

SPEC. CHAR. Branches prickly, furrowed, rather hairy: leaves digitate, 5-divided, membranaceous, puberulous, segments oblong-acuminate, cuspidate: stipulary prickles twin: female spikes axillary, twin, simple, scarcely longer than the petiole: male flowers numerous, greenish white, very fragrant.

Concan. Ghauts. Monghyr. Vendalore. Silhet. Flowering in the rainy season.

(9) D. ACULEATA. *(Linn.)*

Ident. Linn. Spec. 1462.

Engrav. Rheede Mal. vii. t. 37.—Rumph. Amb. v. t. 126.

SPEC. CHAR. Stem prickly, terete: leaves alternate, cordate, acuminate, 7—9-nerved, veins transverse almost simple: male spikes panicled: flowers small, whitish.

Malabar. Flowering in the rainy season.

(10) D. PULCHELLA. *(Roxb.)*

Ident. Roxb. l. c. p. 801.

SPEC. CHAR. Tubers almost round, small: stems herbaceous, twining, terete, glabrous: leaves deeply broad-cordate, acuminate, subulate, 9—11-nerved, glabrous: female spikes axillary, collected together, pendulous.

Chittagong, flowering at the end of the rains.

(11) D. CRISPATA. *(Roxb.)*

Ident. Roxb. l. c. p. 802.

SPEC. CHAR. Tubers almost round: stems annual, twining, terete, 10—15-winged, wings crisp: leaves alternate, broadly cordate: female spikes pendulous, males panicled: flowers alternate, remote.

Interior of Bengal, flowering in the rainy season.

GENUS II. HELMIA.

Diœcia Hexandria. *Sex: Syst:*

Deriv. Named in honor of C. Helm, Archdeacon, an ardent botanist.

GEN. CHAR. Flowers diœcious, very rarely monœcious. *Males.* Perianth rotate or urceolate, campanulate, deeply 6-divided, segments almost equal: stamens 6, sometimes 3, inserted on the perianth (seldom at the bottom) short, very rarely monadelphous: anthers 2-celled, fixed by the back, introrse. *Females.* Perianth superior, 6-parted, segments nearly equal, spreading, seldom reflexed: stamens effete or scarcely any: styline column perspicuous or none: stigmas 3, entire or 2-lobed, plaited upwards: ovary inferior, triangular, 3-celled, ovules 2 in each cell, suspended at different heights from the inner angle: capsule triquetrous, 3-celled, loculicidally 3-valved: seeds twin in the cells, flattened, winged at the base: albumen 2-partible by a large central fissure: embryo spathulate: cotyledon flat.—Twining shrubs: rhizome tuberous, fleshy: leaves petioled, scattered, very rarely sub-opposite, reticulately digito-nerved, entire or ternately trisect: flowers axillary, racemose or spiked, bibracteate at the base.

(1) H. BULBIFERA. *(Kunth.)*

Ident. Kunth Enum. pl. v. 435.

Syn. Dioscorea bulbifera. *Linn.* D. tamnifolia. *Salisb. Parad. t.* 17. D. pulchella. *Hokenhacker pl. Ind. No.* 294.

Engrav. Wight's Icon. t. 878.—Rheede Mal. vii. t. 36.

SPEC. CHAR. Smooth: branches terete: leaves cordate, subrotund, ovate-acuminate, cuspidate, 9-nerved, membranaceous: male spikes axillary, simple, about five together or compound panicled: females about 3 together, longer than the leaf: capsules oblong, smooth, like parchment.

Bombay. Concans. Malabar. Silhet. Canara.

(2) D. DŒMONA. *(Kunth.)*

Ident. Kunth l. c. p. 439.

Syn. Dioscorea Dœmona. *Roxb. fl. Ind. III.* 805.

Engrav. Wight's Icon. t. 811.

SPEC. CHAR. Stems twining, armed: leaves ternate, leaflets obovate-cuneate, 3—5-nerved, very large, acute, entire, villous when young: petioles armed with small prickles: male spikes axillary, compound, drooping, sometimes leaf-bearing, 6—18-inches long: female spikes axillary, solitary, pendulous.

Concan hills. Goruckpore. Flowering in the rains.

(3) H. HIRSUTA. *(Kunth.)*

Ident. Kunth l. c. p. 438.

Syn. Dioscorea hirsuta. *Blume.* Ubium sylvestre. *Rumph.*

Engrav. Rumph. Amb. v. t. 128.—Rheede Mal. vii. t. 51—52.

SPEC. CHAR. Branches glabrate, slightly prickly: leaves membranaceous, slightly hairy on both sides, terminal segment obovate-oblong, 5-nerved, lateral ones dimidiate-cordate-ovate, 6-nerved: petioles slightly villous, petiolets rusty-hirsute: male spikes axillary, solitary, simply composite, villous tomentose: inner segments of the perianth, round ovate, acutish, outer ones 4 times shorter.

Malabar.

(4) H. TOMENTOSA. (*Kunth.*)

Ident. Kunth l. c. p. 439.

Syn. Dioscorea tomentosa. *Roxb. flor. Ind. III.* 805.

Engrav. Wight's Icon. t. 815.

SPEC. CHAR. Herbaceous: tubers irregularly oblong: stems twining, tomentose, slightly armed: leaves alternate, ternate, tomentose: male racemes axillary, composite: flowers tomentose, 3-bracteate at the base.

Circar mountains. Travancore.

ORDER CLIX. ALISMACEÆ.

Flowers hermaphrodite or monœcious: calyx 6-sepalled, regular, much spreading: sepals distinct, outer ones calycine, persistent, inner ones larger, petaloid, withering, deciduous: stamens 6—9—12 or indefinite, hypogynous, free: filaments filiform: anthers 2-celled, more or less extrorse, cells parallel, dehiscing lengthways: ovaries numerous, 1-celled, 1-, seldom 2-ovuled, arranged in a circle or heaped together in heads, distinct, seldom connate at the base, ovules campylotropal: styles as many as the ovaries, continuous, distinct, persistent: stigmas simple: carpels as many as the ovaries, 1-celled, 1-seeded, indehiscent: seeds uncinately reflexed: testa simple, thin, membranaceous: embryo exalbuminous: radicle inferior, next the hilum.—Marshy or aquatic herbs, glabrous, generally stemless: root fasciculately fibrous: leaves petioled, nerved, primary ones sometimes grassy and sessile (phyllodia): petiole sheathing at the base: flowers long-pedicelled, verticillately racemose or panicled, bracteate, white, seldom reddish.

GENUS I. SAGITTARIA.

Monœcia Enneandria. *Sex: Syst:*

Deriv. From *Sagitta* an arrow, referring to a resemblance in the leaves.

Gen. Char. Flowers monœcious: sepals six, outer ones calycine, persistent, inner ones larger, petaloid, deciduous, æstivation imbricated: stamens hypogynous, free: anthers 2-celled, subextrorse, elliptic-oblong, emarginate, 2-lobed at the base and there fixed: cells joined together by a narrow connectivum: ovaries heaped together in heads above a globose receptacle, distinct, compressed at the sides, 1-celled, 1-ovuled: ovule affixed to the base of the cell, erect, campylotropal: styles as many as the ovaries: stigmas obtuse, papillose, carpels shortly beaked with the persistent style: membranaceous, 1-seeded, indehiscent: seed basilar, erect, uncinately plaited, testa membranaceous, very thin: embryo exalbuminous: radicle inferior.—Marshy and aquatic herbs, generally stemless: leaves petioled, most usually sagittate or hastate: scapes many flowered, simple, very rarely paniculately branched: flowers pedicelled, verticillately racemose, white, verticils bracteated, lower ones female, upper ones male.

(1) S. sagittifolia. *(Linn.)*

Ident. Roxb. flor. Ind. III. p. 645.—Spreng. Syst. II. 632.

Engrav. Engl. Bot. II. t. 84.

Spec. Char. Leaves deeply sagittate, acute, basilar lobes acuminate, straight: scape simple, flowers pure white with a purplish base.

Peninsula, flowering from February to April.

(2) S. cordifolia. *(Roxb.)*

Ident. Roxb. l. c. p. 647.

Spec. Char. Leaves very long petioled, ovate, deeply cordate, rounded at the apex, finger-nerved, basilar lobes acutish, spreading: scape simple, very long, racemosely 5—8-flowered at the top, flowers verticilled by threes, hermaphrodite, 9—12-androus, males intermixed, carpels obliquely obovate, girt with a toothed margin, marked on each side with a prominent arched line: flowers small, white.

Silhet. Assam. Coromandel. In tanks near Calcutta. Flowering in the rainy season.

(3) S. OBTUSIFOLIA. *(Linn.)*

Ident. Spreng. l. c. p. 633.—Roxb. l. c. p. 646.

Engrav. Rheede Mal. xi. t. 45.

SPEC. CHAR. Leaves radical, long petioled, ovate-sagittate, basilar lobes divaricate, finely pointed: scapes erect, 5—6-angled, striated, branched and verticilled at the top: flowers numerous, small, white.

Coromandel. Concans. Guzarat. Flowering in the rainy and cold season.

(4) S. TRIANDRA. *(Dalz.)*

Ident. Dalzell Bomb. flora. p. 249.—Hook Journ. Bot. II. 144.

SPEC. CHAR. Leaves long petioled, linear-spathulate, 3-nerved, much longer than the scape, obtusely keeled at the back: scape erect, simple, round, obtusely trigonal at the apex: flowers triandrous, verticilled, short pedicelled, inconspicuous: female flowers on the lower part of the spike.

Malwan district, flowering in August.

ORDER CLX. FLUVIALES.

Flowers naked, males and females in the same or in distinct plants, the one reduced to a simple pistil, the others to a solitary stamen, sometimes heaped together by fours, eights or tens, and bearing pseudo-hermaphrodite flowers: stamen sometimes enclosed in a cup-shaped spathe, very rarely surrounded by a bract: anther sessile or supported by a filament, 1—2 or 4-celled: ovary sessile, rarely stalked, 1-ovuled: ovule erect, descending or pendulous: style 1 or none: stigmas 1—3: fruit more or less juiceless, sometimes sub-drupaceous, 1-seeded, indehiscent: seed erect or suspended: embryo exalbuminous, furnished with a lateral cleft, thickened at the radicular extremity, thinner by the cotyledon and there straight, uncinately curved or spirally bent inwards.—Aquatic herbs, submersed, seldom floating: leaves scattered, very rarely opposite or in three's, usually narrow, stipulate: stipules connate among themselves, or cohering into a sheath together with the petiole: flowers axillary or terminal, solitary, sub-glomerate or spiked.

Sub-Order I. Naiadaceæ.

Style very short: stigmas 3 or 2, elongated: seed erect: embryo straight: pollen globose.—Leaves in three's or opposite, nerveless, repand-toothed.

GENUS 1. NAJAS.

Monœcia Pentandria. *Sex: Syst:*

Deriv. From *Naias*, a water-nymph, alluding to the habitation of the plants.

Gen. Char. Flowers diœcious or monœcious, naked, sessile in the axils of the leaves, solitary: males reduced to a solitary stamen, each inclosed in a cup-shaped spathe: anther sub-sessile, 4-cornered, sharply pointed, 4-celled, bursting the spathe when flowering, sustained by the excrescent filament, and dehiscing at the apex by four revolute valves: pollen sub-globose: female flowers reduced to a pistil, destitute of a spathe: ovary sessile, 1-ovuled, ovule erect: style very short or short, continuous with the ovary: stigmas 2—3, elongated, internally papillose: fruit sub-drupaceous, 1-seeded: seed erect, straight: embryo exalbuminous, straight.—Aquatic herbs, submersed, branched: leaves tern, rarely opposite, sessile, much dilated and sheathing at the base, flat, nerveless, repand-toothed: teeth somewhat thorny.

(1) N. Indica. *(Chamisso.)*

Ident. Cham. in Linnæa, iv. 501.

Syn. Fluvialis Indica, *Pers. syn. II.* 530.—N. dichotoma, *Roxb. flor. Ind. III.* 749. Caullinia Indica, *Willd.*

Spec. Char. Stem round, dichotomous: leaves tern or opposite, elongated, very narrow-linear, remotely denticulate: sheath dentate, ciliated: ovaries axillary, solitary, sessile: style 2-cleft.

Bengal. Tranquebar. Western Coast. Common in tanks. Flowering in the rains.

Sub-Order II. Potamogetoneæ.

Flowers pseudo-hermaphrodite: males surrounded by a bract: stigma sub-sessile, simple: pollen globose.

GENUS II. POTAMOGETON.

Tetrandria Tetra. *Sex: Syst:*

Deriv. From *Potamos*, a river, and *Geiton*, near, alluding to the habitat of the species.

GEN. CHAR. Flowers androgynous, spiked, naked, placed together by eights and bearing a pseudo-hermaphrodite flower, 4-gynous: 4-sepaled, 4-androus, from them four central ones females (pistils), ebracteate, distinct, 4 males at the circumference, reduced to solitary stamens, alternating with the females (pistils), each supported by a broadly spathulate bract: stamen inserted at the short claw of the bract: anther sub-sessile, ovate-cordate, emarginately 2-lobed at the apex, 2-celled, dehiscing extrorsely lengthways: ovary sessile, 1-ovuled: ovule affixed to the ventral suture below the apex: style terminal, short or wanting: stigma introrsely oblique, papillose, entire: fruit drupaceous, lenticular-compressed at the sides, 1-seeded, indehiscent: putamen coriaceous, woody, half-2-celled: embryo exalbuminous: radicle inferior, opposite the hilum.—Caulescent aquatic herbs, submersed or floating: leaves scattered, distichous, the top ones sometimes, very rarely all opposite, stipulate: stipules connate among themselves, distinct from the petiole or leaf, seldom joined together with the petiole into a sheath: spikes spadix-shaped, peduncled, naked, terminal and axillary, emerging while in flower.

(1) P. PERFOLIATUM. *(Linn.)*

Ident. Linn. spec. 182.—Kunth Enum. pl. III. 133.

Syn. P. Loeselii, *Röem. and Schult. syst. III.* 508.

Engrav. Eng. Bot. t. 168.—Cham. in Linn. II. t. 5 fig. 13.

SPEC. CHAR. Stem round, slightly branched; leaves all submersed, of one shaped, sessile, half-stem-clasping with a cordate base, ovate or ovate-lanceolate, obtuse, membranous, pellucid: stipules united into a sheath, embracing the stem: fruit obtusely angled.

Streams near Dapoorie.

(2) P. CRISPUM. *(Linn.)*

Ident. Linn. sp. 183.—Kunth. l. c.—Dalz. Bomb. flor. p. 248.

Syn. P. tuberosum, *Roxb. flor. Ind. I. p.* 452.—P. serratum, *Lam.*

Engrav. Engl. Bot. t. 1012.—Flor. Dan. t. 927.

SPEC. CHAR. Stem branched, rather compresssd: leaves all submersed, uniform, sessile, oblong-linear, obtuse or shortly acuminate, sharply denticulate, waved and crisp on the margin, membranous, pellucid: fruit obliquely and broadly ovate, terminated by a slightly recurved, compressed and subulate peak: flowers green.

Tanks in the Concans. Oudh. Bengal. Flowering in February and March.

(3) P. PECTINATUM. *(Linn.)*

Ident. Linn. sp. 183.—Kunth. l. c. p. 137.

Syn. P. marinum, *Linn.*—P. filiformis, *Pers. syn.*—P. Vaillantii, *Roem et Shult.*—P. tenuifolius, *Humb. et Kunth.*

Engrav. Engl. Bot. t. 323.—Flor. Dan. t. 1746.

SPEC. CHAR. Stem round: all the leaves submersed, extremely narrow, half-round and channelled, divided into tubular compartments, having sheaths at the base: spikes long-peduncled, interrupted: peduncles thread-like.

Plentiful in the large tank at Gogo.

(4) P. INDICUM. *(Roxb.)*

Ident. Roxb. fl. Ind. I. p. 452.—Don. prod. xxi.—Dalz. Bomb. flor. p. 248.

Syn. P. Roxburghianus, *Schult. Mant. III. p.* 367.

SPEC. CHAR. Stem branched, creeping, round, smooth, knotty: leaves alternate, floral ones opposite, petioled, narrow-lanceolate or elliptic-oval, shining, smooth, entire: stipules solitary, axillary, sheathing as long as the petioles, divided to the middle: peduncles solitary, axillary or opposite the leaves, round, thick, smooth, about as long as the cylindric spike: sepals with long claws, roundish, concave, persistent: flowers small, green.

Common in tanks and lakes. Waterholes of the high hill forts of the Western Deccan. Oudh. Flowering in February and March.

GENUS III. SPATHIUM.

Hexandria Tetragynia. *Sex: Syst:*

Deriv. From *Spatha*, a spathe, the flowers are enclosed in a spathe.

GEN. CHAR. Flowers densely sessile on an angular peduncled spadix, surrounded by a 1-leaved, coloured, caducous involucre, each with twin collateral coloured bracts: perianth none: stamens 6, hypogynous: filaments free, subulate, patent: anthers with opposite cells, contiguous: ovary 3—4-celled, 3—4-beaked, beaks erect, stigmatose within: ovules 2—4 ascending from the base of the central angle of the cell, orthotropal : capsule 3—4-celled, 3—4-cleft, introrsely dehiscent, cells 1—4-seeded : seeds erect, ovate, acuminate, testa coriaceous, smooth.—Perennial marshy herbs with a bulbous rhizome : leaves long-petioled, linear-oblong, cordate at the base, nerved, floating, scape obsoletely trigonal : involucre 1- leaved, petioled, cordate : bracts cuneate : capsules smooth or echinate.

(1) S. Chinense. *(Lour.)*

Ident. Lour. Coch. I. 270. Dalz. Bomb. flor. p. 248.

Syn. Aponogeton monostachyon, *Linn. suppl.* 214. *Roxb. flor. Ind. II.* 210.

Engrav. Bot. Repos. t. 406. Roxb. Cor. I. t. 81. Rheede Mal. xi. t. 15.

Spec. Char. Root tuberous : leaves radical, long-petioled, linear-oblong, cordate at the base, pointed, entire, smooth, 3—5-nerved : scapes as long as the leaves : spikes densely flowered : calyx of 2 wedge-shaped concave leaflets : capsules smooth, pointed, 1-celled, 4—8-seeded : flowers small, purplish-white with blue anthers.

Coromandel. Concans. Bengal. Silhet. Tanks in the Dharwar and Belgaum districts. Flowering in the rains.

(2) S. undulatum. *(Voight.)*

Ident. Voight Hort. Calc. p. 694.

Syn. Aponogeton undulatum, *Roxb. l. c.*

Spec. Char. Root tuberous, stoloniferous : leaves radical, submersed or floating, lanceolate, waved, 3—5-nerved : petioles compressed, shorter than the leaves : scapes round, smooth : spikes simple, crowded with flowers : capsules smooth, 1—2-seeded.

Bengal, in sweet water, flowering in the rains.

(3) S. echinatum. *(Roxb.)*

Ident. Roxb. l. c. p. 210 (under Aponogeton.)

Spec. Char. Leaves linear, cordate at the base : spikes single and simple : capsules echinate : seeds about six.

Circars, in shallow fresh waters.

ORDER CLXI. BUTOMACEÆ.

Flowers hermaphrodite, regular : sepals 6, outer ones persistent, inner ones petaloid, usually deciduous, imbricated in æstivation : stamens hypogynous, definite or indefinite : filaments free: anthers 2-celled, fixed by the base, erect, generally moveable, dehiscing lengthways: cells parallel: ovaries 6 or more, orbiculately disposed, separate or more or less coherent at the middle, 1-celled: ovules numerous, fixed to the walls of the reticulately veined cavity, sessile or supported by a short thread, ascending, anatropal or campylotropal: styles continuous, distinct, introrsely stigmatose at the apex, sometimes none, then the stigmas extrorsely adnate to the ovaries: carpels as many as the ovaries, distinct, coriaceous, beaked with the persistent style, 1-celled, many-seeded, dehiscing by the ventral suture: seeds minute, parietal: testa membranaceous: embryo exalbuminous, homotropal, straight or uncinately plaited: radicle looking towards the hilum.—Marshy or aquatic perennial herbs, stemless or caulescent, glabrous: leaves scattered, quite entire, sometimes sessile, linear, sheathing at the base, sometimes petioled, broad, furnished with a petiole sheathing at the base: scapes simple, 1 or umbellately many-flowered at the apex: umbel involucrated with bracts: flowers rose-coloured, white or yellow.

GENUS I. BUTOMOPSIS.

Octandria Triandria. *Sex: Syst.*

Deriv. Plants resembling *Butomus*, which is from *Bous*, an ox, and *Temno*, to cut; it cuts the mouths of cattle.

GEN. CHAR. Same as the Order.

(1) B. LANCEOLATA. *(Kunth.)*

Ident. Kunth Enum. pl. III. p. 165.

Syn. Butomus lanceolatus, *Roxb. flor. Ind. II. p.* 315.

Engrav. Royle Ill. t. 95, fig. 1.

SPEC. CHAR. Leaves radical, long-petioled, lanceolate: scape the length of the leaves, 6—12 flowered: flowers pedicelled, erect, umbellate, middle-sized, white, sepals pale green outside, tipped with rose.

Surat. North West Provinces. Flowering in the rains.

ORDER CLXII. PONTEDERACEÆ.

Flowers hermaphrodite: calyx corollaceous, funnel-shaped or hypocrateriform, limb more or less irregulary 6-cleft, generally sub-bilabiate, sometimes deeply 6-parted, persistent in withering: æstivation spirally convolute: stamens 6, more or less unequal, inserted on the tube of the calyx, sometimes at different heights, sometimes the three outer ones obliterated: anthers 2-celled, fixed by the 2-lobed base, erect, introrse, smaller in the shorter stamens: cells parallely contiguous, dehiscing lengthways: ovary sessile, free, 3-celled: ovules numerous, fixed to 2-lobed placentæ, anatropal, solitary and suspended by the apex when the ovaries are 1-celled by abortion: style simple, terminal: stigma thickish, 3 (?) or 6-lobed: fruit free, either capsular, 3 or pseudo-1-celled, loculicidally 3-valved, valves septiferous and seed-bearing in the middle, or utricular, 1-celled, 1-seeded and indehiscent: seeds ribbed and striated or smooth, marked with a small basal hilum and thickish terminal chalaza: testa thin: embryo cylindric in the axis of densely farinaceous albumen, straight, looking towards the hilum—Marshy and aquatic herbs, creeping with a stem or rhizome, sometimes stemless, perennial, quite glabrous except the calyx: radical fibres and rootlets furnished with a spongiole: leaves long-petioled, more or less fleshy and dilated, very rarely linear and sessile, petioles sheathed at the base: peduncles lateral, very rarely radical or terminal, 1—2-many flowered: flowers sessile or pedicelled, spiked racemose or corymbose, each without bracts, wrapped in a common spathe, slowly more or less remote, furnished below the spathe with a leaf resembling the rest: calyces usually blue or violet, seldom whitish or yellow.

GENUS I. MONOCHORIA.

Hexandria Monogynia. *Sex: Syst:*

Gen. Char. Calyx persistent, sepals oblong, obtuse, spreading, outer ones broader: stamens inserted at the base of the calyx, erect, one more robust: filaments linear-subulate, flattened, the sixth of the larger stamen longer and at one side, towards the middle, spurred with a tooth-shaped subulate ascending appendage: anthers linear or oblong, emarginate at the apex, 2-celled: cells contiguous: ovary free, oblong, sessile, incompletely 3-celled: ovules numerous, fixed to three 2-lobed placentæ, remote from the centre: style longish, persistent: stigma obtuse: capsule ovate, 3-cornered, mucronate with the persistent style, 3-celled, 3-valved, many seeded: seeds minute, elliptic, ribbed lengthways.—Creeping aquatic, glabrous herbs: radical leaves long-petioled, hastate, sagittate or cordate, petioles sheathing at the base: peduncles radical, simple, scapiform, 1-leaved above, racemosely or corymbosely few-many-flowered: flowers blue: spathe 1-leaved below the raceme or corymb, a little remote.

(1) M. HASTÆFOLIA. *(Presl.)*

Ident. Presl. in Reliq. Haenk. II. 128.—Kunth Enum. pl. iv. 133.

Syn. Pontederia hastata, *Linn. Roxb. flor. Ind. II. p.* 121.

Engrav. Roxb. Cor. II. t. 3.

SPEC. CHAR. Leaves triangular or hastate-pointed, many-nerved, smooth and glossy, posterior angles generally obtuse: flower-bearing petioles swollen near the apex and there split for the passage of the raceme: flowers numerous, pedicelled, bright blue-violet.

Margins of tanks in Malabar. Coromandel. Flowering in the rainy and cold season.

(2) M. VAGINALIS. *(Presl.)*

Ident. Presl. l. c.—Kunth l. c. p. 134.

Syn. Pontederia vaginalis, *Burm. Ind. p.* 80. *Roxb. l. c. p.* 121.

Engrav. Roxb. Cor. II. t. 110. Rheede Mal. xi. t. 44. Rumph. Amb. vi. t. 75 fig. 1.

SPEC. CHAR. Leaves narrow-cordate, pointed, smooth, glossy, 5—7-nerved: petioles long, fistulous, smooth, those bearing a raceme swollen about the middle: raceme short-peduncled: flowers about 12, blue hyacinth.

Margins of tanks. Coromandel. Concans. Bengal. Flowering in the rainy and cold season.

(3) M. SAGITTATA. *(Kunth.)*

Ident. Kunth. l. c.

Syn. Pontederia sagittata, *Roxb. l. c. p.* 124.

SPEC. CHAR. Leaves sagittate: umbel sessile: flowers long-pedicelled.

Near Chittagong.

(4). M. DILATATA. *(Kunth.)*

Ident. Kunth l. c.

Syn. Pontederia dilatata, *Buch. in Symes' Ava. Roxb. l. c. p.* 123.

Engrav. Andr. Rep. t. 490.

SPEC. CHAR. Leaves cordate-sagittate, long-petioled, shorter than the floriferous petioles, very acute: flowers umbellately corymbose, pale blue.

Bengal, flowering in the rainy and cold season.

(5) M. PLANTAGINEA. *(Kunth.)*

Ident. Kunth l. c., p. 135.

Syn. Pontederia plantaginea, *Roxb. l. c. p.* 123.

SPEC. CHAR. Diffuse: leaves narrow, cordate: racemes peduncled, 3-flowered.

Silhet. Assam in marshes.

ORDER CLXIII. LILIACEÆ.

Flowers hermaphrodite: calyx 6-sepaled, corollaceous, regular, deciduous or persistent, sepals distinct, equal: æstivation imbricated: stamens 6, inserted at the bottom of the flower or the base of the sepals and shorter than them: filaments distinct, subulate or filiform, beardless, seldom pubescent: anthers 2-celled, dehiscing lengthways introrsely or at either margin: cell parallel, adnate to a narrow dorsal connectivum: ovary free, sessile, 3-celled, cells opposite the outer sepals, ovules numerous, fixed to the central angle, in two rows, horizontal, anatropal: style terminal, sometimes very short, nearly wanting: stigma 3-lobed or 3-cleft, very rarely entire, lobes or segments for the most part plaited: capsule 3-celled, loculicidally 3-valved, central column none: seeds numerous, compressed, superposed: testa membranaceous, thin, sometimes sub-spongiose, brown, rufescent or pale: embryo small, enclosed, axile, straight: radicle next the hilum: albumen sub-cartilaginous or fleshy.—Bulbous herbs: bulb tunicate or scaly: stem herbaceous, erect, simple, very rarely branched above, leafy, 1—2-many flowered at the apex: leaves scattered, opposite or verticilled, sessile, usually narrow, striated or sub-reticulately nerved: flowers usually showy, erect or nodding: peduncles not articulated with the calyx.

GENUS I. METHONICA.

Hexandria Monogynia. *Sex: Syst:*

Gen. Char. Sepals 6, corollaceous, distinct, lanceolate, narrow-clawed at the base, waved at the margin: stamens 6, inserted at the base of the sepals, much spreading, filaments elongated, filiform, straight, anthers broadly linear, deeply emarginate at the base, fixed below the middle, dehiscing lengthways, when open incumbent and slightly curved: ovary free, sessile, obliquely oblong, 3-cornered, 3-celled, ovules in two rows, sub-horizontal, anatropal: style terminal, deflexed, stigma 3-cleft, segments elongated, very narrow, channelled, spreading, recurved: capsule sub-globosely turbinate, coriaceous, 3-celled, carpels splitting by a ventral suture, seed-bearing from either margin, central column none: seeds in two rows, globose, baccate, scarlet: embryo cylindric: radicle centrifugal. —Climbing herbs, branched, root bulbous: leaves scattered, opposite or ternately verticilled, sessile, oblong lanceolate, acuminately cirrhose: peduncles 1-flowered, extra-axillary, somewhat opposite leaved and terminal, elongated: flowers showy.

(1) M. superba. *(Lam.)*

Ident. Lam. encycl. iv. 133.

Syn. Gloriosa superba, *Linn.—Roxb. flor. Ind. II.* 143.

Engrav. Lam. Ill. t. 247.—Red Lil. t. 26.—Rheede Mal. vii. t. 57. Andr. Rep. t. 129.—Bot. Reg. t. 77.

Spec. Char. Leaves tendril-bearing, lower ones oblong, upper ones ovate-lanceolate, undulated: flowers scarlet, yellow at the base.

Malabar and Travancore. Coromandel. Guzerat. Flowering in the rainy season.

GENUS II. LILIUM.

Hexandria Monogynia. *Sex: Syst:*

Deriv. From the Celtic word *Li*, meaning whiteness, on account of the beautiful flowers of the original species.

19

Gen. Char. Sepals 6, regular, deciduous, distinct, often narrow-clawed at the base, spreading or revolute above, with a nectariferous furrow within, above the base either naked or fimbriate-ciliated: æstivation alternative: stamens at the lowest base of the sepals, filaments filiform, subulate at the apex, anthers linear, emarginate or obtuse, 2-lobed at the base, fixed above the base, dehiscing lengthways, when open curved, incumbent: ovary free, 6-furrowed, 3-celled, ovules in 2 rows, horizontal, anatropal: style terminal, cylindric, straight or somewhat curved, deciduous: stigma torosely thickened, 3-cornered, 3-lobed at the apex: capsule sub-coriaceous, oblong or obovate, hexagonal, obtuse at the apex, very shortly and thinly stalked at the base, 3-celled, loculicidally 3-valved above, valves septiferous in the middle, central column none: seeds in two rows, numerous, broadly winged at the margin, brown or yellowish: embryo straight or very slightly sigmoid, more or less shorter than the albumen: radicle next the hilum.—Bulbous herbs: bulb scaly: stem simple, erect, leafy, 1-many-flowered at the apex: flowers peduncled, umbelled, corymbose or racemose, large, showy, erect or nodding: leaves scattered or verticilled, usually narrow.

(1) L. Wallichianum. *(Roem and Schult.)*

Ident. Roem. and Schult. vii. 1689.

Engrav. Wall. tent. 40 t. 29.—Wight's Icon. t. 2035.

Spec. Char. Stem slender, leafy, few or 1-flowered at the apex: leaves scattered, numerous, approximated, linear, acuminate, sessile: flowers hypocrateriform, drooping: tube long, throat campanulate, naked, limb spreading.

Neilgherries. The *L. Neilgherrense* and *L. tubiflorum (R. W.)* are probably mere varieties of the above. Flowering in July and August.

GENUS III. SANSEVIERA.

Hexandria Monogynia. *Sex: Syst:*

Deriv. In honour of M. Sansevier, a Swedish botanist.

Gen. Char. Perianth corollaceous, tubular, 6-cleft to the middle, deciduous, segments sub-spathulate-linear, obtuse, 1-nerved, equal, much spreading: stamens 6, inserted at the throat, exserted, spreading, filaments filiform: anthers 2-celled, linear-oblong, 2-lobed at the apex, 2-cleft at the base, fixed at the middle of the back, introrse: ovary free, sessile, oblong, 3-celled: ovules solitary, sessile, ascending, anatropal: styline column terminal, filiform, erect, exceeding the stamens: stigma capitate: berries 1—3, slightly united, globose, fleshy, 1-seeded: seed globose: embryo albuminous.

—Stemless, perennial, stoloniferous plants: rhizome thick, creeping: leaves radical, lanceolate, thick and hard, often fasciated, sheathing at the base: scape proceeding from the centre of the leaves, bracteate, simple, racemosely many-flowered at the apex: flowers fasciculately heaped together by fours or sixes, bracteolate, greenish-white, or greenish-yellowish: pedicels jointed above the middle: perianth attenuated at the base into the pedicel.

(1) S. Roxburghiana. *(Schult.)*

Ident. Schult syst. vii. 357. Kunth Enum. pl. v. p. 18.

Syn. S. Zeylanica, *Roxb. flor. Ind. II.* 161.

Engrav. Roxb. Cor. II. t. 184.—Rheede Mal. xi. t. 42.

Spec. Char. Leaves deeply channelled, striated, spotted: flowering scape central, higher: flowers numerous, purplish.

Malabar. Travancore. Coromandel. Common in rocky places. Flowering in the rainy season.

GENUS IV. ALOE.

Hexandria Monogynia. *Sex: Syst:*

Deriv. From *Alloeh*, the Arabic name.

Gen. Char. Calyx 6-sepaled, straight or curved, sometimes ventricose at the base, deciduous, outer sepals gibbous at the base, inner ones thinner, free above, spreading or recurved at the apex: stamens hypogynous, enclosed or seldom exserted, filaments filiform, distinct, anthers 2-celled, introrse, deeply 2-cleft at the base: ovary free, sessile, 3-celled: ovules many, biseriate, straight, incumbent on a fleshy cupular cushion, and adnate lengthways: style terminal, thin, 3-furrowed, stigma simple or 3-lobed, papillose: capsule 3-celled, loculicidally 3-valved, valves septiferous in the middle, central column none: seeds unequally triangular or lenticular-compressed, dark, covered with aril at the margins: testa sub-crustaceous, dark: embryo cylindric, straight, axile, scarcely shorter than the fleshy albumen.

(1) A. Indica. *(Royle.)*

Ident. Royle Ill. p. 390.

Syn. A. perfoliata, *Roxb. flor. Ind. II. p.* 167.

Spec. Char. Leaves ensiform, dentate, erect: calyx none: racemes reflexed, cylindric: flowers large, red.

North Western provinces, in dry situations.

GENUS V. UROPETALUM.

Hexandria Monogynia. *Sex: Syst:*

Deriv. From *Oura*, a tail or appendage, and *Petalon*, a petal: the divisions of the flower are lengthened out.

GEN. CHAR. Calyx corollaceous campanulate-tubular, limb 6-parted, regular, persistent, outer segments spreading, inner ones shorter, broader, connate, connivent: stamens 6, inserted on the throat, three opposite the inner segments more deeply inserted, all enclosed, filaments adnate, free and filiform at the apex, anthers 2-celled, introrse, linear, 2-cleft at the base, fixed at the back below the middle: ovary free, sessile, oblong, triangular, 3-celled: ovules 12—22, in two rows, horizontal, anatropal: style erect, teretely 3-cornered, stigma largish, 3-cleft, segments sub-ovate-rotund: capsule parchment-like, short obovate, round at the apex, acutely 3-cornered, 3-celled, loculicidally 3-valved, valves septiferous in the middle: seeds compressed, elliptic-oblong, winged at the margins, dotted, scabrous, black: embryo axile, cylindric, straight, a little shorter than the albumen: radicle touching the hilum.—Bulbous herbs: bulb tunicated: leaves linear, thickish: raceme simple, remote-flowered: pedicels 1-bracteate at the base, bracts exceeding the pedicels: flowers nodding.

(1) U. MONTANUM. *(Dalz.)*

Ident. Dalz. in Hook. Journ. Bot. II. p. 142.—Bomb. flor. p. 250.

SPEC. CHAR. Scape round, 1-foot: leaves linear, folded, as long as the scape: raceme about 8-flowered: bracts scarious, acuminated: capsule stalked: cells 3—4-seeded: flowers white.

Belgaum. Western Deccan, in pastures, flowering in August.

(2) U. CONCANENSE. *(Dalz.)*

Ident. Dalz. l. c.

SPEC. CHAR. Scape 8—10 inches high: leaves half-round, fleshy, filiform, few, deeply grooved above, a half shorter than the scape: raceme drooping, 3—4-flowered: capsule 3-lobed, cells 6-seeded: seeds flat, black, shining and smooth: flowers white.

Rocky places in the Malwan district, flowering in August.

GENUS VI. BARNARDIA.

Hexandria Monogynia. *Sex: Syst:*

Deriv. In honour of E. Barnard, *F.L.S.*

Gen. Char. Calyx corollaceous, 6-sepaled, regular, withering, persistent: sepals distinct, lanceolate-oblong, acute, equal, much spreading: stamens 6, adnate to the base of the sepals and almost equalling them, filaments membranaceous, anthers 2-celled, introrse, oblong, 2-lobed at both ends, fixed by the middle of the back: ovary free, shortly stalked, ovate, 3-celled: ovules solitary, ascending: style erect, subulate, filiform, stigma truncated, simple: capsules oblong, triangular, parchment-like, 3-celled, loculicidally 3-valved, valves septiferous in the middle: seeds linear-oblong, very finely striated, convex at the back: testa chestnut-brown, soluble: embryo axile, cylindric, straight, shorter than the fleshy albumen: radicle touching the hilum.

(1) B. Indica. *(R.W.)*

Ident. Wight's Icon. b. t. 2041.

Spec. Char. Bulbous: leaves lanceolate, channelled towards the base, sub-acuminate at the apex, strongly nerved: scape terete, racemose, longer than the leaves: flowers cernuous, afterwards drooping.

Western slopes of the Neilgherries. Nagpore. Flowering in May.

GENUS VII. URGINIA.

Hexandria Monogynia. *Sex: Syst:*

Gen. Char. Calyx corollaceous, 6-sepaled, regular, deciduous, sepals connate at the base, oblong, obtuse, 1-nerved, equal: stamens 6, inserted at the base of the sepals, filament filiform, equal, slightly dilated towards the base or middle, anthers 2-celled, introrse, linear-oblong, 2-cleft at the base, fixed by the middle of the back: ovary free, sessile, oblong, 3-cornered, 6-furrowed, 3-celled: ovules many, in two rows, horizontal, shortly funiculate, anatropal: style filiform, erect, stigma convex, entire or 3-lobed: capsule chartaceous or membranaceous, elliptic, rounded at the top, 3-cornered, 3-celled, loculicidally 3-valved, many-seeded: seeds flat, winged at the margin, ascending, imbricated upwards: testa membranaceous, black or brown, margin dilated into a wing: embryo axile, cylindric, straight, a little shorter than the albumen: radicle next the hilum.—Bulbous scape-bearing herbs: bulb tunicated: leaves lanceolate or linear, appearing late: raceme simple, pedicels bibracteate at the base.

(1) U. Indica. *(Kunth.)*

Ident. Kunth Enum. pl. iv. p. 333.

Syn. Scilla Indica, *Roxb. flor. Ind. II.* 147.

Engrav. Wight's Icon. t. 2063.

Spec. Char. Leaves narrow, attenuated at the base: racemes simple, exceeding the leaves: flowers remote, solitary, long-pedicelled, lax.

Sandy shores of both Concans. Tuticorin. Rocky places at Covalom near Trevandrum.

(2) U. Coromandeliana. *(R. W.)*

Ident. Wight l. c. t. 2064.

Syn. Scilla Coromandeliana. *Roxb. l. c.*

Spec. Char. Leaves linear, tapering to the point, shorter than the scape: racemes erect, flowers short, pedicelled, supported by a largish scariose bract as long as the pedicel.

Sand hills on the Coromandel coast, flowering in April and May.

(3) U. congesta. *(R. W.)*

Ident. Wight l. c. t. 2064.

Spec. Char. Leaves linear-subulate, about the length of the scape: scape erect, naked: racemes short, compact: flowers short-pedicelled, supported at the base by a short, broadish scariose obtuse bract: sepals lanceolate, the inner slightly smaller: ovary conical: capsules sub-ovate or globose, 3-celled, cells 3—4-seeded, seeds orbicular, bound all round by a broad wing, shining black.

Sea coast.

GENUS VIII. LEDEBOURIA.

Hexandria Monogynia. *Sex: Syst:*

Deriv. Named after M. Ledebour, a botanical author.

Gen. Char. Calyx corollaceous, 6-sepaled, regular, persistent, sepals free, oblong, 1-nerved, campanulately connivent, spreading at the apex: stamens 6, adnate below to the sepals and shorter than them, filaments filiform, anthers 2-celled, introrse, elliptic, 2-lobed at both ends, fixed by the back: ovary free, stalked, depressed-globose, 3-celled: ovules 2 in each cell, fixed at the axis, collateral, ascending, anatropal: style filiform, furrowed, elongated, erect, stigma truncated simple: capsule 3-celled, tripartible: cells 1-seeded, two often abortive.—Bulbous scape-bearing herbs, bulb tunicated: leaves linear, striately nerved, sometimes throwing out a bulb at the top: raceme many-flowered, pedicels 1-bracteate at the base: flowers greenish, bases and pedicels red.

(1) L. HYACINTHINA. *(Roth.)*

Ident. Roth. Nov. Spec. 195.

Syn. Anthericum hyacinthoides. *Willd.* Erythronium Indicum. *Rottl.*

Engrav. Wight's Icon. t. 2040.—Bot. Mag. t. 3226.

SPEC. CHAR. Scapes 1—2, proceeding from the top of the bulb, racemosely-many flowered towards the top: leaves undulate, glabrous, bearing bulbs at the apex: flowers small, bluish, hyacinth-like.

Coimbatore. Coromandel coast. Bundelcund. Southern Concan.

(2) L. MACULATA. *(Dalz.)*

Ident. Dalz. in Hook. Journ. Bot. II. p. 142.—Bomb. flor. 251.

SPEC. CHAR. Leaves obovate, glabrous, wedge-shaped, attenuated into the petiole, purple-spotted and never bearing bulbs: flowers small, bluish, hyacinthine.

Concans. Deccan. Flowering in June.

GENUS IX. ASPHODELUS.

Hexandria Monogynia. *Sex: Syst:*

Deriv. From *A*, privative, and *Sphallo*, to supplant, a flower not to be surpassed.

GEN. CHAR. Calyx 6-sepaled, corollaceous, regular, deciduous, sepals connate at the base, almost equal, spreading: stamens 6, inserted at the base of the sepals, three a little longer, filaments linear, dilated at the base, concave and covering the ovary, anthers 2-celled, oblong, fixed above the 2-lobed base at the back, dehiscing lengthways: ovary free, sessile, sub-globose, 3-celled, ovules twin in the cells, collateral, inverted: style filiform, or sub-clavate, stigma capitately 3-lobed: capsules sub-globose, 3-celled, 3-valved, valves septiferous: seeds 2 in each cell, one often abortive, dimidiately-obovate, 3-sided, transversely wrinkled: embryo axile, cylindric, tapering, slightly curved, parallel to the hilum, the length of the albumen: radicle inferior.—Perennial herbs: leaves radical, subulate, triquetrous or broad linear, sheathing below: stem scapiform, erect, simple, or paniculately branched above, naked: flowers pedicelled, solitary, erect, racemose at the apex of the stems or branches: pedicels 1-bracteate at the base, jointed below the middle: calyx white or whitish.

(1) A. PAUCIFLORUS. *(R.W.)*

Ident. Wight's Icon. t. 2062.

SPEC. CHAR. Leaves fistulous, long-tapering, subulate, pointed: racemes terminal: flowers small, short-pedicelled: seed somewhat triangular, blunt, ovate, pointed.

Sands of the sea coast.

(2) A. CLAVATUS. *(Roxb.)*

Ident. Roxb. flor. Ind. II. 148.

SPEC. CHAR. Stem naked, branched, annual: leaves erect, straight, cylindric, fistular: filaments clavate above the ciliated base: flowers small, white, with brown keels.

Peninsula. Interior of Bengal. Flowering in the cold season.

GENUS X. PHALANGIUM.

Hexandria Monogynia. *Sex: Syst.*

Deriv. From *Phalanx* a venomous spider, whose bite the plants are said to cure.

GEN. CHAR. Calyx 6-sepaled, corollaceous, regular, withering persistent, sepals distinct, 3- seldom 5—9-nerved, much spreading, three inner ones sometimes broader: stamens 6, inserted at the base of the sepals, erect spreading, filaments filiform, beardless, anthers 2-celled, introrse, linear or oblong, emarginate, fixed by the back above the 2-lobed base: ovary free, sessile: ovules numerous, in two rows, horizontal, anatropal: style filiform, erect, stigma thickish, papillose, entire: capsule 3-bodied, 3-furrowed, 3-cornered, loculicidally 3-valved above, valves septiferous in the middle: seeds few, angled, black, shining: testa crustaceous, thin, fragile: embryo axile, slightly curved, almost the length of the fleshy albumen: radicle looking towards the hilum.—Herbs with fascicled roots: stem erect, scapiform, simple or branched above, leafy: leaves narrow, flat, membranaceous, sheathing at the base: flowers pedicelled, solitary, twin or fasciculately heaped together, loosely racemose at the apex of the stem and in the branches, white: pedicels bracteate at the base, articulated above the base.

(1) P. TUBEROSUM. *(Kunth.)*

Ident. Kunth Enum. pl. iv. p. 598.

Syn. Anthericum tuberosum. *Roxb. flor. Ind. II. p.* 149.

Engrav. Wight's Icon. t. 2036.—Roxb. Cor. II. t. 138.

SPEC. CHAR. Roots numerous, fleshy, each terminating in an oblong tuber: leaves radical, sword-shaped, undulated on the margin: scape round, naked: flowers panicled, white.

Circar mountains. Peninsula. Concans. Assam. Flowering in the rainy season.

(2) P. ATTENUATUM. *(R.W.)*

Ident. Wight's Icon. vi. and t. 2037.

SPEC. CHAR. Roots fleshy, not (or rarely) tuberous: leaves all radical, sword-shaped, scarcely waved on the margin, long attenuated on the point, membranaceous: scape round, naked, racemose, longer than the leaves: flowers numerous, 3—4-aggregated in the axils of the scariose bracts: ovary somewhat ovate, ovules numerous, style straight: flowers white.

Coimbatore, flowering in the rains.

(3) P. OLIGOSPERMUM. *(R.W.)*

Ident. Wight l. c. t. 2038.

SPEC. CHAR. Roots fleshy, tuberous: leaves radical, oblong lanceolate, waved on the margin, acute: scape terete, erect, branched: branches racemose: ovary sub-globose, 3-celled, with 2 superposed ovules in each cell: style declining: capsule 3-celled, 3-seeded: seed globose.

Coimbatore, flowering in July and August.

(4) P. PARVIFLORUM. *(R.W.)*

Ident. Wight l. c. t. 2039.

SPEC. CHAR. Roots numerous, fleshy, not tuberous: leaves linear lanceolate, tapering towards the point: scapes several, axillary, slender, ascending, loosely flexuose: flowers small, 3—4-aggregated in the axils of the somewhat remote bracts, short pedicelled: ovary 3-celled, with 2 superposed ovules in each: style simple: capsule 3-celled, cells 1-seeded: seed somewhat globose, concavely umbilicate below, rough: embryo curved.

Coimbatore.

GENUS XI. CHLOROPHYTUM.

Hexandria Monogynia. *Sex: Syst:*

Deriv. From *Chloros*, green, and *Phyton*, a plant, alluding to the appearance of the plants.

GEN. CHAR. Calyx 6-sepaled, corollaceous, regular, persistent: sepals connate at the base, three outer ones 5-nerved, inner ones a little longer, but narrower and thinner, 3-nerved: stamens 6, hypogynous, filaments filiform, glabrous, anthers 2-celled, oblong, emarginately 2-lobed at both ends, fixed at the back above the base, dehiscing lengthways: ovary free, sessile, 3-cornered: ovules many, in two rows: style filiform, erect, stigma truncated, entire: capsule roundish, 3-cornered, 3-lobed at the top, 3-celled, 3-valved: seeds 2—5 in each cell, lenticular-reniform, very finely tubercled: testa thin, crustaceous, adnate to fleshy albumen: embryo cylindric, straight.—Herbs with fascicled roots: fibres usually fleshy: leaves radical, linear or lanceolate, membranaceous or stiff: stem erect, scapiform, simple or paniculately branched: flowers pedicelled, solitary, twin, or collected in fascicles, bracteate, erect, white, greenish externally: pedicels articulated in the middle.

(1) C. ANTHERICOIDEUM. *(Dalz.)*

Ident. Dalz. in Hook. Journ. Bot. II. 141.—Bomb. flor. 251.

SPEC. CHAR. Roots many, tuberous: leaves radical, ensiform, slightly folded, margins waved, shorter than the naked scape, with 2 to 3 very short, simple branches: flowers racemose, solitary or twin: pedicels articulated near the base: filaments covered with minute, papillose vesicles: capsule triquetrous: seeds in each cell 5 to 6, compressed reniform: testa black.

District of Malwan, flowering in July.

(2) C. PARVIFLORUM. *(Dalz.)*

Ident. Dalz. l. c.

SPEC. CHAR. Tubers oblong, pendulous from the fibres: leaves erect, grass-like, linear-folded, striated, longer than the scape: scape simple, few-flowered: flowers solitary or sometimes twin, with acuminate bracts: filaments smooth: anthers green: pedicels jointed in the middle, drooping in fruit: capsule sharply 3-lobed, triangular: seeds in each cell 2—4.

Rocky places near the sea, Malwan district, flowering in July.

(3) C. BREVISCAPUM. *(Dalz.)*

Ident. Dalz. l. c. p. 252.

SPEC. CHAR. Tubers oblong, pendulous from a fibrous root: leaves flat, ensiform, margins undulated, acuminated, attenuated towards the base, striated, pale beneath: scape round, simple or rarely branched, half the length of the leaves: flowers racemose, twin: sepals oblong-acute, reflexed in flowering: pedicels jointed at the top: filaments papillose: capsule triquetrous: cells 1—3-seeded.

Malwan, flowering in July.

(4) C. NIMMONII. *(Dalz.)*

Ident. Dalz. l. c.

SPEC. CHAR. Leaves flat, broad-lanceolate, long-attenuated towards the base, very long, striated, shorter than the round scape: branches of the scape from the axils of sheathing bracts, long, undivided: flowers twin, remote, drooping, racemose: sepals spreading, exterior acute, inner ones obtuse: anthers and filaments papillose: cells of the triquetrous capsule 1-seeded.

Malwan. Ghauts opposite Bombay.

(5) C. GLAUCUM. *(Dalz.)*

Ident. Dalz. l. c.

SPEC. CHAR. Root a spherical depressed fibrous tuber: fibres above the tuber vermiform: leaves recurved, lanceolate acuminate, glaucous, striated, slightly folded, half the length of the rigidly erect scape, which is clothed with sharp sheathing scales: flowers twin, approximated, spreading: pedicels jointed above the middle: anthers and filaments papillose: ovary triquetrous: cells 8-ovuled.

Ghauts, rare.

GENUS XII. DIANELLA.

Hexandria Monogynia. *Sex: Syst:*

Deriv. From Diana, the sylvan goddess, so called from the plants growing in woods.

GEN. CHAR. Perianth corollaceous, deeply 6-parted, deciduous, leaflets oblong, equal: stamens 6, inserted at the base of the perianth, filaments geniculately bent inwards, linear-oblong, 2-lobed at the apex, fixed at the back above the sagittately 2-cleft base, erect, introrse: ovary free, sessile, globosely tricoccous: cells in the shells 5—9, fixed to the inner angle, in two rows, suspended by a short thread, anatropal: styline column terminal, elongated, erect, stigma truncated obtuse, undivided, papillose: berry tricoccous, many-seeded: seeds almost oval, lenticular compressed, hilum naked: testa crustaceous, black, shining, fragile: internal membrane very thin, adhering to fleshy albumen: chalaza clear, orbicular: embryo axile, very small, radicle looking towards the hilum.—Cæspitose plants, caulescent or stemless, sometimes suffruticose: leaves linear-grass-like, often denticulate at the back and margin, sheathing at the base: panicles terminal, solitary, simple or branched, bracteate: flowers pedicelled, usually blue, pedicels drooping, articulated beneath the perianth: bracteoles lateral, more or less remote from the pedicel: anthers very often yellow: berries blue.

(1) D. ENSIFOLIA. *(Aiton.)*

Ident. Ait. Kew (ed. 2), II. 276.—Kunth Enum. pl. v. p. 50.

Syn. D. nemorosa, *Jacq. Schoenbr. I.* 49.—*Roxb. flor. Ind. II.* 161.—Dracæna ensifolia, *Ait. l. c. I.* 454.

Engrav. Wight's Icon. t. 2053.—Red. Lil. t. 1.—Jacq. l. c. t. 94.

SPEC. CHAR. Leaves numerous, long, ensiform: margin prickly, serrulate: keel rough at the base and apex: branches and branchlets of the panicle spreading: pedicels crowded, drooping, nearly as long as the flower.

Courtallum. Malabar mountains.

GENUS XIII. ASPARAGOPSIS.

Hexandria Monogynia. *Sex: Syst:*

Deriv. Plants having the appearance of Asparagus.

GEN. CHAR. Flowers hermaphrodite: perianth corollaceous, deeply 6-parted, persistent, leaflets equal, campanulately connivent: stamens 6, inserted at the base of the leaflets, filaments subulate-filiform or linear, anthers 2-celled, emarginate, fixed at the back above the cordately 2-lobed base, introrse, erect: ovary free, 3-celled, ovules 3—9 in each cell, fixed to a central axis, in two rows, anatropal: styline column terminal, deciduous, stigma 3-cleft, segments recurved: berry globose, by abortion 1—2-seeded: seeds sub-globose: testa thin, black: albumen horny-cartilaginous: embryo transverse to the hilum: radicle remote.—Herbs or undershrubs, branched: leaves scattered, scaliform, often produced at the base into a divaricate spine, surrounding either barren or fertile peduncles or both, the barren ones sharpened, capillaceous, filiform, linear, or subulate, angled, the fertile ones solitary in the fasicles of the barren ones, or twin or more, 1-flowered, bracteolate at the base, nodosely pointed below the apex or at the middle, sometimes racemosely arranged in the bracteolated branchlets.

(1) A. sarmentosa. *(Kunth.)*

Ident. Kunth Enum. pl. v. p. 97.—Dalz. Bomb. flor. p. 246.

Syn. Asparagus sarmentosus, *Linn.*

Engrav. Rheede Mal. x. t. 10.—Red. Lil. t. 460.

Spec. Char. Stems woody, climbing, very much branched: branches grooved, ribbed, branchlets rather rough: thorns subulate, straight, turned downwards: leaves linear-mucronulate: racemes many-flowered, flowers white, berries red.

Guzarat. Deccan hills. Malabar.

(2) A. rubricaulis. *(Kunth.)*

Ident. Kunth Enum. l. c. p. 87.

Syn. Asparagus asiaticus, *Willd.*

Engrav. Wight's Icon. t. 2055.

Spec. Char. Fruticose: branches somewhat 3-cornered, flexuose, purplish, and with the branchlets smooth: thorns spreading recurved: leaves fascicled (25—30), slightly bristle-shaped, sharply mucronulate: peduncles solitary, jointed in the middle: cells of the ovaries 5-ovuled.

Neilgherries. Mysore.

(3) A. floribunda. *(Kunth.)*

Ident. Kunth l. c. p. 98.

Syn. Asparagus racemosus, *Willd.—Roxb. flor. Ind. II.* 151.—A. volubilis, *Ham. Herb.*

Engrav. Wight's Icon. t. 2056.

Spec. Char. Fruticose, very much branched, climbing, younger branches rough, branchlets furrowed, acute-angular: spines subulate, straightish, reflexed: leaflets fascicled (3—6 or more), aciform, triquetrous: racemes twin, many-flowered: cells of the ovary 4-ovuled: styline column 3-cleft at the apex.

Coimbatore, climbing among bushes, and other parts of the Peninsula, flowering in the autumnal rains.

(4) A. ascendens. *(Kunth.)*

Ident. Kunth l. c. p. 102.

Syn. Asparagus ascendens, *Roxb. flor. Ind. II.* 153.

Spec. Char. Herbaceous, erect: spines solitary, straight: leaves fascicled, cylindric: racemes lateral, simple or composite: berries pendulous: flowers white.

Rohilcund, flowering in October and November.

GENUS XIV. DRACÆNA.

Hexandria Monogynia. *Sex: Syst:*

Deriv. From *Drakaina*, a female dragon; the inspissated juice becomes a powder, like the dragon's blood.

Spec. Char. Perianth corollaceous, tubular, deeply 6-cleft, deciduous, segments sub-spathulate linear, obtuse, equal, much spreading or recurved: stamens 6, inserted at the throat of the perianth, exserted, erect spreading, filaments flat, narrow linear, attenuated at the apex, anthers 2-celled, oblong, 2-lobed at the apex, 2-cleft at the base, fixed by the middle of the back, introrse: ovary free, sessile, oblong, 3-celled: ovules solitary, sessile, ascending: styline column filiform, sulcately triangular, erect, exceeding the stamens, stigma 3-lobed, lobes round: berry sub-globose, fleshy, succulent, 1—3-seeded: seeds sub-globose: albumen horny.—Stems arboreous, simple or branched, cicatrised by the fallen leaves: leaves collected at the top of the stem and branches, lanceolate or linear, quite entire, half stem-clasping, glabrous: panicles terminal, solitary, simple or branched, bracteate: flowers pedicelled, solitary, twin, or in three's or five's, racemosely arranged on the branches of the panicle, whitish, greenish or yellowish white: pedicels bracteolate at the base, jointed above.

(1) D. spicata. (*Roxb.*)

Ident. Roxb. flor. Ind. II. p. 157.

Spec. Char. Caulescent: leaves lanceolate, reflexed: spikes terminal: bracts many-flowered: corolla cylindric, at length twisted: flowers pale greenish-yellow.

Chittagong, flowering in the hot season.

(2) D. wallichii. (*Kunth.*)

Ident. Kunth Enum. pl. v. p. 11.

Syn. D. terniflora, *Roxb. l. c.* 159.

Spec. Char. Fruticose: leaves petioled, broadly lanceolate: racemes terminal, solitary, peduncled, erect, somewhat branched at the base: flowers in threes pedicelled, pale greenish-white.

Silhet, flowering in January and February.

(3) D. atropurpurea. *(Roxb.)*

Ident. Roxb. l. c. p. 160.

Spec. Char. Fruticose: erect: leaves lanceolate, acuminate, coloured: panicles terminal: branches few, long, simple, diverging: flowers solitary, pale rose-coloured-white with deep red.

Silhet, flowering in March and April.

(4) D. ensifolia. *(Wall.)*

Ident. Wall. Cat. No. 5143.—Kunth l. c. p. 5.

Spec. Char. Fruticose: leaves sessile, amplexicaul, lanceolate-linear, acuminate: panicles terminal, solitary, simple: branches spreading: flowers in three's.

Silhet.

GENUS XV. OPHIOPOGON.

Hexandria Monogynia. *Sex: Syst:*

Deriv. From *Ophis*, a serpent, and *Pogon*, a beard.

Gen. Char. Perianth 6-leaved, corollaceous, persistent, leaflets oblong, obtuse, inner ones slightly larger: stamens 6, inserted at the bottom of the perianth, equal, filaments free, filiform, anthers 2-celled, emarginate, introrse: ovary free, sessile, tricoccous: ovules 2 in each cell, collateral, erect, anatropal: styline column terminal, thick, 3-cornered, furnished with a triquetrous tube: stigma undivided or 3-cleft, segments papillose: berry globose, 1-seeded: seed globose, smooth, pale rusty, opaque: embryo cylindric, albuminous.

(1) O. Indicum. *(R.W.)*

Ident. Wight's Icon. vi. t. 2050.

Spec. Char. Leaves narrow-linear, acute, sheathing at the base: scape naked, about half the length of the leaves, racemose, secund: bracts subulate, shorter than the pedicels: flowers bell-shaped: berries oval, pale blue when ripe.

Neilgherries. Courtallum. Mysore.

GENUS XVI. PELIOSANTHES.

Hexandria Monogynia. *Sex: Syst:*

Deriv. From *Pelios*, livid, and *Anthos*, a flower.

Gen. Char. Calyx turbinate, adnate to the ovary, limb 6-parted, regular, rotately spreading: stamens 6, inserted at the throat, monadelphous, staminal tube constricted at the mouth, and quite entire, and these internally antheriferous, anthers 2-celled, didymous-sub-rotund, introrse: ovary half-inferior, free, 3-celled: ovules 2 in each cell, collateral, erect, anatropal: stigma sessile, 3-lobed: seeds 1—3, naked.—Stemless herbs: leaves radical, long-petioled, sheathing, oblong-lanceolate, surrounded at the base with dry membranaceous scales: scapes simple, racemosely many-flowered: flowers pedicelled, fascicled, violet-green or greenish: fascicles 3—4-flowered, girt by a dry bract: pedicels bracteolate at the base, articulated towards the apex.

(1) P. Teta *(Andr.)*

Ident. Andr. Bot. Rep. Kunth Enum. pl. v. p. 307.

Syn. Teta viridiflora. *Roxb. flor. Ind. II.* 165.

Engrav. Bot. Rep. t. 605.—Bot. Mag. t. 1302.—Red. Lil. t. 415.

Spec. Char. Leaves lanceolate, acute at both ends; shorter than the racemose scape: segments of the corolla ovate rotund, marginate: flowers green.

Bengal. Silhet.

(2) P. Courtallensis. *(R. W.)*

Ident. Wight's Icon. VI. t. 2051.

Spec. Char. Leaves very long-petioled, lanceolate, acuminate, glabrous: petioles rather shorter than the limb, triangular: scape about the length of the petioles, sub-spicate: bracts subulate, as long as the flowers: calyx campanulate: ovules soon rupturing the walls of the cells when ripe.

Courtallum, in dense woods, flowering in February and March.

(3) P. Neilgherrensis *(R. W.)*

Ident. Wight l. c. t. 2052.

Spec. Char. Leaves lanceolate, tapering at both ends, acuminate, limb about the length of the petiole: scape erect, racemose, shorter than the leaves: flowers drooping, campanulate: ovules usually 4 in each cell, soon rupturing the walls: seed naked, testa fleshy, blue.

Sispara, Western slopes of the Neilgherries, abundant by the road side, flowering at the beginning of the year.

GENUS XVII. TUPISTRA.

Hexandria Monogynia. *Sex: Syst:*

Deriv. Diminutive of *Typis*, a mallet, alluding to the form of the flower.

Gen. Char. Perianth campanulate bowl-shaped, fleshy, coloured, limb 6-parted, slightly irregular, much spreading open: stamens 6, adhering by the whole of the filaments to the tube of the perianth, alternate ones a little longer: anthers 2-celled, cells collateral, distinct at both ends, dehiscing lengthways: pistil free, slightly exceeding the tube of the perianth: ovary oblong, 3-celled, scarcely thicker than the styline column: ovules two in each cell, suspended from the inner angle: styline column thick, 3-furrowed, 3 partible above: stigmas three, large, sub-rotund, convex, furrowed, spreading.

(1) T. nutans. *(Wall.)*

Ident. Wall. in Bot. Reg.—Kunth. Enum. pl. v. p. 318.

Syn. Rohdia nutans. *Schult. Syst. VII.* 1653.

Engrav. Bot. Reg. t. 1223.—Bot. Mag. t. 3054.

Spec. Char. Stemless, herbaceous: leaves radical, petioled, lanceolate: spike shorter than the petioles, nodding: peduncles radical, scapiform, many-flowered: flowers 2-bracteate, yellowish-brown, streaked with purple: filaments distinct.

Borders of Silhet, flowering in December.

ORDER CLXIV. MELANTHACEÆ.

Flowers hermaphrodite: calyx 6-sepaled, regular, usually persistent: sepals distinct, almost equal: æstivation involute: stamens 6: filaments filiform, free: anthers extrorse, fixed by the back looking inwards, 1—2 celled: cells contiguous or distinct with a connectivum, dehiscing lengthways: ovaries three, opposite the outer sepals, joined together by the ventral angles, sometimes adhering to the base of the calyx: ovules numerous, very rarely 2, fixed to the ventral angle, anatropal: styles 3, distinct, sometimes swollen at the summit, sometimes papillosely stigmatose at the thickened apex or the whole length: fruit capsular, 3- or by abortion, 1-celled: carpels at length opening by the ventral suture, sometimes loculicidally

3 valved: valves septiferous in the middle: seeds many, globose, angled or compressed: testa membranaceous, thin, sometimes amplified into a wing: albumen fleshy or sub-cartilaginous: embryo minute, elliptic, oblong or cylindric, next the hilum: radicle centrifugal. Caulescent herbs, often poisonous: roots bulbous, tuberous—fleshy, or fasciculately fibrous: stem simple or branched: leaves scattered, sessile, embracing at the base: flowers usually panicled or racemosely spiked.

GENUS I. DISPORUM.

Hexandria Monogynia. *Sex: Syst:*

Deriv. From *Dis*, twice, and *Poros*, a pore.

GEN. CHAR. Sepals 6, coloured, deciduous, spathulate—lanceolate, distinct, campanulately connivent, saccate, sub-calcarate at the base: stamens 6, inserted at the base of the sepals: filaments subulate: anthers oblong, 2-celled, dehiscing lengthways: ovary sessile, 3-celled: ovules 2 in each cell, fixed to the inner angle, ascending, sessile, anatropal: style 3-cleft: segments stigmatose within, spreading, recurved at the apex: fruit baccate, indehiscent, turbinately 3-cornered, 3-celled, 3- or by abortion 1-seeded: seeds solitary, seldom twin, brown, smooth, convex: hilum naked, basilar, albumen horny: embryo sub-clavate.—Perennial, erect, branched, glabrous herbs: stems angled: leaves scattered, very shortly petioled: flowers terminal in very short 1-leaved branchlets, peduncled, umbellate, nodding: berries black, 3 cornered.

(1) D. CALCARATUM. *(Don.)*

Ident. Don in Proc. Linn. Soc. Nov. 1839.—Kunth Enum. pl. iv. p. 207.

SPEC. CHAR. Umbels peduncled, somewhat 5-flowered: sepals lanceolate, acutish, long-spurred at the base: anthers, filaments and stigmas 3 times longer than the style: leaves ovate-lanceolate, sessile: flowers green.

Khasia mountains.

(2) D. WALLICHII. *(Don.)*

Ident. Don l. c.—Kunth l. c.

SPEC. CHAR. Umbels sessile, somewhat 5-flowered: sepals lanceolate, acuminate: spurs straight, abbreviated: anthers four times shorter than the filaments, style longer than the stigmas: leaves ovate-lanceolate, somewhat petioled: flowers white.

Khasia mountains.

(3) D. Leschenaultianum. *(Don.)*

Ident. Don l. c.—Kunth l. c.

Engrav. Wight's Icon. vi. t. 2048.

Spec. Char. Umbels sessile, 3—5-flowered: sepals ovate-lanceolate, acute, gibbous at the base: anthers scarcely twice shorter than the filaments: style three times longer than the stigmas: leaves ovate, sub-petioled: flowers green.

Neilgherries, flowering in July and August.

(4) D. mysorense. *(R. W.)*

Ident. Wight's Icon. vi. t. 2049.

Spec. Char. Umbels 3—4 flowered, terminal: sepals ovate, cuspidate-acuminate, not gibbous at the base: filaments curved, not dilated at the base, shorter than the sagittate incurved anthers: style much longer than the short, almost inconspicuous, stigmas: leaves almost sessile, broad, ovate-acuminate.

Bababooden Hills. Mysore.

GENUS II. IPHIGENIA.

Hexandria Monogynia. *Sex: Syst:*

Gen. Char. Sepals 6, coloured, deciduous, distinct, equal, stellately much spreading, linear-lanceolate, acuminate, narrowed below and there furrowed internally: stamens hypogynous, three times shorter than the sepals: filaments filiform—subulate, slightly villous: anthers elliptic, cordate at the base and there fixed, flattish at the back looking outwards, 2 celled: cells contiguous, dehiscing lengthways: ovary sessile, obovate, 3-cornered: ovules many, fixed by 2 rows to the inner angle: style very short: stigmas 3, revolute, papillose within: capsule elliptic, terminated by the persistent style, 3-celled, 3-valved, many-seeded: seeds obliquely globose, chestnut brown, smooth: testa thin, membranaceous, adnate to the albumen: embryo small, cylindric-sub-clavate: albumen fleshy.

(1) I. Indica. *(Kunth.)*

Ident. Kunth. Enum. pl. iv. p. 213.

Syn. Melanthium Indicum, *Linn.* Anguillaria Indica, *R. Brown, prod.* 273.

Engrav. Wall. pl. As. rar. III. t. 259.

SPEC. CHAR. Herbaceous, erect, bulbiferous: leaves linear, subulate, longer than the somewhat 3-flowered stem: floral ones lanceolate—linear: petals sub-unguiculate, linear-lanceolate, dark-violet.

Peninsula.

ORDER CLXV. JUNCACEÆ.

Perennial, rarely annual herbs, cæspitose or creeping: culm leafy or leafless, branched at the apex as a cyme, umbel or panicle: leaves sheathing at the base, narrow, terete, channelled or flat: flowers hermaphrodite, small: calyx 6-sepaled, regular, persistent, sepals glumaceous, usually connate quite at the base: stamens 6, inserted at the base of the sepals and opposite to them, very rarely sub-hypogynous, free, persistent: filaments free: anthers 2-celled, dehiscing lengthways, attached by the base: ovary composed of 3 more or less closed carpels, either many-ovuled 3 or with retracted dissepiments 1-celled, or 3-ovuled 1-celled: style terminal, simple, often very short or none: stigmas 3, filiform, distinct or cohering: capsule either many-seeded 3 or falsely 1-celled, or 3-seeded 1-celled: seeds many or three: testa membranaceous, cellulosely reticulated, closely or loosely covering the nucleus: embryo minute, enclosed at the base of thick fleshy albumen: radicle extremity next the hilum.

GENUS I. JUNCUS.

Hexandria Monogynia. *Sex: Syst:*

Deriv. From *Jungo*, to join; ropes were first made from rushes.

GEN. CHAR. Calyx 6-sepaled, regular, persistent: sepals glumaceous, connate at the base, seldom free, spreading, outer ones navicular, inner flattish: stamens perigynous, sometimes the three inner ones obliterated: anthers linear-oblong, 2-celled: ovary many ovuled: style one, often very short: stigmas 3, villous: capsule 3- or the dissepiments very often being retracted, 1-celled, many-seeded, loculicidally 3-valved: testa closely adherent or rather loose, sometimes saccately relaxed on all sides.

(1) J. MONTICOLA. *(Steudel.)*

Ident. Steudel syn. p. 301.

SPEC. CHAR. Culm erect, terete-angular, leafy, often rooting or proliferous towards the base: sheaths elongated, free at the mouth: leaves compressed, nodulose: panicle effuse, compound, primary rays elongated, straight or spreading, seldom horizontal, with 3—4-raylets at the apex: raylets often sending out other divisions: heads of flowers terminal and lateral and sessile in the forks, 10—20-flowered, either naked or with leaflets twice exceeding them: flowers triandrous: sepals nearly equal, lanceolate, acuminate.

Neilgherries.

(2) J. BENGHALENSIS. *(Kunth.)*

Ident. Kunth Enum. III. 360. Steudel l. c. p. 308.

SPEC. CHAR. Culms erect, striated, leafy at the base, 1-leaved above: leaves filiform, channelled: flowers 8, aggregated in heads at the apex of the culm, sheath double, one leaf-bearing: sepals lanceolate, acute, nearly equal.

Bengal.

ORDER CLXVI. COMMELYNACEÆ.

Flowers hermaphrodite: calyx double, each of 3 sepals: outer sepals distinct, persistent, inner ones petaloid, sessile or clawed, distinct or rarely connate into a tube at the base, one often less deformed, caducous or persistent, the unequal sepal of either calyx outermost, embracing the lateral ones: stamens 6, hypogynous or inserted at the base of the inner sepals, opposite the sepals, some often sterile, deciduous: filaments filiform, free, usually bearded: anthers 2-celled, introrse: cells more or less distinct, dehiscing lengthways: ovary free, usually sessile, 3- very rarely 2-celled, cells opposite the outer sepals: ovules usually twin, superposed, 1—2-seriated, inserted at the central angle of the cells, orthotropal: style terminal, simple: stigma simple, obtuse, capitellate, peltately enlarged, excavated or obsoletely 3-lobed: capsule 3—2-celled, 3—2-valved, valves septiferous in the middle, very rarely indehiscent: seeds 2 or 1, compressed angled or quadrate, peltate: testa membranaceous, hardish, reticulate scrobiculate: albumen densely fleshy: embryo antitropal, lying half-buried in a cavity of the albumen remote from the hilum: radicle centrifugal.—Annual or perennial herbs, very rarely undershrubs: root fibrous: stems knotty, simple or branched, erect or procumbent: leaves scattered, simple, entire, flat or channelled, sheathing at the base: flowers white, blue, violet or purple, very seldom yellow, fascicled, umbellate, racemose or panicled, bracteate, sometimes enclosed with spathiform leaves, hooded or plaited.

GENUS I. COMMELYNA.

Triandria Monogynia. *Sex: Syst:*

Deriv. In honour of J. and G. Commelin, famous Dutch Botanists.

Gen. Char. Flowers irregular: sepals 6, distinct, three outer ones unequal, somewhat coloured, persistent; outermost one not similar, navicular, lateral ones larger, concave, three inner ones petaloid, withering, lateral ones longish clawed, round, reniform, dissimilar one smaller, sessile, ovate or lanceolate, embracing the lateral ones in the flower bud: stamens 6, inserted at the base of the sepals, free, three thinner opposite the inner lateral sepals and outer dissimilar one, furnished with thick cruciately 4-cleft anthers, the rest fertile: filaments beardless: anthers 2-celled: cells separated by a narrow connectivum, lateral ones straight, intermediate one larger, arched, sometimes partly metamorphosed: ovary sessile, 3-celled, lateral cells 2-ovuled, ovules superposed: dorsal one smaller, 1-ovuled: style elongated: stigma simple, obtuse, papillose, somewhat 3-lobed: capsule obliquely 3-celled, somewhat 3-valved, lateral cells 2, dorsal one 1-seeded: valves septiferous in the middle: seeds angled, hilum linear.—Branched, rarely simple, herbs, erect or more usually procumbent and creeping: leaves undivided: sheaths entire: peduncles proceeding from the sheaths and often cleaving them in front, 2-cleft above, furnished at the separation of the branches with a folded or hooded leafy spathe, one branch more robust, 2-many-flowered at the apex, enclosed: flowers pedicelled, recurved before and after flowering; the other branch thinner, sometimes sterile, stipitiform, sometimes fertile, exserted, 1-few-flowered at the apex: flowers blue, very rarely yellow, often polygamous.

(1) C. communis. *(Linn.)*

Ident. Linn. sp. 60.—Dalz. Bomb. Flor. p. 252.

Syn. C. polygama. *Willd. Enum.* 67.—C. vulgaris, *Schmiedel.*

Engrav. Schmied. Ic. 158, t. 40, 41.—Red. Lil. t. 206.

SPEC. CHAR. Root fibrous; stems branched, creeping; branchlets marked with a line of hairs; leaves sessile, ovate-lanceolate, acuminate, rounded at the base; margin waved; spathes opposite the leaves, rounded cordate, acute, folded, smooth, with roughish margins; peduncles in the spathe 2, the longer one 1-flowered, the shorter 3-flowered: flowers bright blue.

Common everywhere, flowering in the rains.

(2) C. BENGHALENSIS. *(Linn.)*

Ident. Linn. l. c.—Dalz. l. c. 253.—Roxb. flor. Ind. I. 171.

Syn. C. cucullata, *Linn. Mant.* 176.—C. nervosa, *Burm.*

Engrav. Wight's Icon. t. 2065. Burm. Ind. t. 7, fig. 3.

SPEC. CHAR. Stem branched, creeping, hairy, leaves petioled, ovate-elliptic or cordate-acute, puberulous on both sides: sheaths hairy, with the mouth ciliated: spathes shortly-peduncled, cucullate, turbinate, acute: peduncles twin in each spathe, shorter one 2-flowered, the longer hairy, one-flowered: flowers bright blue.

Common everywhere, flowering in the rains.

(3) C. SALICIFOLIA. *(Roxb.)*

Ident. Roxb. l. c. p. 172.

Syn. C. pedunculosa, *Link.*

SPEC. CHAR. Stem branched, creeping: leaves sessile, linear-lanceolate, acute, glabrous on both sides, scabrous at the margin: sheaths ciliated at the mouth: spathes leaf-opposed, cordate, narrow-acuminate, folded, glabrous: peduncles in the spathe twin, enclosed, somewhat 3-flowered, exserted one 1—2-flowered, slightly hairy: flowers polygamous, azure.

Coromandel. Bengal. Flowering in the rainy season.

(4) C. CÆSPITOSA. *(Roxb.)*

Ident. Roxb. l. c. p. 174.

SPEC. CHAR. Polygamous: creeping: leaves lanceolate: spathe cordate, peduncled, few-flowered: petals nearly equal: capsules 3-celled: cells 1—2-seeded, flowers blue.

Chittagong.

(5) C. DIFFUSA. *(Burm.)*

Ident. Burm. Ind. 18.—Vahl. Enum. II. 169.—Blume En. I. 1.

Engrav. Burm. l. c. t. 7, fig. 2.

SPEC. CHAR. Creeping, diffuse: leaves sessile, ovate-lanceolate, acute: sheaths ciliolate: involucres cordate, leaf-opposed or terminal: pedicels unequal, inner one elongated, 1—2-flowered, the other 3—4-flowered.

Coromandel.

(6) C. POLYSPATHA. *(R. W.)*

Ident. Wight's Icon. vi. l. t. 2066.

SPEC. CHAR. Erect: leaves long-lanceolate, acuminate, glabrous on both sides, paler beneath: sheaths with a line of hairs on one side, setosely hairy on the margin and throat: spathes terminal, 4—8 together, collateral, turbinate, glabrous: pedicel solitary, enclosed, 4—5-flowered: capsule glabrous, 3-celled: cells 1-seeded: flowers light blue.

Mountains near Coimbatore at 3,000 feet, flowering in November.

GENUS II. ANEILEMA.

Triandria Monogynia. *Sex: Syst:*

Deriv. From *A*, without, and *Eilema*, a covering, the involucre is wanting.

GEN. CHAR. Flowers somewhat regular: sepals 6, free, three outer ones navicular, unchanging persistent, three inner ones larger, petaloid, deciduous: stamens 6, of which sometimes 3, sometimes 2—4 are effete, furnished with thick deformed anthers, sometimes 4, of which 2 are sterile: fertile anthers 2-celled, conformable, cells parallel, joined by a narrow connectivum: ovary sessile, 3-celled, ovules 2—5 in each cell, superposed: style elongated: stigma simple: capsule regularly 3-celled, 3-valved: cells 2-few seeded: seeds sessile, angled, fixed to a short hilum.—Branched herbs, erect or diffuse and creeping: leaves resting in an entire sheath: peduncles terminal, corymbosely dichotomous or paniculately branched, bracteate: flowers solitary, pedicelled: pedicels bracteolate at the base: filaments usually beardless, seldom few or always bearded.

(1) A. NUDIFLORUM. *(R. Br.)*

Deriv. R. Brown prod. 271.

Syn. Commelyna nudiflora, *Linn.* Tradescantia Malabarica. *Linn.*

Engrav. Rheede Mal. ix. t. 63.

Spec. Char. Stem creeping, branched, branches erect, smooth: leaves linear-lanceolate, acute, sheathing and ciliated at the base, smooth on both sides, margins a little rough: peduncles 1—2, elongated with several flowers corymbosely arranged at the apex: flowers blue.

Peninsula, common. Bengal. Silhet. Flowering in the rains.

(2) A. compressum. (*Dalz.*)

Ident. Dalz. in Hook. Journ. Bot. III. 138.

Syn. A. secunda, *Wight's Icon. t.* 2075.

Spec. Char. Branched at the base and rooting: branches ascending, compressed, simple, smooth: leaves short, bifarious, ensiform, rather obtuse, a little folded: sheaths hispid all round: peduncles terminal, and from the axils of sheathing bracts, 1 inch long: flowers several, shortly-pedicelled, racemose, exterior sepals oblong, obtuse, smooth: interior rounded, rose-coloured, capsule oblong, 9.seeded.

Malwan. Annamullay forests. Belgaum. Flowering in August and September.

(3) A. ochraceum. (*Dalz*)

Ident. Dalz. l. c.

Spec. Char. Stems erect, simple, round, smooth, leafy: lower leaves ovate-oblong, upper cordate-ovate, acute and smaller: pedicels 6 to 7 together, axillary and terminal, fascicled, articulated in the middle: flowers ochre-yellow: capsule cartilaginous, smooth: cells 7 to 8 seeded: seeds in 2 rows.

Wet rocky places in the South Concan.

(4) A. versicolor. (*Dalz.*)

Ident. Dalz. l. c.

Spec. Char. Branched: branches erect, round, striated, hispid, with spreading hairs: leaves distant, lanceolate-acuminate, smooth, stem-clasping, 5 to 7-nerved beneath: sheaths rather long, a little hispid, furrowed and striated: pedicels axillary, fascicled, 3 to 4 together: flowers ochre-yellow, twice as large as in the preceding: capsule linear, trigonal: cells 7-seeded: seeds in a single row.

Malwan.

(5) A PAUCIFLORUM. *(Dalz.)*

Ident. Dalz. l. c.

Engrav. Wight's Icon. t. 2076.

SPEC. CHAR. Whole plant, except the mouth of the sheaths, smooth: leaves long-linear acuminated, narrow: sheath, of the lower leaves split, the upper suddenly transformed into short sheathing floral bracts: pedicels 1 to 3, from the axils of the bracts, twice articulated in the middle: fertile stamens 2, with orange-coloured anthers: capsule obtusely trigonal: seeds tuberculated, solitary in each cell.

Concans.

(6) A ELATUM. *(Dalz.)*

Ident. Dalz. l. c.

Syn. Commelyna elata, *Vahl.*

Engrav. Wight's Icon. t. 2072.

SPEC. CHAR. Stem erect, round, smooth, leafy: leaves linear-lanceolate, acute, smooth, flat, with white, undulated margins: sheaths entire: peduncles terminal, dichotomously branched, the branches distant and few flowered: flowers in three's: the petaloid sepals obovate cuneate, reflexed.

In dark shady woods of the Concan.

(7) A. CANALICULATUM. *(Dalz.)*

Ident. Dalz. l. c.

Syn. A. paniculatum, *Wight's Icon. t.* 2075.

SPEC. CHAR. Root fibrous: stem simply branched erect, striated, alternately marked on one side with a pubescent line: lower leaves broad-linear lanceolate, upper ones cordate-oblong, all stem-clasping, smooth, channelled in the middle: peduncles terminal and axillary, solitary or twin, dichotomously branched, few flowered: flowers rather long-pedicelled, bifarious, distant: stamens 3, perfect: anthers blue, all the filaments bearded: capsule oblong, acutely trigonal: cells 4 to 5 seeded: seeds in a single row: flowers blue.

South Concan.

(8) A. DEMORPHUM. *(Dalz.)*

Ident. Dalz. l. c.

SPEC. CHAR. Whole plant, except the ciliated mouth of the sheaths, smooth, a little branched at the base: branches erect, round striated, internodes marked on one side with a pubescent line: lower leaves linear-acuminate, upper lanceolate-acute, all stem-clasping: flowers terminal, dichotomously panicled, few: pedicels and branches of the panicle with rounded, cucullate bracts: fertile stamens 3: anthers purple, fertile filaments only bearded, gland bearing: filaments naked.

Southern Concan.

(9) A. SEMITERES. *(Dalz.)*

Ident Dalz. l. c.

Syn. Dichœspermum juncoides, *Wight's Icon. t.* 2078.

SPEC. CHAR. Stem erect, simple, round, smooth, leaves few, subulate, fleshy, half round, sheaths entire: flowers terminal, and from the axils of the uppermost leaf dichotomously panicled, few: peduncles and pedicels red: floral sheaths truncate, one toothed: filaments united at the base.

Western Coast.

(10) A. TUBEROSUM. *(Ham.)*

Ident. Ham. in Wall. Cat. 5207.—Dalz. Bomb. flor. 255.

Syn. Commelyna scapiflora, *Roxb. flor. Ind. I.* 175. Murdania scapiflora, *Royle.*

Engrav. Wight's Icon. t. 2073.

SPEC CHAR. Root perennial, composed of several smooth, elongated tubers: stem none, except the sheathing bases of the leaves, which appear after the flowers: leaves ensiform, waved, acute, smooth: racemes radical, erect, straight, smooth: scape branched above: branches each with a sheathing bract: branchlets with several pedicelled blue flowers, rather large.

Southern Concan.

(11) A. LATIFOLIUM. *(R.W.)*

Ident. Wight l. c. and t. 2072.

SPEC. CHAR. Erect, glabrous: leaves sessile, broad-ovate, cordate, stem-clasping, acute, netted beneath, when dry, with brown veins: sheaths short, glabrous: panicles terminal, rather diffuse: bracts minute: outer sepals lanceolate, inner ones obovate or suborbicular: filaments all bearded: capsule 3-celled, with 3—4-seeds in each cell, seeds angular smooth, depressed above.

Western slopes of the Neilgherries.

(12) A. ENSIFOLIA. *(R. W.)*

Ident. Wight l. c. t. 2074.

SPEC. CHAR. Erect, branched, glabrous, jointed: leaves very long, narrow, sword-shaped, slightly sheathing and stem clasping at the base: primary branches of the panicle umbellate, branched, the branches secundly racemose towards the extremities: flowers fascicled, 3—4 together in the axils of a large obovate caducous bract, opening in succession: sepals ovate, somewhat boat-shaped petals broad-obovate, or sub-orbicular: filaments all bearded, sterile: anthers auricled: capsule ovoid, 3-celled, with 3 rough augular seeds in each.

Courtallum.

(13) A. TERMINALIS. *(R. W.)*

Ident. Wight l. c. t. 2076.

SPEC. CHAR. Procumbent at the base, afterwards ascending: leaves sword-shaped, glabrous: sheath short, loose, ciliate on the margin: floriferous branches few from the upper axils, bearing on the apex a fascicle of close-set short peduncled flowers: sepals ovate obtuse, petals orbicular: stamens 2 fertile, 4 sterile: filaments of the perfect stamens bearded: capsule 3-celled with 2 seeds in each attached to the middle of the axis (ascending and descending), seed roughish, embryo lateral.

Neilgherries.

(14) A. NANA. *(Kunth.)*

Ident. Kunth Enum. pl. iv. p. 65.

Syn. Commelyna Nana, *Roxb.*

Engrav. Wight's Icon. t. 2077.

SPEC. CHAR. Creeping: leaves cordate-lanceolate, stem-clasping: flowers terminal, somewhat panicled, petals equal: capsule 3-celled, many-seeded: cells 3—5-seeded, seed angular or somewhat cylindrical, truncated: flowers bright blue.

Courtallum, Malabar. Coimbatore. Flowering nearly all the year.

(15) A. PAUCIFLORA. *(R. W.)*

Ident. Wight l. c. t. 2077.

SPEC. CHAR. Creeping ,glabrous, except a line of hairs decurrent from the sheaths: leaves sheathing, cordate-ovate, obtuse, slightly waved on the margin, stem-clasping: flowers axillary, solitary or paired, opening in succession, longish peduncled, sepals linear obtuse, petals obovate, exceeding the sepals: filaments all glabrous, fertile stamens about twice the length of the sterile ones, capsule oblong pointed, cells about 5-seeded in a single row.

Quilon. Paulghaut. Flowering in October.

(16) A. VAGINATA. *(R. Br.)*

Ident. R. Br. in Wall. List. No. 5212.

Syn. Commelyna vaginata, *Linn.*

Engrav. Wight l. c. t. 2076.

SPEC. CHAR. Procumbent, diffuse, rooting at the joints, glabrous: leaves sheathing at the base, linear: peduncles lateral and terminal, enclosed in a sheath, 1-flowered, but sometimes 3 flowers from one common sheath: sepals lanceolate: petals orbicular: 2 stamens fertile, 4 sterile antherless, all the filaments glabrous: capsule orbicular, 3-celled: cells one-seeded: oval compressed, somewhat rugous on the margin, depressed on the back: flowers small, blue.

Coromandel. Bengal. Flowering in the rainy season.

GENUS III. DITHYROCARPUS.

Hexandria Monogynia. *Sex: Syst:*

Deriv. From *Dithuros*, double, and *Karpos*, fruit.

GEN. CHAR. Flowers more or less regular: sepals 6, free, persistent: outer ones navicular, inner ones larger, petaloid: stamens 6, hypogynous, beardless, three shorter opposite the inner sepals: anthers 2-celled, all fertile: ovary stalked, 2-celled, ovules solitary: style elongated: stigma sub-capitellate: capsule shortly stalked, compressed didymous, 2-celled, 2-valved: seeds solitary, truncate conical, furrowed lengthways.—Herbs creeping at the base, branches simple, erect: leaves undivided: sheaths entire: panicles terminal, solitary, simple or branched, bracteate: flowers pedicelled, sub-racemose, unilateral, small.

(1) D. PANICULATUS. *(Kunth.)*

Ident. Kunth. Enum. pl. iv. p. 79.

Syn. D. Rothii, *R. W.*—Tradescantia paniculata, *Roxb. flor. Ind. II. p.* 119.

Engrav. Roxb. Cor. II. t. 109.—Wight's Icon. t. 2080.

SPEC. CHAR. Stem creeping: sheaths with the mouth woolly: leaves lanceolate-acuminate: panicle terminal, sub-globose, many-flowered, pubescent: flowers purple blue.

Ghauts. Coromandel coast in moist vallies, flowering in the rains.

(2) D. PETIOLATUS. *(R. W.)*

Ident. Wight l. c. t. 2079.

SPEC. CHAR. Ascending, sparingly branched: leaves sheathing, elliptic-lanceolate, acute, tapering at the base into a longish petiole: sheath ciliated at the margin: flowers secund and with the rachis, villous.

Neilgherries.

(3) D. UNDULATUS. *(R. W.)*

Ident. Wight l. c. t. 2080.

SPEC. CHAR. Ascending: leaves ovate-lanceolate, acuminate, waved on the margin, sheathing: sheaths large, the throat thickly beset with coarse bristly hairs: calyx shaggy, viscid, lobes obovate-obtuse: style curved: capsule 2-celled, 2-seeded.

Station not given.

GENUS IV. CYANOTIS.

Hexandria Monogynia. *Sex: Syst:*

Deriv. From *Kyanos*, blue, and *Ous*, a ear, alluding to the flowers.

GEN CHAR. Flowers somewhat regular: sepals 6, outer ones nearly equal, navicular, connate at the base, persistent, inner ones longer, petaloid, connate by the claws, caducous: stamens 6, almost equal, sub-hypogynous, scarcely adhering to the base of the tube: filaments very long, bearded towards the apex: anthers of the same shape, 2-celled, cells parallel, contiguous: ovary sessile, 3-celled: ovules twin in each cell, superposed, sessile, upper one ascending, lower one descending: style thickened at the top: capsule 3-cornered, 3-celled, membranaceous, 3-valved: seeds twin, superposed, angled. —Annual or perennial herbs, usually diffuse and creeping: leaves entire, sheathing at the base, sheath entire: flowers spicately collected in longish axillary and terminal peduncles, wrapped round with a spathaceous cordate folded leaf, each 1-bracteate externally: bracts falcate, bifariously imbricated: interior calyx blue: flowers sometimes conglomerate by two's or three's or more in the axils of the leaves, interspersed with bracts.

(1) C. HISPIDA. *(Dalz.)*

Ident. Dalz. Hook. Journ. Bot. III. p. 138.—Bomb. flor. p. 255.

SPEC. CHAR. Annual, all hispid, branched at the base: stems erect, round, striated, red: leaves linear, ensiform, fleshy, rather flat: flowers terminal, sessile, capitate, few, with falcate half-cordate bracts: anthers deep violet, filaments with blue hairs all pointing to one side.

On rocks, southern Concan.

(2) C. VIVIPARA. *(Dalz.)*

Ident. Dalz. l. c.

SPEC. CHAR. Epiphytal, stemless, clothed with rufous hairs: radical leaves linear, ensiform, flat, thick, fleshy, fascicled: scapes rising from the root, filiform, rooting and viviparous: peduncles from the nodes of the scape, solitary, alternate, bearing a 3—4-flowered umbel, bibracteate: bracts leafy, oblong, acute: cells of the capsule 2-seeded: valves much recurved after dehiscence: seeds cylindric.

On trees at Parwar Ghaut.

(3) C. ASCENDENS. *(Dalz.)*

Ident. Dalz. l. c. iv. p. 343.

SPEC. CHAR. Root tuberous: stems several, ascending, simple, round, striated, shining: leaves linear, ensiform, glabrous: heads terminal, many-flowered: flowers blue.

Belgaum, in wet grassy places.

(4) C. FASCICULATA. *(Roem. and Schult.)*

Ident. Roem. and Schult. syst. vii. 1152.—Dalz. Bomb. flor. 255.

Syn. Tradescantia fasciculata, *Heyne in Roth. Nov. sp.* 189. C. dichrosticha, *Stocks in Wight Icon. vi.* 2086-7.

SPEC. CHAR. Woolly: stem dichotomous: leaves lanceolate, sub-petioled: head of flowers terminal, few-flowered with about four lanceolate falcate sheaths: flowers rose-coloured, filaments bearded with hairs, of which the lower half are pure white, the upper rose-coloured.

Rocky places in the Deccan. Malabar.

(5) C. TUBEROSA. *(Roem. and Schult.)*

Ident. Roem. and Schult. l. c. 1153.

Syn. Tradescantia tuberosa, *Roxb. flor. Ind. II.* 119.

Engrav. Roxb. Cor. II. t. 108.

SPEC. CHAR. Perennial: root tuberous: stems several, creeping, round: radical leaves 3—4, ensiform, large: stem leaves linear-lanceolate, sheathing, striated, villous and purple beneath: heads of flowers terminal and axillary, solitary or twin, peduncled, imbricated: bracts falcate, ciliated: flowers bluish-purple.

Western Deccan. Coromandel vallies. Flowering in the rains.

(6) C. CRISTATA. *(Roem. and Schult.)*

Ident. Roem. and Schult. l. c. 1150.

Syn. Commelyna cristata, *Linn.*—Tradescantia cristata, *Jacq. Vind.* T. imbricata, *Roxb. flor. Ind. II.* 120.

Engrav. Burm. flor. Ind. t. 7. fig. 4.—Bot. Mag. t. 1435.—Rheede Mal. vii. t. 58.—Wight's Icon. t. 2082.

SPEC. CHAR. Stem diffuse, creeping, marked with alternate pubescent lines: leaves ovate lanceolate, smooth, ciliated: pairs of bracts 6—7, lanceolate, falcate, imbricated, terminal: stamens scarcely longer than the corolla: flowers pale or dark blue.

Peninsula, common, flowering in the rains.

(7) C. AXILLARIS. *(Roem. and Schult.)*

Ident. Roem. and Schult. l. c. 1155.

Syn. Tradescantia axillaris, *Linn. Mant.*—*Roxb. flor. Ind. II.* 118. Commelyna axillaris, *Linn.*

Engrav. Roxb. Cor. II. t. 107.—Rheede Mal. x. t. 13.

SPEC. CHAR. Stem branched, creeping, branches puberulous on one side: leaves linear, acute, smooth, ciliated: sheaths ciliated: flowers axillary in two's or three's, sub-sessile, appearing in succession: flowers largish, deep blue.

Western Deccan. Peninsula, flowering in the rains.

(8) C. PILOSA *(Roem and Schult.)*

Ident. Roem and Schult. l. c.

Syn. Tradescantia pilosa, *Willd.*

Engrav. Wight's Icon. vi. t. 2083.

SPEC. CHAR. Stems scapose, procumbent, spreading, somewhat branched and, with the sheaths and under surface of the leaves, more or less floccose: radical leaves linear, obtuse, villously ciliated, stem leaves smaller: spikes terminal, secund, aggregated, few-flowered: bracts falcate: calyx woolly, filaments densely bearded: ovary pilose: style bearded.

Neilgherries, 6,000 feet, flowering all the year.

(9) C. LONGIFOLIA. *(R. W.)*

Ident. Wight's Icon. vi. t. 2084.

SPEC. CHAR. Leaves radical, ensiform, pubescently ciliate on the margin: stems scapose, branched, with a villous line decurrent from the sheaths: floriferous branches axillary, solitary or aggregated, from the loose sheathing axils of large common bracts: spikes lateral and terminal, imbricated; when lateral furnished with a common bract; partial bracts falcate, villoso-ciliate: calycine lobes of the perianth lanceolate acute, pubescent, limb of the petaloid ones broad obovate, glabrous: filaments long slender, flexuose, densely bearded near the apex: style length of the stamens, glabrous: stigma clavate: capsule small, not half the length of the calyx, sub-globose, pilose on the apex, 3-celled: cells 2-seeded: seed angular, depressed punctuate.

Bolamputty Hills, near Coimbatore; flowering in November and December.

(10) C. LANCEOLATA. *(R. W.)*

Ident. Wight l. c. t. 2085.

SPEC. CHAR. Stems at first procumbent, afterwards ascending or erect, round, succulent: leaves shortly succulent, ovate-lanceolate, acute, slightly villous beneath, ciliate: a line of hairs decurrent from the sheaths, few-flowered: bracts lanceolate acute: calycine lobes lanceolate, acute: petals scarcely connate, obovatè obtuse, scarcely exceeding the calyx: filaments filiform, bearded above the middle: style filiform: stigma simple: capsule obovate, pubescent on the apex, much shorter than the sepals, 3-celled; cells 2-seeded: seed somewhat corrugated.

Eastern Slopes of the Neilgherries, flowering in October and November.

(11) C. ROSEA. *(R. W.)*

Ident. Wight l. c. t. 2086.

SPEC. CHAR. Stems procumbent, rooting at the lower joints, afterwards ascending, succulent, floccosely woolly: leaves sessile on short loose sheaths, cordate-ovate, obtuse, succulent, floccose: peduncles axillary, solitary or two or three from the same axil, longer than the leaves: spike short, imbricated; bracts falcate, woolly: calyx diaphonous, thickly clothed with long woolly hairs: corolla longer than the calyx, deep rose colour: stamens exceeding the corolla, sparingly bearded towards the apex: stigma inflated, clavate: capsule 3-celled with 2 oblong deeply corrugated seeds in each cell.

Near Coimbatore, flowering in November and December.

(12) C. LAWIANA. *(R. W.)*

Ident. Wight l. c. t. 2086.

SPEC. CHAR. Procumbent, diffuse, succulent, villous: leaves sheathing, linear-lanceolate, obtuse, succulent, villous: peduncles axillary, solitary or paired, slender, longer than the leaves: spikes short, few-flowered, woolly: involucral leaf folded, lanceolate-acuminate: bracts falcate, 2—4 pairs: sepals free to the base, lanceolate: filaments simple, bearded near the apex: style and stigma simple: capsule ovate obtuse, hairy on the apex: cells 2-seeded, flowers red.

Dharwar.

(13) C. SARMENTOSA. *(R. W.)*

Ident. Wight l. c. t. 2087.

SPEC. CHAR. Root tuberous: stems long, succulent, pubescent, sarmentose: leaves radical, distichous, linear, blunt, villous: spikes secund, short peduncled, scapose, many-flowered: spathes short, ovate acute: bracts numerous (5—10 pairs), falcate, acute, somewhat woolly: petals connate to near the apex, limb roundish cuspidate: filaments much longer than the perianth, bearded and twined near the apex: style glabrous, twined: stigma sub-capitate: capsule 3-celled, seeds 2, superposed, flowers and stamens pale rose colour.

Bolamputty hills, near Coimbatore.

(14) C. DECUMBENS. *(R. W.)*

Ident. Wight l. c. t. 2088.

SPEC. CHAR. Decumbent, very branchy, woolly all over, especially the sheaths of the leaves: leaves linear lanceolate, bluntish: above sparingly, beneath densely woolly; sheaths short, loose: peduncles axillary and terminal, solitary or two or three aggregated, longer than the leaves: spikes short: 4—6 pairs of imbricating falcate bracts: calyx 3-parted, woolly, as long as the capsule: filaments bearded, simple: style glabrous, twined at the apex: capsule furnished on the apex with a tuft of rigid hairs.

Quilon, Malabar.

(15) C. vaginata. *(R. W.)*

Ident. Wight l. c. t. 2088.

Spec. Char. Erect or ascending, very ramous: lower part of the stem clothed with the persistent sheaths of aborted or fallen leaves: leaves sessile, somewhat stem-clasping, ovate-lanceolate, acute, clothed on both sides with long slender hairs: peduncles axillary and terminal, solitary or aggregated: spikes 10—14 flowered: calyx lobes lanceolate acute: filaments simple, bearded: stigma, sub-capitate: capsule 3-celled, 3-valved, valves deciduous, separating from the persistent 3-lobed placenta: seeds 2 in each cell, superposed.

Malabar.

(16) C. papilionacea. *(Roem. and Schult.)*

Ident. Roem. and Schult. l. c. p. 1151.

Syn. Tradescantia papilionacea, *Linn. Mant.* Tillandsia decumbens, *Forsk, descr.* Commelyna papilionacea, *Burm.*

Engrav. Burm. Ind. t. 7, fig. 1.—Wight l. c. t. 2089.

Spec. Char. Stem creeping, leaves linear lanceolate; pilose beneath, ciliate near the base: sheaths short, loose: peduncles axillary, terminal, pilose on one side, solitary or two or three aggregated, about the length of the leaves: spike 4—12 flowered: bracts 2—6 pairs, ciliate, falcate: filaments bearded, simple: stigma, clavate: valves of the capsule separating from the persistent axile placenta.

Malabar.

(17) C. Burmanniana. *(R. W.)*

Ident. Wight l. c. t. 2089.

Spec. Char. Creeping, diffuse, branched: branches filiform, pilose: leaves sheathing, sessile, ovate lanceolate, obtuse, villous: peduncles axillary and terminal, solitary or aggregated, longer than the leaves: spikes secund, 3—12 or more flowered: bracts 4—6 pairs, falcate, ciliate; lobes of the calyx lanceolate acute: filaments bearded: style simple, not tumid at the apex: stigma sub-capitate: placenta separating from the valves of the capsule, persistent, lobes subulate.

Quilon, Malabar.

GENUS V. ACLISIA.

Hexandria Monogynia. *Sex: Syst:*

Gen. Char. Sepals 6, elliptic, obtuse, three outer ones connate at the base, persistent, inner ones a little less, petaloid, deciduous:

stamens 6, beardless, three posterior ones fertile; anthers adnate by the back; three anterior ones a little shorter, terminated by a gland: ovary globose: style filiform, hooked at the apex: berry juiceless, globose, fragile: seeds numerous, arranged in six rows, fixed to coarsely toothed central placentæ, discoid-angled, crowned at the flattened apex with an immersed umbo, shining, marked all round with little lobes.

(1) A. Indica. *(R. W.)*

Ident. Wight's Icon. vi. t. 2068.

Spec. Char. Perennial: stem erect, simple, and with the panicle pubescent: leaves sheathing at the base, petioled, ovate-lanceolate, taperingly acuminate, acute, glabrous, except the petiole and sheath: panicle long-peduncled, loose: branches racemose, spreading or slightly reflexed: petals obovate-orbicular, larger than the sepals: fruit globose, pale blue: cells 8-seeded in two rows: seed quadangular, depressed.

Malabar. Western slopes of the Neilgherries, flowering in the rainy season.

GENUS VI. DICHÆSPERMUM.

Hexandria Monogynia. *Sex: Syst:*

Gen. Char. Perianth 6-parted, 3 exterior lobes calycine, 3 inner ones petaloid: stamens 6, three calycine fertile, petaline ones barren: filaments bearded or glabrous: ovary 3-celled: style simple, stigma capitate: capsule 3-valved, 3-celled: valves septiferous: 2 rows of superposed seeds in each cell: seed angular, smooth: embryo depressed in the middle of the back.—Herbaceous erect or procumbent ramous plants: leaves scarcely sheathing: inflorescence panicled, terminal, or axillary and lateral: seed, when dry, brownish: flowers blue.

(1) D. lanceolatum. *(R. W.)*

Ident. Wight's Icon. vi. t. 2078.

Spec. Char. Procumbent at the base, rooting, afterwards erect, glabrous: leaves linear-lanceolate, bluntish: panicles terminal, racemose, branches flexuose: pedicels from the axils of loose cucullate bracts: all filaments hairy near the base: capsule oblong, 3-celled, each cell having 20 seeds in each row.

Near Quilon in marshy soil. Malabar.

(2) D. REPENS. *(R.W.)*

Ident. Wight l. c. t. 2078.

SPEC. CHAR. Procumbent, rooting at the joints, glabrous except a decurrent line of hairs from the insertion of the leaves: leaves scarcely sheathing, sessile, ovate-lanceolate, sub-acute: flowers axillary, 2 or 3 from each axil: filaments glabrous: capsule ovate, cells about 8-seeded in two rows.

Quilon in low wet ground, flowering from October to December.

GENUS VII. DICTYOSPERMUM.

Triandria Monogynia. *Sex: Syst:*

Deriv. From *Dictyon*, a net, and *Sperma*, seed.

GEN. CHAR. Perianth 6-parted, 3 outer lobes calycine, inner ones petaloid, all withering: stamens 3, rarely 5, all fertile, middle one opposite the odd petal, slightly dissimilar, when 5, two sterile opposite the lateral petals: ovary 3-celled, with 1 ovule in each: ovule attached to the middle of the axis, horizontal: style filiform, stigma capitate: capsule 3-celled, 3-valved: valves septiferous: seed solitary, oblong, somewhat convex, reticulate on the back: embryo lateral: albumen horny, white.—Herbaceous erect plants: stems simple: leaves sheathing at the base, entire: inflorescence panicled, terminal: flowers solitary, or two or three aggregated in a short sheathing bract, pedicelled: filaments beardless.

(1) D. MONTANUM. *(R.W.)*

Ident. Wight's Icon. vi. t. 2069.

SPEC. CHAR. Erect: leaves longish-petioled, lanceolate, acuminate, round, glabrous except on the margins: sheaths pubescent, truncated: panicle lax, terminal: branches slender, bearing a few flowers on the extremities: petals somewhat larger than the sepals: petaline stamen modified, filaments longer, and cells of the anther somewhat divaricated: style simple: stigma capitate: capsule globose, smooth, shining, papery, fragile: seed corrugately reticulated on the back.

Courtallum. Eastern slopes of the Neilgherries, in damp shady woods, and on banks of streams.

(2) D. OVALIFOLIUM. *(R.W.)*

Ident. Wight l. c. t. 2070.

SPEC. CHAR. Erect: leaves sheathing, short-petioled, oval, acuminate, acute, shortly pubescent on both sides: panicles terminal, sessile, compact, many-flowered: flowers short-pedicelled, at length drooping: sepals and petals about equal, orbicular: filament of the petaline stamen longer than the others, at length spirally convolute: anthers all similar: style short, stigma simple: capsule obsoletely 3-angled, seed reticulate on the back.

Western slopes of the Neilgherries.

(3) D. PROTENSUM. *(R.W.)*

Ident. Wight l. c. t. 2071.

SPEC. CHAR. Erect, pubescent: leaves vaginate, sessile, lanceolate, acuminate: sheaths loose, sub-truncated, ciliated, and like the upper surface of the leaves, sprinkled with bristly hairs: panicles axillary and terminal, long-peduncled: flowers pedicelled, 2—3 aggregated in the axils of cucullate bracts: sepals and petals about equal, shorter than the stamens: filaments filiform: anther of the petaline stamen larger: two sterile stamens: style filiform, stigma capitate: capsule pedicelled, hispid, unequal-sided.

Courtallum.

GENUS VIII. HETEROCARPUS.

Hexandria Monogynia. *Sex: Syst.*

GEN. CHAR. Flowers irregular: perianth 6-parted: 3 outer lobes calycine, 3 inner ones petaloid: anterior calycine lobes obovate, obtuse, connate to near the apex, much larger than the posterior: anterior petaloid lobe sub-sessile, obovate, spathulate, lateral ones unguiculate: stamens 6, filaments glabrous: 3 anterior anthers pollen-bearing, the middle one somewhat deformed, 3 posterior ones sterile: ovary 3-celled, two posterior cells minute, empty, afterwards changing into a rigid curved podocarp, anterior larger 1-ovuled: capsule 1-celled, attached by a groove on the back to the podocarp, indehiscent: seed one, oval: embryo lateral.—Diffuse, herbaceous branched plants: leaves sheathing, entire: peduncles springing from the sheaths, filiform, forked at the apex within the spathe: posterior branch much longer, exserted, bearing on the point a single male flower: anterior enclosed, recurved, 4—5-flowered: spathes cordate, acuminate, folded, sub-coriaceous, ciliated: flowers yellow.

(1) H. HIRSUTUS. *(R.W.)*

Ident. Wight's Icon. vi. t. 2067.

SPEC. CHAR. Diffuse: everywhere pilose, especially on the sheaths and under surfaces of the leaves: sheaths long: leaves linear-lanceolate, acute: spathe long acuminate, ciliate at the base.

Neilgherries, flowering in August and September.

(2) H. GLABER. *(R. W.)*

Ident. Wight l. c. t. 2067.

SPEC. CHAR. Procumbent, diffuse, rooting at the joints, glabrous, except decurrent lines of hairs from the insertions of the leaves and sheaths: leaves lanceolate, obtuse, glabrous: sheaths pubescent: peduncles about the length or a little longer than the leaves, filiform: involucre cordate, acuminate, ciliate at the base: flowers deep orange yellow.

Palghaut jungles. Bolamputty hills. Flowering in October and November.

GENUS IX. FLAGELLARIA.

Hexandria Trigynia. *Sex: Syst:*

Deriv. From *Flagellum*, a whip, alluding to the long flexible branches.

GEN. CHAR. Calyx 6-parted, coloured, persistent: inner segments larger: stamens 6, hypogynous: filaments filiform, free: anthers oblong, fixed by the back, 2-celled, dehiscing lengthways: ovary free, sessile, 3-celled: ovules solitary, basilar, sessile, anatropal: stigmas 3, sessile, filiform, spreading: drupe pea-shaped, crowned by the stigmas, 1-seeded: seed sub-globose: testa membranaceous, thin: hilum basilar: chalaza terminal orbicular: embryo lenticular: very small, half-immersed in mealy albumen: radicle inferior.

(1) F. INDICA. *(Linn.)*

Ident. Linn. sp. 475.—Roxb. flor. Ind. II. 154.

Engrav. Rheede Mal. vii. t. 53.—Rumph. Amb. v. t. 59.—Red. Lil. t. 257.

SPEC. CHAR. Perennial, scandent: leaves narrow, ending in long slender spiral tendrils, contracted and sheathing at the base: flowers terminal, panicled, bracteolate, white, inconspicuous: berries globose, red, smooth, pulpy, 1-seeded, with two abortive ovules.

Rocks near the sea, South Concan. Peninsula. Silhet. Flowering in the rains.

ORDER CLXVII. XYRIDACEÆ.

Flowers densely spiked, hermaphrodite, surrounded by a single scale: calyx double, each 3-sepaled: outer lateral sepals keeled, glumaceous, persistent, anterior more tender and larger, coloured, encircling the inner calyx in the bud together with the genitals, like a cup, soon caducous, inner ones petaloid, very long clawed, equal: claws free, cohering by the assistance of the staminodes except at the top, seldom connate into a tube: laminæ staminiferous at the base, much spreading: fertile stamens 3, free: anthers 2-celled, posticous: cells elongated, contiguous, dehiscing lengthways: staminodes 3, alternating with the fertile stamens, hypogynous, free, filiform, 2-cleft and feathery at the apex: ovary free, sessile, 1—3-celled: ovules numerous, sessile or erect with longish threads, orthotropal: style terminal, 3-cleft at the apex, stigmas simple: capsule membranaceous or papery, 1—3-celled, loculicidally 3-valved: seeds numerous, erect, elliptic or oblong, usually slightly ribbed, seldom sessile and angled: testa coriaceous: embryo very small, lenticular, antitropal: albumen fleshy.—Stemless, perennial, marshy herbs: roots fascicled: leaves iris-shaped, seldom grassy, linear or filiform: peduncles scapiform, simple, wrapped at the base by an open sheath, terminated by a solitary few-many flowered spike: scales imbricated on all sides, outer ones sometimes empty and dissimilar: flowers yellow, seldom blue or violet.

GENUS I. XYRIS.

Triandria Monogynia. *Sex: Syst.*

Deriv. From *Xyros*, acute, the leaves terminate in points.

Gen. Char. Same as in the Order.

(1) X. Wallichii. *(Kunth.)*

Ident. Kunth Enum. pl. iv. p. 16.

Spec. Char. Leaves gladiate-linear, acute, membranaceous, the edges obsoletely scabrous: peduncles filiform, 2-edged, glabrous, equalling or a little exceeding the leaves: spike oblong, few-flowered: scales oblong, marked above on the back with a paler lanceolate scraped area, inner ones somewhat keeled and recurved, outer ones shorter, rounded at the apex, empty: outer lateral sepals broad spathulate, acutish, keeled, dry membranaceous, brownish: flowers yellow.

Silhet.

(2) X. ANCEPS. (*Lam.*)

Ident. Lam. Ill. I. 132.—Vahl. Enum. II. 205.—Kunth l. c. p. 17.

SPEC. CHAR. Peduncles many, 1 foot and more, 2-edged, smooth: leaves narrow, very stiff, 3—4-times less than the twisted peduncles: spike sub-globose: scales roundish, convex, emarginate: outer lateral sepals navicular, attenuated below: anthers 3-teethed at the apex, surrounded at the base with twin penicilliform corpuscules: style deeply 3-cleft, segments dilated above, denticulate at the apex: flowers yellow.

Malabar.

(3) X. LAPPACEA. (*Heyne.*)

Ident. Heyne herb.—Mart. in Wall. pl. As. rar. III. 30.

SPEC. CHAR. Scapes teretely angular, beyond one foot, slightly exceeding the linear acute leaves marked with 7 thick nerves: capitula few-flowered, globose: bracts oblong, of the same colour at the back, apex shortly mucronate, rough.

Coromandel.

(4) X. PAUCIFLORA. (*Willd.*)

Ident. Willd. spec. I. 255.—Kunth l. c.—Mart. l. c. 29.

SPEC. CHAR. Leaves narrow-linear, edges slightly scabrous, glabrous: peduncles twice exceeding the leaves, angular, sheathed below by the leaf: spikes ovate-sub-globose, many-flowered: scales obovate, rounded at the top, shining, convex at the back, somewhat keeled at the top and marked with an ashy triangular scraped area: outer lateral sepals keeled: flowers yellow.

Coromandel. Silhet.

(5) X. WALKERI. (*R.W.*)

Ident. Wight Cat. h. 2373.—Kunth l. c. p. 19.

SPEC. CHAR. Leaves linear, sharply mucronate, sulcately nerved, finely scabrous at the edges: peduncles exceeding the leaves, smooth, 2-edged, finely scabrous at the angles, furnished below with a leafless sheath: spikes ovate, many-flowered: scales broadly obovate, round at the apex, brown, ash-coloured above on the back: outer lateral sepals obovate, keeled, lacerately hairy at the apex, narrowly winged with a keel, wing hispidly spinous at the margin.

Peninsula.

(6) X. ROBUSTA. *(Mart.)*

Ident. Mart. in Wall. Pl. As. rar. III. 30.—Kunth l. c.

SPEC. CHAR. Leaves linear, acutish, glabrous: peduncles terete, sulcated, sharp angled, sheathed by the leaf beneath, exceeding the leaves, spikes ovate or oblong, many-flowered: scales ovate, obtuse, of the same colour, brown, opaque, glabrous: outer lateral sepals narrow, keeled, acute, keel-winged, wing narrow, lacinulate fimbriate.

Silhet.

(7) X. INDICA. *(Linn.)*

Ident. Linn. Zeyl. 14.—Roxb. flor. Ind. I. 179.

Engrav. Rheede Mal. ix. t. 7.

SPEC. CHAR. Glabrous: peduncles terete, sulcate, sharp angled, sheathed below by the leaf, exceeding the sub-gladiate linear acute leaves: spikes elliptic, many-flowered: scales broadly obovate, rounded at the apex, of the same colour, shining: outer lateral sepals narrow, keeled, obtuse, keel-winged above: wing narrow, entire: flowers yellow.

South Concan. Coromandel. Bengal. Flowering in November and December.

(1) X. NILAGIRIENSIS. *(Steudel.)*

Ident. Steudel syn. p. 288.

SPEC. CHAR. Peduncles terete, somewhat angled, compressed at the base and there furnished with a long-sheathed leaflet: radical leaves long and broadly sheathed, very narrow, 2—3-times shorter than the petiole: spike ovate or sub-rotund, elliptic: scales broadly ovate, shining chestnut, slightly paler at the margin, obtuse at the apex.

Neilgherries.

(9) X. ORYZETORUM. *(Miq.)*

Ident. Miq. in Herb. Ind. or. Hohen. 369.—Steudel l. c.

SPEC. CHAR. Scapes angular, sheathing-leafy at the base: leaves flat, linear, narrow, denticulate at the margin: spike ovate: scales broadly ovate, obtuse, chestnut, ashy pubescent at the apex: capsule somewhat triquetrous, 1-celled: seeds very numerous, oblong, pellucid, striated.

Mangalore.

ORDER CLXVIII. ORCHIDACEÆ.

Perennial herbs growing on trunks of trees, rocks and stones, as well as in the earth: roots fibrous, fascicled, fleshy or tubercle-shaped: stems none, either elongated annual, or more frequently perennial woody, forming a rhizome or jointed sheathed branches: leaves almost always sheathing, sometimes articulated with the stalk, membranaceous, coriaceous, terete, even hard and plaited, always undivided, sometimes rough with small cartilaginous teeth, paralled veined, never serrated: flowers hermaphrodite, irregular, very various in shape, spiked or racemose, seldom solitary, sometimes racemosely panicled, always supported by a solitary bract: perianth herbaceous or petaloid, membranaceous or fleshy, closed or reflexed, persistent and withering or articulated with the ovary and deciduous: parts arranged in a double row, free or cohering in various ways, frequently resupinate by the twisting of the ovary: sepals 3, either equal at the base, or variously prolonged and expanded, two lateral anterior by the twisting of the ovary, the third dorsal next to the axis, rarely surrounded by a calyx: petals usually 3, very rarely 1, placed between the sepals, larger or smaller: lateral ones usually resembling the dorsal sepal, seldom altogether different in form: third posticous, but very often standing in front by the twisting of the ovary, polymorphous, called the lip, usually larger than the rest and the form altogether different, sometimes produced at the base into a spur, or affecting a horn with the foot of the column and prolonged bases of the lateral sepals, sometimes altogether connate with the column, undivided or 3-lobed, sometimes increased by a fleshy appendage rising from the stigma, column consisting of the stamens and style consolidated into a solid body, the latter being next the lip, the former near the dorsal sepal: stamens 3, opposite the sepals, central one only bearing anthers, except in Cypripedium, when the central is abortive, and the two lateral ones perfect: anthers 1—2-celled, cells separated by 2—4-partitions, erect at the summit of the column, or turned downwards, or at the back: pollen powdery or granular, or cohering in wedges bound by some elastic substance, or consolidated into waxy masses, the latter free or adherent to a gland, belonging to the beak of the stigma: ovary inferior, 1-celled, consisting of 6 carpels, of which three opposite the petals bear many seeded didymous parietal placentæ without stigmas, and three opposite the sepals are produced in as many stigmas but without placentæ: style not distinct except in Cypripedium and certain Neottieæ: stigmas usually confluent in a hollow mucous disc: the dorsal stigma having on the upper edge one or two glands, often extended into a beak, or hollowed out into pouches or prolonged into two parallel diverging arms, the lateral stigmas usually obsolete: capsule seldom indehiscent, fleshy, pod-shaped, very often breaking up into six dry woody stiff valves, of which three only bear seeds: seeds very numerous, minute, enwrapped in a loose netty skin, sometimes compressed into a circular wing: embryo exalbuminous, solid, fleshy: chalaza at the apex, radicle next the hilum.

GENUS I. MICROSTYLIS.

Gynandria Monandria. *Sex: Syst:*

Deriv. From *Micros*, small, and *Style*, a column.

Gen. Char. Sepals spreading, free, lateral ones equal at the base, usually shorter: petals spreading, linear or filiform: lip much spreading, forming a right angle with the column, hollow at the base, sagittate or auricled, quite entire or toothed, tubercles none: column small, seldom a little elongated, furnished with teeth or two ears at the apex: anther 2-celled: pollen masses 4, collateral. —Terrestrial or epiphytous herbs: leaves plicate or membranaceous, seldom thickened at the base: flowers herbaceous, yellowish or of two colours.

(1) M. versicolor. *(Lindl.)*

Ident. Lindl. gen. and sp. p. 21.

Engrav. Wight's Icon. t. 901.

Spec. Char. Stem leafy: leaves cordate or ovate oblong, abruptly petioled, undulated, plaited: lip transverse, dentated on the margin, cucullate, slightly overlapping at the base: column bicornate at the apex: sepals and petals secund.

Neilgherries and other elevated stations in grassy pastures.

(2) M. Rheedii. *(Lindl.)*

Ident. Lindl. l. c.

Syn. Epidendrum resupinatum *Forst.* Malaxis Rheedii, *Willd.*

Engrav. Wight l. c. t. 902.

Spec. Char. Stem leafy: leaves oblong-lanceolate, plaited: lip truncated, dentate, largely overlapping at the base.

Pulney mountains among pasture.

(3) M. luteola. *(R. W.)*

Ident. Wight l. c. t. 1632.

Spec. Char. Stem leafy at the base: leaves ovate, sub-cordate at the base, acute, plicate: sepals obovate, obtuse, the middle one narrower: petals linear, obtuse, emarginate: lip somewhat 2-lobed, lobes broad, spreading, fimbriate-dentate: flowers yellow.

Ootacamund, Neilgherries. Flowering in August.

(4) M. Wallichii. *(Lindl.)*

Ident. Lindl. l. c. p. 20.

Spec. Char. Stem leafy: leaves oblong, acuminate, raceme elongated, few flowered: sepals oblong-linear: petals filiform: lip oval, slightly 2-cleft at the apex: flowers bluish.

Silhet.

(5) M. biaurita. *(Lindl.)*

Ident. Lindl. l. c.

Spec. Char. Stem leafy: leaves ovate-oblong, acuminate: raceme dense, many flowered: lip acuminate, obtuse, quite entire, 2-crested at the base: wings of the column petaloid: lateral sepals and petals secund.

Pundua, Silhet.

GENUS II. COTTONIA.

Gynandria Monandria. *Sex: Syst.*

Deriv. Named after Major F. Cotton, Madras Engineers, an ardent promoter of Botany.

Gen. Char. Perianth spreading: sepals broad-obovate, obtuse: petals smaller, sub-lanceolate, cuneate at the base: lip ecalcarate, constricted in the middle, sub-panduriform, upper half larger, sub-orbicular, emarginate, cuspidate in the sinus, lower half orbicular, with 2 tubercles at the base: column erect, clavate, margins dilated, membranous in front: anther 2-celled, with a long blunt rostellum: pollen-masses 2, unequally 2-lobed, posterior lobes smaller: caudicle filiform, gland orbicular: capsule long, clavate, drooping.

(1) C. MACROSTACHYS. *(R.W.)*

Ident. Wight's Icon. v. t. 1755.

Syn. Vanda peduncularis. *Lindl. gen. and sp. p.* 216.

Engrav. Paxt. flower garden, III t. 253.

SPEC. CHAR. Caulescent, epiphytal: leaves linear, distichous, obliquely emarginate: peduncles very long, bearing a few-flowered short racemes at the apex: lip purple with yellow borders, velvetty, furnished with bristly knobs and appendages.

Warree Country. Chorla Ghaut. Neilgherries. Near Tellicherry, Malabar.

GENUS III. LIPARIS.

Gynandria Monandria. *Sex: Syst:*

GEN. CHAR. Sepals spreading, free, lateral ones equal at the base, usually shorter: petals narrower than the sepals, seldom equal, linear or filiform: lip ascending or erect, a little accrete at the base with the column, usually with two tubercles above the base, entire, sometimes mucronate but not lobed: column elongated, half-terete, incurved, marginate at the top.—Terrestrial or epiphytous herbs: leaves concrete at the base into a pseudo-bulb, sometimes membranaceous plicate, or sub-coriaceous with the veins less distinct: scape terete or angled, or two-edged: flowers small, herbaceous, racemose, seldom yellow or white.

(1) L. OLIVACEA. *(Lindl.)*

Ident. Lindl. gen. and sp. p. 27.

Engrav. Wight's Icon. t. 903.

SPEC. CHAR. Leaves binate or solitary, roundish, cordate or oblong, acuminated, plicate, shorter than the erect many-flowered raceme: scape terete at the base: lip obovate, retuse, with a mucro, bituberculate at the base: sepals obtuse, lateral ones resting on the lip.

Pulney mountains, on rocky clifts.

(2) L. ATROPURPUREA. *(Lindl.)*

Ident. Lindl. l. c. p. 28.

Engrav. Wight l. c. t. 904.

SPEC. CHAR. Leaves two or three, roundish, acuminated, petiolated, plaited, obliquely cucullate at the base, about as long as the erect few-flowered raceme: labellum oblong, obtuse, recurved, crenulate: lateral sepals oblong-lanceolate, oblique: petals long filiform: flowers purple.

Pulney mountains, among rocky clifts.

(3) L. WALKERIÆ. *(Graham.)*

Ident. Grah. Bot. Mag. No. 3770.

Engrav. Wight l. c. t. 905.

SPEC. CHAR. Leaves two or three, roundish ovate, acute, petioled, plicate, oblique at the base, cucullate, shorter than the erect many-flowered raceme: peduncles angled: lip roundish, reflexed, crenulated: sepals spreading, oblong, margins revolute: the germen and filiform petals equal.

Courtallum.

(4) L. LONGIPES. *(Lindl.)*

Ident. Lindl. l. c. p. 30.

Engrav. Wight l. c. t. 906.

SPEC. CHAR. Pseudo-bulbs long, terete, 2-leaved: leaves ensiform lanceolate: raceme straight, many-flowered: scape ancipitous: lip ovate acute, without tubercles, the length of the column: sepals ovate: petals linear.

Courtallum, flowering in July and August. Mountains of Eastern Bengal.

(5) L. BILOBA. *(R. W.)*

Ident. Wight l. c. t. 1633.

SPEC. CHAR. Leaves two or three, ovate acute, undulate, plicate, cucullate: raceme erect, few-flowered: sepals ovate, acute: petals narrow linear, blunt-pointed: lip spreading, deeply 2-lobed: flowers dull plumb colour.

Neilgherries, nestling among the moss on the branches of trees, flowering in July and August.

(6) L. elliptica. (R. W.)

Ident. Wight l. c. t. 1735.

Spec. Char. Pseudo-bulbs oval, compressed, costate on one side, 2-edged, truncated at the apex, 2-leaved: leaves elliptic, cuspidate, nerved, sub-plicate, about half the length of the scape: scape sub-erect, raceme many-flowered: bracts ovate, subulate, about the length of the ovary: sepals nearly equal, ovate-elliptic, cuspidate: petals narrow, linear, pointed: lip irregularly 3-lobed: lobes undulated, pointed, the middle one larger: flowers greenish-yellow, approaching to straw-colour.

On branches of trees about Conoor, Neilgherries, flowering from August to October.

(7) L. odorata. (Lindl.)

Ident. Lindl. l. c. p. 26.

Syn. Malaxis odorata, *Willd.*

Engrav Rheede Mal. xii. t. 28.

Spec. Char. Leaves oblong-lanceolate, plicate: raceme erect, many-flowered: scape 3-cornered: lip ovate, hollow: flowers yellowish-green, fragrant.

Malabar.

(8) L. luteola. (Lindl.)

Ident. Lindl. l. c. p. 32.

Spec. Char. Pseudo-bulbs very small, sheathed: leaves twin, linear-lanceolate, shorter than the flexuose few-flowered raceme: scape tapering: lip obovate, retuse, incumbent on a column winged at the top: single callus of the base obsolete: bracts ovate, acuminate, decurrent: pedicels many times longer than the flowers.

Pundua mountains, nestling in moss.

GENUS IV. OTOCHILUS.

Gynandria Monandria. *Sex: Syst:*

Deriv. From *Ous*, *otos*, an ear, and *Cheilos*, a lip, alluding to the little ear-like appendages at the base of the lip.

Gen. Char. Sepals and petals equal, free, spreading: lip 3-lobed, lateral lobes ear-shaped, embracing the base of the column, intermediate one spreading, elongated, conformable to the sepals, crests none: column elongated, club-shaped, half-terete: anther terminal, 2-celled, middle dissepiment 2-parted and hence 2-valved: pollen masses 4, incumbent, cohering with granular matter at the base.—Herbs creeping on trees, destitute of a rhizome, but with pseudo-bulbs, always bearing young plants from the side of their own apex: racemes many-flowered from the side of the pseudo-bulbs, sheathed at the base: stigma with the upper lip ovate, drawn out.

(1) O. porrecta. *(Lindl.)*

Ident. Lindl. gen. and sp. p. 36.

Spec. Char. Pseudo-bulbs elongated, fusiform: leaves oblong-lanceolate, plicate: bracts linear: sepals and petals acute: ears of the tip obscurely denticulate.

Pundua.

GENUS V. ERIA.

Gynandria Monandria. *Sex: Syst:*

Deriv. From *Erion*, wool, alluding to the flower.

Gen. Char. Sepals half-spreading or closed, unequal, woolly or glabrous externally, lateral ones very unequal at the base, connate with the foot of the column, emulating the spur: petals equal to or less than the upper sepal: lip articulated with the lengthened base of the column, 3-lobed, seldom sub-entire, hooded, with a callous or crested disc: column much drawn out at the base: anther terminal, 2-celled, cells obsoletely 4-locellate: pollen masses 8, sometimes altogether free, sometimes cohering with an elastic material imitating a gland.—Herbs growing on trees: stems fleshy, sheathed, marked with the scars of the leaves: leaves usually plicate: racemes simple, erect, bracts usually dilated: flowers sometimes conspicuous.

(1) E. polystachya. *(Ach. Rich.)*

Ident. Wight's Icon. t. 1635.

Spec. Char. Stem thickened, resembling a pseudo-bulb at the base, loosely sheathed: leaves terminal from oblong-elliptic acute to obovate-elliptic: spikes axillary about the length of the leaves, erect, clothed with short pubescence: bracts lanceolate, acute: sepals ovate, attenuated at the point, pubescent, exceeding the lanceolate petals: lip ovate-lanceolate, about half the length of the petals.

Western slopes of the Neilgherries, flowering in August and Sepember.

(2) E. pubescens. *(R. W.)*

Ident. Wight l. c. t. 1634.

Spec. Char. Stem leafy, short, clothed at the base with sheathing scales: leaves lanceolate, tapering at both ends, marked with strong longitudinal veins: racemes slender, drooping: rachis and pedicels pubescent: flowers resupinate: bracts as long as the pedicels, lanceolate-acuminate: sepals and petals a little longer than the lip, glabrous, falcate, attenuated towards the point, 3-nerved: lip oblong, 3-nerved, sub-coriaceous at the base, contracted in the middle: limb lanceolate, acute, margins membranous, reflexed: flowers white, perianth tipped with pink.

Western slopes of the Neilgherries, flowering in August and September.

(3) E. pauciflora. *(R. W.)*

Ident. Wight l. c. t. 1636.

Spec. Char. Cæspitose, stems erect, succulent, jointed, thickened at the apex, with a leaf at each joint, last joint thickened, tuberous, surmounted by two leaves, from between which rises the short 1- or 3-flowered raceme: leaves ovate, oblong, obtuse: flowers longish pedicelled: sepals about equal or slightly longer than the narrow linear petals: lip somewhat corrugated, furnished with two lamellæ near the base: flowers pure white.

Moist rocks below the Kaitie falls, Neilgherries, flowering in August and September.

(4) E. reticosa. *(R. W.)*

Ident. Wight l. c. t. 1637.

Syn. E. braccata, *Lindl. in Journ. Proc. Linn. Soc. III. p.* 46. E. uniflora, *Dalz. in Hook. Journ. Bot. IV. III.*

Spec. Char. Cæspitose, stemless: pseudo-bulbs orbicular, depressed, enclosed in a net-like sack: leaves about two, elliptic, spreading: scape filiform, 1-flowered, furnished at the apex with a large somewhat boat-shaped bractea: flowers large, resupinate, expanding: sepals and petals about equal, exceeding the obscurely 3-lobed lip: flowers pure white, lip and column yellow, bract brownish.

Branches of trees about Pycarrah, Neilgherries, flowering in May and June.

(5) E. MICROCHILOS. *(Lindl.)*

Ident. Lindl. l. c.—Dalz. Bomb. flor. p. 262.

Syn. Dendrobium macrochilos, *Dalz. l. c. III.* 345.

SPEC. CHAR. Pseudo-bulbs deeply bi-lobed; lobes orbicular, much depressed, reticulated, with a white skin; leaves 3 to 4, linear, rather obtuse, rather flattened towards the top, narrowed at the base, and there streaking the flowering scape: flowers spiked, alternate, secund, minute, of a straw-colour; capsule sessile, ovate, smooth; sepals acuminated from a broad base: petals similar; lip ovate, undivided, half their length.

On trees in the Warree Country, Western Coast, flowering in August.

(6) E. DALZELLI. *(Lindl.)*

Ident. Lindl. l. c.—Dalz. Bomb. flor. l. c.

Syn. Dendrobium Dalzelli, *Hook. Journ. Bot.* D. fimbriatum, *Hook. Journ. IV.* 292. D. filiforme, *R. W.*

Engrav. Wight l. c. t. 1642.

SPEC. CHAR. Cæspitose: pseudo-bulbs depressed, flattened, sub-orbicular, netted on the surface: leaves 2—3, ovate, oblong, slightly cuspidate: raceme erect, filiform, 2—3 to many-flowered: bracts ovate, acute, longer than the ovary: sepals much attenuated, subulate, pointed, dilated at the base, adnate to the process of the column, forming a short obtuse saccate spur: petals about equalling the sepals and nearly twice as long as the narrow ovate lip: flowers straw colour.

Neilgherries and Iyamullay Hills, near Coimbatore. Southern Concan and Ghauts, on and in hollows of trees.

(7) E. PANICULATA. *(Lindl.)*

Ident. Lindl. gen. and sp. p. 65.

Engrav. Wall. pl. As. rar. t. t. 36.

SPEC. CHAR. Leaves linear-lanceolate, acuminate, glaucous beneath: stems terete, pendulous, elongated: racemes terminal, aggregated, cylindric, many-flowered: sepals woolly, ovate, obtuse and with the smaller petals guttate: lip 3-lobed, callous at the base and apex: lobes guttate, intermediate one truncated.

Pundua.

(8) E. PUMILA. *(Lindl.)*

Ident. Lindl. l. c. p. 68.

SPEC. CHAR. Leaves twin, linear-lanceolate, plicate: stems terete, erect, almost equal: sepals and petals acuminate, somewhat hairy at the base: lip 3-lobed, not callous, lateral lobes subulate, spreading, middle one ovate: spikes capitate, lateral, sub-sessile: ovary pubescent: flowers small, slightly tinged with pink.

Pundua.

GENUS VI. PHOLIDOTA.

Gynandria Monandria. *Sex: Syst:*

Deriv. From *Pholis*, a scale, and *Ous*, *otos*, an ear, alluding to the scaly ear-like bracts of the spike.

GEN. CHAR. Flowers sub-globose: sepals equal, distinct: petals less: lip hooded ventricose, 3-lobed or undivided: parallel with the column: column continuous with the ovary, half-terete or winged, clinandrium hooded: anther bilabiate 2- or 4-valved: pollen masses 4, globose, distinct.—Epiphytous herbs with a fleshy articulated or pseudo-bulbiferous rhizome: leaves plicate: spikes terminal, usually imbricated and nodding.

(1) P. IMBRICATA. *(Lindl.)*

Ident. Lindl. gen. and sp. p. 36.

Syn. Ptilocnema bracteatum, *Don prod.* 33.

Engrav. Wight's Icon. t. 907.—Hooker Flora Exotica t. 138.

SPEC. CHAR. Pseudo-bulbs ovate, oblong, obtuse, somewhat angled: leaves solitary, oblong lanceolate, plicate, acute: spikes the length of the leaves, pendulous; bracteas membranaceous, concave, imbricated: lateral sepals ovate, carinate: lip sub-globose cucullate, lateral lobes small, erect, intermediate 1—2-lobed, cordate.

Courtallum. Chittagong. Khasia Hills. Flowering in September and October.

(2) P. ARTICULATA. *(Lindl.)*

Ident. Lindl. l. c.

SPEC. CHAR. Rhizome fleshy, jointed, ascending: leaves twin or more, oval, plaited, almost entire at the apex: spikes lax, drooping, as long as the leaves: bracts oblong, concave: sepals ovate: lip hooded, entire, rounded at the apex, flat: flowers white, base of the apex of the lip yellow.

Pundua.

GENUS VII. JOSEPHIA.

Gynandria Monandria. *Sex: Syst:*

Deriv. Named after Dr. Joseph Dalton Hooker, the eminent Botanist.

GEN. CHAR. Perianth globose, closed: sepals equal, ovate, sub-orbicular, lateral ones incumbent on the lip: petals obovate, oblong, obtuse, a little shorter than the sepals: lip connate with the base of the column, fleshy, ventricose at the base, ecalcarate, constricted in the middle, limb entire, sub-orbicular, emarginate: column erect, clavate, half-round: anther imperfectly 2-celled: pollen-masses 4, parallel, oblong, clavate, sessile on the dilated shield-like gland.—Epiphytic plants: leaves long-petioled, coriaceous: scapes erect, panicled, many-flowered: flowers congested towards the ends of the branches, pedicelled and furnished with a minute ovate acute persistent bract.

(1) J. LANCEOLATA. *(R. W.)*

Ident. Wight's Icon. v. t. 1742.

SPEC. CHAR. Leaves elliptic-lanceolate, acute at both ends: scapes a little longer than the leaves, naked, panicled: branches of the panicle racemose: flowers whitish, tinged with purple, lip reddish lilac.

Branches of trees below Neddiwuttum, Neilgherries; flowering in August and September.

(2) J. LATIFOLIA. *(R. W.)*

Ident. Wight l. c. t. 1743.

SPEC. CHAR. Leaves broad-oval, very obtuse or round above, tapering below into the longish sulcated petiole: scape panicled, about twice the length of the leaves, scaly, branches of the panicle short: flowers congested, sub-capitate.

Branches of trees on the Pulney mountains, flowering in August and September. The flowers of this curious genus are annually renewed on the old scapes.

GENUS VIII. CŒLOGYNE.

Gynandria Monandria. *Sex: Syst:*

Deriv. From *Koilos*, hollow, and *Gyne*, female, alluding to the form of the stigma.

GEN. CHAR. Sepals connivent or spreading, free, equal, petaloid, usually obtuse at the base: petals of the same form or much narrower: lip hooded, 3-lobed or undivided, petaloid, often saccate at the base, veins 2—3 or more, parallel, crested, sometimes connate with the base of the column: column erect, free, winged, membranaceo-marginate at the apex: stigma prominent, deeply excavated, 2-lipped: pollen masses 4, free, incumbent, cohering with granular matter: anther inserted below the top of the column, moveable, scarcely deciduous.—Epiphytous or terrestrial, pseudo-bulbous: leaves 1—2-nerved: racemes, or solitary flowers, terminal, often bursting from horny scales: flowers white, rose, yellowish or spotted with brown, even greenish, very often showy.

(1) C. Gardneriana. *(Lindl.)*

Ident. Lindl. in Wall. pl. As. rar. I. p. 33, t. 38: fol. orch. 1854, p. 1—2. gen. and sp. p. 41.

Syn. C. trisaccata, *Griff. Itin. notes p.* 72.

Spec. Char. Pseudo-bulbs elongated, ampullaceous, tapering: leaves lanceolate, acuminated, long-petioled: racemes nodding, dense-flowered, terminal and radical, much shorter than the leaves: bracts broad, oblong, hooded, sterile ones fleshy, floriferous ones petaloid, persistent: flowers closed: sepals oblong, keeled, saccate at the base: petals linear-oblong: lip denticulate, with 2 sacs at the base, middle lobe 2-lobed, less than the lateral ones: crest double, evanescent below the middle: flowers large pure white with a yellowish stain at the end of the lip.

Khasia. The flowers seldom expand, but are placed on long nodding racemes supported by fleshy snow-white bracts.

(2) C. breviscapa. *(Lindl.)*

Ident. Lindl. fol. orch. l. c. p. 4.

Syn. C. angustifolia, *Wight's Icon. t.* 1641.

Spec. Char. Pseudo-bulbs ovate, corrugated, 1-leaved: leaves narrow-lanceolate, coriaceous, petioled: scapes few-flowered, very upright, imbricately scaled at the base: bracts broad, oblong, concave, persistent: lateral lobes of the lip obtuse, intermediate one twice as large, sub-rotund, apiculate, with two flexuose veins thickened at the apex, the intermediate one filiform: column denticulate at the apex only: flowers white, lip tinged with yellow.

Neilgherries, on branches of trees in clumps of forests near Neddiwuttum.

(3) C. odoratissima. *(Lindl.)*

Ident. Lindl. gen. and sp. p. 41; fol. orch. p. 5.

Engrav. Wight l. c. t. 1640.

Spec. Char. Pseudo-bulbs ovate, furrowed: leaves 1—2, membranaceous, nerved, shorter than the erect, 2—3-flowered raceme: bracts narrow, cymbiform, divaricate: middle lobe of the 3-crested 3-lobed lip obtuse, sub-rotund, lateral ones shorter, flat: flowers pure white, very fragrant.

Dodabetta. Neilgherries. Flowering from May to October.

(4) C. OCHRACEA. *(Lindl.)*

Ident. Lindl. Bot. Reg. 1846; fol. orch. l. c. p. 5.

Engrav. Lindl. ut supra t. 69.—Bot. Mag. t. 4661.

SPEC. CHAR. Pseudo-bulbs ovate, 4-cornered at the apex: leaves narrow lanceolate, narrowed into the petiole, longer than the few-flowered raceme, which is sheathed at the base by shining scales nodding at the apex: sepals and petals narrow-lanceolate: lateral lobes of the 3-lobed lip which is pubescent within rotund, intermediate one acuminate obtuse, sinus denticulate or entire, with two straightish entire plates which disappear within the middle of the apex, a short elevated line with a tooth-bearing apex being interjacent near the base: flowers pure white with bright orange yellow blotches on the lip, very fragrant.

Khasia.

(5) C. GLANDULOSA. *(Lindl.)*

Ident. Lindl. fol. orch. l. c. p. 6.

Syn. C. nervosa, *Wight l. c. t.* 1638.

SPEC. CHAR. Pseudo-bulbs ovate, furrowed: leaves two, oblong-lanceolate, nerved, sub-sessile, nearly equalling the erect nodding many-flowered raceme: scape loosely sheathed at the base: bracts persistent oblong acute, nearly equal to the flowers: lip ovate-lanceolate, lateral lobes very obtuse, intermediate one tongue-shaped with 3 elevated glandular-toothed lines: column somewhat 2-lobed: flowers pure white, lip tinged with orange, bract reddish brown.

Neilgherries, flowering in May and June.

(6) C. NERVOSA. *(A. Rich.)*

Ident. A. Rich. in Ann. Sc. ser. 2, xv. p. 16.—Lindl. l. c. (not Wight).

SPEC. CHAR. Pseudo-bulbs ovate: leaves two, coriaceous, round-oval, sessile, shorter than the erect 2—4-flowered raceme: bracts cymbiform, spreading, longer than the ovary: sepals and petals oblong, of the same form: lip 3—5-crested, middle lobe ovate acute, lateral ones round obsolete.

Neilgherries, on rocks near Neddiwuttum.

(7) C. corrugata. *(R. W.)*

Ident. Wight l. c. t. 1639.—Lindl. l. c.

Spec. Char. Pseudo-bulbs ovate, very much wrinkled: leaves 2, oblong, membranaceous, undulate, longer than the erect 3-flowered raceme: bracts cymbiform oblong: sepals and petals nearly equal, oblong, acute: lip 3-crested in the middle, lateral lobes acutish, middle one ovate, acuminate, obtuse: flowers pure white, except the crests and veins of the lip, which are yellow.

Khasia. Courtallum. Pulneys. Neilgherries. Flowering in August and September.

(8) C. corymbosa. *(Lindl.)*

Ident. Lindl. l. c. p. 7.

Spec. Char. Pseudo-bulbs oblong, tapering leaves oval, narrowed at the base into a short petiole: racemes 3—4-flowered corymbose from a loose imbricated sheath: bracts soon deciduous: sepals and petals lanceolate: lateral lobes of the lip round, denticulate at the apex, middle one ovate-lanceolate, flat, quite entire: lines 3, elevated, of which two are longer and crumpled, the other shortened, increased at both ends at the sinus of the lip: flowers white, fragrant, lip with red veins on the lower half and six ocellate spots at the base of the lower lobe.

Khasia.

(9) C. brevifolia. *(Lindl.)*

Ident. Lindl. l. c.

Spec. Char. Pseudo-bulbs ovate, sub-angulate, shining: leaves ovate-oblong, acute at both ends, shorter than the few-flowered racemes: raceme lax, erect, bracts deciduous: sepals and petals narrow-lanceolate: lip 3-lobed, pubescent within, lobes round with 2 staightish plates evanescent within the middle of the apex, a very small membranaceous line being added in the lower axis: flowers white with orange spots on each lateral lobe.

Khasia.

(10) C. ocellata. *(Lindl.)*

Ident. Lindl. gen. and sp. p. 40.

Engrav. Bot Mag. t. 3767.

Spec. Char. Pseudobulbs ovate, angled, clothed with shining scales: leaves lanceolate, long narrowed at the base, equalling the straight racemes: bracts soon deciduous: sepals and petals oblong-lanceolate: lateral lobes of the lip truncated, middle one ovate: lines three, elevated, straightish, one shortened toothed, increased at both ends at the sinus of the lip: flowers pure white, lip with two bright orange yellow spots on each lateral lobe, and two others smaller and of the same colour at the base of the middle lobe, besides some lateral streaks of brown: the column is bordered with brilliant orange yellow.

Khasia. Silhet.

(11) C. CRISTATA. (*Lindl.*)

Ident. Lindl. Coll. Bot. p. 33.—Gen. and sp. p. 39.

Syn. Cymbidium speciosissimum, *Don prod. Nep. p.* 35.

Engrav. Bot. Reg. 1841, t. 57.

SPEC. CHAR. Pseudo-bulbs oblong, at length angled: rhizome thick, scaly: leaves linear-lanceolate: raceme erect, 3—5-flowered, shorter than the leaves, sheathed at the base with horny scales: bracts oblong, divaricate, persistent: petals oblong-lanceolate, undulated: lip 3-lobed, crest 3-fold, interrupted, lowest one short, 5-lamellate, middle one many-cleft, pectinate, uppermost one 2-lamellate, toothed, middle lobe round, small, flat, obtusely sub-tridentate: flowers white.

Silhet.

(12) C. BARBATA. (*Griff.*)

Ident. Griff. Itin. not. p.—Notul. p. 280.—Ic. t. 291, fig. 2.—Lind. fol. orch. l. c. p. 9.

SPEC. CHAR. Pseudo-bulbs sub-ampullaceous: leaves oblong-lanceolate, long-petioled, very coriaceous, waxy: scape straight, stiff, imbricated at the apex with coriaceous scales: raceme sub-flexuose, sessile: bracts very large, hooded, soon deciduous: sepals oblong: petals lanceolate: lip 3-lobed, saccate at the base, inner margin and ribs ciliate-fimbriate; flowers pure white with brown hairy fringes at their base.

Khasia.

(13) C. ELATA. (*Lindl.*)

Ident. Lindl. gen. and sp. p. 40; fol. orch. l. c.

Engrav. Wall. pl. As. rar. III. t. 218.—Griff. Icon. t. 290.

SPEC. CHAR. Pseudo-bulbs oblong, angled: leaves oblong, coriaceous, attenuated at the base, long-petioled: scape, stiff, straight, shorter than the leaves, sheathed at the apex with distichous coriaceous scales: raceme straightish, sessile: bracts soon deciduous: petals linear-lanceolate: lip flat, 2-crested in the middle, middle lobe cordate-ovate, crenulate, lateral ones obsolete: flowers white, stained with yellow near the point of the lip, with an unpleasant smell: crests of the middle lobe rich orange yellow.

Silhet.

(14) C. PROLIFERA. *(Lindl.)*

Ident. Lindl. l. c.

SPEC. CHAR. Pseudo-bulbs elongated, somewhat compressed, tapering: leaves lanceolate, long-petioled: scape terminal, slender, erect, twice as long as the leaves, usually proliferous, closely sheathed under each raceme by distichous scales: bracts deciduous: sepals oblong, of two colours: petals linear: middle lobe of the lip retuse denticulate, lateral ones very obtuse with two continuous elevated lines: flowers greenish-yellow.

Khasia.

(15) C. FLAVIDA. *(J. D. Hooker.)*

Ident. Lindl. fol. orch. l. c. p. 10.

SPEC. CHAR. Pseudo-bulbs ovate, somewhat angled: leaves lanceolate, petioled: scape terminal, slender, erect, nearly equal to the leaves, proliferous, closely sheathed by distichous scales under each raceme: bracts deciduous: sepals ovate: petals filiform: lip oblong, very obtuse, lateral lobes dwarf, obtuse, imbricating the middle cordate one: lines two, elevated, passing into the sinus: column almost wingless: flowers pale green.

Khasia.

(16) C. LONGIPES. *(Lindl.)*

Ident. Lindl. l. c.

SPEC. CHAR. Pseudo-bulbs cylindric, tapering: leaves lanceolate, very acute, narrowed into a slender petiole: scape terminal, filiform, longer than the leaves, proliferous, closely sheathed under each raceme by distichous scales: bracts deciduous: sepals ovate: petals filiform: lateral lobes of the lip obtuse, divergent, middle one obovate-sub-rotund: lines 2, elevated, decurrent at the base: column broadly winged.

Khasia.

(17) C. FUSCESCENS. *(Lindl.)*

Ident. Lindl. gen. and sp. p. 41.

Syn. C. brunnea, *Lindl. in Gardn. Chron.* 1848 *p.* 71 *with fig.*

SPEC. CHAR. Pseudo-bulbs long, tapering: leaves broad, oblong, plicate, acute at both ends: raceme nodding, few-flowered: bracts deciduous: petals acuminate, linear: middle lobe of the lip ovate, acute, waved, large, lateral ones dwarf: lines 3, elevated near the base: flowers brownish green: lip with four cinnamon spots, one on each of the small lateral lobes, and two at the base of the middle lobes: elevated lines of the crest reddish orange.

Khasia.

(18) C. FIMBRIATA. *(Lindl.)*

Ident. Lindl. in Bot. Reg. 1838: *misc.* 172—fol. orch. l. c. p. 12.

Engrav. Bot. Reg. t. 868. Bot. Cab. t. 1425.

SPEC. CHAR. Pseudo-bulbs sub-rotund-oblong, not striated: leaves oval-lanceolate, waved, acute, longer than the peduncle, which is sheathed at the base and few-flowered: bracts concave, cartilaginous, deciduous, longer than the flowers: petals filiform, reflexed: laterai lobes of the lip round, denticulate in the front, middle one narrower ovate, fimbriated with brown hairs: plates 2, elevated, straight, slightly denticulate: flowers pale olive brown, with the lip paler, fasciated, crested and fimbriated with dark purple.

Khasia mountains.

(19) C. FULIGINOSA. *(Lindl.)*

Ident. Lindl. in Lodd. Cab. fol. orch. l. c. p. 12.

Engrav. Bot. Mag. t. 4440.

SPEC. CHAR. Pseudo-bulbs narrow, fusiform, rhizome branched, ascending: leaves lanceolate, waved, longer than the raceme: bracts deciduous: petals filiform: lateral lobes of the lip scarcely broader than the middle one, acute, fimbriated in the front, middle one oblong, retuse, fimbriated: plates 2, flexuose, suddenly interrupted towards the base: flowers orange-yellow, lip brown.

Khasia mountains.

(20) C. DIPHYLLA. *(Lindl.)*

Ident. Lindl. fol. orch. l, c. p. 15.

Syn. Pleione diphylla, *Lindl. in Paxton's fl. Gard. t.* 51.

SPEC. CHAR. Pseudo-bulbs oblong, constricted in the middle: leaves twin, narrow, sub-coriaceous, acuminate: peduncle three times longer than the flower: bract obtuse, inflated, apiculated, the length of the ovary: lip obtusely 3-lobed, emarginate, with 5—7 interrupted fimbriated veins: flowers white, lip stained and lined inside with violet and crimson, with 7—9 lines of yellow fringes.

Khasia.

(21) C. MACULATA. *(Lindl.)*

Ident. Lindl. in Wall. pl. as. rar. I. 45—fol. orch. l. c.

Syn. Pleione maculata, *Lindl. in Paxton l. c.*

Engrav. Wall. l. c. t. 53.—Bot. Mag. t. 4691. Paxton l. c. t. 39, fig. I.

SPEC. CHAR. Pseudo-bulbs of one colour, umbonate, thick, narrowed at the base: bract short, sub-rotund, hooded, inflated: sepals and petals oval, acute: lip round, quite entire, emarginate, with 7-bearded lines: flowers pure white, lip yellow on the disc and marked with crimson streaks at the edge.

Khasia, on trunks of trees. Assam.

(22) C. PRÆCOX. *(Lindl.)*

Ident. Lindl. gen. and sp. p. 43—fol. orch. l. c. p. 16—17.

Syn. Epidendrum præcox. *Smith Ex. flor. t.* 97.—Pleione præcox, *Don prod. p.* 37.—C Wallichiana, *Griffith notul. p.* 402.

Engrav. Bot. Mag. t. 4496.

SPEC. CHAR. Pseudo-bulbs turbinate, umbonate: leaves 3-many-nerved with tubercled sheaths: bracts obovate, longer than the ovary: lip sub-repand, 2-cleft at the apex, apical half torn: veins of the disc 5, dentate-crested: middle segments of the 4-parted clinandrium inflexed: flowers deep rose-coloured.

Var. a. Leaves green: bracts very deciduous.

Var. b. *Wallichiana.*—Leaves green: bracts deciduous: lip plaited and toothed at the end, not lacerated, with the teeth of the crests very short and confined to the disc.—C. Wallichiana, *Lindl. gen. and sp. p.* 43.—*Bot. Mag.* 1840. *t.* 24.

A. Khasia. B. Pundua.

GENUS IX. CORYMBIS.

Gynandria Monandria. *Sex: Syst:*

GEN. CHAR. Sepals linear, dilated at the apex, spreading: dorsal one deeply adnate to the base of the column, lateral ones equal at the base, connate: petals of the same form, free: lip (dorsal) linear, channelled, embracing the column, with two elevated lines running out into curved callosities, limb membranaceous, dilated with two callosities at the base: column club-shaped, tapering, much elongated after flowering: stigma ovate, 2-cleft: pollen masses 4, twin, powdery: caudicle bristly: gland almost quadrate: anther dorsal, ovate, muticous: capsule ribbed, crowned by the very long hardened style.

(1) C. DISTICHA. *(Lindl.)*

Ident. Lindl. fol. orch. 1854, p. 1.—Thouars hist. des pl. orch. Afr. tt. 37—38.

Syn. Centrosis? corymbosa, *Thouars l. c.* Macrostylis disticha, *Kuhl and Hasselt, g. and s. orch.* (1827).

SPEC. CHAR. Terrestial, arundinaceous: leaves membranaceous, plicate, sheathing: racemes brachiate, axillary: flowers sub-secund, pale; whitish-green, fragrant.

Madras. Assam.

GENUS X. IONE.

Gynandria Monandria. *Sex: Syst:*

Gen. Char. Sepals membranaceous, equal at the base, 2-lipped: lateral ones parallel, usually connate, placed under the lip: petals dwarf: lip posticous, entire, larger or equal to the sepals, membranaceous at the margin, striated in the middle, fleshy, usually produced into a dagger-shaped apex: column dwarf, half-terete, free, muticous, drawn out at the base: pollen masses 4, adnate in pairs to 2 distinct cartilaginous oval glands.—Epiphytes, pseudobulbous: leaves solitary, coriaceous: scape radical, spiked: bracts membranaceous, sometimes spathaceous, longer than the flowers.

(1) I. Khasiana. *(Lindl.)*

Ident. Lindl. fol. orch. 1853, p. 3.

Syn. Dipodium Khasiyanum, *Griff. not. p.* 354: *ic. t.* 327, *fig.* 2.

Spec. Char. Leaves linear-oblong, emarginate, equalling the filiform scape: spike flexuose: bracts lax, narrow, distant, equalling the flowers: lateral sepals connate: petals round, serrulate: lip panduriform-rhomboid obtuse, middle one serrated, quite entire in front with two lines elevated as far as the middle: flowers small, sepals white streaked with violet, lip deep violet with two white streaks.

Khasia hills.

(2) I. candida. *(Lindl.)*

Ident. Lindl. l. c.

Spec. Char. Leaves linear-oblong, emarginate, equalling the filiform scapes: spikes sub-flexuose: bracts shorter than the flowers: sepals all free: petals ovate, acute, ciliate-fimbriate: lip ovate, fimbriated at the base, serrulate towards the apex, drawn out into a long thick apex: flowers pure white.

Khasia hills.

GENUS XI. BOLBOPHYLLUM.

Gynandria Monandria. *Sex: Syst:*

Deriv. From *Bolbos*, a bulb, and *Phyllon*, a leaf; the leaves always spring from a pseudo-bulb.

Gen. Char. Sepals erect, acuminate, almost equal, lateral ones connate with the foot of the column and oblique at the base: petals dwarf: lip articulated with the foot of the column, clawed, usually entire and posticous: column dwarf, 2-toothed or horned in front: anther 1—2-celled: pollen masses 4, free, very unequal, sometimes connate in one, or else cohering by pairs, one of either pair minute lobuliform.—Epiphytes: rhizome creeping, pseudo-bulbiferous: leaves coriaceous; veinless: racemes radical.

(1) B. UMBELLATUM. *(Lindl.)*

Ident. Lindl. gen. and sp. p. 56.

SPEC. CHAR. Pseudo-bulbs ovate, elongated, sub-angulate: leaves solitary, linear-lorate, obtuse, emarginate: scapes three times shorter than the leaves: flowers corymbose: lateral sepals oblique falcate, obtuse, larger: petals ovate, obtuse: lip cordate, ovate, folded upon itself, entire: column marginate, 2-horned: flowers dull dirty yellow spotted brown.

Khasia hills.

(2) B. NEILGHERRENSE. *(R. W.)*

Ident. Wight's Icon. v. t. 1650.

SPEC. CHAR. Pseudo-bulbs ovate, sub-angular: leaves oblong, elliptic, obtuse, emarginate: spikes cylindric, shorter than the leaves: flowers numerous, congested: bract lanceolate, acute: petals ovate-acuminate, sub-denticulate: lip 3-lobed, lateral ones spreading, triangular, acute, much smaller than the broad ovate obtuse, somewhat tongue-shaped hispid middle one: sepals dull brownish-yellow, lip brownish-green, sprinkled with short hairs.

Neilgherries. Malabar.

(3) B. FUSCOPURPUREUM. *(R. W.)*

Ident. Wight l. c. t. 1651.

SPEC. CHAR. Pseudo-bulbs ovate, angular, congested: leaves broadly-elliptic, contracted at both ends, emarginate: raceme much longer than the leaves, 4—6-flowered, drooping towards the apex: flowers longish-pedicelled: lateral sepals about twice as large as the ovate-lanceolate posterior one: petals ovate at the base, prolonged into a long filiform acumen, terminating in a little fleshy nob: lip 3-lobed, lateral lobes short-obovate or sub-spathulate, middle one fleshy, nearly equalling the sepals, sub-spathulate or tongue-shaped, entire, hispid: flowers dark reddish-brown, lip brownish-purple.

Neilgherries, on trees and rocks along the banks of the Kartairy river, and on the north-western slopes.

(4) B. TREMULUM. *(R.W.)*

Ident. Wight l. c. t. 1749.

SPEC. CHAR. Pseudo-bulbs ovate: leaves ovate, lanceolate, acute: scape straight: bracts small, ovate, acute: sepals ovate-lanceolate, acute, pubescent: petals rhomb-ovate, small, densely ciliated: lip articulated with the prolonged base of the column, linear, obtuse, the back towards the apex covered with long tremulous hairs: flowers yellow, passing into purple towards the margins of the sepals, lip purple.

Wynaud on trees.

GENUS XII. LIMATODES.

Gynandria Monandria. *Sex: Syst:*

GEN. CHAR. Perianth erect, spreading, nearly equal, free: lip free, undivided, spurred, limb swollen internally: column erect, half-terete: anther 2-celled, cells somewhat quadrilocellate: pollen masses 8, obovate: caudicle short, filiform, gland minute.—Terrestrial: stems tumid at the base: leaves broad-lanceolate, nerved, membranaceous: peduncles lateral, solitary, few-flowered: flowers white.

(1) L. GRACILIS. *(Lindl.)*

Ident. Lindl. fol. orch. 1854, p. 1.

Syn. Calanthe gracilis, *Lindl. gen. and sp. p.* 251.

Engrav. Bot. Mag. p. 4714.

SPEC. CHAR. Racemes many-flowered, pubescent, shorter than the leaves: spur none: flowers pale yellow.

Silhet. Khasia.

(2) L. MISHMENSIS. *(Lindl.)*

Ident. Lindl. in Paxt. fl. gard. sub. t. 81: fol. orch. l. c.

SPEC. CHAR. Raceme few-flowered, long-peduncled, shorter than the leafy stem: flowers glabrous: lip obovate, obtuse, 4-lobed, ramentaceous on the axis: spur incurved.

Assam, on the lower ranges of the Mishmee hills.

GENUS XIII. LUISIA.

Gynandria Monandria. *Sex: Syst:*

GEN. CHAR. Sepals herbaceous, linear, lateral ones placed under the lip, dorsal one less: petals dissimilar, thinner, usually longer, very much spreading or vaulted: lip undivided, usually auricled, continuous with the column, hanging down, inappendiculate, convex or concave and constricted in the middle: column dwarf, fleshy, apodous: stigma anticous, circular: beak obtuse, obsolete: pollen masses two, waxy, posticously hollowed out: caudicle broad, short, triangular: gland membranaceous, replicate: anther sub-rotund, 2-celled: valvelets barren.—Caulescent, erect epiphytes, rushy: leaves tapering, stiff: flowers small, obscurely green or purplish.

(1) L. volucris. *(Lindl.)*

Ident. Lindl. fol. orch. 1853.

Spec. Char. Spikes very short, few-flowered: dorsal sepal straight, linear, hooded: petals almost three times longer, much spreading, linear, sub-spathulate: lip bi-auricled, with a caudate oblong convex lamina.

Khasia. The flowers look like little birds with narrow wings or petals.

(2) L. tenuifolia. *(Blume.)*

Ident. Blume Museum, 64.—Lindl. orch. l. c. p. 2.

Syn. Cymbidium tenuifolium, *Lindl. gen. and sp. p.* 167.—Birchea teretifolia, *A. Rich. ann. sc.* 1841, *t.* 10.—Luisia Birchea, *Blume l. c.*

Engrav. Rheede Mal. xii. t. 5.

Spec. Char. Petals twice longer than the dorsal sepal: lateral sepals mucronulate below the apex: lip oblong, 2-eared, convex, 3-furrowed, 2-lobed at the apex: sepals and petals yellowish green, lip pale green, painted with purple.

Neilgherries. Malabar. Khasia.

(3) L. trichorhiza. *(Blume.)*

Ident. Blume Museum, 63.—Lindl. l. c.

Syn. Vanda (?) trichorhiza, *Hook. ex. bot. t.* 72. Cymbidium triste, *Hooker in Bot. Mag. t.* 3648.

Spec. Char. Raceme few-flowered: petals a little longer than the dorsal sepal: lateral sepals deeply keeled: lip convex oblong, round, 2-eared at the base, interrupted above the base: younger roots pubescent: flowers dull dirty purple, or with white sepals and petals.

Khasia. Neilgherries.

(4) L. BRACHYSTACHYS. *(Blume.)*

Ident. Blume Rumphia, 64.—Lindl. l. c. p. 3.

Syn. Mesoclastes brachystachys, *Lindl. gen. and sp. p.* 45.—Cymbidium triste, *Roxb. flor. Ind. III. p.* 461.

Engrav. Wight's Icon. t. 1689.

SPEC. CHAR. Racemes sessile: sepals and petals nearly equal: lip concave, constricted in the middle, furrowed at the ovate apex: flowers pale pink, or yellowish, or greenish yellow, lip dark, with a few yellowish spots.

Peninsula. Delta of the Ganges. Silhet. Khasia. Flowering in March and April.

GENUS XIV. PANISEA.

Gynandria Monandria. *Sex: Syst:*

GEN. CHAR. Sepals membranaceous, lateral ones obtuse or oblique at the base: petals of the same form, a little smaller: lip undivided, membranaceous, altogether bald, sigmoid at the base, altogether free: column as in Cœlogyne: pollen masses four, collateral, waxy: caudicle and gland none: anther membranaceous, moveable, 2-celled, inserted below the apex of the column.—Pseudo-bulbous cæspitose epiphytes: leaves usually grassy, always thin: racemes radical, erect, 1-many-flowered: bracts membranaceous: flowers middle-sized, pale.

(1) P. REFLEXA. *(Lindl.)*

Ident. Lindl. fol. orch.

Syn. Androgyne, *Griff. Notul. III.* 279.

SPEC. CHAR. Leaves oval, solitary, long-petioled, much longer than the nodding racemes: bracts ovate, bristly-acuminate, longer than the pedicels: sepals and petals reflexed: lip linear, spathulate, margin crisp towards the base, white, with yellow spots near the base.

Assam, on oaks. Khasia.

GENUS XV. SARCOPODIUM.

Gynandria Monandria. *Sex: Syst:*

GEN. CHAR. Sepals ringent, coriaceous or fleshy, lateral ones drawn out at the base, adnate to the foot of the column, dorsal one equal or smaller: petals smaller: lip dwarf, articulated with the lengthened base of the column, fleshy, moveable, channelled, subcordate at the base, sometimes increased by three short plates, sometimes inappendiculate: column dwarf, half-terete, muticous, produced at the base into a foot: stigma a pit excavated under the beak: pollen masses 4, collateral, almost equal, waxy, altogether free: anther 2-celled.—Pseudo-bulbous epiphytes: leaves solitary, coriaceous: flowers solitary or few, conspicuous, peduncles radical.

(1) S. amplum. (*Lindl.*)

Ident. Lindl. in Paxt. fl. gard: gleanings No. 199.—fol. orch. 1853.

Syn. Dendrobium amplum. *Wall.—Lindl. gen. and sp. p.* 74.

Engrav. Wall. pl. As. rar. I. t. 29. Griff. Icon. t. 304.

Spec. Char. Pseudo-bulbs ovate, scaly, 2-leaved: leaves oblong, emarginate, petioled: peduncle much longer than the petaloid bracts: sepals ovate, acuminate, obtuse: petals narrower: lip cordate, sessile, 3-lobed, lamellate at the base: lateral lobes shortened, round, middle one ovate, acute: flowers straw-coloured, spotted internally, 3 inches wide: lip with 3 lamellæ in the middle, central one shorter, middle lobe deep purple.

Pundua. Khasia hills.

(2) S. fuscescens. (*Lindl.*)

Ident. Lindl. fol. orch. 1853.

Syn. Dendrobium fuscescens, *Griff. Icon. t.* 309.

Spec. Char. Pseudo-bulbs ovate, acuminate, scaly, 2-leaved: leaves oblong-lanceolate, emarginate, petioled, half-twisted at the apex: peduncle much longer than the membranaceous bracts, sepals oblong-lanceolate, very acuminate, reflexed: petals very narrow: lip 3-lobed, sessile, lamellate at the base, lateral lobes oblong, longer than the column, intermediate one ovate, acuminate: sepals and petals brownish flesh-colour: lateral lobes of lip chestnut, middle one purplish towards the base, crests white: column with two pale orange spots in front.

Khasia hills.

(3) S. striatum. (*Lindl.*)

Ident. Lindl. fol. orch. l.c. p. 5.

Syn. Dendrobium striatum, *Griff. Notul. p.* 318.

Spec. Char. Pseudo-bulbs sub-globose, 1-leaved: leaves oblong, flat, emarginate, nearly equalling the linear petiole: racemes few-flowered, weak, prostrate, loosely bracteate: sepals ovate, nearly equal: petals linear, much spreading, obtuse: lip lanceolate, quite entire, obsoletely toothed on both sides at the base: flowers very small, greenish, lined and dotted with sanguine: lip greenish-white, with 3 sanguine lines and crimson lateral veins.

Khasia.

(4) S. AFFINE. *(Lindl.)*

Ident. Lindl. in Paxt. l. c.—fol. orch. l. c. p. 5.

Syn.. Bolbophyllum affine, *Wall. Cat. Lindl. gen. and sp. p.* 48.

SPEC. CHAR. Pseudo-bulbs oblong, tapering: leaves coriaceous, stiff, oblong, solitary, petioled, emarginate: flowers solitary: sepals and petals equal, ovate-lanceolate: lip fleshy, ovate-lanceolate, obtuse, quite entire: perianth white, streaked with red: lip red-brown: column yellow.

Khasia hills.

(5) S. LEOPARDINUM. *(Lindl.)*

Ident. Lindl. in Paxton l. c.—fol. orch. l. c.

Syn. Dendrobium leopardinum, *Wall. tent. I. p.* 39 *t.* 38 Bolbophyllum leopardinum, *Lindl. in Wall. Cat.*

SPEC. CHAR. Pseudo-bulbs cæspitose, ovate-oblong: leaves coriaceous, stiff, oblong, solitary, petioled: flowers fascicled, globose campanulate: sepals ovate, guttate, almost equal: petals smaller of the same form: lip fleshy, ovate, obtuse, quite entire, denticulate at both sides at the base: flowers pale yellowish-brown, closely dotted with purple: lip deep purple.

Khasia mountains.

(6) S. GRIFFITHII. *(Lindl.)*

Ident. Lindl. fol. orch. l. c. p. 6.

Engrav. Bolbophylli sp. *Griffith Icon. t.* 296, *fig.* 2.

SPEC. CHAR. Pseudo-bulbs oblong: leaves oval, emarginate: bract small, membranaceous, obtuse, hooded: flowers sub-globose: sepals and petals small, ovate, concave: lip ovate: flowers fleshy, whitish, with numerous rosy-purple blotches: lip white, similarly blotched: column white.

Khasia hills.

GENUS XVI. VANDA.

Gynandria Monandria. *Sex: Syst.*

Deriv. Vandà is the Sanscrit name of the original species.

Gen. Char. Sepals flattened, all equal and narrowed at the base, usually petaloid: petals of the same form usually twisted at the base: lip saccate at the base or spurred, continuous with the base of the apodous column, fleshy, usually much shorter than the sepals, somewhat 3-lobed or entire, usually callous before the spur, auricles dwarf or obsolete: column thick, dwarf, free, apodous: clinandrium vertical: stigma transverse: beak obtuse or retuse: pollen masses waxy, plano-convex, twin, or 2 deeply partite: caudicle lorate or cuneate, longer than the pollinia: gland large, sub-rotund or triangular: anther ovate, 2-celled, valvelets half free.—Epiphytes: leaves coriaceous, distichous, oblique at the apex: flowers usually racemose, conspicuous: peduncles lateral.

(1) V. Roxburghii. *(R. Br.)*

Ident. R. Brown in Bot. Reg. t. 506.—Lindl. gen. and sp. p. 215.

Syn. Cymbidium tesseloides, *Roxb. flor. Ind. III. p.* 463.

Engrav. Bot. Mag. t. 2245.—Paxt. fl. garden t. 42, fig. 2.—Wight's Icon. t. 916.

Spec. Char. Stem short thick: leaves obliquely 3-toothed at the apex: racemes erect, longer than the leaves: sepals and petals oblong-obovate, wavy, tessellated, obtuse: middle lobe of the lip convex, ovate, emarginate, very obtuse, channelled, obtusely callous before the spur, auricles acuminate, nearly equalling the column: flowers largish, tessellated, lip blue.

Mango trees in Bengal, flowering nearly all the year.

(2) V. teres. *(Lindl.)*

Ident. Lindl. in Wall. Cat. No. 7324; fol. orch. 1853, p. 7.

Engrav. Bot. Reg. t. 1809.—Bot. Mag. t. 4114.

Spec. Char. Scandent: leaves tapering: racemes ascending, somewhat 2-flowered, equalling the leaves: sepals oblong, obtuse, uppermost one erect, lateral ones half-twisted, placed under the lip, petals larger, sub-orbiculate, wavy: lip very large, hooded, pubescent, dilated at the apex, round, emarginate, auricles sub-rotund very large, incurved: spur large, funnel-shaped: sepals white, petals sanguine with a white border, lip sanguine, strongly veined, yellow on the upper surface, and speckled with crimson.

Jungles in Silhet. Chittagong. Khasia hills. Flowering in April and May.

(3) V. SPATHULATA. *(Spreng.)*

Ident. Spreng. Syst. III. p. 719.—Lindl. gen. and sp. p. 216.

Engrav. Wight's Icon. t. 915.

SPEC. CHAR. Stem elongated: leaves ovate-oblong, obtuse, obliquely emarginate: peduncles naked, distantly sheathed, erect, many-flowered, much longer than the leaves and stem: sepals and petals oblong, obtuse, flat: lip rhomboid, incurved at the top, crested in the middle, bicallous at the base within the acutely conical spur, auricles retuse: ovary 6-winged: leaves and flower-stalks marked with golden spots: flowers golden yellow.

Mysore. Malabar. Common in jungles in Travancore.

(4) V. CŒRULEA. *(Griff.)*

Ident. Griffith MSS. Itin. notes p. 88.—Lindl. fol. orch. l. c. p. 8.

Engrav. Bot. Reg. 1847, t. 30.—Paxton's flower garden t. 36.

SPEC. CHAR. Leaves coriaceous, equal at the apex, truncated, with a concave sinus, lateral lobes acute: spikes dense, erect, many-flowered: bracts oblong, concave, very obtuse, membranaceous: sepals and petals twisted at the base, azure, membranaceous, oblong, very obtuse, flat, sub-unguiculate: lip coriaceous, linear-oblong, divergently 2-lobed at the apex, obtuse, 3-lamellate through the axis: auricles triangular, acuminate: spur curved, obtuse, smooth within: flowers bright blue.

Khasia hills.

(5) V. ALPINA. *(Lindl.)*

Ident. Lindl. fol. orch. l. c. p. 10.

Engrav. Luisia alpina, *Lindley in Bot. Reg.* 1838, *misc.* 101.

SPEC. CHAR. Leaves channelled, recurved, obliquely 2-lobed, a small mucro usually intermediate: racemes sub-sessile, erect, 2—3-flowered: sepals oblong, thickened below the apex: petals a little smaller: lip oblong, concave, naked, gibbous below the apex, emarginate: auricles confluent with the lamina: flowers small, pale green: lip yellowish, streaked with dull purple: basal hollow deep purple.

Khasia hills.

(6) V. (?) PULCHELLA. *(R. W.)*

Ident. Wight l. c. t. 1671.

SPEC. CHAR. Leaves narrow, strap-shaped, deeply 2-cleft at the apex, segments divaricate: racemes short, many-flowered: sepals and petals equal, obovate, cuneate: lip 3-lobed, lateral lobes short, obtuse, middle one ovate, fimbriated, with a large inflated sack at the base: flowers green or yellowish, passing into white dashed with purple.

Kartairy falls, Neilgherries, pendulous from trees.

GENUS XVII. OBERONIA.

Gynandria Monandria. *Sex: Syst:*

GEN. CHAR. Sepals spreading or reflexed, usually equal, free: petals smaller than the sepals, agreeing with them in shape or linear, sometimes eroded: lip ascending, not articulated with the column, various in shape, usually elongated, always more or less distinctly 4-lobed: lateral lobes sometimes dentiform, intermediate ones almost connate: column very small, free, with an elevated stigma: anther 2-celled: pollen masses 2, pyriform, solid.—Herbs growing on trees and rocks, usually stemless, leaves always distichous: scape usually two-edged: flowers sometimes verticillate on a very long raceme, sometimes alternate, green or yellow.

(1) O. BRUNONIANA. *(R. W.)*

Ident. Wight's Icon. t. 1622.

SPEC. CHAR. Leaves ensiform, succulent, nearly as long as the raceme: stem compressed at the base, furnished near the apex with a short narrow falcate sheathing leaf or common bract: raceme compact: bracts ovate, denticulate, acute: sepals ovate, obtuse, reflexed, a little longer than the narrow lanceolate petals: lip entire, broad, cordate at the base, obtusely 3-lobed at the apex, the middle one small or sometimes obsolete: lip and sepals dark brownish, petals pale yellowish.

Iyamullay hills, near Coimbatore, flowering in June and July.

(2) O. PLATYCAULON. *(R. W).*

Ident. Wight l. c. t. 1623.

SPEC. CHAR. Leaves long, narrow ensiform; stem flatly compressed, nearly as broad as the leaves: raceme lax, flowers longish pedicelled: bracts ovate, acute, the length of the ovary, fimbriate on the margin: sepals ovate, lanceolate, acute: petals narrow, linear, narrower and slightly shorter than the sepals: lip 3-lobed, lateral ones obtuse, middle larger, 3-toothed, middle one the least: flowers whitish or pale yellow.

Pulney mountains, flowering in September.

(3) O. Lindleyana. *(R. W.)*

Ident. Wight l. c. t. 1624.

Spec. Char. Leaves ensiform, short, very succulent, slightly falcate: stem compressed: spike drooping towards the apex, densely covered with innumerable small sessile flowers: bracts ovate, somewhat obtuse, sub-denticulate on the margin: sepals broad, ovate, obtuse, entire: petals narrow-linear: lip broad cordate at the base, crenate, 2-lobed at the apex, with a minute tooth between, all furnished with minute numerous opaque dots: flowers straw-colour, lip dull orange.

Iyamullay hills, near Coimbatore, flowering in August and September.

(4) O. denticulata. *(R. W.)*

Ident. Wight l. c. t. 1625.

Spec. Char. Leaves broad ensiform: stem short, fleshy, compressed: spike very long, closely covered with minute, sessile flowers: bracts ovate, serrate-dentate: sepals and petals almost equal, ovate, obtuse, reflexed: lip irregularly triangular, denticulate, somewhat 2-lobed at the apex, each lobe bi-denticulate: flowers dark orange.

Iyamullay hills, near Coimbatore, flowering in July and August.

(5) O. verticillata. *(R. W.)*

Ident. Wight l. c. t. 1626.

Spec. Char. Leaves narrow ensiform, sub-falcate: raceme erect or inclined, short-peduncled: flowers verticelled: bracts ovate, lanceolate, acute, fimbriated on the margin: sepals short, broad, ovate, obtuse: petals sub-obovate, obtuse, longer than the sepals: lip oblong, slightly cordate at the base, 2-lobed at the apex, lobes broad, roundish, spreading, slightly crenulate on the margin: ovary and sepals pale green, perianth dull orange.

Pulney mountains, Neilgherries, on branches of trees, flowering between July and October.

(6) O. Wightiana. *(Lindl.)*

Ident. Lindl. in Herb. Wight.

Engrav. Wight l. c. t. 1627.

Spec. Char. Leaves broad ensiform, acute: racemes very long, drooping towards the apex: flowers scattered, short pedicelled: bracts broad, ovate at the base, shorter than the linear obtuse petals: lip 3-lobed, lateral lobes strap-like, embracing the base of the column, middle one prolonged, ending in two obovate-spathulate spreading lobes, crenulate on the margin: flowers pale green.

Neilgherries and Pulney mountains, flowering in August and September.

(7) O. Arnottiana. *(R. W.)*

Ident. Wight l. c. t. 1628.

Spec. Char. Leaves ensiform, sub-falcate, succulent: racemes erect or slightly inclined towards the apex, scarcely drooping: flowers alternate, longish pedicelled: bracts ovate, acute, ciliated, somewhat sheathing at the base: sepals ovate, acute, about the length of the narrow-linear petals: lip cordate at the base, 3-lobed, lateral lobes broad ovate, obtuse, middle one prolonged, forked at the apex: flowers pale green.

Neilgherries and Pulney mountains, flowering in September.

(8) O. iridifolia. *(Lindl.)*

Ident. Lindl. gen. and sp. p. 15.

Syn. Malaxis ensiformis, *Sm.*—Cymbidium iridifolium *Roxb. flor. Ind. III. p.* 458.

Spec. Char. Leaves broad ensiform: raceme long, two-edged at the base, many-flowered: flowers verticillate: bracts fimbriated: sepals reflexed: petals eroded: lip sub-ovate, obtuse, fimbriated, hollow at the base, obsoletely 4-lobed: flowers yellow.

Silhet, Khasia hills, on trees; flowering in October and November.

(9) O. bicornis. *(Lindl.)*

Ident. Lindl. and sp. l. c. p. 16.

Spec. Char. Leaves short, somewhat waved, ovate: racemes many-flowered, nodding: flowers sub-verticillate: petals ovate: lip truncated, sub-lunate, 2-horned at the base: sepals spreading, lateral ones shorter.

Silhet.

GENUS XVIII. CHILOSCHISTA.

Gynandria Monandria. *Sex: Syst:*

Deriv. From *Cheilos,* a lip, and *Schistos,* cut, alluding to the divisions of the lip.

GEN. CHAR. Perianth somewhat closed: petals larger than the sepals, adnate with the lateral sepals to the prolonged base of the column: lip articulated with the claw of the column, bipartite, crested in the middle: column very small, erect, half-terete: pollen masses two: caudicle short, subulate,gland very small.

(1) C. USNEOIDES. *(Lindl.)*

Ident. Lindl. gen. and sp. p. 219.

Syn. Epidendum usneoides, *Don. flor. Nep. p.* 37.

Engrav. Wight's Icon. t. 1741.

SPEC. CHAR. Low herbaceous hairy leafless epiphyhyte: roots flattened, green: spikes erect: flowers whitish, or cream-coloured.

Wynaad. Northern slopes of the Neilgherries, on branches of trees, flowering in April.

GENUS XIX. APORUM.

Gynandria Monandria. *Sex: Syst:*

Deriv. From *Aporux,* a running shoot, alluding to the appearance of the plants.

GEN. CHAR. Sepals fleshy, erect, lateral ones larger, oblique, connate with the base of the column: petals smaller than the uppermost sepal: lip articulated with the foot of the column, posticous, undivided or 3-lobed, limb crested, callous or naked: column half-terete, far drawn out at the base: anther sessile, 2-celled, sometimes membranaceous at the apex: pollen masses 4, collateral by pairs.—Caulescent epiphytes: leaves distichous, equitant, 2-edged: flowers somewhat solitary, bursting from membranaceous scales.

(1) A. ANCEPS. *(Lindl.)*

Ident. Lindl. gen. and sp. p. 71. Roxb. flor. Ind. III. p. 487.

Syn. Dendrobium anceps, *Swz. Willd.*

Engrav. Bot. Reg. t. 1239.—Bot. Mag. t. 3608.

SPEC. CHAR. Leaves shaped like a scalpel, fleshy, acute: flowers solitary or twin: sepals fleshy: lateral ones ovate, spreading, upper one larger: lip posticous, unguiculate, without callosities, inappendiculate, cuneate, emarginate, crenulate: stems pendulous: flowers green, lip slightly coloured.

On trees, especially at the estuaries of rivers. Soonderbunds; flowering in the hot season.

GENUS XX. AGGEIANTHUS.

Gynandria Monandria. *Sex: Syst:*

Deriv. From *Aggeion*, a vase, and *Anthos*, a flower, alluding to the shape of that organ.

GEN. CHAR. Sepals equal, cohering, tubular, the lateral ones connate with the prolonged base of the column: petals shorter than the sepals, spathulate unguiculate, inclosed within the tube of the calyx: lip articulated with the prolonged base of the column, broad ovate rounded, papillosely hispid at the apex, truncated and furnished at the base with a subulate tooth-like process, 3-nerved in the axis: column erect, concave above: anther 2-celled, cells obsoletely 4-celled with 4, (or by abortion ?) fewer obovate pollinia in each.—Stemless plants, pseudo-bulbs aggregated, depressed flattened, netted all over: leaves small, 2—5, sheathing, ovate, acute, membranaceous: flowers tubular, vase-shaped, dull brick-red colour, externally glabrous, pilose within: petals obovate, spathulate with a longish claw, pubescent: the lip when spread out is somewhat trowel-shaped at the base and orbicular at the point.

(1) A. MARCHANTIOIDES. (*R. W.*

Ident. Wight Icon. v. t. 1737.

Growing in broad patches (somewhat resembling a Marchanta) on moist rocks on the Iyamully Hills towards Paulghat, flowering in July and August.

GENUS XXI. LICHENORA.

Gynandria Monandria. *Sex: Syst:*

GEN. CHAR. Sepals adhering at the base, posterior one larger, somewhat galeate: lateral ones connate with the prolonged base of the column, ovate, obtuse: petals linear, lanceolate, shorter than the sepals: lip sub-rhombeo-ovate acutish, articulated with the long base of the column: anther terminal, 2-celled, with 4 pollinia in each.—Stemless plants: pseudo-bulbs thin, flat, adhering like lichens to the branch on which they grow: leaves paired, broad-ovate, sub-orbicular, cuspidate-pointed, reticulately veined, large in proportion to the rest of the plant, glabrous: flowers axillary, paired, short pedicelled, hairy: bract obovate, somewhat boat-shaped, densely ciliate, lateral sepals hairy within

(1) L. Jerdoniana. *(R.W.)*

Ident. Wight's Icon. t. 1738.

Spec. Char. Leaves green, afterwards changing to purplish-brown: flowers tawny-coloured.

Malabar mountains, on branches of trees.

GENUS XXII. DENDROBIUM.

Gynandria Monandria. *Sex: Syst:*

Deriv. From *Dendron,* a tree, and *Bios* life; the species are generally found upon trees.

Gen. Char. Sepals membranaceous, erect or spreading, lateral ones larger, oblique, connate with the base of the column: petals usually larger than the uppermost sepal, sometimes smaller, always membranaceous: lip articulated or connate with the foot of the column, always sessile, undivided or 3-lobed, usually membranaceous, sometimes appendiculate: column half-terete, lengthened out at the base: anther 2-celled: pollen masses 4, collateral in pairs.—Epiphytous herbs, sometimes caulescent, sometimes with a creeping pseudo-bulbiferous rhizome: leaves flat, usually veined: flowers solitary, fascicled or racemose, showy.

(1) D. Pierardi. *(Roxb.)*

Ident. Lindl. gen. and sp. p. 79.

Engrav. Wight's Icon. t. 908.—Hook. ex. flora. t. 9.—Bot. Reg. t. 1756.—Bot. Mag. t. 2584.

Spec. Char. Stems pendulous, glabrous: leaves ovate-lanceolate, acute: flowers in pairs, forming a spurious raceme: sepals acuminate, membranaceous: petals larger than the upper sepal, acuminate: lip dilated, cucullate, somewhat truncated, ciliated: flowers large, pale yellow.

Chittagong, Soonderbunds, Silhet; flowering in the hot season.

(2) D. Heyneanum. *(Lindl.)*

Ident. Lindl. l. c. p. 90.

Syn. D. chlorops. *Lind. in Bot. Reg.* 1844.—*Dalz. Bomb. flor. p.* 261.

Engrav. Wight l. c. t. 909.

Spec. Char. Stem erect, flexuose, clavate, clothed with the lax sheaths of the leaves: leaves linear-lanceolate, acute: racemes axillary spreading, many-flowered : bracteas minute ovate : sepals and petals ovate-lanceolate, acute, about equal: lip 3-lobed, united with the base of the column, callosity on the disk longitudinal : lateral lobes acute, the middle one roundish, fleshy, inciso crenate.

Branches of trees in Malabar.

(3) D. BARBATULUM. *(Lindl.)*

Ident. Lindl. l. c. p. 84.

Engrav. Wight l. c. t. 910.

SPEC. CHAR. Stems terete, aphyllous : racemes lateral and terminal, many-flowered : sepals ovate acuminate : petals obovate, acute, larger than the upper sepal : lip flat, obovate obtuse, apiculate, entire, bearded at the base : flowers pale straw-coloured.

Trees in Malabar, Concans. Flowering in the cold season.

(4) D. HUMILE. *(R. W.)*

Ident. Wight l. c. t. 1643.

Syn. D. microbolbon, *A. Rich. Ann. Soc. Nat.* xv. *t.* 8.

SPEC. CHAR. Cæspitose : pseudo-bulbs ovate, covered with the sheaths of fallen leaves, leaves often wanting, when present one or two from the apex of the bulb, linear-lanceolate, about the length of the scape : raceme erect, 4—8-flowered : bracts small, linear, subulate : lateral sepals acute, sub-falcate, forming with the process of the column an acute spur, posterior divaricate-lanceolate : petals lanceolate, narrower than the posterior sepal : lip large, 3-lobed, middle lobe crenulate, crisp, sub-orbicular, lateral ones entire, or slightly crenate : flowers greenish-yellow, tipped with pink, lip pink, with darker crimson lines.

Iyamullay hills, on trees. Flowering in July and August.

(5) D. JERDONIANUM. *(R. W.)*

Ident. Wight l. c. t. 1644.

SPEC. CHAR. Erect, stems jointed, thickening upwards, internodes about the length of the leaves : leaves ovate-lanceolate, succulent, forked at the apex : racemes axillary, short, 2—3-flowered : bracts minute : flowers long pedicelled, calcarate : lateral sepals much produced at the base, posterior ones and petals equal, all linear lanceolate, acute : lip sinuately undulated on the margin, obovate, forming with the long base of the column a short conical spur : flowers deep orange-colour, lip conforming, or a little redder.

Coorg Jungles, Iyamullay hills. Flowering in August and September.

(6) D. ALBUM. *(R. W.)*

Ident. Wight l. c. t. 1645.

SPEC. CHAR. Erect, jointed: stems enlarging from the base to the apex, internodes much shorter than the leaves: leaves oblong, elliptic, acuminate: flowers axillary, paired, long peduncled: sepals ovate, acute: lateral ones falcate: petals obovate-elliptic, obtuse, larger than the posterior sepal: lip 3-lobed, lateral lobes entire, obtuse, middle one cucullate, ovate, acute, saccate at the base, ciliate: flowers pure white.

Iyamullay hills, flowering in September.

(7) D. RAMOSISSIMUM. *(R. W.)*

Ident. Wight l. c. t. 1648.

SPEC. CHAR. Erect, ramous, lower part of the stem naked, smooth, dark, shining, brownish-coloured, ramuli leafy: leaves narrow, linear-lanceolate, acute: racemes terminal, short, few-flowered: flowers small: sepals ovate, acute, lanceolate, broader than the lanceolate acute, entire petals: lip oblong, obtuse, contracted near the apex, forming a sub-orbicular terminal lobe: flowers yellow.

Coorg Jungles.

(8) D. GRAMINIFOLIUM. *(R. W.)*

Ident. Wight l. c. t. 1649.

SPEC. CHAR. Rhizome creeping, stems ascending, leafy: leaves sheathing at the base, linear, lanceolate, acute: raceme terminal, slender, 4—6-flowered, flexuose: bracts much shorter than the pedicels, ovate, acute: flowers calcarate: sepals and petals equal, acute: petals narrow, lanceolate: lip cucullate, 3-lobed: lateral lobes small, blunt, middle one orbicular, crenate, somewhat crisp on the margin: claw united with the prolonged process of the column forming a conical spur: flowers white.

Courtallum, flowering in August and September.

(9) D. LAWIANUM. *(Lindl.)*

Ident. Lindl. in proc. Linn. Soc. III. p. 10.—Dalz. Bomb. flor. 260.

Syn. Dendrobium roseum, *Dalz. in Hook. Journ. Bot. IV.* 291.

SPEC. CHAR. Young stems fleshy, ascending: leaves membranaceous, lanceolate-acute: flowering stem leafless, concealed under lax membranaceous sheaths: sepals and petals ovate, rather obtuse: lip a little larger, of the same shape, concave: flowers in pairs, of a beautiful shining rose-colour.

On trees on the Southern Ghauts.

(10) D. Macræi. (*Lindl.*)

Ident. Lindl. gen. and sp. p. 75.—Dalz. Bomb. flor. p. 260.

Spec. Char. Much branched: stems many, long and pendulous, knotty, and with many oblong pseudo-bulbs: leaf 1, terminal, short-oblong on the terminating pseudo-bulb: flowers solitary at the base of the leaf, one in front and one behind, small, white: middle lobe of the lip much dilated, and the disk with 2 longitudinal fleshy crests.

On Jambool trees at the Ram Ghaut, flowering in August and September.

(11) D. longicornu. (*Lindl.*)

Ident. Lindl. l. c. p. 80.

Spec. Char. Stems erect, hispid, flexuose: leaves ovate-lanceolate, very oblique at the apex: flowers fascicled or solitary, terminal: bracts ovate-acuminate, hispid, much shorter than the pedicel: lateral sepals connate into a long acuminate spur: petals conformable to the upper sepal: lip infundibular, hooded, entire, dentate, growing to the foot of the column: flowers white, lip yellow.

Silhet, flowering in April.

(12) D. formosum. (*Roxb.*)

Ident. Roxb. flor. Ind. III. p. 485.—Lindl. l. c. p. 81.

Engrav. Wall. pl. As. rar. I. t. 39.—Bot. Reg. 1839, t. 64. Paxt. vi. t. 49.

Spec. Char. Stems terete, pendulous, hairy: leaves distichous, ovate, obliquely emarginate at the apex, obtuse: raceme short, terminal, 4—5-flowered: bracts short, ovate: sepals oblong, acute, lateral ones lengthened at the base, petals twice broader, acute: lip obovate, dilated, retuse, connate with the base of the column into an obtuse spur: flowers very large, pure white, fragrant, middle lip yellow.

Khasia hills, flowering in April and May.

(13) D. ramosum. (*Lindl.*)

Ident. Lindl. l. c. p. 82.

Spec. Char. Stems pendulous, slender, branched, glabrous: leaves lanceolate-acuminate, quite entire at the apex: flowers subracemose: bracts membranaceous, reflexed, obtuse: lateral sepals obtuse, connate into a straight elongated horn: petals smaller: lip hooded, acute, crisp.

Pundua.

(14) D. PULCHELLUM. *(Roxb.)*

Ident. Roxb. l. c. p. 486.—Lindl. l. c. p. 83.

SPEC. CHAR. Stems pendulous: leaves oblong-lanceolate, sub-plicate: racemes lateral, straight, many-flowered: bracts short, ovate, obtuse: sepals ovate-acuminate, somewhat ribbed: petals oblong, obtuse, thinner and broader: lip clawed, shell-shaped, very obtuse, ciliated, shorter than the petals: sepals white, petals rose: lip yellowish with a red-orange spot at the base.

On trees and stones in the Khasia hills, flowering in May and June.

(15) D. PUMILUM. *(Roxb.)*

Ident. Roxb. l. c. p. 479.

SPEC. CHAR. Parasitic, stemless: leaves 3—4, rising from each bulb, lanceolate, smooth, fleshy: scapes from the base of the bulb: raceme villous, bearing many erect flowers: inner two petals linear: lip recurved, lamina somewhat 3-lobed: flowers yellow.

Chittagong forests, flowering in the rains.

(16) D. PENDULUM. *(Roxb.)*

Ident. Roxb. l. c. p. 484.

SPEC. CHAR. Stems simple, pendulous, contracted at the joints and base, when old leafless: leaves bifarious, linear: flowers in pairs from the joints of the old leafless stem, drooping: petals nearly equal, lanceolate: lip sub-orbicular, short-clawed: capsules clavate, obscurely 6-ribbed.

Chittagong forests, flowering in the hot season.

GENUS XXIII. MYCARANTHES.

Gynandria Monandria. *Sex: Syst:*

GEN. CHAR. Sepals closed or patent, equal or unequal, woolly outside, lateral ones adnate to the foot of the column, not oblique: petals smaller: lip articulated with the prolonged base of the column, 3-lobed, hooded, disc crested or appendiculate: column dwarf, base prolonged, margins winged bent inwardly: anther terminal, 2-celled, cells 4-locellate: pollen masses 8, small, ovate. —Caulescent herbs, growing on trees or rocks: leaves fleshy or coriaceous, not plicate: racemes terminal, many-flowered.

(1) M. STRICTA. *(Lindl.)*

Ident. Lindl. gen. and sp. p. 63.

Syn. Eria stricta, *Lindl. Coll. Bot. t.* 41, *B.*

Engrav. Wight's Icon. t. 1733.

SPEC. CHAR. Stem terete: spike secund, densely many-flowered: lip with a scrotiform callosity in the middle: perianth woolly, short: leaves 1—2, linear-lanceolate, sessile: flowers glaucous outside, pale ochre-yellow inside.

Assam. Khasia.

GENUS XXIV. PHREATIA.

Gynandria Monandria. *Sex: Syst:*

GEN. CHAR. Sepals connivent, almost equal, lateral ones connate with the prolonged base of the column: petals smaller, conformable: lip entire, fleshy, articulated with the foot of the column: column dwarf, clinandrium deeply immersed: margin membranaceous, almost entire: anther enclosed within the clinandrium, 2-celled, cells obsoletely 4-pitted: pollen masses 8, spherical, cohering with viscid matter.—Cæspitose, epiphytous, pseudo-bulbous herbs: leaves not plicate: scapes radical.

(1) P. UNIFLORA. *(R. W.)*

Ident. Wight's Icon. v. t. 1734.

SPEC. CHAR. Repent: pseudo-bulbs globose, about 2-leaved: leaves obovate, cuspidate: scape longer than the leaves, 1-flowered: bract large, cordate-ovate, acuminate: lip lanceolate-acuminate, 2-nerved.

Khasia hills.

GENUS XXV. ACAMPE.

Gynandria Monandria. *Sex: Syst:*

GEN. CHAR. Sepals fleshy, brittle, flattened out, all equal at the base, the lateral ones slightly adnate to the spur of the lip, dorsal one a little larger or more remote: petals of the same form as the sepals, always straight: lip fleshy, fragile, saccate or spurred, adnate to the footless column, undivided, auricled, often increased within the bag by an elevated linea or plate and hairs: column thick, dwarf, footless, anticous angles usually produced into a mucro: clinandrium vertical: stigma transverse, sub-rotund, beak short, obscure, emarginate: pollen masses waxy, twin: caudicle subulate, longer than the pollen masses: gland small, sub-rotund: anther ovate, 2-celled, valves half free.—Herbaceous epiphytes: leaves coriaceous, distichous, oblique at the apex: flowers densely racemose, fleshy, brittle, yellow spotted: peduncles short, stiff, lateral bracts broad, short, for a long time persistent.

(1) A. Wightiana. *(Lindl.)*

Ident. Lindley fol. orchid. 1853, p. 2.

Syn. Vanda Wightiana, *Wight's. Icon. t.* 1670.

Spec. Char. Leaves obliquely 2-lobed: racemes dense, sessile, dwarf: sepals and petals very obtuse: lip ovate, obtuse, fimbriated, two-horned at the base: spur hairy within: flowers yellowish, dashed with dark crimson or purplish spots: lip nearly white, with a red line at the base of the lamina.

Wild on trees, Iyamullay hills. Malabar.

(2) A. congesta. *(Lindl.)*

Ident. Lindl. l. c.

Syn. Vanda congesta, *Lindl. in Bot. Reg.* 1839, *Misc.* 94.

Spec Char. Leaves elongated, channelled, obliquely 2-lobed, with an interjacent mucro: racemes sub-sessile, dwarf: lip rhomboid, acutangular, papillose, middle line elevated: spur hairy within, elevated line mucronate above: flowers small, yellow and brown.

Southern Peninsula.

(3) A. papillosa. *(Lindl.)*

Ident. Lindl. l. c.

Syn. Saccolabium papillosum, *Lindl. gen. and sp. orch. p.* 222. —Cymbidium prœmorsum, *Swarz. Nov. Act. Ups. b.* 75, *Willd. iv.* 103.—Epidendrum prœmorsum, *Roxb.*—Aerides undulatum, *Sm. in Rees. Cycl.*

Engrav. Rheede Mal. xii. t. 4.—Roxb. Cor. I. t. 43.—Bot. Reg. t. 1552.

Spec. Char. Stem elongated, branched: leaves obtuse, obliquely emarginate, with an interjacent mucro: racemes sessile, dwarf: lip ovate, oblong, papillose, elevated in the middle, spur hairy within: auricles confluent in front: flowers small, variegated with red and yellow: lip white.

Malabar. East Bengal and Chittagong. Circars. Flowering in the hot season.

(4) A. CEPHALOTES. *(Lindl.)*

Ident. Lindl. l. c. p. 3.

SPEC. CHAR. Racemes capitate, shorter than the stiff scaly peduncle: lip ovate, sub-cordate, papillose, crumpled, spur short conical, villous within: auricles fleshy, confluent: flowers yellowish green, with transverse bars of brown purple, posterior lip very pale rose with deeper spots, much fimbriated on the disc.

Silhet, on the plains.

(5) A. EXCAVATA. *(Lindl.)*

Ident. Lindl. l. c.

SPEC. CHAR. Leaves straight, flat, one lobe truncated, toothed, the other longer, round: racemes sessile, dwarf: sepals and petals narrow, dorsal one larger: lip ovate, acute, excavated, base 1-toothed, spur hairy within.

Western India. Concan. Colour of flowers unknown.

GENUS XXVI. PHAJUS.

Gynandria Monandria. *Sex: Syst:*

Deriv. From *Phaios*, shining, alluding to the beauty of some of the species.

GEN. CHAR. Sepals and petals nearly equal, spreading, free: lip usually hooded, adnate with the base of the column, spurred, entire or 3-lobed, usually keeled above, lamellose or crested: column erect, continuous with the ovary, semi-terete, marginate, elongated: anther 8-celled: pollen masses 8, almost equal.—Terrestrial: caulescent or stemless: leaves broad, plicate: scapes radical: flowers showy.

(1) P. GRANDIFOLIUS. *(Lour.)*

Ident. Lour. flor. Coch.—Lindl. gen. and sp. p. 126.

Syn. Limodorum Tankervilliæ, *Ait.—Roxb. flor. Ind. III.* 466. —L. Incarvillei, *Pers. Syn.*—Pachyne spectabilis, *Salisb.*—Bletia Tankervilliæ, *R. Br. in Hort. Kew.*

Engrav. Bot. Mag. 44, t. 1924.

SPEC. CHAR. Stemless: leaves oblong-lanceolate, acute: sepals and petals oblong-lanceolate, two-coloured within: lip oblong, hooded, entire, crisp, emarginate at the apex: spur curved, emarginate: flowers large, above sulphur, densely marked with rust-coloured dots, underneath white, the lip whitish-yellowish, variegated rose and purple.

Khasia hills, flowering in March and April.

(2) P. Wallichii. *(Lindl.)*

Ident. Lindl. l. c.

Engrav. Wall. pl. as. rar. II. t. 158.

Spec. Char. Stemless: leaves oblong-lanceolate, acute: sepals and petals lanceolate and with the hooded crisp entire, lip very acuminate: spur curved, emarginate: bracts acuminate: flowers large, brown, lip yellowish-white, variegated with rose.

Khasia hills, flowering in March.

(3) P. veratrifolius. *(Lindl.)*

Ident. Lindl. l. c. p. 127.

Syn. Dendrobium veratrifolium, *Roxb. H. B. p.* 63.

Spec. Char. Caulescent: leaves oblong-lanceolate, acuminate: sepals and petals linear-oblong, acutish: lip obovate-oblong, crisp, entire, repand, emarginate at the apex: spur straight, conical, obtuse: flowers yellow.

Silhet.

(4) P. maculatus. *(Lindl.)*

Ident. Lindl. l. c.

Syn. Bletia Woodfordii, *Hook.*

Engrav. Wall. in Bibl. Anglo-Indica, t. 1147.—Bot. Mag. 54, t. 2719.

Spec. Char. Caulescent: leaves ovate-lanceolate, acuminated, spotted: sepals and petals oblong, obtuse: lobes of the 3-lobed lip plicate-crenated at the apex: lateral ones rounded, much smaller than the ovate obtuse middle one: spur straight, oblong, obtuse: flowers yellow, lip spotted brown-purple at the tops of the lobes: column hairy.

Khasia hills.

(5) P. albus. *(Lindl.)*

Ident. Lindl. l. c. p. 128.

Engrav Wall. pl. As. rar. II. t. 198.

Spec. Char. Caulescent: leaves oblong-lanceolate, acute, glaucous beneath: sepals and petals oblong-lanceolate, acute, nearly equal: lip oblong, hooded, denticulate, rounded at the top: disc 5-crested: spur straightish, emarginate: flowers very large, white, fragrant, lip purple-veined with a yellow disc.

Khasia hills, flowering in April and May.

GENUS XXVII. CYTHERIS.

Gynandria Monandria. *Sex: Syst:*

Gen. Char. Sepals spreading, nearly equal: lateral ones adnate at the base to the spur, upper one parallel with the broader membranaceous petals, recurved: lip spurred, flat, 3-lobed, disc crested: column short, winged, clavate: anther membranaceous, 2-celled: pollen masses 8, equal.

(1) C. cordifolia. *(Lindl.)*

Ident. Lindl. gen. and sp. p. 129.

Spec. Char. Terrestrial: stem thin, clothed with lax membranaceous sheaths: leaves cordate, oblong, acuminate, 5-plicate, long-petioled: bracts linear, acute: spur short, clavate, very obtuse: lip oblong, narrowed at the base, lateral lobes entire, much smaller than the middle one, with three approximated elevated sub-undulated lines in the middle, free at the apex: scape terminal: flowers small.

Khasia hills.

GENUS XXVIII. APATURIA.

Gynandria Monandria. *Sex: Syst:*

Gen. Char. Sepals spreading, pubescent, lateral ones sometimes larger, oblique at the base: petals narrower, spreading: lip clawed, articulated with the more or less prolonged base of the column, ventricose at the base, fleshy, 3-lobed at the apex, disc crested: column terete, clavate, arched, clinandrium winged: anther 4—8-celled: pollen masses 8.—Terrestrial, leafless: scapes clothed with scarious filamentous sheaths: bracts membranaceous: flowers racemose, pendulous, pubescent.

(1) A. senilis. *(Lindl.)*

Ident. Lindl. gen. and sp. p. 130.

Syn. A. Lindleyana, *Wight's Icon. v. t.* 1662.

Spec. Char. Petals linear-oblong: veins three, distant, lateral lobes of the lip sub-falcate, intermediate one ovate, undulated, a little longer : three glandular lines, of which the lateral ones are larger, elevated, and run out to the top of the lip as far as the margin.

Khasia hills.

(2) A. Smithiana. *(Lindl.)*

Ident. Lindl. l. c. p. 131.

Spec. Char. Petals spathulate, clawed, 3-veined in the middle: lateral lobes of the lip obtuse, intermediate one roundish, emarginate: five elevated lines, undulated, clavately ending in the centre of the middle lobe: raceme many-flowered.

Kudjiree Ghaut in Oude.

GENUS XXIX. EUPHROBOSCES.

Gynandria Triandria. *Sex: Syst:*

Gen. Char. Perianth posticous, connivent, fleshy: sepals linear-oblong, lateral ones keeled: petals narrow-lanceolate, reflexed at the apex: lip simple, entire, semi-convolute, continuous with the oblique base of the column: column vertical, attenuated in front into a long two-legged rostellum: stigma vertical: anther (anthers ?) dorsal, beaked: pollen masses 8, waxy, globose, with a long caudicle and linear gland.

(1) E. pigmæa. *(Griffith.)*

Ident. Griff. in Calc. Journ. Nat. Hist. v. 371—2.

Engrav. Wight's Icon. v. t. 1732.

Spec. Char. Epiphytous, cæspitose: pseudo-bulbs turbinate, new ones 3—4-leaved: leaves fleshy, oblong, emarginate: scape sub-clavate, erect: flowers spiked, 1-bracteate, minute, greenish.

Malabar Ghauts.

GENUS XXX. ANIA.

Gynandria Monandria. *Sex: Syst:*

Gen. Char. Sepals and petals linear-lanceolate, equal, connivent: lip connate with the base of the column into a spur or bag, 3-lobed, flat, lamellate in the middle: column winged, elongated, erect: anther 6—8-celled: pollen masses 8, of which four are smaller in the other species — Epiphytes with a creeping rhizome: leaves plicate, membranaceous, solitary: scape many-flowered.

(1) A. LATIFOLIA. *(Lindl.)*

Ident. Lindl. gen. and sp. p. 130.

Engrav. Wight's Icon. t. 914.

SPEC. CHAR. Leaves oblong, plicate, shorter than the scape: lip unguiculate, 3-lobed, cohering with the elongated base of the column: lateral lobes obtuse, shorter than the roundish ovate acute middle one, the claws furnished with three truncated lamellæ terminating below the sinus of the lobes, that of the middle one 5-toothed, the lateral ones shorter.

Silhet. Pulney mountains.

GENUS XXXI. CIRRHOPETALUM.

Gynandria Monandria. *Sex: Syst:*

Deriv. From *Cirrhos*, a tendril, and *Petalon*, a petal, alluding to the form of the flowers.

GEN. CHAR. Sepals ringent, lateral ones acuminate, very oblique, adnate to the column, much longer than the upper one: petals dwarf, apiculate: lip entire, articulated with the base of the column: column very small, lengthened out at the base, with 2 petaloid horns at the apex: anther 2-celled: pollen masses four, of which 2 inner ones are much smaller, lamelliform.—Epiphytous herbs: rhizome creeping, bearing 1-leaved pseudo-bulbs: leaves coriaceous, veinless: flowers densely racemose, sometimes radiate, at the apex of a radical scape.

(1) C. ROXBURGHII. *(Lindl.)*

Ident. Lindl. gen. and sp. p. 58.

Syn. Aerides radiatum, *Roxb. flor. Ind. III. p.* 476.

Engrav. Wall. pl. As. rar. I. t. 67.

SPEC. CHAR. Petals ciliated, acute: sepals all acuminated: leaves lanceolate: umbel radiate, many-flowered: flowers yellow, upper sepal and petals purple-veined.

Trees at the mouths of the Ganges, flowering in June and July.

(2) C. FIMBRIATUM. *(Hook.)*

Ident. Hook. Bot. Mag.—Lindl. in Bot. Reg. 1839, p. 72.—Dalz. Bomb. flor. p. 261.

Engrav. Wight's Icon. t. 1655.

SPEC. CHAR. Leafless: pseudo-bulbs cæspitose, irregularly angular, depressed: scapes slender, erect, furnished with remote adpressed scales: umbels orbicular: lateral sepals long, linear, cohering to near the point, posterior one ovate-acuminate and with the conformable but smaller petals fimbriate on the margin: lip ovate, obtuse, fleshy, shorter than the petals: lateral sepals often cohering, cream-coloured with darker lines, petals, lip and posterior petal red.

Parwar Ghaut on trees, Coorg forests. This curious species has been called the "Umbrella Orchis," from its peculiar inflorescence.

(3) C. ALBIDUM. *(R. W.)*

Ident. Wight l. c. t. 1653.

SPEC. CHAR. Leaves oblong-elliptic, obtuse, emarginate: flowers umbelled: scape about the length of the leaves: bracts somewhat boat-shaped, shorter than the pedicels: sepals acuminate, posterior one a little shorter than the lateral ones: petals broad, ovate, obtuse: lip short, fleshy, sub-sagittate: flowers very pale, greenish-yellow or nearly cream colour.

On moist rocks near Kotergherry, flowering in August and September.

(4) C. NEILGHERRENSE. *(R. W.)*

Ident. Wight l. c. t. 1654.

SPEC. CHAR. Leaves linear, obtuse, emarginate, 3-nerved: scape shorter than the leaves, umbelled, 6—8-flowered: lateral sepals very long, broad ovate at the base, tapering to a point, posterior one ovate, acute, nearly twice the length of the broad sub-ovate blunt petals: lip cordate, ovate, short, recurved, hairy on the back: prolonged base of the column pubescent within: flowers at first pale greenish-yellow, tinged with pink, marked with darker lines, afterwards becoming reddish or light rusty coloured: process of the column red.

Neilgherries, on moist rocks below Kaity.

GENUS XXXII. SPATHOGLOTTIS.

Gynandria Monandria. *Sex: Syst:*

Deriv. From *Spathe*, a spathe, and *Glotta*, a tongue.

GEN. CHAR. Sepals spreading, free, equal: petals a little broader and more membranaceous, spreading or connivent: lip articulated with the base of the column, sometimes saccate, 3-partite, intermediate segment clawed, tubercled or crested at u usually 1-toothed on both sides: column winged or peta : anther 2-celled: pollen masses eight.—Terrestrial herbs: cor subterraneous: leaves ensiform, plicate: flowers yellowish.

(1) S. PUBESCENS. *(Lindl.)*

Ident. Lindl. gen. and sp. p. 120.

Engrav. Wight's Icon. t. 1739.

SPEC. CHAR. Leaves binate, linear-lanceolate, narrow at the base, striated, shorter than the erect scape: raceme secund, bracteate: bracts minute, acute: sepals ovate acute: petals oblong: lip saccate at the base, the lateral lobes oblong, erect, middle one with three keel-like appendages, two tubercles at the base, cuneate, and a little longer: peduncles, sepals and ovary pubescent: flowers dirty yellow, lip slightly violet at the base.

Khasia hills.

GENUS XXXIII. BLETIA.

Gynandria Monandria. *Sex: Syst.*

Deriv. Named after Don Louis Blet, a Spanish physician and botanist.

GEN. CHAR. Sepals spreading, equal: petals spreading or connivent, almost equal: lip hooded, articulated with the base of the column, sometimes saccate at the base, 3-lobed, disc usually lamellate or tubercled: column elongated, semi-terete: anther fleshy, 8-celled: pollen masses 8, equal, cohering to 4 powdery caudicles. —Sub-terrestrial herbs: leaves ensiform, plicate: scapes racemose, many-flowered: flowers usually showy.

(1) B. OBCORDATA. *(Lindl.)*

Ident. Lindl. gen. and sp. p. 123.

SPEC. CHAR. Caulescent: sepals and petals linear, equal, obtuse, lateral lobes of the spreading lip abbreviated, rounded, intermediate one obcordate: scape lateral, many-flowered, racemose: leaves oblong-lanceolate, acuminate: flowers ochre, lip slightly veined with red.

Silhet.

GENUS XXXIV. ARUNDINA.

Gynandria Monandria. *Sex: Syst:*

Deriv. From *Arundo*, a reed, a resemblance in the stems.

GEN. CHAR. Sepals linear-lanceolate, equal, slightly connate at the base, spreading: lip convolute around the column, not articulated with it, 3-lobed or entire, crested in the middle or with sohe elevated lines: column straight, parallel with the lip, half-terete, club-shaped.—Caulescent, terrestrial herbs: leaves distichous, ensiform, plicate: flowers purple, showy.

(1) A. BAMBUSIFOLIA. *(Lindl.)*

Ident. Lindl. gen. and sp. p. 125.

Syn. Bletia graminifolia, *Don. prod. flor. nep. p.* 29. Cymbidium bambusifolium, *Roxb. flor. Ind. III. p.* 460.

Engrav. Wight's Icon. t. 1661.

SPEC. CHAR. Lip furnished within with two fleshy undulated crested plates, and a short straight intermediate one: lateral lobes short, entire or sub-obsolete, middle one 2-lobed, segments divaricating, crisp: petals lanceolate, leaves acuminate: flowers rosy, lip a lively red-purple.

Silhet. Chittagong. Vailey Mullay in Travancore. Malabar. Flowering in the hot season.

GENUS XXXV. GEODORUM.

Gynandria Monandria. *Sex: Syst:*

Deriv. From *Ge*, the earth, and *Doron*, a gift.

GEN. CHAR. Perianth connivent: sepals and petal free, subsecund, somewhat equal: lip hooded-ventricose, sessile, not jointed with the column, saccate towards the base: column short, erect, half-terete: anther 2-lipped: pollen masses 2, posticously 2-lobed, caudicle very short, gland transverse.—Terrestrial, tuberous: leaves plicate: racemes recurved at the apex.

(1) G. PURPUREUM. *(R. Br.)*

Ident. R. Br. in Hort. Kew, ed. 2. 5, 207.—Lindl. gen. and sp. p. 175.

Syn. Limodorum nutans, *Roxb.*—Malaxis nutans, *Willd.*

Engrav. Roxb. Cor. I. t. 40.

SPEC. CHAR. Scape longer than the leaf: raceme pendulous: flowers alternate: lip ovate, acute, painted: flowers rose-coloured.

Moist vallies among the Circar mountains, flowering in the rainy season.

(2) G. DILATATUM. *(R. Br.)*

Ident. R. Br. l. c.—Lindl. l. c.

Syn. Limodorum recurvum, *Roxb. Swz.* — *Willd.* Malaxis cernua, *Willd.*—G. pallidum, *Don. prod. nep.* 31.

Engrav. Wight's Icon. t. 912.—Bot. Reg. t. 675.—Roxb. Cor. I. t. 39.—Rheede Mal. xi. t. 35. (?)

SPEC. CHAR. Scape shorter than the leaves: spike pendulous: flowers heaped together: lip somewhat spurred, dilated at the apex, crenulate: whitish flowers marked with pink streaks and yellow.

Moist vallies among the Circar mountains. Malabar. Coimbatore. Silhet. Flowering in June and July.

(3) G. RARIFLORUM. *(Lindl.)*

Ident. Lindl. fol. orch. 1854, p. 2.

SPEC. CHAR. Leaves long-petioled: scape shorter: sheaths and bracts small, herbaceous: raceme rare: lip scrotiform at the base, ovate, obtuse, emarginate, with a very small 2-toothed callosity, the rest naked.

Assam.

(4) G. CANDIDUM. *(Wall.)*

Ident. Wall. Cat. No. 7374.—Lindl. l. c. p. 3.

Syn. Limodorum candidum, *Roxb. flor. Ind. III. p.* 470.

Var. a. Very small: leaves sessile: sepals and petals very acute: lip ovate, with a slightly dilated emarginate point, with a pair of large callosities near the sac: flowers white. Silhet.

Var. b. Leaves with long stalks: lip wider at the point and wrinkled: flowers white, smaller. Khasia.

(5) G. CITRINUM. *(Jacks.)*

Ident. Jackson in Bot. Rep. t. 626.—Lindl. gen. and sp. p. 176.

SPEC. CHAR. Scape shorter than the leaves: spike pendulous: flowers congested: lip somewhat spurred at the base, obtuse at the apex, quite entire: flowers pale yellow.

Chittagong.

GENUS XXXVI. CYMBIDIUM.

Gynandria Monandria. *Sex: Syst:*

Deriv. The diminutive of *Cymba*, a boat, alluding to the shape of the lip.

Gen. Char. Perianth flattened out: sepals and petals almost equal, free: lip sessile, free, without a spur, concave, articulated with the base of the column or slightly connate, undivided or 3-lobed: column erect, half-terete: anther 2-celled: pollen masses 2, usually posticously 2-lobed, sub-sessile into a somewhat triangular gland.

(1) C. cyperifolium. *(Wall.)*

Ident. Lindl. gen. and sp. p. 163.

Spec. Char. Leaves linear-ensiform, acute, striated, 3-ribbed, longer than the straight scapes: bracts leafy, acuminate, longer than the ovaries: sepals and petals linear-oblong, acute, striated: lateral lobes of the 3-lobed channelled lip acute, intermediate one ovate, refracted: plates almost parallel, continuous: flowers green purplish at the base, lip pale green, plate 2—4 times purple-spotted.

Silhet.

(2) C. giganteum. *(Wall.)*

Ident. Lindl. l. c.

Syn. Limodorum longifolium, *Buch.*

Spec. Char. Leaves ensiform, striated, acute, longer than the drooping many-flowered raceme: bracts minute: sepals oblong and with the linear-lanceolate petals acute: lateral lobes of the 3-lobed lip small, acute, pubescent at the base, intermediate one much larger, ovate, acute, undulated, bearded in the middle: plates arched, connate at the apex, hairy: flowers brownish-purple, margined with yellow.

Khasia hills, flowering in March.

(3) C. aloifolium. *(Swartz.)*

Ident. Swartz Nov. Act. Ups. vi. 73.—Lindl. l. c. p. 165.

Syn. Epidendrum aloifolium, *Linn. sp.* 1350.—Aerides Borassi, *Rees Cycl. suppl.*

Engrav. Bot. Mag. xi. t. 387.—Rheede Mal. xii. t. 8.—Wight's Icon. t. 1687-8.

SPEC. CHAR. Leaves long ensiform, coriaceous, oblique, obtuse: racemes pendulous, many-flowered: bracts minute: petals and sepals lanceolate, somewhat obtuse: lip revolute: lateral lobes acute, middle one oblong, obtuse: petals and sepals yellowish-red, lip dark lilac, tending to purple.

On branches of trees and Palms throughout the Peninsula. Salsette. Garrow hills. Khasia mountains. Flowering in March and April.

(4) C. ERECTUM. *(R.W.)*

Ident. Wight l. c. t. 1753.

SPEC. CHAR. Leaves ligulate, succulent, rigid, deeply and obliquely emarginate: racemes erect, many-flowered: bracts small, fleshy: sepals linear, somewhat obtuse, narrower than the lanceolate acute petals: lip 3-lobed, middle one pubescent, and revolute at the apex, lateral ones acute: plates linear, straight: flowers reddish-yellow, deepening to purple along the middle line, limb of the lip purplish-red, yellowish near the base.

Iyamally hills, near Coimbatore, flowering in August and September.

(5) C. PENDULUM. *(Swartz.)*

Ident. Swartz l. c.—Lindl. l. c. p. 165.

Syn. Epidendrum pendulum, *Roxb. flor. Ind. III. p.* 458.

Engrav. Roxb. Cor. I. t. 44.

SPEC. CHAR. Leaves ensiform, coriaceous, obliquely obtuse: racemes pendulous, many-flowered: bracts minute: petals and sepals linear-oblong, obtuse: lateral lobes of the 3-lobed lip acute, intermediate one ovate, acute: plates continuous, approximate, confluent at the apex: flowers striated with red and yellow.

Silhet. Peninsula. Flowering in the hot season.

(6). C. APHYLLUM. *(Swartz.)*

Ident. Roxb. flor. Ind. III. p. 462.

Engrav. Roxb. Cor. I. t. 41.

SPEC. CHAR. Roots fibrous: stems several, simple, diffuse or pendulous, naked, round, jointed at every inch, at each joint a small membranaceous scale, leafless: flowers sessile, single, issuing from the joints: lip large, incurved at the sides near the base, outer portion 6-parted: margins curled, waved ciliated, pale sulphur.

Dry rocky hills, rare.

(7) C. ALATUM. *(Roxb.)*

Ident. Roxb. l. c. p. 459.

SPEC. CHAR. Stems bulbiform, aggregated: leaf solitary from the apex of each bulb, lanceolar: scapes rising from the base of the bulbs, drooping, many-flowered: column much incurved: lamina 2-lobed: flowers small, tinged with rusty red.

Chittagong forests, flowering in April and May.

GENUS XXXVII. ACANTHOPHIPPIUM.

Gynandria Monandria. *Sex: Syst:*

GEN. CHAR. Perianth ventricose: sepals agglutinated, lateral ones to the claw of the column, dorsal one vaulted with the spathulate petals: lip clawed, elastically articulated with the prolonged base of the column, limb 3-lobed undivided, folded upon itself: disc lamellate: anther fleshy, 2-celled: pollen masses 8, unequal, sessile.—Terrestrial, sub-caulescent: stem bulbous below, sheathed: leaves oblong-lanceolate, plicate: peduncle sheathed, few-flowered: flowers showy.

(1) A. SILHETENSE. *(Lindl.)*

Ident. Lindl. gen. and sp. p. 177.

SPEC. CHAR. Petals oblong-lanceolate, acutish: lateral lobes of the lip acute: perianth obovate: leaves very large, white.

Silhet. Khasia hills.

GENUS XXXVIII. CYRTOPERA.

Gynandria Monandria. *Sex: Syst:*

GEN. CHAR. Perianth flattened out, sepals and petals ascending, almost equal, connate with the prolonged claw of the column: lip without a spur, concave, sub-ventricose, 3-lobed, veins of the axis callous or crested or tubercled: column semi-terete, margined: anther 1—2-celled: pollen masses 2, posticously 2-lobed, caudicle short, sub-triangular.—Terrestrial: leaved plicate: stems fleshy, fusiform elongated, or abbreirated flowers racemose, showy, scapes radical.

(1) C. CULLENII. *(R. W.)*

Ident. Wight's Icon. v. t. 1754.

SPEC. CHAR. Leaves oblong-lanceolate, acute, plaited: scape slender, angular, somewhat drooping towards the apex: flowers numerous, yellow, loosely racemed, long-pedicelled, bracts ovate, subulate: sepals sub-obovate lanceolate, narrower than the obovate very obtuse petals: middle lobe of lip smaller, 3-crested.

Travancore forests, flowering in the rains.

(2) C. Fusca. *(R. W.)*

Ident. Wight's Icon. l. c. t. 1690.

Spec. Char. Leaves long lanceolate, plicate: scape straight, many-flowered: sepals linear-lanceolate, acute, longer than the broader ovate-lanceolate petals: lip obsoletely 3-lobed, lateral lobes short, roundish, middle one oblong, undulate, pointed, the disc covered with minute papillæ: base of the column prolonged, obtuse, forming with the lip a large inflated spurious spur: sepals dull reddish brown or lilac, ascending, petals and lip much paler.

On rocky clefts among turf by the Kartairy falls, near Kaity, Neilgherries, flowering in May and June; also on hills near Conoor.

GENUS XXXIX. CRYPTOCHILUS.

Gynandria Monandria. *Sex: Syst.*

Deriv. From *Kryptos*, hidden, and *Cheilos*, a lip.

Gen. Char. Perianth tubular, contracted at the throat, gibbous at the base in front: sepals almost entirely connate, free at the apex only: petals free, a little smaller: lip undivided, free, continuous with the prolonged base of the column: column semi-terete, clinandrium 4-toothed: anther 2-celled: pollen masses 8, adhering by four pairs to a common gland.—Terrestrial: pseudo-bulbs aggregated: leaves semi-coriaceous, striated: spike secund, many-flowered: flowers blood red, pubescent.

(1) C. sanguinea. *(Wall.)*

Ident. Lindl. gen. and sp. p. 193.

Engrav. Wight's Icon. t. 1757.—Wall. tent. flor. nep. t. 26.

Khasia mountains.

GENUS XL. EULOPHIA.

Gynandria Monandria. *Sex: Syst:*

Deriv. From *Eulophos*, a handsome crest, alluding to the lip bearing elevated lines or ridges.

Gen. Char. Perianth flattened out, sepals and petals ascending, almost equal, either altogether free or connate with the more or less drawn out stalk of the column: lip horned, or shortly spurred, sessile, veins crested, bearded or quite smooth: usually trilobed, or undivided: column half-terete, marginate: anther 1—2-celled: pollen masses 2, posticously 2-lobed, or hollow, caudicle linear short, gland transverse.—Terrestrial, pseudo-bulbous herbs: leaves long, membranaceous, plicate or many times ribbed: scapes radical, many-flowered.

(1) E. VIRENS. *(R. Brown.)*

Ident. Lindl. gen. and sp. p. 182.

Syn. Serapias epidendræa, *Retz. obs. vi.* 65.. Limodorum virens, *Roxb. Willd.* L. epidendroides, *Willd.*

Engrav. Wight's Icon. t. 913.—Roxb. cor. I. t. 38. Rheede Mal. xii. t. 25.

SPEC. CHAR. Leaves grass-like, linear-lanceolate, shorter than the branched scape: sepals and petals oblong, obtuse, narrower at the base, tessellated: lip 3-lobed, bearded, lateral lobes shorter, middle one ovate obtuse with an erect conical spur: flowers greenish-yellow striated.

Coromandel. Bengal. Clefts of rocks near Coimbatore. Malabar. Flowering in the cold season.

(2) E. BRACTEOSA. *(Lindl.)*

Ident. Lindl. l. c. p. 181.

SPEC. CHAR. Leaves oblong-lanceolate, plicate, longer than the terminal scape: bracts leafy, almost equalling the flowers: sepals and petals fleshy, oblong, acute: lip oblong, channelled, retuse at the apex, undulate, elevated, veined, glandularly bearded towards the apex: spur bent inwards, tumid, acutish.

Chittagong.

(3) E. CARINATA. *(Lindl.)*

Ident. Lindl. l. c. p. 183.

Syn. Limodorum carinatum. *Willd.*

Engrav. Rheede Mal. xii. t. 26.

SPEC. CHAR. Leaves linear, folded inwards, fleshy, easily fractured: scape simple: lip concave, spathulate, repand at the apex: spur without a keel.

Malabar.

(4) E. CAMPESTRIS. *(Wall.)*

Ident. Lindl. l. c. p. 185.

SPEC. CHAR. Sepals and petals linear-spathulate, rather obtuse: lip oblong, 3-lobed, veined: intermediate lobe rounded, transverse, crenulate, with 3 short lines bearded at the base: spur short, conical, incurved: flowers secund, drooping, brown purple, lip whitish rosy at the margins.

Bhurtpore, Oude.

(5) E. RAMENTACEA. *(Lindl.)*

Ident. Lindl. l. c.

Engrav. Wight l. c. t. 1666.

SPEC. CHAR. Leafless: bracts subulate, shorter than the ovary: flowers erect: sepals and petals linear, spathulate, acute: lip 3-lobed, the middle lobe undulated, obtuse: plates of the disk 3, broken or torn towards the point: spur obtuse, conical.

Coorg, Mysore.

(6) E. MACROSTACHYA. *(Lindl.)*

Ident. Lindl. l. c. p. 183.

Engrav. Wight l. c. t. 1667—68.

SPEC. CHAR. Leaves oblong, acuminated at both ends, plaited, somewhat 3-ribbed: scape simple, radical, longer than the leaves: sepals linear, lanceolate, acuminate: petals conformable, broader, sub-undulate: lip sub-orbicular 3-lobed, lateral lobes about the length of the shortened, deeply-cleft middle one: two short petals near the base: spur short, roundish, obtuse, inflated: flowers greenish-yellow, lateral: lobes of the lip tinged and streaked with crimson lines, the middle lobes yellow.

Eastern slopes of the Neilgherries.

GENUS XLI. CALANTHE.

Gynandria Monandria. *Sex: Syst.*

Deriv. From *Kalos*, beautiful, and *Anthos*, a flower.

GEN. CHAR. Perianth flattened out, free, or lateral sepals slightly adnate to the lip: lip connate with the column, lobed or entire, spurred or muticous, lamellated or tubercled with a disc: column short, beak usually rostrate: pollen masses 8, much attenuated at the base, adhering by fours to a bi-parted gland.—Terrestrial: scapes erect, many-flowered: leaves broad, folded: flowers white, or lilac, rarely yellow.

(1) C. PUBERULA. *(Lindl.)*

Ident. Lindl. gen. and sp. p. 252.—fol. orch. 1854, p. 2.

Engrav. Griff. Icon. t. 313.

SPEC. CHAR. Scape equal to the leaves, loosely racemose : bracts linear-lanceolate longer than the ovary : sepals ovate lateral oblique : petals linear : lip hastate without an appendage or spur, lateral lobes somewhat falcate, middle one lanceolate : flowers rose-colour, with linear yellowish petals and a purple lip.

Silhet mountains. Khasia. Assam. The middle lobe of the lip varies from linear-lanceolate and entire to obovate-oblong, or lanceolate and serrate.

(2) C. CLAVATA. *(Lindl.)*

Ident. Lindl. l. c. p. 251.—fol. orch. l. c. p. 5.

SPEC. CHAR. Scape shorter than the leaves : raceme congested, drooping, long bracteated : lip sub-orbiculate, mucronate, quite entire with two callosities at the base : spur club-shaped, furrowed, straight : flowers primrose.

Silhet. Khasia.

(3) C. MASUCA. *(Lindl.)*

Ident. Lindl. l. c. p. 249.—fol. orch. p. 6.

Syn. Calanthe emarginata, *Wight* Bletia Masuca, *Don. prod. Nep. p.* 30.

Engrav. Wight's Icon. t. 918.—Bot. Reg. t. 37.—Bot. Mag. t. 4541.

SPEC. CHAR. Scape erect, longer than the broad oblong petioled acuminated leaves : racemes lax, many-flowered : lip 3-lobed, 2-crested at the base : lateral lobes adpressed, middle one retuse, transverse : spur pendulous, clavate, twice longer than the pubescent ovary : flowers large, purple, with 3 long rugged white or orange-coloured callosities on the base of the lip.

Neilgherries.

(4) C. ANGUSTA. *(Lindl.)*

Ident. Lindl. fol. orch. l. c. p. 7.

SPEC. CHAR. Raceme tomentose, dense, narrow : lateral lobes of the lip less than the intermediate 2-parted one : warts few, gyrate : spur somewhat club-shaped, apex inflexed, a little longer than the ovary.

Khasia.

(5) C. VAGINATA. *(Lindl.)*

Ident. Lindl. l. c. p. 7.

SPEC. CHAR. Scape densely imbricated with sheaths: raceme dense, conical, tomentose: bracts longer than the flowers: segments of the 4-lobed lip equally broad, obtuse, crest warty, antrorsely hispid: spur longer than the lip.

Assam.

(6) C. PEROTETTII. *(A. Rich.)*

Ident. A. Rich. in Ann. Sc. ser. 2, xv. 68.—Lindl. fol. orch. l. c.

Engrav. Wight l. c. t. 1664.

SPEC. CHAR. Leaves elliptic, plicate, acute: scape longer than the leaves furnished with distant sheathing scales: raceme lax: bracts ovate-lanceolate, length of the ovary: sepals and petals nearly equal, ovate, obtuse: lip 3-lobed, lateral lobes lanceolate, middle one much larger, truncately 2—3-lobed, lobes spreading: spur slender, straight, longer or about the length of the lip: flowers light lilac, lip with a deeper tinge.

Neilgherries, flowering in July and August.

(7) C. VERATRIFOLIA. *(R. Br.)*

Ident. R. Br. in Bot. Reg. t. 720.—Lindl. l. c. p. 8. Gen. and sp. p. 249.

Syn. Amblyglottis flava, *Blume.* C. comosa, *Rchb. f. in Linn.* xix. 374. Limodorum veratrifolium, *Willd. sp. iv.* 122.

Engrav. Griff. Icon. t. 283, fig. 4.—Rumph. Amb. vi. t. 52, fig. 2.—Blume bidjr. 370, t. 64.

SPEC. CHAR. Scape straight, longer than the oblong acute leaves: bracts oblong, concave: racemes dense, many-flowered: lip 4-lobed, furrowed and glandular at the base: spur filiform, pendulous, a little longer than the lip: flowers pure white.

Peninsula, Neilgherries. There are varieties, one a dwarf form with a dirty brown lip and pale purple central stain, and another with white flowers changing to buff.

(8) C. ALISMÆFOLIA. *(Lindl.)*

Ident. Lindl. l. c. p. 8—9.

SPEC. CHAR. Leaves ovate-sub-rotund, very long petioled, glaucescent beneath: lateral segments of the 4-lobed lip linear, intermediate one deeply obcordate, callus very large, fleshy, bright yellow, tubercled near the base: spur scarcely equal to the lip: flowers white tinged with pink, except the sepals, which are roundish and somewhat green.

Khasia.

(9) C. densiflora. *(Lindl.)*

Ident. Lindl. gen. and sp. p. 250.—fol. orch. p. 9.

Engrav. Bot. Reg. t. 1646.

Spec. Char. Scape loosely sheathed much shorter than the leaves: lip obovate, obtuse, 2-lobed, slightly connate with the elongated column: spur long, straight, pendulous, clavate at the apex: flowers apricot-yellow.

Silhet. Assam. Khasia.

GENUS XLII. SUNIPIA.

Gynandria Monandria. *Sex: Syst:*

Deriv. From *Sunipiang*, an Indian word.

Gen. Char. Sepals cartilaginous, equal, ringent: lateral ones placed under the lip, separated from the dorsal one at the base: petals dwarf: lip posticous, entire, sessile, less than the sepals, fleshy, concave, inappendiculate: column dwarf, free, muticous, scarcely lengthened out at the base: pollen masses 4, adnate by pairs to 2 distinct caudicles contiguous at the apex: gland none: anther affixed by the back, vertically 4-valved.—Pseudo-bulbous epiphyte: leaves solitary, coriaceous: scape radical, spiked at the apex: bracts membranaceous, spathaceous, longer than the flowers.

(1) S. scariosa. *(Lindl.)*

Ident. Lindl. in Wall. Cat. No. 7373.—Gen. and sp. p. 179.

Syn. Ornithidium bracteatum, *Wall. Mss.*

Engrav. Lindl. Sert. orch. frontisp. f. 8.

Spec. Char. Pseudo-bulbs small, ovate, slightly elongated: flowers white, stained with pink: lip destitute of fringes.

Khasia hills.

GENUS XLIII. SARCANTHUS.

Gynandria Monandria. *Sex: Syst:*

Deriv. From *Sarx* flesh, and *Anthos* a flower.

Gen. Char. Perianth flattened: sepals and petals almost equal: lip short spurred, 3-lobed, fleshy, articulated with the column: spur half 2-celled within: column erect, half-terete: anther 2-celled: pollen masses 2, posticously lobed, caudicle and gland various.—Caulescent epiphytes: leaves distichous, flat or terete: racemes leaf-opposed: flowers showy.

(1) S. PENINSULARIS. *(Dalz.)*

Ident. Dalzell in Hook. Journ. Bot. III. p. 343.

Syn. S. pauciflorus, *Wight Icon. t.* 1747.

SPEC. CHAR. Stem simple, terete, flexuose, leafy, pendulous: leaves linear-acuminate, thick, coriaceous, a little 3-edged: racemes half the length of the leaves: spur as long as the flower, horn-like, obtuse, pendulous, completely bilocular, the throat closed by two tubercles: lip short, entire, ovate, obtuse, thick, fleshy, erect, painted white and violet.

On trees near Kirwee in the Warree country, Malabar; flowering in July and August.

(2) S. FILIFORMIS. *(R. W.)*

Ident. Wight l. c. v. t. 1684.

SPEC. CHAR. Pendulous: leaves terete, filiform: spike simple, ascending, much shorter than the leaves: sepals narrow-lanceolate, posterior one larger: petals ovate, orbicular, obtuse, much longer than the sepals: lip 3-lobed, lateral lobes erect, obtuse, middle one ovate, acute, reflexed: spur slightly recurved, obtuse, as long as the flower: capsule sub-cylindrical, clavate: flowers orange-yellow streaked with darker crimson lines.

Annamullay forests, flowering in September and October.

(3) S. ROSEUS. *(R. W.)*

Ident. Wight l. c. t. 1685.

SPEC. CHAR. Pendulous: leaves round, subulate, firm: racemes spicate, ascending, compact: anterior sepal lanceolate, acute, posterior one linear, obtuse: petals broad, orbicular: spur straight, inflated at the point, produced into an ovate acute fleshy plate, with a large globose callosity at the base, gland of the pollen large: capsule small, ovate: flowers rose-coloured, petals green at the base within.

Neilgherries, flowering in August and September.

GENUS XLIV. PODOCHILUS.

Gynandria Monandria. *Sex: Syst:*

Deriv. From *Pous* a foot, and *Cheilos* a lip the latter is jointed with the foot of the column.

GEN. CHAR.—Perianth closed: sepals connate at the base, lateral ones broader connate with the prolonged claw of the column: petals narrower, free: lip elastically articulated with the foot of the column, entire, clawed: column recumbent on the ovary, clinandrium 2-horned, membranaceous: anther almost dorsal, 2-celled: pollen masses 4, caudicles 2, membranaceous, convolute.—Caulescent epiphytes: leaves distichous, small: flowers small, solitary or spiked, usually terminal.

(1) P. MICROPHYLLUS. *(Lindl.)*

Ident. Lindl. gen. and sp. p. 234.

SPEC. CHAR. Leaves narrow ovate, acute, obliquely twisted: petals obtuse: lip sagittate, emarginate: rostellum obtuse: gland roundish: petals obovate, obtuse, smaller than the sepals: flowers very minute.

Silhet.

(2) P. MALABARICUS. *(R. W.)*

Ident. Wight's Icon. v. t. 1748—2.

SPEC. CHAR. Leaves short, fleshy, imbricating, obtuse: spikes terminal, short, few-flowered, drooping: bracts broad-ovate, somewhat cuspidate: petals lanceolate, lateral sepals connate, forming a short ventricose spurious spur: lip entire, constricted in the middle, upper half linear-lanceolate, obtuse.

Malabar, flowering in the rainy season.

GENUS XLV. AERIDES.

Gynandria Monandria. *Sex: Syst:*

Deriv. From *Aer*, the air, alluding to their habits.

GEN. CHAR. Perianth spreading or closed: lateral sepals usually oblique at the base, connate with the prolonged claw of the column: lip articulated with the claw of the column, saccate or spurred, 3-lobed: lateral lobes dwarf: limb hooded, or subulate, or abbreviate-tumid, or somewhat forked: column recumbent on the ovary, short, wingless: anther 2-celled: pollen masses 2, furrowed: caudicle broad or filiform, gland peltate, roundish.—Caulescent epiphytes: stems somewhat simple, rooting: leaves distichous, coriaceous, or somewhat fleshy: flowers racemose or spiked.

(1) A. WIGHTIANUM. *(Lindl.)*

Ident. Lindl. gen. and sp. p. 238.

Syn. Vanda parviflora, *Lindl. in Bot. Reg.* 1844, *misc.* 57.

Engrav. Wight's Icon. t. 1669.

SPEC. CHAR. Leaves strap-shaped, oblique at the base, 2-lobed at the apex with a tooth between: racemes straight, simple, many-flowered, longer than the leaves: sepals and petals oval, anterior ones larger: lip funnel-shaped: lateral lobes adnate to the foot of the column, middle one sub-cuneate, roundish, 3-lobed at the apex: disc crested with several crisp lines: spur short, conical: middle lobe of the lip deep lilac: capsules club-shaped, 6-angled: flowers yellow.

South Concan. Hills near Coimbatore, flowering in August and September.

(2) A. CRISPUM. *(Lindl.)*

Ident. Lindl. l. c. p. 239.

Syn. A. Brookei, *Bot. Reg.* 1841.—Saccolabium speciosum, *Wight l. c. t.* 1674-5.

Engrav. Bot. Reg. t. 55.

SPEC. CHAR. Leaves strap-shaped, obliquely emarginate at the apex: panicle large, lateral branches few-flowered, terminal one long, drooping, many-flowered: sepals broad, ovate-elliptic, obtuse: petals rhombeo-spathulate, lip 3-lobed, lateral ones small, orbicular, middle one sub-triangular, crenate, truncated at the apex, spur tapering, shorter than the lip, hooked outwards: fruit short, ob-conical: flowers rose-coloured, lip more intense.

Southern Concan. Warree country. Courtallum. Palghaut forests. Flowering in July and August.

(3) A. LINDLEYANUM. *(R. W.)*

Ident. Wight l. c. t. 1677.—Dalz. Bomb. flor. p. 265.

SPEC. CHAR. Leaves fleshy, coriaceous, linear-oblong, oblique, deeply emarginate at the apex: racemes erect, few-flowered: sepals and petals obovate, sub-orbicular: anterior sepals somewhat larger, and like the lip, thick and coriaceous: lip 3-lobed, attached to the point of the prolonged base of the column, lateral lobes small, ovate, ventricose above, crisp on the margins, with a large fleshy lobe at the base, closing the spur: spur short, rigid, inflexed under the laminæ: capsules large, obovate, long-pedicelled: flowers pinkish-lilac, lip deeper coloured, very fragrant.

Near Vingorla. Warree country. Kaitie falls. Hills near Coonoor. Neilgherries. Flowering nearly all the year.

(4) A. MACULOSUM. *(Lindl.)*

Ident. Lindl. Bot. Reg. 1845, and t. 58.—Dalz. l. c. p. 266.

SPEC. CHAR. Leaves coriaceous, plain, oblique at the apex, obtuse: racemes dense, nodding, sub-paniculate: sepals round-oblong, petals the same, double the breadth: lip ovate, entire, with a tooth on each side at the base and a tubercle between: flowers spotted all over with light purple, on a pale rose-coloured ground.

Concan forests, common.

(5) A. CYLINDRICUM. *(Lindl.)*

Ident. Lindl. l. c. p. 240.

Engrav. Wight l. c. t. 1744.

SPEC. CHAR. Leaves round, somewhat cylindrical: racemes short, about 2-flowered: sepals ovate, obtuse, petals oblong, broader: lip hooded, funnel-shaped, lateral lobes oblong, obtuse, adnate to the ovate, obtuse, fleshy middle one: spur straight, conical: flowers white or slightly tinged with red, lip reddish, middle lobe yellow at the base.

Iyamullay hills. Coimbatore. Flowering in August and September.

(6) A. ODORATUM. *(Lour.)*

Ident. Lour. flor. Coch. p. 525.—Lindl. l. c. p. 239.

Syn. A. cornutum, *Roxb. flor. Ind. III. p.* 472.

Engrav. Bot. Reg. 18, t. 1485.

SPEC. CHAR. Leaves flaccid, obtuse, oblique: racemes pendulous, many-flowered, longer than the leaves: lateral segments of the hooded funnel-shaped lip erect, cuneate, rounded, middle one ovate, acute, inflexed: spur conical, incurved: flowers large, white, with a tinge of rose, fragrant.

Chittagong. Dacca. Khasia hills. Flowering in April.

(7) A. AFFINE. *(Wall.)*

Ident. Lindl. l. c.

SPEC. CHAR. Leaves channelled, somewhat recurved, retuse, mucronate: racemes cylindric, many-flowered, erect, equal to the leaves: sepals oblong, obtuse: petals the same, larger: lip larger than the rest, ovate, membranaceous, obsoletely 3-lobed, claw saccate, geniculate: spur small, horned, almost opposite the lamina: flowers rose, with a few darker spots.

Khasia hills, flowering in the hot season.

(8) A. TESSELATUM. *(R.W.)*

Ident. Wight in Wall. Cat.—Lindl. l. c. p. 240.

Syn. Epidendrum tesselatum, *Roxb.*—Cymbidium tesselatum, *Willd.*

Engrav. Roxb. Cor. I. t. 42.

SPEC. CHAR. Leaves lorate, truncated at the apex, rounded, somewhat equal-sided: racemes few-flowered, horizontal, shorter than the leaves: petals and sepals patent, clawed, obovate, obtuse, crisp, tesselated: spur of the lip straight, conical, lamina ovate, convex, teeth lateral, erect, acuminate, the length of the column: flowers greenish-yellow.

On trees in the Circar mountains.

(9) A. (?) SUAVEOLENS. *(Roxb.)*

Ident. Roxb. l. c. p. 473.

SPEC. CHAR. Caulescent: stems rooting: leaves bifarious, linear, bidentate: racemes lateral, filiform, drooping: lamina horn-shaped, unguiculate, with two oblong erect lobes at the base: flowers yellow, purple-spotted, fragrant.

Chittagong forests, flowering all the year.

(10) A. (?) ROSTRATUM. *(Roxb.)*

Ident. Roxb. l. c. p. 474.

SPEC. CHAR. Caulescent: leaves bifarious, linear, channelled, præmorse at the apex: racemes lateral, longer than the leaves: lip clavate, sac conical from the apex of the lamina: column beaked, with a recurved white apex in addition: flowers rose.

Silhet forests.

(11) A. (?) MULTIFLORUM. *(Roxb.)*

Ident. Roxb. l. c. p. 475.

SPEC. CHAR. Caulescent: leaves bifariously imbricated, linear, channelled, obliquely emarginate, with a hooded acumen: racemes axillary or lateral, longer than the leaves, sometimes compound: the lower 2 outer petals rounded, lip with broad-cordate lamina, with a short obtuse horn beneath: capsules triquetrous: flowers light purple and white, purple dotted.

Silhet, flowering in the hot season.

GENUS XLVI. APETALON.

Gynandria Monandria. *Sex: Syst:*

Deriv. From *A* derivative and *Petalon* a petal.

GEN. CHAR. Perianth bilabiate: posterior sepal large, 3-lobed, lobes very obtuse, middle one larger, somewhat obovate-orbicular: anterior ones resting on the lip, cohering nearly half their length, the two forming a single, sub-orbicular cleft sepal: petals none: lip shorter than the sepals, broad, truncated at the apex, disc fleshy and punctuate, margins petaloid: column erect, clavate: anther terminal, 2-celled: pollen masses granular.

(1) A. MINUTUM. *(R. W.)*

Ident. Wight's Icon. v. t. 1758—1.

SPEC. CHAR. Whole plant about 3 inches high, leafless (?): scape erect, furnished with a few scales bearing 3—4 globose, apparently unexpanding, flowers at the apex: bracts ovate, large in proportion to the plant.

Near Sultan's Battery in Coorg, under a clump of Bamboos.

GENUS XLVII. PLATANTHERA.

Gynandria Monandria. *Sex: Syst:*

GEN CHAR. Flowers galeate: sepals nearly equal, upper one connivent with the petals into a kind of fork, lateral ones converging or reflexed: petals erect, nearly equal to the sepal: lip anterior, spurred, entire or undivided, connate with the base of the column: anther with the cells diverging at the base: glands naked: stigma with the upper lip (beak) flat, adnate to the anther: processes fleshy.—Herbs with the habit and nature of the genus Orchis.

(1) P. LUTEA. *(R. W.)*

Ident. Wight's Icon. t. 919.

SPEC. CHAR. Stem erect, lower half clothed with sheathing scales, above leafy: leaves ovate-lanceolate, acute: bracts leafy, ovate, cucullate, acuminated, equalling the flowers: sepals ovate obtuse, lateral ones ascending: petals smaller, linear-lanceolate: lip 3-lobed, about the length of the sepals, lobes obtuse, entire, lateral ones smaller: spur pendulous, clavate, somewhat shorter than the ovary: flowers yellow.

Pulney mountains, among long grass.

(2) P. Susannæ. *(Lindl.)*

Ident. Lindl. gen. and sp. p. 295.

Syn. Orchis Susannæ, *Linn. Willd. Lour. fl. Coch.*—Habenaria Susannæ, *R. Br. prod. Blume.*—O. gigantea, *Smith.*—H. gigantea, *Don. prod.* 24.

Engrav. Wight l. c. t. 920.—Rumph. Amb. v. t. 99, fig. 2.—Smith Exot. Bot. 100.—Hook. Bot. Mag. t. 3374.

Spec. Char. Stem leafy, about 3-flowered: leaves ovate-oblong, acute, upper ones cucullate, acuminated, sepals ovate obtuse, lateral ones oblique, the dorsal one rhomboid: petals linear-acute: lip 3-parted, lateral lobes truncated, many-cleft, the middle one linear: spur double its length: flowers greenish-white or white.

Pulney mountains. Concans and Ghauts.

(3) P. brachyphylla. *(Lindl.)*

Ident. Lindl. l. c. p. 293.

Engrav. Wight l. c. t. 1694.

Spec. Char. Leaves 2, radical, fleshy, reniform orbicular: scape clothed with acuminate scales: bracts ovate-acuminate, cucullate, as long as the flowers: sepals ovate, roundish, upper ones obtuse, lateral ones acute: petals smaller, ovate: lip deeply 3-cleft, shorter than the clavate spur: ovary beaked: flowers white, spur greenish.

Hills around Jooneer. Neilgherries and other Alpine localities. Flowering in June and July.

(4) P. (?) iantha. *(R. W.)*

Ident. Wight l. c. t. 1692.

Spec. Char. Stem leafy: leaves broad, cordate-ovate, obtuse, stem-clasping, diminishing in size towards the apex where they resemble large bracts: flowers solitary, sessile, posterior larger sepal and petals united, helmet-like, ovate obtuse, lateral ones falcate, longer than the lanceolate acute petals: lip broad obcordate, apiculate, limb equalling the claw, pubescent at the base: spur short, conical. Flowers deep lilac, leaves similarly tinged and striated with darker lines.

Neilgherries, in pastures. Malabar. Flowering from August to September.

(5) P. (?) affinis. *(R. W.)*

Ident. Wight l. c. t. 1693.

Spec. Char. Stem leafy, leaves ovate, acute, sessile, 3-nerved, diminishing in size towards the apex, flowers small, axillary, sessile: sepals and petals galeate: posterior sepal ovate, scarcely exceeding the length of the narrower lanceolate acute petals: anterior sepals slightly exceeding the posterior: lip broad, obovate, slightly pointed, disc pubescent: claw ciliated: spur short, inflated.

Pulney mountains, flowering in September. Wight considers this and the preceding species might with greater propriety to referred to the genus *Gymnadenia.*

(6) P. uniflora. *(Lindl.)*

Ident. Lindl. l. c. p. 295.

Syn. Habenaria uniflora, *D. Don. flor. nep. p.* 25.

Spec. Char. Lip very large, sub-orbiculate: leaflets of the perianth oval, obtuse: spurs almost twice as long as the ovary: flowers small, yellow.

Khasia hills, flowering from August till October.

GENUS XLVIII. PERISTYLUS.

Gynandria Monandria. *Sex: Syst:*

Gen. Char. Same as in Platanthera, except that the calyx is campanulate and the spur very short and usually scrotiform.

(1) P. plantagineus. *(Lindl.)*

Ident. Lindl. gen. and sp. p. 300.

Engrav. Wight's Icon. v. t. 921.

Spec. Char. Leaves erect, oblong-lanceolate, acute, almost as long as the spike: sepals ovate: petals roundish obtuse: lip roundish, obtusely 3-toothed: spur spheroid: flowers small, white.

Moist pastures in the Palghaut forests, flowering in May and June.

(2) P. Lawii. *(R. W.)*

dent. Wight l. c. t. 1695.

Spec. Char. Stem loosely sheathed at the base, 3—4-leaved in the middle, above naked: leaves oblong-lanceolate, acute, scape exceeding the leaves, thin: sepals linear-lanceolate, obtuse, narrower than the petals, lip equalling the sepals, 3-lobed at the apex, lobes all equal: spur short, bladdery.

Belgaum.

(3) P. goodyeroides. *(Lindl.)*

Ident. Lindl. l. c. p. 299.

Syn. Habenaria goodyeroides, *D. Don. prod. nep. p.* 25.

Engrav. Bot. Mag. t. 3397.

Spec. Char. Stem erect, round, leafy, upper leaves gradually increasing in size: flowers small, white, in a densely crowded spike, furnished with lanceolate bracts.

South Concan, flowering in the rains.

(4) P. elatus. *(Dalz.)*

Ident. Dalzell in Hook. Journ. Bot. III. p. 344.

Spec. Char. Stem vaginate at the base, leafy in the middle: leaves few, spreading, elliptic, lower ones obtuse, stem-clasping, upper longer, acute, with a callous mucro, all shorter than the scape, abruptly passing off into acuminate scales: upper sepal rounded, lateral oblong, hooded at the apex, with a mucro on the back: petals longer, lip almost entire, rounded like the petals: spur spheroidal, scrotiform: bracts lanceolate, acuminate, longer than the flower: spike cylindric, many-flowered: flowers small, crowded.

Malwan, flowering in July.

(5) P. spiralis. *(A. Rich.)*

Ident. Wight l. c. t. 1696.

Spec. Char. Stem slender, leafless at the base, loosely sheathing: leaves 3—4, elliptic-lanceolate, acute, sheathing at the base: scape above clothed with acuminate scales passing into bracts: spike spiral, flowers small: bracts lanceolate-acuminate, as long as the flowers: sepals ovate, oblong, obtuse: petals lanceolate, acute: lip saccate at the base, 3-cleft, fleshy, lobes linear-obtuse: flowers greenish-white.

Neilgherries in pastures.

(6) P. Richardianus. *(R. W.)*

Ident. Wight l. c. t. 1697.

Spec. Char. Stem leafy from the base: leaves ovate, lanceolate, acute, scarcely sheathing at the base: spike somewhat compact: bracts broad, ovate, shorter than the ovary: sepals and petals equal: lip 3-lobed, lateral lobes filiform, subulate, erect, longer than the sepals, middle one short, fleshy, conical, blunt-pointed, furrowed in front, shorter than the inflated bladdery spur: flowers greenish-white.

Neilgherries in pastures.

(7) P. exilis. *(R. W.)*

Ident. Wight l. c. t. 1698.

Syn. P. robustior *Wight l. c. t.* 1699.

Spec. Char. Stem naked or slightly sheathed at the base, leafy in the middle: leaves lanceolate, acuminate, acute, tapering at the base into a short petiole, slightly sheathing: scape very long and slender, furnished with a few remote scales: flowers numerous: bracts ovate, acute, about half the length of the ovary: sepals and petals ovate, bluntish, about equal: lip concave at the base, 3-lobed, lateral lobes long, filiform, acute, cirrhate at the point, middle one much shorter, straight: spur short, inflated at the apex, with a narrow neck.

Pulney mountains, flowering in September.

GENUS XLIX. CÆLOGLOSSUM.

Gynandria Monandria. *Sex: Syst:*

Deriv. From *Koilos* hollow, and *Glossa*, a tongue.

Gen. Char. Sepals connivent, equal, free: petals conformable, adnate to the claw of the lip: lip fleshy, clawed, spurred, 3-parted, disc usually tubercled: claw very fleshy, concave, ascending, margin sometimes eroded and glandular, usually (or always) bearing 2 fleshy clavate processes springing from the mouth of the spur, parallel, adnate: anther small, shorter than the cavity of the claw, lobes ascending from the base, adnate to a short 3-toothed beak: glands naked.—Herbs: roots testiculate, stem leafy or sheathing: flowers minute.

(1) C. densum. *(Lindl.)*

Ident. Lindl. gen. and sp. p. 302.

Spec. Char. Stem leafy: leaves lanceolate, acuminate, sensibly decreasing: spike oblong, dense: bracts acuminate equalling the flowers: lateral segments of the lip bristly, middle one linear, shorter: claw thickened at the margin, undulate: spur pendulous, twice longer than the lip.

Silhet.

(2) C. SECUNDUM. *(Lindl.)*

Ident. Lindl. l. c. p. 303.

SPEC. CHAR. Stem leafy: leaves oblong-lanceolate, acuminate, flat: spike dense, secund: bracts ovate-lanceolate, bristly acuminate, leafy, longer than the flowers: lateral segments of the lip filiform, middle one linear, 3 times shorter: claw linear, eroded at the margin: spur scrotiform, apiculated.

Mysore hills.

(4) C. LUTEUM. *(Dalz.)*

Ident. Dalzell in Hook. Journ. Bot. II. p. 263.

Syn. Habenaria peristyloides, *Wight Icon. t.* 1702.

SPEC. CHAR. Leaves few, linear, acuminate, congested near the base: scape clothed with a few ovate-acuminate scales: spike very slender, many-flowered: bracts acuminate, half the length of the ovary: lip callous at the base: lateral segments filiform, twice the length of the middle tongue-shaped segment: spur filiform, cylindric, as long as the ovary: flowers yellow.

Near Malwan, flowering in August.

GENUS L. ATE.

Gynandria Monandria. *Sex: Syst:*

GEN. CHAR. Perianth of Platanthera: anther with diverging bases, attenuated, adnate to the stigmatic channels: glands naked: processes fleshy, free, with a horny spathulate deflexed channelled lamina interposed: sterile anthers narrowed from a broad base, almost the length of the fertile one, thickened at the apex.—Herbs with a tubercled root: stems leafy: flowers herbaceous, galeate.

(1) A. VIRENS. *(Lindl.)*

Ident. Lindl. gen. and sp. p. 326.

Engrav. Wight's Icon. t. 928.

SPEC. CHAR. Leaves ovate, acuminate, occupying the whole stem, suddenly changed into bracts: raceme secund, lax, 4—6-

flowered, bracts leafy, longer than the ovary: flowers green, galeate: sepals ovate, acuminate, lateral ones reflexed, upper one forming a helmet with the petals: petals pubescent, twice broader than the sepal, 2-cleft, segments acuminate, anterior one shorter: lip pendulous, pubescent, 3-cleft, longer than the sepals, lobes linear-acuminate, equal: spur filiform, length of the ovary, obtuse.

Dindigul mountains.

GENUS LI. SATYRIUM.

Gynandria Monandria. *Sex: Syst:*

GEN. CHAR. Perianth ringent, lower lip made from the sepals and petals, upper from a galeate 2-spurred or 2-saccate labellum: column sessile or elongated: anther resupinate, cells parallel or diverging: glands of the pollen masses naked, separate: stigma 2-lipped: upper lip large, exceeding the lower.—Herbs with the habit of Orchis: roots testiculate.

(1) S. NEPALENSE. *(Don.)*

Ident. Lindl. gen. and sp. p. 340.

Engrav. Wight's Icon. t. 929.

SPEC. CHAR. Radical leaves oblong-lanceolate, acute, sheaths inflated, acuminated, distant: spike lax, many-flowered: bracts ovate-acuminate, reflexed, length of the flowers: lateral sepals oblong, middle one and the petals glabrous: lip helmet shaped, crested above: spurs filiform, longer than the ovaries: flowers rose-coloured.

Neilgherries and Pulney mountains, in pastures.

(2) S. PERROTTETIANUM. *(A. Rich.)*

Ident. A. Richard in Wight's Icon. t. 1716.

SPEC. CHAR. Cauline leaves sessile, broad, ovate, acute, plaited, loosely sheathing at the base, diminishing above: flowers loosely spiked: bracts longer than the flowers, ovate-oblong, acute, erect or often reflexed: lateral sepals ovate-lanceolate, acute, middle one linear-oblong: petals linear, obtuse: spur the length of the ovary, stalk of the stigma (gynostem) round, longish: flowers and bracts deep pink.

Neilgherries, in low moist pastures.

(3) S. albiflorum. *(Rich.)*

Ident. Rich. l. c.

Engrav. Wight l. c. t. 1717.

Spec. Char. Cauline leaves ovate-oblong, acute, sessile, sheathing at the base, gradually passing into ovate acute bracts: spikes round, compact: bracts the length of the flowers, ovate-oblong, acute, reflexed: lateral sepals thick, oblique, unequal-sided, subfalcate, obtuse: middle one obovate, oblong, obtuse: petals linear, obtuse: spurs length of the ovary, gynostem short: upper lip of the stigma 2-lobed, lobes very obtuse: flowers white, bracts greenish-red.

Neilgherries, in moist pastures, flowering from July to September.

(4) S. Wightianum. *(Lindl.)*

Ident. Lindl. gen. and sp. p. 340.

Engrav. Wight l. c. t. 1718.

Spec. Char. Stem naked at the base, sheathed: cauline leaves ovate, acute, somewhat coriaceous, sessile, loosely sheathing at the base: spike dense: bracts the length of the flowers, broad, ovate, acute: lateral sepals oblique, ovate, obtuse, middle one narrower: petals narrower, obtuse: spurs shorter than the ovary: upper lip of the stigma obtuse, scarcely emarginate, gynostem short: flowers deep pink, bracts dull lilac.

Neilgherries, flowering from July to September.

GENUS LII. PODANTHERA.

Gynandria Monandria. *Sex: Syst:*

Gen. Char. Sepals and petals equal, narrow-lanceolate: lip calcarate, sessile, ovate-elliptic, acute, 3-crested on the disc, eroso-dentate towards the apex: spur short, clavate: column short, truncated in front: posteriorly the thick fleshy filament is produced into an arched crest-like foot to the anther: anther 2-celled: pollen masses granular, with a longish slender caudicle.

(1) P. pallida. *(R.W.)*

Ident. Wight's Icon. v. t. 1759.

Spec. Char. Herbaceous, leafless, apparently parasitic and colourless: scape 12—15 inches high, many-flowered, clothed with short sheathing scales: bracts lanceolate, about the length of the pedicels: lip large, marked with a few pale pink spots: capsule ovate, nearly the length of the sepals.

Wynaud forests, in black vegetable soil.

GENUS LIII. DIPLOCENTRUM.

Gynandria Monandria. *Sex: Syst:*

Deriv. From *Diplos*, double, and *Kentron*, a spur.

Gen. Char. Perianth almost closed, free: upper sepal much smaller than the oblique lateral ones: petals a little larger than the upper sepal: lip articulated with the column, undivided, with 2 spurs: column minute, semi-terete, beak obtuse: pollen masses 2, caudicle subulate, gland very large, concave.—Epiphytes: caulescent: leaves folded on themselves, fleshy, recurved: racemes panicled, recurved: flowers minute: spurs short, obconical, incurved.

(1) D. longifolium. *(R.W.)*

Ident. Wight's Icon. v. t. 1681.

Spec. Char. Leaves linear, strap-shaped, channelled, obtuse, oblique, the apex emarginate: racemes axillary, erect, sparingly branched, longer than the leaves: sepals and petals ovate, nearly all equal, obtuse: lip entire, undulated, obtuse or emarginate: capsules obovate, penduleus, connectivum prolonged into a flat very obtuse appendage with the cells at the base: sepals and petals dull brownish, tinged with pink, lip dull pinkish-lilac.

On branches of trees, Neilgherries and Iyamullay hills, flowering in June and July.

(2) D. congestum. *(R.W.)*

Ident. Wight l. c. t. 1682.

Spec. Char. Leaves short, sub-elliptic, oblong, deeply emarginate, or 2-lobed at the apex: racemes longer than leaves, axillary, sparingly branched, erect, many-flowered: flowers congested, small: sepals and petals ovate: lateral sepals oblique, larger than the petals: lip ovate, tapering, truncated at the point: connectivum of the anther prolonged, truncated at the apex: caudicle long subulate: gland very large, somewhat 2-lobed.

On branches of trees, Iyamullay hills, flowering during the rainy season.

GENUS LIV. CAMAROTIS.

Gynandria Monandria. *Sex: Syst:*

Gen. Char. Perianth flattened out: lateral sepals connate with the back of the lip, free at the apex: petals a little smaller, free: lip obovate, channelled, 1-chambered at the apex, appendiculate:

column erect, terete, free, very long sigmoid-rostrate: anther dorsal, apiculate, half 2-celled: pollen masses 2: caudicle very long, subulate: rostellum forficate:—Caulescent: leaves distichous, coriaceous: racemes axillary, many-flowered.

(1) C. purpurea. *(Lindl.)*

Ident. Lindl. gen. and sp. orch. p. 219.

Spec. Char. Leaves emarginate, oblong-linear, almost equal at the apex: lip at the apex under the subulate inflexed appendage, furnished with a foramen, which is the mouth of the calceiform chamber constituting the whole top of the lip, the sides of the lip a little agglutinated, but the margins spreading: flowers pale purple, more intense at the top.

Silhet.

GENUS LV. MICROPERA.

Gynandria Monandria. *Sex: Syst.*

Gen. Char. Perianth equal, spreading, lateral sepals adnate to the base of the lip: lip continuous with the base of the column, calceiform, slightly 3-lobed, intermediate lobe smaller, lateral ones erect: column short, beak large inflexed: pollen masses 2, caudicle subulate.—Epiphytes, caulescent: leaves distichous, linear, arcuate, equal at the apex, emarginate: spikes lateral, horizontal, shorter than the leaves: flowers citron.

(1) M. pallida. *(Lindl.)*

Ident. Lindl. gen. and sp. orch. p. 219.

Syn. Aerides pallidum, *Roxb.*

Spec. Char. Caulescent: leaves broadly linear, oblique at the apex, somewhat 3-toothed: racemes short, 8—15-flowered: capsules narrow, tapering: flowers middle-sized, pale yellow.

Silhet. Chittagong. Flowering in May and June.

(2) M. maculata. *(Dalz.)*

Ident. Dalzell in Hook. Journ. Bot. III. p. 282.

Spec. Char. Almost stemless: leaves flat, linear-oblong, narrow towards the base, obliquely emarginate towards the apex, mucronate: racemes basal and axillary, simple, solitary, elongated, erect, many-flowered from the base, twice the length of the leaves: sepals and petals about equal, obovate, lip painted with white and rose-colour, and furnished with 2 horns on the sides which lean backwards: spur shorter than the flower, saccate, obtuse, pointing forwards, hairy within, and lying under a 3-lobed lamina, lip in front calceiform, with the front leather turned backwards, white at the base: sepals and petals yellow, with a purple spot in the centre.

Tulkut ghaut, flowering in May.

GENUS LVI. POLYSTACHYA.

Gynandria Monandria. *Sex: Syst:*

Deriv. From *Polys* many, and *Stachys* a spike.

GEN. CHAR. Sepals erect, acute, lateral ones larger, connate with the lengthened base of the column: petals smaller: lip sessile, articulated with the base of the column, 3-lobed: column half-terete, short: anther 2-celled: pollen-masses 4, collateral, equal, cohering by pairs.—Caulescent epiphytes, sometimes pseudo-bulbous: leaves slightly nerved: flowers panicled, small, flower-buds trigonal.

(1) P. LUTEOLA. *(Hooker.)*

Ident. Hooker Exot. flor. t. 103.—Lindl. gen. and sp. p. 73.

Syn. Epidendrum minutum, *Aubl.*—Cranichis luteola, *Swartz flor. Ind. Occ. III.* 1433.—Dendrobium polystachyon, *Willd. et al. auct.* P. mauritiana, *Spreng.*

Engrav. Wight's Icon. t. 1678. Thouars Orch. Afr. t. 85.

SPEC. CHAR. Leaves oblong-lanceolate, many-nerved, shorter than the scape: spike panicled: ovaries glabrous: flowers pale yellow.

Iyamullay hills near Coimbatore, on branches of trees, flowering in August and September.

(2) P. PURPUREA. *(R. W.)*

Ident. Wight l. c. t. 1679.

SPEC. CHAR. Leaves coriaceous, linear-oblong, obtuse, emarginate, shorter than the scape: flowers and ovaries glabrous: lip pubescent within: gland of the pollen scutelliform, orbicular, caudicle short: capsules ovoid: flowers purplish or dark lilac, lip much paler.

Iyamullay hills, 3000 feet, on branches of trees, flowering in June.

GENUS LVII. SACCOLABIUM.

Gynandria Monandria. *Sex: Syst.*

Deriv. From *Saccus* a bag, and *Labium* a lip.

Gen. Char. Perianth flattened out, spreading: sepals equalling the petals, lateral ones usually larger: lip undivided, spurred, accrete to the base of the column: column erect, half-terete, beak subulate: anther half-2-celled: pollen-masses 2, sub-globose, caudicle elongated, gland minute.—Epiphytous herbs, caulescent: leaves distichous, coriaceous, usually oblique at the apex: flowers axillary, racemose or solitary.

(1) S. Wightianum. *(Lindl.)*

Ident. Lindl. gen. and sp. p. 221.

Engrav. Wight's Icon. t. 917.

Spec. Char. Leaves channelled, narrow, obtuse, fleshy, almost equal at the apex: racemes erect, branched, longer than the leaves: sepals and petals ovate, obtuse: lip with a cylindrical obtuse bent spur: limb furnished at the base with a 2-lobed fleshy callosity, lateral lobes rounded: capsules 3-winged and 3-furrowed: flowers rose-coloured.

Trees on the Pulney mountains.

(2) S. micranthum. *(Lindl.)*

Ident. Lindl. l. c. p. 220.

Spec. Char. Leaves oblong-lorate, oblique at the apex, obtuse, deeply 2-lobed: racemes nodding, dense-flowered, shorter than the leaves: sepals sub-rotund-ovate, petals linear obtuse, spur of the lip roundish: lamina obovate, obtuse or acute, furnished at the base with a reflexed callosity: flowers violet, lip deep rose-coloured.

Silhet.

(3) S. densiflorum. *(Lindl.)*

Ident. Lindl. l. c. p. 220.

Spec. Char. Leaves lorate-oblong, oblique at the apex, obtuse, emarginate: racemes dense, cylindric, equal to or shorter than the leaves: flowers externally scabrous: upper sepal forked, lip funnel-shaped: top of the spur ventricose: lamina acuminate: sepals and petals rosy brick-colour internally, white in the middle, brown without: lip yellowish, pubescent in front.

Silhet, on trees and stones.

(4) S. GUTTATUM. *(Lindl.)*

Ident. Lindl. l. c.

Syn. Epidendrum retusum, *Linn.* Limodorum retusum, *Swarz Nov. act. Ups. vi.* 80. Aerides retusum, *Willd.* Sarcanthus guttatus, *Lindl. in Bot. Rep.* A. guttatum, *Roxb. flor. Ind. III. p.* 471.

Engrav. Wight l. c. t. 1745-6. Bot. Reg. t. 1443.—Rheede Mal. xii. t. I.

SPEC. CHAR. Leaves linear, channelled, denticulate, truncated or præmorse at the apex: racemes pendulous, densely many-flowered: posterior sepal ovate, lateral ones unequal-sided, about twice the breadth of the lanceolate acute petals: spur saccate, compressed, conical, hairy on the throat: lamina of the lip broad, obcordate-cuneate, spreading: flowers pale pink, dotted with deeper coloured spots, lip deeper pink.

Salsette. Concans. Peninsula. Chittagong. Assam. Flowering in the hot and rainy season.

(5) S. PRÆMORSUM. *(Lindl.)*

Ident. Lindl. l. c. p. 221.

Syn. Aerides præmorsum, *Willd.* Rhyncostylis præmorsa, *Blume.*

Engrav. Rheede Mal. xii. t. 2.

SPEC. CHAR. Leaves radical, linear, channelled, præmorse at the apex, cuspidate: racemes very long: spur of the lip funnel-shaped, obtuse, recurved: lamina ovate, acute.

Malabar.

(6) S. RINGENS. *(Lindl.)*

Ident. Lindl. l. c.

SPEC. CHAR. Raceme somewhat branched, straight, thickish, many-flowered: perianth ringent: sepals ovate, acute, petals a little smaller: spur of the lip funnel-shaped, obtuse, incurved: lamina 3-lobed, callous at the base: lateral lobes dwarf, rounded, middle one ovate, acute.

Near Madras.

(7) S. UNDULATUM. *(Lindl.)*

Ident. Lindl. l. c. p. 222.

SPEC. CHAR. Stemless: leaves narrow lorate, undulate, acuminate, oblique at the apex, obtuse: racemes short, many-flowered: sepals ovate-oblong, acute, petals twice as narrow: spur of the lip oblong, somewhat inflated at the top: lamina oblong, obtuse, very lightly 3-lobed: flowers small.

Silhet.

(8) S. CALCEOLARE. *(Lindl.)*

Ident. Lindl. l. c.

Syn. Gastrochilus calceolaris, *Don prod. Nep.* 32. Aerides calceolare, *Sm. in Rees. Cycl.*

SPEC. CHAR. Almost stemless: leaves lorate, acuminate, obliquely 2-toothed at the apex: corymbs many-flowered, short peduncled: sepals and petals obovate-oblong, obtuse: spur of the lip inflated, orbicular: lamina lunate, rotund, ciliated: sepals and petals yellow marked with purple spots, lip white, lamina dotted at the base yellow and scarlet.

Silhet.

(9) S. RAMOSUM. *(Lindl.)*

Ident. Lindl. l. c. p. 224.

SPEC CHAR. Leaves narrow, flat, arcuate, obliquely præmorse at the apex, eroded: racemes much branched, erect, longer than the leaves: branches divaricated, sepals obovate-oblong, obtuse: petals obovate, narrower: spur of the lip conical, sub-arcuate, obtuse, dentate at the margin: lamina oblong, rounded, with 2 lateral obsolete lobes: petals and sepals pale brick-colour, yellowish at the margins, lip white tinged with rose.

Delta of the Ganges on trees.

(10) S. VIRIDIFLORUM. *(Lindl.)*

Ident. Lindl. in proc. Linn. Soc. III. p. 36.

SPEC. CHAR. Stemless: leaves 2, oblong, flat, obtuse, emarginate: peduncle 2-sheathed, lateral, few-flowered, shorter than the leaves: sepals and petals unguiculate, obtuse: lip oval, equal to the incurved spur: flowers fleshy, greenish-white, lip white and rose colour.

Western ghauts.

(11) S. PANICULATUM. *(R. W.)*

Ident. Wight l. c. t. 1676.

SPEC. CHAR. Leaves strap-shaped, somewhat channelled, obliquely 2-lobed at the apex: panicles racemose, many-flowered, much longer than the leaves: sepals and petals sub-orbicular, obovate obtuse, petals smaller, lip ovate, attenuate towards the point, with 2 small sub-orbicular lobes at the base, and a fleshy gland-like appendage closing the throat of the spur: spur conical, about the length of the lip: flowers nearly white, lightly tinged with pink, lip streaked with crimson.

Iyamullay hills, on trees, flowering in September and October.

GENUS LVIII. TÆNIOPHYLLUM.

Gynandria Monandria. *Sex: Syst:*

Deriv. From *Taina*, a fillet or ribbon, and *Phyllon*, a leaf.

Gen. Char. Perianth connivent: sepals connate at the base, lateral ones adnate to the lip: lip spurred, growing to the base of the column, limb entire: spur inappendiculate: column dwarf, erect, rostellum ovate: anther half 2-valved: pollen masses 4, caudicle capillary, gland very minute.—Very minute, stemless epiphytes: leaves fascicled, linear, flat, fasciolate: flowers spiked, bracteolate, very minute.

(1) T. (?) Jerdonianum. *(R. W.)*

Ident. Wight's Icon. v. t. 1756.

Spec. Char. Leaves linear; spikes branched, many-flowered: bracts ovate, acute, exceeding the pedicel: sepals broad ovate: petals narrow, linear-lanceolate: spur large, saccate, lip undulate: gland largish, elongated.

Malabar, on branches of trees. Probably belongs to another genus.

GENUS LIX. ŒCEOCLADES.

Gynandria Monandria. *Sex: Syst:*

Deriv. From *Oikos*, a habitation, and *Klados*, a branch.

Gen. Char. Perianth spreading, or ringent, or connivent, free, not secund: lip free, sessile, articulate with the column, naked or bilamellate at the base, spurred: spur curved, often obconical, plate lobed, hooded or plaited, or concave: column often elongated, half-terete: anther 2-celled: pollen masses 2, furrowed, caudicle narrow, gland minute.—Stemless or caulescent epiphytes, sometimes pseudo-bulbous: leaves coriaceous, or seldom membranaceous, never plicate: flowers usually minute.

(1) Œ. PANICULATA. *(Lindl.)*

Ident. Lindl. gen. and sp. p. 236.

SPEC. CHAR. Caulescent: leaves oblong, 2-lobed at the apex, eroded: panicles lateral, twice longer than the leaves: upper sepal acute, galeate, shorter than the lateral ones: petals smaller than the upper sepal, acute: lip sinuate, cordate, long acuminated at the apex: spur short, ventricose: flowers minute, dirty coloured without, within tawny margined with yellow: lip yellow.

Goalpara. Silhet.

(2) Œ. AMPULLACEA. *(Lindl.)*

Ident. Lindl. in. Wall. Cat.

Syn. Saccolabium rubrum, *Lindl. gen. and sp. p.* 222.—Aerides ampullaceum, *Roxb.*

SPEC. CHAR. Leaves channelled, arcuate, 2-toothed at the apex: racemes erect, many-flowered: sepals and petals ovate: spur of the lip cylindric, obtuse, incurved, plate oval, acuminate, somewhat fleshy at the apex, bicorniculate at the base: flower rose-coloured.
Khasia hills, flowering in May and June.

(3) Œ. FLEXUOSA. *(Lindl.)*

Ident. Lindl. gen. and sp. p. 236.

SPEC. CHAR. Almost stemless: leaves linear-lorate, very oblique at the apex, somewhat 2-lobed, eroded: panicles flexuose, erect, divaricate: sepals and petals obovate-oblong: lip oblong, obtuse, repand, hairy within: spur conical, incurved, longer than the plate: teeth of the margin 2, acute: flowers minute, petals and sepals yellow, rose within: lip white palely fasciated with rose.

On trees at the Delta of the Ganges.

(4) Œ. PUSILLA. *(Lindl.)*

Ident. Lindl. l. c. p. 237.

SPEC. CHAR. Somewhat stemless: leaves obovate-oblong, equal at the apex, acute, 2-lobed, racemes ascending, slender, longer than the leaves: sepals obovate, obtuse: petals of the same form, smaller: lip hastate-triangular: spur infundibuliform, longer than the incurved lip: flowers minute.

Silhet forests.

GENUS LX. HABENARIA.

Gynandria Monandria. *Sex: Syst:*

Deriv. From *Habena,* a rein or thong, alluding to the long strap-shaped spur.

GEN. CHAR. Perianth of the Orchis: spur elongated: column free, reclinate: anther with the bases of the cells loosened, diverging, and adherent to the channels of the stigma: glands naked: beak flat, adnate to the anther: stigmatic processes fleshy, two, projecting beyond the anther, usually adnate to the mouth of the spur, various in form.

(1) H. LINDLEYANA. *(R. W.)*

Ident. Wight's Icon. t. 922.

SPEC. CHAR. Leaves few, distant, roundish ovate cordate, acuminated: raceme many-flowered: bracts leafy, equalling the flowers: posterior sepal truncated at the apex, lateral ones ovate acute: petals 2-parted, segments linear subulate, about equal: lip 3-parted, middle segment the longest.

Pulney mountains in pasture.

(2) H. HEYNEANA. *(Lindl.)*

Ident. Lindl. gen. and sp. p. 320.

Engrav. Wight l. c. t. 923.

SPEC. CHAR. Leaves narrow oval, acute: raceme lax, secund, few-flowered: bracts leafy, cucullated, somewhat ventricose, acuminated, longer than the flowers: lip 3-parted, segments about equal the length of the sepals, middle one narrow oval, lateral ones filiform, incurved: sepals and petals about the same length, connivent: spur pendulous, filiform, shorter than the ovary: flowers pale yellowish green.

Neilgherries in pasture.

(3) H. RARIFLORA. *(A. Rich.)*

Ident. Richard Ann. des Sc. xv. p. 70.

Engrav. Wight l. c. t, 924.

SPEC. CHAR. Leaves oblong-lanceolate, acute, plicate, occupying the lower part of the stem: stem 1—2-flowered: flowers long-peduncled, bracteate: bracts convolute, oval, acute, usually shorter than the peduncle: petals oval-oblong, acuminate, with a longer linear appendage: lip 3-parted, lateral segments the longest, linear-subulate, somewhat spreading: spur longer than the ovary, processes of the stigma long, obtuse.

Neilgherries, on clifts near Kaity Waterfall.

(4) H. LONGICALCARATA. *(A. Rich.)*

Ident. Rich. l. c.

Engrav. Wight l. c. t. 925.

SPEC. CHAR. Radical leaves numerous, oblong-elliptic, acute: upper leafless part of the stem clothed with the sheaths of numerous depauperated leaves: flowers 1—2, large, long peduncled: bracteas convolute, oval acuminated, length of the peduncle: sepals diverging, petals erect, lanceolate: lip trifid, middle segment lanceolate narrow: lateral ones broad, truncate crenate: spur very long, two or three times the length of the ovary and peduncle.

Pulney mountains. Neilgherries (rare).

(5) H. CRINIFERA. *(Lindl.)*

Ident. Lindl. l. c. p. 323.

Engrav. Wight l. c. t. 926.

SPEC. CHAR. Radical leaves oblong lanceolate, spike many-flowered: bracteas acuminate, about one-third the length of the ovaries: lip 4 times longer than the sepals, unguiculate at the base, limb 4-parted, lobes much acuminated, upper sepal and petals galeate: spur curved, compressed, clavate, longer than the lip.

Locality not given.

(6) H. MONTANA. *(A. Rich.)*

Ident. Rich. l. c. p. 73.

Engrav. Wight l. c. t. 927.

SPEC. CHAR. Stem erect, scaly at the base: leaves sheathing, oblong lanceolate, acute, sub-plicate, 4—5, perfect, approximate, the rest passing into long lanceolate very acute sheathing scales: racemes few, 4—5-flowered, lax: bracteas oblong-linear, very acute, shorter than the very long ovary: sepals glabrous: lip three cleft, middle lobe lanceolate acute, lateral ones broader, truncated, irregularly cut on the margins, stigmatic processes obtuse, short: spur longer than the ovary.

Pulney mountains. Kaity waterfall. Neilgherries.

(7) H. ROTUNDIFOLIA. *(Lindl.)*

Ident. Lindl. l. c. p. 306.—Dalz. Bomb. flor. p. 267.

SPEC. CHAR. Leaf solitary, radical, cordate, sub-rotund: raceme 3—5-flowered: petals 2-cleft, anterior segment subulate: lip 3-partite, divisions nearly equal, middle one broader: flowers white.

Between Ram Ghaut and Belgaum. Sewnere fort. Flowering in July and August.

(8) H. DIGITATA. *(Lindl.)*

Ident. Lindl. l. c. p. 307.—Dalz. l. c.

Syn. H. trinervia, *Wight's Icon. t.* 1701.

SPEC. CHAR. Leaves ovate-oblong, acute, undulate: raceme long, many-flowered: petals 2-parted, divisions linear: lip 3-partite, divisions linear: flowers greenish-white.

Island of Caranjah. Khasia hills. Flowering in July.

(9) H. GRAMINEA. *(Lindl.)*

Ident. Lindl. l. c. p. 318.

SPEC. CHAR. Leaves radical, linear, acuminated, much shorter than the straight filiform scape: raceme lax, few-flowered: bracts scale-shaped, acute, scarcely longer than the pedicel of the ovary: segments of the 3-parted lip the length of the sepals, filiform, nearly equal: spur compressed, clavate, the length of the ovary.

Khasia hills.

(10) H. VIRIDIFLORA. *(R. Br.)*

Ident. R. Brown prod. in Annot. Lindl. l. c. p. 319.

Syn. Orchis viridiflora. *Willd.*

Engrav. Wight l. c. t. 1705.

SPEC. CHAR. Leaves radical, narrow, acute, recurved: raceme lax, many-flowered: bracts subulate, the length of the pedicels: petals ovate, sepals larger, similar: lip 3-parted, a little longer than the sepals, lateral lobes horizontal, filiform, middle one longer: spur filiform, pendulous, the length of the ovary.

Peninsula.

(11) H. MARGINATA. *(Colebr.)*

Ident. Colebrook in Hook. Exot. Pl. t. 136.—Lindl. l. c. p. 320.—Dalz. l. c. p. 268.

SPEC. CHAR. Radical leaves cordate-oblong with a white margin: raceme dense, many-flowered: lip 3-parted, lateral divisions linear-acuminate, middle one lanceolate, obtuse, shorter: flowers deep yellow.

Caranjah. Ghauts around Jooneer. Bengal.

(12) H. CEPHALOTES. *(Lindl.)*

Ident. Lindl. l. c.

Engrav. Wight l. c. t. 1711.

Spec. Char. Leaves oblong-acuminate, channelled: raceme oblong, densely many-flowered: bracts hooded, acuminate, longer than the ovary: lip 3-lobed, pubescent, middle lobe linear-acute, lateral ones roundish, fimbriate-ciliate: upper sepals and petals converging, galeate, pubescent, anterior sepals sub-triangular, tomentose within, twice as large: spur pendulous, clavate at the apex, longer than the lip: flowers white.

Neilgherries, in pastures, flowering in August and September.

(13) H. plantaginea. *(Lindl.)*

Ident. Lindl. l. c. p. 323.

Syn. Orchis platyphyllos, *Roxb.*

Engrav. Wight l. c. t. 1710.

Spec. Char. Radical leaves oblong, acute or obtuse: spike lax, secund: bracts membranaceous, acute: lip 3-cleft, roundish, middle lobe linear, acute, lateral ones broad, denticulate, about equal: sepals about equal, ascending: spur filiform, pendulous, longer than the beaked ovary: flowers white, spur green.

Hills between Tinnevelly and Travancore. Iyamullay hills. Monghyr. Bombay.

(14) H. platyphylla. *(Spreng.)*

Ident. Spreng. Syst. III. 690.

Syn. Orchis plantaginea, *Roxb.*—O. platyphyllos, *Willd.*—O. Roxburghii, *Pers. Syn. II.* 503.

Engrav. Roxb. Cor. I. t. 37.—Wight l. c. t. 1709.

Spec. Char. Radical leaves orbicular, acute, horizontal: spike dense, many-flowered: bracts bristly-acuminated, half the length of the ovary: lip 3-toothed, middle tooth linear-acute, lateral ones short, toothless: sepals equal: spur filiform, very long, thickened at the point: flowers white.

Neilgherries. Iyamullays. Circars. Flowering from July to September.

(15) H. commelinifolia. *(Wall.)*

Ident. Lindl. l. c. p. 325.

Syn.. Orchis commelinifolia, *Roxb.*

Spec. Char. Leaves oblong-lanceolate, flat: spike loose, many-flowered: bracts leafy, acuminated, ciliated, nearly equal to the long-beaked ovary: lip 3-cleft, lateral segments bristly divaricate, middle one linear-acuminate, longer: petals oblong, and with upper hooded sepal galeate, lateral ones reflexed, triangular, roundish: spur filiform, clavate, twice longer than the ovary: flowers white.

Peninsula. Bengal. Flowering in July and August.

(16) H. affinis. *(R. W.)*

Ident. Wight l. c. t. 1707.

Spec. Char. Radical leaves elliptic-lanceolate, pointed, tapering below into a short sheathing petiole: stem clothed with ovate acuminated leafy scales: raceme lax, many-flowered: bracts acute, shorter than the ovary: sepals and petals about equal, posterior sepal galeate, anterior ones reflexed: lip 3-cleft, longer than the sepals: lateral lobes subulate, middle one narrow-lanceolate: spur incurved or even hooked at the point, filiform, a little more than the length of the ovary.

Belgaum. (?)

(17) H. foliosa. *(A. Rich.)*

Ident. A. Richard in Wight's Icon. v. t. 1700.

Spec. Char. Stem leafless at the base, sheathing, sheaths loose: leaves elliptic, acute, sheathing at the base, decreasing in size above: spikes dense, bracts ovate, acute, convolute at the base, longer than the ovary: sepals ovate, posterior one broader and shorter than the lanceolate lateral ones: petals deeply 2-cleft, anterior lobe thinner and shorter: lip 3-parted to the base, lobes filiform, subulate, equal: fleshy processes of the column obtuse: spur inflated, the length of the ovary: flowers greenish or dirty white, petals green.

Neilgherries, on elevated dry knolls among stunted grass, flowering in July and August.

(18) H. elliptica. *(R. W.)*

Ident. Wight l. c. t. 1706.

Spec. Char. Radical leaves elliptic-lanceolate, acute, attenuated at the base, those above bract-like, smaller, sub-cucullate, acuminate: bracts ovate, lanceolate, acuminate, acute, about the length of the ovary: raceme lax, many-flowered: sepals ovate, anterior ones reflexed, larger than the posterior one and petals: petals broad-ovate, obtuse, about the length of the anterior sepals: lip 3-cleft, lobes equal: spur filiform, pendulous, the length of the ovary: flowers greenish-white.

Pulney mountains, in pastures, flowering in September.

(19) H. ovalifolia. *(R.W.)*

Ident. Wight l. c. t. 1708.

Spec. Char. Radical leaves sheathing at the base, oval, acute above, attenuated below into the petiole: stem clothed with a few distant scales: racemes lax, many-flowered: bracts ovate, acute, shorter than the ovary: sepals and petals about equal, posterior ones galeate, anterior one reflexed, deeply 3-cleft, lobes lanceolate, lateral ones reflexed, pendulous, middle one ascending, erect: spur filiform: flowers dull pale pea-green.

Malabar and Annamally hills, flowering in July and August.

(20) H. fimbriata. *(R.W.)*

Ident. Wight l. c. t. 1712.

Spec. Char. Stem leafy throughout: leaves ovate-acuminate, channelled: raceme short, compact, many-flowered: bracts ovate, acuminate, the lower ones leafy, somewhat hooded, longer than the ovary, upper ones shorter: sepals broad, ovate-cordate, obtuse, posterior one galeate, lateral ones sub-oblique, spreading: lip orbicular, 3-lobed, middle lobe dentate, obtuse, lateral ones broad, half-orbicular, fimbriated on the margins: spur filiform, longer than the ovary: flowers white.

Neilgherries, flowering in July and August.

(21) H. Richardiana. *(R.W.)*

Ident. Wight l. c. t. 1713.

Spec. Char. Stem leafy at the base, scaly above: leaves ovate, somewhat sheathing, acute: raceme short, lax few-flowered: bracts ovate-lanceolate, acute, membranous, shorter than the ovary: sepals ovate, posterior one shorter, galeate, acute, lateral one oblique, reflexed, obtuse: petals broad ovate, obtuse, erect: lip 3-cleft, middle lobe dentate, entire, shorter than the lanceolate, diverging, acute, fimbriated lateral ones: spur filiform, pendulous, longer than the ovary: flowers white, diverging from the axis.

Neilgherries and Anamullies, on rocky ground among grass.

(22) H. decipiens. *(R.W.)*

Ident. Wight l. c. t. 927.

Spec. Char. Stem leafy at the base, furnished with lanceolate, much acuminated, acute scales: leaves linear-lanceolate, acute: raceme lax, 4—6-flowered: bracts ovate-lanceolate, long acuminate, shorter than the ovary: posterior sepal and shorter petals converging, galeate, lateral ones larger, oblique, falcate, reflexed: lip 3-cleft, middle lobes straight, pointed, rough, shorter than the broader half-lanceolate, denticulate lateral ones: ovary attenuated at both ends, ventricose in the middle, scarcely half the length of the filiform long spur: flowers white.

Pulney monntains. Malabar. Neilgherries.

(23) H. MODESTA. (*Dalz.*)

Ident. Dalz. in Hook. Journ. Bot. II. p. 262.

SPEC. CHAR. Stem leafy at the base, naked above: bracts half the length of the ovary: lip 3-cleft, lateral divisions linear-lanceolate, free, spreading, middle one ovate obtuse, shorter, introrse, cohering with the apices of the petals and the upper sepal, and concealing the column: spur filiform, a little longer than the ovary: flowers greenish-white.

Salsette, flowering in August.

(24) H. CARANJENSIS. (*Dalz.*)

Ident. Dalz. l. c.

SPEC. CHAR. Lower leaves somewhat rounded, upper oblong-lanceolate, 3-nerved: bracts acuminated, shorter than the ovary: upper sepal rounded, petals half-ovate, obtuse: lip 3-parted, middle division oblong, rather obtuse, lateral ones shorter, cuneate, truncated: spur clavate, shorter than the ovary: flowers small, yellow.

Island of Caranjah.

(25) H. CANDIDA. (*Dalz.*)

Ident. Dalz. l. c.

SPEC. CHAR. Stem 1 foot, leafy: leaves sheathing at the base, linear-lanceolate, acute, mucronate, 3—5-nerved, changing above into floral bracts, which are longer than the ovary: upper sepal ovate, obtuse, lateral ones oblong: petals entire, oblong, rather acute: lip 3-cleft, middle one broad-lanceolate, obtuse, lateral linear-falcate, all the same length: spur slender, filiform, shorter than the ovary: flowers few, white.

Southern Concan.

(26) H. SUAVEOLENS. (*Dalz.*)

Ident Dalz. l. c.

SPEC. CHAR. Stem half a foot, leafy only at the base: leaves lanceolate, acute, erect, folded, half the length of the scape: scape angled, 1-bracteate in the middle, few-flowered: floral bracts foliaceous, ovate-lanceolate, acute, sheathing, as long as the ovary:

upper sepal broad-lanceolate, rather acute: lateral sepals falcate, acute, deflexed in flowering: petals and sepals alike: lip 3-cleft: middle segment linear-acute, lateral broader and shorter, obliquely truncated and denticulate at the apex: spur pendulous, filiform, as long as the ovary.

Vingorla and Malwan.

(27) H. DIPHYLLA. *(Dalz.)*

Ident. Dalz. l. c.

Syn. H. Jerdoniana, *Wight Icon. t.* 1715.

SPEC. CHAR. Six inches in height: leaves two, radical, fleshy, orbicular: cordate at the base, obscurely 7-nerved, pressing flat on the ground: cauline bracts subulate, floral ones half the length of the ovary: upper sepal broad-ovate, 3-nerved, lateral ovate-acute, spreading: petals linear, falcate, acute: lip 3-divided, segments filiform, lateral longer, ascending, reflexed, spirally twisted at the apex: spur pendulous, filiform, shorter than the ovary: flowers few, distant, greenish-white.

Southern Concan.

GENUS LXI. DIPLOMERIS.

Gynandria Monandria. *Sex: Syst:*

Deriv. From *Diplos* double, and *Meros* a part, alluding to the lip.

GEN. CHAR. Perianth campanulate, spurred: sepals smaller than the petals and undivided lip: anther horizontal, bases of the cells prolonged, free, distant: glands naked: stigma with the upper lip (beak) very large, membranaceous, dilated, flat: two processes fleshy, collateral, stretched out, sometimes cohering, simulating a lower lip.—Low few-leaved herbs: stems naked or 1-scaled: bracts hooded, somewhat solitary: roots bearing tubercles.

(1) D. PULCHELLA. *(Don.)*

Ident. Don prodr. Nep. 26. Lindl. gen. and sp. p. 330.

Syn. Paragnathis pulchella, *Spreng.*—Diplochilos longifolium, *Lindl. in Wall. Cat.*

Engrav. Bot. Reg. t. 1499.

SPEC. CHAR. Stem 2—3-leaved, somewhat 2-flowered: leaves ensiform, glabrous: bracts ovate, cucullate, acute: sepals ovate-lanceolate, acute: petals longer, twice as large, ovate-oblong: lip obcordate, mucronate, flat: spur straight, compressed: anther almost resupinate.

Khasia hills.

GENUS LXII. DISPERIS.

Gynandria Monandria. *Sex: Syst:*

Gen. Char. Perianth ringent: upper sepal cohering with the petals into a helmet, lateral ones saccate, patent, free, or connate: lip clawed, adnate to the face of the column, ascending between the lobes of the anther, appendage usually villous at the apex, inflexed above the column: anther resupinate, or supine, even erect: glands naked: stigma narrow, transverse, divaricated, two arms cartilaginous, often twisted.—Small herbs, usually villous: stems 1-few-flowered, 1—2-leaved: roots testiculate and tuberous.

(1) D. Neilgherrensis. *(R. W.)*

Ident. Wight's Icon. v. t. 1719.

Spec. Char. Stem erect, 3—4-flowered: leaves cordate, acute, crenate, stem-clasping: posterior sepals and petals cohering, reflexed on the margins, lateral sepals spathulate, spreading, undulate on the margin, sub-cuspidate, pubescent at the base: lip fleshy, ascending, concealing the column, dilated, deeply 2-lobed above, ending below in an orbicular cuspidate appendage: flowers pale reddish-white, spotted with crimson points.

Neilgherries, in woods on large mossy stones, flowering in July and August.

(2) D. tripetaloidea. *(Lindl.)*

Ident. Lindl. gen. and sp. p. 371.

Engrav. Wight l. c. t. 930.

Spec. Char. Stem erect, 2—4-flowered: leaves cordate-oblong, acute: sepals glabrous, lateral ones pendulous, sessile, connate at the base, pitted behind the base: lip filiform: pubescent, dilated-round at the apex, appendage very small, concave.

Coonoor. Goodaloor Ghaut. Neilgherries.

GENUS LXIII. POGONIA.

Gynandria Monandria. *Sex: Syst:*

Deriv. From *Pogon* a beard, alluding to the fringed lip of the flowers.

Gen. Char. Perianth irregular, sub-ringent, spreading, sepals and petals free, of the same or different shapes: lip free, without callosities, parallel with the elongated column, petaloid, 3-lobed, disc lamellate, crested or villous: column elongated, clavate, marginate, or half-terete, apex somewhat auricled: anther stalked, 2-celled: pollen masses 2, furrowed.—Terrestrial herbs: tubercles spherical, terminating a descending stem.

(1) P. JULIANA. *(Wall.)*

Ident. Lindl. gen. and sp. p. 414.

Syn. Epipactis Juliana, *Roxb.*

SPEC. CHAR. Leaf cordate, 7-nerved: whole plant stained purple: scape 1-flowered: lateral lobes of the lip dwarf, rounded, middle one somewhat rhomboid, quite entire, acute, hairy at the base: sepals and petals linear-lanceolate, purplish-green: lip much broader, white or very pale pink, mottled with bright red.

Bengal, in grass in shady places, flowering in June.

(2) P. CARINATA. *(Lindl.)*

Ident. Lindl. l. c.

Syn. Epipactis carinata, *Roxb.*

Engrav. Wight's Icon. t. 1720.

SPEC. CHAR. Leaf cordate, 7-nerved: scape many-flowered: lip rhomboid, somewhat 3-lobed, veined, woolly within, middle lobe crenate: flowers large, drooping: sepals and petals unilateral, linear-lanceolate, pale green: lip with purple veins and spots upon a pale greenish yellow ground: bracts ensiform, as long as the peduncle and ovary together.

Bengal, in grass. Coorg. Concan jungles. Flowering in December and January.

(3) P. BIFLORA. *(R. W.)*

Ident. Wight l. c. v. t. 1758—2.

SPEC. CHAR. Scape about 2-flowered: sepals and petals lanceolate: lip obovate-rhomboid, obsoletely 3-lobed, glabrous: lateral lobes short, obtuse, middle one large, undulate, slightly retuse at the apex: lip pale pink, sepals and petals white.

Wynaud.

(4) P. PLICATA. *(Lindl.)*

Ident. Lindl. l. c. p. 415.

Syn. Epipactis plicata, *Roxb.*

SPEC. CHAR. Leaves rusty-coloured above, greener beneath, bristly: scape usually 2-flowered, sheathed by 2—3 scales: lip sub-cylindric, margins incurved into a tube connecting the column: lamina 2-lobed: flowers yellowish-green, lip rose-coloured.

Bengal, under the shade of Bamboos, flowering in June. Roxburgh states that the plant is propagated by suckers from the apex of the petiole, just below the leaf, and under the surface of the soil.

(5) P. FLABELLIFORMIS. *(Lindl.)*

Ident. Lindl. l. c. Dalz. Bomb. flor. p. 270.

Syn. *Gaudich. in it. Freyc. p.* 422, *t.* 35. Nervilia Aragoana.

SPEC. CHAR. Leaves cordate-subrotund, repand, membranaceous, many-nerved: scape many-flowered, racemose: flowers at length pendulous: lateral lobes of the 3-lobed lip dwarf, middle one oblong, obtuse, undulated, crisp, hairy: flowers numerous, apparently white.

Concan. Dharwar, in thickest and shadiest forests.

GENUS LXIV. VANILLA.

Gynandria Monandria. *Sex: Syst:*

Deriv. An alteration of *Vaynilla*, which is a diminutive of *Vaina*, a Spanish word signifying a sheath, in reference to the cylindrical pod being like the sheath of a knife.

GEN. CHAR. Perianth spreading at the apex only, articulated with the ovary, usually channelled: sepals and petals almost equal, of the same shape, free at the base: lip connate with the column, entire, concave, bearded in the middle: column elongated, wingless: anther terminal, with a lid: pollen masses two, 2-lobed, granular: fruit siliqua-shaped, fleshy, dehiscing from the side, placentæ 3—6, seed-bearing: seeds globose, testa crustaceous, fragile.—Climbing herbs: stems terete: leaves articulated with the stem, fleshy, sub-cordate at the base: flowers fleshy: fruit in some species aromatic, abounding in essential oil.

(1) V. APHYLLA. *(Blume.)*

Ident. Lindl. gen. and sp. p. 436.—Blume bijdr. 422.

Engrav. Wight's Icon. t. 931.—Rumph. amb. I. t. 68.

SPEC. CHAR. Leafless: peduncles 3 or many-flowered: limb of the lip undulated, obtuse, bearded in the middle: anthers 2-lobed: fruit cylindrical: flowers green, lip violet, fragrant.

Trevandrum, Travancore, climbing among bushes.

GENUS LXV. TRIPLEURA.

Gynandria Monandria. *Sex: Syst:*

GEN. CHAR. Perianth flattened, cruciate, as if 4-leaved, upper sepal broad, agglutinated to the petals, lateral ones linear very patent: lip posterior, free, concave: column terete, very short, furnished behind with two membranaceous horn-shaped processes: anther sub-rotund, apiculate, terminal.

(1) T. PALLIDA. *(Lindl.)*

Ident. Lindl. gen. and sp. p. 452.

SPEC. CHAR. Terrestrial, glabrous, caulescent: stem very slender, erect, lower leaves withered, remote, upper ones apparently clustered, linear, acute, revolute at the edges: scape smooth, terminal, with 4 membranous acuminate scales, not sheathing at the base: flowers very small, smooth, white, spike dense, cylindric.

Silhet.

GENUS LXVI. CNEMIDIA.

Gynandria Monandria. *Sex: Syst:*

GEN. CHAR. Perianth connivent: lateral sepals half-connate, base produced into a spurious spur: lip posterior, free, spurred, channelled, acuminate: column terete, acuminated at the apex, beak acuminate, 2-cleft: anther subulate: pollen masses 2, caudicle subulate.—Caulescent, leafy, stiff, branched herbs: stems or branches 2-leaved, loosely sheathed at the base: leaves broad, plaited, sheathing, as if opposite: racemes dense, peduncle terminal, altogether naked, shorter than the leaves: bracts stiff.

(1) C. ANGULOSA. *(Lindl.)*

Ident. Lindl. gen. and sp. p. 463.

SPEC. CHAR. Leaves ovate-oblong, acuminate: sepals ovate, acute, keeled, lateral ones connate beyond the middle.

Khasia hills. Courtallum.

GENUS LXVII. SPIRANTHES.

Gynandria Monandria. *Sex: Syst:*

Deriv. From *Speira* a spiral, and *Anthos* a flower, alluding to the arrangement of the flowers.

GEN. CHAR. Perianth ringent: lateral sepals placed on the lip, oblique at the base and decurrent into the ovary, dorsal one agglutinated to the petals: lip affixed to the foot of the prolonged column, clawed, seldom sessile, oblong, usually dilated at the apex, sometimes 3-lobed, always furnished with 2 callosities below the middle, oppressed to the column, and adhering to it the margins bent inwards: column obliquely terminating the top of the ovary, terete: stigma ovate, prolonged into an acuminate, afterwards 2-cleft, or obtuse emarginate, seldom horny undivided beak: anther dorsal, acuminate or obtuse, sometimes apiculated with a membrane, 2-celled : clinandrium membranaceous on both sides, margined : pollen masses 2, powdery, 2-partite, fixed to a common oblong gland.—Terrestrial herbs, usually small-flowered, and glandular-pubescent: roots fascicled: leaves radical, sometimes caulescent, sometimes altogether deficient: flowers spiked, spiral.

(1) S. Australis. *(Lindl.)*

Ident. Lindl. gen. and sp. p. 464.

Syn. Neottia crispata, *Blume. bijdr.* 406. N. flexuosa, *Smith in Rees Cycl. (var.)* S. flexuosa, *Lindl. in Bot. Reg.* 823. *Spreng. syst. (var.)* N. Australis, *R. Brown prod.* 319. *Don flor. Nep.* 27. *(var.)* N. parviflora, *Smith in Rees (var.)* S. parviflora, *Lindl. l. c. (var.)* S. pudica, *Lindl. Coll. Bot. t.* 30. *Spreng. syst. (var.)* Aristotelia Spiralis, *Lour. flor. Coch. (var.)* Neottia Sinensis, *Pers. syn. (var.)*

Engrav. Wight's Icon. t. 1724.

Spec. Char. Radical and cauline leaves linear or linear-lanceolate, obtuse or acute, sometimes ensiform : flowers spiral, glabrous or oftener pubescent: bracts ovate, longer than the ovary: lip oblong, dilated at the apex, crisp, pubescent above : flowers white.

Neilgherries, in pastures. Western Ghauts. Flowering from June till October.

GENUS LXVIII. ZEUXINE.

Gynandria Monandria. *Sex: Syst:*

Gen. Char. Perianth ringent: lateral sepals placed on the lip, seldom connate, dorsal one convex at the base, agglutinated with the petals: lip ventricose at the base, connate to the column, bicallous within, limb undivided, shorter than the sepals, often fleshy : column short, terete, glandular swollen on both sides (always?), anther dorsal, 2-celled, clinandrium usually membranaceous margined: pollen masses granular 2, 2-lobed, caudicle common.—Terrestrial caulescent herbs: leaves linear, scattered: spike terminal, sessile between the leaves or scarcely peduncled.

(1) Z. sulcata. *(Lindl.)*

Ident. Lindl. gen. and sp. p. 485.

Syn. Pterygodium sulcatum, *Roxb. flor. Ind. III. p.* 452.

Engrav. Bot. Reg. t. 1618.

Spec. Char. Leaves linear-lanceolate, acuminate, aggregated, equal to the stem: spike dense, sub-sessile: lip reniform at the apex: flowers small, white.

In pastures near Calcutta; flowering in the cold season.

(2) Z. brevifolia. *(R. W.)*

Ident. Wight's Icon. v. t. 1725.

Spec. Char. Leaves narrow-linear, lower ones slightly sheathed: spike short, compact: bracts linear-acute, longer than the flowers: limb of the lip sub-orbicular, cuspidate.

Mysore, flowering in the cold season.

(3) Z. robusta. *(R. W.)*

Ident. Wight l. c. t. 1726.

Spec. Char. Leaves broad at the base, stem-clasping, or slightly sheathing, approximated, 3-nerved, acute: spike long: bracts broad, foliaceous, longer than the flowers.

Mysore, flowering in the cold season.

(4) Z. emarginata. *(Lindl.)*

Ident. Lindl. l. c.

Syn. Adenostylis emarginata, *Blume. bijdr.*

Spec. Char. Leaves linear-acute, scattered: spike dense, sub-sessile: lip dilated at the apex, emarginate, bright yellow: flowers white: stems reddish.

Peninsula.

(5) Z. goodyeroides. *(Lindl.)*

Ident. Lindl. l. c. p. 486.

Spec. Char. Leaves ovate-lanceolate, petioled, pale in the middle: sheaths of the scape 2, distant, petaloid, acuminate: spike pubescent, rare: lateral sepals very patent: limb of the lip membranaceous, sub-rotund.

Assam (?)

GENUS LXIX. MONOCHILUS.

Gynandria Monandria. *Sex: Syst:*

Deriv. From *Monos* single, and *Cheilos* a lip.

Gen. Char. Perianth conical, connivent: lateral sepals free, placed on the lip, dorsal one agglutinated to the petals: lip connate with the column, ventricose at the base, callous within, limb membranaceous, flattened out, cleft, much longer than the sepals: column short, terete, glandular swollen on either side: anther dorsal, 2-celled: clinandrium marginate: pollen masses 2, granular, 2-lobed, gland and caudicle common.

(1) M. longilabre. *(Lindl.)*

Ident. Lindl. gen. and sp. p. 487. Dalz. Bomb. flor. p. 271.

Syn. M. affinis, *Wight's Icon. t.* 1728.

Spec. Char. Stem pilose: leaves ovate, petioled, nerved: scape furnished with sheathing scales: spike secund, few-flowered: bracts roundish, hooded, acuminate, membranaceous, as long as the pubescent ovary: sepals ovate-acute: petals rounded at the apex: lobes of the lip oblong, coarsely crenate with two involute subulate callosities: flowers white.

On Chorla Ghaut. Courtallum. Flowering in August and December.

GENUS LXX. CHEIROSTYLIS.

Gynandria Monandria. *Sex: Syst:*

Gen. Char. Flowers ringent: sepals all connate, lateral ones placed on the lip: petals agglutinate to the dorsal sepal: lip free cleft, keeled at the base, bicallous within: column erect, terete, free, processes or arms two, free or adnate, erect or stretched out from the increased front: stigma 2-parted: anther dorsal, acuminate: pollen masses four, powdery, adnate to the linear acute gland.—Terrestrial herbs, very small: leaves petioled, ovate: scape distantly sheathed: spikes few-flowered.

(1) C. flabellata. *(R. W.)*

Ident. Wight's Icon. v. t. 1727. Dalz. Bomb. flor. p. 271.

Syn. Goodyera flabellata, *Rich. in Ann. Soc. Nat.* xv. *t.* 12.

Spec. Char. Leaves brownish, ovate, 3-nerved, acute, reticulately veined: scape pilose, few-flowered at the apex: lip orbicular, limb spreading, deeply 2-cleft: lobes digitately 4—5-cleft, claw with 2 callosities at the base: flowers white.

Chorla Ghaut. Neilgherries. Coonoor. Flowering in the cold season. The leaves are almost transparent, and most beautifully veined.

(2) C. PUSILLA. *(Lindl.)*

Ident. Lindl. gen. and sp. p. 489.

SPEC. CHAR. Very small: leaves ovate, aristate-acuminate: flowers quite glabrous: segments of the lip oblong, toothed at the apex: petals clawed, rhomboid at the apex: arms of the column ascending, adnate: flowers in pairs.

Khasia hills, among moss.

GENUS LXXI. GOODYERA.

Gynandria Monandria. *Sex: Syst.*

GEN. CHAR. Sepals herbaceous, lateral ones placed on the lip, dorsal one agglutinated with the petals into a helmet: lip free or connate with the column, ventricose or concave, without callosities, undivided: column dwarf, straight, terete: stigma membranaceous, rounded or beaked: anther dorsal: pollen masses two, sectile.—Terrestrial, caulescent herbs: roots succulent, fibrous: leaves narrowed into a sheathed petiole: flowers spicate, usually pubescent.

(1) G. PROCERA. *(Hooker.)*

Ident. Hooker Exotic Flora, t. 39. Lindl. gen. and sp. p. 493.

Syn. Neottia procera, *Ker. in Bot. Reg. t.* 639.

SPEC. CHAR. Caulescent, glabrous: leaves lanceolate, acuminate, shorter than the scape: spike dense, elongated, cylindric: bracts ovate acuminate longer than the ovary: flowers sub-globose: sepals and petals roundish convex, obtuse: lip ventricose, callous at the apex, apiculate, villous within: upper angles of the column acuminated: flowers white.

Silhet, flowering in the cold season. Burliar, Eastern slopes of the Neilgherries. Courtallum. Malabar.

(2) G. OVALIFOLIA. *(R. W.)*

Ident. Wight's Icon. v. t. 1730.

SPEC. CHAR. Roots creeping: leaves ovate-acuminate, or oval, short-pointed: petiole dilated: spikes long, slender, thinnish, pubescent: lower bracts as long as the ovaries, acute: sepals somewhat pubescent, ovate-acute: lip shorter than the sepals, 3-toothed at the point, furnished within with a fimbriated appendage: ovary cylindrical, pilose: flowers white with a reddish tinge externally.

Courtallum, in dense forests, flowering in August and September.

GENUS LXXII. TROPIDIA.

Gynandria Monandria. *Sex: Syst:*

Gen. Char. Perianth closed: sepals herbaceous, glabrous, lateral ones larger, obliquely produced at the base, like a false spur: dorsal one shorter, free from the petals: petals free, resembling the dorsal sepal: lip free, sessile, ventricose, constricted at the apex, and abruptly expanded into a hooded small limb, within the margin increased at both sides by a thin plate: column elongated, terete, free: beak acute: lower lip of the stigma thickened: clinandrium excavated far below the stigma: anther dorsal, parallel with the stigma, keeled, muticous: pollen masses four, coherent into two powdery 2-lobed masses: caudicle short.—Herb with the appearance of grass: leaves sessile in a long sheath, altogether grassy: spike small, conical, sub-sessile: flowers minute, green.

(1) T. curculigoides. *(Lindl.)*

Ident. Lindl. gen. and sp. p. 497.

Spec. Char. Glabrous: stem straight, thin, striated, scarcely solid: leaves linear-lanceolate, very acuminate, sessile, upper ones smaller, gradually changing into bracts: spike many-flowered: upper bracts bristly: lateral sepals ovate-lanceolate, semi-cordate at the base, upper one shorter and narrower: petals lanceolate, sub-falcate: flowers green.

Khasia hills.

GENUS LXXIII. ANŒCTOCHILUS.

Gynandria Monandria. *Sex: Syst:*

Deriv. From *Anoiktos* opened, and *Cheilos* a lip, alluding to the spreading apex of that organ.

Gen. Char. Perianth ringent: upper sepal agglutinated with the petals into a helmet, lateral ones spreading, unequal at the base, resting on the lip: lip connate at the base with the column, ventricosely spurred, claw stiff channelled, bent inwards, fimbriate: limb 2-lobed, spreading: callosities two at the bottom of the scrotum: column short, margins membranaceous, dilated, involute, resembling a bilamellate appendage: stigma bicallous at the base: pollen masses two, powdery, somewhat 2-lobed, caudicles short, gland oblong.—Herbs: roots fibrous, rhizome filiform, subterraneous: stems leafy: leaves nerved, of different colours, veins usually shining with gold: flowers spiked, loose, glandularly hairy.

(1) A. Roxburghii. *(Lindl.)*

Ident. Lindl. gen. and sp. p. 499.

Syn. Chrysobaphus Roxburghii, *Wall. tent. flor. nep. t.* 27.

Engrav. Wall. l. c.—Bot. Reg. t. 2010.

Spec. Char. Leaves painted, ovate, acute, of two colours: spike many-flowered and with the sepals pubescent: margin of the lip bristly, many-cleft, sagittate at the base: bag conical, emarginate.

Shady forests in Silhet. Khasia. Assam.

(2) A. brevilabris. *(Lindl.)*

Ident. Lindl. l. c.

Spec. Char. Leaves painted, rotund-ovate, of two colours: spike lax, many-flowered, hairy: bracts spreading, ovate, bristly acute, shorter than the ovary: sepals pubescent: margin of the lip pinnatifidly toothed, lamina shorter, sagittate at the base: bag marginate.

Assam.

(3) A. lanceolatus. *(Lindl.)*

Ident. Lindl. l. c.

Spec. Char. Leaves ovate-lanceolate, of one colour: spike dense, many-flowered, hairy: bracts erect, longer than the flowers: sepals glabrous: margin of the lip interruptedly dentate-fimbriate, the length of the lamina, bag double.

Assam. Khasia.

(4) A. setaceus. *(Blume.)*

Ident. Lindl. l. c.

Engrav. Wight's Icon. v. t. 1731.—Bot. Reg. t. 2010.

Spec. Char. Leaves coloured, ovate or oval acute, two-coloured, dark brown, traversed with netted golden coloured veins: spikes straight, few-flowered, and like the sepals, pubescent: lip many-cleft, bristly on the margins, rounded at the base: bag conical, emarginate: sepals greenish-white, edged and tipped with red, lip white.

Travancore mountains at 4,500 feet. I believe this which I have found at the above locality, to be identical with the Ceylon plant.

GENUS LXXIV. CYPRIPEDIUM.

Gynandria Diandria. *Sex: Syst:*

Deriv. From *Kupris* a name of Venus, and *Pedion* a slipper, Venus or Ladies' slipper.

Gen. Char. Perianth patent: lateral sepals connate or distinct, superposed on the lip: petals free, usually narrower: lip inflated, margin auricled on both sides, bent inwards: column dwarf: stamens 3, one sterile central dilated inflexed, two fertile lateral: anthers hidden under the sterile stamen, sub-rotund, 2-celled: pollen pulticeo-granular: style somewhat free, terete, terminated by a disk-shaped stigma.—Terrestrial herbs: leaves radical or cauline, coriaceous or plaited: flowers racemose or panicled, showy.

(1) C. venustum. *(Wall.)*

Ident. Lindl. gen. and sp. p. 530.

Engrav. Bot. Mag. t. 2129.—Hooker Exot. flor. t. 35.

Spec. Char. Stemless: leaves coriaceous, ligulate, channelled, spotted, somewhat scabrous: scape pubescent: bract more than twice shorter than the ovary: sterile stamen cuneate: anterior sepal lanceolate, shorter than the lip, dorsal one sub-rotund-ovate, acuminate: petals linear-oblong, obtuse, bearded: mouth of the oblong lip bent inwards at both sides, and increased by an acute erect lobe: flowers greenish, inside of the petals purple, lip yellowish, netted with green veins.

Silhet, flowering in the cold season.

(2) C. insigne. *(Wall.)*

Ident. Lindl. l. c.

Engrav. Lindl. Coll. Bot. t. 32.—Hooker Exot. flor. t. 34.—Lodd. Bot. Cab. t. 1321.

Spec. Char. Stemless: leaves coriaceous, linear-ligulate, weak, channelled at the base: scape tomentose: bract almost equal to the ovary: sterile stamen obcordate, pubescent: anterior sepal obtuse, almost equalling the lip, dorsal one forked oblong, undulated, emarginate: petals linear-obovate, sub-undulate, bearded at the base, pubescent externally: mouth of the oblong lip bent inwards at both sides, and increased by an erect obtuse lobe: flowers pale green: upper sepal large, broad, white-edged and spotted with brownish-purple: lip deep yellow.

Khasia hills. Silhet. Flowering in the cold season.

Note.—I discovered a new species, C. Drurii, *(Beddome,)* on the Travancore mountains at 4—5000 feet, which flowered in March, 1867. The Genus had hitherto been, unrepresented in Southern India.

ORDER CLXIX. BURMANNIACEÆ.

Perianth tubular, adhering, 6-toothed, three inner teeth smaller, sometimes the outer ones winged or keeled at the back: stamens 3, inserted in the tube opposite the petals: anthers sessile, 2-celled, opening transversely: connectivum 2-lobed, fleshy: ovary adherent, 1—3-celled, with three simple and parietal, or double and axile placentæ: ovules very numerous: capsule surmounted by the persistent calyx, 1—3-celled, dehiscing vertically or horizontally, or indehiscent, or by a single cleft into a boat-shaped pericarp: seeds numerous, very small: testa loose or tight: albumen none.—Herbaceous plants: leaves tufted, radical, or wanting: stem slender, naked: flowers terminal, sessile upon a 2—3-branched rachis, or solitary.

GENUS I. BURMANNIA.

Triandria Monogynia. *Sex: Syst:*

Deriv. Named in honour of J. D. Burmann, a famous Dutch botanist and author.

GEN. CHAR. Tube of the perianth connate with the ovary, tapering or 3-winged, limb 6-cleft: stamens opposite the inner segments of the perianth: ovary 3-celled: style filiform, stigmas 3, globose, dilated or 2-lobed: capsule 3-celled incompletely loculicidally 3-valved at the apex: seeds fusiform, slightly striated.

(1) B. TRIFLORA. *(Roxb.)*

Ident. Roxb. flor. Ind. II. 117.—Dalz. Bomb. flor. p. 271.

SPEC. CHAR. Flowers 1—3 in a terminal head: scape 4—6 inches, filiform, quadrangular with 3—4-remote stem-clasping pointed bracts: flowers minute, purple: wings of the perianth half-oval.

At the hot-springs, near Mahar.

ORDER CLXX. MUSACEÆ.

Flowers spathaceous: perianth 6-parted, adherent, petaloid, in two rows, irregular: stamens 6, inserted on the middle of the divisions, some abortive: anthers linear, turned inwards, 2-celled, usually with a membranous petaloid crest: ovary inferior, 3-celled, many (rarely 3) seeded: ovules anatropal: style simple: stigma 3-lobed: fruit either a 3-celled capsule with a loculicidal dehiscence, or succulent and indehiscent: seeds sometimes surrounded by hairs: embryo orthotropal, oblong-linear, or mushroom-shaped: radicle next the hilum: albumen mealy.—Stemless or nearly stemless plants: leaves sheathing at the base, usually very large, with finely paralleled' veins diverging from the mid-rib to the margin.

GENUS I. MUSA.

Hexandria Monogynia. *Sex: Syst:*

Deriv. From Mooza the Indian name of the fruit.

GEN. CHAR. Perianth epigynous, 2-lipped, lower lip tubular, 5-lobed at the apex, upper concave: stamens 6, one abortive: ovary inferior 3-celled: ovules many in two rows, horizontal: style thick: stigma funnel-shaped clavate, shortly 6-lobed: berry oblong, angular, 3-celled: seeds numerous, nestling in pulp.

(1) M. ORNATA. *(Roxb.)*

Ident. Roxb. flor. Ind. I. 666.

Syn. M. rosacea, *Jacq. Hort. Schoenbr. iv. and t.* 445.

Engrav. Bot. Cab. t. 615.—Reg. ix. t. 706.

SPEC. CHAR. Root perennial, stems 3—5 feet: leaves linear-oblong: spadix erect: spathes deciduous, 3-flowered, lanceolate: fruit linear-oblong, slightly incurved, small: seeds black, tubercled: pulp none: flowers purple yellow-white.

Precipitous crags, Western coast. Chittagong.

(2) M. SUPERBA. *(Roxb.)*

Ident. Roxb. l. c.

Engrav. Roxb. Cor. III. t. 223.—Wight's Icon. t. 2017-18.

SPEC. CHAR. Root bulbous with an annual short spurious stem: leaves petioled lanceolate: spadix terminal, drooping: spathes broad-cordate, smooth, ferruginous: flowers numerous in each spathe: berry oblong, and dry when ripe: flowers pale.

Dindigul. Western coast. Flowering in the rains.

(3) M. Paradisiaca. *(Linn.)*

Ident. Spreng. syst. I. p. 833.

Syn. M. sapientum, *Roxb. l. c. p.* 663.

Engrav. Roxb. Cor. III. t. 275.—Rheede Mal. I. t. 12, 13, 14. —Rumph. Amb. I. t. 60.

Spec. Char. Spadix drooping, spathes ovate, deciduous, smooth, crimson inside, 6 or 8 of those nearest the spadix embracing a double row of female-hermaphrodite flowers, the rest expanding in succession embracing the male-hermaphrodite ones, always deciduous: outer sepal unequally 5-toothed at the apex, inner one smaller, both deeply concave, emarginate at the apex, incurved and ensiform at the point: ovary oblong, 3-celled, with 4—6 rows of ovules in each cell: style cylindric: stigma 3-lobed, large, clammy: fruit oblong, tapering to each end, 5-ribbed, 3-celled, partitions soft and pulpy: seeds numerous, round, turbinate, tubercled.

Forests of Chittagong. The common cultivated plantain is a variety of this species.

ORDER CLXXI. MARANTACEÆ.

Calyx 3-sepaled: corolla tubular, irregular, 2-whorled, outer whorl 3-parted, nearly equal, inner one very irregular, one of the lateral segments usually coloured, dissimilar to the rest: stamens 3, distinct, one lateral, one fertile: filament petaloid, entire or 2-lobed, 1 lobe antheriferous: anther 1-celled, opening lengthways: ovary 1—3-celled, ovules solitary, erect, and campylotropal, or numerous, anatropal and attached to the axis of each cell: style petaloid: stigma hollow, hooded, curved inwards: fruit a capsule: seeds round exarillate: albumen hard: embryo straight, naked: radicle next the hilum.—Herbs, not aromatic: rhizome usually tuberous, abounding in starch: stem often branched: leaves simple, sheathing, with a single mid-rib: flowers on spikes, racemes or panicles, terminal or radical, proceeding from among spathaceous bracts, usually in pairs.

GENUS I. PHRYNIUM.

Monandria Monogynia. *Sex: Syst:*

Deriv. From *Phrynos* a frog, the plants inhabit marshes.

GEN. CHAR. Calyx 3-leaved: lip of the 6-parted corolla smaller than the segments, 2-lobed: filament short, inserted on the inner lateral segment of the corolla: anther terminal: ovary inferior, 3-celled: ovules solitary, basilar, campylotropal: style hooked above, stigma incurved: capsule 3-celled, loculicidally 3-valved: seeds solitary in the cells, uncinate: albumen horny: embryo straight. — Perennial herbs: root creeping, leaves long-petioled: stem none or with a 1-leaved or leafy apex: inflorescence radical or terminal, spicately capitate or loosely capitate or panicled.

(1) P. CAPITATUM. *(Willd.)*

Ident. Willd. sp. I. 17.—Roxb. flor. Ind. I. p. 8.

Syn. Phyllodes placentaria, *Lour.*

Engrav. Rheede Mal. XI. t. 34.—Wight's Icon. t. 2016.

SPEC. CHAR. Root tuberous: stem none: leaves radical, oblong-entire, smooth: petioles longer than the leaves, slender and round, flower-bearing: flowers numerous, collected into a largish sessile head, bursting from the anterior margin of the jointed petioles, pale rose.

Concan jungles. Chittagong. Silhet. Assam. Flowering in the rainy season.

(2) P. PARVIFLORUM. *(Roxb.)*

Ident. Roxb. flor. Ind. I. p. 7.

SPEC. CHAR. Stemless: root tuberous, hairy: leaves long-petioled, elliptic-oval, entire, acute: heads of flowers sub-globose, sessile, bursting from the inner side of the petiole near the middle, composed of many imbricated sessile distichous, single or compound spikes: outer bracts broad-ovate, larger, smooth, all acute-pointed: flowers in pairs, inconspicuous, yellow.

Eastern parts of Bengal, flowering at the beginning of the rains.

(3) P. IMBRICATUM. *(Roxb.)*

Ident. Roxb. l. c. p. 6.

SPEC. CHAR. Leaves radical, long-petioled, tapering at both ends, lanceolate, finely acuminate: flower-bearing petioles with a hairy joint near the middle, the spike bursting through a slit 2—3 inches long: spike short-peduncled, linear-oblong, imbricated: outer bracts oval, truncated, with the transverse apex many-toothed, smooth, each embracing several small pale pink flowers opening successively.

Chittagong, flowering in March and April.

GENUS II. MARANTA.

Monandria Monogynia. *Sex: Syst:*

Deriv. Named after B. Maranti, a Venetian physician and Botanist who died in 1554.

GEN. CHAR. Calyx 3-leaved: outer petals equal, more deeply distinct, lip 2-cleft: filament petaloid, 2-parted, one antheriferous, the other segment encircling the style: ovary inferior, 1-celled: ovule 1, basilar, campylotropal: style fleshy, incurved, stigma sub-trigonal: berry 1-seeded: seed uncinate globose, testa hard, wrinkled: albumen horny.—Herbs: stem herbaceous or suffrutescent, panicled: inflorescence terminal, spiked or racemose.

(1) M. DICHOTOMA. *(Wall.)*

Ident. Wall. Cat.

Syn. Phrynium dichotomum, *Roxb. flor. Ind. I. p.* 2. Donax arundinastrum, *Lour.*

Engrav. Rumph. Amb. iv. t. 7.

SPEC. CHAR. Stems 3—6-feet, very smooth: branches numerous, dichotomous, jointed at each division: leaves alternate, petioled, ovate-cordate, smooth, entire with sheathing petioles: racemes terminal, usually solitary, jointed, slightly flexuose: flowers in pairs on a common pedicel from the alternate joints of the rachis: large, pure white.

Coromandel. Bengal. Silhet. Assam. Flowering in the hot season.

(2) M. VIRGATA. *(Wall.)*

Ident. Wall. Cat.

Syn. Phrynium virgatum, *Roxb. flor. Ind. I. p.* 4.

Engrav. Wight's Icon. t. 2015.

SPEC. CHAR. Stems simple, jointed, and knotted at the joints: leaves distichous, lanceolate: panicles terminal, loose, branches filiform: flowers scattered, paired, small: fruit hairy.

Courtallum. Malabar. Bolamputty. Travancore mountains.

ORDER CLXXII. ZINGIBERACEÆ.

Flowers hermaphrodite, irregular: perianth double, outer one shorter, usually coloured, tubular, limb 3-toothed or 3-cleft, inner one corollaceous, tubular, segments of the 6-parted limb in two rows, 3 outer rows nearly equal, or two lateral ones equal, the third dissimilar, inner lateral ones very rarely agreeing with the outer ones, usually very minute, lip larger, entire or 2—3-lobed: stamen inserted on the outer segment of the corolla: filament linear, usually produced beyond the cells of the anther, undivided or lobed: anther 2-celled, terminal, cells parallel, adnate by the back, dehiscing lengthways: ovary inferior, 3-celled: ovules many, 1- or 2-rowed in the central angle of the cells, horizontal, anatropal: style filiform: stigma thickened, often hollow: capsule crowned with the perianth, membranaceous, sometimes baccate, 3-celled, loculicidally 3-valved: seeds solitary in the cells, erect, or many when the fruit in 3-celled, naked or surrounded with a short aril: testa cartilaginous: albumen mealy: embryo orthotropal.—Herbs with a creeping or tuberous rhizome, perennial, stemless or caulescent: leaves sometimes all radical, or cauline, alternate, simple, petioled, the petiole forming a sheath, cleft lengthways: furnished with a ligula at the mouth or naked, limb quite entire, middle nerve strong: inflorescence radical or terminal, densely or loosely spiked, racemose or panicled.

GENUS I. GLOBBA.

Monandria Monogynia. *Sex: Syst:*

Gen. Char. Calyx 3-cleft: tube of the corolla slender, inner lateral segments narrow, denticulate, lip larger, entire, tubulated with the filament: filament keeled not produced beyond the anther: ovary inferior, 1-celled: ovules numerous in three parietal placentæ, ascending, anatropal: style filiform, passing between the cells of the anther: stigma funnel-shaped: capsule 1-celled, 3-valved, bearing seeds in the middle: seeds numerous, arillate.—Low annual herbs: leaves distichous, membranaceous, lanceolate, sheaths cleft: inflorescence terminal, loosely fascicled, racemose or spiked.

(1) G. MARANTINOIDES. *(R. W.)*

Ident. Wight's Icon. vi. and t. 2001.

Syn. G. marantina, *Linn.* *Willd. sp. I.* 153.

Spec. Char. Root tuberous: stem 12—18 inches: leaves bifarious, broad-lanceolate, acute, smooth above, villous and whitish beneath, margins waved: spike terminal, solitary, strobiliform, oblong: bracts ovate-cordate with a small bulb in the axil: flowers slender, bright yellow, fragrant, tube long and slender.

Warree country. Annamullay forests. Flowering in August and September.

(2) G. OPHIOGLOSSA. *(R. W.)*

Ident. Wight l. c. t. 2002.

Spec. Char. Leaves short-petioled, acuminate, glabrous: panicle terminal: lip linear pointed, deeply cleft: inner lobes (petals) linear-lanceolate: capsule globose, smooth.

Malabar. Annamullay hills.

(3) G. SALTATORIA. *(Roscoe.)*

Ident. Roscoe Scit.

Syn. G. radicalis, *Roxb.* G. subulata, *Roxb. flor. Ind. I. p.* 81. G. purpurea, *Andr. Bot. Rep.* Mantisia saltatoria, *Sims.*

Engrav. Roxb. Cor. III t. 230. Andr. Bot. Rep. x. t. 615. Bot. Mag. 32 t. 1320.

Spec. Char. Roots fusiform: stems bending to one side, 1—2-feet: leaves bifarious, sessile on their sheaths, lanceolate, point filiform, withering, villous on both sides: sheaths smooth, keeled: ligula truncated: scapes radical, often several, sheathed: panicle erect, 1-foot including the scape, purple, branches simple, long, diverging, bearing in succession numerous alternate sessile, small purple and yellow flowers: bracts smooth, purple, of the branches oblong, of the flowers cordate: tube of the corolla long and slender, lower half horizontal, upper erect, flower dropping at the angle, the lower half withering, border single, 3-parted, upper division erect, pressing on the back of the filament, oblong, boat-shaped, lower two divisions obliquely cordate, reflexed: lip cuneate, deeply 2-parted, deep orange yellow: filament very long, afterwards revolute, grooved on the inside with two very long slender flat subulate recurved diverging wings near the base: anther double with reniform wings at the sides: ovary oval with nine longitudinal ridges, seeds numerous: capsule globular, six-ridged, 1-celled, 3-valved, opening from the top: seeds villous, oblong.

Chittagong, flowering in the hot season. From the peculiar and fantastic shapes assumed by the flowers, this plant has been called "Opera girls."

(4) G. SPATHULATA. *(Roxb.)*

Ident. Roxb. l. c. p. 83.

SPEC. CHAR. Panicles radical, erect, oblong, 8—12-inches, branches diverging: bracts oval and oblong, concave, with a larger one to each branch and one to each flower: tube of the corolla slender, villous, curved, border 3-lobed, lobes equal, oblong, lip cuneate, yellow: filament long, slender, recurved with a spathulate diverging wing on each side near the base: anther with a semi-lunar wing on each side: ovary 1-celled, many-ovuled: flowers numerous.

Khasia hills, flowering in April.

GENUS II. COSTUS.

Monandria Monogynia. *Sex: Syst:*

Deriv. From the Arabic name *Gosth.*

GEN. CHAR. Calyx tubular, 3-cleft: tube of the corolla funnel-shaped, outer segments of the limb equal, connivent, inner lateral ones none: lip very large, campanulate, cleft at the back: filament petaloid, long and broadly produced above the intra-marginal anther: ovary inferior, 3-celled: ovules numerous, horizontal, anatropal: style filiform, passing between the cells of the anther: stigma bilamellate, furnished at the base with 2-small horns.—Herbs with creeping tuberous roots: leaves fleshy, petiolar sheaths produced above the insertion of the leaf into an obliquely truncated ochrea: inflorescence spiked, terminal or rarely radical, imbricated with bracts.

(1) C. SPECIOSUS. *(Smith.)*

Ident. Roxb. flor. Ind. I. p. 69.

Syn. Hellenia grandiflora. *Rets* Amomum hirsutum, *Lam.* Banksia speciosa, *Koen.*

Engrav. Rheede Mal. xi. t. 8. Wight's Icon. t. 2014.

SPEC. CHAR. Stem somewhat spiral: leaves sub-sessile, spirally arranged, oblong, cuspidate, softly villous beneath: bracts obovate, obtuse, scarlet: flowers very large, pure white.

Coromandel. Travancore. Western coast. Bengal. Flowering in the rainy season.

GENUS III. ZINGIBER.

Monandria Monogynia. *Sex: Syst:*

Deriv. The Indian name.

GEN. CHAR. Calyx tubular: tube of the corolla short, outer segments of the limb equal, inner lateral ones none, lip 3-lobed: filament elongated above the muticous anther into a simple incurved beak: ovary inferior, 3-celled: ovules numerous, horizontal, anatropal: style filiform, wrapped round by the filament: stigma funnel-shaped: capsule sub-baccate, 3-celled, 3-valved: seeds arillate, nestling in pulp.—Herbs: roots tuberous, jointed, creeping: stems annual: leaves membranaceous, distichous with closed sheaths: spikes strobiliform, radical, solitary, composed of many 1-flowered bracts.

(1) Z. SQUARROSUM. *(Roxb.)*

Ident. Roxb. flor. Ind. I. p. 54.

Engrav. Wight's Icon. t. 2004.

SPEC. CHAR. Leaves lanceolar: spikes squarrose, half immersed in the earth: bracts linear, with a long, waved, tapering point: lip 2-cleft at the apex: flowers pink, the inner lip of the corolla speckled purple-red and yellow.

Annamullays. Bolamputty hills, near Coimbatore. Flowering from July to November.

(2) Z. ZERUMBET. *(Smith.)*

Ident. Roxb. flor. Ind. I. p. 47.

Syn. Z. spurium, *Koen. in. Retz. obs. III. p.* 60.—Amomum Zerumbet, *Willd.*—A. sylvestre, *Lam.*—A. spurium, *Gmel.*

Engrav. Wight l. c. t. 2003.—Rheede Mal. xi. t. 13.—Sm. Exot. bot. II. t. 112.

SPEC. CHAR. Stems declinate: leaves sessile, lanceolar: spike long-peduncled, oval, compact, obtuse: bracts broad-obovate, obtuse, margins coloured: flowers pale sulphur.

Annamullays. Peninsula. Bengal. Western forests, Flowering in August and September.

(3) Z. CASSUMUNAR. *(Roxb.)*

Ident. Roxb. flor. Ind. I. 49.

Syn. Z. purpureum, *Rosc. in Trans. Linn. Soc.*

Engrav. Bot. Mag. t. 1426.—Andr. Bot. Rep. t. 558.

SPEC. CHAR. Root tuberous: stems erect, round, 3—5-feet: leaves bifarious, linear-lanceolate: scapes radical, 6—12-inches long: spikes oblong, strobiliform, closely imbricated with numerous obovate acuminate villous bracts: flowers large, pale sulphur.

Concans. Behar. Silhet. Bengal. Flowering in July and August.

(4) Z. NIMMONII. *(Dalz.)*

Ident. Dalz. in Hook. Journ. Bot. iv. p. 341.

Syn. Z. panduratum, *Roxb. flor. Ind. I. p.* 55.

SPEC CHAR. Leaves lanceolate-acuminate, short-petioled, paler and covered with a fine web below: spike ascending, short-peduncled, ovate, scarcely rising above the ground: bracts linear-oblong or lanceolate, inner ones 2-cleft, outer divisions of the corolla yellowish red, lip 3-lobed, middle one ovate, rounded.

Concans, flowering in the rains.

(5) Z. CERNUUM. *(Dalz.)*

Ident. Dalz. l. c. p. 342.

SPEC. CHAR. Stem somewhat curved: leaves narrow-elliptic, acuminate, glabrous: spikes ovate-obtuse, very shortly peduncled, scarcely rising above ground: bracts ovate or oblong, inner ones shortly 3-cleft, middle lobe of the lip ovate, deeply 2-cleft, variegated with white and pink, lateral lobes yellow and pink.

Ram Ghaut, flowering in July.

(6) Z. MACROSTACHYUM. *(Dalz.)*

Ident. Dalz. l. c.

SPEC. CHAR. Stem red, pubescent: leaves lanceolate, acuminate, paler and pubescent beneath: spikes 1—2 from the root, cylindric-elongated, long-peduncled: bracts obovate-acute: flowers white, lip 3-lobed: middle one rounded, emarginate, marked with diverging purple lines: capsule obovate, pubescent, red.

Ram Ghaut, flowering in July.

(7) Z. ROSEUM. *(Roscoe.)*

Ident. Roscoe in Trans. Linn. Soc. viii. 348.—Roxb. l. c. p. 50.

Engrav. Roxb. Cor. II. 126.

SPEC. CHAR. Stems several, 2—3-feet: leaves short-petioled, lanceolate, acute: spikes remote from the stems, imbricated with lax reddish, one-flowered bracts: flowers solitary, red and yellow: interior bract linear, obtuse and notched at the apex: corolla bright red.

Northern Circars, flowering during the rains.

(8) Z. RUBENS. *(Roxb.)*

Ident. Roxb. l. c. p. 53.

SPEC. CHAR. Stems 2—4-feet: leaves sessile, lanceolate: ligula large, membranaceous: spikes several, sub-obovate, fastigiate, loosely imbricated with numerous straight, erect, linear-lanceolate, acute, involute, red exterior bracts, inner bracts shorter, irregularly 3-toothed: corolla tube long, slender, segments of the outer border linear-lanceolate, acute, red: lip ovate-oblong, entire, speckled red and yellow.

Rungpore district, flowering in August.

(9) Z. CAPITATUM. *(Roxb.)*

Ident. Roxb. l. c. p. 55.

SPEC. CHAR. Stems erect, round, 2—3-feet: leaves narrow-lanceolate, acute, smooth above, slightly hairy beneath: spike terminal, sessile on the mouth of the sheaths of the upper leaves, linear-oblong, somewhat cone-shaped: bracts in pairs, 1-flowered, permanent, outer one lanceolate, concave, erect, longer than the corolla tube, inner ovate, shorter, enveloping the ovary, calyx and nearly the whole of the corolla: lip of the corolla 3-lobed, middle lobe very large, round, lateral ones expanding: anther with a very long curved beak: flowers large, pure yellow.

Rohilcund, flowering in the rains.

(10) Z. ELATUM. *(Roxb.)*

Ident. Roxb. l. c. p. 57.

SPEC. CHAR. Stems straight, 4—5-feet: leaves linear, recurved, smooth above, softly hairy beneath: sheaths slightly hairy: spikes terminal, solitary, narrow-lanceolate, compactly imbricated with lanceolate 1-flowered bracts, the latter hairy outside: calyx white, smooth, mouth unequally toothed: corolla bright yellow: filaments with a long curved beak crowning the linear 2-lobed anther.

Interior of Bengal, flowering in July and August.

GENUS IV. HEDYCHIUM.

Monandria Monogynia. *Sex: Syst:*

Deriv. From *Hedys* sweet, and *Chion* snow, alluding to the fragrant white flowers.

Gen. Char. Calyx tubular, 3-toothed: tube of the corolla long, slender, outer segments of the limb narrow, equal, inner ones of the same shape or a little shorter, lip greater, undivided or emarginate or 2-cleft: filament filiform, anther terminal, incumbent, emarginate at both ends: style filiform, stigma funnel-shaped: ovary inferior, 3-celled: ovules numerous, horizontal, anatropal: capsule 3-celled, 3-valved: seeds arillate.—Caulescent herbs: roots tuberous, jointed, horizontal: leaves sessile in half-stem-clasping sheaths: inflorescence terminal, spiked, imbricated with spathes: flowers fascicled with involute bracts.

(1) H. scaposum. *(Nimmo.)*

Ident. Nimmo in Grah. Cat. p. 205.—Dalz. Bomb. flor. p. 273.

Syn. Monolophus scaposus, *Dalz. in Hook. Journ. Bot. II.* 143.

Engrav. Wight's Icon. vi. t. 2030.

Spec. Char. Root with small oblong tubers hanging from the fibres: leaves lanceolate, long-acuminated, long-petioled: scape erect, round, a little leafy: spike terminal, compact, imbricated, many-flowered: flowers in pairs with a lanceolate pure white bract: outer petals oblong, reflexed, inner very large, round, cordate: lip 2-cleft at the apex.

Banks of rivulets, South Concan. Malabar.

(2) H. flavescens. *(Roscoe.)*

Ident. Roscoe Scit.

Engrav. Bot. Cab. t. 723.—Bot. Mag. t. 2378.—Wight l. c. t. 2008-9.

Spec. Char. Leaves lanceolate-acuminate, villous beneath, the acumen withering: spike capitate, imbricate: exterior bracts broad, obtuse, ciliated at the apex: inner ones cylindrical, 2—3-flowered: lip broad, 2-lobed, as long as the filament: flowers pale yellow.

Neilgherries, flowering in the rains.

(3) H. coronarium. *(Willd.)*

Ident. Roxb. flor. Ind. p. 10.

Engrav. Wight l. c. t. 2010.—Bot. Cab. t. 507, t. 51.—Bot. Mag. t. 708.—Smith Exot. Bot. t. 107.

Spec. Char. Leaves lanceolate, pubescent beneath: spike capitate, imbricated: bracts broad-ovate, acute: lip orbicular, 2-cleft at the apex, longer than the filament: flowers pure white, fragrant.

Neilgherries. Coromandel. Assam. Silhet. Flowering in the rains.

(4) H. venustum. *(R.W.)*

Ident. Wight l. c. vi. t. 2012.

Spec. Char. Leaves long-petioled, lanceolate acute: spike drooping, lax: bracts linear obtuse, margined: lobes of the perianth narrow, outer somewhat lanceolate, interior linear, all longer than the stamen: lip deeply cleft, lobes lanceolate.

Coorg.

(5) H. cernuum. *(R.W.)*

Ident. Wight l. c. vi. t. 2011.

Spec. Char. Leaves short-petioled, long-lanceolate, acutely acuminate: spike nodding, loose: bracts narrow, obtuse: lobes of the perianth narrow-linear, longer than the stamen: lip lanceolate, 2-cleft at the apex: capsule globose, hairy, dark red or orange.

Burlear, Neilgherries, on the banks of a stream.

(6) H. angustifolium. *(Roxb.)*

Ident. Roxb. l. c. p. 13.

Syn. H. aurantiacum, *Roscoe.*

Engrav. Roxb. Cor. II. t. 157.—Bot. Mag. t. 2078.

Spec. Char. Leaves linear-lanceolate, almost filiform, pointed: spike terminal, erect, rigid, 6—18-inches, smooth: fascicles of flowers usually three-fold, spreading: outer bracts cylindric, linear: flowers small, dull red.

Chittagong. Silhet. Flowering in June.

(7) H. flavum. *(Roxb.)*

Ident. Roxb. l. c. p. 12.

Engrav. Bot. Cab. t. 1604.—Bot. Mag. t. 3039.—Bot. Cab. t. 1785.

Spec. Char. Stems 2—3-feet: leaves lanceolate, finely acuminated, smooth: sheaths with a large stipule rising far above the mouth: spike terminal, solitary, erect, oblong, imbricated: flowers numerous, large, yellow: outer bracts oval or oblong, obtuse, finely nerved, 3—4-flowered, inner, one to each flower, much smaller.

Vallies in the Khasia hills, flowering in June.

(8) H. GRACILE. (*Roxb.*)

Ident. Roxb. l. c. p. 14.

Syn. H. glaucum, *Roscoe.*

Engrav. Roxb. Cor. III. t. 250.

SPEC. CHAR. Slender, about 3-feet: leaves lanceolate: spikes terminal, open: flowers solitary, scattered: segments of the 2-cleft sessile lip semi-lanceolate, remaining segments of the corolla linear: flowers white, with scarlet filaments.

Khasia hills, flowering in the rains.

(9) H. SPECIOSUM. (*Wall.*)

Ident. Roxb. l. c. Ed. Car. I. p. 13.

Engrav. Wall. pl. As. rar. III. t. 285.

SPEC. CHAR. Leaves oblong-lanceolate, somewhat waved, attenuated at both ends: spikes elongated, open: fascicles of flowers approximated, 2-flowered: lip entire, acute: flowers pale sulphur.

Khasia hills, flowering in the rains.

(10) H. VILLOSUM. (*Wall.*)

Ident. Roxb. l. c. p. 13 (not *Roscoe*).

SPEC. CHAR. Leaves oblong-lanceolate, glaucous beneath: spikes elongated, villous, open: fascicles close packed, somewhat 3-flowered: lip 2-cleft, equalling the petals: flowers pale yellow, very fragrant.

Khasia hills, flowering in the rains.

GENUS V. CURCUMA.

Monandria Monogynia. *Sex: Syst:*

Deriv. From the Arabic name *Kurkum.*

GEN. CHAR. Calyx tubular, 3-toothed: tube of the corolla dilated upwards, outer segments of the limb of the same shape as the inner lateral ones, lip larger, spreading: filament dilated like a petal, keeled, 3-lobed at the apex, middle lobe terminated by the

2-spurred anther: ovary inferior, 3-celled: ovules numerous, horizontal, anatropal: style filiform, stigma capitate: capsule 3-celled, 3-valved: seeds arillate.—Stemless herbs: roots perennial, palmately tuberous: leaves herbaceous, petioles sheathing, bifarious: scape simple, lateral or central: spike simple, erect, comose, imbricated below with saccate bracts: flowers yellowish, approximated by threes or fives between each bract, bracteolate.

(1) C. AROMATICA. *(Salisb.)*

Ident. Roscoe Scit.

Syn. C. Zedoaria, *Roxb. flor. Ind. I.* 23.

Engrav. Wight's Icon. t. 2005.

SPEC. CHAR. Bulbs small and with the long palmate tubers inwardly yellow: leaves broad lanceolar, sessile on their sheaths, silky underneath: whole plant a uniform green, except the spike: bracts pale green below, passing into pink and almost crimson: outer perianth pink, inner and lip yellow.

Malabar. Peninsula. Concans. Flowering in the hot season.

(2) C. NEILGHERRENSIS. *(R. W.)*

Ident. Wight l. c. t. 2006.

SPEC. CHAR. Leaves scarcely petioled, lanceolate, somewhat cuspidate, glabrous: spikes scarcely rising above the ground, compact: limb of the bracts prolonged, sub-lanceolate, obtuse, longer than the flowers, reflexed: outer lobes of the perianth linear cuspidate, inner ones obovate-lanceolate, obtuse, lip broad, sub-orbicular, 2-toothed at the apex: anther spurs short: capsule globose, glabrous, crowned with the withered remains of the flower: terminal tuft of the spike deep pink, lower bracts pale yellow, changing to greenish flowers, deep yellow, especially the lip.

Neilgherries, near Neddiwuttum, flowering in April and May.

(3) C. ANGUSTIFOLIA. *(Roxb.)*

Ident. Roxb. flor. Ind. I. p. 31.

SPEC. CHAR. Root with small oval tubers hanging to the fibres: leaves narrow lanceolar, very acute, smooth on both sides: petioles 6—12-inches long: spike radical, crowned with a tuft of oval purple bracts: flowers longer than the bracts, bright yellow.

Ram Ghaut. Banks of the Sona at Nagpore, appearing at the beginning of the rains.

(4) C. DECIPIENS. *(Dalz.)*

Ident. Dalz. in Hook. Journ. Bot. II. p. 144.

SPEC. CHAR. Root with numerous almond-shaped tubers hanging from the fibres: earlier scapes lateral, later central, 6—8-inches long: leaves broadly oval, glabrous, rarely velvetty beneath, long-petioled: floral bracts saccate, purple: flowers twin, purple, the lip 2-cleft, with curled margins.

Malwan, flowering from June to August.

(5) C. ZEDOARIA, *(Roscoe.)*

Ident. Roscoe Scit. (not *Roxb*).

Syn. Curcuma Zerumbet, *Roxb. flor. Ind. I. p.* 20. Amomum Zerumbet, *Koen.*

Engrav. Bot. Mag. t. 1546.—Roxb. Cor. III. t. 201. Rheede Mal. xi. t. 7.

SPEC. CHAR. Stemless: leaves 4—6-together, broad-lanceolate, finely acuminated, smooth, purple in the centre: scape 5—6-inches long, surrounded by a few lax green sheaths: spike tufted, covered with imbricated oblong bracts containing each 3—4 yellow sessile flowers, upper ones usually sterile, deeper crimson or purple than those containing the flowers.

Chittagong, flowering in April.

(6) C. AMADA. *(Roxb.)*

Ident. Roxb. flor. Ind. I. p. 33.

SPEC. CHAR. Tubers palmate, inwardly pale yellow: leaves long-petioled, broad-lanceolate, smooth: spikes central, cylindric, crowned with a tuft of pale abortive bracts: flowers small, yellow.

Concans. Guzerat. Flowering in the rains.

(7) C. PSEUDOMONTANA. *(J. Grah.)*

Ident. Grah. Cat. Bomb. plants, p. 210.

SPEC. CHAR. Tubers round, white inside: leaves with the petiole 2—3-feet long, tapering at both ends: scape central: coma of a beautiful dark rose-colour, waved: flowers yellow, of about equal length.

Concans, flowering in September.

(8) C. CAULINA. *(J. Grah.)*

Ident. Grah. Cat. l. c.—Dalz. Bomb. flor. p. 275.

SPEC. CHAR. Root with large oblong tubers, white inside: radical leaves short petioled: scape central, leafy, 3-feet: upper leaves on the stem alternate, frequently tinged with a beautiful red: coma white: bracts green, large, loose, oval: flowers yellow, longer than the bracts.

Mahableshwur hills.

(9) C. FERRUGINEA. *(Roxb.)*

Ident. Roxb. l. c. p. 27.

Syn. C. amarissima, *Roscoe.*

SPEC. CHAR. Leaves broad-lanceolate with a rusty tinge running down the middle: sheaths of the scapes rusty red: roots pale yellow, fragrant: flowers few, large, outer border red, inner deep yellow: bracts of the fertile part of the spike rusty, of the coma bright crimson.

Bengal, flowering in April and May.

(10) C. RUBESCENS. *(Roxb.)*

Ident. Roxb. l. c. p. 28.

SPEC. CHAR. Leaves broad-lanceolate, cuspidate, smooth, strongly marked with parallel veins, nerves and ribs red: petioles and sheaths channelled, deep red: scape lateral, cylindric, invested in dark reddish sheaths: spike tufted, erect: flowers small, bright yellow, fragrant.

Bengal. Travancore. Flowering in April and May. All the plant has a pleasant aromatic smell, particularly the root,

(11) C. LEUCORRHIZA. *(Roxb.)*

Ident. Roxb. l. c. p. 30.

SPEC. CHAR. Bulbs ovate: palmate tubers long and far-spreading: leaves broad-lanceolate, smooth: spikes lateral, few-flowered: flowers the length of the bracts, outer border slightly tinged with pink, inner yellow.

Forests of Behar, flowering in the rains.

(12) C. MONTANA. *(Roxb.)*

Ident. Roxb. l. c. p. 35.

Engrav. Roxb. Cor. II. t. 151.

SPEC. CHAR. Leaves radical, oval, pointed, finely veined: spikes rising from the centre of the petioles, lower bracts roundish, upper oblong, waved, rose-coloured, usually without flowers: flowers green, with a rose-coloured tuft.

Circar mountains, flowering in the rains.

(13) C. reclinata. *(Roxb.)*

Ident. Roxb. l. c. p. 36.

Spec. Char. Root with oval tubers: leaves radical, 2 on each side of the spike, with the lower sheathing part of the petioles reclinate, oblong, acute: petioles deeply channelled: spike rising from the centre of the leaves, loosely imbricated above with large, ovate, coloured bracts: flowers small, dull dark pink, lower segment of the inner border tinged with yellow.

Hindostan, flowering in the rains.

GENUS VI. ALPINIA.

Monandria Monogynia. *Sex: Syst:*

Deriv. Named in honour of Prosper Alpini, an Italian botanist.

Gen. Char. Calyx tubular, loose, bursting at the apex: tube of the corolla short, outer segments of the limb equal, inner lateral ones tooth-shaped or none, lip large, flattened out, entire, or 2—3-lobed: filament linear, not produced beyond the cells of the emarginate muticous anther: ovary inferior, 3-celled, ovules numerous, horizontal, anatropal: style filiform, passing between the cells of the anther: stigma capitately three cornered: capsule baccate, 3-celled, indehiscent: seeds many or few by abortion, arillate.—Herbs: roots thick, tuberous, horizontal, stems many, perennial: leaves bifarious: sheath cleft, ligulate: inflorescence terminating the stem, panicled or loosely racemose or spiked.

(1) A. Rheedii. *(R. W.)*

Ident. Wight's Icon. vi. and t. 2026.

Engrav. Rheede Mal. xi. t. 14.

Spec. Char. Leaves sub-sessile from broad lanceolate obtuse to lanceolate cuspidate: panicle terminal, erect, many-flowered: outer series linear, obtuse, somewhat concave, lip unguiculate, sub-orbicular, 2-lobed, claw with two dilatations at the base, each ending in a subulate point: capsules slightly downy.

Malabar. Courtallum.

(2) A. nutans. *(Roscoe.)*

Ident. Roxb. flor. Ind. I. p. 65.

Syn. A. auriculata, *Rosc. Scit.*—Costus Zerumbet, *Pers.*—Globba nutans, *Linn.*—G. sylvestris, *Rumph.*

Engrav. Wight l. c. t. 2027.—Bot. Mag. t. 1903.—Andr. Bot. Repos. t. 360.

Spec. Char. Leaves lanceolar, short-petioled, smooth: racemes compound by the lower pedicels being two or three flowered, drooping: lip large, ovate, cordate, obscurely 3-lobed at the base: middle lobe curled on the margin: ovary hairy, oval, 3-celled: capsule slightly hairy: flowers rose, lip orange on a dark crimson ground.

Silhet. Coromandel. Flowering in April and May.

(3) A. calcarata. *(Roscoe.)*

Ident. Roxb. flor. Ind. I. p. 69.

Engrav. Wight l. c. t. 2028.—Bot. Reg. t. 141.—Bot. Rep. t. 241.

Spec. Char. Root stoloniferous, fragrant: stems oblique: leaves short-petioled, narrow lanceolar, finely acuminated, smooth on both sides: racemes terminal, solitary, erect, compound: flowers numerous, large, lip ovate-oblong, deeply coloured with purple veins on a yellow ground.

South Concan, flowering in the hot season.

(4) A. Allughas. *(Roscoe.)*

Ident. Roscoe in Linn. Trans. viii. 346.—Roxb. flor. Ind. I. 61.

Syn. Hellenia Allughas, *Linn.*—Heritiera Allughas, *Koen.*

Engrav. Rheede Mal. xi. t. 14.—Bot. Rep. t. 501.

Spec. Char. Stem erect, slightly compressed, entirely covered with the sheaths of the leaves: leaves oblong, glabrous, paler beneath: panicle terminal, bending to one side: flowers numerous, large, rose-coloured: capsule globular, smooth, black when ripe.

South Concan. Coromandel. Silhet. Assam. Flowering in June and July.

(5) A. Galanga. *(Willd.)*

Ident. Willd. sp. I. R.—Roxb. flor. Ind. I. p. 59.

Syn. Maranta Galanga, *Linn.*—Amomum Galanga, *Lour.*

Engrav. Rumph. Amb. v. t. 63.

Spec. Char. Root perennial: stems erect, round, smooth, 6—7-

feet, leafy in the upper part: leaves lanceolar, smooth on both sides, margins white and somewhat callous: panicle terminal, erect, oblong, branched: flowers greenish-white: fruit obovate, smooth, deep orange red.

Wag Donger, Warree Country. Chittagong. Silhet. Flowering April and May.

(6) A. Malaccensis. *(Roscoe.)*

Ident. Roscoe in Trans. Linn. Soc. 8, 345.—Roxb. l. c. p. 64.

Syn. Maranta Malaccensis, *Linn.*—Galanga Malaccensis, *Rumph.*—A. petiolaris, *Soland.*

Engrav. Bot. Reg. iv. t. 328.

Spec. Char. Leaves lanceolate, petioled, villous beneath: raceme terminal, simple: lip obscurely 3-lobed with two spurs at the base, lateral lobes incurved: capsules obliquely spheroidal: flowers large, pure white with the lip orange-crimson.

Chittagong, flowering in April and May.

GENUS VII. KŒMPFERIA.

Monandria Monogynia. *Sex: Syst.*

Deriv. Named after E. Kœmpfer, a German naturalist.

Gen. Char. Calyx tubular, cleft, tube of the corolla filiform, outer segments of the limb narrow, equal, lateral ones spreading, posticous ones forked, inner ones much larger, lip flat: filaments short, keeled, expanded above the muticous anther into a 2-cleft crest: ovary inferior, 3-celled: ovules numerous, horizontal, anatropal: style filiform, stigma urceolate, ciliated: capsule 3-celled, 3-valved: seeds arillate.—Herbs: bracts usually bifariously imbricated, seldom saccate.

(1) K. rotunda. *(Willd.)*

Ident. Roxb. flor. Ind. I. p. 16.

Engrav. Wight's Icon. t. 2029.—Bot. Mag. t. 920.—Rheede Mal. xi. t. 9.

Spec. Char. Leaves oblong, coloured: spike radical, appearing before the leaves: lateral lobes of the corolla obovate-lanceolate, acute: lip deeply 2-cleft, lobes obovate, very obtuse, crest of the anther linear, forked, with a small tooth between: flowers large, purplish-white.

Malabar.

(2) K. Galanga. *(Linn.)*

Ident. Roxb. flor. Ind. I. p. 15.

Syn. Alpinia sessilis, *Koen.*

Engrav. Bot. Mag. t. 850. Rheede Mal. xi. t. 41.

Spec. Char. Stem none : leaves spreading flat on the ground, round ovate-cordate, margins waved, upper surface somewhat woolly towards the base : flowers fascicled, 6—12 within the sheath of the leaves, expanding in succession, pure white with a purple spot on the centre of each of the divisions of the inner series : bracts 3 to each flower, linear, acute, half the length of the tube of the corolla.

Peninsula. Bengal. Flowering in the rains.

(3) K. angustifolia. *(Roxb.)*

Ident. Roxb. l. c. p. 17.

Engrav Redout, Lil. vii. t. 389.

Spec. Char. Leaves radical, linear-lanceolate, waved : spikes hidden in the centre of the leaves : upper two segments of the inner border of the corolla linear, oblong, obtuse : flowers white, tinged with purple towards the apex, lip lilac, middle dark purple.

Bengal, flowering in the rains.

GENUS VIII. ELETTARIA.

Monandria Monogynia. *Sex: Syst:*

Gen. Char. Calyx tubular, 3-toothed : tube of the corolla long, filiform, outer lateral segments of the limb narrower than the posticous ones, inner lateral ones very small, shaped like small teeth, lip very large, flat : filament flattened, undivided, truncately emarginate not produced above the cells of the muticous anther : ovary inferior, 3-celled : ovules numerous, horizontal, anatropal, style filiform, passing between the cells of the anther : stigma funnel-shaped : capsules 3-celled, 3-valved : seeds arillate.—Herbs with the habit of Amomum : inflorescence radical, densely or loosely spiked, bracteate.

(1) E. cannæcarpa. *(R. W.)*

Ident. Wight's Icon. vi. t. 2007.

Spec. Char. Stems 6 feet, procumbent and rooting at the base, underground shoots bearing the spikes, leaves lanceolate, acutely acuminate, glabrous : floriferous stems clothed with sheathing scariose leaves, at length ascending: spikes short, ovate: bracts lanceolate, red: perianth hairy on the throat and lip: outer lobes obovate-lanceolate, sub-cuspidate, inner reduced to two subulate teeth or spurs: lip oval, bicuspidate: filament produced beyond the anther: capsule globose, echinate, dark brownish purple: perianth yellow.

Hooliculdroog, Neilgherries, in dense forests, flowering in May.

(2) E. CARDAMOMUM. *(Maton.)*

Ident. White and Maton Linn. Soc. Trans. x. p. 254.

Syn. Alpinia Cardamomum, *Roxb.* A. repens, *Roscoe.* A. racemosum, *Lam.*

Engrav. Roxb. Cor. III. t. 226. Rheede Mal. xi. t. 4—5.

SPEC. CHAR. Stem 6—9-feet enveloped in the sheaths: leaves lanceolate-acuminate, sub-sessile, 1—2-feet long: sheaths slightly villous: scapes several, flexuose, jointed, branched: flowers alternate, solitary at each point of the racemes: outer divisions of the corolla oblong, concave, inner lip obovate, curled at the margins, apex 3-lobed, marked in the centre with purple violet stripes: flowers pale greenish-white.

Hilly parts of Travancore and Wynaad. Coorg. Nuggur. Flowering in the rains. Produces the well-known Cardamoms.

(3) E. COSTATA. *(Voight.)*

Ident. Voight Hort. Calc. p. 568.

Syn. Alpinia Cardamomum Medium, *Roxb. l. c. p.* 74. A. media, *Spreng.*

Engrav. Roxb. Cor. III. t. 252.

SPEC. CHAR. Leaves lanceolate, villous underneath: spikes radical, lax: lip ovate-lanceolate: capsule pedicelled, ovate-oblong, conical, 9-winged: flowers large, red, fragrant.

Khasia hills, flowering in June.

(4) E. LINGUIFORMIS. *(Schult.)*

Ident. Schult Mant.

Syn. Alpinia linguiformis, *Roxb.*

Engrav. Roxb. Cor. III. t. 276.

SPEC. CHAR. Leaves lanceolate, smooth on both sides: spikes radical, linear, rather open: lip tongue-shaped, 2-cleft, base broad, without spurs, sides incurved: flowers red, lip yellow, and down the centre slightly red.

Interior of Bengal, flowering in the rains.

GENUS IX. AMOMUM.

Monandria Monogynia. *Sex: Syst:*

Deriv. From *A,* privative, and *Momos,* impurity, alluding to the counter-poison qualities some species are supposed to possess.

GEN. CHAR. Calyx tubular, 3-cleft at the apex, tube of the corolla short, outer lateral segments of the limb narrower than the posticous one, inner lateral ones none: lip very large, flattened out: filament flat, produced at the sides and apex beyond the muticous anther, increased by two small lobes, terminal lobe 2-cleft: ovary inferior, 3-celled: ovules horizontal, numerous, anatropal: style filiform, hidden between the cells of the anther: stigma funnel-shaped: capsule usually baccate, 3-celled, 3-valved: seeds arillate.—Herbs: roots jointed, creeping, bifarious, membranaceous: sheaths cleft: inflorescence radical, loosely imbricated.

(1) A. DEALBATUM. *(Roxb.)*

Ident. Roxb. flor. Ind. I. p. 43.

SPEC. CHAR. Stems numerous, 3—5-feet: leaves broad-lanceolate, villous beneath: spikes radical: bracts lanceolate, obtuse, outer border vaulted: lip round oval, crest of one broad truncated lobe: capsules ovate-oblong, 9-winged: flowers white, middle of lip yellow.

Chittagong. Silhet. Flowering in March and April.

(2) A. SUBULATUM. *(Roxb.)*

Ident. Roxb. l. c. p. 44.

Engrav. Roxb. Cor. III. t. 277.

SPEC. CHAR. Leaves lanceolate, smooth: spikes ovate, echinated with the long subulate points of the bracts, calyx and upper segment of the outer border of the corolla: lip oblong: flowers large, yellow.

Khasia hills, flowering in March and April.

(3) A. SERICEUM. *(Roxb.)*

Ident. Roxb. l. c. p. 46.

SPEC. CHAR. Leaves lanceolate, white silky beneath: racemes radical, sub-globular, branched: lip obovate, spurred at the base: flowers white, the centre of the lip variegated with pink veins on a yellow ground.

Khasia hills, flowering in the rains.

GENUS X. MONOLOPHUS.

Monandria Monogynia. *Sex: Syst:*

Deriv. From *Monos*, single, and *Lophos*, a crest.

Gen. Char. Calyx tubular, cleft: tube of the corolla long, filiform, outer segments of the limb equal, lateral ones erect, posticous one deflexed, inner lateral ones broader, spreading, lip 2-cleft: filament linear, flattened out, produced above the muticous anther into an obtuse, undivided, reflexed ligula: ovary inferior, 3-celled: ovules many: style filiform: stigma funnel-shaped.—Caulescent herbs: root simple, fibrous: leaves oblong, petioled: spike terminal, wrapped at the base by a nerved spathe.

(1) M. secundus. (*Wall.*)

Ident. Wall. in Roxb. flor. Ind. ed. Car. I. p. 19.

Syn. Costus secundus, *Spreng.*

Spec. Char. Stem sheathed: leaves petioled, ovate, acuminate: spike terminal, drooping, few-flowered, unilateral: lip obcordate.

Khasia hills.

(2) M. linearis. (*Wall.*)

Ident. Wall. in Roxb. l. c. p. 20.

Syn. Costus linearis, *Spreng.*

Spec. Char. Leaves sessile, linear-lanceolate, cuspidate: ligula 2-cleft: flowers terminal, few.

Khasia hills.

ORDER CLXXIII. AMARYLLIDACEÆ.

Flowers hermaphrodite: perianth superior, corollaceous, 6-leaved, regular or irregular, sometimes crowned at the throat, withering persistent, or deciduous: leaflets connate below, equal or inner ones of different dimension and shape: æstivation imbricated: stamens 6, opposite the sepals and more or less deeply adnate to them, equal or alternate, longer, erect, sometimes irregular and declinate: filaments distinct or connate by their dilated bases into a faucial crown: anthers 2-celled, anticous, fixed at the back above the base or at the middle, moveable, erect and then usually deeply perforated for the reception of the filament: cells dehiscing lengthways: ovary adnate its whole length to the base of the perianth, 3-celled: ovules numerous, attached by two rows to the inner angle, horizontal, anatropal, sometimes two collateral or solitary, ascending, very rarely pendulous: styline column terminal, channelled fistular, generally 3-cornered: stigma obtuse, capitellate, 3-lobed or cleft: fruit 3, sometimes by abortion 2—1-celled, 1—many-seeded, usually capsular, loculicidally 3-valved, rarely indehiscent and pulpy within or baccate: seeds globose, oblong, angular, compressed or flat: testa membranaceous or crustaceous, pale or dark, sometimes greatly swelling, fleshy, clothed with a green adherent skin in place of a testa: albumen fleshy, hardish, sometimes succulent: embryo cylindric, straightish, axile: radicle extremity reaching the hilum. — Plants usually with bulbs and scapes: bulb tunicate: scape simple, 1—many-flowered at the apex: flowers umbelled, pedicelled or sessile, involucrated by a 1—many-leaved spathe: bracts distinct, erect, cernuous or pendulous, usually showy, often fragrant: some caulescent, furnished with fibrous or tuberous fascicled roots: flowers terminal, cymose or spiked, bracteated: leaves simple-nerved, entire, sheathing at the base, in the bulbiferous ones often narrow, lorate, in the caulescent ones scattered, sometimes dentately spinous at the margin.

GENUS I. CRINUM

Hexandria Monogynia. *Sex: Syst:*

Deriv. From *Krinon*, the Greek name for the lily.

Gen Char. Perianth superior, corollaceous, tube elongated, slender, throat not enlarged, limb 6-parted, segments almost equal, erect, spreading or reflexed: stamens 6, inserted at the top of the tube, elongated: filaments filiform, spreading or declinate: anthers linear, versatile: ovary inferior, 3-celled: ovules numerous, in 2 rows, horizontal, anatropal: styline column filiform, erect or inclined: stigma obtuse, obsoletely 3-lobed or 3-cleft: capsule membranaceous, depressed spherical, 3- or by abortion, 1—2-celled, irregularly bursting: seeds few or solitary, angular, sub-globose, often changed into fleshy small bulbs.—Bulb-bearing herbs with scapes: bulb tunicated, columnar or spherical: leaves in many rows: scape solid, umbellately many-flowered: spathe 2-leaved: flowers pedicelled or sessile, intermixed with linear ramentaceous bracts.

(1) C. Roxburghii. *(Dalz.)*

Ident. Dalz. Bomb. flor. p. 275.

Syn. C. Asiaticum, *Roxb. flor. Ind. II.* 127 (not *Willd*). C. defixum, *Ker.*

Engrav. Bot. Mag. t. 2208.

Spec. Char. Root bulbous with a fusiform crown: stem none: leaves radical, linear concave, without a keel: margins smooth: scapes as long as the leaves, a little compressed, smooth: spathe with filiform bracts among the flowers: flowers large, white, sub-sessile: berry sub-globose.

Banks of Deccan rivers. Coromandel. Concans. Flowering in October.

(2) C. Asiaticum. *(Linn.)*

Ident. Linn. sp. 419. Dalz. l. c.

Syn. C. toxicarium, *Roxb. l. c.* C. brevifolium, *Roxb. l. c.* C. bracteatum, *Willd.* C. declinatum, *Herb. Amaryll.*

Engrav. Bot. Mag. t. 1073.—Bot. Reg. t. 179.—Bot. Mag. t. 2231.—Wight's Icon. t. 2021—22.

Spec. Char. Caulescent or stemless: leaves linear-lanceolate, very smooth: margins entire, striated beneath, 3—4-feet long: scaped axillary, shorter than the leaves, a little compressed: flowers numerous, 12—50 in an umbel, white, not fragrant: berries roundish.

Concans. Lower Bengal. Silhet. Flowering nearly all the year.

(3) C. augustum. *(Roxb.)*

Ident. Roxb. flor. Ind. II. 136.—Dalz. l. c.

Syn. C. canaliculatum, *Roxb. l. c.*

Engrav. Bot. Mag. t. 2397.—Bot. Reg. t. 679.

Spec. Char. Bulb columnar, mostly above ground: leaves lanceolate, channelled, linearly tapering, 3—5-feet long: scapes lateral from the axils of the outermost leaves and nearly as long: umbels of 30—40 pedicelled flowers, white or rosy, fragrant.

Banks of Gutpurba and Mulpurba rivers.

(4) C. AMŒNUM. *(Roxb.)*

Ident. Roxb. l. c. p. 127.—Kunth Enum. pl. v. p. 562.

SPEC. CHAR. Bulb spherical without an elongated neck: leaves 1—2-feet, broad, a little channelled, margin obsoletely scabrous: flowers 4—8-sessile, white.

Silhet, flowering nearly all the year.

(5) C. PRATENSE. *(Herb.)*

Ident. Herb. Amaryll. 256.

Syn. C. longifolium, *Roxb. l. c. p.* 130.

SPEC. CHAR. Bulb ovate or spherical: leaves lorate, flaccidly recumbent: umbel sessile, many-flowered: flowers large, white, fragrant.

Interior of Bengal. Silhet. Flowering in the rainy season.

(6) C. ORNATUM. *(Herb.)*

Ident. Herb. l. c.

Syn. C. zeylanicum, *Linn.* C. latifolium, *Roxb.* C. Herbertianum, *Wall. pl. As. rar. II.* 145. Amaryllis zeylanica, *Linn.* A. latifolia, *Herit.* C. speciosum, *Herb.* C. Moluccanum, *Roxb.* A. Moluccana, *Ker.* C. Careyanum, *Herb.*

Engrav. Bot. Mag. 1171.—Bot. Rep. 478.—Rheede Mal. xi. t. 39.—Bot. Mag. t. 2217.—Bot. Mag. t. 2292, 2466. Wight's Icon. t. 2019—20.

SPEC. CHAR. Bulb spherical: caudex slender: leaves undulated: umbel somewhat 20-flowered: segments of the perianth broad, striated externally: cells many-seeded: flowers large, white, streaked with purple, with a purple tube, sometimes reddish or pale rose, fragrant.

Peninsula. Bengal. Coromandel. Flowering in the rainy season.

GENUS II. PANCRATIUM.

Hexandria Monogynia. *Sex: Syst:*

Deriv. From *Pan* all, and *Kratys* potent, alluding to their supposed medicinal virtues.

GEN. CHAR. Perianth superior, corollaceous, withering persistent, tube elongated, straight: throat funnel-shaped enlarged, limb 6-parted, segments almost equal, spreading: faucial crown turbinate-infundibular, 6-lobed, very far adnate to the limb, stameniferous between the entire or 2-cleft lobes: stamens 6, erect-connivent, equal: filaments subulate-filiform, decurrent: anthers linear-oblong, fixed by the middle of the back, incumbent: ovary inferior, 3-cornered, 3-celled: ovules numerous in two rows, ascending: styline column filiform: stigma clavate, 3-cornered, entire: capsule membranaceous, 3-cornered, 3-celled, 3-valved, many-seeded: seeds sub-globose: testa black, crustaceous: embryo cylindric, straight, axile, shorter than the fleshy albumen: radicle extremity reaching the filum,—Maritime bulbous and scape-bearing herbs, bulb tunicated: leaves lorate-linear or lanceolate: scape solid, many-flowered: spathe 2-valved: flowers pedicelled or sessile, mixed up with linear bracteoles, erect, white, externally green.

(1) P. PARVUM. *(Dalz.)*

Ident. Dalz. in Hook. Journ. Bot. II. p. 144.

SPEC. CHAR. Leaves linear striated, rather flat, attenuated towards the base: scape compressed, striated, 3—4-flowered: corolla tube very long and slender: corona half the length of the limb, 12-toothed: flowers white: capsule ovate, 3-lobed, seeds few in each cell.

Concan and Ghaut hills, flowering in June.

(2) P. VERECUNDUM. *(Soland.)*

Ident. Spreng. syst. II. p. 46.

Syn. P. biflorum and triflorum, *Roxb. flor. Ind. II.* 125.

Engrav. Wight's Icon. t. 2023.—Bot. Reg. t. 413.

SPEC. CHAR. Leaves linear-acute: limb of the corolla shorter than the tube: divisions of the corona alternately deeper: stamens incurved, 2—3 times longer than the segments of the crown: flowers pure white.

Coimbatore, flowering in the rainy season.

(3) P. MALABATHRICUM. *(Herb.)*

Ident. Herb. Amaryll. 202, 206.—Kunth Enum. pl. v. 661.

Engrav. Rheede Mal. xi. t. 46.

SPEC. CHAR. Leaves oblong-linear, acuminate, keeled: segments of the perianth linear, erect: crown with 2-teethed sinuses, base adnate to the segments: flowers white.

Malabar.

ORDER CLXXIV. HYPOXIDACEÆ.

Flowers hermaphrodite: perianth corollaceous, adherent to the ovary, limb 6-parted: stamens 6, inserted at the base of the segments of the perianth: filaments distinct: anthers incurved, 2-celled, erect, dehiscing lengthways: ovary 3-celled, cells opposite the sepals: style terminal, simple: stigmas distinct or combined: ovules numerous, axile, amphitropal: fruit indehiscent, dry or baccate, 1—3-celled: seeds numerous, roundish, with a lateral hilum and beaked strophiole: embryo in the axis of fleshy albumen: radicle remote from the hilum. —Perennial herbs with tuberous or fibrous roots: leaves springing from the root and crown, linear, entire, plaited: scapes simple or branched.

GENUS I. HYPOXIS.

Hexandria Monogynia. *Sex: Syst.*

Deriv. From *Hypo*, beneath, and *Oxys*, sharp, referring to the base of the capsule.

GEN. CHAR. Perianth corolline, tube connate with the ovary, limb 6-parted, persistent: stamens 6: ovary inferior, 3-celled: ovules in two rows: style free: stigmas 3, adnate to the corners of the style, seldom distinct: capsule crowned with the withered limb, 3-celled, not valved: seeds numerous.—Perennial herbs: flowers in a bract-shaped or sub-glumaceous 2-valved spathe.

(1) H. LEPTOSTACHYA. *(R.W.)*

Ident. Wight's Icon. vi. and t. 2045.

SPEC. CHAR. Leaves long-petioled, lanceolate, acute at both ends, glabrous above, sprinkled with longish lax hairs beneath: scape short, slender, corymbose, lower flowers hermaphrodite: pedicels filiform, and with the ovary and exterior sepals, hairy: sepals sub-obovate, obtuse: capsules few-seeded.

Malabar, flowering in June.

(2) H. TRICHOCARPA. *(R.W.)*

Ident. Wight l. c. t. 2045.

SPEC. CHAR. Leaves long-petioled, lanceolate, acute at both

ends, glabrous above, loosely hairy beneath: scapes racemose and with the pedicels and ovary densely covered with long coarse brownish hairs: sepals ovate lanceolate, hairy on the back.

Malabar.

GENUS II. CURCULIGO.

Hexandria Monogynia. *Sex: Syst:*

Deriv. From *Curculio* a weevil; the seeds have a process resembling the beak of that animal.

Gen. Char. Perianth corolline, tube ventricose with the ovary, persistent, connate with the style, limb 6-parted, flat, deciduous: stamens 6, segments of the limb inserted low down: ovary inferior, 3-celled: ovules in 2 or more rows, amphitropal: style connate with the tube of the perianth, free at the apex: stigmas 3: berry apiculated with the tube of the perianth, by abortion 1—2-seeded: seeds few, distinguished by fleshy pulpous strophioles: lateral umbilicus beak-shaped.—Perennial herbs: roots tuberous, fleshy: all the leaves radical, ensiform: flowers radical or fascicled or subspicate in a simple scape, enclosed in a convolute 1-leaved membranaceous spathe.

(1) C. Malabarica. *(R.W.)*

Ident. Wight's Icon. vi. and t. 2043.

Spec. Char. Leaves long-petioled, linear-lanceolate, tapering at both ends, glabrous: scape racemose, the lower flowers only hermaphrodite, all clothed with long soft pubescence: bracts ovate, tapering from the base, subulate, pointed: anthers deeply sagittate, stigma large, 3-lobed.

Quilon. Mahableshwur. Common on the Ghauts.

(2) C. brevifolia. *(Ait.)*

Ident. Ait. Hort. Kew.—Dalz. Bomb. flor. p. 276.

Engrav. Wight l. c. t. 2043.

Spec. Char. Leaves sessile or short-petioled, narrow linear lanceolate, sprinkled with long soft hairs: scape short: lower flowers only hermaphrodite: tube long, slender, pubescent: bracts ovate, lanceolate, and with the perianth clothed with long loose hairs: lobes of the limb of the perianth lanceolate: stigma deeply 3-lobed: flowers bright yellow.

Neilgherries. Annamullays. Western Ghauts. Flowering in the rains.

(3) C. GRAMINIFOLIA. *(Nimmo.)*

Ident. Nimmo in Grah. Cat. p. 215.—Dalz. l. c. p. 276.

SPEC. CHAR. Leaves very narrow, keeled: flowers solitary on very long slender peduncles.

Khandalla. Belgaum.

(4) C. ORCHIOIDES. *(Gœrtn.)*

Ident. Gœrtn. fr. I. p. 63.—Spreng. syst. II. p. 60.—Roxb. flor. Ind. II. p. 144.

Engrav. Bot. Mag. t. 1076.—Rheede Mal. xii. t. 59.—Roxb. Cor. I. t. 13.

SPEC. CHAR. Leaves linear, subulate, 3-nerved: scape racemose: flowers smallish, yellow.

Coromandel. Silhet. Assam. Flowering nearly all the year.

(5) C. RECURVATA. *(Dryand.)*

Ident. Spreng. syst. l. c.—Roxb. l. c. p. 145.

Syn. Molineria recurvata, *Herb. Am. p.* 83.

Engrav. Bot. Reg. t. 770.

SPEC. CHAR. Leaves oblong, attenuated at both ends, long-petioled: scape hirsute: flowers capitate, bracteated, nodding: tube of the flower very short: flowers yellow.

Bengal. Silhet. Coromandel. Flowering in the rainy season.

ORDER CLXXV. TACCACEÆ.

Flowers hermaphrodite: perianth corolline, tube cylindric, connate with the ovary, limb superior, 6-parted, segments in two rows, all spreading or reflexed, persistent: stamens 6, inserted at the bottom of the segments: filaments petaloid, concave or forkedly hooded at the apex: anthers 2-celled, introrse, cells separate, parallel, free at the top, erect or inflexed, dehiscing lengthways: ovary inferior, 1-celled: ovules numerous, anatropal or horizontal: styline column short, thick, 3-furrowed: stigma orbiculate or depressed capitate, radiately

3-cleft: berry umbilicated to the persistent perianth, 1—or incompletely 3-celled: seeds ovate, angular or lunate: testa coriaceous, striated: hilum basilar or ventral: embryo ovoid, enclosed at the base of fleshy albumen.

GENUS I. TACCA.

Hexandria Monogynia. *Sex: Syst:*

Deriv. The Malay name.

GEN. CHAR. Same as in the Order.

(1) T. PINNATIFIDA. *(Forst.)*

Ident. Forst. pl. exs. No. 28.—Prod. No. 209.—Roxb. flor. Ind. II. 172.

SPEC. CHAR. Root tuberous: radical leaves petioled, 3-parted, segments 2—3-parted and finally pinnatifid with waved margins: petioles 1—3-feet long: scape radical, round, naked, twice the length of the petioles: umbel simple, 10-flowered: flowers long pedicelled, drooping, greenish, mixed with several long threads.

Concans, flowering in the rains.

(2) T. LŒVIS. *(Roxb.)*

Ident. Roxb. flor. Ind. II. 171.

SPEC. CHAR. Leaves oblong, acuminated: petioles and scapes glabrous: leaflets of the involucre sessile, equal, ovate, finely acuminate: flowers greenish-grey violet.

Silhet. Goalpara. Flowering in the rains.

(3) T. ASPERA. *(Roxb).*

Ident. Roxb. l. c. p. 169.

Syn. T. integrifolia, *Ker.*

Engrav. Roxb. Cor. III. t. 257.

SPEC. CHAR. Leaves oblong, acuminate: petioles and scapes scabrous: outer leaflets of the involucre stem-clasping, broadly ovate-lanceolate, reflexed, inner ones much longer, broadly petioled, galeate, oval-ventricose: flowers greenish, purple and yellow.

Chittagong, flowering in the rains.

ORDER CLXXVI. HYDROCHARIDACEÆ.

Flowers diœcious, occasionally hermaphrodite: enclosed in a spathe before flowering. Male flowers pedicelled, perianth 6-leaved, outer three leaflets calycine, inner ones petaloid, smaller: stamens inserted at the bottom of the perianth, in many rows: filaments free, sometimes 2-forked at the apex: anthers introrse, 2-celled, ovate-globose or linear: cells dehiscing lengthways: rudimentary ovary occupying the centre of the flower: female and hermaphrodite flowers solitary within a tubular, sometimes cleft spathe, sessile: tube of the perianth connate with the ovary: stamens rarely fertile: ovary inferior, 1—6-celled: ovules ascending: style very short: stigmas 3—6, deeply 2-cleft: fruit dry or succulent, indehiscent, 1—more celled: seeds without albumen, embryo undivided.

GENUS I. HYDRILLA.

Diœcia Triandria. *Sex: Syst:*

Gen. Char. Flowers diœcious: *Males.* Spathe sessile, 1-flowered: flower pedicelled: perianth 6-parted, inner segments cuneate-oblong: stamens 3, opposite the outer segments of the perianth. *Females.* Spathe tubular, throat oblique, flower sessile: outer segments of the calyx spathulate-oblong, inner petaloid, smaller: ovary 1-celled: ovules numerous: style bristle-shaped, elongated, connate with the tube of the perianth: stigmas 3, linear-lanceolate, undivided: berry somewhat 3-cornered, 1-celled: seeds few, cylindric.

(1) H. verticillata. *(Rich.)*

Ident. L. C. Rich. Mem. d'Inst. II. p. 61, t. 2.

Syn. Serpicula verticillata, *Roxb. flor. Ind. III. p.* 578.—Vallisneria verticillata, *do.*—Udora verticillata, *Spreng.*—Hottonia serrata, *Willd.*

Spec. Char. Aquatic, with long slender stems: leaves small, verticilled, sessile, oblong, serrulate: calyx muricated: flowers small, whitish.

Common in tanks throughout the country, flowering in the rains.

GENUS II. VALLISNERIA.

Diœcia Diandria. *Sex: Syst:*

Deriv. Named after Antonio Vallisneri, an Italian botanist.

Gen. Char. Flowers diœcious: *Male.* Spathe terminating the very short scape, unequally 3-valved, many-flowered: flowers shortly pedicelled, heaped together upon a conical receptacle: perianth 3-parted, valvate in æstivation: staminodes 4, petal-shaped, three unequal, fourth alternate to the sepals: stamens 3, by abortion 2—1: anthers sub-globose, cells contiguous. *Female.* Spathe terminating a very long filiform scape, tubular, throat 2-cleft: flower solitary, sessile: limb of the calyx 3-parted: staminodes 3, one usually 2-cleft: ovary 1-celled: ovules numerous, anatropal: style almost none: stigmas 3 large, often 2-cleft: berry cylindric, crowned with the limb of the calyx, 1-celled: seeds cylindric.—Perennial, stemless, aquatic herbs: leaves sheathing at the base, serrulate at the apex.

(1) V. alternifolia. *(Roxb.)*

Ident. Roxb. flor. Ind. III. p. 750.—Dalz. Bomb. flor. p. 277.

Syn. Nechamandra Roxburghii, *Planch. Ann. Soc. Nat. xi. p.* 79.

Engrav. Hook. Bot. Misc. III. t. xi.

Spec. Char. Aquatic, submersed: leaves alternate, grassy, stem-clasping, acute, many-nerved, minutely serrulate: stamens 2: ovary ovate-lanceolate: ovules parietal.

Common in tanks everywhere, flowering in the rains.

(2) V. spiralis. *(Linn.)*

Ident. R. Br. prod. 201.

Syn. V. spiraloides, *Roxb.*—V. Jacquiniana, *Spreng.*

Spec. Char. Leaves linear obtuse, quite entire, glabrous, nerved: scape spiral.

Coromandel in tanks. Patna. Flowering in the rains.

GENUS III. BLYXA.

Diœcia Octandria. *Sex: Syst:*

Gen. Char. Flowers diœcious. *Males.* Spathe terminating a short scape, throat 2-cleft, many-flowered, flowers pedicelled: perianth 6-parted: stamens 3—8, filaments filiform: anthers oblong, apiculated, cells joined by a narrow connectivum: rudiment of the superior ovary sub-globose: style bristly, 3-cleft. *Females.* Spathe as in the male, 1-flowered, flower sessile: tube of the perianth elongated, connate at the base with the ovary: ovary 1-celled: ovules numerous, ascending, anatropal: style filiform, connate with the tube of the perianth, apex shortly exserted, free: stigmas 3, linear, entire: berry cylindric, 1-celled: seeds numerous.—Perennial herbs inhabiting streams: leaves radical, sheathing at the base, linear, quite entire: scapes 2-edged: flowers emersed.

(1) B. OCTANDRA. *(Rich.)*

Ident. L. C. Rich. Mem. d'Inst. II. p. 63.

Syn. Vallisneria octandra, *Roxb. flor. Ind. III. p.* 752.

Engrav. Rich. l. c. t. 4, 5.—Roxb. Cor. II. t. 165.

SPEC. CHAR. Leaves linear, acute: male flowers octandrous, female scape straight: capsule 2-celled: flowers small, white.

Coromandel. Bengal. Flowering in the rains.

GENUS IV. OTTELIA.

Hexandria Hexagynia. *Sex: Syst:*

Deriv. The Malabar name Latinised.

GEN. CHAR. Flowers hermaphrodite: spathe terminating the scape, tubular-winged, throat 2-cleft, 1-flowered: flower sessile: tube of the perianth connate with the ovary, limb 6-parted, outer segments calycine oblong, inner petaloid, obovate: stamens 6—12: filaments cuneate-oblong: anthers fixed by the base, linear, cells separated by a narrow connectivum: ovary connate with the tube of the ovary, 6—8-celled: ovaries numerous, ascending, anatropal: stigmas 6, sessile, linear, 2-cleft or 2-parted: berry crowned with the limb of the perianth, oblong, slightly tapering, incompletely 6—8-celled: seeds ovate.—Perennial aquatic herbs: leaves radical, long-petioled, cordate: petioles dilated at the base, sheathing: fruit hidden within the spathe.

(1) O. ALISMOIDES. *(Pers.)*

Ident. Pers. syn. I. p. 400.

Syn. Stratiotes alismoides, *Linn.*—Damasonium Indicum, *Willd. Roxb. flor. Ind. II. p.* 216.

Engrav. Smith Exot. Bot. I. t. 15.—Roxb. Cor. II. t. 185.—Bot. Mag. t. 1201.—Rheede Mal. xi. t. 46.

Spec. Char. Leaves large, oblong, cordate, usually growing under water: petioles 3-sided: calyx spathaceous, winged: flowers white, longitudinally veined.

Common in tanks throughout the country, flowering in the rains.

ORDER CLXXVII. PALMACEÆ.

Flowers monœcious or polygamo-diœcious, seldom hermaphrodite, sometimes more or less immersed in the hollows of a spadix, often 3-bracteate, the 2 inner bracts opposite: calyx double, either of the 3 sepals, persistent, inner ones valvate or imbricately convolute: stamens 6, opposite the sepals, perigynous or hypogynous on a fleshy torus, rudimentary in the female flowers: filaments free, or connate below: anthers sub-linear, fixed by the back, 2-celled, dehiscing lengthways: ovaries three, rudimentary or none in the male flowers: ovules solitary, erect, orthotropal: styles as many as the ovaries, very short, connate into one: stigmas simple, undivided: fruit drupaceous or baccate, surrounded by the persistent calyx, sometimes 1—3-celled with connate carpels, sometimes three-fold with distinct carpels: cells or carpels 1-seeded: seed filling the cell, ovate or spherical: mesocarp fleshy or fibrous: albumen thick, cartilaginous, horny or woody, milky, dry or oily, solid or carved out of the ventral or central cavity, sometimes ruminated: embryo undivided, conical or cylindric.

GENUS I. ARECA.

Monœcia Decandria. *Sex: Syst:*

Deriv. The Malabar name Latinised.

Gen. Char. Flowers monœcious on the same spadix, sessile in the depressions of the rhachis, bracteate: males uppermost or below twin surrounding single females: spathe double, either complete. *Males.*—Outer calyx 3-parted, segments keeled: inner 3-sepaled: sepals lanceolate, valvate: stamens 3—6—12: filaments subulate, cohering at the base: anthers sagittate. *Females.*—Either calyx 3-sepaled, sepals convolute-imbricated: rudiments of stamens: ovary ovate, 3-celled; stigmas 3, sessile, spreading: drupe berry-shaped, 1-seeded: sarcocarp fibrous: putamen thin, crustaceous or membranaceous, connate with the testa: albumen ruminated, horny: embryo basilar, or lateral near the base.—Stem tall, slender, or sub-flexuose, ringed, polished, unarmed or prickly: fronds all terminal, pinnate, pinnæ spreading like a comb, lanceolate, acuminate, upper ones often confluent and præmorse at the apex: rhachis unarmed or prickley: petioles far sheathing, base cylindric: spadixes springing below the lower leaves, simply or duplicately branched, seldom simple, branches fastigiate: spathes membranaceous or fibrous, coriaceous: bracts and bracteoles sometimes inconspicuous: fruit oval or rarely globose.

(1) A. TRIANDRA. *(Roxb.)*

Ident. Roxb. flor. Ind. III. 617.

Engrav. Mart. Palm. 171, t. 149.

SPEC. CHAR. Unarmed: stem tall, stoloniferous: pinnæ oblong-linear or linear, lower ones ensiform-acuminate, upper ones often confluent, truncated, toothed: spadix much branched, erect: male flowers twin in one row, triandrous: fruit oblong, size of an olive, sparingly pulpy, deep orange, at length red.

Chittagong. Silhet. Flowering from May to January.

GENUS II. SEAFORTHIA.

Polygamia Monœcia. *Sex: Syst:*

Deriv. In honour of Francis, Lord Seaforth, a patron of Botany.

GEN. CHAR. Flowers polygamo-monœcious on a branched spadix, sessile, bracteolate, males upper or twin below surrounding single females: spathe double, inner complete. *Males.*—Outer calyx 3-sepaled, sepals ovate, imbricated, inner 3-cleft, segments oblong, valvate: stamens numerous, filaments filiform, free: anthers linear, sub-sagittate. *Females.*—Calyx as in the male: sepals imbricate-convolute: ovary 1-celled, 1-ovuled, ovule erect: style very short, terminal: stigma 3-lobed or capitate: berry 1-seeded: albumen ruminated: embryo basilar.—Unarmed: stem ringed: fronds large, pinnate: pinnæ reduplicate, eroded: spadixes below the fronds, lateral, simply or doubly branched: flowers for the most part green: berries oval: seed mostly striated or furrowed.

(1) S. Dicksonii. *(Mart.)*

Ident. Mart. Palm. 184.

Syn. Areca Dicksonii, *Roxb. flor. Ind. III.* 616.

Spec. Char. Stem middle-sized, slender: pinnæ linear-lanceolate, folded, truncated, præmorse, uppermost ones confluent: spadix refracted, simply branched: flowers distichous: calyces of the males subulate, a little shorter than the ovate-acuminate petals: stamens 30: stamens of the females abortive, six, penicillate at the apex: berries ovate acutish.

Forests of Malabar.

(2) S. gracilis. *(Mart.)*

Ident. Mart. Palm. 185.

Syn. Areca gracilis, *Roxb. l. c.*

Spec. Char. Stem middle-sized, arundinaceous, tufted: pinnæ folded: lower ones linear, long falcate-acuminate, terminal ones confluent, truncated, shortly cleft: segments 2-toothed: rhachis and nerves minutely scurfy beneath: spadix simple, bent back: male flowers polyandrous: petals cordate, acute, many times exceeding the calyx: berries narrow-oblong, acute.

Chittagong. Silhet. Assam. Flowering from February to March.

GENUS III. HARINA.

Monœcia Hexandria. *Sex: Syst:*

Gen. Char. Flowers monœcious on the same spadix, sessile, bracteate, females below bibracteolate among many males: spathes many, basilar, incomplete. *Males.*—Outer calyx thickened, subcylindric, 3-denticulate, inner 3-sepaled, sepals valvate: stamens 6, filaments short, free, anthers linear. *Females.*—Outer calyx urceolate, 3-cleft, inner 3-sepaled: no rudimentary stamens: ovary 2, seldom 3-celled: stigmas 2—3, connate: berry 2—3-seeded: seeds convex at the back, flat below: albumen cartilaginous: embryo dorsal.

(1) H. caryotides. *(Hamilt.)*

Ident. Hamilt. in Wern. Soc. v. 317.

Syn. Wallichia caryotides, *Roxb. Cor. III.* 91. Wrightia caryotides, *Roxb. flor. Ind. III.* 621.

Engrav. Mart. Palm. t. 136.—Roxb. Cor. t. 295.

SPEC. CHAR. Stem subterraneous: fronds simply pinnate, pinnæ cuneate, præmorse: spadix intra-foliaceous, a cubit long, terminal, at first erect, then nodding: flowers pale yellowish, rubicund at the apex, small: berry ovate-oblong, dry.

Chittagong. Assam. Flowering in the rains.

GENUS IV. CARYOTA.

Monœcia Enneandria. *Sex: Syst:*

Deriv. The Greeks gave the name to a species of Date.

GEN. CHAR. Flowers monœcious on the same spadix, sessile, males almost without bracts, twin with the bibracteolate female in the middle: spathes basilar, complete. *Males.*—Outer calyx 3-sepaled, sepals imbricated, thickened at the back, inner deeply 3-parted, segments valvate: stamens numerous: filaments very short, connate into an urceolus at the base: anthers linear, fixed by the base: rudimentary pistil none. *Females.*—Calyx as in the male, sepals imbricated: effete stamens 3, club-shaped, or none: pistil simple: stigma acute, either double or triple, stigmas connate into a pyramid: ovules solitary: berry 1—2-seeded: seeds convex at the back: albumen horny, ruminated.—Tall palms: stem ringed: all the fronds terminal, bipinnate: pinnulæ dimidiate-flabelliform or cuneate-triangular, præmorse-dentate in front and sometimes cleft: petioles sheathing: spadices springing between the leaves, large, pendulous, simply fastigiately branched, branches many, flowering downwards: caudex dying out after the fructification of the lowest, propagating, however, by lateral suckers: flowers coriaceous, green: fruit sub-globose, sparingly fleshy, purplish black or green.

(I) C. URENS. *(Linn.)*

Ident. Linn. Zeyl. 369.—sp. 1660.—Roxb. flor. Ind. III. 625.

Engrav. Lam. Ill. t. 897.—Mart. Palm. t. 107—108.—Rheede Mal. I. t. xi.

SPEC. CHAR. Stem 60 feet, straight, cylindric: adult plant bearing suckers towards the end of flowering: pinnules membranaceous coriaceous, obliquely triangular or dimidiate-rhomboid, cuneate downwards, the outer side more produced, unequally toothed in front: stamens of male flowers 18—32: berries depresso-globose, 2-seeded: at first green, then yellowish or reddish, sparingly fleshy, burning.

Malabar. Coromandel. Bengal. Flowering nearly all the year.

GENUS V. CALAMUS.

Hexandria Monogynia. *Sex: Syst:*

Deriv. From *Kalam*, a reed in Arabic.

Gen. Char. Flowers diœcious or polygamo-diœcious, spathellulate on the catkins of a spadix: spadix sheathed with many incomplete spathes. *Males.*—Outer calyx 3-toothed or cleft, inner 3-parted or 3-sepaled: stamens 6, very rarely fewer: filaments connate at the base: anthers sagittate. *Females.*—Calyx as in the male: stamens 6, rudimentary, connate into an urceolus: ovary 3-celled: ovules erect: stigmas 3, sessile: berry 1, very rarely 2—3-seeded, coated with imbricated retrorse scales: albumen horny: embryo sub-basilar.—Stems simple, often cæspitose, slender, weak, very long, usually wandering far and wide over trees and shrubs, alternately and remotely leafy, terete, narrow-ringed, unarmed, polished, shining, younger ones often besmeared with a glutinous substance, flexible, tough and elastic: fronds lateral, long sheathing: rhachis lax, often altogether leafless, exhibiting straight slender tendrils or attenuated into a tendril-shaped acumen: prickles frequent, smaller ones common on margin and nerves of the pinnæ: spadices terminal, lateral by the increasing stem, sheathed with incomplete cylindric spathes, distichously panicle-branched: flowers distichous on the ultimate branches, amentaceous with bracts and spathiform bracteoles, distinct, very small, rose-coloured or greenish: berries globose or elliptic, brown or yellowish.

(1) C. latifolius. *(Roxb.)*

Ident. Roxb. flor. Ind. III. p. 775.—Mart. Palm. 208.

Spec. Char. Stem scandent, much elongated: fronds bearing tendrils: pinnæ broad-lanceolate many-nerved, fascicled, erect, polished, convex: prickles of the sheaths very broad, flat, sub-verticilled: male spadix supra-decompound.

Chittagong, flowering in November and December.

(2) C. Rotang. *(Linn.)*

Ident. Linn. sp. 463.—Roxb. l. c. 777.

Engrav. Mart. Palm. 208, t. 116, fig. 8.

Spec. Char. Stem scandent: fronds without tendrils, pinnæ somewhat equi-distant, linear-lanceolate, acuminate: prickles of the sheathes frequent, compressed, straight, of the rhachis straight and recurved, of the spathes and tendrils bent: spadix compound: male calyx 3-cleft, campanulate, a half shorter than the broad-triangular segments of the corolla: berries ovate-sub-globose, size of a small cherry.

Moist jungles in Bengal and Peninsula, flowering in the rains.

(3) C. Pseudo-Rotang. *(Mart.)*

Ident. Mart. Palm. 209, t. 116, fig. 6.

Spec. Char. Stem scandent: fronds without tendrils, pinnæ linear lanceolate, fascicled aggregate: prickles of the sheaths and whitish tomentose rhachis subulate, straight, of the spathes and tendrils bent: spadices compound branched, abortive ones whip-shaped: berries globose.

Coromandel forests.

(4) C. fasciculatus. *(Roxb.)*

Ident. Roxb. l. c. p. 779.—Mart. Palm. 209.

Spec. Char. Stem scandent, elongated: fronds without tendrils: pinnæ aggregated into many distsnt-fascicles, ensiform: prickles of the fronds straight, scattered and confluent: spadix decompound, abortive ones whip-shaped: berries ovate.

Cuttack. Bengal.

(5) C. polygamus. *(Roxb.)*

Ident. Roxb. l. c. p. 780.—Mart. Palm. 210.

Spec. Char. Polygamous: stem scandent: fronds without tendrils: pinnæ linear, posterior ones aggregated into 3 or 4 distant fascicles, anterior ones solitary, alternate or opposite: male and hermaphrodite flowers on one and the same supra-decompound spadix, abortive spadices whip-shaped.

Chittagong.

(6) C. extensus. *(Roxb.)*

Ident. Roxb. l. c. p. 777.—Mart. Palm. 210, t. 116, fig. 4.

Spec. Char. Stem scandent, elongated: fronds with tendrils: pinnæ alternate, remote, equi-distant, narrow-lanceolate: prickles slender, straight, somewhat verticelled: berries of the compound female spadix globose, acute at the top, pale.

Silhet.

(7) C. gracilis. *(Roxb.)*

Ident.. Roxb. l. c. p. 781.—Mart. Palm. 210.

Spec. Char. Stem scandent: fronds without tendrils, reflexed: pinnæ narrow-lanceolate, shining, 6 to 12 fascicled together: prickles of the sheaths straight, thin, of the rusty tomentose rhachis, tendrils and spathes bent: spadices compound: berries globose.

Chittagong forests, flowering in May and June.

(6) C. QUINQUENERVIUS. *(Roxb.)*

Ident. Roxb. l. c.—Mart. Palm. 210.

SPEC. CHAR. Stem scandent, elongated: fronds with tendrils: pinnæ few, remote, equi-distant, lanceolate, 5-nerved, prickles rare, separate, short, strong: spadix decompound.

Silhet.

(9) C. GURUBA. *(Hamilt.)*

Ident. Mart. Palm. 211.

SPEC. CHAR. Stem scandent: fronds without tendrils: pinnæ equi-distant, linear: acute: rhachis rusty-villous: prickles of the rhachis and male decompound, spadix bent: calyx campanulate, 3-cleft, twice shorter than the lanceolate petals.

Rungpoor

(10) C. TENUIS. *(Roxb.)*

Ident. Roxb. l. c. p. 780.—Mart. Palm. 212.

SPEC. CHAR. Polygamous: stem scandent: fronds without tendrils: pinnæ numerous, alternate, equi-distant, linear, 3-nerved, acute, shining, prickly: flowers of the decompound spadix, males and hermaphrodite, consociated together in a small spathe: calyx and corolla urceolate, abortive calyx whip-shaped.

Chittagong.

(11) C. HUMILIS. *(Roxb.)*

Ident. Roxb. l. c. p. 773.—Mart. Palm. 213.

SPEC. CHAR. Cœspitose-frutescent, destitute of stem and tendrils: pinnæ of the fronds lanceolate, polished, many nerved: prickles rare, long, robust.

Chittagong.

(12) C. ERECTUS. *(Roxb.)*

Ident. Roxb, l. c. p. 774.—Mart. Palm. 217.

SPEC. CHAR. Stem erect, 15-feet, not climbing: fronds without tendrils: pinnæ linear-lanceolate, equi-distant, prickles somewhat verticelled: spadix compound: berries compound.

Silhet.

GENUS VI. BORASSUS.

Diœcia Hexandria. *Sex: Syst:*

Deriv. A name given by Linnaus to the spathe of a certain species of Date.

Gen. Char. Flowers diœcious on a spadix sheathed with many incomplete spathes. *Males.*—Catkins cylindric from the coalition of densely imbricated scales: flowers bracteate, aggregated in two rows in the depressions, emerging by degrees: outer calyx 3-cleft, inner 3-parted: stamens 6: filaments connate at the base: anthers sagittate. *Females.*—Catkins fewer, less densely scaled: flowers solitary between the scales, bracts in pairs, at first altogether overlapped by fours or more: outer calyx 3-, inner 6-sepaled: abortive stamens 6: ovary 3, rarely 2—4-celled: stigmas as many as the cells, sessile: drupe 3-, seldom 2—4-stoned: sarcocarp fleshy, fibrous: stones of the drupe obcordate, compressed, woody and fibrous: albumen cartilaginous: embryo vertical.

(1) B. flabelliformis. *(Linn.)*

Ident. Linn. flor. Zeyl. 395.—Roxb. flor. Ind. III. p. 790.

Engrav. Rheede Mal. I. t. 9, 10.—Roxb. Cor. I. t. 71, 72.—Mart. Palm. t. 108, 121, 162.

Spec. Char. Stem 30—100-feet: fronds terminal: leaves very large, fan-shaped, segments 2-cleft at the apex: petioles serrated and spinous on the margins: fruit large, spherical, obscurely brown when ripe.

Malabar and Travancore, in sandy places towards the south. Coromandel. Bengal. Flowering in the hot season.

GENUS VII. BENTINCKIA.

Monœcia Hexandria. *Sex: Syst:*

Deriv. In honour of Lord W. Bentinck; some time Governor-General of India.

Gen. Char. Flowers monœcious in distinct spadices or seldom polygamous: spathes two or more, membranaceous, basilar, lowest ones complete: flowers in the depressions of the rhachis, at length emerging: a few males alternately distichous, females solitary: either calyx 3-sepaled. *Males.*—Stamens 6, filaments distinct: anthers linear: rudiment of a pistil. *Females.*—Stamens 6, without anthers: ovary 3-celled: stigmas 3, sessile: berry spherical, succulent, 1-seeded: sarcocarp from woody branched fibres: endocarp papyraceous: nucleus furrowed: albumen solid: embryo sub-basilar.

(1) B. Condapanna. *(Berry.)*

Ident. Berry in Roxb. flor. Ind. III. 621.—Mart. Palm. 165, 229, and t. 139.

Spec. Char. Stem thin, reed-like, about 20 feet: fronds terminal, pinnate: pinnæ reduplicate: inner spathe opening lengthways: spadix bursting below the fronds, branched, coloured: flowers very small, in a sub-glumaceous joint, reddish: berries purplish, very small.

Mountains of Travancore, flowering in the rainy season.

GENUS VIII. CORYPHA.

Hexandria Monogynia. *Sex: Syst.*

Deriv. From *Coryphe* the summit; the leaves are only at the tops of the trees.

Gen. Char. Flowers hermaphrodite, sessile on a spadix surrounded by many incomplete spathes, bracteated: calyx double, outer one cup-shaped, 3-denticulate, inner 3-sepaled: sepals valvate: stamens 6: filaments dilated at the base: anthers ovate: ovaries three, cohering: styles subulate, caulescent: stigma simple: berry usually single, 1-seeded: albumen equal: embryo vertical.—Stem ringed: fronds all terminal, large, palmately flabelliform, segments cleft at the apex: flowers very small: berries yellowish or greenish.

(1) C. Taliera. *(Roxb.)*

Ident. Roxb. flor. Ind. II. p. 174.

Syn. Taliera Bengalensis, *Spreng. syst. II.* 18.

Engrav. Mart. Palm. t. 127, fig. I.—Roxb. Cor. III. t. 255, 256.

Spec. Char. Stem 30-feet: fronds orbicular, palmately pinnatifid, segments 40—50 pairs: spadix ovate-pyramidal, erect, very large, 20-feet: flowers white, fragrant: berries ovate-globose, olive or yellowish-green.

Bengal, flowering in March and April.

(2) C. umbraculifera. *(Linn.)*

Ident. Linn. sp. 1657.—Roxb. flor. Ind. II. p. 177.

Engrav. Loud. Gard. Mag. No. 18, fig. 19.—Rheede Mal. III. t. 1—12.—Mart. Palm. t. 108, and t. 127.

Spec. Char. Stem 60—70-feet, smooth: fronds sub-lunate-orbicular, palmately pinnatifid: segments of 40 pairs: spadix pyramidal, erect, equal to half the length of the stem: flowers green-yellowish, very fragrant: berries spherical, smooth, green, succulent, oily.

Malabar, in rocky mountainous places.

(3) C. ELATA. *(Roxb.)*

Ident. Roxb. l. c. p. 175.—Mart. Palm. 233.

SPEC. CHAR. Fronds sub-orbicular-lunate, cordate at the base, palmately cleft: segments ensiform, 40—50 pairs: spadix globose, equalling in height the 4th or 5th part of the stem: stem 70 feet: berries olive.

Bengal, flowering in March and April.

GENUS IX. LICUALA.

Hexandria Monogynia. *Sex: Syst:*

Deriv. The name of one of the species in the Macassar language.

GEN. CHAR. Flowers hermaphrodite, sessile or very shortly pedicelled on an alternately branched spadix, sheathed with many incomplete spathes, bracteated: outer calyx campanulate, 3-cleft, inner 3-parted: stamens 6, filaments connate into a somewhat repand cupula, very shortly free at the apex: anthers sagittate: ovaries 3, slightly cohering at the base and truncated top: style trigonal: stigma 3-toothed: drupe simple by abortion, 1-seeded, putamen thin: albumen horny: embryo ventral.—Low palms: stem somewhat reed-like: fronds terminal, digitate or palmately flabelliform: spadix hirsute: flowers usually silky-pubescent: fruit very small, usually yellow.

(1) L. PELTATA. *(Roxb.)*

Ident. Roxb. flor. Ind. II. p. 179.

Engrav. Mart. Palm. t. 134, 162.

SPEC. CHAR. Stem 5—8-feet, curved, thin, smooth, rough towards the top with the remains of the petioles: fronds peltate, digitately-flabelliform, petioles prickly on the whole of the margin: leaflets long-cuneiform, many-nerved, middle one usually broader: teeth triangular, unequally sharply 3-cleft: spadix exceeding the leaflets: flower-bearing branches simple, testaceo-tomentose: fruit oblong-obovate, succulent, orange, dotted.

Chittagong. Silhet. Assam. Flowering in November.

GENUS X. PHŒNIX.

Diœcia Hexandria. *Sex: Syst:*

Deriv. The Greek name for the Date.

Gen. Char. Flowers diœcious, sessile on a branched spadix surrounded by a complete simple spathe, bracteate. *Males.*—Outer calyx cup-shaped, 3-toothed, inner 3-sepaled, valvate in æstivation: stamens 6, (rarely 3 or 9): filaments very short, almost none: anthers linear, erect. *Females.*—Outer calyx cupular, 3-toothed, inner 3-sepaled, sepals imbricated: ovaries 3, globose-ovate, distinct, one ripening: ovules erect: stigmas sessile, hooked: berry 1-seeded: sarcocarp soft: endocarp thin, membranaceous: seed linear-oblong, with a ventral longitudinal furrow: albumen horny: embryo dorsal or almost basilar.—Stem middle-sized or almost none, ringed: fronds terminal, pinnate, pinnæ narrow, stiffish, arranged in bundles, quite entire or shortly 2-cleft, lowest ones contracted into subulate spines: spadices bursting from between the fronds, surrounded by a 2-edged woody spathe: peduncle compressed, flower-bearing branches sub-fastigiate: flowers coriaceous, supported by very small membranaceous bracts: berries yellowish or purplish, endocarp white.

(1) P. sylvestris. *(Roxb.)*

Ident. Roxb. flor. Ind. III. p. 787.

Syn. Elate sylvestris, *Linn.*

Engrav. Mart. Palm. t. 136.—Rheede Mal. III. t. 22—25.

Spec. Char. Stem long, thickish: pinnæ arranged in sub-opposite fascicles, ensiform, terminated by a spine, tetrastichous.

Common throughout the country, flowering in March.

(2) P. paludosa. *(Roxb.)*

Ident. Roxb. l. c. p. 789.

Engrav. Mart. Palm. t. 136.

Spec. Char. Stem straight, 6—16-feet, sub-arboreous: pinnæ solitary, ensiform, flaccid, bifarious: embryo in the base of the seed.

Forests bordering the Delta of the Ganges. Soonderbunds. Flowering in the hot season.

(3) P. FARINIFERA. *(Roxb.)*

Ident. Roxb. l. c. p. 758, and Cor. I. t. 74.

SPEC. CHAR. Almost stemless: fronds pinnate, pinnæ opposite, stiff, terminated by a spine.

Dry barren places in the Peninsula, flowering in January and February.

(4) P. ACAULIS. *(Roxb.)*

Ident. Roxb. l. c. p. 783.

SPEC. CHAR. Stemless: fronds radical, pinnate: pinnæ plicate, ensiform, arranged in sub-opposite fascicles, lower ones thorny.

Behar, flowering in November and December.

GENUS XI. COCOS.

Monœcia Hexandria. *Sex: Syst:*

Deriv. From the Portuguese word *Coco,* the end of the nut resembles a monkey's head.

GEN. CHAR. Flowers monœcious on the same spadix, sessile, bracteate, males more in the upper part, females more in the lower: spathe simple, woody, fusiform or club-shaped. *Males.*—Either calyx 3-sepaled, outer sepals lanceolate, keeled, usually connate at the base, inner membranaceous or fleshy, erect or connivent: stamens 6 from a basilar torus, for the most part enclosed: filaments subulate, anthers linear, sub-sagittate, erect: rudimentary ovary scarcely any. *Females.*—Calyx membranaceous or parchment-like, either of 3 sepals, outer ones sub-orbicular or ovate, imbricated, inner membranaceous: ovary ovate, 1-celled, sometimes surrounded by 6 abortive scale-shaped stamens: style very short or none: stigmas 3, at first connivent, afterwards revolute: drupe ovate, elliptic or ovate sub-trigonal, 1-seeded: mesocarp thick, fibrous, dry: putamen bony, 3-porous at the base: albumen equal or obsoletely radiate, almond-like or cartilaginous, hollow in the middle.

(1) C. NUCIFERA. *(Linn.)*

Ident. Linn. Flor. Zeyl.—Roxb. flor. Ind. III. p. 614.

Engrav. Roxb. Cor. I. t. 73. Mart. Palm. t. 62, 65, and t. 88, fig. 3—6. Rheede Mal. I. t. 1—4.

SPEC. CHAR. Stem tall, flexuose, thickened at the base: fronds spreading: pinnæ linear-lanceolate, acuminate: female flowers sub-globose: drupes very large, ovate 3-cornered.

Common on all the shores of the Peninsula, flowering nearly all the year.

ORDER CLXXVIII. PANDANACEÆ.

Flowers monœcious or diœcious, sometimes polygamous, densely packed on simple or branched spadices, spathe 1 or more leaved, usually coloured, persistent or deciduous. *Males.*—Calyx none or regular: stamens numerous: filaments filiform: anthers terminal, 2—4-celled, dehiscing lengthways. *Females.*—Ovaries almost naked, 1-celled: ovules solitary, ascending, anatropal: style none or sometimes lateral from the base of the ovary: stigma terminal, sessile, undivided: fruit baccate or drupaceous, cells one or many-seeded: seeds very small, usually furnished with a fleshy tubercle-shaped cord: albumen copious, fleshy or horny: embryo very small, enclosed at the base of the albumen: radicle next the hilum, inferior.—Stems usually arborescent, straight, decumbent, sometimes stoloniferous or rooting: leaves packed close together, alternate, usually imbricated, simple, long, pinnate or palmatifid, half-sheathing with the petiole.

GENUS I. PANDANUS.

Diœcia Monandria. *Sex: Syst:*

Deriv. From *Pandang*, a word in the Malay language, meaning conspicuous.

GEN. CHAR. Flowers diœcious. *Males.*—Spadix compound, thyrsoid: stamens numerous, packed close: anthers 2-celled. *Females.*—Spadix simple: ovaries numerous, densely packed together, free or connate in ranks, 1-ovuled: ovule ascending from the base of the parietal placenta: stigmas sessile, distinct: drupe fibrous, 1-seeded: putamen bony: seed erect: testa membranaceous: raphis filiform, obsolete.—Stem arboreous, straight, often bearing suckers: leaves imbricated in three rows, long linear-lanceolate, stem-clasping, usually spinous at the margins: spathes packed close, often coloured, projecting the spadices from the axil.

(1) P. ODORATISSIMUS. *(Linn.)*

Ident. Linn. Suppl. 424.—Roxb. flor. Ind. III. p. 738.

Syn. P. vera. *Rumph.*—Keura odorifera, *Forsk. descr.* 172.

Engrav. Rheede Mal. II. t. 1—5.

Spec. Char. Shrub, 10—12-feet: branches simple, undivided: leaves linear, rib and margins spinous: spines green: male spadices spiked, bracts white, distinct: females solitary: fruit sub-globose, peduncled: drupes turbinate filled with a many-celled putamen: stigmas oval, sessile: flowers small, very fragrant.

Sandy places near the sea coast, flowering in the rainy season.

(2) P. fascicularis. *(Lam.)*

Ident. Lam. Encycl. I. 372.—Willd. Spec. iv. 646.

Engrav. Rheede Mal. II. t. 6.

Spec. Char. Shrubby: leaves spinous at the back and on the margin: spines distant: fruit oblong, solitary: drupes fascicled.

Malabar.

(3) P. fœtidus. *(Roscoe.)*

Ident. Roxb. flor. Ind. III. p. 742.

Spec. Char. Shrubby, 5—6-feet: racemes partial, or male thyrses simple: ovaries distinct: drupes cuspidate-spinous: nuts 1-celled: flowers fetid-smelling.

Bengal, flowering in the cold season.

(4) P. furcatus. *(Roxb.)*

Ident. Roxb. l. c. p. 774.

Engrav. Rheede Mal. II. t. 8.

Spec. Char. Shrubby: leaves broad-lanceolate, margin and keel prickly-serrulate: drupe of the oblong compound fruit cuneate, crowned with a smooth, acuminate, incurved, forked spine: nuts 1-celled.

Chittagong. Malabar.

GENUS II. NIPA.

Monœcia Hexandria. *Sex: Syst:*

Deriv. The name given to the plant in the Moluccas.

Gen. Chár. Flowers monœcious on a branched spadix, branches surrounded by a spathe, lateral ones amentiform, male: upper ones female, compact in a capitulum. *Males.*—Calyx 1-bracteate, 6-sepaled, sepals linear, reflexed: stamens 6: filaments connate into a column: anthers extrorse, 2-celled. *Females.*—Calyx none: ovaries many, compact into a head, obliquely truncated, 1-celled, glabrous, 3-ovuled: stigmas 3, sessile: drupes irregular, fibrous, 1-celled, 1—2-seeded: seed bony: embryo basilar.

(1) N. FRUTICANS. *(Thunb.)*

Ident. Thunb. in Act. Holm. 1782, p. 231.—Roxb. flor. Ind. III. 650.

Syn. Cocos Nypa. *Lour. Coch.* 694.

Engrav. Mart. Palm. t. 108.

SPEC. CHAR. Palm-shaped: stem low: fronds terminal, pinnate, unarmed: pinnæ lanceolate-linear, acerose-dentate: petioles stem-clasping at the base: male flowers very minute: fruits aggregated into a large capitulum.

Soonderbuns.

ORDER CLXXIX. PISTIACEÆ.

Spadix connate with the spathe, not distinct: flowers appearing from the margin of the fronds, naked, the males remote from the solitary female: stamens definite, often monadelphous: ovary 1-celled: ovules many, erect on a basilar or sub-lateral placenta, orthotropal: style distinct: fruit membranous or capsular, 1 or more seeded: seeds albuminous: embryo antitropal.—Aquatic floating herbs: leaves entire, many nerved, lobed.

GENUS I. LEMNA.

Monœcia Monandria. *Sex: Syst:*

Deriv. From *Lepis*, a scale, in reference to the form of the plants.

GEN. CHAR. Male flowers 2, one more precocious in development than the other: filaments filiform, recurved: ovary 1-celled, ovule erect, horizontal, half-anatropal: style elongated, recurved: utricle 1-seeded, indehiscent: seed affixed in the bottom, horizontal, transverse: embryo conical: radicle lateral, remote from the hilum.—Small herbs inhabiting stagnant or gently flowing waters: fronds 1-rooted, dehiscing with twin basilar clefts: flowers proceeding from a lateral cleft.

(1) L. TRISULCA. *(Linn.)*

Ident. Linn. spec. 1376.

Syn. L. cruciata, *Roxb. flor. Ind. III. p.* 566.

SPEC. CHAR. Fronds very frequent, cruciately joined together, stalked, oblong-lanceolate, denticulate towards the apex, thin, submersed, floriferous ones floating: radicles solitary.

Bengal, under the surface of water in tanks in extensive interwoven masses.

(2) L. GLOBOSA. *(Roxb.)*

Ident. Roxb. flor Ind. III. p. 565.

SPEC. CHAR. Fronds solitary or occasionally joined together by pairs, globular, without roots, each the size almost of a grain of sand.

Bengal. Bombay. Forms a green scum on the surface of stagnant water.

GENUS II. PISTIA.

Polyandria Hexandria. *Sex: Syst:*

GEN. CHAR. Spathe tubular at the base, connate with the spadix, limb spreading, increased by a process wrapping the spadix above: spadix interruptedly androgynous, female at the base, male at the free apex: anthers 3—8 adnate to the thickened apex of the spadix, sub-globose, dehiscing by a transverse furrow: ovary 1, obliquely seated at the base of the adnate spadix, 1-celled: ovules many, sub-horizontal from a parietal placenta near the base, orthotropal: style terminal, thick: stigma sub-cyathiform: berry 1-celled, many or by abortion few-seeded: seeds pyriform, smooth: testa coriaceous, thick: embryo cylindric, enclosed in the apex of albumen: radicle opposite the hilum.—Aquatic herbs, free, floating, flagelliferous: roots fibrous: leaves sessile, expanding like the petals of a rose, quite entire, nerved: spadix axillary, solitary, supported by a short scape.

(1) P. STRATIOTES. *(Linn.)*

Ident. Linn. Zeyl. No. 322.—Roxb. flor. Ind. III. p. 131.

Engrav. Rumph. Amb. vi. t. 74, fig. 2.—Rheede Mal. xi. t. 32. —Roxb. Cor. III. t. 268.

SPEC. CHAR. Leaves roundly obcordate, waved at the margin: nerves lamelliform, confluent in a basilar truncated area: flowers pale yellow.

Malabar. Travancore. Coromandel. Common in tanks. Flowering nearly all the year.

(1) P. ÆGYPTIACA. *(Schleid.)*

Ident. Schleiden in Bot. Zeit. 1838, No. 3, p. 19.

Syn. P. stratiotes, *Delile*, 20.—Stratiotes ægyptia, *Moris hist. III. t.* 4.

SPEC. CHAR. Leaves cuneate-obcordate: nerves a little prominent, uniting in a minute basilar area.

Coromandel.

(3) P. CRISPITA. *(Blume.)*

Ident. Blume Rumphia I. 78-79 (ex parte). Schleid. l. c.

SPEC. CHAR. Leaves obcordate: narrow-cuneiform: nerves simple, free as far as the base.

Pondicherry.

ORDER CLXXX. ARACEÆ.

Herbaceous plants with tubers or creeping rhizome, stemless or caulescent, or under-shrubs: leaves usually collected together above the rhizome or at the apex of the stem, alternate: petioles sheathing, nerves of the leaf palmate, pedate or peltate, often cut at the base, cordate or hastate, quite entire or variously dissected, convolute in vernation: scape radical or axillary, enclosed by sheaths at the base of the leaves, ending in an undivided spadix: spadix sessile or stalked in the axil of a 1-leafed, often coloured, persistent or deciduous spathe, sometimes all beset with flowers, sometimes ending in a barren appendage: flowers usually unisexual, seldom hermaphrodite, frequently androgynous, the females in the lower, the males sessile in the upper part of the spadix, continuous or separated by a sterile interstice: perianth none or rudimentary in the hermaphrodite flowers: stamens numerous, free or variously connate: anthers extrorse, usually 2-celled, cells immersed in a thick connectivium, dehiscing lengthways, or by a cleft or pore of the vertex: ovaries most frequently aggregated, free or connate, 1—many-celled: ovules solitary, or many, basilar or parietal, erect sessile, or ascending from cords, seldom anatropal: style none or simple: stigma capitate or discoid, undivided or lobed: fruit baccate, indehiscent, 1—many-celled, 1—many-seeded: seeds sub-globose or angled: testa coriaceous, usually thick: albumen fleshy, mealy, copious.

GENUS I. CRYPTOCORYNE.

Monœcia Diandria. *Sex: Syst:*

Deriv. From *Kruptos* hidden, and *Coryne* a club, alluding to the shape of the flowers.

GEN. CHAR. Spathe shortly tubular at the base, limb elongated, the fold closing a tube, connate with the top of the spadix, transversely 2-celled: spadix enclosed, interruptedly androgynous, naked in the middle: anthers many, sessile at the top of the spadix, with two pores on their summit: ovaries 6 or more, verticilled round the base of the spadix, many-ovuled: ovules affixed to the inner angle, sub-horizontal, orthotropal: styles as many as the ovaries, distinct, diverging radiately: stigmas discoid: berry many-celled, umbilicate: seeds many in the cells: embryo albuminous.

(1) C. SPIRALIS. *(Fischer.)*

Ident. Fisch. MSS. — Wydler in Linnæa, v. 428. — Schott. Meletemata, I. 16.

Syn. Arum spirale, *Retz. obs. I.* 30.—Ambrosinia spiralis, *Roxb. flor. Ind. III. p.* 492.

Engrav. Blume Rumphia, I. 84, t. 36.—Bot. Mag. t. 2220.—Lodd. Bot. Cab. t. 525.—Wight's Icon. t. 773.

SPEC. CHAR. Leaves linear-lanceolate: spathe sessile, much shorter than the leaves, spirally twisted.

Banks and ponds of rivers on the coast of Coromandel, Deccan, and the Concans, flowering in the rainy season.

(2) C. RETROSPIRALIS. *(Fischer.)*

Ident. Fisch. l. c.—Kunth. Enum. pl. III. p. 12.

Syn. Ambrosinia retrospiralis, *Roxb. l. c. p.* 492.

Engrav. Wight l. c. t. 772.

SPEC. CHAR. Leaves linear-lanceolate: spathe first twisted to the right and there closed, then to the left and there open: capsule 5-celled, 5-valved.

Northern parts of Bengal, in mud soil.

(3) C. CILIATA. *(Fischer.)*

Ident. Fisch. l. c.—Schott. Meletemata I. 16.

Syn. Ambrosinia ciliata, *Roxb. flor. Ind. III. p.* 491.

Engrav. Roxb. Cor. t. 262.—Wight l. c. t. 775.

SPEC. CHAR. Leaves long-petioled, oblong-lanceolate: spathe peduncled, long-tubular, fimbriated at the apex: capsule 6-celled.

Bengal, in marshy ground and beds of streams and tanks, flowering in the rainy season.

(4) C. ROXBURGHII. *(Dalz.)*

Ident. Dalz. Bomb. Flor. p. 257.

Syn. C. unilocularis, *Kunth.*—Ambrosinia unilocularis, *Roxb flor. Ind. III. p.* 493.

Engrav. Wight l. c. t. 774.

SPEC. CHAR. Roots fibrous, stoloniferous: leaves radical, erect, ensiform, smooth, a little curled on the margin, 8 to 12 inches long: scape about an inch long, smooth, compressed: spathe as long as the leaves, erect, twisted like a screw to a very fine point, beautifully spotted inside with very dark purple: capsule coriaceous, conical, 5-celled: seeds very numerous.

Banks of streams and other wet places, common; flowering in October.

GENUS II. ARISÆMA.

Monœcia Heptandria. *Sex: Syst:*

GEN. CHAR. Spathe convolute at the base, limb fornicate or flattish: spadix unisexual below, increased above with rudimentary organs, naked with an exserted or enclosed apex: anthers verticillate in distinct filaments, cells separate or opposite, dehiscing by a transverse pore or cleft: ovaries many, free: ovules 2—6, erect, orthotropal: style short or nearly none: stigma capitato-peltate or depresso-hemispherical: berries 1—few-seeded: seeds sub-globose: testa coriaceous or membranaceous: embryo albuminous.—Perennial plants with a tuberous rhizome, stemless or caulescent, the petioles of the leaves sheathing at the base and concrete with a central scape: leaves (very rarely undivided) sometimes peltatisect, sometimes pedate or palmatipartite, segments sessile or stalked, quite entire, or rarely eroso-serrate, sub-reticulately veined.

(1) A. Murrayii.

Ident. Dalz. Bomb. Flor. p. 258.

Engrav. Bot. Mag. t. 4388.

Spec. Char. Tubers the size of small potatoes: leaves peltate, divided, segments 5 to 6, ovate-lanceolate, acuminate: lower part of the spathe green, forming a wide tube, upper ovate-convex, somewhat cucullate, acuminate: spadix subulate, bent, scarcely longer than the tube of the spathe.

Mahableshwur, flowering in May, before the leaves.

(2) A. erubescens. *(Schott.)*

Ident. Schott. Meletem. I. 17.—Dalz. l. c.

Syn. Arum erubescens, *Wall. pl. as. rar. II. t.* 156.

Spec. Char. Leaves peltate, divided, segments 10 to 12, sessile, linear-lanceolate, acuminated, entire, remotely veined: spadix club-shaped, rather obtuse, shorter than the acuminated sub-fornicate spathe.

Between Ram Ghaut and Belgaum, flowering in the rains.

(3) A. curvatum. *(Kunth.)*

Ident. Kunth. Enum. pl. III. p. 20.

Syn. Arum curvatum, *Roxb. flor. Ind. III.* 506.

Spec. Char. Stemless: leaflets 10 to 12, lanceolate: spathe fornicate, half the length of the curved spadix: roots tuberous: leaves with very long petioles: leaflets entire, glabrous.

Western coast.

(4) A. Leschenaultii. *(Blume.)*

Ident. Blume Rumphia I. 93.—Kunth. Enum. pl. III. p. 16.

Spec. Char. Leaves peltatisect, segments 10—12, sessile, oblong, acuminate, eroded, parallel-veined: spadix club-shaped, obtuse, shorter than the acuminated sub-fornicate spathe.

Neilgherries.

(5) A. echinatum. *(Schott.)*

Ident. Schott. Meletem. I. 17.—Blume l. c. p. 94.

Syn. Arum echinatum, *Wall.*

Engrav. Wall. pl. As. rar. II. t. 136.

SPEC. CHAR. Leaves peltatisect, segments 7—8, sessile, oblong-lanceolate, acuminate: spadix club-shaped, obtuse, flattish at the apex, shorter than the sub-fornicate, subulate, much acuminated spathe.

Interior of Bengal.

(6) A. TORTUOSUM. *(Schott.)*

Ident. Schott. l. c.—Blume l. c. p. 106.

Syn. Arum tortuosum, *Wall.*

Engrav. Wall. pl. As. rar. II. t. 114.

SPEC. CHAR. Leaves pedatisect, segments 7—19, lateral ones sessile, intermediate ones somewhat ansate, lanceolate-elliptic, acute, sub-repand: spadix subulate, tortuously ascending, exceeding the acute fornicate spathe.

Neilgherries.

(7) A. GRACILE. *(Kunth.)*

Ident. Kunth. Enum. pl. III. p. 21.

Syn. Arum gracile, *Roxb. flor. Ind. III. p.* 505.

Engrav. Wight's Icon. t. 793.—Rheede Mal. xi. t. 21.

SPEC. CHAR. Stemless: leaves deeply 3-parted or sub-ternate, lobes acute, the middle one oblong, lateral ones semi-hastate: spathe flagelliform, the length of the ffagelliform spadix: nectarial scales simple and revolute.

Silhet.

GENUS III. TYPHONIUM.

Monœcia Enneandria. *Sex: Syst:*

GEN. CHAR. Spathe convolute at the base: spadix interruptedly androgynous below, rudimentary organs collected below the stamens, apex subulate: anthers distinct: cells opposite, dehiscing lengthways: ovaries many, free: ovule 1, basilar, erect from a longish thread, orthotropal: stigma terminal, sessile, depresso-hemispherical: berries 1-seeded: seed sub-globose, erect, sessile: testa coriaceous, thick, wrinkled: embryo albuminous: radicle superior.—Stemless herbs with a tuberous rhizome: leaves simultaneous, long-petioled, nerved, cordate or hastate, entire: scape long exserted from the sheathing bases of the leaves: spathe of the same colour.

(1) T. DIVARICATUM. *(Decaisne.)*

Ident. Decaisne descr. herb. Timor. 39.

Syn. Arum divaricatum, *Blume.* A. Orixense, *R. Br. prod.* 336 *(ex parte).* A. trilobatum, *Thunb. Jap.* 234. A. divaricatum, *Linn. Roxb. flor. Ind. III. p.* 503. Arisarum Amboinicum, *Rumph.*

Engrav. Lodd. Bot. Cab. t. 422.—Bot. Mag. t. 339 and 2324. Rumph. Amb. 5 t. 110, fig. 2.—Wight's Icon. 790.

SPEC. CHAR. Stemless: leaves cordate-hastate, entire or 3-cleft, lobes of the base rounded: spathe ovate-oblong above, reflexed, longer than the subulate spadix: rudimentary organs glomerate, bristle-shaped: filaments incurved.

Malabar.

(2) T. CUSPIDATUM. *(Decaisne.)*

Ident. Decaisne l. c.—Kunth Enum. pl. III. p. 26.

Syn. Arum cuspidatum, *Blume.*

Engrav. Blume Rumphia I. t. 30, fig. 1, 2.—Rheede Mal. xi. t. 20.

SPEC. CHAR. Leaves hastate, entire: spathe linear-lanceolate above, reflexed, nearly equalling the subulate spadix: rudimentary organs lax, bristle or scale-shaped.

Malabar.

(3) T. FLAGELLIFORME. *(Blume.)*

Ident. Blume Rumphia I. 134.—Kunth. l. c.

Syn. Arum flagelliforme, *Roxb. flor. Ind. III.* 502.

Engrav. Lodd. Bot. Cab. t. 396.—Wight's Icon. t. 791.

SPEC. CHAR. Stemless: leaves ovate, undivided or 3-parted: spathe narrow-lanceolate above, reflexed, equalling the spadix.

Bengal.

(4) T. BULBIFERUM. *(Dalz.)*

Ident. Dalz. in Hook. Journ. Bot. iv. 113.—Bomb. Flor. p. 258.

SPEC. CHAR. Leaves 2, cordate-hastate, mucronulate, long-petioled, shining beneath: petioles 3 times longer than the leaf, striated, bulb-bearing at the apex: spathe narrow-linear, pale rose: spadix as long as the spathe, filiform: ovules 6, erect, stalked, fixed to the base of the ovary.

Southern Concan, flowering in June.

GENUS IV. SAUROMATUM.

Monœcia Enneandria. *Sex: Syst:*

Gen. Char. Spathe tubular at the base, limb flat, spreading: spadix interruptedly androgynous below, rudimentary organs scattered below the stamens, apex sub-clavate: anthers sessile, distinct: cells opposite, somewhat obliquely dehiscing by a small cleft: ovaries many, free, 1-celled: ovules 2, basilar, erect from short threads, orthotropal: stigma terminal, sessile, depresso hemispherical: berries 1-seeded.—Herbs with a globose, fleshy, large, rooting tuber: scape radical, very short, scaly at the base: spathe spotted: leaf appearing late, pedatipartite, many-lobed.

(1) S. sessiliflorum. *(Schott.)*

Ident. Kunth Enum. pl. III. p. 28.

Syn. Arum sessiliflorum, *Roxb. flor. Ind. III.* 507.

Engrav. Wight's Icon. t. 800.

Spec. Char. Stemless: leaves pedate: leaflets about 9, broad-lanceolate, entire: spathes sessile, bursting out when the plant is destitute of flowers, revolute, twice exceeding the long, conical, erect, acute spadix: nectarial filaments club-shaped: anthers 2-lobed: berries 1—2-seeded.

Around Cawnpore, flowering in the hot weather.

GENUS V. AMORPHOPHALLUS.

Monœcia Polyandria. *Sex: Syst:*

Gen. Char. Spathe convolute at the base, limb flat, spreading: spadix continuously androgynous below, rudimentary organs none: sterile appendage elongated, smooth or depresso-dilated, warty: anthers distinct, furnished with a very short filament: cells 2, opposite, dehiscing at the apex by a double pore: ovaries many, free, 2—3—4-celled: ovules solitary in the cells, basilar, anatropal: style distinct or none: stigma sometimes capitately undivided, sometimes emarginate or depresso-lobate: berries distinct, 1 few-seeded: seed exalbuminous.—Herbs with a fleshy rooting tuber: scape radical, short: leaves appearing late, sub-solitary, bi-pinnatifid-decompound.

(1) A. campanulatus. *(Blume.)*

Ident. Blume in Decaisne descr. herb. Timor. 38: in Rumphia I. 139.

Syn. Arum Rumphii, *Gaud. in Freyc. voy.* A. campanulatum *Roxb. flor. Ind. III.* 509. Tacca phallifera, *Rumph.* Candarum Rumphii, Roxburghii et Hookeri, *Schott. Melet. I.* 17.

Engrav. Wight's Icon. t. 785. Blume Rumphia I. t. 32, 33. Bot. Mag. t. 2812. Rumph. Amb. v. t. 113, fig. 2.

Spec. Char. Stemless: leaves decompound: flowers sessile with respect to the surface of the ground, and appearing when the plant is destitute of leaves: spathe the length of the spadix, campanulate, with curled margins, no nectary: club broad ovate, lobate: anthers 2-celled.

Coromandel. This species is much cultivated in the northern Circars and other parts of the Peninsula for the sake of its nutritious roots. The flowers are very small and appear in June.

(2) A. bulbifer. *(Blume.)*

Ident. Blume l. c. 148.—Kunth Enum. pl. III. p. 34.

Syn. Arum bulbiferum, *Roxb. l. c. p.* 510. Pythonium bulbiferum, *Schott Melet. I.* 18.

Engrav. Wight l. c. t. 783. Bot. Mag. t. 2072—2508.

Spec. Char. Root tuberous, stemless: leaves decompound, bulb-bearing: spathe ovate, obtuse, rather longer than the cylindric spadix, no nectaries.

Bengal: plentiful in woods in the vicinity of Calcutta, flowering in May.

(3) A. sylvaticus. *(Kunth.)*

Ident. Kunth l. c. p. 34.—Dalz. Bomb. Flor. p. 259.

Syn. Arum sylvaticum, *Roxb. l. c. p.* 511.

Engrav. Wight l. c. t. 802.

Spec. Char. Leaves supra-decompound: leaflets lanceolate: spadix straight, two or three times longer than the short gibbous campanulate spathe: anthers 2-celled.

Circar mountains, flowering in the wet season.

(4) A. margaritifer. *(Kunth.)*

Ident. Kunth l. c. p. 34.

Syn. Arum margaritiferum, *Roxb. l. c. p.* 512.

Engrav. Wight l. c. t. 795.

Spec. Char. Herbaceous, stemless: leaves trifid with entire

lanceolate pinnatifid segments: spathe campanulate equalling the obtuse spadix: nectaries like large pearls.

Hindostan, flowering in May and June.

(5) A. DUBIUS. *(Blume)*

Ident. Blume Rumphia I. 142.—Kunth l. c. p. 32.

Syn. Dracunculus Zeylanicus, *Tournef. Burm. thes. Zeyl.* 90.

Engrav. Rheede Mal. xi. t. 18.

SPEC. CHAR. Petioles glabrous: spathe longer than the spadix which is round obtuse above.

Malabar.

(6) A. GIGANTEUS. *(Blume.)*

Ident. Blume l. c. 144.—Kunth l. c. p. 33.

Engrav. Rheede Mal. xi. t. 19.

SPEC. CHAR. Petioles rough with warts: spathe ovate, slightly obtuse, spreading above, a little exceeding the cylindric fusiform spadix: anthers heaped together without order.

Malabar.

(7) A. LYRATUS. *(Kunth.)*

Ident. Kunth l. c.

Syn. Arum lyratum, *Roxb. l. c. p.* 508.

SPEC. CHAR. Stemless: leaves long-petioled, tripinnatifid, divisions unequal, outer ones broader, acute, obliquely oblong, lower ones narrow and obtuse: leaflets lyrate, glabrous: berries red, 1-seeded,

Circar mountains.

GENUS VI. REMUSATIA.

Monœcia Enneandria. *Sex: Syst:*

GEN. CHAR. Spathe convolute at the base, limb bent back, expanded: spadix interruptedly androgynous: rudimentary organs below the ovaries and stamens: stamens connate by two's or three's: column of filaments shortish: anthers 2-celled, connate at the back: cells arranged verticillately, widely gaping at the apex: ovaries many, free, with 3 incomplete septa, united at the apex, incompletely 3-celled: ovules numerous, affixed to the dissepiments, horizontal from longish threads, orthotropal: stigma sessile, depressed orbicular.

(1) R. VIVIPARA. *(Schott.)*

Ident. Schott Meletem, I. 18.

Syn. Caladium viviparum. *Nees ab Esenb.*—Arum viviparum, *Roxb. l. c. p.* 496.

Engrav. Lodd. Bot. Cab. t. 281.—Rheede Mal. xii. t. 9.—Wight's Icon. t. 798, 900.

SPEC. CHAR. Stemless; leaves peltate, cordate, acuminate: root flagelliferous and these runners bearing scaly viviferous bulbs in clusters.

Malabar. Courtallum. Flowering in August and September.

GENUS VII. COLOCASIA.

Monœcia Heptandria. *Sex: Syst:*

GEN. CHAR. Spathe straight or hooded: spadix interruptedly androgynous: rudimentary organs below and even above the stamens, appendage sterile club-shaped or acuminate: anthers 2-celled, cells contiguous, open by a common pore at the apex: ovaries many, free, 1-celled, ovules affixed near the base to 3 parietal placentæ, erect, orthotropal: style very short: stigma sub-capitate.—Herbs with a tuberous rhizome or caulescent: leaves peltate. peduncles (scapes) somewhat solitary or many in the same axil, shortened, sheathed.

(1) C. ANTIQUORUM. *(Schott)*

Ident. Scott. Meletem, I. 18.

Syn. Arum Colocasia, *Linn. Roxb. flor. Ind. III. p.* 494.

Engrav. Rumph. Amb. v. t. 110, fig.—Wight's Icon. t. 786, 1.

SPEC. CHAR. Stemless: leaves peltate, ovate-repand, semi-bifid at the base: scape shorter than the petioles: spathe much longer than the spadix, cylindric, erect: club sub-cylindrical, length of the antheriferous part of the receptacle: anthers many celled.

Marshy grounds in the Tanjore district. Much cultivated in Bengal. Flowering in the rainy season.

(2) C. NYMPHÆIFOLIA. *(Kunth.)*

Ident. Kunth Enum. pl. III. p. 37.

Syn. Caladium nymphæifolium, *Ventenat cels.* 30.—Arum nymphæifolium, *Roxb. l. c. p.* 495.

Engrav. Wight l. c. t. 786, 2.

SPEC. CHAR. Stemless: leaves peltate, ovate-repand, semi-bifid at the base: scape shorter than the petioles: spathe much longer than the spadix, sub-cylindrical, erect: club slender acute, scarcely half the length of the antheriferous part of the receptacle: anthers many celled.

Malabar and South Concans, flowering in the rainy season.

(3) C. cucullata. *(Schott.)*

Ident. Schott. Meletem. I. 18.

Syn. Arum cucullatum, *Lour. Coch.—Roxb. l. c. p.* 501. Caladium cucullatum, *Pers. syn. II.* 575.

Engrav. Wight l. c. t. 787.

Spec. Char. Caulescent, branched: leaves sub-peltate, cordate, acute, lobes finely rounded, convex or concave: scape half the length of the petioles: spadix cylindrical, nearly as long as the cymbiform spathe.

Bengal, flowering in the rains.

(4) C. montana. *(Kunth.)*

Ident. Kunth. Enum. pl. III. p. 40.

Syn. Arum montanum, *Roxb. l. c. p.* 497.

Engrav. Wight l, c. t. 796.

Spec. Char. Stemless: root a sub-cylindrical tuber: leaves cordate, repand, polished: spadix nearly as long as the cucullate coloured spathe: anthers many-celled.

Mountainous parts of the Northern Circars. Root poisonous. Flowering in the rains.

(5) C. fornicata. *(Kumth.)*

Ident. Kunth. l. c. p. 41.

Syn. Arum fornicatum, *Roxb. l. c. p.* 501.

Engrav. Wight l. c. t. 789.

Spec. Char. Caulescent: leaves peltate, narrow cordate, lobes angled, rounded: spadix club-shaped, upper half of the spathe vaulted, equalling the spadix: berries 1—3-seeded.

Bengal Chittagong. Flowering in the rains.

(6) C. virosa. *(Kunth.)*

Ident. Kunth. l. c.

Syn. Calla virosa, *Roxb. l. c. p.* 517.

Engrav. Wight l. c. t. 808.

Spec. Char. Caulescent: leaves peltate, ovate, slightly waved, undivided at the base: spadix 1-4th the length of the subulate spathe with the female flowers at the base: anthers many-celled.

Chittagong, flowering in September and Ooctober.

GENUS VIII. HOMALONEMA.

Monœcia Heptandria. *Sex: Syst:*

Deriv. From *Homalos* regular, and *Nema* a filament

Gen. Char. Spathe opening, at length shut: spadix androgynous: rudimentary stamens mixed with the ovaries: sterile appendage none: anthers many, sessile: ovaries numerous, free, 3-celled, ovules numerous, ascending from the central angle of the cells, orthotropal: stigma sessile, 3-cleft, concave.—Sub-caulescent herbs: leaves cordate or sagittate: peduncles short: spathe aromatic.

(1) H. aromaticum. *(Schott.)*

Ident. Schott. Meletem, I. 20.

Syn. Calla aromatica, *Roxb. flor. Ind. III. p.* 513. Zantedeschia aromatica, *Spreng.* C. occulta, *Lodd.*

Engrav. Wight's Icon. t. 805.—Sims Bot. Mag. t. 2279.—Lodd. Bot. Cab. t. 12.

Spec. Char. Caulescent: leaves sub-sagittate, cordate-acuminate, lobes rounded and divaricate: spadix cylindric, obtuse, equalling the spathe, above male, below females with abortive stamens intermixed: anthers many-celled.

Chittagong.

(2) H. rubescens. *(Kunth.)*

Ident. Kunth. Enum. pl. III. p. 57.

Syn. Calla rubescens, *Roxb. l. c. p.* 515.

Engrav. Rumph. Amb. v. 111, fig. 2.—Wight l. c. t. 807.

SPEC. CHAR. Leaves cordate, bifid at the base: spathe contracted, acute, equalling the spadix, lower third of the spadix covered with germs and clavate corpuscules intermixed, upper two-thirds covered with anthers only.

Chittagong.

GENUS IX. SCINDAPSUS.

Tetrandria Monogynia. *Sex: Syst:*

GEN. CHAR. Spathe open, afterwards expanded, deciduous: spadix sessile, female at the base, above pseudo-hermaphrodite: stamens placed round the ovaries in the upper part of the spadix: filaments cuneate, compressed: anthers terminal, 2-celled: cells divaricate, adnate, dehiscing lengthways: ovaries 1-celled, ovules solitary or twin, basilar, erect, campylotropal: stigma sessile, oblong: berry 1-seeded: seed uncinate: embryo exalbuminous.—Stem scandent: leaves perforated, laciniate or pinnatifid: petioles channelled: stipular sheaths opposite the leaf, deciduous: spathes yellowish or dirty purple.

(1) S. PEEPLA. *(Schott.)*

Ident. Schott. Meletem. I. 21.

Syn. Pothos Peepla, *Roxb. flor. Ind. I. p.* 454.

Engrav. Wight's Icon. t. 780.

SPEC. CHAR. Perennial, sub-parasitic, rooting on trees: leaves long-petioled, oblong acuminate: flowers sub-terminal: florets apetalous.

Silhet, flowering in April and May.

(2) S. PERTUSUS. *(Schott.)*

Ident. Schott. l. c.

Syn. Pothos pertusus, *Roxb. l. c. p.* 455.

Engrav. Rheede Mal. xii. t. 20, 21.—Wight l. c. 781.

SPEC. CHAR. Scandent, sub-parasitic, rooting on trees: leaves cordate, perforated on one side and pinnatifid on the other: anther 2-lobed.

Mountains of Coromandel. Courtallum.

(3) S. OFFICINALIS. *(Schott.)*

Ident. Schott. l. c.

Syn. Pothos officinalis, *Roxb. l. c. p.* 452.

Engrav. Wight l. c. t. 778.

SPEC. CHAR. Perennial, epiphytic, stems rooting: leaves oblong, cordate, entire: flowers terminal: florets naked, octandrous: berries 1-seeded.

Bengal.

(4) S. DECURSIVUS. *(Schott.)*

Ident. Schott. l. c.

Syn. Pothos decursus, *Roxb. l. c. p.* 456.

Engrav. Wall. pl. As. rar. II. t. 192.—Wight l. c. t. 779.

SPEC. CHAR. Perennial, rooting on trees, smooth: leaves somewhat decursively pinnate, segments falcate, cuspidate: flowers lateral or axillary, long peduncled.

Silhet, flowering in the hot season.

GENUS X. POTHOS.

Tetrandria Monogynia. *Sex: Syst:*

Deriv. A Cingalese name.

GEN. CHAR. Spathe reflexed, persistent: spadix, stalked, sub-globose, beset with hermaphrodite flowers: sepals 4: stamens 4, opposite the sepals: filaments linear, flattened: anthers 2-celled: ovary 1-celled: ovules 1—3, basilar, campylotropal: stigma sessile, umbilicate: berry 1—2-seeded: seeds exalbuminous.

(1) SCANDENS. *(Linn.)*

Ident. Linn. spec. 1374.—Roxb. flor. Ind. I. p. 451.

Engrav. Bot. Reg. t. 1337.—Hook. Icon. t. 175.—Wight's Icon. t. 776.—Rheede Mal. vii. t. 40.—Rumph. Amb. v. t. 184, fig. 1—3.

SPEC. CHAR. Rooting epiphyte: leaves more or less long-petioled, lanceolate or oblong-lanceolate, narrow-acuminate, obtusely rounded at the base and there articulated with a winged petiole: spadix axillary, solitary, peduncled, recurved, sub-globose: spathe ovate, acute, boat-shaped, reflexed.

Malabar. Chittagong.

GENUS XI. LASIA.

Tetrandria Monogynia. *Sex: Syst:*

Gen. Char. Spathe elongated, opened, at length shut: spadix sessile, shortened, cylindric, beset with hermaphrodite flowers: stamens four opposite the four sepals: filaments linear, flattened: anthers 2-celled: ovary 1-ovuled, ovules pendulous from the top of the cell, campylotropal: stigma sessile, sub-truncate: berry muricated, 1-seeded: seed exalbuminous.—Herbs, almost stemless, erect or decumbent, bristling all over with sharp prickles: leaves pinnatifid: petioles sheathed at the base.

(1) L. Loureirii. *(Schott.)*

Ident. Schott Meletem, I. 21.

Syn. L. aculeata, *Lour. Coch.* I. 103.—Pothos Lasia, *Roxb. flor. Ind. I. p.* 458.

Spec. Char. Stemless: leaves long-petioled, petioles and scapes armed with short curved prickles: scapes almost equalling the leaf: spathe very long, subulate, twisted.

Circar mountains. Silhet. Flowering in December.

(2) L. heterophylla. *(Schott.)*

Ident. Schott l. c.

Syn. Pothos heterophylla, *Roxb. l. c. p.* 457.

Engrav. Wight l. c. t. 777.

Spec. Char. Caulescent, creeping, armed: leaves from cordate-sagittate to pinnatifid: spathe erect, spiral, many times longer than the short cylindric spadix: florets tetra-petalous.

Bengal.

GENUS XII. TAPINOCARPUS.

Tetrandria Monogynia. *Sex: Syst:*

Gen. Char. Spathe convolute at the base, limb narrow elongated, acuminated, flat, spreading: spadix below interruptedly androgynous, cylindric at the apex, slender, nearly equalling the spathe: anthers distinct, sessile, cells cylindric parallel, much larger than the connectivum, dehiscing by a pore at the apex: ovaries, many, free, obconical, verticelled around the base of the spadix, biserial, 1-celled: ovules in the cells 6, cords longish, spongiose, 2—3 basilar, erect, rest pendulous from the apex: stigma sessile, depressed-hemispherical.

(1) T. Indicus. *(Dalz.)*

Ident. Dalz. in Hook. Journ. Bot. III. p. 346.

Spec. Char. Stemless: root small, tuberous, perennial: leaves long-petioled, cordate-hastate, entire, basal lobes obtuse: scape long-exserted: spathe convolute at the base, above narrow-elongated, acuminate, flat: spadix cylindric above, slender, as long as the spathe: scape in fruit twisted and bent downwards, the fruit resting on the ground.

Vingorla, flowering in the rainy season.

GENUS XIII. LAGENANDRA.

Polyandria Monogynia. *Sex: Syst:*

Gen. Char. Spathe tubulose at the base, the middle cleft somewhat closed, from the middle much attenuated, subulate, valve almost closing the tube, connate with the mucronate vertex of the spadix: spadix enclosed, interruptedly androgynous, middle naked filiform: stamens numerous, collected together at the hemispherical top of the spadix, sessile, spirally arranged: anthers didymous, 2-celled, cells lageniform: ovaries numerous, verticelled round the base of the spadix, free, obconical, angled by mutual pressure, softly echinulate around the apex, 1-celled, ovules 4—8 erect on a basilar placenta: stigma sessile, flat, discoid, 5-cornered, papillose: capsules (ripe) a little fleshy, collected together at the apex of the scape, forming a head a finger in diameter: seeds cylindric-oblong, furrowed, hilum fleshy, integument of the seed breaking: embryo cylindric in copious horny albumen.

(1) L. toxicaria. *(Dalz.)*

Ident. Dalzell l. c. p. 289.

Spec. Char Marshy, 3-feet, root or rhizome thick, creeping: leaves long-petioled, oblong, obtuse, entire, coriaceous, large: sheaths stipulary, opposite the leaf: scapes axillary, solitary, compressed: spathe longer than the scape, tubular at the base, attenuated into a long slender apex: fruit compound: seeds minute.

Marshes of South Concan. Belgaum. It is a deadly poison. Flowering in February.

ORDER CLXXXI. TYPHACEÆ.

Male and female flowers in distinct spadices of the same plant, narrowly contracted, some to a simple pistil, some reduced to a naked stamen, mostly barren: fertile stamens sometimes solitary, sometimes approximated by twos or fours and connate with the filaments, intermixed with more numerous scale-shaped sterile stamens: filament long: anthers 2-celled, dehiscing lengthways, fixed by the base, erect, cells contiguous, parallel: pistils sessile or stalked, each surrounded by sterile stamens: ovary 1-ovuled, ovule pendulous from the apex of the cell: style one: stigma tongue-shaped, unilateral, elongated: fruit 1-seeded, a juiceless drupe, indehiscent: seed inserted: testa very thin, membranaceous: embryo straight, cylindric, in the axis of fleshy albumen, furnished with a lateral cleft: radicle superior, looking towards the hilum.—Marshy herbs: stem simple, seldom branched above, terete, without knots, leafy: leaves scattered, narrow-linear, horizontal, sheathing at the base: spadices super-posed at the top of the stem or branches, dense flowered, globose or cylindric, upper males, lower females.

GENUS I. TYPHA.

Monœcia Triandria. *Sex: Syst:*

Deriv. From *Typhos* a marsh, the habitat of the species.

Gen. Char. Spadices two, cylindric, pannose, lower female, upper male, one sometimes double: fertile stamens approximated by twos or fours, surrounded by the more numerous sterile ones: pistils long-stalked, 1-celled: style long, capillaceous: fruit subdrupaceous: the rest as in the order.

(1) T. angustifolia. *(Linn.)*

Ident. Linn. Spec. 1377.—Roxb. flor. Ind. III. p. 567.

Engrav. Engl. Bot. t. 1456.—Flor. Dan. t. 815.

Spec. Char. Leaves linear, somewhat channelled below, exceeding the flower-bearing stem: male spadix remote from the female, both cylindric.

Peninsula. Bengal. Flowering in the rainy season.

(2) T. elephantina. *(Roxb.)*

Ident. Roxb. l. c. p. 566.

SPEC. CHAR. Leaves ensiform, obtuse, the length of the stem: male ament distinct from the female, interstice of 2—3 fingers: filaments solitary, 1—3 antheriferous at the apex.

Margins of tanks and beds of rivers throughout India, flowering nearly all the year.

ORDER CLXXXII. ERIOCAULACEÆ.

Flowers capitate, sometimes diœcious, bracteated, calyx double: ovary 3-celled, superior, surrounded by a 2—3-teethed or lobed membranous tube: ovules solitary, orthotropal: style very short: stigmas equal in number to the cells of the ovary: capsule loculicidally dehiscing: seeds solitary, pendulous, covered with wings or rows of hairs: embryo more or less lenticular, lying upon albumen at the extremity of the seed opposite the hilum.—Perennial marshy plants, stemless, scape-bearing, or caulescent, sometimes suffrutescent: leaves fistular, quite entire, radical ones packed close, cauline ones scattered: flowers very small.

GENUS I. ERIOCAULON.

Triandria Trigynia. *Sex Syst:*

Deriv. From *Erion* wool, and *Caulon* a stem.

GEN. CHAR. Flowers capitate, androgynous, bracteate, central ones male, marginal ones female, the former longish pedicelled: calyx double, outer 3-sepaled, lateral sepals keeled, boat-shaped, inner tubular or trumpet-shaped, limb bilabiately 3-lobed: stamens 6, very rarely 3, inserted on the limb of the inner calyx, three alternate opposite the sepals and adnate to them: anthers 2-celled, introrse: female flowers very shortly pedicelled: calyx double, 3-sepaled, persistent, outer one often remote from the inner one, more or less regular: ovary sessile, 3-coccous, cocci 1-ovuled: style one: stigmas 3, simple: capsule 3-coccous, loculicidally dehiscing: seeds mostly ribbed.—Marshy stemless plants: leaves grassy, quite entire, sometimes fistular: peduncles simple, scapiform, sulcately angular, sheathed at the base, 1-headed at the apex: capitules involucrated with empty bracts: receptacle hairy: bracts surrounding the flowers and calyxes, usually white with thickish white opaque hairs.

(1) E. SETACEUM. *(Lynn.)*

Ident. Linn. spec. 129.—Mart. in Wall. pl. As. rar. III. 29.

Syn. Randalia Malabarica, *Petiv. Gazophyl. t.* 33, *fi.* 10.

Engrav. Rheede Mal. xii. t. 68.

SPEC. CHAR. Stem simple, elongated, submersed, very densely leafy: leaves capillaceous, bi-fistular, pellucid, peduncles and sheaths glabrous, the latter much shorter than the leaf, the former 6-furrowed: heads of flowers glabrous: involucrating bracts broadly ovate, round at the top, floral ones short-acuminate: male flowers hexandrous, females trigynous.

Bengal. Peninsula. Flowering in the rains.

(2) E. HAMILTONIANUM. *(Mart.)*

Ident. Mart. l. c. p. 29.

SPEC. CHAR. Glabrous: scapes striated: leaves linear-lanceolate acuminate, much smaller than the scapes: heads of flowers globose, shining, testaceous, glabrous: bracts oblong, involucral ones slightly obtuse, inner ones shortly mucronulate: female calyces scarcely broader than the corollas.

Goalpara.

(3) E. LUZULÆFOLIUM. *(Mart.)*

Ident. Mart. l. c. p. 28.

SPEC. CHAR. Rhizome perpendicular, short, simple, with a leafy apex: leaves sub-ensiform linear, narrow-acute, pellucid, glabrous, exceeding the sheaths: peduncles 5-furrowed, glabrous: heads of flowers whitish villous: involucral bracts obovate, rounded at the apex, floral ones spathulate, acute: male flowers hexandrous, female ones trigynous.

Silhet.

(4) E. ARGENTEUM. *(M.art.)*

Ident. Mart. l. c. p. 28.

SPEC CHAR. Stemless: leaves linear from a broad base, narrow acute, not pellucid, stiffish, densely beset above with very short adpressed hairs, exceeding the glabrous sheaths: peduncles 6-furrowed: heads of flowers snow-white villous: involucral bracts obovate, round at the top, floral ones acuminate: male flowers hexandrous, female trigynous.

Bengal in rice-fields.

32

(5) E. Brownianum. *(Wall.)*

Ident. Wall. pl. As. rar. II. 25, t. 248.

Spec. Char. Stemless: leaves long, grassy linear, narrow at the top, many-nerved, not pellucid, pubescent on both sides, exceeding the softly villous pubescent sheaths: peduncles sulcately 7 angled, sparingly puberulous, slowly glabrate, scarcely exceeding the leaves: heads of flowers hemispherical or globose, white villous: involucral bracts obovate, round at the top, glabrous, floral ones rhomb-cuneate, acute: male flowers hexandrous, females trigynous.

Silhet.

(6) E. consanguineum. *(Kunth.)*

Ident. Kunth Enum. pl. III. p. 566.

Spec. Char. Stemless: leaves grassy linear, narrow acutish, very finely nerved, scarcely pellucid, peduncles and sheaths glabrous: peduncles furrowed, 5-angular, exceeding the leaves: heads of flowers depressed globose, white powdery: involucral bracts obovate, round at the top, glabrous, floral ones sub-rhomb-cuneate, acute: male flowers hexandrous, female trigynous: seeds lineolate.

Peninsula.

(7) E. melaleucum. *(Mart.)*

Ident. Mart. l. c. p. 29.

Spec. Char. Rhizome annual: scape striated, longer than the leaves: leaves narrow linear, acute, sheaths transversely truncated: heads of flowers globose: bracts oblong, darkish: perianths blackish, bearded above with white hairs.

Coromandel.

(8) E. sexangulare. *(Linn.)*

Ident. Linn. Zeyl. p. 49.

Syn. E. minimum, *Lam. Encycl. III.* 275. Leucocephala spathacea, *Roxb. flor. Ind. III.* 613.

Spec. Char. Stemless: leaves narrow-linear, subulate, 3-nerved, pellucid: peduncles and sheaths glabrous, the latter half the length of the leaf: peduncles 5-furrowed: heads of flowers glabrous, involucral bracts oblong, obtuse: male flowers hexandrous, female trigynous.

Bengal. Peninsula. Western Coast. Flowering in the rains.

(9) E. quinquangulare. *(Linn.)*

Ident. Linn. Zeyl. p. 48.

Syn. Leucocephala graminifolia, *Roxb. l. c. p.* 612.—Sphacrochloa quinquangularis, *Beauv. and Desv. in Ann. des Scien. Nat.* xiii. 47.

Spec. Char. Stemless: leaves grassy, linear, sharp, 7—11-nerved, pellucid, minutely and obscurely strigose: sheaths shorter than the leaf and with the peduncles glabrous, the latter 5-furrowed.

Rice fields throughout the country.

(10) E. Wallichianum. *(Mart.)*

Ident. Mart. l. c. p. 26, t. 249.

Spec. Char. Stemless: leaves grassy linear, narrow acute, many-nerved, sub-pellucid: peduncles and sheaths glabrous: peduncles furrowed, 5-angled, twice the length of the leaves: leaves membranous: sheathes lax, membranaceous: seeds with small hairs in rows.

Peninsula. Western coast.

(11) E. odoratum. *(Dalz.)*

Ident. Dalz. in Hook. Journ. Bot. III. p. 280.

Spec. Char. Stemless: leaves subulate, recurved, 7-nerved, 1-inch long: sheaths as long as the leaf: peduncles several, 5-angular, 6 inches high, twisted, filiform, glabrous: heads of flowers snow-white: involucral bracts very short, obovate-cuneate, scarious: floral ones rhomb-cuneate, clothed with opaque white hairs at the apex.

Stagnant water at Malwan, flowering in September.

(12) E. cuspidatum. *(Dalz.)*

Ident. Dalz. l. c.

Spec. Char. Stemless: leaves linear ensiform, very obtuse, cuspidate, 7—9-nerved, glabrous, one-third the length of the sheath: peduncles 7-angled, glabrous: heads of flowers white, villous: involucral bracts ovate, shorter than the head, floral ones obovate, cuneate, incurved and rounded at the apex.

Between Vingorla and Malwan.

(13) E. pygmœum. *(Dalz.)*

Ident. Dalz. l. c.

Spec. Char. Stemless: leaves flat, linear, acuminate, 7-nerved, twice the length of the sheath and as long as the peduncles: sheaths striated, glabrous, acuminated and split at the apex: peduncles several, 3—4-angled: involucral bracts lanceolate-acuminate, minutely striated, 3—4-times longer than the head, spreading.

Near Malwan.

(14) E. Dalzelli. *(Dalz.)*

Ident. Dalz. l. c. p. 280.—Bomb. flor. p. 280.

Spec. Char. Stem simple, elongated, submersed, densely leafy: leaves linear, flat, attenuated into a bristly pointed acumen, 7-nerved, twice the length of the sheath: sheaths striated, glabrous, lacerated at the apex: peduncles terete, 10-furrowed, twice the length of the leaf.

On sunken stones in the rivulets of South Concan, flowering in the rains.

(15) E. Rouxianum. *(Steudel.)*

Ident. Steudel Syn. II. p. 270.—Dalz. l. c. p. 316.

Spec. Char. Cæspitose: stem very short: leaves linear-lanceolate, rather obtuse, 9—11-nerved, rather obtuse at the apex, subpellucid, twice the length of the tumid sheaths: heads of flowers snow-white, villous, a little shorter than the involucre.

Bombay.

(16) E. heterolepis. *(Steudel.)*

Ident. Steudel l. c. 271. Dalz. l. c.

Spec. Char. Cæspitose: stem very short: leaves lanceolate, rather obtuse, 9—11-nerved, scarcely one inch long: sheaths short, tumid, membranous, divided at the apex: involucral bracts in two rows, scarious, outer ones oblong-lanceolate, deciduous, interior ones ovate-obtuse, much shorter than the flower heads: floral bracts cuneate-ovate, ciliated at the apex.

Bombay.

(17) E. Nilagirense. *(Steudel.)*

Ident. Steudel l. c.

Spec. Char. Stemless: scapes 1—3-leaved at the base, somewhat twisted, angularly furrowed, hairy pubescent: leaves narrow-linear, many-nerved, narrowly fenestrate-pellucid between the nerves, hairy pubescent: capitules hemispherical, white-villous: involucral bracts broad-ovate, obtuse, darkish, hairy, floral ones triquetous from a narrow longish base, naked at the bottom: scales hairy.

Neilgherries.

(18) E. robustum. *(Steudel.)*

Ident. Steudel l. c.

Spec. Char. Stemless: radical leaves cæspitose, furnished at the base with soft wool, lanceolate, glaucous, not pellucid, folded and twisted towards the apex, more or less distinctly spoon-shaped at the top, dilated, sometimes two twined together: scape erect, clothed with two sheaths from the base to the middle, cohering with a tubular base, free at the top, twisted, furrowed: capitule solitary, spherical, concave at the base: involucral bracts oblong-ovate, here and there denticulate at the margin: male flowers hexandrous, anthers brown, ovary exactly tricoccous.

Neilgherries.

(19) E. LANCEOLATUM. *(Miq.)*

Ident. Miq. in Steudel l. c.

SPEC. CHAR. Stemless, cæspitose: leaves broad-lanceolate, very thinly striated, 2—3-times shorter than the scapes: sheaths almost equalling the leaves, leafy, acuminate: capitules depressed-globose, white, hairy: involucral bracts ovate-lanceolate, hairy at the back and ciliated, floral ones oblong ciliated: achenium ovate, very obtusely angled.

Mangalore.

(20) E. BRACTEOSUM. *(Steudel.)*

Ident. Steudel l. c. p. 272.

SPEC. CHAR. Stemless: radical leaves cæspitose, packed together, oblong-lanceolate, striated, not pellucid, twice shorter than the sheath clothing the base of the stem: scape solitary, erect, furrowed, somewhat twisted: capitule terminal, solitary, spherical, involucral bracts scariose, oblong, much shorter than the capitule, floral ones linear, hairy, obscurely green: flowers tetrandrous covered like the bracts with longish hairs.

Neilgherries.

ORDER CLXXXIII. CYPERACEÆ.

Flowers hermaphrodite or diclinous, naked or furnished with a calyx, each surrounded by a scale, congested into a many, few, or 1-flowered spike, lower ones often reduced to an empty scale: calyx, when present, rudimentary, sepals 6 or more, bristle-shaped, thorny, scabrous, or plumose, sometimes very thin, capillary, sometimes out of six all or three alternately scale-shaped: stamens three, opposite the sepals, seldom fewer (2 or 1) or more (4, 6, 8, or 12): filaments elongated after fecundation, sometimes very long, persistent: anthers 2-celled, undivided at the top, acute or mucronate, fixed by the base, linear: ovary compressed, usually triangular, 1-celled: ovule straight, inverted, adnate to a cord its whole length: styles 3, seldom 2, more or less connate below: fruit 1-seeded, indehiscent, lenticular, plano-convex, triangular, cylindric or globose, smooth, tubercled, wrinkled or striated: pericarp membranaceous, crustaceous or bony: seed erect: albumen conformable to the seed: embryo enclosed in the base of the albumen: radicle looking towards the hilum: plumula inconspicuous.—Roots fibrous: stem (culm) triangular, seldom terete or many-angled, for the most part without knots, often umbellately branched at the top: leaves grassy, sheathing at the base, sometimes reduced to a sheath: sheaths entire, sometimes cleft by age: spikes capitate or spicately congested, seldom solitary.

SECT. I. CYPEREÆ.

GENUS I. CYPERUS.

Triandria Monogynia. *Sex: Syst:*

GEN. CHAR. Spikes many-flowered: scales distichously imbricated, all flower-bearing, equal, sometimes some of the lower ones smaller, empty: bristles or scales none: stamens 3, seldom 1—2: style 3, seldom 2-cleft, deciduous: achenium triangular or seldom compressed, often mucronated with the persistent base of the style. —Culms foliate, seldom leafless: leaves grassy, usually flat: spikes fascicled, capitate or umbellate, umbels single, compound or supra-decompound.

(1) C. PUNCTATUS. *(Roxb.)*

Ident. Roxb. flor. Ind. I. p. 193.—Kunth En. pl. II. p. 4.

Syn. C. pulvinatus, *N. ab. E. et. Mey. in Wight Contrib. Bot. p*, 74 (partly).

SPEC. CHAR. Culms triangular, glabrous, leafy at the base: leaves equalling the culm, narrow, flat, thorny, scabrous towards the top: umbel 4—5-rayed, rays unequal, 4—9-spiked at the top: involucre 3-leaved, very long: spikes digitately fascicled, much spreading, oblong, compressed, 14—21-flowered: scales roundish-obovate, round at the top, emarginate, slightly recurved, mucronate, keeled, somewhat 5-nerved, pale straw, rusty lineolate at the back: stamens two: style 2-cleft: achenium obovate, compressed at the sides, rounded at the top, somewhat retuse, pale brown, 3 times shorter than the scale.

Peninsula.

(2) C. PUMILUS. *(Linn.)*

Ident. Linn. Amœn. Acad. iv. 302.—Vahl. En. II. 330.—N. ab. E. l. c. p. 74.

Syn. Pycreus pumilus, *N. ab. E. Linnæa. ix.* 283.

SPEC. CHAR. Rays of the compound umbel straight: spikelets packed in ovate spikes, reflexed, spreading, oblong, slightly compressed, 8—18-flowered: scales ovate, pale at the sides, nerved, green at the keel, mucronate, mucro spreading: style 2-cleft: caryopsis obovate, compressed, retuse, slightly dotted: leaflets of the 3—5-leaved involucre 2—3, longer than the umbel, broadish, flat, and with the cauline ones equalling the culm or exceeding it, smooth: culm leafy at the base, triquetrous, smooth: root fibrous.

Peninsula.

(3) C. VULGARIS. *(Sieb.)*

Ident. Sieb. herb. Maurit. No. 14.—Kunth l. c. p. 4.

Syn. C. conglomeratus, *Vahl.*—C. strictus, *Lam. Ill. I.* 146.—C. globosus, *Vahl.*—C. curvatus, *Vahl.*—C. capillaris, *Koen in Roxb. l. c.*—*N. ab. E. in Wight p.* 76.—*Dalz. Bomb. flor. p.* 283.—C. divaricatus, *Lam.*—C. flavidus, *Vahl.*—C. lanceolatus, *Seib. l. c. No.* 32.

SPEC. CHAR. Culms triangular, leafy at the base: root fibrous: leaves filiform, as long as or shorter than the culm: involucre 3-leaved, filiform: umbel small, usually composed of one sessile spikelet and two pedicelled ones: spikelets linear, many-flowered, diandrous: scales membranaceous, obtuse: seed compressed, dark-coloured.

Deccan. Peninsula.

(4) C. ERAGROSTIS. *(Vahl.)*

Ident. Vahl. l. c. 322.—Kunth l. c. p. 7.

Syn. C. cruentus, *Retz.*; *Roxb. flor. Ind. I.* 196.—C. sanguinolentus, *N. ab. E. in Wight p.* 75.—C. albidus, *Lam.*; *Ill.*—C. pumilus, *Rottb. gram.* 28, *t.* 9, *fig.* 4.—C. nitidus, *Lam.*

SPEC. CHAR. Culms triangular, creeping at the base: leaves shorter than the culm, keeled, flat: umbel 4—7-rayed, rays 3—8-spiked, one commonly very short: involucre 3-leaved, usually exceeding the umbel: spikes spicately fascicled, broad linear or oblong, compressed, 16—24-flowered: scales broadly ovate, obtuse, muticous, keeled boat-shaped, margins brightly or chestnut sanguineous, keel green: style very long: achenium roundish, compressed at the sides, apiculate, very finely dotted, chestnut or dark-brown, 2—4 times shorter than the scale.

Nathpur. Bengal.

(5) C. ATER. (*Vahl.*)

Ident. Vahl. l. c.—Kunth l. c.—Dalz. Bomb. flor. p. 283.

Syn. C. pumilus, *Rottb. gram.*

SPEC. CHAR. Culm triangular, smooth: leaves linear-lanceolate, smooth on the margin: umbel about 6-rayed: rays unequal with 4—15 spikelets at the top, the longer ones 3-divided: involucre 3—4-leaved, longer than the umbel: spikelets spicately fascicled, oblong-lanceolate, acute, compressed, shining and almost black: scales ovate-elliptic, obtuse, muticous, keeled boat-shaped, sides chestnut sanguineous above.

Deccan.

(6) C. STRAMINEUS. (*N. ab. E.*)

Ident. N. ab. E. in Wight Contrib. p. 74.

SPEC. CHAR. Culm filiform, compressed, glabrous: leaves almost equalling the culm, narrow, flat, scabrous at the upper margin: spikes 5—6, alternately and spicately arranged at the apex of the culm, linear or oblong-linear, acute, compressed, 20—40-flowered, straw yellow: involucre 2—3-leaved, very long: scales broadly ovate, keeled, acutely sub-mucronate: stamens 2: achenium round obovate, compressed at the sides, transversely wrinkled, chestnut, slightly shining, nearly 3 times shorter than the scale.

Silhet.

(7) C. POLYSTACHYUS. (*Rottb.*)

Ident. Rottb. gram. 39, t. xi. fig. 1.—Kunth l. c. p. 13.—Roxb. flor. Ind. I. 193.—N. ab. E. in Wight p. 75.

Syn. C. fascicularis, *Lam. Ill.*—C. paniculatus, *Rottb. l. c.* 40.—C. olidus, *Vahl. Enum. II.* 333.

SPEC. CHAR. Culm triangular, glabrous, leafy at the base: leaves shorter than the culm, flat and keeled, rough on the margins: umbel several rayed, rays branched, corymbiform at the apex, many-spiked, most frequently abbreviated: involucre 3—6 leaved: spikes fascicled corymbiform, linear-lanceolate, compressed, 20—22-flowered: scales ovate-elliptic, keeled, shortly mucronate: keel 3-nerved, green: stamens 2.

Common everywhere.

(8) C. puncticulatus. *(Vahl.)*

Ident. Vahl. l. c. 348.—Kunth. l. c. p. 15.

Syn. C. inundatus, *Roxb. N. ab. E. in Wight. p.* 76. — C. diluvialis, *Schult.*—C. procerus, *Roxb.*

Spec. Char. Tall: culm triangular, glabrous: leaves stiff, keeled flat, somewhat scabrous on the margin and keel: umbel decompound, somewhat 8-rayed, large, diffuse: rays bracteately 3—5-cleft, branches many-spiked: spikes spicately arranged, much spreading, broadly linear, 20—26-flowered: involucre 3-leaved, very long: scales roundish-elliptic, shortly mucronate, keeled: stamens 2: achenium obliquely sub-cordate, compressed at the sides, dotted and slightly scabrous, bright chestnut, shorter by half than the scale.

Peninsula. Bengal.

(9) C. tortuosus. *(Koen.)*

Ident. Koen. in Roxb. flor. Ind. I. p. 197.—Kunth l. c.—Wight Contrib. p. 75.

Spec. Char. Umbel compound: spikelets linear, incurved, 20—40-flowered: scales oval, mucronulate, chestnut: stamens 2: caryopsis obovate, lenticular, compressed, smooth: involucre 3-leaved, exceeding the umbel, leaflets spreading: leaves sub-radical, shorter than the smooth triangular culm, keeled, spirally sheathing the base of the culm.

Circars, in moist meadows.

(10) C. mucronatus. *(Rottb.)*

Ident. Rottb. gram. xix. t. 8, fig. 4.—Roxb. l. c.—N. ab. E. in Wight p. 72.—Kunth l. c. p. 17.

Syn. C. lateralis, *Roxb.—N. ab. E. l. c. p.* 73, *(Var.)*—C. lævigatus, *Linn. Mant.—Rottb. l. c. (Var.)*—C. pleuranthus, *N. ab. E. l. c. p.* 73.

Spec. Char. Creeping, stoloniferous: culms terete, 3-cornered at the apex, 1-leaved at the base: leaf erect, short, flat: spikes 2—30, fascicled and congested, seldom solitary, broadly linear, sometimes oblong, 15—30-flowered, sometimes arched: involucre somewhat 2-leaved, one leaflet erect, continuing the culm, exceeding the spikes: scales broadly ovate, concave, obtuse, upper ones acutish: stamens 3: achenia compressed, plano-convex, oblong, elliptic or sub-rotund, dotted, strawy-brown, one-third shorter than the scale.

Coromandel, and other moist localities in the Peninsula.

(11) C. PYGMŒUS. (Rottb.)

Ident. Rottb. gram. xx. t. 14, fig. 4, 5.—Kunth l. c. p. 18.—N. ab. E. in Wight p. 72.

Syn. C. squarrosus, *Roxb.*—C. diffusus, *Roxb.*

Engrav Rottb. l. c.—Rheede Mal. xii. t. 54.

SPEC. CHAR. Culms cæspitose, triangular, glabrous, leafy at the base: leaves longer than the culm, keeled and flat, scabrous at the margin: heads of flowers solitary, ovate-globose, glomerate (sometimes in threes or fours): involucre 4—7-leaved, very long: spikes lanceolate, 10—16—24-flowered: scales oblong, acutely mucronate, convex and keeled, 3-nerved: achenium oblong, terminated by the persistent style, convex and obtusely angled externally, brownish, one-third shorter than the scale.

Peninsula.

(12) C. ALOPECUROIDES. (Rottb.)

Ident. Rottb. gram. xxxviii.—R. Brown prod. 217.—Kunth l. c. p. 19.—Wight Contrib. p. 76.—Dalz. Bomb. flor. p. 282.

Engrav. Rottb. l. c. t. 8, fig. 2.

SPEC. CHAR. Culms triangular, glabrous: leaves flat, scabrous on the margin: umbel decompound, about 9-rayed, rays very unequal: umbellets 3 — 7-rayed, partial rays densely covered with spikes on every side, forming elongated cylindrical compound spikes: involucre 3—5-leaved, longer than the umbel, partial about 18-flowered: scales broad-elliptic, mucronate, obsoletely 7-nerved.

Western coast.

(13) C. CASTANEUS. (Willd.)

Ident. Willd. sp. I. 278.—Wight Contrib. p. 79.—Roxb. flor. Ind. I. 195.

SPEC. CHAR. Culms triangular and with the leaves glabrous, convolute and bristly: umbel many-rayed: rays of many spikes: involucre many-leaved, equalling the umbel: scales sharply keeled, recurved mucronate: flowers monandrous: achenium oblong, triangular, very finely tuberceled and dotted, brown, a half shorter than the scale.

In moist sandy pastures of the Peninsula.

(14) C. ANGUSTIFOLIUS. ((Hamilt.)

Ident. Wight Contrib. l. c.—Kunth l. c. p. 21.

SPEC. CHAR. Culms furrowed and with the leaves glabrous, narrow, convolute: umbels few-rayed, shorter than the 5-leaved involucre, rays many-spiked: spikes linear, compressed, 14—20-flowered: scales sharply keeled, recurved and mucronately awned: flowers diandrous: achenium obovate, triangular, very finely tubercled and dotted, brown, a half shorter than the scale.

Lower Bengal.

(15) SQUARROSUS. *(Linn.)*

Ident. Linn. Am. Acad. iv. 303.—Wight l.c. p. 75.

Syn. C. Maderaspatanus, *Willd.*

Engrav. Rottb. gram. 25, t. 6, fig. 3.

SPEC. CHAR. Leaves linear, keeled, glabrous, longer than the culm: umbel 3—5-rayed, rays very unequal, many-spiked: spikes clustered, 10—11-flowered: involucre very long: scales sharply keeled, 3-nerved, mucronate: flowers monandrous: achenium linear, triangular, 1-third shorter than the scale.

Peninsula.

(16) C. ARISTATUS. *(Rottb.)*

Ident. Rottb. gram. 23.—Roxb. flor. Ind. I. 190.—Wight Contrib. p. 78.

Syn. C. capitatus, *Burm. Ind.* 21.—C. intricatus, *Linn. Mant.* 182.—Scirpus Lappaceus, *Lam. Ill. I.* 139.—C. versicolor, *Wight Contrib. p.* 78.

Engrav. Rottb. l. c. t. 6, fig. I.

SPEC. CHAR. Leaves linear, keeled, glabrous, almost equalling the triquetrous culm: umbel depauperated, 1—4-rayed, rays very unequal, many-spiked: spikes fasciculato-capitate, 8—10-flowered: capitules oblong or elliptic-globose: involucre 3—4-leaved, very long: scales 7—8-nerved, acuminately awned, awns hooked: achenium oblong, triangular, brown, very finely dotted, 3-times shorter than the scale.

Moist pastures of the Peninsula. Sandy places at Negapatam.

(17) C. COMPRESSUS. *(Linn).*

Ident. Linn. sp. 68.—Kunth l. c. p. 23.—Roxb. l. c. 194.—Wight Contrib. p. 76.

Syn. C. pectinatus, *Roxb.*—C. Coromandelianus, *Spreng.*—C. pectiniformis, *Schult. Mant. Wight l. c. p.* 77.

Engrav. Rottb. gram. 27, t. 9, fig. 3.

SPEC. CHAR. Leaves glabrous, flat, longer than the triangular culm, younger ones serrulated on the margin: umbel 1—6-rayed, rays 3—6-spiked at the top, very unequal, one almost undeveloped: involucre 3—6-leaved, very long: spikes lanceolate and linear, compressed, 24—36-flowered: scales keeled, acute and mucronate, many-nerved, green: achenium obovate, triquetrous, one-third the length of the scale.

Deccan. Coromandel.

(18) C. Silletensis. *(N. ab. E.)*

Ident. Nees ab. Esen. in Wight Contrib. p. 79.

Spec. Char. Culm triquetrous, glabrous: leaves flat, scabrous at the margin: umbel compound, many-rayed: involucre 4—5-leaves, very long: spikes fascicled and capitate, oblong, compressed, 10—13-flowered: scales ovate, boat-shaped, obsoletely 3-nerved: achenium elliptic, triangular, mucronate, a half shorter than the scale.

Silhet.

(19)* C. Haspan. *(Linn.)*

Ident. Linn. sp. 66.—Roxb. l. c. 210.—Wight l. c. p. 80.

Syn. C. autumnalis, *Vahl.*—Scirpus autumnalis, *Linn. Mant.*—C. gracilis, *Muelhenb. gram.* 18.—C. leptos, *Schult.*—C. nudus, *Humb. et Kunth Nov. gen.*—C. tunicatus, *Schult. Mant. II.* 115.—C. juncoides, *Lam. Ill. I.* 147.—C. complanatus, *Willd.*

Engrav. Rottb. gram. 36, t. 6, fig. 1.—58, t. 17, fig. 3.

Spec. Char. Culm triquetrous at the base, sometimes sheathed and leafless, or leafy: leaves linear, flat, glabrous: umbel decompound, lax: involucre 2-leaved, usually shorter than the umbel: spikes in threes, or fascicled and clustered, linear compressed, 18—30-flowered: scales somewhat keeled, navicular, 3-nerved: achenium obovate, rounded, pointed, rough with minute tubercles.

Peninsula.

(20) C. difformis. *(Linn.)*

Ident. Linn. sp. 67.—Roxb. l. c. p. 195.—Wight Contrib. p. 88.

Engrav. Rottb. l. c. 24, t. 9, fig.—Sibth. flor. græc. I. t. 46.

Spec. Char. Culm triquetrous: leaves flat, glabrous: umbels simple or compound, 3—11-rayed: involucre 2—3-leaved, very long: spikes densely clustered into globular heads, linear-compressed, 8—25-flowered: scales orbicular, reniform, retuse, blunt, 3-nerved at the back: achenium obovate-elliptic, triangular, as long as the scale.

Peninsula.

(21) C. Iria. *(Linn.)*

Ident. Linn. sp. 67.—Rottb. gram. 41.—Roxb. l. c. p. 201.—Wight Contrib. p. 87.

Syn. C. Santonici, *Rottb.*—C. panicoides, *Lam. Ill. I.* 145.

Engrav. Rottb. l. c. 41, t. 9, fig. I.

Spec. Char. Culm triquetrous, glabrous: leaves flat, flaccid, rough on the margins: umbel 6—8-rayed: involucre very long, 3—4-leaved: rays very unequal, branched and fascicled at the apex: spikes linear-compressed, 8—20-flowered, flowers distant: scales rounded, obovate-emarginate, very shortly mucronate, 5-nerved: achenium elliptic, triangular, mucronate, as long as the scale.

Deccan.

(22) C. coronarius. *(Kunth.)*

Ident. Kunth l. c. p. 44.

Syn. Scirpus coronarius, *Vahl. En. II.* 261.—Isolepis coronaria, *Roem. and Schult. syst. II.* 113.

Spec. Char. Rhizome creeping: culms filiform, triangular, glabrous, leafy at the base: leaves shorter than the culm, stiffish, very narrow, keeled: spikes many, capitately congested, roundish ovate, obtuse, compressed, many-flowered: involucre 4—5-leaved, much exceeding the capitulum: scales ovate-lanceolate, obtuse, convex and keeled, keel prominent above: achenium oblong, trigonal, very finely dotted, a half shorter than the scale.

Bengal.

(23) C. niveus. *(Retz.)*

Ident. Retz. obs. v. 12.—Roxb. l. c. p. 191.—Wight Contrib. p. 78.

Spec. Char. Rhizome creeping: culm slender, triangular, glabrous: leaves short, narrow: spikes 10—12, capitately aggregated, oblong, compressed, 38—40-flowered: involucre 2-leaved, exceeding the spikes, keeled, stiff: scales approximated, ovate, compressed and navicular, keeled, compressed at the top, 13-nerved, dirty straw: achenium obovate-roundish, equilateral, smooth, 3—4-times shorter than the scale.

Rajahmundry. Midnapore.

(24) C. arenarius. *(Retz.)*

Ident. Retz. obs. iv. 9.—Wight Contrib. p. 77.—Dalz. l. c. p. 284.

Spec. Char. Stem long, descending, covered with brown fibrous remains of withered sheaths: branches solitary, lateral, their bases covered with many-nerved mucronate sheaths: culms round, short, smooth with 3—4 glaucous retro-curved channelled mucronate leaves, much longer than the culm: sheaths a white thin membrane uniting the margins of the leaf, truncated at the apex: spikelets 12—15 in a dense head, ovate-obtuse, subtended by bracts of which two lower ones long and leafy: seed obovate, smooth, trigonal: scales ovate, mucronate, membranous, with reddish brown striæ: styles three, long, pointed.

Sands on the sea-shores of the Peninsula.

(25) C. cephalotes. *(Vahl.)*

Ident. Vahl. l. c. 311.—Kunth l. c. p. 48.

Syn. C. monocephalus, *Roxb.* Anosporum monocephalum, *N. ab. E. in Wight Contrib. p.* 92.

Spec. Char. Creeping: culm triangular, glabrous, 2-leaved at the base: leaves equalling the culm, stiff, flat, scabrous at the margin: capitule solitary, ovate-sub-globose, many-spiked: involucre 3—4-leaved, much exceeding the capitulum: spikes numerous, compact, ovate, compressed, 14—16-flowered: scales much approximated, and closely imbricated, ovate, acutely sub-mucronate, compressed and boat-shaped, keeled above (keel a little scabrous), many-nerved, brownish: fruit (unripe) ovate-oblong, attenuated at the apex into the style, internally flat, outwardly convex angular, chestnut brown, spongy and whitish below.

Bengal. Silhet. Peninsula.

(26) C. tuberosus. *(Rottb.)*

Ident. Rottb. Gram. 28.—Vahl. l. c. 340.—Roxb. l. c. p. 203.

Syn. C. stoloniferus, *Retz. Wight Contrib. p.* 81. C. spadiceus *Lam. Ill.*

Engrav. Rottb. l. c. t. 7, fig. 1.

Spec. Char. Glaucous: root tuberous, stoloniferous: culm triangular, glabrous, leafy at the base: leaves as long as the culm, rigid, flat, keel and margin rough: umbel simple, about 8-rayed, rays 3—9-spiked, involucre 3-leaved, very long: spikes fascicled, linear-compressed, 18—24-flowered: scales ovate-obtuse, 7-nerved:

achenium somewhat rounded, elliptic, obsoletely dotted, half the length of the scale.

Peninsula.

(27) C. PROCERULUS. *(N. ab. E.)*

Ident. Nees ab. Esenb. in Wight Contrib. p. 82.

SPEC. CHAR. Umbel decompound, contracted : rays very unequal, larger ones 3-cleft : spikelets spicately approximated, spreading lanceolate-linear, somewhat 30-flowered, compressed : scales ovate, muticous : bracts in the place of involucels alternate, linear, ovate at the base : caryopsis short, obovate, 3-cornered, mucronate, dotted and wrinkled : leaflets of the 3—5-leaved involucre 1—2, longer than the umbel and with the linear leaves equalling the culm, flat, flaccid, scabrous at the margin : culm leafy at the base, trigonal, smooth : root bulbous.

Peninsula.

(28) C. ARTICULATUS. *(Linn.)*

Ident. Linn. sp. 66.—Rottb. Gram. 26.—Vahl. l. c. 301.—Wight Contrib. p. 80.

Syn. C. articulatus et nodosus, *Willd.*—C. niloticus, *Forsk. Vahl. II.* 302.—C. nudus, *Roxb.* I. p. 191—C. gymnos, *Roem. and Schult.*—C. flavescens, *Sieb. Agrost. n.* 107.

SPEC. CHAR. Culm terete, chequered with transverse dissepiments, leafless, sheathing at the base, glabrous : umbel compound, many-rayed : involucre 2—3-scaled, very short : spikes 3—14, spicately fascicled, elongated, linear, compressed, 30—40-flowered : scales convex boat-shaped, obtuse, 5—7-nerved at the back : stamens 3 : style very long : achenium oblong, triangular, mucronate, three times shorter than the scale : rhacheola winged.

Peninsula.

(29) C. SEMINUDUS. *(Roxb.)*

Ident. Roxb. l. c. p. 187.—Wight Contrib. p. 80.

Syn. C. Kœnigii, *Vahl.*

SPEC. CHAR. Culm terete, equal, leafless, sheathing at the base, glabrous : umbel compound, somewhat corymbose, somewhat 10-rayed : involucre somewhat 3-leaved, short : spikes 3—8, spicately fascicled, elongated, linear, compressed, 28—33-flowered : scales convex-navicular, obtuse, 5-nerved, rusty red : style very long : rhacheola winged, wings at length loosening.

Silhet.

(30) C. CORYMBOSUS. *(Rottb.)*

Ident. Rottb. Gram. 42.—Vahl. l. c. II. 347.

Syn. Papyrus corymbosus, *N. ab. E. Wight. Contrib.* 89.—C. tegetum, *Roxb.*—C. monophyllus, *Vahl.*

Engrav. Rottb. l. c. t. 7, fig. 4.

SPEC. CHAR. Culm triangular, leafless, sheathing at the base, glabrous: umbel compound, corymbiform, somewhat 7-rayed, longer rays brachiately branched: involucre somewhat 4-leaved, twice exceeding the umbel: leaflets flat, scabrous at the margin: spikes 4—12, spicately fascicled, patent, linear, compressed, 12—32-flowered: scales oblong, rounded emarginate at the apex, keeled and boat-shaped, 5-nerved, rusty, keel green: achenium oblong, triquetrous, nearly 3 times shorter than the scale: wings of the rhacheola slowly becoming rusty and loosening.

Peninsula.

(31) C. DEHISCENS. *(N. ab. E.)*

Ident. Nees ab. Esen. in Wight Contrib. p. 89 (under Papyrus).

SPEC. CHAR. Culm 1-leaved at the base, triquetrous above: umbel decompound, rays slender, 2—3-cleft: spikelets 5—6-paired, approximate, alternate, linear, 12—16-flowered: scales oblong, obtuse, spreading: involucels bracteal, small, lanceolate, scale-shaped: involucre 3-leaved exceeding the umbel: inner small scales soluble.

Peninsula.

(32) C. TEGETIFORMIS. *(Roxb.)*

Ident. Roxb. Hort. Beng.—Kunth l. c. p. 56.

Syn. Papyrus tegetiformis, *Arn. in Wight Contrib. p.* 89. C. nudus, *Roxb. flor. Ind. I. p.* 213.

SPEC. CHAR. Culm trigonal, leafless, sheathed at the base, glabrous: umbel compound, many-rayed: involucre 3-leaved, short, scale-shaped: spikes 6—11, spicately fascicled, linear, compressed, 8—12-flowered, scales obtuse, convex-navicular, 3-nerved at the back, green: style very long: rhacheola winged.

Bengal.

(33) C. PANGOREI. *(Rottb.)*

Ident. Rottb. Gram. 31.—Vahl. l. c. 345.

Syn. Papyrus Pangorei, *Wight Contrib. p.* 88.

Engrav. Rottb. l. c. t. 7, fig. 3.

Spec. Char. Culm triangular, glabrous: umbel compound, many-rayed: rays brachiately branched at the top, branches alternate, 2—14-spiked: involucre 3-leaved, leaflets nearly equal, flat, scabrous at the margin, the length of the umbel: spikes spicately fascicled, linear, compressed, 16—18-flowered: scales ovate-oblong, obtuse, obsoletely 5-nerved, keeled and boat-shaped, muticous: achenium oblong, triangular, a half shorter than the scale: wings of the rhacheola chestnut, slowly loosening.

Peninsula.

(34) C. tenuiflorus. *(Rottb.)*

Ident. Rottb. Gram. 30.—Vahl. Enum. II. 347.—Wight Contrib. p. 82.

Syn. C. incurvatus, *Roxb.*—C. torosus, *Vahl.*—C. strigosus, *Roxb.*

Engrav. Rottb. l. c. t. 14, fig. 1.

Spec. Char. Root creeping: culm triquetrous, leafy below, glabrous: leaves shorter than the culm, flat, 5-nerved: umbel compound, corymbiform, somewhat 7-rayed, rays brachiately branched: involucre 4-leaved, exceeding the umbel: spikes 2—8, spicately fascicled, narrow-linear, compressed, 16—24-flowered: scales ovate-obtuse, keeled and navicular, muticous: achenium oval, 3-cornered, smooth: rhacheola winged.

Peninsula. Deccan.

(35) C. rotundus. *(Linn.)*

Ident. Linn. syst. 98.—Flor. Zeyl. 36.—Vahl. Enum. II. 343. —Roxb. flor. Ind. I. 197.

Syn. C. hexastachyos, *Rottb. Wight Contrib. p.* 81.—C. Hydra, *Vahl.*—C. tetrastachyos, *Vahl.*—C. bicolor, *Vahl.*—C. litoralis, *Sieb. Agrost.* 109.—C. bulbosus, *Vahl. Wight Contrib. p.* 80.—C. Jemenicus, *Willd.*—C. procerus (*var. Benghalensis*), *Roxb.*

Engrav. Rottb. l. c. t. 14, fig. 2.

Spec. Char. Root fibrous, here and there throwing out a tuber: culm triangular, glabrous, leafy below, bulbously thickened at the base: leaves commonly shorter than the culm, flat, scabrous at the margin: umbel 3—8-rayed, rays either simple and 3—10-spiked at the apex or 3-cleft at the apex and many-spiked: involucre 2—3-leaved, exceeding the umbel: spikes spicately fascicled, linear, compressed, 10—50-flowered: scales ovate, muticous or shortly mucronate, keeled and boat-shaped, 7-nerved and green at the back: style deeply 3-cleft: achenium obovate, triquetrous, dotted: rhacheola glassy winged.

Peninsula.

(36) C. VENUSTUS. *(R. Br.)*

Ident. Brown Prod. 217.—Wight Contrib. p. 86.

Syn. C. auricomus, *Spreng. syst. I.* 230.—C. Xanthocomus, *Link.*—C. fastigiatus, *Rottb.*—Papyrus venustus, *Nees. ab. Esenb. in Linnœa x.* 138.

Engrav. Rheede Mal. xii. t. 42.—Rottb. l. c. t. 7, fig. 2.

SPEC. CHAR. Culm triquetrous, leafy at the base, glabrous: leaves 3-nerved, flat, scabrous at the margin: umbel compound, many-rayed, rays somewhat digitately branched at the apex: involucre 5-leaved, very long: spikes spicately arranged in long branches, patent, narrow linear, compressed, 10—16-flowered: scales keeled and boat-shaped, ovate, mucronate, lineolate: style exserted: achenium oblong, slightly arched, externally convex-angular, very finely dotted, a half shorter than the scale.

Peninsula.

(37) C. EXALTATUS. *(Retz.)*

Ident. Retz. obs. v. 11.—Vahl. Enum. II. 366.—Wight Contrib. p. 84.

Syn. C. altus, *N. ab. E. in Wight l. c.*—C. alopecuroides, *Roxb.*—C. canaliculatus, *Retz.*

SPEC. CHAR. Culm triangular, glabrous, leafy at the base: leaves flat, serrulate-scabrous at the margin: umbel compound or decompound, many-rayed: involucre 3—4-leaved, very long: ochreæ 2-cleft: spikes numerous, spicately arranged, lanceolate-linear, compressed, 20—24-flowered: scales roundish-ovate, keeled and navicular, mucronate, obsoletely 7-nerved: achenium elliptic, triangular, 2—3 times shorter than the scale.

Peninsula. Lower Bengal.

(38) C. VERTICILLATUS. *(Roxb.)*

Ident. Roxb. flor. Ind. I. 206.—Wight Contrib. p. 87.

SPEC. CHAR. Culm leafy, trigonal: umbel decompound and supra-decompound: spikelets spiked, packed together, linear-subulate, 8—9-flowered, shortly bracteolate, and with the lowest partial spikes very patent: scales ovate, slightly obtuse with a mucro, 7-nerved at the back, sides yellow: involucels linear, almost equalling the umbel: leaflets of the many-leaved involucre commonly exceeding the umbel and with the leaves broad-linear, serrulate-scabrous at the margin.

Peninsula.

(39) C. PROCERUS. *(Vahl.)*

Ident. Vahl. herb.—Kunth l. c. p. 72.—Wight Contrib. p. 83?

Syn. C. carnosus, *Wight l. c.*—C. tenuiflorus, *Roxb.*

SPEC. CHAR. Culm triquetrous, leafy at the base: leaves longer than the culm, keeled, spongy and thickish: umbel compound, many-rayed, rays brachiately branched above, flexuose: spikes spicately arranged, distichous, much spreading, linear, compressed, many-flowered: involucre 3-leaved, leaflets scabrous on the margin and keel, one very long: scales ovate, elliptic, rounded at the apex, 9-nerved, keeled and navicular, pale-chestnut: achenium obovate, triangular: a half shorter than the scale.

Peninsula.

(40) C. RETZII. *(N. ab. E.)*

Ident. Nees. ab. Esenb. in Wight Contrib. p. 82.

Syn. C. Pangorei, *Kœn. in Retz. obs. iv.* 10.

SPEC. CHAR. Umbel decompound and supra-decompound, spreading: larger rays 3-cleft at the apex: spikelets spicate, approximated, alternate, patent, lanceolate-linear, somewhat 20-flowered, compressed: scales ovate, attenuated at the apex, acute, muticous, rusty: bracts alternate instead of involucels, bristly from a broadish base, exceeding the ochreolæ: caryopsis oval-3-cornered: one or the other leaflet of the 3-leaved involucre longer than the umbel and with the leaves linear, flattish, smooth: culm triquetrous, smooth, leafy at the base.

Peninsula.

(41) C. WALLICHII. *(N. ab. E.)*

Ident. Nees. ab. E. l. c. p. 83.

SPEC. CHAR. Culm triquetrous, scabrous at the angles above, leafless: umbel compound, many-rayed: rays brachiately 3—7-cleft at the apex: involucre somewhat 4-leaved, exceeding the umbel: spikes 5—15, spicately arranged, distichous, linear, compressed, 11—15-flowered: scales ovate-roundish, convex-navicular, 5—7-nerved at the back: achenium obovate-elliptic, triquetrous, mucronate, almost a half shorter than the scale.

Lower Bengal.

(42) C. PENNATUS. *(Lam.)*

Ident. Lam. Ill. I. 144. Vahl. Enum. II. 305.

Syn. C. canescens, *Vahl. Wight. Contrib. p.* 84. C. parviflorus, *Vahl.*

Spec. Char. Greenish-glaucous: culm trigonal, leafy at the base, leaves equalling or exceeding the culm, stiff, flat, scabrous at the margin: umbel compound, 6—8-rayed, rays brachiately branched at the apex, beset on all sides with oblong-lanceolate, 6—10-flowered, very patent spikes, and bearing divaricated spikelets: involucre 5—6-leaved, very long: rhacheola flexuose, alternately excavated and winged: scales ovate-elliptic, boat-shaped, keeled above, very shortly mucronate below the apex, 9—11-nerved, subcoriaceous, pale: achenium obovate, triangular, 2—3-times shorter than the scale.

Peninsula.

(43) C. dilutus. *(Vahl.)*

Ident. Vahl. Enum. II. 357.

Syn. Mariscus dilutus, *Nees ab. Esenb. in Wight Contrib. p.* 90.—C. compactus, *Retz.*—C. congestus, *Poir.*—C. spinulosus, *Roxb.*

Spec. Char. Culm trigonal, leafy: leaves flat, somewhat spongiose, serrulate-scabrous at the margin and keel: umbel compound, very patent, many-rayed: umbellets 4—12-rayed, rays much spreading, many-spiked at the apex: involucre 5—7-leaved, very long: involucels 3—5-leaved, almost equalling the umbellet: spikes spicately capitate, slender, 4—6-flowered, much spreading: scales oblong, obtuse, keeled, 7-nerved, boat-shaped, rusty purplish: achenium oblong, acuminate-mucronate, triangular, pale rusty, a half shorter than the scale.

Peninsula.

(44) C. distans. *(Linn.)*

Ident. Linn. suppl. 103.—Vahl. Enum. II. 362.—Wight Contrib. p. 88.—Roxb. flor. Ind. I. 207.

Syn. C. elatus, *Rottb. gram.*—C. nutans, *Sieb. herb. Maur. No.* 32.—C. laxus, *Vahl.*—C. lucidus, *Sieb. Agrost.*

Engrav. Jacq. Ic. II. t. 299.—Beauv. flor. I. 35, t. 20.—Rottb. l. c. t. 10.

Spec. Char. Culm triangular, glabrous, leafy at the base: leaves equalling the culm, flat, scabrous at the margin: umbel decompound, umbellets many-rayed, partial rays 2—3-leaved: branches 5-spiked: involucre 5—8-leaved, very long: spikes filiform, roundish, 9—14-flowered: scales obovate-elliptic, rounded at the apex.

Peninsula.

(45) C. Kyllingioides. *(Vahl.)*

Ident. Vahl. Enum. II. 312.—Kunth l. c. p. 94.

Syn. C. dubius, *Rottb. gram.* 20. *Roxb. flor. Ind. I.* 188.—C. mollis, *Poir.*—C. capitatus, *Poir.*—C. capitellatus, *Schult. Mant. II.* 101.

Engrav. Rottb. l. c. t. 4, fig. 5.

Spec. Char. Culm triquetrous, leafy at the base, and there somewhat bulbous and thickened: leaves linear, keeled and flat, margin rough above, membranaceous, nearly equalling the culm: capitule solitary, ovate-sub-globose, densely glomerated with numerous spikes: involucre 4-leaved, very long: spikes ovate-oblong, 6—8-flowered: scales much approximated, roundish-ovate, sub-cordate, keeled and boat-shaped, many-nerved: achenium elliptic, triquetrous, brown, a half or third shorter than the scale.

Peninsula.

(46) C. pusillus. *(Vahl.)*

Ident. Vahl. Enum. II. 203.

Syn. C. pygmæus, *Retz. obs.* iv. 9.

Spec. Char. Culm terete: leaves radical, twice as long as the culm, filiform: umbel compound, partial rays 5—6, 4—6-flowered: spikelets lanceolate: involucre 4-leaved, longer than the umbel.

Tranquebar.

(47) C. umbellatus. *(Burm.)*

Ident. Burm. Ind. 21, t. 9, fig. I.—Roxb. flor. Ind. I. 208.

Spec. Char. Root fibrous: culms erect, 4—6-feet, smooth, bluntly angled, leafy at the base: leaves long, one equalling the culm: involucre 3—6-leaved, leaflets unequal, the largest 2—3-feet: umbel decompound, with many unequal rays: spikelets numerous, spiked, alternate, 3—4-flowered: seed elliptic, triangular.

Deccan.

(48) C. Wightii. *(N. ab. E.)*

Ident. Nees ab. Esenb. in Wight Contrib. p. 78.

Spec. Char. Spikelets globose-capitate, oblong-lanceolate, compressed, 10—30-flowered: scales closely imbricated, ovate, attenuated into a subulate recurved acumen, finely nerved and striated: caryopsis obovate, trigonal, ashy: involucre 2—3-leaved, one leaflet almost twice longer than the capitule: leaves narrow-linear, plaited and channelled: culm flaccid, triquetrous, longer than the leaves: root fibrous.

Peninsula.

(49) C. PERTENUIS. *(Roxb.)*

Ident. Roxb. flor. Ind. I. 202.—Wight Contrib. p. 83.

SPEC. CHAR. Culm 3—4-feet, trigonal above: leaves few, radical, shorter than the culm: umbel compound and decompound: involucre nearly equalling the umbel: spikelets lanceolate, many-flowered: caryopsis 3-cornered.

Near Calcutta.

(50) C. ROXBURGHII. *(N. ab. E)*

Ident. Nees ab. Esenb. in Wight Contrib. p. 84.

Syn. C. elatus, *Roxb.*

SPEC. CHAR. Umbel decompound and supra-decompound, contracted: rays elongated, compressed and trigonal, fascicled and umbelled from many fastigiate cylindric sub-sessile spikes: spikelets imbricated, linear, ebracteolate, 12—16-flowered: scales closely imbricated, embracing, roundish-ovate, obtuse with a small mucro: caryopsis oblong, 3-cornered, acute at both ends, smooth: leaflets of the many-leaved involucre twin, outer ones largest and with the radical leaves broad: involucels narrow, shorter than the umbellet: culm triquetrous, angles rough above, sides concave.

Coromandel. Bengal.

(51) C. ROYLEI. *(W. Arnott.)*

Ident. Arn. in Wight Contrib. p. 85.

Syn. C. digitatus, *Nees ab. Esenb. in Wight l. c.*

SPEC. CHAR. Umbel compound, many-rayed, rays compressed, straight, umbelled at the apex by 5—6 nearly equal erect, terete, densely imbricated spikes: spikelets lanceolate, compressed, ebracteate, 4—14-flowered: scales ovate, obtuse, mucronate, yellow, 3-nerved at the back: caryopsis oval, smooth, triquetrous: involucels 2-leaved, shorter than the umbellet: involucre 6-leaved: leaflets 4, longer than the umbel, linear: culm trigonal, smooth,

Silhet.

(52) C. NILAGIRICUS. *(Hochst.)*

Ident. Hochst in Herb. Hohenhack, No. 945.—Steudel syn. pl. Cyp. p. 2.

SPEC. CHAR. Root ascending, fibrous: culm $1\frac{1}{2}$ foot, triquetrous, striated, smooth, thin, leafy below: leaves linear, narrow, flat, smooth, shorter than the culm: involucre few-leaved, leaflets resembling the stem ones, many times longer than the contracted umbel, one or the other ray elongated, rest more or less sessile, floriferous from the base: spikelets linear, flattened, 20—30-flowered: scales ovate, concave, obtuse at the apex, muticous or terminated by a very short mucronule, brown-rusty, nerveless except the keel, white-membranaceous at the margin, at length lacinulate-dentate: achenium three times shorter than the scale, ovate, scarcely triquetrous, a little dotted and warty.

Neilgherries.

(53) C. ATROFERRUGINEUS. *(Steudel.)*

Ident. Steudel l. c.

SPEC. CHAR. Culm triquetrous, slender, erect, smooth, leafy below: leaves narrow, shorter than or longer than the culm, slightly scabrous above at the margin, rest smooth: leaflets of the few-leaved involucre twin, many times exceeding the umbel, third (when present) equalling it: umbel few-rayed, somewhat close packed, rays from the base or more above somewhat distichously spiked: spikelets somewhat linear-lanceolate, 8—15-flowered: scales ovate, obtuse, dark-rusty, a little shining, nerveless except the dark greenish keel: achenium somewhat compressed, ovate, brownish, very thinly dotted.

Neilgherries.

(54) C. TENUISPICA. *(Steudel.)*

Ident. Steudel l. c. p. 11.

SPEC. CHAR. Root cæspitiferous: culms erect, flat-compressed, striated: leaves 1—2 towards the base of the culm, sheathed, flat, smooth, striated, shorter than the culm: leaflets of the 2—3-leaved involucre unequal, shorter than the umbel, rays of the many-nerved umbel unequal, umbelluliferous at the apex, raylets simple or again umbellulate, rays and raylets compressed, smooth: spikelets very thin, many-flowered: scales yellowish-rusty, linear, truncated, obtuse, muticous, easily deciduous: achenium somewhat spherical, slightly dotted, wrinkled, white.

Near Mangalore.

(55) C. PETRÆUS. *(Hochst.)*

Ident. Hochst in Herb. Hohenhack, No. 1293.—Steudel l. c. p. 29.

SPEC. CHAR. Root cæspitiferous: culms very low, compressed and triquetrous, scales at the base membranaceous, thin, ovate, pellucid, muticous, or terminated by a leaf: leaves shorter than the culm, linear, sub-cartilaginous at the margin, very minutely serrulate and slightly scabrous, more or less equalling the culm: leaflets of the involucre 2—4, shorter than the few-spiked umbel: spikes sessile, compressed, 4—8, oblong-linear, 16—30-flowered: scales many- (7—11) -nerved, keeled, red-rusty, mucronulate: style 3-cleft: achenium triquetrous, chestnut brown, many times shorter than the scales.

Neilgherries.

(56) C. ORYZETICOLA. *(Steudel.)*

Ident. Steudel l. c. p. 37.

SPEC. CHAR. Culm lofty, acutely triquetrous: involucre many-leaved: leaflets exceeding or nearly so the very large compound umbel, remotely serrulate-scabrous at the keel and margin: rays sessile and very long peduncled, umbellate at the apex: involucels linear, remotely scabrous, shorter than the umbellet, raylets alternately brachiate-spike-bearing: spikelets narrow linear, elongated, 30—60-flowered, furnished at the base with 2—3 acute or bristly-acuminate bracteoles: scales ovate, rusty yellow, sharp pointed: achenium triquetrous, 2—3-times shorter than the scale.

Rice-fields near Mangalore.

(57) C. RACEMOSUS. *(Retz.)*

Ident. Retz. obs. vi. 20.—Vahl. Enum. II. 355.—Wight Contrib. p. 85.

Syn. C. digitatus *Roxb.*

SPEC. CHAR. Umbel decompound, fastigiate, many-rayed, rays half-terete, straight, common and partial ones umbelled at the apex from many sessile, linear, straight spikes: spikelets imbricated, linear-lanceolate, compressed, somewhat ebracteolate, 5—10-flowered: scales ovate, mucronate, tawny or rufous at the back: caryopsis oval, white, inner side concave: involucre 10-leaved, erect: leaflets attenuated from a broader base, scabrous at the margin, longer than the umbel: involucels leafy, exceeding or equalling the umbel: radical leaflets broad-linear, longer than the firm and tall culm.

Peninsula.

(58) C. MITIS. *(Steudel.)*

Ident. Steudel l. c. p. 316.

SPEC. CHAR. Culm leafy at the base, naked upwards, all parts smooth: leaves sheathed linear, acute, quite glabrous, shorter than the culm: leaflets of the involucre unequal, longer ones exceeding the umbel, similar to the stem leaves, narrower ones (2—3) shorter than the umbel: rays of the umbel unequal, very short, all spiculate at the apex, sometimes furnished at the base with minute bristly involucels: spikelets thin, somewhat compressed, and loosely many-flowered, upper ones oblong-ovate, slightly obtuse, somewhat lightly 5-nerved, rusty-yellowish, much larger than the achenium.

Bengal.

GENUS II. MARISCUS.

Triandria Monogynia. *Sex Syst:*

Deriv. From a Celtic term, signifying a Marsh, in allusion to the habitat of the species.

Gen. Char. Spikes 1—2, seldom 3—5-flowered: scales distichous, lower ones empty: bristles and small scales none: stamens 3: ovary triangular: style 3-cleft, deciduous: achenium triangular, received into the cavity of the rhacheola, often mucronulate.—Culms triangular, leafy at the base: capitules or compound spikes, sometimes solitary, sometimes fasciculately congested, or arranged by umbels.

(1) M. umbellatus. *(Vahl.)*

Ident. Vahl. Enum. II. 376.—Wight Contrib. p. 90.

Syn. Scirpus cyperoides, *Linn. Mant.* 181.—Kyllingia umbellata, *Linn. Suppl. Roxb.*—K. Sumatrensis, *Retz. obs.* iv. 13.—M. cyperinus, *Wight l. c.*—M. pictus, *Wight l. c.*

Engrav. Rheede Mal. xii. t. 63.—Rottb. Gram. 15, t. 4, fig. 2.

Spec. Char. Culm glabrous: leaves longer than the culm, membranaceous, scabrous at the margin and keel: spikes compound, 11—16, unequally peduncled and sessile, umbelled: involucre many-leaved, very long: proper spikes very closely congested, fructiferous ones much spreading and reflexed, linear-lanceolate, 1-(rarely 2—3)-flowered: scales elliptic, rounded at the apex, muticous: achenium oblong, slightly curved internally, shorter than the scale.

Peninsula.

(2) M. paniceus. *(Link. ?)*

Ident. Link Hort. Berol. I. 323.—Wight Contrib. p. 89.

Syn. M. biglumis, *Gærtn.*—Kyllingia panicea, *Linn. Suppl.* 105.

Engrav. Rottb. Gram. 15, t. 4, fig. 1.

Spec. Char. Culm slender: spikes in threes or fours, oblong, sessile and peduncled: spikelets at first subulate, falcately recurved, afterwards ovate-oblong, trigonal, erect, spreading, apex subulate recurved: two lowest small scales of the spikelets equal, ovate, inferior one acute: involucre 2—4-leaved, longer than the umbel.

Peninsula.

(3) M. Kyllingioides. *(Steudel.)*

Ident. Steudel l. c. p. 60.

Spec. Char. Culm erect, triquetrous, somewhat compressed, ½—1-foot, striated, very smooth, leafy towards the base: leaves flat, narrow, much shorter than the culm, very smooth: leaflets of the involucre about 3, serrulate-scabrous, much longer than the simple ovate-oblong capitulum: spikelets obliquely ovate, 1-flowered: scales fertile and sterile combining at the base, many-nerved, nerves coloured, keel green, bristlets remote 2—3, ending at the apex into a recurved mucro: achenium lenticular, roundish: slightly striated and dotted.

Neilgherries.

(4) M. leptochloides. *(Steudel.)*

Ident. Steudel l. c. p. 317.

Spec. Char. Culm obtusely triquetrous, smooth, 2-feet, long-sheathed at the base: sheaths lax, membranaceous with a hyaline margin, striated, smooth: leaves linear, almost equalling the culm, scabrous at the edges: leaflets of the 3—5-leaved involucre very long, similar to the stem leaves, quite scabrous at the edge, many times exceeding the compound umbel: rays 3—5, umbellulate at the apex: involucels equalling the raylets, very scabrous, spiculate even to the base, thin: spikes imbricated, small, 2—3-flowered: scales (lower ones shorter) oblong, acute, nerved, dirty brown, greenish at the keel.

Serampore, Bengal.

GENUS III. COURTOISIA.

Triandria Monogynia. *Sex: Syst:*

Char Gen. Spikes 1—2-flowered, compressed: scales 3—4, lowest one small, channelled, empty, rest distichous, keeled and boat-shaped, winged at the keel, of these one empty: bristles and small scales none: stamens 3: style 3-cleft, pyramidate and thickened at the base, continuous with the ovary: achenium lanceolate-oblong, triangular, beaked with the persistent pyramidate continuous base of the style.—Culm slender, triangular, striated, leafy at the base: leaves long, linear, flat, membranaceous, scabrous at the margin: umbel compound, many rayed: capitules sub-globose, many-spiked: involucre 4-leaved, very long: scales rusty, mucronate at the apex.

(1) C. CYPEROIDES. *(N. ab. E.)*

Ident. Nees ab. Esenb. in Wight Contrib. p. 92.

Syn. Kyllingia cyperoides, *Roxb.*—Mariscus cyperoides, *Dietr. Spec. II.*, 348.

Peninsula.

GENUS IV. KYLLINGIA.

Triandria Monogynia. *Sex: Syst:*

Deriv. Named after P. Kylling, a Danish botanist, who died in 1696.

GEN. CHAR. Spikes compressed, 1—2-flowered, upper flower male, seldom 3-flowered: scales distichous, fertile ones keeled, sterile (2 lower ones) small: bristles and small scales none: stamens 1—3: ovary compressed at the sides: style 2-cleft, deciduous: achenium compressed at the sides, pointed.—Culms leafy at the base, very seldom leafless: leaves grassy: capitules solitary, seldom twin or in threes, compact, involucrate.

(1) K. MONOCEPHALA. *(Linn.)*

Ident. Linn. Suppl. 104.—Vahl. II. 379.—Roxb. flor. Ind. I. 185.—Wight Contrib. p. 91.

Syn. Schœnus coloratus, *Linn.*—Scirpus cephalotes, *Vind. Jacq. I.* 42.

Engrav. Rottb. Gram. 13, t. 4, fig. 4.

SPEC. CHAR. Creeping: culms erect, triangular, leafy at the base: leaves membranaceous, flat, ciliolate with fine spines at the margin and keel: capitule solitary, globose, dense: involucre 3—4-leaved, very long: spikes 1-flowered: upper scales equal, compressed and boat-shaped, thick and crested above, crest ciliated, sharply mucronate, purple-dotted, 7-nerved, upper one more deeply inserted: stamens 2: achenium elliptic, straw-yellow.

Peninsula.

(2) K. BREVIFOLIA. *(Rottb.)*

Ident. Rottb. Gram. 13.—Vahl. Enum. II. 380.—Wight Contrib. p. 91.

Engrav. Rottb. l. c. t. 4, fig. 3.

Spec. Char. Culms 1-leaved at the base, leaf shorter flat: capitule solitary, globose: involucre 3-leaved, far exceeding the capitule: spikes 1-flowered, obliquely ovate, compressed: scales keeled, mucronate, 5-nerved, upper one exceeding the lower: stamens 3: achenium roundish-obovate, mucronate, nearly three times shorter than the scale.

Peninsula.

(3) K. melanosperma. *(N. ab. E.)*

Ident. Nees ab. Esenb. in Wight Contrib. p. 91.

Spec. Char. Capitule simple, ovate-roundish, sessile, densely compact, spikelets 1-flowered, triandrous: scales ovate-lanceolate, acuminate, 7-nerved, nerves in threes, lateral ones ribbed-shaped, keel serrated with fine spines: caryopsis oblong, side somewhat ribbed, dotted, black: involucre 3—4-leaved, much longer than the capitulum, margin rough: leaves very short: culm winged and triquetrous.

Peninsula.

(4) K. triceps. *(Rottb.)*

Ident. Rottb. Gram. 14, t. 4, fig. 6.—Vahl. Enum. II. 381.—Wight Contrib. p. 91.

Syn. K. nivea, *Pers.*—Scirpus glomeratus, *Linn.*—Schœnus niveus, *Linn.*

Engrav. Rheede Mal. xii. t. 52.

Spec. Char. Creeping: culms leafy at the base: leaves equalling or exceeding the culm, membranaceous, flat, rough with fine spines at the margin: capitules somewhat in threes, dense, middle one sub-globose-elliptic, lateral ones smaller: involucre 3—4-leaved, very long: spikes obliquely lanceolate, compressed, 1-flowered: fertile scales keeled, sharply sub-mucronate, lower one 7, upper 5-nerved: stamens 2: achenium oblong, mucronulate, a little shorter than the scale.

Peninsula.

(5) K. gracilis. *(Wall.)*

Ident. Wall. Cat. 3443.—Kunth l. c. p. 134.

Spec. Char. Creeping: culms erect, elongated, leafy at the base: leaves shorter than the culm, flat, membranaceous, rough with fine spines at the margin: capitule solitary, cylindric-oblong, 1-flowered: two upper scales broadly ovate, keeled and boat-shaped, mucronate, upper 5, lower 7-nerved: stamens 2: achenium obovate-elliptic, compressed, rounded at the apex, pointed, straw-white, a half shorter than the scale.

Lower Bengal.

GENUS V. REMIREA.

Triandria Monogynia. *Sex: Syst:*

Deriv. Its name in Guiana.

GEN. CHAR. Spikes 1-flowered: scales about four, distichously imbricated, broadly ovate, convex, three lower ones gradually shorter, empty, obtuse, terminal one acutely mucronate, fertile: bristles and small scales none: stamens 3: style 3-cleft, equal at the base: achenium trigonal, mucronate with the persistent base of the style, located in the terminal thickened tuberous hollow joint of the rhacheola and wrapped round with scales.—Maritime plants: culms branched, creeping, branches erect, densely leafy everywhere: leaves stiff, channelled, patent: capitules terminal, 1—3, conglomerated from numerous imbricated spikes, involucrated with many leaves.

(1) R. PEDUNCULATA. *(R. Br.)*

Ident. R. Brown prod. 236.—Kunth l. c. p. 139.

Syn. R. Wightiana, *N. ab. E. in Wight Contrib. p.* 92.

SPEC. CHAR. Capitules peduncled.

Peninsula.

SECTION II. SCIRPEÆ.

GENUS. VI. ELEOCHARIS.

Triandria Monogynia. *Sex: Syst:*

Deriv. From *Helos*, a marsh, and *Chairo*, I delight, alluding to the habitat of the species.

GEN. CHAR. Spikes many- seldom few -flowered: scales imbricated on all sides, conforming, very few of the lower ones empty: calyx—bristles six, more or less, very frequently retrorsely hispid, very seldom none: stamens three: style 3- seldom 2-cleft, dilated at the base: achenium triangular or lenticular, crowned with the persistent base of the style.—Culms sheathed, leafless, 1-spiked.

(1) E. CHÆTARIA. *(Roem. and Schultz.)*

Ident. Roem. and Schult. syst. II. 154.—Kunth l. c. p. 140.

Syn. Cyperus setaceus, *Retz. obs. v.* 10.—*Vahl. II.* 305.—*Roxb. flor. Ind. I.* 190.—Scirpus chætarius, *Spreng.*—Chætocyperus Limnocharis, *Wight Contrib. p.* 96.—C. setaceus, *Nees. ab. Esenb. in Linnœa ix.* 289.—S. pygmæus, *Lam. Ill. I.* 139.

SPEC. CHAR. Culms cæspitose, bristly, furrowed and angular: spike solitary, ovate, obtuse, slightly compressed, ebracteate, 2—4-flowered: scales 4—6, broadly ovate, rounded at the apex, muticous, keeled and boat-shaped: style 3-cleft: achenium obovate, triangular cancellate, opaque, beaked with the shortened triangular obtuse base of the style, which is decurrent at the angles: bristles six, retrorsely spinous, whitish.

Coromandel.

(2) E. CAPITATA. *(Brown.)*

Ident. R. Br. prod. 225.

Syn. Scirpus capitatus, *Willd.*—*Vahl.*—*Roxb.*—S. Cariboeus, *Rottb.*—Eleogenus capitatus, *Wight Contrib. p.* 112.

Engrav. Rottb. gram. 46, t. 15, fig. 3.

SPEC. CHAR. Root fibrous: culms cæspitose, filiform, furrowed: spike solitary, erect, ovate-sub-globose, obtuse, ebracteate: scales elliptic, rounded at the apex, convex, 1-nerved, nerve green, evanescent at the top: style deeply 2-cleft: achenium obovate, swollen lenticular, smooth, dark chestnut, shining, terminated by a small abbreviated pale tubercle: bristles 7—1, retrorsely spinous, rusty; a little exceeding the fruit.

Peninsula. Lower Bengal.

(3) E. ATROPURPUREA. *(Kunth.)*

Ident. Kunth l. c. p. 151.

Syn. Scirpus atropurpureus, *Retz. obs. v.* 14.—*Vahl. En. II.* 249.—Eleogenus atropurpureus, *Wight Contrib. p.* 113.—Isolepis atropurpureus, *Roem. and Schult. syst. II.* 106.

SPEC. CHAR. Root fibrous: culms cæspitose, filiform, striated: spike, erect, ovate, obtuse, ebracteate: scales ovate-elliptic, rounded at the apex, muticous, 1-nerved, keeled and concave, sanguineous at the back: style deeply 2-cleft: achenium obovate, swollen and lenticular, smooth, dark-chestnut, shining, terminated by a small abbreviated pale tubercle: bristles 4, retrorsely spinous, whitish, almost equalling the fruit.

Moist pastures of the Peninsula.

(4) E. PLANTAGINEA. (*Brown.*)

Ident. R. Br. prod. 224.—Kunth l. c. p. 153.

Syn. Scirpus plantagineus, *Retz. obs. v.* 14.—*Vahl.*—*Roxb.*—S. plantaginoides, *Rottb. gram.* 45.—Limnochloa plantaginea, *Wight Contrib. p.* 114.

Engrav. Rottb. l. c. t. 15, fig. 2.

SPEC. CHAR. Culms tapering, chequered with transverse dissepiments, sheathing at the base: spike cylindric: scales broad, rounded at the top, finely nerved, palish green, saffron-dotted: style unequally 3-cleft: bristles 7, retrorsely spinous.

Stagnant waters in the Peninsula. Lower Bengal.

(5) E. TUMIDA. (*Schult.*)

Ident. Schult. Mart. II. 86.—Kunth. l. c. p. 154.

Syn. Scirpus tumidus, *Roxb.*—Limnochloa tumida, *Wight Contrib. p.* 114.

SPEC. CHAR. Culms 2—3-feet, terete, regularly intercepted: spike terminal, cylindric: scales broadly lanceolate: seeds with simple bristles.

Peninsula.

(6) E. FISTULOSA. (*Schult.*)

Ident. Schult. Mart. II.

Syn. Limnocharis fistulosa, *Nees ab Esenb in Linnœa.*—Scirpus acutangulus, *Roxb.*—E. acutangula, *Schult. l. c.* 91.—Limnochloa acutangula, *Wight l. c. p.* 114.

SPEC. CHAR. Culms triquetrous, sheathed at the base: spike cylindric: scales broad, rounded at the apex, somewhat keeled at the back, many-nerved: style 2-cleft: achenium roundish-obovate, biconvex-lenticular, many-ribbed, finely striated transversely, pale, terminated by the short-conical flattened rusty base of the style: bristles six, retrorsely spinous, exceeding the fruit.

Stagnant waters of the Peninsula. Bengal.

(7). E. MEDIA. (*Schult.*)

Ident. Schult. Mart. II. 91.

Syn. Scirpus medius, *Roxb.*—Limnochloa media, *Wight l. c. p.* 114.

SPEC. CHAR. Culms 1—2-feet, triangular: spike terminal, subcylindric: scales obtuse: seeds bristly.

Peninsula. Circar hills.

(8) E. SPIRALIS. *(Brown.)*

Ident. R. Br. prod. 224.—Kunth l. c. p. 155.

Syn. Scirpus spiralis, *Rottb. gram.* 45.—*Vahl.*—*Roxb.*—Limnochloa spiralis *Wight l. c. p.* 114.

Engrav. Rottb. gram. t. 15, fig. I.

SPEC. CHAR. Culms triquetrous: spike cylindric: scales spiral, broad, very obsoletely many-nerved, truncated at the apex: style 3-cleft: achenium obovate, swollen lenticular, very finely cancellate, terminated by the flattened conical continuous base of the style: surrounded by five small bristles a half shorter.

Stagnant waters of the Peninsula.

GENUS. VII. SCIRPUS.

Triandria Monogynia. *Sex: Syst:*

Deriv. From the Celtic *Cirs*, rushes.

GEN. CHAR. Spikes many- seldom few-flowered: scales imbricated on all sides: calyx rudimentary: bristles 6, seldom fewer, retrorsely hispid with spines, sometimes either smooth or antrorsely hispid or plumose: stamens 3, very rarely fewer: style 3-, seldom 2-cleft: achenium compressed or triangular, obtuse or often mucronated with the persistent base of the style.—Spikes solitary, thin, capitately conglomerate, fascicled or more or less compound-umbelled.

(1) S. JUNCOIDES. *(Roxb.)*

Ident. Roxb. flor. Ind. I. 216.—Kunth l. c. p. 160.

Syn. S. junciformis, *Wight Contrib. p.* 112.—Eleocharis juncoides, *Schult. Mart. II.* 90.

SPEC. CHAR. Culms cæspitose, sheathed: spikes somewhat in three's, congested, sessile, ovate: involucre 1-leaved, continuing the culm, very long: scales somewhat keeled and convex, acute and sub-mucronulate, greenish at the apex: style 2-cleft: achenium obovate, flat and convex, mucronate, obsoletely and transversely undulated and wrinkled, brown, shining: bristles 4—6, retrorsely spinous, brownish.

Lower Bengal. Silhet. Peninsula.

(2) S. WALLICHII. *(N. ab. E.)*

Ident. Nees. ab. Esenb. in Wight Contrib. p. 112. Kunth l. c.

SPEC. CHAR. Culms cæspitose, slender, sheathed, leafless: spikes somewhat twin, sessile, ovate-oblong, acute: involucre 1-leaved, continuing the culm, very long: scales somewhat keeled and convex, acutely acuminate, pale brownish, greenish at the apex: style 2-cleft: achenium roundish-obovate, mucronate, flat and convex: bristles four, retrorsely spinous.

Silhet.

(3) S. MUCRONATUS. *(Linn.)*

Ident. Linn. spec. I. 73.—Vahl.—R. Br. prod.—Kunth l. c. p. 161.

Syn. S. glomeratus, *Scop. Carn.* 63.—S. triangulatus, *Roxb.*—*Wight Contrib. p.* 111.

Engrav. Host. Gram. iv. t. 68.

SPEC. CHAR. Culm triquetrous, sheathed, leafless: spikes many, capitately conglomerate, sessile, ovate-oblong: involucre 1-leaved, continuous with the culm, keeled and triquetrous, much spreading and reflexed: scales acute or mucronate, keeled and convex: style 3-cleft: achenium obovate-roundish, internally flat, outwardly convex and angled, mucronate, obsoletely transversely undulated and wrinkled, shining: bristles 6, retrorsely spinous.

Chittagong. Silhet.

(4) S. SUBULATUS. *(Vahl.)*

Ident. Vahl. Enum. II. 268.—Dalz. Bomb. flor. p. 288.

Syn. S. pectinatus, *Roxb.*—Malacochæte pectinata, *Wight Contrib. p.* 110.

SPEC. CHAR. Culm round, 3-cornered at the apex, sheathed, leafless: umbel irregularly compound: involucre 1-leaved, 3-cornered, subulate, as long as the umbel: spikes solitary, ovate-oblong, obtuse.

Peninsula, in sandy localities.

(5) S. KYSOOR. *(Roxb.)*

Ident. Roxb. flor. Ind. I. 235.—Dalz. l. c.

Syn. Rhyncospora Kysoor, *Dietr. spec. II.* 74.

SPEC. CHAR. Culms 5—6-feet, triangular, hispid: umbel supradecompound: spikes ovate: seed oblong, triangular: bristles 5, villous.

Bengal. Western Coast.

(6) S. GROSSUS. *(Linn.)*

Ident. Linn. suppl. 104.—Retz.—Vahl.—Roxb.

Syn. Hymenochæte grossa, *Wight Contrib. p.* 110.

SPEC. CHAR. Culm triquetrous, leafy at the base: umbel supra-decompound, cyme-shaped: involucre somewhat 3-leaved, very long, scabrous at the margin: spikes solitary, ovate-elliptic, obtuse: scales keeled and convex, sub-mucronulate: style 3-cleft: achenium obovate, smooth: bristles 5, retrorsely spinous, hooked at the apex, brown.

Peninsula, in stagnant waters.

(7) S. MARITIMUS. *(Linn.)*

Ident. Linn. spec. I. 74.—N. ab. E. in Wight Contrib. p. 111.

Syn. Scirpus corymbosus, *Forskh. descr.*—S. glaucus, *Lam.—Ill.*—S. macrostachys, *do.*—S. robustus, *Pursh.*—S. capensis, *Burm.—Vahl.*—S. tridentatus, *Roxb.* S. affinis, *Roth.—Wight l. c. iii.*

Engrav. Linn. flor. Dan. t. 937.—Engl. Bot. t. 542.—Host. gram. III. t. 67.

SPEC. CHAR. Creeping: culms triquetrous: leaves flat, rough on the margin, longer than the culm: umbel simple, few-rayed: rays very unequal, 1-many-spiked, sometimes capitate-contracted: involucre 3—4-leaved, very long: spikes ovate-oblong, or cylindric: scales 2-lobed at the apex, mucronate.

Peninsula.

GENUS VIII. ERIOPHORUM.

Triandria Monogynia. *Sex: Syst:*

Deriv. From *Erion* wool, and *Phoreo* I bear, alluding to the calyx.

GEN. CHAR. Spikes many-flowered: scales imbricated on all sides, some lower ones empty: calyx consisting of many lamelliform, smooth, persistent hairs, far exceeding the scales, and appearing as down or coma: stamens 3, seldom fewer: style 3-cleft, elongated, deciduous: achenium mucronate or muticous, either flattish or more or less convex-angular.—Spikes solitary, fasciculate or supra-decompound, umbelled.

(1) E. COMOSUM. *(Wall.)*

Ident. Wall. Cat. 3446.—Dalz. Bomb. flor. p. 289.—N. ab E. in Wight Contrib. p. 110.

Syn. Scirpus comosus, *Roxb.*—E. arundinaceum, *N. ab E. l. c. p.* 111.—S. elongatus, *Ham. in Don. prod.* 40.

Spec. Char. Root fibrous: culms cæspitose, erect, round, trigonous above, smooth: leaves rigid, narrow, keeled, folded, 3-cornered at the apex, rough on the margin, twice as long as the culm: involucre very long, about 5-leaved: corymb supra-decompound, umbellate: scales ovate-oblong, mucronate, 1-nerved, somewhat keeled and convex.

Ravines in the Western Deccan, near Jooneer.

GENUS IX. FUIRENA.

Triandria Monogynia. *Sex: Syst:*

Deriv. In honour of J. Fuiren, a Danish botanist.

Gen. Char. Spikes many-flowered: scales everywhere imbricated, very few of the outer ones empty: calyx, of 3 small scales alternating with the angles of the ovary, commonly with as many bristles between, increasing and persistent in fruit: stamens 3: style 3-cleft: achenium triangular, mucronate or beaked with the persistent base of the style, covered by small scales and persistent small bristles.—Culm 3—5-angled: spikes solitary, in threes or capitate-congested, axillary and terminal, sometimes arranged as umbels: scales convex, mucronate or awned below the rounded apex, membranaceous, externally pubescent or hirsutely-pilose, commonly greenish azure above.

(1) F. Wallichiana. *(Wall.)*

Ident. Wall. Cat. No. 3545.—Kunth l. c. p. 182.

Spec. Char. Culms acutely triangular, villous at the apex: sheaths triangular, glabrous: leaves slightly rigid, scabrous at the margin: spikes somewhat in fours, glomerately congested at the top of the culm, ovate, acute: scales mucronate and keeled, 3-nerved, pubescent: small scales and bristles none: ovary attenuated and somewhat beaked at the apex, glabrous.

Hurdwar.

(2) F. glomerata. *(Lam.)*

Ident. Lam. Ill. I. 150.—Vahl.

Syn. Scirpus ciliaris, *Linn. Mant.* 182.—F. Rottboellii, *Wight Contrib. p.* 94.

Engrav. Rottb. gram. 55 t. 17.

SPEC. CHAR. Culm obliquely tetragonal, and with the sheaths glabrous: leaves ciliately hairy at the margin: peduncles 3—5-spiked, terminal and axillary, solitary and twin, short: spikes sessile, ovate, obtuse: scales mucronate and somewhat awned, 3 nerved, pubescent; small scales long-clawed, broad, 3-lobed at the apex, somewhat hastate at the base, 3-nerved, glabrous: bristlets minute, retrorsely hispidulous: achenium strongly mucronate, mucro glabrous.

Peninsula.

(3) F. UNCINATA. *(Wall.)*

Ident. Wall. Cat. No. 3534[d].—Kunth l. c. p. 184.

Syn. Scirpus uncinatus, *Willd. Vahl.*—Isolepis uncinata *Roem. and Schult. II.* 111.—F. ciliaris, *Wight Contrib. p.* 93.

SPEC. CHAR. Culms diffuse, sheaths and leaves pilose: capitules axillary, solitary, peduncled, terminal ones twin, the other sessile: spikes few-flowered: scales keeled, mucronate and somewhat awned, costately 7-nerved, pubescent, ciliated: small scales clawed, ovate, 3-nerved, ciliated, hispidulous and villous at the apex and slightly awned, awn retrorsely spinous: achenium long-mucronate.

Coromandel shores. Silhet. Peninsula.

(4) F. PENTAGONA. *(W. and A.)*

Ident. Wight and Arnott Contrib. Bot. p. 93.

SPEC. CHAR. Culms glabrous, sheaths acutely 5-angular: peduncles terminal and axillary, somewhat twin, one 1-headed, the other longer, 2—3-headed: capitules many-spiked, one sessile, 1—2 shortly pedicelled: spikes ovate, acute: scales mucronate and somewhat awned, 3-nerved, pubescent: small scales clawed, somewhat obcordate, with a hooked mucronule: bristlets none: achenium strongly mucronate, mucro hairyish.

Peninsula.

(5) F. CUSPIDATA. *(Kunth.)*

Ident. Kunth l. c. p. 187.—Dalz. Bomb. flor. p. 286.

Syn. Scirpus cuspidatus, *Roth. sp.* 31.

SPEC. CHAR. Root stoloniferous: culms leafy, sheaths sharply triangular, the mouths membranous: leaves twice the length of the sheaths, spreading, rigid, linear-subulate, keeled: spikelets about 8, or in twos or threes, ovoid, oblong, on pedicels of different lengths: general involucre of one rigid ciliated leaf, partial ones shorter than the umbel: spikelets greenish, all puberulous: glumes with blood-red streaks with transmitted light.

Watery places in the Deccan.

GENUS X. ISOLEPIS.

Triandria Monogynia. *Sex: Syst:*

Deriv. From *Isos* equal, and *Lepis* a scale.

GEN. CHAR. Spikes many, seldom few-flowered: scales everywhere imbricated, all flower-bearing or very few of the outer ones empty: bristles and small calycine scales none: stamens 3: style 3- seldom 2-cleft, equal at the base, deciduous: achenium triangular, mucronate with the persistent base of the style or muticous.—Culms leafy or leafless: spikes solitary, twin, in threes or more, capitate-conglomerate: glomerules solitary or more, arranged in a simple or compound umbel.

(1) I. CURVULA. *(Kunth.)*

Ident. Kunth Enum. pl. II. 189.

Syn. Eleogiton curvulus, *N. ab E. in Wight Contrib. p.* 110.

SPEC. CHAR. Culm branched, leafy, flaccid, creeping or floating: leaves fascicled, linear, acutish, 3-nerved, incurved, almost equalling the striated incurved culm: spikes solitary, terminal: scales roundish, truncated, lower ones shorter than the spike: stamens 2: caryopsis obovate, lenticular, smooth.

Peninsula.

(2) I. SUPINA. *(Brown.)*

Ident. R. Br. prod. 221.—N. ab E. in Wight l. c. p. 107.

Syn. Scirpus supinus, *Linn. Vahl. Roxb.*—S. lateralis, *Retz.* Schœnus junceus, *Willd. phyt. I.* 2.—Scirpus erectus, *Poir.*

Engrav. Host. gram. III. t. 64.—Willd. l. c. t. 1, fig. 4.

SPEC. CHAR. Culms cæspitose, procumbent or erect, striated, somewhat 1-leaved at the base, glabrous: leaf short, channelled: spikes 2—10, conglomerate, sessile, ovate-oblong, acute: involucre 1-leaved, continuing the culm, very long, channelled at the base: scales keeled and boat-shaped, broadly ovate, obtuse, mucronate: achenium turbinate roundish, internally flat, outwardly convex-angular, mucronate.

Lower Bengal. Silhet.

(3) I. ARTICULATA. (*N. ab. E.*)

Ident. N. ab. E. in Wight l. c. p. 108.

Syn. Scirpus articulatus, *Linn.—Rottb. Gram.* 45. *Roxb.* S. fistulosus, *Forsk.*

Engrav. Rheede Mal. I. t. 71

SPEC. CHAR. Culms tapering, sheathed, leafless: spikes numerous, capitately-conglomerate, ovate-oblong: involucre 1-leaved, continuing and much exceeding the culm in length, fistular, somewhat articulated with transverse necks: scales ovate, acutish, keeled and convex: achenium roundish, obovate, triquetrous, umbonate, smooth.

Stagnant waters of the Peninsula.

(4) I. PRÆLONGATUS. (*N. ab. E.*)

Ident. Nees ab. Esen. in Wight l. c. p. 108.

Syn. Scirpus prælongatus, *Poir.*—S. sub-articulatus, *Roxb.*

SPEC. CHAR. Culms terete, sheathed, leafless: spikes numerous, capitately conglomerate, ovate, acute: involucre 1-leaved, continuing the culm, very long, fistular, obsoletely sub-articulate with transverse dissepiments: scales broadly ovate, acute, keeled and convex: achenium obovate, triquetrous, mucronate.

Peninsula. Silhet.

(5) I. INCURVATA. (*N. ab E.*)

Ident. Nees ab. Esen. l. c. p. 108.

Syn. Scirpus incurvatus, *Roxb.*—Eleocharis incurvata, *Schult. Mant. II.* 92.

SPEC. CHAR. Spikes ovate-oblong, capitate: capitule in appearance lateral, broadly ambient near the base of the culm: involucre much longer than the culm, terete, intensely articulated: scales ovate, obtuse: caryopsis obovate, 3-cornered.

Moist places near Calcutta.

(6) I. SQUARROSA. (*Roem. and Schult.*)

Ident. Roem. and Schult. Syst. II. 3. Wight Contrib. p. 106.

Syn. Scirpus squarrosus, *Linn. Mant.* 181. *Vahl. Roxb.*

Engrav. Rottb. Gram. 49 t. 17, fig. 5.—Rheede Mal. xii. t. 38.

GEN. CHAR. Culms filiform, 3-cornered, glabrous: leaves shorter than the culm, capillaceous: spikes somewhat in threes, sessile, oblong, obtuse: involucre 2-leaved, very long: scales convex, obovate-cuneate, acuminate and awned at the apex, recurved, somewhat 5-nerved: stamen one: style 3-partite: achenium elliptic, flat and acute-angled, somewhat pointed, very finely dotted, brown opaque.

Dry sandy pastures in the Peninsula.

(7) I. DIPSACEA. *(Roem. and Schult.)*

Ident. Roem. and Schult, Syst. II. 119.

Syn. Scirpus dipsaceus, *Rottb. Gram.* 56. *Vahl.* Echinolytrum dipsaceum *Desv. Journ.* iv. 20. *Wight Contrib. p.* 96.

Engrav. Desv. l. c. t. 1 et. 117.—Rottb. l. c. t. 12, fig. 1.

SPEC. CHAR. Culms cæspitose, bristly, 3-cornered, 1-leaved: leaves short, bristly-capillaceous, glabrous: umbel simple, 2—10-rayed, rays unequal, divaricate, 1-spiked, one very short, almost none: involucre 3—5-leaved, almost equalling the umbel: spikes elliptic, obtuse: scales somewhat keeled and convex, oblong lanceolate, acuminately awned and recurved at the apex: stamens 2: style 2-cleft: achenium oblong, slightly compressed parallel to the scale, everywhere, especially at the sides, beset with flattish stalked soft glands, somewhat dotted.

Peninsula.

(8) I. BARBATA. *(Brown,)*

Ident. R. Br. prod. 222.—Wight Contrib. p. 109.

Syn. Scirpus barbatus, *Rottb. Gram.* 52.—S. antarcticus, *Vahl. Roxb.*—S. capillaris, *Linn.*—S. monander, *Roxb.*—Fimbristylis monandra, *Schult.*

Engrav. Burm. Zeyl. t. 47, fig. 2.—Rottb. l. c. t. 17, fig. 4.

SPEC. CHAR. Culm cæspitose, bristly-filiform, furrowed, leafy at the base: leaves shorter than the culm, capillaceous, scabrous: sheaths pilosely bearded at the mouth: capitulum 3, many-spiked, solitary, roundish: involucre 3—4-leaved: more or less exceeding the capitulum: spikes oblong, acute: scales boat-shaped, ovate, mucronate: stamen one: style 3-cleft: achenium roundish-obovate, flat and convex-angular, very finely tubercled and dotted.

Peninsula.

(9) I. CAPILLARIS. *(Roem. and Schult.)*

Ident. Roem. and Schult. Syst. II. 118.

Syn. Scirpus densus, *Roxb.*—I. densa, *Wight Contrib. p.* 109.—S. capillaris, *Linn.*

Spec. Char. Culms cæspitose, filiform-bristly, furrowed and angled, glabrous or slightly scabrous; leaves shorter than the culm, filiform-capillaceous, channelled, externally furrowed, scabrous at the margin: sheaths bearded on the mouth: umbel simple or compound, depauperated: rays 3—5, very unequal, 1—3-spiked: spikes ovate-oblong, pedicelled, central ones sessile: involucre 2-leaved, variable in length: scales boat-shaped, broadly ovate, obtuse, muticous, lower ones mucronulate: achenium roundish-obovate, triangular, terminated by a depressed tubercle.

Lower Bengal. Khasia hills.

(10) I. gracilis. *(N. ab. E.)*

Ident. Nees ab. Esenb. in Wight Contrib. p. 109.

Spec. Char. Spikelets oblong, angled, capitately twin or in threes: capitules collected or simply aggregated into a compound or decompound depressed and spreading umbel: scales trifarious, ovate, deeply keeled, mucronate-acute, rufous-brown: caryopsis obovate, 3-cornered, transversely wrinkled, yellowish: leaflets of the involucre and involucel subulate-cuspidate from an ovate scariose base, shorter or longer than the umbel and umbellet: culm filiform, 3-cornered, compressed: sheaths dehiscing at the apex, villous: leaves bristly.

Peninsula.

(11) I. bellula. *(Steudel.)*

Ident. Steudel l. c. p. 318.

Spec. Char. Culms and leaves bristly, dwarf, stiffish, smooth, glabrous, reddish, fructiferous ones 2—3-times elongated: lowest leaves springing at the base from a loose sheath: spike lateral, solitary, terete-cylindric, obtuse, very densely imbricated on all sides: scales somewhat triangular-ovate, hardish, sub-acute, a little exceeding the oblong obtuse, blueish achenium.

Bengal.

GENUS XII. FIMBRISTYLIS.

Triandria Monogynia. *Sex: Syst:*

Deriv. From *Fimbria* a fringe, and *Stylus* the style, the style is fringed.

Gen. Char. Spikes many-flowered: spikes imbricated on all sides, scarcely any of the lower ones empty: bristles and small calycine scales none: stamens three: style 2- seldom 3-cleft, bulbous and thickened at the base, often ciliated, deciduous: achenium lenticular, seldom triangular, naked and muticous at the apex, surrounded at the base by a minute annular membranaceous adnate disc.—Culms leafy: spikes solitary, twin, capitately conglomerate or umbellate, umbel more or less compound: scales usually keeled, 3-nerved at the keel, articulated at the base, deciduous, lateral lobelets persistent.

(1) F. polytrichoides. *(Vahl.)*

Ident. Vahl. En. II. 249.—Nees ab. Esenb. in Wight Contrib. p. 96.

Syn. Scirpus polytrichoides, *Retz. obs.* 411.—S. scaber, *Roxb.*—F. scaber, *Schult. Mant.* II. 59.—Eleogiton scabra, *Dietr. Spec. II.* 99.

Spec. Char. Culms cæspitose, filiform, glabrous, 1-leaved at the base: leaves short, linear-bristly, glabrous: spike solitary, erect, ovate-oblong, obtuse, supported by a short subulate bract: scales ovate-oblong, obtuse, muticous, 1-nerved: style 2-cleft, ciliolate at the apex: achenium obovate, biconvex, rounded at the apex, rough with very minute glands.

Peninsula.

(2) F. schænoides. *(Vahl.)*

Ident. Vahl. l. c. 286.—N. ab. E. l. c. p. 97.

Syn. Scirpus Schænoides, *Retz.*—S. monostachys, *Roxb.*—Isolepis monostachya, *Schult. Mant II.* 61.—Eleogiton monostachya, *Dietr. Spec. l. c.*

Spec. Char. Culms cæspitose, filiform, leafy at the base: leaves shorter than the culm, linear filiform, scabrous at the margin: spikes solitary, erect, seldom 2—3, one sessile, rest pedicelled, ovate, obtuse: involucre 1-leaved, short, often none: scales very broadly roundish-ovate, sometimes sub-mucronate, many-nerved: style 2-cleft: achenium obovate, lenticular, umbonate, whitish or brown.

Peninsula.

(3) F. bispicata. *(N. ab E.)*

Ident. Nees ab Esenb. in Wight Contrib. p. 97.

Syn. Scirpus bispicatus, *Roxb.*—Isolepis tristachya, *Schult. l. c.*—S. tristachyus, *Roxb.*

Ident. Culms filiform, stiff, furrowed, leafy at the base: leaves shorter than the culm, linear-filiform, channelled, scabrous at the margin: spikes 1—3, one sessile, rest pedicelled, cylindric-oblong, acute: involucre 1-leaved, very long: scales ovate-elliptic, mucronulate: achenium long-stalked, obovate-roundish, lenticular-compressed, scarcely umbonate.

Peninsula. Bengal.

(4) F. ARGENTEA. *(Vahl.)*

Ident. Vahl. l. c. 294.—N. ab E. l. c. p. 100.

Syn. Scirpus argenteus, *Rottb. gram.* 51.—*Roxb.*—S. monander, *Rottb. l. c.* 50.—S. nanus, *Poir.*

Engrav. Rottb. l. c. t. 17, fig. 6, and t. 14, fig. 3.

SPEC. CHAR. Glaucous: culms cæspitose, filiform, leafy at the base: leaves linear-filiform, channelled, scabrous at the margin: spikes numerous, capitately congested, sessile, cylindric-oblong, acute: involucre somewhat 3-leaved, very long: scales ovate, acute, 3-nerved at the back: style 2-cleft: achenium roundish-obovate, swollen lenticular, pointed.

Peninsula.

(5) F. ALBICANS. *(N. ab E.)*

Ident. Nees ab Esenb., l. c. p. 100.

SPEC. CHAR. Spikelets capitate, oblong: scales membranaceous, oblong, acute, monandrous: caryopsis obovate, transversely tubercled and waved: involucre 2—3-leaved, somewhat twice as long as the capitule: radical leaves linear, obtuse, flat, recurved, shorter than the compressed culm.

Peninsula.

(6) F. SQUARROSA. *(Vahl.)*

Ident. Vahl. Enum. II. 289.

Syn. Isolepis hirta, *Humb. et Kunth Nov. gen. I.* 224.—F. hirta, *Roem. and Schult. II.* 99.—F. comata, *Wight Contrib. p.* 102.—Scirpus æstivalis, *Wall. in Annot. ad Roxb. flor. I.* 230.

SPEC. CHAR. Culms cæspitose, leafy at the base: leaves very narrow, flat, beneath or on both sides together with the sheaths pubescent: umbel compound, many-rayed, rays very unequal, 1—6-spiked: involucre about 4-leaved, almost equalling the umbel: spikes oblong, squarrose, long-pedicelled, divaricate, central ones sessile: scales ovate, mucronate and somewhat awned: stamen one: style 2-cleft, bulbous and thickened at the base, and there villous on both sides: achenium obovate-roundish, lenticular and compressed, sub-umbonate.

Lower Bengal. Silhet.

(7) F. DICHOTOMA. *(Vahl.)*

Ident. Vahl. l. c. 287.

Syn. Scirpus dichotomus, *Rottb. gram.* 57.—F. pallescens, *Roxb. Wight Contrib. p.* 101.—Isolepis pallescens, *Dietr. spec.*

Engrav. Rottb. l. c. t. 13, fig. 1.

SPEC. CHAR. Glaucous: culms cæspitose, leafy at the base: leaves equalling the culm, narrow linear, flat, scabrous at the margin, glabrous or softly pubescent: sheaths pubescent: umbel supra-decompound, many-rayed, rays unequal: involucre 5—6-leaved, exceeding the umbel: spikes solitary in threes, central one sessile, rest pedicelled, oblong, acute: scales keeled, broadly ovate, mucronate, glabrous, beset with rusty lineolæ and dots: stamen one: style 2-cleft: achenium obovate, lenticular, umbonate, cancellate, rusty or whitish, pearly shining.

Lower Bengal. Peninsnla.

(8) F. ÆSTIVALIS. *(Vahl.)*

Ident. Vahl. En. II. 288.—Wight Contrib. p. 102.

Syn. Scirpus æstivalis, *Retz. obs.* iv. 12.—*Roxb.*

SPEC. CHAR. Glaucous: culms cæspitose, filiform, furrowed, leafy at the base: leaves almost equalling the culm, narrow-linear, flat and with the sheaths softly pubescent: umbel supra-decompound, many-rayed: rays very unequal: involucre many-leaved, exceeding the umbel: spikes solitary in threes, central one sessile, oblong-lanceolate, acute, somewhat squarrose: scales keeled, ovate, long mucronate: achenium obovate-elliptic, lenticular-biconvex, sub-umbonate.

Peninsula.

(9) F. COMPLANATA. *(Link.)*

Ident. Link. Hort. I. 292.

Syn. Scirpus complanatus, *Retz. obs.* v. 14. *Vahl. Roxb.*—Isolepis complanata, *Roem. and Schult. syst. II.* 119.—Trichelostylis complanata, *Wight Contrib. p.* 103.—I. Willdenowii, *Roem. and Schult. l. c.* 120.—Cyperus complanatus, *Willd.*—F. autumnalis, (*var.* Indica) *Roth.*—S. anceps, *Roxb.*—I. anceps, *Dietr. spec. II.* 125.

SPEC. CHAR. Culms compressed, leafy at the base: leaves shorter than the culm, linear, obliquely acute, above scabrous at the margin: sheaths compressed, distichous: umbel irregular supra-decompound: involucre 2-leaved, shorter than the umbel:

spikes lanceolate, central ones sessile: scales keeled, ovate, mucronulate, 3-nerved at the back, rusty and marked with a riper double zone: stamens 3: style 3-cleft: achenium obovate, trigonal, almost umbonate, very obsoletely dotted.

Peninsula.

(10) F. SCABERRIMA. *(N. ab E.)*

Ident. Nees ab Esenb. in Wight Contrib. p. 102.

SPEC. CHAR. Culms compressed, furrowed, scabrous: leaves shorter than the culm, linear, flat, scabrous at the margin: umbel decompound, many-rayed: rays very unequal, glabrous: involucre 2-leaved, exceeding the umbel: spikes ovate-oblong, acute, central ones sessile: scales keeled and boat-shaped, ovate, mucronulate below the apex, 3-nerved at the back: stamens 3: style 2-cleft: achenium roundish-obovate, lenticular-biconvex, scabrous with obsolete tubercles.

Silhet. Peninsula.

(11) F. QUINQUANGULARIS. *(Kunth.)*

Ident. Kunth Enum. pl. II. p. 229.

Syn. Scirpus quinquangularis, *Vahl. Roxb.* — Trichelostylis quinquangularis, *Wight Contrib. p.* 104.—S. pentagonus, *Roxb.*

SPEC. CHAR. Culms cæspitose, 5-angled, leafy at the base, sometimes leafless: leaves linear, flat, acute, scabrous above at the margin: sheaths compressed, distichous: umbel irregular supra-decompound: involucre somewhat 5-leaved, bristly, short: spikes ovate, acute, central ones sessile: scales keeled, broadly ovate, mucronulate, 3-nerved at the back and marked with a double rusty zone: stamen one: style 3-cleft: achenium roundish, 3-cornered, umbonate, transversely striated, tubercled and muriculate.

Peninsula. Lower Bengal.

(12) F. SALBUNDIA. *(Kunth.)*

Ident. Kunth l. c. p. 230.

Syn. Trichelostylis salbundia, *Wight Contrib. p.* 105.

SPEC. CHAR. Culms cæspitose, rigid, acutely 5-angular, sheathed at the base, leafless: umbel irregularly supra-decompound: involucre somewhat 3-leaved, subulate, short: spikes elliptic, central one sessile: scales keeled, broadly ovate, rounded at the apex, muticous, 3-nerved at the back, keel rusty: stamens 3: style 3-cleft: achenium truncately obovate, obtusely keeled.

Silhet.

(13) F. MILIACEA. *(Vahl.)*

Ident. Vahl. Enum. II. 287.

Syn. Scirpus miliaceus, *Linn.—Burm. Ind.*—Trichelostylis miliacea, *Wight Contrib. p.* 103.—S. tetragonus, *Poir.—Roxb.*—F. tetragona, *Dietr. spec. II.* 152.—T. tetragona, *Wight l. c. p.* 104.—S. Benghalensis, *Pers. syn. I.* 68.—F. Benghalensis, *Roem. and Schult.*

Engrav. Burm. Ind. t. 9, fig. 2.—Rottb. gram. 57, t. 5, fig. 2.

SPEC. CHAR. Culms cæspitose, compressed, quadragonal, leafy at the base, glabrous: leaves distichous, narrow-linear, ensiform: sheaths compressed: umbel irregularly supra-decompound, with 3 to 4 rays: involucre and involucels 2-leaved, short, subulate: spikes sub-globose, central ones sessile: scales broadly ovate, rounded and blunt at the apex.

Moist pastures in the Peninsula. Silhet.

(14) F. COMMUNIS. *(Kunth.)*

Ident. Kunth l. c. p. 234.

Syn. F. diphylla, *Vahl.—Wight Contrib. p.* 100. — Scirpus diphyllus, *Retz.*—S. miliaceus, *Roxb.*—Isolepis curvifolia, *Schult.*—Trichostelis curvifolia, *Wight Contrib.* 105. *(Annot.)*—F. ovalis, *Wight l. c. p.* 98.—F. cincta, *Wight l. c.*—F. pilosa, *Vahl.*—F. tomentosa, *Wight l. c.* 100.—F. rigidula, *Wight l. c. p.* 99.—F. podocarpa, *Wight l. c. p.* 98.—F. Royeniana, *Wight l. c. p.* 99.

SPEC. CHAR. Cæspitose: glaucous: glabrous or pubescent: culms furrowed: leaves narrow linear, flat: umbel compound or decompound, usually few-rayed: involucre 2—5-leaved: spikes ovate-lanceolate, ovate or elliptic, acute: scales very broadly ovate, shortly mucronate: style 2-cleft: achenium bi-convex, umbonate, finely cancellate.

Peninsula.

(15) F. FERRUGINEA. *(Vahl.)*

Ident. Vahl. Enum. II. 291.—Dalz. Bomb. flor. p. 287.

Syn. Scirpus ferrugineus, *Linn.*—S. debilis, *Lam. Ill. I.* 141.—F. arvensis, *Vahl.*—F. Tranquebariensis, *Roth.*

SPEC. CHAR. Culm erect, compressed, triangular above, smooth: sheaths pubescent: leaves short, narrow-linear, roughish on the margins: umbel simple or compound: rays very unequal, with 1 to 5 spikelets: involucre 1 to 2-leaved, shorter than the umbel:

spikelets ovate-oblong, acute, central ones sessile: scales ovate-elliptic, mucronate under the apex, ferruginous, a little hoary and puberulous: stamens 2: style bifid: seed obovate, umbonate, dark-coloured, shining.

Banks of streams in the Deccan.

(16) F. LATIFOLIA. *(Kunth.)*

Ident. Kunth l. c. p. 239.

Syn. Trichelostylis latifolia, *Wight Contrib. p.* 106.

SPEC. CHAR. Involucre 2—3-leaved, subulate, much shorter than the decompound, contracted, loose umbel: culm furrowed and angular, compressed above, slender: leaves broad-linear, obtuse, glaucous, twisted: spikelets capitate, in threes or fives, ovate, angular: scales ovate, obtuse, keeled, very finely roughened: style bulbous at the base: ovary 3-cornered.

Peninsula.

(17) F. CHÆTORHIZA. *(Kunth.)*

Ident. Kunth l. c. p. 240.

Syn. Trichelostylis chætorhiza, *Wight Contrib. p.* 106.

SPEC. CHAR. Involucre 2—3-leaved, subulate from a membranaceous base, much shorter than the straight, erect, decompound umbel: culm compressed and 3-cornered straight: leaves narrow linear, recurved, obtuse, shorter than the culm: spikelets subcapitate, ovate: scales obtusely keeled, acutish, smooth: caryopsis obovate, 3-cornered, white, tubercled: rhizome thick, creeping, fibrous.

Peninsula.

(18) F. TORTA. *(Kunth.)*

Ident. Kunth l. c. p. 241.

Syn. Trichelostylis torta, *Wight Contrib. p.* 105.

SPEC. CHAR. Involucre 2—3-leaved, linear from a membranaceous base, obtuse, much shorter than the loose 2-rayed decompound umbel: culm furrowed and angular, slightly compressed: leaves linear, recurved, mucronate from a rounded apex, stiffish, twisted: spikelets in threes, sessile or short pedicelled, oblong: scales obtuse, with white margins, triandrous: caryopsis obovate, 3-cornered, white, tubercled: rhizome creeping, fibrous, fibres whip-like.

Peninsula.

(19) F. Wightiana. (*N. ab. E.*)

Ident. Nees ab. Esenb. in Wight Contrib. p. 99.

Spec. Char. Umbel decompound, rounded, dense: umbellets many-flowered, compact: involucre 2-leaved, much shorter than the umbel: spikelets elliptic, obtuse: scales closely imbricated, broadly ovate, very obtuse, testaceous, white membranaceous at the margin, very finely 3-nerved at the back, diandrous: style beardless: caryopsis obovate, flat-convex, rough with small tubercles: leaves linear, stiff, channelled, scabrous at the margin: culm furrowed and angular at the base, compressed at the apex, longer than the leaves.

Peninsula.

(20) F. tenuissima. (*Steudel.*)

Ident. Steudel l. c. p. 109.

Spec. Char. Culms thin, somewhat compressed, sheathed at the base, sheaths hairy at the mouth: leaves capillary, flattish, shorter than the culm: leaflets of the involucre 2—3, somewhat bristly: umbellet capitate, composed of 2—5-aggregated spikes: spikes oblong-sessile: scales ovate, concave, keeled, mucronulate: achenium ovate-triquetrous with the angles somewhat elevated, white, smooth.

Bengal.

(21) F. Griffithiana. (*Steudel,*)

Ident. Steudel l. c. p. 110.

Spec. Char. Culms low, striated, puberulous, at the base from the sheaths densely pubescent, leafy: leaves flattish, very narrow, more or less shorter than the culm: involucres of the compound and decompound umbel more or less shorter than the umbel itself, rays unequal: involucels oblong, somewhat bristly-acuminate, short, densely pubescent: spikes thin, acute, lengthening after the very easily deciduous lower scales, lowest scales persistent, all ovate, acutish, pale: style 2-cleft: achenium ovate, not angled, smooth, whitish.

Bengal.

(22) F. uliginosa. (*Hochst.*)

Ident. Hochst. in Herb. Hohenhack, 1295. Steudel l. c. p. 109.

Spec. Char. Root fibrous, thickened into a woody densely cæspitiferous rhizome: culms filiform, striated, leafy at the base, smooth: radical and stem leaves very narrow-linear, flat or keeled and concave, a little curved, acute, scabrous at the edge, three times shorter than the culm: capitulum compact, spikes 5—8, closely sessile, ovate-oblong: involucre 1—2-leaved, scale-shaped with a narrow short leaf-shaped appendage, equalling the capitulum: scales ovate-oblong, obtuse, rusty, mucronulate: achenium obtusely triquetrous, whitish.

Neilgherries.

(23) F. oxylepis. *(Steudel.)*

Ident. Steudel l. c. p. 110.

Spec. Char. Culms unequal, erect, smooth, compressed and flat, thin, with the whole plant pale rufescent: leaves flat, very narrow, more or less shorter than the culm: involucres of the somewhat simple umbel shorter than the umbel itself, rays usually 1—3-spiculate: spikes oblong, acutish: scales ovate, somewhat angular in the middle, acutely mucronate: style 2—3-cleft: achenium roundish-ovate, obtuse, whitish or brown, everywhere slightly warty and tubercled.

Near Serampore.

(24) F. capillacea. *(Hochst.)*

Ident. Hochst. in Herb. Hohenhack, 939.—Steudel l. c. p. 111.

Spec. Char. Culms bristly, compressed, striated, erect, smooth: leaves bristly, shorter than the culm, acute, pale green, smooth: sheaths beset with hairs at the mouth: involucrè somewhat 3-leaved: leaflets scaly, small, usually terminated by a much shorter third leaflet: umbel simple, 3—4-rayed with a sessile spikelet, rays seldom 2-cleft: spikelets in the solitary rays oblong, 5—9-flowered: scales rusty: style and 3-cleft stigma fimbriated: achenium obtusely triquetrous, ovate.

Neilgherries.

(25) F. glabra. *(Hochst.)*

Ident. Hochst. in Steudel l. c. p. 111.

Spec. Char. Culms erect, filiform, striated, smooth, leafy at the base: leaves flat, linear, obtuse, 2—3-times shorter than the culm, glabrous: rays of the very simple umbel 3—6, longer than the 2-leaved involucre: spikes linear, very thin, narrow: florets imbricated, soon deciduous at the base: scales ovate, rusty, scariose at the edges: style 2-cleft, fimbriated, base remarkably bulbous: achenium white, triquetrous, sparingly warty.

Mangalore.

(26) F. MONTICOLA. *(Hochst.)*

Ident. Hochst. l. c.

SPEC. CHAR. Culms erect, flattened, striated, very slightly rough-serrulate at the margin: sheaths thin, glabrous, terminated by a short linear flattish leaflet: leaflets of the involucre about three, linear from a scaly ovate base, scarcely the length of the raylets: umbel simple, 3—4-rayed, rarely one or the other ray again radiolate: spikes very shortly peduncled or sessile, linear-oblong, 8—12-flowered: scales ovate, very shortly mucronulate, rusty chestnut: style and stigmas fimbriated: achenium triquetrous, ovate, silvery, shining, warty.

Neilgherries.

(27) F. SIMILIS. *(Steudel.)*

Ident. Steudel l. c. p. 112.

SPEC. CHAR. Culms erect, flexuose, somewhat triquetrous, smooth, sheathed and leafy at the base: sheaths sparingly but densely hairy at the mouth, striated: leaves narrow, linear, obtuse, asperulous at the margin: leaflets of the involucre nearly equalling the very simple 3—5-rayed umbel: rays 1-spiculate: spikes oblong-ovate: scales ovate, concave, rounded, obtuse, pale rusty, scarcely mucronulate at the apex, of one colour, easily deciduous: style 2-cleft: achenium ovate, striated lengthways, with thin white lines between the striæ.

Bengal.

(28) F. BOECKELERI. *(Steudel.)*

Ident. Steudel l. c. p. 113.

SPEC. CHAR. Culms compressed, thin, erect, smooth, 1½ foot: sheaths at the base lax, leafless: leaves from the upper sheaths linear, narrow, flat, scabrous above, nearly equalling the culm: leaflets of the involucre 1—2, shorter than the compound and decompound umbel: involucels small, scaly, more or less bristly acuminate or none: rays thin, compressed, raylets 1-spiculate: spikelets ovate-oblong: scales ovate, keeled and concave, rusty, very shortly mucronulate: style 3-cleft: achenium ovate, much shorter than the scale, whitish, warted and tubercled.

Bengal.

(29) F. FLACCIDA. *(Steudel.)*

Ident. Steudel l. c.

SPEC. CHAR. Culm compressed, striated, weak, and with the leaves slightly flaccid, base leafy: leaves flattish, smooth, shorter than the culm: leaflets of the involucre bristly from a broader base, many times shorter than the umbel: rays simple or 3-spiked at the apex and then again involucelled: spikelets oblong, many-flowered: scales brown-rusty, oblong, obtuse: style 3-cleft: achenium triquetrous, slightly verrucose at the angles, white.

Bengal. (?)

(30) F. TENERA. *(Schult.)*

Ident. Schult. Mant. II. 57.

Syn. Scirpus tenellus, *Roxb.*—Trichelostylis tenella, *Wight Contrib. p.* 103.

SPEC. CHAR. Culm filiform, angular, slightly compressed: umbel sub-compound: rays 3—1-spiked: spikelets ovate-oblong, middle one of the rays sessile, lateral ones long-peduncled, patent: scales ovate, acute with a mucronule, keeled, glandular-dotted, brownish: caryopsis obovate, obtusely 3-cornered, coarsely tubercled, white: involucre 2—3-leaved, much shorter than the umbel: leaves linear-filiform, and with the culm scabrous at the apex.

Peninsula.

GENUS II. ABILGAARDIA.

Triandria Monogynia. *Sex: Syst:*

Deriv. Named after Professor Abilgaard, of Copenhagen.

GEN. CHAR. Spikes many-flowered: scales distichous, fructiferous ones bifarious by the twisting of the rhacheola, keeled, deciduous, very few of the lower ones empty: bristles and calycine scales none: stamens 1—3: style 3-cleft, pyramidately thickened at the base, articulated with the ovary, deciduous: achenium somewhat pear-shaped, triangular or trigonal, umbonate.—Culms leafy at the base, seldom leafless: spikes solitary, twin, tern, congested in heads or umbelled: umbel simple or supra-decompound.

(1) A. MONOSTACHYA. *(Vahl.)*

Ident. Vahl. Enum. II. 296.

Syn. Cyperus monostachyus, *Linn. Rottb.*—A. Rottboelliana, *Wight Contrib. p.* 95.—Scirpus Schænoides, *Roxb.*—C. Cariboeus et Indicus, *Pers. Syn. I.* 65.—A. Indica, *Nees ab. Esenb. in Linnœa* ix. 289.

Engrav. Rottb. Gram. 18, t. 13, fig. 3.

Spec. Char. Glaucous-green: culms furrowed: leaves acute: spikes solitary, very rarely twin: achenia more or less tuberculose, varying in size.

Dry pastures in the Peninsula.

(2) A. tristachya. (*Vahl.*)

Ident. Vahl. l. c. 297.—Wight Contrib. p. 96.

Syn. Cyperus triflorus, *Linn.*—Schœnus cyperoides, *Retz.*

Spec. Char. Culms triangular, furrowed, glabrous: leaves shorter, channelled, smooth: spikes 3 or 4, umbellate, one sessile, rest pedicelled, oblong, acute, compressed, fructiferous ones spirally twisted: involucre about 1-leaved, short, stiff, scabrous at the margin: scales compressed and keeled, broadly ovate, sharply mucronate, obsoletely 9-nerved at the back: achenium roundish-pyriform, stalked, trigonal, pointed, very finely reticulated, tubercled and rough.

Peninsula.

SECT. III. HYPOLYTREÆ.

GENUS XIII. LIPOCARPHA.

Triandria Monogynia. *Sex: Syst:*

Gen. Char. Spikes many-flowered: scales imbricated on every side, spathulate, deciduous, some lower ones empty: inner proper scales 2, parallel to the outer larger one, nearly equal, very thinly membranaceous, enclosing the flower and more slowly the fruit: inner one broader, embracing the outer: calyx none: stamens one, seldom 2: style 2—3-cleft: achenium flattish internally, convex and obtuse angled outwardly, pointed or acuminately beaked, wrapped in their own scales, one (scale) deciduous with them.—Culms simple, somewhat triangular, leafy at the base: spikes very many, aggregated in heads at the top of the culm, involucrate.

(1) L. argentea. (*Brown.*)

Ident. Brown Congo 40.—Kunth Enum. II. p. 266.

Syn. Hypœlyptum argenteum, *Vahl.*—Scirpus Senegalensis, *Lam. Ill. I.* 140.—Tunga lœvigata, *Roxb.*—Hypolyhum lœvigatum, *Spreng.*—L. lœvigata, *Wight Contrib. p.* 92.

Spec. Char. Culms trigonal: leaves shorter, stiff, keeled and flat, glabrous: spikes 3—7, ovate, obtuse: involucre 2—4-leaved, very long : scales spathulate, somewhat 5-nerved, whitish : stamen one : achenium pointed.

Peninsula.

(2) L. SPHACILATA. *(Kunth.)*

Ident. Kunth l. c. p. 267.

Syn. Hypœlyptum sphacelatum, *Vahl.*—Tunga triceps, *Roxb.*—L. triceps, *Wight Contrib. p.* 92.

SPEC. CHAR. Culm compressed and trigonal, leafy at the base: leaves shorter, flat, glabrous : spikes tern, congested, ovate, obtuse : involucre 2-leaved, very long : scales spathulate, acutish, somewhat 7-nerved : stamen one : style 3-cleft : achenium elliptic, acuminately beaked, triangular, cinnamon.

Peninsula.

GENUS XIV. HEMICARPHA.

Triandria Monogynia. *Sex: Syst.*

GEN. CHAR. Spikes many-flowered : scales everywhere imbricated, obovate-cuneate, deciduous : proper inner scale one, smaller, lateral, very thin, glossy, embracing the flower : calyx none : stamen one, somewhat lateral : style 2-cleft : achenium elliptic-oblong, terete, umbonate, impressed and dotted, wrapped round by the glassy scale.—Very small, culms cæspitose, leafy at the base and leaves bristly : spike solitary, ovate, obtuse, sessile : involucre 1-leaved, continuing the culm.

(1) H. ISOLEPIS. *(N. ab. E.)*

Ident. Nees ab. Esenb. in Wight Contrib. p. 92.

Syn. Scirpus hemisphericus, *Roth.* —Isolepis hemispherica *Dietr. Spec. II.* 109.

Peninsula.

GENUS XV. HYPOLYTRUM.

Triandria Monogynia. *Sex : Syst :*

GEN. CHAR. Spikes tapering, many-flowered : scales imbricated on every side, persistent, some lower ones empty : proper inner scales 2, keeled and compressed, contrary to the outer larger one, calyx none : stamens 2—3 : style 2-cleft : achenium bony, beaked with the conical base of the style, a little compressed, swollen-lenticular, exceeding the scale.—Culms triquetrous, leafy : spikes capitately fascicled or arranged in panicled corymbs.

(1) H. LATIFOLIUM. *(Rich.)*

Ident. Rich. in Pers. Syn. I. 70.

Syn. H. giganteum, *Wight Contrib. p.* 93.—Tunga diandra, *Roxb.*—Schœnus nemorum, *Vahl.*

Engrav. Rheede Mal. xii. t. 58.

SPEC. CHAR. Culms triangular, leafy : leaves longer, broadly linear, flat, 3-nerved, stiffish, spinous-serrulate at the margin and middle-nerved beneath : corymbs paniculately arranged at the apex of the culm : leaves distinct : spikes cylindric oblong : scales rounded at the apex, sub-mucronate, proper ones free, ciliated at the keel : stamens 2 : fruit ovate, roundish, confluent with the acute conical base of the style.

Peninsula.

SECT. IV. RHYNCOSPOREÆ.

GENUS XVI. RHYNCOSPORA.

Triandria Monogynia. *Sex : Syst :*

Deriv. From *Rhyncos* a beak, and *Sporos* a seed.

GEN. CHAR. Spikes 1—9-flowered : flowers either all hermaphrodite or lower one hermaphrodite (or female), the rest males : scales everywhere imbricated, 1-nerved, often mucronate and awned, lower ones smaller, empty : calyx rudimentary : bristles 6, often more or fewer, sometimes minute or quite obliterated : stamens 3, very rarely 2—1 : style more or less deeply 2-cleft, dilated and thickened at the base : achenium biconvex, beaked with the hardened conical or subulate persistent base of the style.—Culms leafy : spikes capitate, corymbose or panicled, usually rusty-brown : scales deciduous.

(1) R. ARTICULATA. *(Schult.)*

Ident. Schult. Mant. II. 49.—Dalz. Bomb. flor. p. 288.

Syn. Schœnus articulatus, *Roxb.*—Cephaloschœnus articulatus, *Wight Contrib.* 115.

SPEC. CHAR. Spikelets sub-capitate: heads fascicled, corymbose: corymbs axillary, decompound, terminal one supra-decompound, many-flowered, erect: bracts setaceous: leaves broad-linear.

Peninsula.

SECT. V. SCLERINEÆ.

GENUS XVII. SCLERIA.

Triandria Monogynia. *Sex: Syst:*

Deriv. From *Scleros* hard, alluding to the fruit.

GEN. CHAR. Monœcious: male spikes intermixed with the fewer female or androgynous ones, many-flowered: scales imbricated, outer ones somewhat distichous, empty: stamens 3, seldom 2—1: female spikes 1-flowered: scales few: style undivided: androgynous spikes very like the females, many-flowered: lower flower female, rest males: achenium stony or crustaceous and fragile, supported by a disc: disc more or less 3-lobed, often ciliated, fimbriated, serrated and cut, or cut and many-cleft, slowly bipartible: upper part adnate to the fruit, lower to the bottom of the spike.—Culms triangular, leafy: leaves 3—5-nerved, somewhat plaited, usually grassy, rigid: sheaths in front (at the side opposite the origin of the leaf) usually prolonged into a more or less elongated strap: spikes panicled, fascicled, racemose or verticillately spiked, females sessile, males usually pedicelled, more numerous.

(1) S. LITHOSPERMA. *(Willd.)*

Ident. Willd. Sp. iv. 316.—Wight Contrib. p. 117.

Syn. Scirpus lithospermus, *Linn.*—S. tenuis, *Roth.*

Engrav. Rheede Mal. xii. t. 48.

SPEC. CHAR. Glaucous: culms slender, triquetrous: leaves narrow-linear, scabrous on the margin: sheaths triquetrous: strap short, rounded: peduncles axillary and terminal, simple or branched, few-spiked: spikes in twos or threes: achenium ovate-elliptic.

Peninsula.

(2) S. TESSELLATA. *(Willd.)*

Ident. Willd. Spec. iv. 315.—Wight Contrib. p. 118.

Syn. S. biflora, *Roxb.*

SPEC. CHAR. Culms triquetrous: leaves flat, serrulate and scabrous at the margin, sub-membranaceous: sheaths triquetrous, puberulous: strap short, rounded, stiff: panicles axillary and terminal, simple, bracteate, androgynous: bracts long, subulate: male flowers triandrous: achenium sub-globose, mucronate, tessellated and cancellate, milky-whitish, hairyish at the prominent margins, opaque.

Peninsula. Lower Bengal.

(3) S. PERGRACILIS. *(Kunth.)*

Ident. Kunth Enum. pl. II. p. 354.

Syn. Hypoporum pergracile, *Wight Contrib. p.* 118.

SPEC. CHAR. Culms and sheaths triquetrous: leaves narrow-linear, scabrous at the margin: spike compound, interruptedly glomerate, slender: proper spikes congested by threes or twos, somewhat 5-flowered, lower flower female, rest males: scales mucronate: achenium depresso-globose, umbonate and somewhat mucronate, trigonal, sub-echinate and tubercled, milky-white, shining: strap none.

Silhet.

(4) S. ORIZOIDES. *(Presl.)*

Ident. Presl. in Rel. Haenk. III. 201.—Wight Contrib. p. 116.

SPEC. CHAR. Culm triquetrous: leaves slightly scabrous at the margin: sheaths winged and triquetrous: panicle terminal, fastigiate: rachis scabrous: spikelets solitary, sessile, longer than the bract: glumes ovate, acute, 1-nerved, glabrous: fruit globose, very smooth, very shortly apiculate.

Peninsula.

(5) S. SUMATRENSIS. *(Retz.)*

Ident. Retz. obs. v. 19.—Wight Contrib. p. 116.

SPEC. CHAR. Culms triquetrous, glabrous: leaves rigid, elongated, linear, very narrow at the apex, puberulous beneath, scabrous at the margin: sheaths triangular, puberulous, approximated by threes, purplish, mouth truncated and rounded, fimbriate-ciliate: panicles axillary and terminal, branched, pyramidal, androgynous: achenium globose, reticulated, ashy-dark: disc obsoletely 3-lobed, lobes waved and crenated.

Peninsula.

(6) S. ANDROGYNA. *(N. ab E.)*

Ident. Nees ab Esenb. in Wight Contrib. p. 117.

SPEC. CHAR. Culm triquetrous: sheaths triquetrous, keels scabrous: lobelet leaf-opposed, rounded: leaves alternate: corymbs axillary and terminal, stiff, constituting an elongated panicle: spikelets some male, some androgynous: third scale female, the fourth embracing the male 2-flowered spikelet: nuts ovate, acute, smooth, white: disc deeply 3-lobed, entire.

Peninsula.

(7) S. PARVULA. *(Steudĕl.)*

Ident. Steudel l. c. p. 174.

Syn. S. uliginosa, *Hochst. herb. Ind. Hohen.* 1295.

SPEC. CHAR. Culms simple or somewhat branched, erect, triquetrous, glabrous: sheaths sub-truncate at the mouth, slightly hairy: leaves narrow, linear-lanceolate, slightly scabrous at the edge, here and there ciliated, unequal, longer ones exceeding the culm: raceme or panicle depauperated, terminal, few-flowered: fruits globose, tesselated reticulate, white, scarcely mucronulate at the apex: disc 3-lobed, lobes entire, obtuse.

Neilgherries.

SECT. VI. CARICINEÆ.

GENUS. XVIII. CAREX.

Triandria Monogynia. *Sex: Syst:*

Deriv. From *Careo* to be without, the upper spikes are destitute of seeds.

GEN. CHAR. Spikes androgynous or monœcious, very rarely diœcious, males simple, females somewhat compound: scales imbricated on all sides, 1-flowered: bristles and calycine scales none: stamens three: pistil embraced by another inner scale which is keeled at the margins and bearing a utricle: style 2—3-cleft: stigma elongated, exserted: achenium lenticular, flat-convex, or triangular, tunicated by an increased bladder-shaped scale.—Cæspitose herbs, sometimes creeping: culms triangular, simple, seldom branched: leaves grassy, usually scabrous at the keel and margin: spikes axillary and terminal, solitary, twin, in threes or more, arranged as a fascicle, capitule, spike or panicle.

(1) C. nubigena. *(Don.)*

Ident. Don. flor. Nepal. 42.—Wight Contrib. p. 120.

Spec. Char. Spike compound, oblong, from many approximated ovate spikelets: bracts leafy-cuspidate from a truncated membranaceous base, leaflet of the lower ones longer than the spikelet or spike: fruit erect, ovate or oval, flat-convex, striated at the back, margin naked or denticulate: beak short, 2-toothed: stigmas two: scales ovate, cuspidate, a little shorter than the fruit: culm obtusely 3-cornered, smooth: leaves linear-narrow, keeled or convolute, scabrous at the margin.

Peninsula.

(2) C. cæspititia. *(Nees ab Esenb.)*

Ident. N. ab E. in Wight Contrib. p. 127.

Spec. Char. Male spike one, oblong, cylindric: females in threes, somewhat approximated, smaller, appressed, cylindric: bracts leafy, without sheaths, angles of the culm and leaves serrulate-scabrous at the margin, lowest one a little remote: stigmas twin: perigynium glabrous, obtuse, mouth entire: scales ovate-oblong, obtuse, females smaller, green, males marked on both sides with a ferruginous vitta.

Silhet.

(3) C. longicruris. *(Nees ab Esenb.)*

Ident. N. ab E. l. c. p. 124.

Spec. Char. Spikelets fascicled, peduncled, compound or simple, lax, males at the top: upper and partial bracteal sheaths bristle-bearing: stigmas two, capillary, very long: fruit oval, biconvex, beaked, younger ones ciliate-serrate at the margins: female scales alternate, spreading, oval oblong, mucronate-acute, yellowish-red: culm slender: leaves long, linear, straight, scabrous above.

Peninsula.

(4) C. longipes. *(Don.)*

Ident. Don. flor. Nep. 43.—Wight Contrib. p. 124.

Spec. Char. Spikes many, alternate, narrowly cylindric, lax, males at the top: lower ones sometimes compound at the base, peduncle long exserted: stigmas twin, elongated: fruit broadly oval, nerved and striated, long-beaked: beak 2-cleft at the apex:

scales oblong, awned, yellow, equalling the fruit: culm slender: leaves narrow, scabrous and with the bracteal ones elongated.

Peninsula.

(5) C. PHACOTA. *(Spreng.)*

Ident. Spreng. syst. III. 826.—Wight Contrib. p. 126.

Syn. C. lenticularis, *Don. flor. Nep.* 43.

SPEC. CHAR. Spikes cylindric, somewhat in fives, approximate, nodding: lower ones females, males at the top, terminal one, and twin terminal ones male: bracts leafy, without sheaths: stigmas two: fruit obovate, cuneate at the base, very shortly rostellate, papillosely shining, depressed: scales obcordate, bristly-awned from the sinus: female awn longer than the scale and fruit: culm very narrowly triquetrous: leaves and bracts exceeding the culm, linear, flat, scabrous at the margin and keel.

Peninsula.

(6) C. WALLICHIANA. *(Prescott.)*

Ident. N. ab Esenb. in Wight Contrib. p. 129.

SPEC. CHAR. Male spikes in threes: females twin, remote, subsessile, erect, cylindric: bracts leafy, almost without sheaths, long: stigmas tern: perigynium of the flower strongly 2-toothed, hairy: scales oblong-lanceolate, acuminate, somewhat awned, pale-green, males broader, repand, membranaceous.

Oude.

(7) C. DONIANA. *(Spreng.)*

Ident. Spreng. syst. III. 825.—Wight Contrib. p. 128.

Syn. C. chlorostachys, *Don. flor. Nep.* 43.

SPEC. CHAR. Female spikelets in threes or fours, slightly erect, cylindric, short-peduncled, male solitary: lower bracts leafy, without sheaths: fruit spreading, ovate-lanceolate, margin acute, attenuated into a flat 2-toothed beak, obsoletely nerved, glabrous: scales subulate-lanceolate from a broader base, scabrous, white-membranaceous, narrow, shorter than the fruit: leaves linear, flat, scabrous at the margin: culm triquetrous.

Silhet.

(8) C. SPECIOSA. *(Kunth.)*

Ident. Kunth Enum. pl. II. 504.

Syn. C. concolor, *Wight Contrib. p.* 125.

SPEC. CHAR. Spikelets somewhat in threes, very distant, one sub-radical and one intermediate androgynous, linear, males above, long-peduncled, short-sheathed, uppermost one naked: stigmas 3: fruit coarse, ventricosely 3-cornered, beaked, densely and finely striated, twice longer than the rhomb-ovate, obtuse scales: culm 3-cornered: leaves broadish-linear, flat, very acute, longer than the culm.

Rajmahal.

(9) C. MYOSURUS. *(N. ab E.)*

Ident. Nees ab Esenb. in Wight Contrib. p. 122.

SPEC. CHAR. Spikes compound, axillary, exserted, peduncled: spikelets alternate, elongated, curved, many-flowered, above males: stigmas 3: fruit trigonal, gibbous, attenuated at the base: beak short, 2-cleft: segments præmorse: scales conformable, ovate, membranaceous at the margin, lower ones quadrifarious, upper ones from the middle males: leaves linear, long, scabrous at the edges.

Dindigul hills.

(10) C. RAMOSA. *(Schkuhr.)*

Ident. Schkuhr. Car. II. 40.

Syn. C. cruciata, *Wight Contrib. p.* 124.

SPEC. CHAR. Corymbs supra-decompound, divaricate, androgynous, peduncled, remote: spikes filiform, slender, above males: stigmas 2: fruit lanceolate-triquetrous, beaked, bipartite, pubescent, larger than the lanceolate mucronate scale.

Peninsula.

(11) C. MEIOGYNA. *(N. ab E.)*

Ident. Nees ab Esenb. in Wight Contrib. p. 125.

SPEC. CHAR. Spikes compound, axillary, lower ones exserted-peduncled: spikelets alternate, approximated, terete, acute, loosely scaly at the base, female: stigmas 3: female scales smaller, ovate-lanceolate, sub-acute, males more, closely imbricated, ovate, obtuse, brown: leaves broadish linear, flat, floral ones usually exceeding their own spikes.

Peninsula.

(12) C. INDICA. *(Linn.)*

Ident. Linn. Mant. 574.—Willd.—Wight Contrib. p. 123.

Spec. Char. Spikes somewhat decompound, subpinnate, axillary, lower ones exserted-peduncled: rhachis angular, very scabrous: spikelets alternate, sub-distichous, terete, acute, females at the base: stigmas 3: fruit trigonal-ovate, beaked, scabrous: scales nearly equal, imbricated, ovate, mucronate, females a little longer, mucronate, scabrous: leaves broadish-linear, scabrous at the edges, floral ones exceeding their own spikes.

Peninsula.

(13) C. filicina. *(N. ab E.)*

Ident. Nees ab Esenb. in Wight Contrib. 123.

Spec. Char. Spikes pinnately decompound and supra-decompound, androgynous, peduncled, dense: spikelets male above, below loosely female: stigmas 3: fruit lanceolate, subulate-rostrate, longer than the ovate scales: leaves broad, scabrous.

Peninsula.

(14) C. Lindleyana. *(N. ab E.)*

Ident. Nees ab Esenb. l. c. p. 122.

Spec. Char. Spikes decompound-glomerate, oval, lower ones long-peduncled, solitary or twin, upper ones confluent: rachis strigose: spikelets ovate, males at the apex: stigmas tern: fruit trigonal, ovate, glabrous, beaked, longer than the ovate, acuminate-awned scale: leaves narrow, serrulate-scabrous at the apex, shorter than the culm.

Peninsula.

(15) C. Wightiana. *(N. ab. E.)*

Ident. Nees. ab. Esenb. l. c. p. 122.

Spec. Char. Spikes decompound-glomerate, oblong: lower ones long-peduncled, upper ones confluent: rhachis glabrous: spikelets oblong, imbricated, males at the extreme apex: stigmas 3: fruit erect, trigonal, oval, scabrous between the nerves, beaked, twice longer than the acute, striated, oval scale: leaves broad-linear, very scabrous and with the bracts exceeding the culm.

Peninsula.

(16) C. rhaphidocarpa. *(N. ab. E.)*

Ident. Nees. ab. Esenb. l. c. p. 122.

SPEC. CHAR. Spikes compound and decompound, oblong, solitary or twin, lowest one long-peduncled, rest somewhat enclosed-peduncled, upper ones confluent: rhachis hirsute: spikelets alternate, approximate, ovate, few-flowered, males at the extreme apex: stigmas 3: fruit patent, oblong, trigonal, long-beaked, subulate-acuminate scale: leaves linear, beneath and with the sheaths hairy.

Peninsula.

(17) C. BACCANS. *(N. ab. E.)*

Ident. Nees. ab. Esenb. l. c. p. 122.

SPEC. CHAR. Spikelets compound, enclosed-peduncled, lower ones remote: rhachis triquetrous, scabrous, stiff: spikelets cylindric, males at the top, lower ones of the spikes twin or in three's: stigmas 3: fruit ovate, inflated, gibbous and angular at the back, short-beaked, patent recurved, nearly equalling the ovate, bristly cuspidate scale: all the bracts leafy, and with the leaves broadish-linear, scabrous at the edges, equalling the triquetrous culm.

Peninsula.

(18) C. LIGULATA. *(N. ab. E.)*

Ident. Nees. ab. Esenb. l. c. p. 127.

SPEC. CHAR. Male spike solitary, females somewhat in fives, approximate, exserted-peduncled, erect, narrow-cylindric: stigmas tern: fruit oblong, trigonal-gibbous, beaked, roughish pubescent, 2-nerved: scales ovate, females short-awned, muticous: culm trigonal, leafy at the apex: leaves and bracts sheathed and ligulate, flat, longer than the culm.

Peninsula.

(19) C. SPICULATA. *(Boott.)*

Ident. Boott. Caric. nov. 139.—Steudel l. c. p. 188.

SPEC. CHAR. Culm slender, firm, smooth, 2-feet, base covered with rusty lacerated sheaths: leaves equalling the culm: spikes 4—5, cylindric, pale, erect, androgynous, males at the apex, upper ones approximated, sessile, lowest one somewhat remote, peduncled: stigmas 3: fruit triquetrous-elliptic, cylindric-beaked, 2-cleft, stalked, longer than the lanceolate acuminate or hispid-cuspidate scale.

Khasia hills.

(20) C. MERCARENSIS. *(Hochst.)*

Ident. Hochst. in Herb.—Hohenhack Ind. or. 943.—Stendel l. c. p. 194.

Spec. Char. Root strongly fibrous: culm triangular, smooth, slender, leafy, 1—2-feet: radical and stem leaves flat, narrow, scabrous at the margin, shorter than the culm, long acuminated at the almost filiform apex: panicles axillary and terminal, peduncled, branches simple or branched: spikes lax, 8—15-flowered, males at the apex: female scales ovate, aristulate, spreading, a little shorter than the utricles: utricles ovate-triquetrous, striated lengthways, smooth or rough, long-beaked, beak shortly or scarcely 2-cleft: male scales narrower.

Neilgherries. Near Mercara.

(21) C. leucantha. *(Boott.)*

Ident. Boott. l. c. 135.—Steudel l. c. p. 195.

Spec. Char. Stem slender, 2—3-feet, leafy at the base: spike decompound from small androgynous spikelets: males at the apex, terminal, and beneath at the apex of the peduncles congested and sessile, axillary: partial spikes 4—6, alternate, more or less compound, lower ones remote, peduncled, upper approximated, sessile, abbreviated: stigmas 3: fruit trigonal-elliptic, acuminated, beaked, deeply and obliquely cleft, scabrous, twice longer than the ovate, hispidly mucronate scale.

Peninsula.

(22) C. macrophylla. *(Hochst.)*

Ident. Hochst. l. c. 942.—Stendel l. c. p. 207.

Spec. Char. Root strongly fibrous, supporting a 1-culmed leafy turf: leaves numerous, radical, very long, linear, long acuminated, scabrous at the edge, green glaucescent: culm triquetrous, leafy, bearing from sheaths, fasicled unequal simple once-divided very slender androgynous spikes, females below: scales hyaline, linear-lanceolate, middle nerve lengthed into a short scabrous awn: stamens 3, elongated, almost equalling the scale: female scales similar to the males, inner scale elongated, forming a utricle embracing the style up to the division.

Neilgherries.

(23) C. nilagerica. *(Hochst.)*

Ident. Hochst. l. c. 1290.—Steudel l. c. p. 207.

Spec. Char. Root fibrous, thickened into a somewhat bulbous woody rhizome: culm erect, triquetrous, smooth, leafy, 1-foot: radical and stem leaves linear lanceolate, a little scabrous, more or less equalling the culm: panicles axillary and a terminal one, small, forming a compound panicle: spikes androgynous, males at the apex: scales ovate-lanceolate, acute: stigmas 3, fruit lanceolate-triquetrous, curved, beaked, roughish, beak exceeding the scale.

Neilgherries.

(24) C. PLATYCARPA. *(Hochst.)*

Ident. Hochst. l. c. 1292.—Steudel l. c. p. 214.

SPEC. CHAR. Culm acutely triquetrous, smooth or slightly scabrous towards the apex, leafy below the spikelets: leaf of the lowest spikelet much exceeding all (5—8) the spikelets, rest smaller, glaucescent: spikes axillary, all peduncled, somewhat nodding, terminal one male, rest female, cylindric, dense, many-flowered: style 2-cleft: fruit imbricated, compressed, ovate, very shortly mucronate, dark brown, white margined: scales narrow mucronate from an obtuse apex, scabrous mucronule equalling or exceeding the fruit.

Neilgherries.

(25) C. GEMELLA. *(Hochst.)*

Ident. Hochst. l. c. 942.—Steudel l. c. p. 214.

SPEC. CHAR. Culm thin, triquetrous, leafy at the base and there covered by scariose sheaths: leaves linear, flat, very narrow, a little shorter than the culm, scabrous at the margin: bracts leafy, smaller by degrees: terminal spikes 2, male, thin, females 8, more or less peduncled, males usually at the apex: female scales oblong, acute, shorter than the oblong-ovate beaked fruit.

Neilgherries.

(26) C. OLIVACEA. *(Boott.)*

Ident. Boott. Car. nov. 138.—Steudel l. c. p. 232.

SPEC. CHAR. Culm triquetrous, below strong, smooth, above slender, 2-feet: uppermost bracts narrower, seldom shorter than the spikelet, inner ones far exceeding the culm: spikes 6—8, elongated, cylindric, alternate, remote, males 2, rusty, peduncled, unequal, females 4—5, males at the apex, tawny olive, very long bracteate, lowest one remote: fruit elliptic, acuminately beaked, 2-toothed, ventricose, wrinkled, divaricate, shorter and broader than the lanceolate, hispidly awned scale.

Assam.

ORDER CLXXXIV. GRAMINACEÆ.

Annual or perennial herbs, seldom undershrubs, very rarely aborescent: rhizome fibrous, sometimes bulbous or woody and thickened: culms cylindric, fistular, articulated with annular tumid, seldom contracted knots: leaves solitary, sheathing at each joint, the dilated petiole embracing the stem and forming a sheath, the sheath very rarely narrowed at its exit into a flattened or tubular petiole: the blade usually narrow, seldom dilated, always undivided, nerves parallel: stipule axillary at the conjunction of the sheath with the culm, more or less short, membranaceous, ligula seldom none: flowers usually green, seldom coloured, hermaphrodite, monœcious, polygamous, very seldom diœcious, arranged in 1—many-flowered spikelets and forming a spike, thyrse, raceme, capitule or panicle: calyx most frequently 2-valved (glumes), seldom 1-valved or none: perianth (corolla) somewhat similar to the glumes, 2-valved, seldom 1-valved: valvelets (paleæ) dissimilar, outer one (inferior) usually keeled, 1—3-many-nerved, muticous or awned, inner one (superior) usually 2-nerved, muticous, seldom awned, sometimes deficient: small scales hypogynous, succulent, minute, irregular, 2—3, sometimes none: stamens hypogynous, three, seldom solitary or two or 6, very rarely 4 or 6 or indefinite: anthers 2-celled, 2-forked, dehiscing lengthways: ovary 1-celled, 1-ovuled: styles usually two, distinct or connate at the base, sometimes 1 or 3: stigmas plumose or hispidulous: fruit a caryopsis, free or adnate to the valvelets: pericarp adnate to the seed, thin, papery membranaceous, seldom crustaceous: albumen mealy: embryo attached at the base of the outer side of the albumen: cotyledon scutelliform, scooped out externally with a longitudinal furrow: plumula naked, enclosed by its own sheath.

SECT, I. ORYZEÆ.

Spikelets 1-flowered: glumes either none or rudimental, very rarely equal in length to the valvelets, but much narrower: lower valvelets 5—7, upper 3—5-nerved.

GENUS I. ORYZA.

Hexandria Digynia. *Sex: Syst:*

Deriv. From the Arabic word, *Eruz.*

GEN. CHAR. Panicle: spikes 1-flowered: glumes two, small,

membranaceous, slightly concave, muticous: valvelets 2, chartaceo-coriaceous, compressed and keeled, nearly equal in length, closed, lower one much broader, usually awned at the apex: awn straight, somewhat jointed at the base: stamens 6: ovary glabrous: styles 2, terminal: stigmas plumose with branched hairs: scalelets 2, glabrous, somewhat fleshy: caryopsis glabrous, oblong, enclosed by the valvelets.—Leaves flat: panicle branched: spikelets racemosely arranged in branchlets, jointed with the pedicel, compressed, hispid.

(1) O. SATIVA. *(Linn.)*

Ident. Roxb. flor. Ind. II. 200.

Engrav. Lam. Ill. t. 264.—Beauv. Agr. t. vii. fig. 7—8.

SPEC. CHAR. Culm erect: leaves linear, elongated, scabrous: panicle racemose, contracted, branches scabrous, glumes lanceolate, pale, adpressed: valvelets beset with long hairs, one muticous, the other usually awned.

Circars. The wild rice plant from which all the cultivated varieties have sprung is found in and on the borders of lakes in the Circars. The grain is gathered and eaten by the richer classes in the Rajahmundry districts, it being considered a great dainty and realising a high price.

GENUS II. BLEPHAROCHLOA.

Hexandria Digynia. *Sex: Syst:*

Deriv. From *Blepharon* a fringe, and *Chloa* grass.

GEN. CHAR. Spikelets hermaphrodite, 1-flowered: glumes (or paleæ) 2, compressed, keeled, muticous, obtusely mucronate, very shortly stalked, lower one 5-nerved, middle nerve and marginal ones denticulate-ciliate, upper shorter, 3-nerved, keel denticulate-ciliate: scalelets 2, fleshy, scimitar-shaped: stamens 6: ovary sessile: stigmas long, plumose.

(1) B. CILIATA. *(Steudel.)*

Ident. Steudel Syn. pl. gram. p. 4.

Syn. Zizania ciliata, *Spreng.—Griff. in Journ. As. Soc. v.* t. 25, fig. I.—Leersia ciliata, *Roxb. flor. Ind. II.* 207.—Pharus ciliatus, *Retz.*

SPEC. CHAR. Culms slender, far creeping at the base, smooth: joints cylindric, pubescent: leaves somewhat glaucescent, linear, acute, lineate above, scabrous: spikes few, distant, somewhat secund, alternately arranged in a nodding panicle: spikelets solitary articulated at the cup-shaped apex of a curved pedicel.

Stagnant waters at Jumalpore, Eastern Bengal.

GENUS III. POTAMOCHLOA.

Hexandria Digynia. *Sex: Syst:*

Deriv. From *Potamos* a river and *Chloa* grass.

Gen. Char. Spikelets hermaphrodite, 1-flowered: glumes (or paleæ) 2, sessile, continuous to the apex of the pedicel, scarcely compressed; lower one larger, 5-nerved, terminating in a straight awn, nerves denticulate-ciliate, upper muticous, acuminate, 3-nerved, keel denticulate-scabrous: scalelets 2, large, fleshy, glabrous or ciliated at the apex: stamens 6: filaments long-exserted: ovary sessile: styles two, stigmas plumose.

(1) P. aristata. *(Griffith.)*

Ident. Griffith l. c. t. 24, fig. 2.

Syn. Leersia aristata, *Roxb. l. c.*—Pharus aristatus, *Retz.*—Hygroryza aristata, *Nees.*—Zizania aristata, *Kunth.*

Engrav. Rheede Mal. x. t. 12.

Spec. Char. Densely cæspitose, floating: submersed culms very long, here and there capillaceous rooting, emersed culms glabrous: sheaths submersed and half emersed, very callous, thickened, somewhat inflated, emersed ones longer, cylindric: leaves lanceolate, cordate at the base, obtuse, somewhat hooded at the apex, stiff, scabrous: panicle erect, lowest branches sub-verticelled, spikelets somewhat secund, lower ones twin, unequally pedicelled, upper ones solitary on longer club-shaped pedicels, marked with a red ring.

Floating on deep standing waters near Calcutta. Jumalpoor, Eastern Bengal. Flowering in the cold season. Malabar. Peninsula.

SECT. II. PHALARIDEÆ.

Spikelets hermaphrodite, polygamous seldom monœcious, sometimes 1-flowered, with or without the stipitiform rudiment of another upper flower, sometimes 2-flowered, either flower hermaphrodite or male, sometimes 2—3-flowered, terminal flower fertile, rest incomplete: glumes usually equal: paleæ often shining, hardened in fruit: styles or stigmas elongated into many.

GENUS IV. COIX.

Monœcia Triandria. *Sex: Syst:*

Gen. Char. Flowers monœcious: males loosely spiked, issuing from a common ovate, inflated, thickly coriaceous, at length bony involucre, apex pervious: glumes 2, membranaceous, muticous, upper one 2-keeled: scalelets 2, glabrous: stamens 3: female flower enclosed in an involucre, basilar: spikelets 2-flowered, lower flower neuter: glumes fleshy, concave, muticous, neutral one 1-valved: perfect one valvelets 2, upper one 2-nerved: scalelets none: style one: stigmas 2—3, elongated, hairy, rudimentary stamens minute: caryopsis sub-globose, at length free within the involucre.

(1) C. LACRYMA. *(Linn.)*

Ident. Roxb. l. c. III. p. 568.

Syn. Lithagrostis Lacryma Jobi, *Tournef.*

Engrav. Bot. Mag. t. 2479.—Rheede Mal. xii. t. 70.—Beauv. Agrost. t. 24, fig. 5.—Kunth l. c. suppl. t. 3, 4.

SPEC. CHAR. Culm branched, full of pith, half-terete above, obtuse: spikelets axillary, peduncled, not involucrate: fruit ovate: root annual.

Peninsula. Bengal. Flowering in the rainy season. The hardened involucres are known as *Job's tears.*

(2) C. BARBATA. *(Roxb.)*

Ident. Roxb. l. c. p. 569.—Dalz. Bomb. flor. p. 289.

SPEC. CHAR. Roots annual: culms erect, cernuous at the apex, branched, jointed, smooth, furrowed, not piped, 3—6-feet: leaves sheathing, narrow, keeled, margins armed with small prickles and clothed with numerous stiff white hairs: mouths of the sheaths slightly bearded: spikes numerous, pedicelled, terminal, and from the exterior axils forming a large linear panicle, collected in fascicles of from 2 to 6 on a common peduncle: involucre of one hard, glossy, valve, allowing free egress to the male spike and enclosing the female flower.

High hills around Jooneer. Circars. Bengal. Flowering in the rainy season.

(3) C. GIGANTEA. *(Koen.)*

Ident. Roxb. l. c. p. 570.

SPEC. CHAR. Culm erect, branched, round, smooth, jointed, 8—15-feet: upper side and margins of the leaves hispid: sheaths smooth: spikes pedicelled, pedicels long, filiform, naked, not jointed: involucre ovate, perforated at the top for the male spike to pass through, smooth, glossy, hard, male spikes drooping, three-fold, middle one pedicelled.

Circar vallies. Bengal. Flowering in the rains.

(4) C. AQUATICA. *(Roxb.)*

Ident. Roxb. l. c. p. 571.

SPEC. CHAR. Floating and creeping, 50—100-feet: stems perennial, jointed, round, smooth, filled with pith, rooting at the joints, extreme shoots emersed 4—5-feet above the water and bearing the leaves and flowers: lower leaves linear-lanceolate, upper ones ensiform, all acute, margins hispid: spikes terminal, and from the exterior axils peduncled, solitary or in pairs, drooping: female flowers usually solitary at the base of the male spikes: involucre turbinate, perforated, glumes within the involucre 6—7 valved: ovary oblong: male flowers 3-fold, two lateral ones sessile, middle one pedicelled: seed turbinate, smooth, dull pearl colour, size of a pea.

Lakes in lower Bengal, flowering in the rains.

(5) C. HETEROCLITA. *(Roxb.)*

Ident. Roxb. l. c. p. 572.

SPEC. CHAR. Erect, branched: spikes terminal, single or paired, when two, one is male, the other androgynous, with a jointed rhachis and its five or six female flowers bracteate.

Eastern Bengal, flowering in the rains.

SECT. III. PANICEÆ.

Spikelets solitary, twin or more, 1—2-flowered: lower flower incomplete: glumes thinner than the valvelets: floret 2-valved: valvelets more or less coriaceous or chartaceous, lower half involving the upper, persistent in fruit: caryopsis compressed parallel to the embryo.

GENUS V. PASPALUM.

Triandria Digynia. *Sex: Syst:*

Deriv. From the Greek term for a species of Millet.

GEN. CHAR. Spikelets in simple, solitary, or digitate or alternate or loosely panicled racemes, unilateral, or regularly 2—3—4-serial, more or less imbricated, sessile or short-pedicelled, closed, hermaphrodite, 2-flowered, the partial axis usually flattened, sometimes leafy: lower flower 1-paleaceous, neuter, membranaceous, muticous, upper one 2-paleaceous hermaphrodite: glume single, superior, the length of the neutral flower: flower hermaphrodite: paleæ 2, coriaceous, muticous, lower one concave, embracing the 2-nerved upper one: stamens 3: ovary glabrous: styles 2, terminal, free: stigmas brush-shaped: hypogynous scales 2, entire, glabrous, fleshy, truncated or dolabriform: caryopsis oblong or orbicular, a little depressed, glabrous, enclosed by the hardened paleæ.

(1) P. SCROBICULATUM. *(Linn.)*

Ident. Linn. Sp. 330.—Roxb. flor. Ind. I. 278.

Syn. P. Kora, *Willd. Roxb. l. c. p.* 279.—P. frumentaceum, *Rottl.*—P. Commersonii, *Lam. Ill. I.* 175.—P. orbiculare, *Forst. Brown Prod.* 188.

Engrav. Trin. Ic. t. 143.—Willd. Hort. 7, t. 74.

SPEC. CHAR. Root fibrous: culm branched, erect, 1—2-feet: sheaths glabrous or hirsute at the base, ciliated: ligula very short, rounded: leaves linear, sub-acuminate, glabrous: racemes 2—3, approximated, alternate: spikelets biserial, short-pedicelled, oblong-roundish, acutish: glumes 5—7-nerved, upper one scrobiculate at the sides.

Peninsula.

(2) P. METZII. *(Steud.)*

Ident. Steud. l. c. p. 21.

SPEC. CHAR. Root fibrous: culm simple or branched, glabrous, leafy: sheaths elongated, covering the culm, scarcely hairy at the mouths: ligula membranaceous, short, torn: leaves long, flat, lanceolate, attenuated into a long acumen, smooth, often waved and slightly plaited on one side: spikes 2, seldom ternate, sub-alternate, erect: spikelets biserial, sessile, imbricated, almost lineal, ovate, obtuse, yellowish golden.

Neilgherries.

(3) P. DISTICHUM. *(Burm.)*

Ident. Burm. Ind. 23.

Syn. P. longiflorum, *Retz. Roxb. l. c. p.* 279.

Engrav. Rheede Mal. xii. t. 44.—Beauv. flor. t. 85.

SPEC. CHAR. Culm creeping at the base: ligula hairy: leaves rolled inwards, distichous, and with the sheaths glabrous: racemes twin, conjugate, divaricately horizontal: spikelets in two rows: axis equalling in breadth the solitary spikelets.

Peninsula, in pastures.

(4) P. BIFARIUM. *(Edgew.)*

Ident. Edgeworth in Journ. As. Soc., 1852. 187.

SPEC. CHAR. Culms decumbent, glabrous: sheaths acutely keeled, much longer than the internodes: leaves usually approximated, bifarious, linear-lanceolate, acute, quite glabrous, glaucescent, narrow margined: ligula membranaceous, decurrent into the edge of the sheath: floriferous culms terminal: racemes conjugate, secund, diverging: rhachis flat, herbaceous-margined: spikelets 3: pedicels unequal, of the two upper flowers more or less adnate to the rhachis, swollen at the apex, cup-shaped, glabrous, smooth: glumes two, pubescent, unequal, scarcely exceeding the florets: valvelets hardened in fruit, shining, ovate.

Banda district. (?)

(5) P. NEMATODES. *(Schult.)*

Ident. Schult. Mant. II. 171.—Steud. l. c. p. 33.

Syn. Milium filiforme, *Roxb. l. c. I.* 314.—Helopus filiculmis, *Nees.*

SPEC. CHAR. Creeping, glabrous: culm flower-bearing, erect, tapering: leaves short with a stipulary process at the throat of the sheath: racemes 2—3, sessile, secund erect: axis somewhat membranaceous and waved: spikelets alternate, solitary, in two rows: glumes stiff, glabrous, muticous.

Pasture ground in the Peninsula, flowering in the rainy season.

GENUS VI. PANICUM.

Triandria Digynia. *Sex Syst:*

Deriv. Either from *Panis* bread, or *Panicula* a panicle.

GEN. CHAR. Spikelets 2-flowered, naked: upper flower hermaphrodite, lower 1—2-paleaceous male, or neuter muticous, membraceous: glumes 2, unequal, membranaceous, concave, muticous: valvelets of the hermaphrodite flower 2, coriaceous, very rarely membranaceous, concave muticous, lower embracing the equal-nerved upper one: stamens 3: ovary glabrous: styles 2, terminal, elongated: stigmas penicillate, hairs simple denticulate: hypogynous scales 2, fleshy, dolabriform or truncated, 2—3-lobed, glabrous, collateral: caryopsis slightly compressed parallel to the embryo, closely enclosed by the paleæ, free: inflorescence a raceme, thyrse, or panicle.

(1) P. corymbosum. *(Roxb.)*

Ident. Roxb. flor. Ind. I. 292.

Syn. Paspalum corymbosum, *Kunth.*

Spec. Char. Culms creeping, floating, emersed at the apex, branched, 2—3-feet: leaves linear, hairs stiff, white: sheaths bristly: racemes about 15, loosely fascicled, corymbose, closely floriferous: spikelets twin, sub-lineal, linear-oblong, acute, pubescent at the sides: lower glume none, upper very small.

Standing water among the Circar vallies, growing to a large size.

(2) P. dilatatum. *(Steudel.)*

Ident. Steudel Syn. pl. Gram. p. 39.

Syn. P. extensum, *Nees in Wight herb. No.* 1045—47.

Spec. Char. Culm creeping at the base, branched, and with the sheaths glabrous, hairy at the mouth: leaves lanceolate-linear, waved at the margin, glabrous or sparingly hairy: racemes many, verticillately corymbose, elongated, hirsute at the insertions: spikelets approximated, twin, one sub-sessile, one short pedicelled, pedicels beardless and with the broadish rachis serrulate, scabrous at the margin: lower glume obsolete, upper one lanceolate, 3-nerved, 3 times shorter than the lanceolate acute 7-nerved floret, pubescent at the edge.

Courtallum.

(3) P. pseudo-setaria. *(Steud.)*

Ident. Steudel l. c.

Syn. Digitaria stricta, *Roth.*—Setaria stricta, *Kunth.*

Spec. Char. Culm erect, filiform, and with the sheaths glabrous, the latter hairy at the mouth: leaves linear, elongated, striated, sparingly scattered with long hairs: ligula short, cut and ciliated: spikes somewhat fasciculate-panicled, very long, bristly, bearded at the base: common rhachis furrowed and angled, hairy at the springing of the spikelets, partial ones somewhat triquetrous, serrulate at the edge: spikelets oval, pubescent at the margin, extrorsely half-involucrated at the base with a bundle of bristles: outer glume very small, ovate, very obtuse.

Bengal.

(4) P. Wallichianum. *(W. and A.)*

Ident. Wight and Arnott ex Nees MS.—Steudel l. c. 41.

Spec. Char. Culm branched, creeping at the base, slender, glabrous: sheaths at the sides and with the leaves above villous, the latter waved at the edge, glaucous beneath: racemes many alternate or verticilled: rhachis sparingly villous: pedicels 2-flowered, somewhat lax: lower glume obsolete, truncated or obliquely 1-toothed, upper one oblong, equalling the florets, 3-nerved: neuter valvelet 7-nerved, slightly villous at the circumference, interstices whitish-silky.

Peninsula.

(5) P. conjugatum. *(Roxb.)*

Ident. Roxb. l. c. 288.

Syn. Digitaria conjugata, *Schult.*

Spec. Char. Somewhat creeping, thin, softly villous: spikes twin, conjugate, secund: flowers solitary, sessile, muticous: glumes 3-nerved: corolla furnished with a neutral accessory valvelet: leaves softly hairy: sheaths large, downy.

Coromandel. Western coast.

(6) P. cimicinum. *(Retz.)*

Ident. Retz. obs. III. 9.—Roxb. l. c. 291.

Syn. Urochloa cimicina, *Kunth l. c.* 31.—Milium cimicinum, *Linn. Mant.* 184.—Axonopus cimicinus, *Beauv. agrost.* 42.

Spec. Char. Culms erect or ascending: sheaths with scattered hairs: leaves lanceolate from an ovate base, smooth, ciliated: spikes in fives, digitate: spikelets solitary, or in twos or threes: glumes 3-nerved, the upper one densely ciliated on the margin: outer palea terminated by an awn.

Peninsula.

(7) P. Burmanni. *(Retz.)*

Ident. Retz. l. c. 10.—Roxb. l. c. p. 295.

Syn. Oplismenus Burmanni, *Beauv. agrost.* 54.—P. hirtellum, *Burm.*—Orthopogon Burmanni, *R. Br. prod.* 194.—P. bromoides, *Lam. Enc.* iv. 742.—P. album, *Poir.*—O. albus, *Roem. and Schult.* Echinochloa hirtella, *Schult. Mant. II.* 269.—O. Humboldtianus, *Nees ab Esenb. in Mart. Bras. II.* 264.—O. Brasiliensis, *Raddi. agrost. Bras.* 400.

Engrav. Trin. Ic. 17, t. 193.—Burm. Ind. t. 12, fig. I.

Spec. Char. Culms creeping, branched, extremities erect: leaves lanceolate, waved, hairy: sheaths half the length of the joints, very hairy: spikes compound, secund, erect: spikelets 4—8, alternate, secund, adpressed: flowers generally paired, 1 sessile, the other pedicelled: glumes hairy, long-awned.

Generally found under the shade of trees.

(8) P. Peninsulanum. *(Steud.)*

Ident. Steudel l. c. p. 44.

Syn. Oplismenus decompositus, *Nees in Endl. prod. flor. Norf.* 19.—P. compositum, *Rottl. herb.*

Spec. Char. Culm creeping at the base and with the branch elongated, knots hairy: sheaths striated without tubercles, margin mouth and ovate-oblong leaves at the base, ciliated: spikes 8—12, alternate, erect, compound at the base, approximate: spikelets packed together: pedicels long-bearded: glumes glabrous, equal, lower one bearing bristles, upper one obsoletely mucronulate, neuter floret 1-valved.

Peninsula.

(9) P. acuminatissimum. *(Steud.)*

Ident. Steudel l. c. p. 45.

Syn. Oplismenus compositus, *var. Wight herb.*

Spec. Char. Culm branched, ascending, marked below with a hairy line, knots glabrous: sheaths ciliated at the edge and mouth: leaves narrow-lanceolate, very acuminate, scabrous: spikes about 12, distant, few-flowered, hairy at their origin, upper ones fascicle-shaped: lower glume larger long-bristly, upper one and the valvelet of the neuter floret short-bristly, bristles purple.

Peninsula.

(10) P. elatius. *(Linn. fil.)*

Ident. Linn. suppl. 107.

Syn. Oplismenus elatior, *Roem. and Schult. II.* 483.

Spec. Char. Culm erect, stiff: leaves grassy, elongated: spike compound, incurved: rhachis triquetrous: spikelets 12 or more, ovate-oblong, adpressed, remote, alternate, seldom opposite: glumes awned, neuter valvelet mucronate.

Malabar.

(11) P. colonum. *(Linn.)*

Ident. Linn. sp. 84.

Syn. Oplismenus colonus, *Humb. and Kunth Nov. gen. I.* 109.

Engrav. Trin. Ic. xiv. t. 160.—Beauv. agr. t. x. fig. 6.

Spec. Char. Culms below resting on the ground and rooting, above sub-erect, branched, a little compressed, smooth: leaves short, smooth, tapering from the base to a sharp point: spikes compound, secund, 7—9, alternate, distant, spikelets in four series: glumes scabrous, mucronate, unequal, 3-nerved.

Common in cultivated fields.

(12) P. dubium. *(Steud.)*

Ident.. Steudel l. c. p. 46.

Syn. Echinochloa dubia, *Roem. and Schult. I.* 479—Oplismenus dubius, *Kunth.*

Spec. Char. Culms cæspitose, angular, flexuose, glabrous: leaves linear, acuminate-bristly and with the sheaths glabrous: panicles sub-spicate, compound, spikes alternate: spikelets muticous and the awned, hispid, 3—5-nerved: rhachis furrowed and angular, flexuose.

. Coromandel.

(13) P. cuspidatum. *(Roxb.)*

Ident. Roxb. l. c. p. 298.

Spec. Char. Cæspitose, creeping, all glabrous: culms branched, 2-feet: leaves linear, ensiform, coloured at the edges: ligula none: racemes simple, alternate, spikelets twin and solitary, subulate-mucronate, strigulose at the edges: seeds cuspidate.

Bengal, flowering in April.

(14) P. Royleanum. *(Nees.)*

Ident. Nees Ms. et in Royle herb.—Steudel l. c. p. 47.

Spec. Char. Culm straight and with the linear acuminate leaves pubescently hairy: raceme compound, straight linear-elongated, and with the partial short appressed ones secund-flowered, lower ones sub-verticilled: common rhachis furrowed, spikelets twin, oblong, scabrous, naked at the base: glumes acute, lower one 3-keeled, third part shorter than the florets, upper one 5-nerved, hispidulous, longer than the male 2-valved slightly hermaphrodite, lanceolate, roughish floret.

Bengal.

(15) P. Crus Galli. *(Linn.)*

Ident. Linn. sp. 83, 84.

Syn. P. Crus Corvi, *Roxb.*—Echinochloa C. galli, et E. C. Corvi, *Roem. and Schult.*—Oplismenus C. galli, *Beauv.*

Engrav. Beauv. Agr. t. xi. fig. 2.—Engl. Bot. t. 876.—Curt. flor. Lond. t. 8.—Host. gram. II. t. 19 and t. 51.

Spec. Char. Culms filiform, creeping at the base, above nearly erect: leaves soft, downy: spikes compound, alternate, secund: flowers imbricated in two rows: glumes and outer paleæ of the neuter floret hispid, awned or mucronate.

Surat. Bengal.

(16) P. stagninum. *(Retz.)*

Ident. Retz. obs. v. 17.—Roxb. l. c. p. 295.

Syn. Oplismenus stagninus, *Kunth.*—Echinochloa stagnina, *Roem. and Schult.*.

Spec. Char. Culms 1—4-feet, ascending: leaves soft and smooth: mouth of the sheaths ciliated: spike compound, erect: partial ones alternate: spikelets ovate-oblong, tubercled, bristly and ciliated: lower glume ovate-elliptic, acute, a half shorter than the flower, upper one awned.

In wet cultivated ground, flowering in the rainy season.

(17) P. hispidulum. *(Retz.)*

Ident. Retz. in Nees flor. Austr. Afr. 57.—Roxb. l. c. 303.

Syn. P. crus corvi, *Thumb. flor. Jap.*

Spec. Char. Culm ascending, branched: sheaths and linear-acuminate leaves glabrous: ligula none: raceme compound, erect: rays alternate, bearded at the base and insertion of the spikelets: spikelets quadrifarious, packed together, ovate, hispidulous, sub-sessile: lower glume three times shorter than the spikelet, broadly cordate, acute, 3-nerved, upper one short-mucronate or bristly 5-nerved, caudate-bristly: hermaphrodite, oval, very smooth, rostellate.

Bengal, flowering in the rainy season. Roxburgh suggests this may be *P. frumentaceum* in a wild state.

(18) P. lanceolatum. *(Retz.)*

Ident. Retz. obs. v. 17.—Roxb. l. c. p. 294.

Syn. Oplismenus lanceolatus, *Kunth.*—Echinochloa lanceolata, *Roem. and Schult.*—P. aristatum, *Retz.*

Spec. Char. Culms creeping, branched, extremities sub-erect: leaves lanceolate-acuminate, waved, very unequal-sided: mouths of the sheaths bearded: panicle terminal, naked, consisting of distant, spreading spikes: florets sessile, solitary, subtended by a few long hairs: lower glume narrow, ending in a long purple awn, upper broader, oblong and mucronate.

Foot of the Ghauts, under trees. Bengal.

(19) P. Benghalense. *(Spreng.)*

Ident. Spreng. syst. I. 311.

Syn. P. strictum, *Roxb. l. c. p.* 303.—Oplismenus strictus, *Schult.*

Spec. Char. Culms straight, especially hairy at the joints, 2—3-feet: sheaths hirsute, beset at the throat with long soft white hairs: leaves attenuated from a broad base, acuminate, somewhat hairy: spikes compound, cylindric, straight: spikelets numerous, 1-serial, expanded: glumes hairy, acute: corolla 3-valved, inner one awned.

Bengal, in dry barren places.

(20) P. asperum. *(Wight.)*

Ident. Wight herb. No. 52a.—Steudel l. c. p. 49.

Spec. Char. Culm thickened below the spike: leaves narrow, attenuated and with the sheaths very rough with small muriciform bristlets: panicle spicately branched, compound: partial spikes approximated, spreading, 4—8-spiked: spikelets alternate, distant or solitary, lanceolate-subulate: upper glume finely prolonged into a longish subulate acumen.

Peninsula. (?)

(21) P. glaucum. *(Linn.)*

Ident. Linn. sp. 83.—Steudel l. c. p. 50.—Griff. Notulæ. 35.

Syn. Setaria glauca, *Beauv. agrost.* 51.—Pennisetum glaucum, *Brown prod. I.* 195.—Pan. penicillatum, *N. ab E. in Mart. Bras.* —Pan. flavescens, *Moench.*—Pan. lutescens, *Weig. obs.* 20.—Pan. pumilum, *Poir.*—Setaria pumila, *Roem. and Schult.*

Engrav. Schreb. gram. t. 25.—Host. gram. II. t. 16.—Trin. Ic. 17, t. 195.

Spec. Char. Culm erect, branched: leaves internally slightly scabrous, sub-glaucescent, scabrous at the margin: spike cylindric:

involucre with many bristles, much longer than the 1—4-nous spikelets: glumes glabrous: hermaphrodite floret transversely waved: male 2-paleaceous.

Jellanghey, near the banks of the Ganges. Western coast. A variety of this, with the involucels of a reddish colour and the fertile florets transversely and deeply wrinkled and shining, is one of the commonest grasses on the table-land of Mahableshwur where it is called "Kolara," *(Dalz. Bomb. flor. p.* 293-4.*)*

(22) P. HELVOLUM. *(Linn.)*

Ident. Linn. suppl. 107.

Syn. Pennisetum helvolum, *R. Brown prod.* 195.—Panicum glaucum, *Roxb.*—Setaria helvola, *Roem. and Schult.*

SPEC. CHAR. Culm branched, 6-feet, sterile branches shorter: leaves towards the base, above beset with spreading white hairs: spike simple, about 7-inches, florets without order: involucels 1-flowered, bristles fascicled, greyish-yellow: hermaphrodite flower striated lengthways.

Bengal, on cultivated land.

(23) P. TOMENTOSUM. *(Roxb.)*

Ident. Roxb. flor. Ind. I. 301.

Syn. Setaria tomentosa, *Kunth.*—Oplismenus tomentosus, *Schult.*

SPEC CHAR. Cæspitose: culms ascending, almost erect: leaves covered with soft long hairs: sheaths bearded at the throat: racemes composed of 10—12 oblong, alternate, 6—8-flowered spikes: involucels bristly, intermixed, hispid: seed ovate, transversely wrinkled.

A delicate rare species growing in dry pastures.

(24) P. CANALICULATUM. *(Nees.)*

Ident. Nees in litt. et Wight herb.—Steudel l. c. p. 55.

Syn. P. Myurum, *Wight herb.*—Aira interrupta, *Rottl. Klein. herb.*

SPEC. CHAR. Culm slender, ascending: leaves linear-acuminate, flat, and with the sheaths hairy: raceme narrow, lax, compound at the base: branchlets appressed, few-flowered, thin: spikelets alternate on the lower branchlets, on the upper rhachis twin or fascicled, ovate-lanceolate, glabrous: glumes almost equal, obtuse, twice exceeding the florets, larger one 2-valved, lower valvelet deeply plaited introrsely in the middle, upper one broad with inflexed margins: hermaphrodite floret smaller, lanceolate acuminate, transversely wrinkled, rough.

Peninsula. (?)

(25) P. Helopus. *(Trin.)*

Ident. Trin. Ic. t. 183.—Steudel l. c. p. 57.

Syn. P. hirsutum, *Roxb.* — P. Kœnigii, *Spreng.* — Urochloa pubescens, *Kunth En. I.* 74.

Spec. Char. Culm 1—2-feet, decumbent, rooting, ascending, knots bearded: sheaths hairy: racemes alternate, much longer than the interstices: spikelets somewhat solitary, loosely imbricated, ovate, acute, densely pubescent hairy: lower glume 4-times shorter than the florets, hermaphrodite one acuminate, wrinkled.

Pastures and borders of cultivated ground.

(26) P. grossarium. *(Linn.)*

Ident. Linn. Sp. I. 349.—Roxb. l. c. p. 297.—Griff. Not. p. 36.

Syn. P. Careyanum, *Nees ab. Esenb. in Mart. Bras. II.* 118. *adnot. Kunth. l. c. p.* 89.

Spec. Char. Spike compound: common ones (6—12) secund-flowered, alternate: spikelets solitary, ovate, glabrous, sub-sessile: neuter floret 2-valved: caryopsis oblong, transversely wrinkled: culm creeping: leaves ovate-lanceolate, softly pubescent.

Bengal, in rice fields and fresh pastures.

(27) P. Canaræ. *(Steudel.)*

Ident. Steudel l. c. p. 58.

Spec. Char. Culms rooting at the base, many or solitary, ascending, erect, thin, glabrous: leaves ovate or oblong-lanceolate, acute, nerved, ciliated, and with the sheaths hairy: raceme compound, racemules solitary or twin, alternate, 1-sided, 1—2-serial: spikelets ovate, hairy: glumes costately 3—5-nerved, almost equal, the length of the hermaphrodite one, the latter orbiculate-compressed, very thinly silver-dotted.

Canara.

(28) P. flavidum. (*Retz.*)

Ident. Retz. obs. iv. 15.

Syn. P. brizoides, *Roxb.* (not *Retz.*)—P. granulare, *Lam.*

Engrav. Trin. Ic. t. 159, 158.

Spec. Char. Culm slender, erect, simple: leaves linear, glabrous: racemes 6—12, alternate, much shorter than the instertices, by degrees shorter: spikelets solitary, in 2 rows, somewhat roundish-oblong, acutish, glabrous: lower glume rounded, upper ones a little shorter than the florets, hermaphrodite ones hooked at the apex, a little wrinkled.

Bengal. Peninsula. Both in wet and dry situations. Parts of the plant are often tinged with purple.

(29) P. fluitans. (*Retz.*)

Ident. Retz. obs. III. 8, l. v. 13.—Vahl.—Willd.—Roxb. l. c. p. 297.

Spec. Char. Culms 2—3-feet, creeping at the base: leaves long and smooth: mouths of the sheaths bearded and sub-ciliate: spike compound, partial ones alternate, adpressed: spikelets bifarious, elliptic: lower glume very short and truncated, upper obovate, rounded, a little shorter than the paleæ: lower flower neuter, 1-valved: seed elliptic, acute, minutely wrinkled.

Moist rich soil. Bengal. Peninsula.

(30) P. brizoides. (*Jacq.*)

Ident. Jacq. Eclog. Gram. I. t. 2.—N. ab. E. in Mart. Bras. II. 115.—Dalz. Bomb. flor. p. 290.

Spec. Char. Culms near the base resting on the ground, above ascending, compressed, smooth: leaves bifarious, smooth: mouths of the sheaths bearded: spikes compound: spikelets bifarious, ovate, ventricose: glumes ovate, lower one-third-shorter than the flower, upper a little shorter than the flower: seed ovate, obtuse, smooth.

Near Surat.

(31) P. Javanicum.

Ident. Poir Enc. Suppl. iv. 274.

Syn. Urochloa panicoides, *Beauv. Agrost.* 52, *t.* ii., *fig.* 1.—*Dalz. Bomb. flor. p.* 290.—Milium sanguinale, *Roxb.*

Engrav. Burm. Ind. t. 10, fig. 1.

SPEC. CHAR. Culms creeping near the base, the rest erect, smooth, one-and-a-half foot high : leaves long, narrow, smooth: racemes sub-digitate, 3—8 : spikelets alternate in two series, unequally pedicelled : glumes glabrous : sheaths hairy.

Western coast.

(32) P. PYRAMIDALE. *(Lam.)*

Ident. Lam. Encycl. iv. 745.—Kunth l. c. p. 93.

SPEC. CHAR. Leaves linear, glabrous, scabrous at the margin with small spines : spikes numerous, somewhat verticillately spiked at the top of the culm, spreading : spikelets unilateral, in 4 series : glumes unequal, scabrous with spines on the nerves : male flower 2-paleaceous, hermaphrodite slightly striated, glabrous, shining.

Bengal.

(33) P. LEPTOCHLOA. *(Nees.)*

Ident. Nees Ms.—Steudel l. c. p. 62.

Syn. Leptochloa (?) panicoides, *Wight Herb. No.* 125.

SPEC. CHAR. Leaves linear, elongated, glabrous, knots yellow: raceme compound, dense, partial ones approximated, alternate, straight, hairy at the base : rhachis furrowed : spikelets solitary or twin, short-pedicelled, ovate-lanceolate, polygamous : glumes cuspidate, lower one smaller : keel hispidly scabrous, upper one 5-nerved : lower valvelet of the 2-valvet floret 3-nerved, smooth, hermaphrodite one twice shorter than the male, lower valvelet emarginate.

Peninsula.

(34) P. PROSTRATUM. *(Lam.)*

Ident. Lam. Encycl. iv. 745.—Dalz. l. c.

Syn. P. procumbens, *Nees Agr. Bras.* 109.—P. setigerum, *Retz. Roxb. l. c.* 299.—P. cæspitosum, *Swartz.*

SPEC. CHAR. Culm creeping, branched, 1—2-feet, nodes pubescent : sheaths glabrous or ciliated : leaves lanceolate from a cordate base, ciliated at the base, 1—2-inches long : racemes 4—15, crowded, alternate, much longer than the interstices : spikelets twin and solitary, oval, acute, smooth : lower glume a quarter the length of the flowers : hermaphrodite floret cuspidate-mucronate, slightly wrinkled.

About Surat. Bengal.

(35) P. NILAGIRICUM. *(Steud.)*

Ident. Steudel l. c. p. 62.

SPEC. CHAR. Culm prostrate at the base, rooting, branched, ascending, 2—3-feet, leafy, angular, pubescent, densely hairy at the knots: sheaths striated, elongated, pubescent: leaves lanceolate, hairy: rays of the panicle alternate, lower ones bifoliolate, upper ones solitary, spreading, 10—15-spiculate: rhachis hairy: spikelets glabrous, ovate, sub-gibbous at the apex: lower glume minute, 4 times shorter than the spikelet, upper one almost equalling the neuter valvelet, glabrous: caryopsis slightly striated and dotted lengthways.

Neilgherries.

(36) P. OXYPHYLLUM. *(Hochst.)*

Ident. Steudel l. c. p. 65.—Hohenhack. herb. Ind. Or. N. 627.

SPEC. CHAR. Culm branched or seldom simple, glabrous: sheaths striated, hairy at the edges and mouth: leaves lanceolate, very acute, striated, sparingly hairy or glabrous: rays of the spreading panicle solitary, remotish, paniculate, upper ones more approximated, racemiform: spikelets ovate, obtuse, glabrous: glumes unequal, shorter than the floret: hermaphrodite shining, very smooth.

Canara.

(37) P. INTERRUPTUM. *(Willd.)*

Ident. Willd. spec. I. 351.—Roxb. l. c. p. 305.—Dalz. l. c. 316.

Syn. P. inundatum? *Kunth.*

SPEC. CHAR. Culm under the water, floating, thick, ascending, several feet high: sheaths longer than the joints, smooth: leaves smooth, narrow: raceme spike-like, slender, cylindric, erect, 4—8-inches: florets small, green, smooth, short-pedicelled, crowded all round the rhachis, oblong: glumes 5—7-nerved, lower one roundish and perfoliate: neuter floret 2-paleaceous: anthers purple, long-exserted.

A large species clothing the margins of tanks throughout the Concan. Bengal.

(38) P. CURVATUM. *(Linn.)*

Ident. Linn. syst. xii. 730.—Roxb. l. c. p. 289.

SPEC. CHAR. Culm slender, erect or ascending: leaves lanceolate-linear, acuminate, hairy above, sheaths ciliated at the edge: rays of the compound raceme flexuose, erect: pedicels equalling or exceeding the spikelet, 1-flowered: spikelets oblong-lanceolate, incurved, nervose-striated, glabrous: lower glume minute, ovate, almost nerveless, upper one 11-nerved, a little longer than either 1-valved 5-nerved floret: hermaphrodite ovate, smooth.

Borders of tanks.

(39) P. REMOTUM. *(Retz.)*

Ident. Retz. obs. iv. 17.

SPEC. CHAR. Culm branched, creeping at the base, ascending, apex slender: leaves linear-acuminate, and with the sheaths glabrous: raceme decompound, lax, partial ones alternate, thin, secund, scabrous: spikelets twin, distant, oval, puberulous: pedicels longish, naked: glumes unequal, obtuse: lower one twice shorter: neuter floret 2-valved: hermaphrodite one oblong, muticous, transversely lightly waved and wrinkled, striated lengthways, equalling the upper glume.

Peninsula.

(40) P. PALUDOSUM. *(Roxb.)*

Ident. Roxb. l. c. p. 302.

Syn. P. natans, *Koen. Trin. diss. II.* 737.

SPEC. CHAR. Culm branched, erect, swollen under the water, and there emitting roots from the joints: leaves linear, glaucescent, hispid, sheaths bearded at the mouth: panicle oval, diffuse, thin, composed of scattered, sub-alternate ramous branches, angles sharp, finely pointed: flowers oblong, twin, partial pedicels unequal: seed oblong, smooth, brown.

Usually growing in water in the Circar vallies.

(41) P. MULTIBRACHIATUM. *(Hochst.)*

Ident. Hochst in Steudel l. c. p. 74.

SPEC. CHAR. Culm sub-prostrate at the base, branched, rooting, almost entirely sheathed, naked below the panicle, terete, glabrous: sheaths and leaves more or less hairy from very minute tubercles: ligula thin, membranaceous, exserted: leaves linear-lanceolate, often plicately waved at the edges, here and there as if stipulated by small leaflets in the axils: panicles straightish, lower rays 4—5-nate verticelled, upper ones scattered, all erect, simple, racemose, sparingly hairy: spikelets unequally pedicelled, longer or shorter than the pedicels themselves: spikelets varying between green and violet, ovate-lanceolate, acute: glumes a little unequal, 5—7-nerved: hermaphrodite floret shorter than the glumes.

Neilgherries.

(42) P. MOVAIENSE. *(Steud.)*

Ident. Steudel l. c. p. 78.

Syn. P. concinnum, *Edgw. in. As. Journ.* 1852, *p.* 79.

SPEC. CHAR. Creeping: culms tapering, glabrous: knots hairy, lower ones rooting: lower sheaths hairy, upper glabrous, ciliated at the edges only, closely involving the culm, throat ciliated: ligula ciliated: leaves as if petioled, flat, bearded with long hairs at the base, rest glabrous, very scabrous, serrulate at the margin: panicles sub-decompound, secund, branches secund, racemose or solitary, sessile or 1—2-pedicelled: rhachis scabrous-angular, rhachilla scabrous-pubescent: spikelets solitary, all short-pedicelled, jointed at the apex of the pedicel, 2-flowered: glumes 2, outer very small, ovate, membranaceous at the apex, lower one ovate, acute, 3—5-nerved, hairy externally: male or neutral floret 2—valved; outer valvelet a little longer than the lower glume, 3-nerved, ciliated, apex and margin hyaline acutish, inner one hyaline, oblong, 2-nerved, valvelets of the hermaphrodite shining, obtuse, very smooth.

Near Movai, Banda district.

(43) P. triflorum. *(Edgew.)*

Ident. Edgew. l. c.

Spec. Char. Annual, creeping, softly pubescent: culms decumbent, half-terete, pubescent: sheaths lax: ligula short ciliated: leaves oblong-linear, sub-cordate at the base, shortly acuminated at the apex: panicle few-branched, tomentose, racemes straight, sub-alternate, diverging: rhachis and rhachilla excavated, back tomentose, angles scabrous, pedicels hairy, bristles few, fulcrate: spikelets twin or solitary, one sub-sessile, broadly ovate, acute, 3-flowered, (seldom 2-flowered): glumes 2, outer one somewhat decurrent, obscurely 3-nerved, inner one broadly ovate, 5-nerved: flowers 2 (or one) neutral, male flower between the neutral, lower flower neutral, 1- rarely 2-valved, outer valvelet 5-nerved, acute, inner one oblong, margin involute, 2-toothed: valvelets of the hermaphrodite flower wrinkled, outer one concave, 3-nerved.

Stony places near Banda.

(44) P. Mangaloricum. *(Steudel.)*

Ident. Steudel l. c. p. 78.

Spec. Char. Culm erect, branched at the base, rooting, quite glabrous: knots thickened: leaves glaucescent, sub-cordate at the base, and with a few scattered hairs, lanceolate, long-acuminate, scabrous at the edges: panicle erect, spreading, rays fascicled and solitary, branched, erect-patent: small rays more or less flexuose, 1—2-spiculate: spikelets ovate: lower glume exceeding half the spikelet, 3-nerved, upper equalling the neutral and hermaphrodite floret.

Near Mangalore.

(45) P. Courtallense. *(Nees.)*

Ident. Nees et Wall. in Steud. l. c. p. 83.—Wight Herb. 1011-13.

Spec. Char. Culm creeping at the base and with the knots glabrous: sheaths ciliated at the margin and mouth: leaves cordate-lanceolate, ciliated: panicle capillary, erect: rachis and rays slightly scabrous, divided nearly from the middle, pedicels long: spikelets oval almost obovate when in fruit, with few scattered small bristles: glumes mucronate below the apex, and with the florets nearly equal, lower one somewhat 5-nerved, upper and the valvelet of the neutral 1-valved floret 5-nerved.

Courtallum.

(46) P. Indicum. *(Linn.)*

Ident. Linn. Mant. 184.—Roxb. l. c. 285.

Engrav. Trin. Ic. 17, t. 197.

Spec. Char. Culm prostrate, thin, branched: sheaths glabrous: leaves linear, glabrous or scattered above with a few hairs: thyrses very narrow, rays simple, very short, shorter than the spikelet: spikelets ovate, acute, glabrous: lower glume a half shorter than the florets, 3-upper ones 7—11-nerved.

Coromandel.

(47) P. trigonum. *(Retz.)*

Ident. Retz. obs. III. 9.—Roxb. l. c. p. 308.

Syn. P. patens, *Burm. Ind. t.* 10, *fig.* 2.

Spec. Char. Culm prostrate, rooting, leafy: leaves narrow, glabrous: panicle small, erect, peduncles few, slightly flexuose, 2-flowered: glumes unequal, obtuse, hispid, 1-flowered: seed 3-cornered.

Pasture ground under the shade of trees.

(48) P. megalanthum. *(Steud.)*

Ident. Steudel l. c. p. 93.

Syn. Tricholœna Wightii, *Nees MS. Herb. Wight No.* 1097.

Spec. Char. Culm erect from a base curved inwards: leaves linear, sheaths and knots pubescent: panicle a little dense: spikelets large: upper glume and valvelet of the male flower bristly below the 2-lobed apex, woolly, middle wool longer, exceeding the apex, shorter than the bristle, fastigiate, connivent: lower glume clearly distant from the male floret, oblong, truncated, somewhat convolute.

Courtallum.

(49) P. ELEGANS. *(Dalz.)*

Ident. Dalz. Bomb. flor. p. 291, (under Isachne.)

SPEC. CHAR. Culms 8-inches, geniculate below: sheaths ciliated and with the apex bristly: leaves deeply striated, and minutely serrulate on the margin: flowers panicled: panicle consisting of slender, alternate, undulating branchlets: florets solitary, pedicelled, globular: glumes green with red margins, tuberculated and bristly, 2-flowered, both flowers perfect, plano-convex.

Margins of rivulets in the Deccan.

(50) P. NODIBARBATUM. *(Hochst.)*

Ident. Steudel l. c. p. 95.

SPEC. CHAR. Stem ascending, simple, glabrous, hairy at the knots, bearded: sheaths striated, ciliate at the edges, rest glabrous: margin of the ligula ciliated: leaves rounded and half stem-clasping at the base, lanceolate, acute, sparingly hairy or glabrescent: panicle spreading, ovate: rays and radioles capillary, flexuose, 1-spiculate at the apex: spikelets glabrous: glumes and neuter valvelets exceeding the smooth florets.

Neilgherries.

(51) P. METZII. *(Hochst.)*

Ident. Hochst in Steudel l. c. p. 95.

SPEC. CHAR. Culm decumbent at the base, rooting, ascending, simple, pubescent at the somewhat tumid knots: sheaths striated and with the leaves hairy: ligula short, membranaceous, hairy: leaves oblong or ovate-lanceolate, short-acute at the apex, subcordate and stem-clasping at the base, whitish at the margin: panicle spreading, ovate, rays and radioles angled, hairy: spikelets sessile and pedicelled, glume and neuter floret hairy, hermaphrodite glabrous.

Neilgherries.

(52) P. BRACHYGLUME. *(Hochst.)*

Ident. Hochst in Steudel l. c.

SPEC. CHAR. Root fibrous: culm weak, simple, or branched, glabrous, puberulous at the knots: sheaths striated, hairyish at the mouth: leaves lanceolate, small, acute, striated, glabrous: raceme compound, racemules alternate, few-flowered, intervals shorter, erect, or adpressed to the rhachis: spikelets small: glumes nearly equal, ovate, acute, bright green at the back, whitish at the margin, twice shorter than the oblong, very smooth hermaphrodite one.

Neilgherries.

(53) C. Kunthianum. *(W. and A.)*

Ident. Wight and Arnott in Herb. Wight.—Steudel l. c. 96.

Spec. Char. Culm creeping: leaves ovate-lanceolate, subcordate and with the sheaths tuberculated and hirsute: ligula bristly: panicle small, oval, stiff: branchlets alternate, 4—5, patent, somewhat 6-flowered: two lower pedicels somewhat 2-flowered, two upper ones 1-flowered: spikelets very small, ovate, monœcious, lower floret hermaphrodite—male, smooth, upper one stalked, female, hairy: glumes exceeding the florets, hirsute from tubercles towards the apex.

Peninsula.

(54) P. æquatum. *(Nees.)*

Ident. Nees Ms.—Steudel l. c. p. 98.

Syn. P. patens, *Roxb. l. c.* 305.

Spec. Char. Culm branched, creeping: sheaths ciliated at the margins: leaves cordate-ovate, cuspidate, puberulous: panicle short, oval, somewhat decompound, rhachis and branchlets stiffish, glabrous, the latter with yellow scars, fasciculately branched from the base: glumes and florets equal, lower florets male, 2-valved, upper hermaphrodite, hispidulous at the back.

Shady pasture ground.

(55) P. Roxburghii. *(Spreng.)*

Ident. Spreng. Syst. I. 320.

Syn. P. tenellum, *Roxb. l. c.* 306.—P. trypheron, *Schult. Mant. II.* 244.

Spec. Char. Culm branched, rooting at the knots, ascending: leaves cordate at the base, elongated, softly hairy: panicles oblong, branches expanded, capillary: spikelets solitary, remote, small, oval: valvelets secund: seed oval, glabrous, 5-nerved.

Pasture ground and borders of cultivation.

(56) P. serrulatum. *(Roxb.)*

Ident. Roxb. l. c. p. 307.

SPEC. CHAR. Culms erect, branched: leaves sub-cordate at the base, ensiform, attenuated at the apex, serrulate at the margin: sheaths glabrous: panicle erect, spike-like: branches erect, linear, branched, sub-remote: spikelets lanceolate, glumes very acute: florets hermaphrodite: seed oblong, glabrous.

Moist vallies in the Peninsula.

(57) P. ULIGINOSUM. *(Roxb.)*

Ident. Roxb. l. c. p. 308.

SPEC. CHAR. Culms erect, branched, rooting at the base, glabrous, 2—3-feet: leaves short, acute, somewhat pubescent: sheaths bearded at the throat: panicle erect, ovate, thin: branches compressed: flowers solitary, polygamous: glumes cuspidate.

Moist borders of rice-fields and wet grounds.

(58) P. TENUE. *(Roxb.)*

Ident. Roxb. l. c. p. 310.

SPEC. CHAR. Culm ascending, branched, 1—6-feet: leaves large, hairy above, bristly at the edge, acute: sheaths hairy, bearded at the throat: racemes of the erect panicle sub-secund, alternate, compound: florets twin on a common hairy pedicel: partial pedicels unequal: glumes many-nerved: seed ovate, transversely waved.

Circar mountains.

(59) P. MONTANUM. *(Roxb.)*

Ident. Roxb. l. c. p. 313.

SPEC. CHAR. Culm erect, 3—4-feet, somewhat woody: leaves lanceolate, unequally divided by the nerve, striated lengthways, ciliated below at the throat of the sheath: branches of the oblong panicle capillary, straight: spikelets small, ovate, remote: seed glabrous, 3-nerved at the back.

Circar mountains.

(60) P. CILIARE. *(Retz.)*

Ident. Retz. obs. iv. 16.—Roxb. l. c. 293.

Syn. Digitaria ciliaris, *Pers. Syn.*—D. commutata, *Schult.*

Engrav. Host. Gram. iv. t. 15.

SPEC. CHAR. Spikes 4—5, digitate, undivided: leaves lanceolate, waved, rather hairy: sheaths smooth: florets imbricated: outer valve of the glume very minute, nerveless: inner one half the length of the flower.

Western coast. Peninsula. Bengal.

(61) P. Egyptiacum. *(Retz.)*

Ident. Retz. obs. III. 8.—Roxb. l. c. 293.

Syn. Digitaria Egyptiaca, *Willd.*—P. filiforme, *Jacq. obs. III.* 18.

Engrav. Jacq. l. c. t. 70.

Spec. Char. Creeping at the base: spikes 4—8, corymbose, smooth: florets twin, unequally pedicelled: accessory valve of the glume minute or wanting, the rest unequal, nerved and ciliated on the margin.

Western Coast. Peninsula. A scarce grass in India.

(62) P. Nepalense. *(Spreng.)*

Ident. Spreng. syst. I. 321.—Dalz. l. c. p. 291.

Syn. P. nervosum, *Roxb. l. c.* 311.

Spec. Char. Erect, 4—5-feet: leaves lanceolate, plicate, 1-foot in length, 2 inches in breadth: mouths of the sheaths bearded: panicle thin, branches long, simple, filiform, remote: florets solitary or twin, or in threes, pedicelled, with a long awn often springing from the pedicel, smooth.

Western side of the Ghauts.

(63) P. geniculatum. *(Griffith.)*

Ident. Griffith notulæ p. III. p. 41. (under Isachne.)

Spec. Char. Decumbent at the base and rooting, joints hirsute, swollen: sheaths short, pubescent, ciliated and bearded at the throat: leaves short, lanceolate, somewhat stem-clasping at the base, hairy at the margins, scabrous: panicle slender, ovate, flowers solitary as if 2-lipped: peduncles somewhat cartilaginous at the base: upper flower female with rudimentary stamens.

Near Osunpoor, Bengal. This and the following species are included by Griffiths under *Isachne*, a genus which only differs from *Panicum* by the female floret being superior and with rudimentary stamens. Brown in his Prodomus makes *Isachne* a section of the Genus *Panicum*, in which he is followed by Steudel and others.

(64.) P. STIGMATOSA. *(Griffith.)*

Ident. Griff. l. c. p. 42.

SPEC. CHAR. Culm somewhat simple, glabrous at the knots: sheaths ciliated at the edge and with the necks bearded: leaves lanceolate-acuminate, cordate at the base, rough on both sides: panicle effuse, slightly scabrous: branchlets 3-flowered, glumes nearly equal: male floret exceeding the female: paleæ of the female flower minutely pubescent, the outer one ciliate.

Boorea Barak, a little below Luckipoor, on the banks of the river.

(65) P. VERTICILLATUM. *(Linn.)*

Ident. Linn. sp. 82.—Dalz. Bomb. flor. p. 294.

Syn. Setaria verticillata, *Beauv. Agrost.* 51. Pennisetum verticillatum, *Brown prod.* 195.

Engrav. Eng. Bot. t. 874.—Host. Gram II. t. 13. Trin. Ic. 17 t. 202.

SPEC. CHAR. Culms below resting on the ground and rooting, above weak, leaning to one side, smooth: leaves sheathing, linear-lanceolate, a little downy, margins hispid, mouths of the sheaths hairy: spikes cylindric, compound sub-verticelled: bristles of the involucels reversely hispid: hermaphrodite florets rather smooth.

Common about rubbish heaps in the Peninsula.

GENUS VII. MILIUM.

Triandria Digynia. *Sex: Syst:*

Deriv. From *Mille* a thousand, alluding to the immense number of seeds produced by it.

GEN. CHAR. Inflorescense panicled: spikelets hermaphrodite, elliptic-oblong, acutish, 1-flowered: glumes membranaceous equalling or slightly exceeding the floret: perianth sessile, elliptic or lanceolate-oblong, papery and somewhat coriaceous, muticous, the lower palea overlapping the upper one: hypogynous scales either ovate acute, or unequally denticulate, or cuneiform emarginate: ovary oblong, glabrous: styles two: stigmas branched-plumose: stamens three, anthers linear: caryopsis oblong, slightly compressed, free.

(1) M. RAMOSUM. *(Linn.)*

Ident. Linn. sp. I. 361.—Roxb. flor. Ind. I. 315. Griffith notulæ p. III. p. 15.

Syn. Paspalum annulatum, *Fluegge Monogr.* 133. Helopus lævis, *Trin. in Spreng. N. Entd. II.* 49. Agrostis ramosa, *Poir encycl.* H. annulatus, *Nees. ab. Esenb. in Mart. Bras. II.* 17.

Engrav. Trin. Ic. 12. t. 133.

Spec. Char. Creeping: culms 1—4 feet, spreading near the base and there rooting at the joints: leaves smooth: panicle oval, very thin, composed of a few, 4—8-compound, spreading, racemes: rhachis of the racemes 3-sided: flowers paired on common pedicels: valves of the calyx equal, pointed, very hairy.

Growing in large tufts on moist pasture ground Bengal, on the Jellinghey river.

GENUS VIII. PENNISETUM.

Triandria Monogynia. *Sex: Syst:*

Deriv. From *Penna* a feather, and *Setum* a bristle.

Gen. Char. Thyrse simple: spikelets lanceolate, acute, closely involucrated with bristles, solitary or 2—4 within the involucel, sessile or pedicelled: involucre deciduous with the spikelet: bristles of the involucre unequal, in most exceeding the spikelet, hispid or plumose: glumes 2, or the lower one being suppressed, solitary: lower floret neuter or male, 1—2-valved, muticous or rarely caudulate: upper floret hermaphrodite, ovate-lanceolate, acute or acuminate, membranaceous or chartaceous, afterwards firmer than the glumes: hypogynous scales none or situate outside the upper valvelet: ovary glabrous: styles usually connate below: stigmas plumose: stamens 3, anthers linear: caryopsis oblong.

(1) P. alopecuros. *(Nees.)*

Ident. Nees Ms. (under Gymnothrix). Steudel l. c. p. 102.

Syn. Gymnothrix cenchroides, *Wight herb. No.* 66. Cenchrus hordeiformis, *Rottl. herb.*

Spec. Char. Leaves narrow-linear, bearded at the base on both sides: spike elongated, interrupted at the base: larger bristles of the unequal sub-sessile 1-flowered involucre twice longer than the spikelet, rest equal or shorter: lower glume ovate, 6 times shorter than the spikelet, upper one ovate-oblong, twice shorter than the same, the latter 5-nerved at the base: neuter floret 9-nerved: styles deeply connate.

Peninsula?

(2) P. Hohenhackeri. *(Hochst.)*

Ident. Hochst in herb.—Hohenhack. No.—Steudel l. c. p. 103.

Spec. Char. Root strongly fibrous : culm erect, simple, straight, 2—feet or more, glabrous : sheaths broadly sheathing, compressed, striated, glabrous, hairy at the mouth and lowest base : leaves narrow, folded upon themselves, stiff, quite glabrous, narrowed-bristly, equal to or shorter than the culm, a little scabrous at the edges : ligula hairy at the edges : spike solitary, a little loose, bristles unequal, partly longer partly shorter than the spikelet: spikelets sessile : lower glume 4 times shorter than the spikelet, ovate-lanceolate, obscurely 3-nerved, upper one equal in length to the floret, 3-nerved at the apex, glaucous, hermaphrodite valvelet smooth, quite glabrous : style long-exserted.

Neilgherries.

(3) P. imberbe. *(Edgw.)*

Ident. Edgeworth in As. Journ. 1852, p. 184.—Steudel l. c. p. 104.

Spec. Char. Erect, branched : culms and knots quite glabrous : sheaths glabrous : ligula short, torn and ciliated : leaves sub-petiolate, bearded with a few hairs, broadish, very acuminate, scabrous above, smooth below, serrulate at the edges : spikes terminal and axillary, cylindric, lax : rhachis compressed, winged on both sides, involucre sessile, bristles connected at the base, unequal in an almost simple row, one more than twice longer than the rest : spikelet solitary, 1-flowered : glumes two, deeply purple-red, glabrous, outer one longer acute, inner 3-toothed, margins involute glassy : valvelets pale, acute, ciliated at the apex, afterwards hardened embracing the seed.

Gurhrampore.

(4) P. araneosum. *(Edgew.)*

Ident. Edgew. l. c. p. 180.

Spec. Char. Erect : culms geniculate, rooting, and with the knots glabrous : lower sheaths pubescent, glabrous : ligula ciliate-membranaceous : leaves broadish, flat, glabrous, bearded near the base with very few long scattered lairs, smooth below, scabrous above, serrulate at the edges : spikes terminal : involucres many-bristled in a double row, outer bristles smaller, inner very unequal, cohering near the middle with long cobweb-like hairs, naked and hispid at the apex, one twice longer than the rest, bispiculate : one spikelet sessile, 2-flowered, the other pedicelled 1-flowered : outer glume of the sessile flower twice shorter than the flower, very long, cobweb-ciliated, inner one 3—5-nerved, shortly mucronate : lower flower neuter or male, 1—2-valved, outer valvelet truncated, ciliolate at the apex, equalling the glume, 3-nerved, glandular-dotted, the other valvelet oblong, ciliated at the apex, often wanting.

Mountains near Banda.

(5) P. HOLCOIDES. *(Schult.)*

Ident. Schult Mant. II. 148.

Syn. Panicum holcoides, *Roxb. l. c. p.* 285.

SPEC. CHAR. Culms branched, erect, 2—4-feet, glabrous: sheaths bearded at the throat: involucels numerous, scattered, 1-flowered, bristles alternately longer, woolly, and another shorter and smooth: flowers sometimes polygamous: lower glume minute, upper 3-toothed at the apex.

Mountain tracts, growing on cultivated lands.

(6) P. AUREUM. *(Link.)*

Ident. Link. H. Berol. I. 215.—Dalz. Bomb. flor. p. 294.

SPEC. CHAR. Culm 2-feet and with the bases of the leaves much compressed: leaves much longer than the culm, margins at the base ciliated: spike 2—3 inches long, imbricated on all sides: bristles of the involucre rough, elongated, rigid, yellowish.

Common everywhere in the Deccan.

GENUS IX. CENCHRUS.

Triandria Digynia. *Sex: Syst:*

Deriv. The oriental name of the Millet.

GEN. CHAR. Thyrse simple: spikelets sessile, 1—5, within an involucre: glumes 2 (lower one sometimes suppressed), membranaceous, acute, lower one small, more or less shorter than the florets, 3—5-nerved: lower floret neuter or male, membranaceous, 1—2-valved: upper floret hermaphrodite, sub-chartaceous: upper valvelet closely embracing the lower: involucre consisting of bristly or thorny-partite coriaceous segments, more or less connate at the base into a solid disc: caryopsis oblong, rather hard.

(1) C. RAMOSISSIMUS. *(Poir.)*

Ident. Poir. Encyc. suppl. v. 51.—Dalz. Bomb. flor. p. 294.

SPEC. CHAR. Root fibrous and bulbous: culm branched above, sub-scandent, smooth, round: leaves flat, narrow, finely acuminated, rough on the inner surface, slightly hairy: spikes terminal, solitary on the sub-corymbose branches of the culm, cylindric-oblong: spikelets 2—4 in each involucre, ovate, acute, 2-flowered; involucre hard, coriaceous, 10—12-divided, divisions stiff, lanceolate-acute, unequal, smooth, beaded at the base on the inside, as long as the spikelets.

Hedges in Guzarat.

(2) C. BIFLORUS. *(Roxb.)*

Ident. Roxb. l. c. p. 233.—Dalz. l. c.

SPEC. CHAR. Culms branched from the base, spreading: leaves elongated, slender, roughish: mouths of the sheaths a little hairy: spikes terminal, solitary, cylindric, 3—4 inches long, involucres with only two spikelets, segments subulate, hooked, hairy within, barbed and pungent.

Sandy sea-shores at Gogo and Domus. Dry parts of the Coromandel coast.

GENUS X. TRACHYOZUS.

Triandria Digynia. *Sex: Syst:*

Deriv. From *Trachys* rough, and *Ozos* a branch or twig.

GEN. CHAR. Racemes simple, 1—2, approximated: partial axis flattened, articulated, at each joint spikelets (usually 4) subfascicled, sessile, lower spikelets complete: glumes 3-nerved, lower one more than twice shorter than the florets, coriaceous, lanceolate, often recurved, upper one a little longer, membranaceous, dagger-shaped, adpressed, a little villous below: neuter florets 2-valved, lower valve largest, coriaceous, oval, cuspidate-acuminate, margins inflexed, 13-nerved: upper very minute, oblong, obtuse, nerveless: hermaphrodite more than half shorter than the neuter, chartaceous, ovate-lanceolate, very acute: lower palea 3-nerved, wrapping round the upper one: outermost spikelet composed of some coriaceous, barren, more or less incurved paleæ.

(1) T. MURICATA. *(Pers.)*

Ident. Pers. syn. I. 85, (under Trachys.)—Steudel l. c. p. 112.

Syn. T. mucronata, *Beauv.* — Cenchrus muricatus, *Linn.* — Trachystachys geminata, *A. Dietr. spec. II.* 16.—Panicum squarrosum, *Retz. Roxb. l. c. p.* 288.—P. dimidiatum, *Burm.*

Engrav. Beauv. agrost. t. 21, fig. 7.—Schreb. gram. II. t. 34. —Roxb. Cor. t. 206.—Burm. Ind. t. 8, fig. 3.

SPEC. CHAR. Culm procumbent, ascending, branched, 1-foot or more: leaves linear-lanceolate, sheaths and knots more or less hairy.

Dry sandy ground near the sea.

GENUS XI. LAPPAGO.

Triandria Digynia. *Sex: Syst:*

Deriv. From *Lappa* burdock, because of its rough prickly flowers.

GEN. CHAR. Thyrse cylindric, composed of 2—5-flowered fascicles or thyrsules: partial axis very short, raylets approximate-alternate, very short: spikelets fascicled, in twos or fives, 2-flowered-hemigamous, stiff: lower glume none, upper small, membranaceous, nerveless: neuter floret 1-valved, large, oval, acute, 5-nerved, thickly glochidiate-echinate: hermaphrodite one chartaceous, scarcely shorter than the neuter, lanceolate, acute, lower palea 3-nerved, wrapping round the upper more tender one: hypogynous scales 2, truncated, prolonged into a small tooth: caryopsis oblong.

(1) L. ALIENA. *(Spreng.)*

Ident. Spreng. N. Ent. II. 15.—Dalz. Bomb. flor. p. 295.

Syn. L. biflora, *Roxb. l. c. p.* 281.—Tragus occidentalis, *Nees.*

SPEC. CHAR. Culms pressing on the earth, rooting from the joints, 6—12-inches long, branched: leaves short, margins ciliated and waved, glaucous, mouths of the sheaths bearded: racemes terminal, simple: pedicels short, diverging, 2-flowered: flowers lanceolate, echinated on the back or outside, diverging on all sides round the rhachis, the prickles pointing in five different directions.

Dry pastures on the Coromandel coast.

GENUS XII. SPINIFEX.

Dioecia Triandria. *Sex: Syst:*

Deriv. From *Spina* a thorn; alluding to the prickly nature of the plant.

GEN. CHAR. Capitules or floral fascicles terminal and axillary, large, composed of many densely fascicled axes: males and fructiferous one in distinct plants: male plants sometimes loosely, sometimes closely thyrse-flowered, all below longer or shorter, flowerless: each spikelet sessile at the tooth of the axis, ovate: glumes 2, 7—9-nerved, inner one a little shorter: florets 2, sessile, males 2-valved, the substance of the glumes, valves equal acute, lower 2—7-, upper 2-nerved: anthers 3: axes of the fructiferous plant capitate, 1-flowered, rest as in the male but commonly longer: spikelet solitary, sessile at the base of the axis, lanceolate: glumes 2, equal, acuminate, 7—9-nerved: lower floret neuter, 1—2-valved, lower valve 5-nerved, upper, when present, very small: hermaphrodite equalling the neuter: lower valve 3-nerved, embracing the upper: styles two, connate at the base, elongated: fruit oval.

(1) S. SQUARROSUS. *(Linn.)*

Ident. Linn. Mant. 300.

Syn. Stipa spinifex, *Linn. Mant.* 34.

Engrav. Rheede Mal. xii. t. 75.

SPEC. CHAR. Frutescent: culms large, glaucous, fasciculate-leafy at the knots: leaves convolute, recurved-patent, stiff, pungent: sheaths woolly at the mouth the rest striated, with the spikelets and leaves glabrous: male axes floriferous: bracts of the capitules fascicled, very large, involucres mucronate.

Sandy shores of the Peninsula, on both coasts.

GENUS XIII. LOPHOLEPIS.

Monœcia Triandria. *Sex: Syst:*

Deriv. From *Lophos* a crest, and *Lepis* a scale.

GEN. CHAR. Spikelets monœcious or polygamous, congested into a terminal, linear-cylindric, erect, many-flowered raceme: rhachis straight, pedicels thickened upwards, ciliated, jointed at the geniculate base: paleæ 2, laterally compressed, minutely elevate-dotted, acutely keeled: awns diaphanous, pectinate-ciliate, increased by ciliæ, hooked at the apex, outer one globose at the base, paleæ-shaped, 2-crested, inner much smaller, furnished with a strong tooth below the apex, 1-crested beneath: caryopsis covered with hardened paleæ, oblong, sub-acuminate, gibbous at the base above, depressed below.

(1) L. ORNITHOCEPHALA. *(Hook.)*

Ident. Hook. Bot. Misc. II. t. 76, (under Hollböllia.)

SPEC. CHAR. Root fibrous: culms cæspitose, erect from a decumbent base: leaves flat, stiffish, undulated, cartilaginous-margined, scabrous.

Pulney hills.

GENUS XIV. ARUNDINELLA.

Triandria Digynia. *Sex: Syst:*

GEN. CHAR. Panicle compound: spikelets solitary or twin, while closed lanceolate-ovate: glumes 3—5-nerved, usually acuminate, lower one shorter: lower floret male, seldom neuter, 2-valved, the substance of the glumes, muticous: upper hermaphrodite or female, coriaceous, ovate-lanceolate, girt at the base with shortish hairs, simply or 2-cleft, awned at the apex, awn often long, usually twisted, geniculate, sometimes very short: lower valve closely embracing the upper: stigmas plumose: caryopsis oval, beardless.

(1) A. CILIATA. *(Roxb.)*

Ident. Roxb. l. c. p. 318 (under Holcus).

SPEC. CHAR. Erect, hairy: panicle linear, hirsute: glumes papillose, ciliated, 2-flowered: flowers sessile: one hermaphrodite, awned, the other male, muticous.

Coromandel.

(2) A. NERVOSA. *(Roxb.)*

Ident. Roxb. l. c.

SPEC. CHAR. Erect, hairy: panicle oblong: glumes 3—5-nerved, cuspidate, 2-flowered: flowers sessile: one hermaphrodite, awned, the other male and muticous.

Coromandel.

(3) A. HIRSUTA. *(Nees.)*

Ident. Nees Ms. in Steudel l. c. p. 115.

SPEC. CHAR. Culm with few knots, 1—2-feet: sheaths shorter than the internode, hirsute with the linear flat leaves: knots glabrous: spikelets subulate-acuminate: glumes hirsute: fertile floret smooth.

Courtallum.

(4) A. FUSCATA. *(Nees.)*

Ident. Nees l. c.

SPEC. CHAR. Leaves shorter than the culm, linear-lanceolate, and with the sheaths softly hirsute from tubercles: panicles oblong or lanceolate, contracted, rays floriferous from the base, short: glumes glabrous, with elevated nerves, lower one a fourth shorter: fertile floret finely asperulous.

Peninsula.

(5) A. Khasiana. *(Nees.)*

Ident. Nees Ms.—Steudel l. c. p. 115.

Spec. Char. Culm and raceme straight, glabrous: knots and sheaths bearded at the mouth: leaves 7-nerved, serrulate-scabrous at the margin: middle rays of the panicle verticillate: spikelets purple-brown: glumes subulate, 5-nerved, lateral nerves approximated, scattered with hairs: fertile floret smooth, equalling the lower male: lower valve deeply 2-cleft: divisions filiform at the apex, bristle slightly exceeding the glumes.

Khasia hills.

(6) A. mesophylla. *(Nees.)*

Ident. Nees Ms.—Steudel l. c.

Spec. Char. Whole plant hirsute from tubercles: leaves lanceolate, flat: raceme compound: partial racemules, alternate, short: spikelets secund, in four rows, imbricated: pedicels very short, somewhat 2-flowered: glumes hirsute: lower valve of the upper floret 2-bristled, awn exserted.

Courtallum.

(7) A. setifera. *(Steudel.)*

Ident. Steudel l. c.

Syn. A. hirsuta, *Hochst. in Herb. Hohenhack. Ind. No.* 920.

Spec. Char. Root strongly fibrous: culm erect, 1-foot, glabrous: sheaths long, densely hairy at the margin, ciliated at the mouth: leaves linear-lanceolate, elongated, hairy on the blade from scattered tubercles, on the margin from bristly, usually twin approximated tubercles: panicle erect-spreading: rays twin at the base: spikelets solitary, lanceolate, spreading at the apex, pedicelled: glumes 2, ovate-lanceolate, acuminate, nearly equal, hairy at the back, 5-nerved: sterile floret monandrous, equalling the upper glume, fertile one twice shorter, 2-cleft at the apex, very finely bristly: awn geniculate, exceeding the florets.

Neilgherries.

(8) A. purpurea. *(Hochst.)*

Ident. Hochst. in Herb. Hohenhack. Ind. No. 928.—Steudel l. c.

Spec. Char. Culm erect, simple, glabrous, more or less hairy towards the top, ligula very short, or in its place the margin hairy: sheaths elongated, hairy: leaves lanceolate, many-striated, hairyish or at length glabrate, acuminate: panicle erect, straight: rhachis and rhacheoles angular, hairy: rays half verticelled, erect, floriferous from the base, pedicels stiffish, shorter than the purplish spikelet: lower glume shorter, ovate-lanceolate, keeled, strongly 1-nerved on both sides, upper one keeled, ovate-oblong, 2-nerved towards the margin on both sides: awn twisted, geniculate, a little exceeding the glumes, fugacious.

Neilgherries.

(9) A. pilosa. *(Hochst.)*

Ident. Hochst l. c. No. 647. Steudel l. c. p. 116.

Spec. Char. Root fibrous, somewhat cæspitiferous: culms erect, simple, terete, furrowed, sparingly hairy, the sheaths densely so from glands: leaves lanceolate, shorter than the culm, similarly hairy: panicles green, rays alternately fasciculately half-verticelled, somewhat paniculately compound: glumes very acuminate, 3-nerved, exceeding the florets: either floret sessile, one hermaphrodite awned, the other larger, muticous.

Mercara in Coorg.

(10) A. tenella. *(Nees.)*

Ident. Nees Ms.—Dalz. l. c. p. 292.—Steudel l. c.

Spec. Char. Culms several from the same root: sheaths ciliate along the margins: leaves few, a little narrowed at the base, tender, acuminated at the apex, sparingly hairy on both sides: panicle very slender: pedicels long, capillary, solitary or more frequently twin on the branches of the panicle: spikelets 2-flowered, lower flower barren, upper fertile: glumes lanceolate-acuminate, unequal, upper one larger, long-acuminated, minutely 2-cleft at the apex, with 3—5 green veins clothed with hairs rising from glands: paleæ of the lower flower membranous, and, like the glumes of the upper flower, much smaller, dark brown, scabrous at the apex, with two tufts of bristly hairs at the base: lower paleæ 2-cleft at the apex, furnished with a long bent awn.

Mahableshwur, common under shrubs and trees,

(11) A. stricta. *(Nees.)*

Ident. Dalz. l. c. p. 293.—Hook. Kew Gard. Misc. II. 102.

Spec. Char. Culms 1—3-feet, rigid, wiry, smooth, round: nodes elongated: sheaths smooth, woolly at the apex: leaves few, finely pointed, shortly pubescent on the upper side, striated:

margins serrulate: flowers panicled: branchlets sub-verticelled: spikelets solitary, racemed: pedicels pubescent: florets pale-purple, smooth: glumes unequal, lower smaller, ovate-acuminate, strongly 3-nerved, upper acuminate, 5-nerved, twice the length: lower paleæ of upper flower slightly 2-cleft, with a short twisted awn.

Mahableshwur.

(12) A. GIGANTEA. (*Dalz.*)

Ident. Dalz. l. c.

SPEC. CHAR. Culms erect, round, smooth, 6-feet, thickish at the base, branched at all the lower joints: nodes much swollen, covered by the tomentose base of the sheaths, which are ciliated along the margins and about half the length of the joints: leaves finely attenuated to a point, scabrous and deeply striated above, sparingly hairy: panicle very delicate and large: pedicels solitary or paired, very slender, scabrous: flowers similar to the preceding.

Foot of the Ghauts, Kineshwur.

(13) A. SPICATA. (*Dalz.*)

Ident. Dalz. l. c.

SPEC. CHAR. Culms erect, 1-foot: leaves ensiform and, with the sheaths, clothed with stiff, spreading hairs: spike terminal, cylindric, densely flowered: lower glume herbaceo-membranous, with 3 green veins, lanceolate, subulate, a little pilose, upper long-attenuated and folded, and concealing within it the awn of the hermaphrodite flower.

Mahableshwur hills, common.

GENUS XV. MIQUELIA.

Triandria Digynia. *Sex: Syst:*

GEN. CHAR. Raceme compound: spikelets twin or solitary, homogamous or one incomplete, conforming, sub-sessile or one of the twins pedicellate: glume single, adverse to the rhachis, membranaceous, 3-nerved: lower floret neuter, 1-valved, 3-nerved, larger than the glume, upper one hermaphrodite, sessile, 2-valved: lower valve embracing the upper, smooth, sending out an awn or bristle, (geniculate below the middle,) from the short-toothed apex, susceptible of twisting: upper one shorter, 2-nerved, smooth, back flat, margins bent inwards, apex entire: hypogynous scales 2, small, somewhat fleshy, obovate: stamens 3: ovary glabrous, styles separated at the base, stigmas narrow: caryopsis enclosed in stiffish valves, free, oblong, smooth.

(1) M. Courtallensis. *(Arnot & Nees.)*

Ident. A. and Nees in Nov Act. N. C. xvii. p. 179.—Steudel l. c. p. 119.

Spec. Char. Root creeping: culm procumbent, ascending from a branched leafy base, pubescent at the knots: sheaths glabrous, bearded at the mouth, lower ones ciliated at the margin: ligula short, torn: leaves lanceolate, pubescent: raceme compound or somewhat decompound, rays in three's or four's fascicled, partial rhachis smooth: pedicels naked: spikelets in 3—6 pairs, one almost sessile, the other pedicelled.

Courtallum.

GENUS XVI. THYSSANOLŒNA.

Triandria Digynia. *Sex: Syst:*

Gen. Char. Raceme large, panicled, supra-decompound: spikelets hemiologamous, homogamous, twin or solitary: glumes 2, smaller than the florets, muticous, lower one shorter: lower floret neuter, 1-valved, valve herbaceous, entire, muticous, upper hermaphrodite, 2-valved, lower valve herbaceo-membranaceous, muticous, 3-nerved, long-ciliated, upper smaller, narrower, linear-lanceolate: scales very small, round, quite entire: stigmas penicillate (purple) joined to the base of the style.

(1) T. agrostis. *(Arn. et Nees.)*

Ident. Arn. et Nees N. Act. C. xvii. suppl. I. 182.—Steudel l. c. p. 119.

Syn. Agrostis maxima, *Roxb. I.* 319.

Spec. Char. Root woody: culm erect, strong, 4—12-feet: leaves glabrous, attenuated into a thin acumen: panicle ovate, dense-flowered, rays alternate, branched, filiform, expanded or nodding: glumes 4 times shorter than the densely ciliated florets, ovate.

Peninsula. Mountainous places.

SECT. IV. STIPACEÆ.

Panicle more or less compound: spikelets one-flowered, 1—3-androus: hypogynous scales whorled in three's, often showy: glumes long, membranaceous, muticous or bearing a fine point, lower one smaller: floret inserted on a somewhat strigose callosity, 2-valved, coriaceous, hardening, narrow: lower valve embracing the other smaller one, 3—many-bristled at the apex, or a simple or 3-cleft awn inserted at the joint, base often twisted, in many very long: caryopsis compressed cylindric, enclosed by the floret.

GENUS XVII. ARISTIDA.

Triandria Digynia. *Sex: Syst:*

Deriv. From *Arista,* an ear of corn.

GEN. CHAR. Panicle sometimes much impoverished, racemiform: spikelets 1-flowered, ripe floret separating at the joint from the glumes, callus obconical, bearded: glumes 2, unequal, very often muticous: paleæ 2, lower coriaceous, awned at the apex: awn 3-parted or cleft, sometimes jointed at the base: upper paleæ scarcely exceeding the scales, muticous: filaments adnate through the base to the stalk of the ovary: ovary stalked, glabrous: styles terminal, short, stigmas plumose: scales 2, entire, adnate to the stalk of the ovary: caryopsis terete, involved in the paleæ, free.

(1) A. DEPRESSA. *(Retz.)*

Ident. Retz. obs. iv. p. 22.—Roxb. l. c. p. 351.

SPEC. CHAR. Culm 9—18-inches, ascending or procumbent: leaves rather glaucous: rays of the dense panicle rather contracted and nodding.

Peninsula, in dry barren soil. A troublesome grass: the flowers, which fall off easily, are like barbed arrows (*Dalzell.*)

(2) A. HYSTRIX. *(Linn.)*

Ident. Spreng. syst. I. 267.—Roxb. l. c. p. 350.

Syn. Chætaria hystrix, *Beauv.*

SPEC. CHAR. Root creeping, stoloniferous, branched, culms diffuse, ascending, 10—20-inches: sheaths smooth, striated, bearded in the mouth: leaves rather glaucous, spreading in two ways, convolute, smooth, roughish above: panicle rigid, divisions spreading, angular, bearded at the axis.

Dry barren soil in the Peninsula. Malabar.

(3) A. SETACEA. *(Retz.)*

Ident. Retz. obs. iv. p. 22.—Roxb. l. c. p. 349.

SPEC. CHAR. Rhizome thick: culms erect, firm, 2-feet, usually branched, tumid at the nodes: sheaths smooth: leaves filiform, convolute, flaccid, 3—6-inches long: panicle rather dense, straw-colour, linear, contracted: branches of the panicle solitary or several together: glumes unequal, upper 2-toothed at the apex, mucronate, longer than the subulate inferior one: awns spreading.

On dry hills.

SECT. V. AGROSTIDEÆ.

Spikelets 1-flowered, sometimes with the joint of the secund floret naked, very small: callus either none or obsolete or present, naked or bearded with very short hairs: inflorescence a raceme, thyrse or panicle.

GENUS XVIII. ALOPECURUS.

Triandria Digynia. *Sex: Syst:*

Deriv. From *Alopex*, a fox, and *Oura*, a tail, from which it is called Foxtail grass.

Gen. Char. Thyrse ovate or roundish, oblong, cylindric, dense: spikelets at length deciduous, somewhat compressed: pedicels very short, club-shaped: glumes 2, free or more or less connate, equal: valves 1, seldom 2, lower one nearly equalling the glumes, obtuse or obliquely truncate, 5-nerved, commonly awned at the back: scales none: stamens 2—3: ovary oblong, styles sometimes connate at the base: stigmas linear-narrow: caryopsis oblong, glabrous.

(1) A. diandrus. *(Griff.)*

Ident. Griffith Notulæ, III. p. 11.

Spec. Char. Ascending: culms geniculate, striated: sheaths lax, exceeding the leaves, glirate, glabrous: ligula oblong, entire: leaves linear, narrow, margins scabrous: panicles terminal, spiciform, cylindrically obtuse: florets densely aggregated, lower ones few, upper solitary, all sessile, obliquely fixed and jointed at the apex of incurved pedicels: stamens 2.

Assam, on the sandy banks of the Brahmaputra river.

GENUS XIX. VILFA.

Triandria Digynia. *Sex: Syst:*

Gen. Char. Juba, panicle or thyrse: spikelets 1-flowered: glumes 2, either both or only the upper one equalling the valves or both shorter than them, one or nerveless: valves deciduous, equal, without a callosity, lower 2—nerved, nerves as if approximated into one, obtuse: scales 2, small: ovary glabrous: stigmas plumose: caryopsis free, in a loosening glassy pericarp.

(1) V. Coromandeliana. *(Beauv.)*

Ident. Beauv. Agrost. 16.

Syn. Agrostis Coromandeliana, *Retz.* — Sporobolus Coromandelianus, *Kunth.*

Engrav. Trin. Ic. I. t. 11.

Spec. Char. Culms 4—8-inches: panicle verticelled, branches simple, secund: inner glume as long as the paleæ, outer one minute: ligula hairy: leaves ovate-lanceolate, pointed-acuminate, serrate-ciliated at the margins.

Pasture ground in the Peninsula.

(2) V. diandra. *(Trin.)*

Ident. Trin. Agrost. I. 38.

Syn. Agrostis diandra, *Retz.—Roxb. l. c. p.* 317.

Spec. Char. Culm thin, simple, sheaths a half shorter than the internodes, more or less hairy at the margins: ligula very short, ciliate: leaves linear, compressed: juba contracted: lower rays more or less naked, upper ones floriferous from the base: lower glume more than twice shorter than the valves.

Moist pastures near Calcutta. Western coast.

(3) V. orientalis. *(Nees.)*

Ident. Nees Agrost. Bras. p. 393, (under Agrostis.)

Syn. Agrostis tenacissima, *Roxb.*—A. orientalis, *Nees.*—A. elongata, *Roth.*

Spec. Char. Root somewhat creeping: culm flagelliferous at the base, ascending, slightly branched: ligula very short, ciliated: leaves rolled inwards on the culms of the short branches, distichous, shorter, recurved: rays of the spike-formed juba 3—4, flower-bearing from the base.

Pasture grounds.

(4) V. geniculata. *(Nees.)*

Ident. Nees Ms.—Steudel l. c. p. 156.

Spec. Char. Culm fasciculately branched, geniculate: leaves

flat, linear-lanceolate, and with the sheaths sparingly hairy: raceme compound, narrow, rays short, 2—3-flowered: pedicels longish, florets triandrous: glumes oval, lower one twice shorter than the valves, one sinuate at the side, cuspidate, upper one equalling the valves and with the lower valve obtuse.

Madras.

(5) V. Mangalorica. *(Hochst.)*

Ident. Hochst. in Herb. Hohenhack Ind. Or. 1847, No. 137.—Steudel l. c. p. 159.

Spec. Char. Culm erect, somewhat branched, glabrous: leaves elongated, narrow-acuminate, glabrous: ligula scarcely any: panicle pyramidate, elongated, rays scattered without order, smaller ones capillary, 1—3-flowered at the apex: spikelets pedicelled: glumes very minute, acute: valves nearly equal, obtuse, entire, or scarcely denticulate.

Mangalore.

GENUS XX. TRIACHRYUM.

Triandria Digynia. *Sex: Syst:*

Gen. Char. Panicle: spikelet 1-flowered, muticous: glumes 2, lower smaller, upper equalling the valves: floret inserted in a nodule, 3-valved, valves nearly equal, nerveless, third a little smaller and thinner: stigmas simply plumose: caryopsis free, ovate, compressed or swollen on both sides, mucronulate, obliquely truncate and scrobiculate at the base.

(1) T. Nilagiricum. *(Steudel.)*

Ident. Steudel l. c. p. 176.—Herb. Hohenhack No. 931.

Spec. Char. Root fibrous, densely cæspitiferous: culms erect from a geniculate base, glabrous: sheaths and leaves hairy from tubercles, especially at the edges: leaves lanceolate, acute: ligula scarcely any: panicle very narrow, straight, linear: rays very short, 1—2-flowered: spikelets oblong, lower glume minute, linear, fugacious, upper equalling the pellucid valves: achenium shorter than the valves, ovate-oblong, scarcely triquetrous at the base.

Neilgherries.

GENUS XXI. PEROTIS.

Triandria Digynia. *Sex: Syst:*

Deriv. From *Peros* deficient; alluding to the flower.

Gen. Char. Thyrse: spikelets linear, 1-flowered, at length much spreading: glumes membranaceous, hairyish, running into a bristle much longer than themselves: valves muticous, more than half shorter than the glumes: hypogynous scales 2, shorter than the ovary: ovary obtuse: stigmas simple, plumulose: caryopsis linear, glabrous.

(1) P. latifolia. *(Ait.)*

Ident. Roxb. l. c. p. 233.—Ait. Hort. Kew I. 85.

Syn. Anthoxanthum Indicum, *Linn.* — Saccharum spicatum, *Linn.*—Agrostis spicæformis, *Linn.*

Engrav. Burm. Ind. t. 9, fig. 3.—Rheede Mal. xii. t. 62.

Spec. Char. Root thin and fibrous: culm ascending, 8—10-inches, branched below, slender, nodes and sheaths smooth: leaves acute, linear-oblong, short, margins waved and hispid: racemes terminal, erect, cylindrical, lead-coloured, 3-inches long: spikelets linear-lanceolate, very shortly pedicelled: glumes hairy, terminating in a scabrous awn.

Peninsula, not very common.

SECT. VI. ARUNDINACEÆ.

Spikelets sometimes 1-flowered with or without the pedicel of another flower, sometimes many-flowered: flowers usually beset with long soft hairs or surrounded at the base: glumes and valves 2, the latter often equalling or exceeding the flowers; of the former, the lower awned or muticous.

GENUS XXII. PHRAGMITES.

Triandria Digynia. *Sex: Syst:*

Deriv. From *Phragmos* a hedge; it forms hedges.

Gen. Char. Panicle: spikelets 3—6-flowered: flowers distichous, distant, lowest male, rest hermaphrodite, rhachis beset with long silky hairs: glumes 2, acutish, keeled, shorter than the flowers, membranaceous, unequal, upper one larger: valves 2, membranaceous, lower one very long, narrow-subulate, upper 2-keeled: stamens 3: ovary glabrous: styles elongated: stigmas plumose, hairs thickish, simple, 2-cleft or branched: scales 2, glabrous: caryopsis free.

(1) P. Roxburghii. *(Kunth.)*

Ident. Kunth ex Nees N. Act. N. C. 173.

Syn. Arundo Karka, *Roxb. l. c.* 347.

Spec. Char. Culm branched, leafy: leaves lanceolate, much attenuated, glabrous above, beneath and at the margin scabrous: panicle large, lax, rays and raylets slender, very glabrous: spikelets 3—5-flowered: glumes oblong-lanceolate, acutish or obtuse, lower one twice shorter than the upper glume: lower valve of the lower male floret linear-attenuated, equalling the upper hermaphrodite and subulate florets.

Peninsula. Bengal, on banks of rivulets and lakes.

GENUS XXIII. AMPHIDONAX.

Triandria Digynia. *Sex: Syst:*

Gen. Char. Panicle: spikelets 2—3-flowered, twin, heterogamous or homogamous, polygamo-monœcious, lower ones of the rays all males, of the upper ones either one of each pair or both female: glumes two, keeled, 1-nerved, nearly equal, shorter than the florets or equalling them, spreading, upper one larger: florets conforming, sessile, opposite, when in threes more separated, 2-valved: lower valve lanceolate, long-acuminate, subulate, convolute, hirsute below, 5—7-nerved, membranaceous, upper shorter, lanceolate, obtuse, bidenticulate, 2-nerved at either side, hirsute at the base: scales membranaceous, emarginate-obcordate, or repand at the apex, cuneate at the base: filaments short, anthers long linear, yellowish: vestiges of a pistil in the males conspicuous, of stamens in the females scarcely any, no organs in the neuter spikelets: ovary lanceolate, compressed, glabrous: styles slender, thickened at the base: stigmas ovate, thick, tomentosely brush-shaped: caryopsis free.

(1) A. Heynii. *(Nees.)*

Ident. Nees Ms.—Steudel l. c. p. 197.

Spec. Char. Leaves convolute : panicle lax, nodding : spikelets pale, homogamous, 2-flowered : glumes twice shorter than the floret.

Courtallum.

(2) A. Benghalensis. *(Nees.)*

Ident. Nees l. c.—Steudel l. c.

Syn. Arundo Bengalensis, *Retz.—Roxb. l. c. p.* 348.—Donax Bengalensis, *Beauv.*

Spec. Char. Culm thick, leafy, 6—10-feet, fistular: leaves glabrous, flat, distichous, ensiform : panicle much branched, erect, 2-feet : rays half-verticelled, unequal, branched : spikelets 3—4-flowered : glumes equal, one floret sessile : lower valve subulate-alternate, 3-nerved.

Peninsula. Bengal.

(3) A. bifaria. *(Nees.)*

Ident. Nees l. c.—Steudel l. c.

Syn. Arundo bifaria, *Retz.—Roxb. l. c. p.* 347.

Spec. Char. Culm thick, very leafy : sheaths close, striated, glabrous, covering the culm : ligula very short, semi-lunar : leaves distichous, flat, spreading, linear-lanceolate, attenuated and very acute, thichish, firm, hispid at the edges : panicle oblong, contracted, dense, erect : spikelets 3-flowered : glumes lanceolate-linear, acuminate, nearly equalling the florets : lowest florets short-pedicelled : lower valve lanceolate, 3-nerved, nerves running out into an acumen.

Circars. Bengal.

(4) A. tenella. *(Wight & Arn.)*

Ident. W. and A. in Steudel l. c.

Spec. Char. Leaves narrow-linear, at length folded upon themselves, equalling the culm, striated, sparingly hairy above : panicle dense : spikelets homogamous, 2-flowered : glumes acute, three times shorter than the floret.

Peninsula.

SECT. VII. CHLORIDEÆ.

Spikes or racemes distichous-secund, seldom solitary : spikelets seldom 1, usually many-flowered, upper florets withering : glumes two, persistent on the rhachis : valves 2, usually stiffer, lower one seldom muticous at the apex, commonly with one or several bristles.

GENUS XXIV. MICHROCHLOA.

Triandria Digynia. *Sex: Syst:*

Deriv. From *Micros*, small, and *Chloa*, grass.

Gen. Char. Spike terminal, solitary: spikelets unilateral, 1-flowered: flower sessile: glumes 2, oblong, acutish, nearly equal, muticous: valves 2, shorter than the glumes, very thinly membranaceous, densely hairy externally: lower one broadly ovate, truncated, sub-mucronate, mucro membranaceous, concave, 3-nerved, upper one 2-keeled: stamens 2—3: ovary glabrous: stigmas plumose: hairs simple: scales 2, adnate to the upper valve.

(1) M. setacea. *(R. Br.)*

Ident. Brown Prod. 208.

Syn. Nardus Indica, *Linn.*—Rotboëllia setacea, *Roxb. l. c.* 357.

Engrav. Roxb. Cor. II. t. 132.

Spec. Char. Very small, cæspitose: culms several, filiform, branched: leaves linear, at length folded inwards, scabrous: spike bristly, somewhat incurved, valves densely hairy at the back.

Peninsula, on old walls.

GENUS XXV. SCHŒNEFELDIA.

Triandria Digynia. *Sex: Syst:*

Gen. Char. Spikes solitary or several, 2—4: spikelets unilateral, closely imbricated, sessile, 1-flowered: glumes 2, nearly equal, acute-subulate, keeled, twice exceeding the floret, which is hairy at the base: valves 2, lower long awned below the apex, concave, upper channelled, ciliated or hairy at the back: ovary fusiform: style simple: caryopsis free.

(1) S. pallida. *(Edgew.)*

Ident. Edgew. in Asiat. Journ. 1852, p. 183.

Spec. Char. Annual, branched: sheaths ciliolate at the margins, ligula ciliolate-membranaceous: leaves linear, here and there with a few scattered hairs, at length convolute: spikes twin, secund: rhachis serrulate at the margin: spikelets 1-flowered, sessile, bifarious, glumes 2, persistent, sharply keeled, prolonged at the apex into a small bristle, flower stalked on a silky callosity, bipaleaceous, outer valve larger, involving the other nerveless one, outwardly puberulous, bearing below the apex a very long hispid awn: scales emarginate at the apex: achenium long, azure.

Banda district.

GENUS XXVI. CHLORIS.

Polygamia Monœcia. *Sex: Syst:*

Deriv. From *Chloros*, green, alluding to the colour of the herbage.

Gen. Char. Spikes digitately fascicled, very rarely twin or solitary: spikelets 2—many-flowered, imperfect upwards, unilateral on a common rhachis, alternate, sessile: glumes two, persistent, lower one smaller, upper often mucronate or bristle-bearing: lower florets 1—3, hermaphrodite: lower valve compressed and keeled, chartaceous, emarginate at the apex, 2-cleft or toothed or truncated and from the back of the sinus more or less bristle-bearing: keel and margin often bearded or ciliated, embracing the upper one: imperfect flowers 1 or more, pedicelled: scales glabrous: styles confluent at the base: stigmas plumose with simple hairs: caryopsis elongated, obovate, free.

(1) C. barbata. *(Swartz.)*

Ident. Swartz flor. Ind. Occ. I. 200.—Roxb. l. c. 329.

Syn. Andropogon barbatum, *Linn. Mant.* 302.—C. Caribœa, *Spreng.*

Engrav. Jacq. Ecl. gram. fasc. I. t. 8.—Rheede Mal. xii. t. 51.

Spec. Char. Culm 1-foot, compressed, branched: leaves acute, a little hairy above: spikes digitate, 4—12, spikelets sessile, imbricated, hermaphrodite: corolla ciliated, awned, neuter of 2 awned valves.

Peninsula, very common.

(2) C. tenella. *(Roxb.)*

Ident. Roxb. l. c. p. 329.—Dalz. l. c. p. 296.

Spec. Char. Culms delicate, erect, smooth, 1-foot: leaves smooth, soft: spikes solitary, secund, scarcely 2 inches: spikelets alternate, and alternately pointing two ways: flowers to each calyx 3—5, all perfect: glumes uneqnal, broad-lanceolate, smooth, acute, persistent.

City walls of Surat, elsewhere rare.

(3) C. montana. *(Roxb.)*

Ident. Roxb. l. c. p. 329.

Spec. Char. Spikes digitate, 4—6, secund, connate at the base: hermaphrodite flowers ciliate, awned: awns straw-coloured: valves of the neuter floret 3, muticous.

Mountainous districts in the Peninsula.

(4) C. Roxburghiana. *(Schult.)*

Ident. Schult. Mant. II. 239.

Syn. C. polystachya, *Roxb. l. c. p.* 330.

Spec. Char. Culm somewhat decumbent at the base, ascending, 2-feet: spikes fasciculately umbelled, several (10—20), spikelets somewhat 3-flowered: glumes unequally lanceolate, muticous: lower valve of the sessile hermaphrodite floret ciliated at the margin, awned: two neuter florets peduncled, 1-valved, muticous.

Peninsula.

(5) C. tetrameris. *(Trin.)*

Ident. Trin. Ms. ap. Steudel l. c. p. 206.

Syn. Aira filiformis, *Koen. Roxb. l. c. p.* 326.—Cynodon elongatum, *Trin.*—Digitaria elongata, *Spreng.*

Spec. Char. Culm filiform, roughish, glaucescent: sheaths swollen above, glabrous, sparingly hairy at the mouths, ligula very short: leaves very narrow, linear, retrorsely scabrous: spikes in whorls of four, erect, spreading: spikelets imbricate-erect, lanceolate: glumes very unequal, upper one bristly: lower valve 3-nerved, 2-cleft at the apex, terminated at the middle nerve in an awn 4-times longer than the valve itself.

Peninsula. Bengal.

(6) C. Wightiana. *(Nees.)*

Ident. Nees Ms. Steudel l. c. p. 206.

Syn. C. incompleta, *Wight herb.*

Spec. Char. Culm branched, angular, tubercled above or rough with glands, younger part pubescent, at length glabrescent: sheaths and leaves acute, villous: spikes digitate, 3—5, compact, short: upper glume emarginate-mucronate at the apex, nearly equalling the hermaphrodite floret, the latter rough, densely bearded with villi on the edge above, and below on the back, all the florets ventricose-inflated, neuter ones in whorls of four, bristle-bearing from the base, lower neutral bearded, rest naked, bristles equal, upper hermaphrodite valve broad, flat, lower very shortly 2-toothed at the apex.

Peninsula.

(7) C. digitata. *(Steudel.)*

Ident. Steudel l. c. p. 207.

Syn. Melica digitata, *Roxb. l. c. p.* 326.—C. Roxburghiana, *Edgew. in As. Journ.* 1852, *p.* 183.

Spec. Char. Culms procumbent at the base, ascending, 4—5-feet: leaves above and sheaths at the mouth hairy: spikes 4—5, filiform, digitate, terminal, expanded, hairy at the base: flowers sessile in a double row · glumes unequal, inner one 3—4-times longer, shortly awned: fertile floret single, lower valves awned below the apex and with a rudimentary pedicel.

Hedges and thickets in the Peninsula, and Central India.

GENUS XXVII. LEPTOCHLOA.

Triandria Digynia. *Sex: Syst:*

Deriv. From *Leptos* slender, and *Chloa* grass.

GEN. CHAR. Spikes racemosely arranged: spikelets unilateral, sessile, 2-many-flowered, distichous: glumes 2, keeled, usually shorter than the flowers, muticous: valves 2, lower one 3-nerved, keeled, muticous, mucronate or awned, upper one shorter, 2-keeled: awn straight, not jointed: stigmas penicilliform: scales 2, glabrous: caryopsis oblong.

(1) L. CALYCINA. *(Kunth.)*

Ident. Kunth. Gram. I. 91.—Dalz. l. c. p. 296.

Syn. Eleusine calycina, *Roxb.*

SPEC. CHAR. Culms 2-feet, very leafy: leaves slightly hairy: panicle linear, composed of many sessile, expanding, alternate, secund, short spikes: spikelets on the underside: calyx 3-flowered: glumes equal, twice the length of the flowers, ending in a long sharp dagger.

Banks of the Taptee above Surat. Peninsula.

(2) L. COROMANDELINA. *(Steudel.)*

Ident. Steudel l. c. p. 209.

SPEC. CHAR. Culm thin, simple: leaves lanceolate, acute, scabrous: sheaths slightly scabrous, hairy from scattered glands: ligula scarcely any: rays of the panicle erect, filiform, solitary, alternate or twin, opposite: spikelets very thin, very shortly pedicelled, somewhat 2-flowered, very small: glumes unequal, shorter than the florets, acute: valves stiffish, muticous, 1-nerved, rather obtuse.

Coromandel.

(3) L. VERTICILLATA. *(Kunth.)*

Ident. Kunth Enum. pl. I. p. 272.—Steudel l. c. 210.

Syn. Acrachne verticillata, *W. and A.*—Eleusine verticillata, *Roxb. l. c. p.* 346.

Spec. Char. Culm erect, 1—4-feet: leaves bifarious, large, and with the sheaths sparingly hairy: spikes of the erect compound panicle numerous, verticelled, expanded, linear: spikelets 8—12-flowered: glumes subulate: lower valve terminating in a long mucro: seeds oblong, wrinkled.

Peninsula, in moist pastures.

GENUS XXVIII. ELEUSINE.

Triandria Digynia. *Sex: Syst:*

Deriv. From *Eleusis*, one of the appellations of Ceres.

Gen. Char. Spikes digitately fascicled, seldom 1—2: spikelets sessile, unilateral, 2 many-flowered: flowers distichous: glumes 2, keeled, muticous, shorter than the flowers: lower one interior: paleæ 2, muticous, lower one-keeled, upper 2-keeled: ovary glabrous: stigmas plumose, hairs simple: scales 2, emarginately 2-lobed, glabrous: caryopsis free, pericarp membranaceous, loosening: seed transversely wrinkled.

(1) E. Indica. *(Gœrtn.)*

Ident. Gœrtn. fig. I. p. 8.—Roxb. l. c. p. 345.

Syn. Cynosurus Indicus, *Linn.*—Panicum compressum, *Forsk.*

Engrav. Burm. Zeyl. t. 47, fig. I.—Trin. Ic. t. 71.—Lam. Ill. t. 48, fig. 3.

Spec. Char.—Root fibrous, cæspitiferous: culm compressed, leafy, ½ to 2-feet: sheaths hairy at the mouth: leaves flat, linear, somewhat obtuse, here and there scattered with hairs, or altogether glabrous: ligula short, hairy: spikes straight, linear, somewhat in whorls of four, one usually remote from the rest, rhachis narrow: spikelets about 6-flowered: valves oblong, entire at the apex.

Peninsula. Bengal.

GENUS XXIX. DACTYLOCTENIUM.

Triandria Drigynia. *Sex: Syst:*

Deriv. From *Dactylos* a finger, and *Kteis* a comb, alluding to the digitate spikes.

Gen. Char. Spikes digitately fascicled, very seldom solitary:

spikelets unilateral, 2-many-flowered, secund on the rhachis, distichous: glumes 2, keeled and compressed, somewhat herbaceous, shorter than the florets, upper one sharply cuspidate below the apex: florets sub-membranaceous, lower valve deeply keeled, mucronate from the apex, 3-nerved, upper reflexed at the margin, 2-nerved, shorter: scales 2, truncately 2—3-lobed: ovary glabrous: stigmas plumose with branched hairs: caryopsis free, utriculated, separating into fragments: seed sub-globose, transversely wrinkled.

(1) D. Ægyptiacum. *(Beauv.)*

Ident. Cynosurus ægyptius, *Linn.*—Eleusine ægyptiaca, *Roxb.* —E. cruciata, *Lam.*—D. mucronatum, *Willd.*

Engrav. Rheede Mal. xii. t. 69.—Lam. Ill. t. 48, fig 2.—Trin. Ic. t. 69.

Spec. Char. Root fibrous and cæspitose: culms ascending, proliferous, branched, sometimes rooting, 3—12-inches: spikes short, 2—4, scarcely 1-inch: rhachis terminated by a mucro: spikelets imbricated, 3—5-flowered, awns of the glumes longer than the spikelet.

Common about road-sides.

GENUS XXX. CYNODON.

Triandria Digynia. *Sex: Syst:*

Deriv. From *Kuon* a dog, and *Odous* a tooth.

Gen. Char. Spikes digitate, twin or racemose: spikelets unilateral, somewhat 2-flowered: lower flower hermaphrodite, upper reduced to an awn-shaped pedicel, sometimes none: glumes 2, keeled, muticous, a little unequal: upper (outer) a little larger: valves 2, lower keeled, acute, muticous or shortly mucronate beneath the apex, upper one 2-keeled at the back: styles 3, terminal, stigmas plumose with simple hairs: scales 2, fleshy: caryopsis free.

(1) C. Dactylon. *(Pers.)*

Ident. Pers. syn. I. 85.

Syn. Panicum dactylon, *Linn.* *Roxb. l. c. p.* 289.—Digitaria stolonifera, *Schrad.*—C. stellatus, *Willd.*

Engrav. Engl. Bot. 12, t. 850.—Host. gram. II. t. 18.—Burm. Ind. t. 10, fig. 2.

Spec. Char. Root turfy or stoloniferous: culms creeping, compressed, rooting, branched and giving rise to new plants: leaves distichous and with the sheaths hairy: ligula ciliated: spikes digitate, twin, in threes or fours, linear-smooth.

Common throughout the country. It is known as the Doorba and Hurryalee grass, especially noted as the chief food for cattle.

(2) C. gracilis. *(Nees.)*

Ident. Nees MS.—Steudel l. c. p. 213.

Syn. Leptochloa gracilis, *Wight. herb.*

Spec. Char. Culm branched, very tender: leaves lanceolate, thin: spikes several, racemose, filiform, lower ones sub-opposite: upper glume linear, lower oblong, long-subulate: lower valve acute, villous at the edge and back.

Peninsula.

(3) C. virgatus. *(Nees.)*

Ident. Nees MS.—Steudel l. c.

Spec. Char. Culm creeping at the base, ascending, branched: leaves glabrous, upper sheaths somewhat villous: racemes many, racemose, lower ones sub-verticelled: spikelets glabrous: upper glume and lower valve mucronulate behind the apex.

Peninsula.

GENUS XXXI. MELANOCENCHRIS.

Triandria Digynia. *Sex: Syst:*

Gen. Char. Raceme slender, secund: spikelets 6 or 3-flowered, approximately alternate on a short rhachis, showing an involucrated capitulum: glumes in the lowest spikelets 2, equal, in the upper ones one, bract-shaped, subulate, stiff, hirsute, longer than the florets, membranous-margined; florets 2, when the glume is single, in the axil of the glume and rhachilla, one inner, perfect, sessile, the other stamineous or neuter, pedicelled; third, when present, rudimentary club-shaped: valves 2, lower 3-nerved, 2-cleft-subulate at the apex, with a long intervening bristle 2-cleft at the apex: upper floret conforming, less: scales short, somewhat square, 2-toothed: ovary oblong, smooth, compressed: styles long, filiform: stigmas narrow, shortly puberulous: caryopsis free.

(1) M. Rothiana. *(Nees.)*

Ident. Nees in Ann. Nat. Hist. vii. 221.—Dalz. l. c. 297.

Syn. Pommereullia monoica, *Roth. N. pl. sp.* 33.

Spec. Char. Culms cæspitose, filiform, 4—5-inches, knots bearded: leaves short, rigid, folded, convolute at the apex, mucronate: raceme short, erect: spikelets secund, short: awns dark-coloured.

Common in barren places in the Concan and Deccan.

SECT. VIII. AVENACEÆ.

Inflorescence panicled: spikelets 2-many-flowered: terminal floret often abortive: glumes large more or less surrounding the spikelets, with the lower valve chartaceo-membranaceous or scarious and rather stiff, the former awned in many, awn dorsal or rising beneath the apex and twisting: valve usually 2-cleft at the apex or bristle-bearing.

GENUS XXXII. AIRA.

Triandria Digynia. *Sex: Syst:*

Gen. Char. Spikelets hermaphrodite, 2- seldom 3-flowered: glumes 2, nearly equal, keeled, equalling or exceeding the florets: valves 2, herbaceous, lower sometimes awned above the base or at the back, sometimes entire at the apex, 2-cleft or 4-toothed: scales two, membranaceous: stamens 3: ovary glabrous: stigmas subsessile, terminal, plumose: caryopsis glabrous.

(1) A. Maderaspatana. *(Nees.)*

Ident. Nees MS.—Steudel l. c. p. 221.

Spec. Char. Leaves bristly scabrous: panicle narrow: glumes twice longer than the florets, above and with the florets dotted and scabrous: awn inserted near the base, not exceeding the glumes: lower valves entire.

Madras.

(2) A. filiformis. *(Koen.)*

Ident. Koenig in Roxb. l. c. p. 326.

Spec. Char. Erect, 1-foot: culms naked: leaves ensiform, small: panicles oblong, compound: racemes simple, filiform, expanded, secund, alternate: flowers in a double row: calyx 2-flowered, large.

Peninsula, in moist pastures. Bengal.

GENUS XXXIII. POMMEREULLA.

Triandria Digynia. *Sex: Syst:*

Gen. Char. Spikes terminal, solitary, enveloped at the base by a spathiform leaf: spikelets sub-sessile, about 6-flowered: flowers closely imbricated, 2 lower ones 1-paleaceous neuter, hermaphrodites above similar, terminal one withering: glumes 2, remote from the flowers, very unequal, lower lanceolate, concave, muticous, a little shorter than the spikelet, upper minute subulate: valves 2, lower herbaceous, concave, 4-cleft at the apex, keeled at the back, inner lobes lanceolate-subulate, mucronately awned, outer ones larger, wing-shaped, ovate-oblong: awn divaricate: upper valve 2-keeled: scales 2, sub-falcate: stigmas plumose: caryopsis ovate-elliptic.

(1) P. cornucopiæ. *(Linn. fil.)*

Ident. Linn. sp. I. 314.—Roxb. l. c. p. 331.

Engrav. Roxb. Cor. II. t. 131.—Beauv. Agr. t. 18, fig. 6.

Spec. Char. Glaucescent: root white, stoloniferous: culms several: sheaths imbricated in two rows: leaves lanceolate, slightly obtuse, sometimes sparingly ciliated at the base: spikelets alternate.

A small rare grass, growing under bushes on dry uncultivated ground.

SECT. IX. FESTUCACEÆ.

Spikelets many- (seldom few-) flowered: glumes and paleæ 2, membrano-herbaceous, seldom coriaceous: lower one of the former usually awned: awn not twisted: inflorescence panicled: scales 2, membranaceous or thickish: stamens seldom less than 3: caryopsis free or adherent.

GENUS XXXIV. ERAGROSTIS.

Triandria Digynia. *Sex: Syst:*

Deriv. From *Eros,* love, and *Agrostis,* grass, alluding to the dancing spikelets, whence the English name Love-grass.

Gen. Char. Panicle more or less compound or decompound, occasionally spike-shaped or racemose: spikelets 2 or many-flowered, more or less flattened: glumes 2, shorter than the spikelet, muticous, 1—nerved, deciduous: florets 2-valved: lower valve keeled, 3-nerved: upper reflexed, folded, bifid-toothed or entire, ciliated, long persistent: scales 2: stamens 2—3: stigmas plumose.

(1) E. nutans. (*Retz.*)

Ident. Retz. obs. iv. 19 (under Poa.)—Dalz. l. c. p. 297.

Syn. Poa nutans, *Roxb. l. c. p.* 335.

Spec. Char. Culm erect, smooth, 3—5-feet: leaves narrow-elongated, rough: panicle linear, contracted, 1—2-feet, rays filiform, solitary, twin or several, approximated, adpressed: spikelets 8—14-flowered, pedicelled: seed oblong.

In water-holes in Gujarat. Coromandel. Bengal.

(2) E. ciliata. (*Nees.*)

Ident. Steudel l. c. p. 265.

Syn. Poa ciliaris, *Roxb.* l. c. p.

Spec. Char. Culms erect, rigid, smooth, 1—2-feet: leaves pubescent at the mouth of the sheaths: panicle columnar, 2—4-inches, hairy at the insertion of the branches: spikelets 6—12-flowered, outer valve 3-nerved, cuspidate, margins ciliated: seed obovate-globose, smooth, dark-coloured.

Domus. Dry barren ground in the Peninsula.

(3) E. cynosuroides. (*Retz.*)

Ident. Retz. obs. iv. 20 (under Poa).

Syn. Briza bipinnata, *Linn.*—Uniola bipinnata, *Linn.*—Poa cynosuroides, *Roxb.*

Spec. Char. Root creeping: culm stout, reed-like, clothed at the base with withered sheaths: leaves rigid, flat, or the younger root ones convolute, elongated, nearly a foot long: raceme compound, close, elongated, branches scattered, dense, racemose: spikelets sessile, secund, distichous, 9—50-flowered: florets lanceolate, ovate, shining.

Peninsula. Bengal, in dry barren ground.

(4) E. multiflora. (*Trin.*)

Ident. Trinius in Act. Petrop. vi. 401.

Syn. Poa multiflora, *Roxb.*

Spec. Char. Culm sub-erect, round, smooth, 6—18-inches: leaves short: mouths of the sheaths a little hairy: panicle much longer than the rest of the plant, oblong: branches filiform, short, drooping, simple: spikelets pedicelled, very long, linear, crowded, 50—70-flowered, smooth: glumes obtuse.

Gogo on the Kattywar coast. Bengal.

(5) E. viscosa. *(Trin.)*

Ident. Trinius l. c.—Dalz. l. c. p. 298.

Syn. Poa riparia, *Willd.*—P. viscosa, *Roxb.*

Spec. Char. Culms narrow and with the leaves glabrous: panicle thyrsiform, contracted, elongated, with the branches very short and compound: spikelets oblong, very shortly pedicelled, 6—20-flowered, lower valve most frequently ciliated.

Malabar hill, Bombay. Peninsula. Bengal. It is covered with a viscid resinous substance, having a balsamic odour.

(6) E. bifaria. *(Vahl.)*

Ident. Vahl. symb. II. 19 (under Poa).

Syn. Poa bifaria, *Roxb.*

Engrav. Kunth. gram. I. t. 80.

Spec. Char. Culms erect, simple, slender, 1—2-feet: leaves keeled and folded, stiff, glaucescent, glabrous: sheaths keeled: spike straight, simple, unilateral, distichous: spikelets sessile, alternate, linear-lanceolate, compressed: lower ones 4—11, upper 15—17-flowered.

Mountains and dry localities.

(7) E. cretacea. *(Nees and Arn.)*

Ident. Nees and Arn. MS.—Steudel l. c. p. 264.

Spec. Char. Root of long fibres, turfy: culms erect, low, compressed: leaves narrow, folded: spike simple, rigid, waved, margined: spikelets secund, distichous, incumbent, 4-flowered, sub-oval, convex at both ends, almost cartilaginous: glumes equal, 2-furrowed at the keel: lower valve ovate, obtuse, 3-nerved.

Madras.

(8) E. punctata. *(Linn.)*

Ident. Linn. sp. I. 395 (under Poa).

Syn. Poa punctata, *Roxb.*

Spec. Char. Culm erect, simple: leaves small, glabrous: sheaths bearded at the mouth: rays of the oblong panicle simple, expanded: lower ones verticilled: spikelets rather remote, linear, 12—14-flowered: seed oblique, oblong.

Bengal, in tufts on pasture ground.

(9) E. Mangalorica. *(Hochst.)*

Ident. Hochst. in Herb. Hohenhack Ind. Or. N. 262.—Steudel l. c. p. 265.

Spec. Char. Culm erect, geniculate, with knots and very short leaves glabrous: sheaths hairy at the mouth: rays of the contracted panicle solitary, irregularly distributed on the rhachis, almost floriferous from the base, not hairy: spikelets 8—14-flowered, rufescent, valves ciliated at the edges, ovate, obtuse, smooth at the keel, 1-nerved at the side.

Mangalore.

(10) E. tenella. *(Linn.)*

Ident. Linn. sp. I. 395 (under Poa).

Syn. Poa tenella, *Roxb.*

Spec. Char. Erect: culms prostrate below, branched, 1—2-feet: leaves smooth, scabrous at the margin, hairy at the throat of the sheath: panicle spreading, linear-oblong, verticillate, pedicels hairy at the base: spikelets very small, 4—6-flowered, nodding.

Peninsula. Bengal.

(11) E. plumosa. *(Retz.)*

Ident. Retz. obs. iv. 20 (under Poa).

Syn. Poa plumosa, *Roxb.*—P. decipiens, *Link.*

Spec. Char. Culms filiform, branched, spreading at the base, erect above, 1—2-feet: leaves linear, long hairy at the throat of the sheath: rays of the ovate-oblong diffuse panicle scattered, horizontal, hairy at the insertions: spikelets depending, pedicelled, 4—6-flowered: inner valves ciliated.

Bengal. Peninsula. In tufts on pasture ground.

(12) E. stenophylla. *(Hochst.)*

Ident. Hochst. in Herb. Hohenhack. Ind. Or. N. 664.—Steudel l. c.

Spec. Char. Culm simple, striated, straight, especially leafy at the base: leaves linear, very narrow, somewhat convolute, glabrous: sheaths striated, hairy at the mouth: ligula very short, scarcely any: panicle erect, contracted, rays fascicled, erect, almost adpressed to the culm, racemosely panicled: spikelets linear, 12—20-flowered: florets rather loose, smooth, lower valve twice as narrow as the outer one, very thinly serrulate.

Canara.

(13) E. PROCERA. *(Roxb.)*

Ident. Roxb. l. c. p. 332 (under Poa).

SPEC. CHAR. Culms branched, 3—5-feet: leaves elongated, slender, scabrous: ligula long, lacerated, membranaceous: rays of the large panicle elongated, simple, filiform: spikelets pedicelled, rather remote, linear, many-flowered.

Peninsula, in moist rich soil.

(14) E. KOENIGII. *(Kunth.)*

Ident. Kunth En. pl. I. p. 346 (under Poa).

Syn. Poa interrupta, *Roxb. l. c. p.* 335.

SPEC. CHAR. Culms terete, glabrous, 1—3-feet, erect: leaves narrow, elongated, scabrous and glabrous: rays of the erect linear panicle short, remotely fascicled, or twin or even solitary: spikelets pedicelled, minute, 6—12-flowered: seed obcordate.

Borders of rice-fields.

(15) E. DIARRHENA. *(Steudel.)*

Ident. Steudel l. c. p. 266.

Syn. Poa diandra, *Roxb.*—P. diarrhena, *Roem. and Schult.*

SPEC. CHAR. Root turfy: culms erect, slightly branched, 3—6-feet: leaves elongated, attenuated into a long acumen: rays of the linear panicle (half the entire plant in length) scattered, compound, expanded: spikelets lanceolate, small, 4—8-flowered, slightly obtuse, diandrous.

Bengal, flowering in the cold season.

(16) E. ELEGANTULA. *(Nees.)*

Ident. Nees in Steudel l. c.

Syn. Poa elegans, *Roxb.*—P. elegantula, *Kunth.*

SPEC. CHAR. Culm erect, simple, 1—3-feet: leaves few, small, bearded at the throat, rest glabrous: rays of the nodding oblong panicle solitary, rather remote, adpressed: spikelets pedicelled, 8—12-flowered, purplish: outer valve of the corolla 3-nerved: seed globose, brown.

Bengal, in moist pastures.

(17) E. FLEXUOSA. *(Roxb.)*

Ident. Roxb. l. c. p. 339 (under Poa).

Syn. Poa Roxburghiana, *Schult.*—P. tortuosa, *Spreng.*

Spec. Char. Culm sub-erect, flexuose, glabrous: leaves flat: sheaths hairy at the mouth: rays of the nodding, ovate, close-packed, elongated panicle (usually exceeding half the plant in length) solitary, alternate, somewhat horizontal, branched: gland in each axil brown, hairy: spikelets lanceolate, 20-flowered: seed brown.

Bengal.

(18) E. paniculata. (*Roxb.*)

Ident. Roxb. l. c. p. 340 (under Poa).

Spec. Char. Culm sub-erect, 2—4-feet: leaves long, very hairy at the mouth of the sheaths: rays of the oblong panicle very numerous, filiform, expanded, hairy at the insertions: spikelets long-pedicelled, 4—16-flowered: glumes ciliated: outer valve rounded at the apex, inner obsoletely ciliated at the back.

Bengal.

(19) E. Gangetica. (*Roxb.*)

Ident. Roxb. l. c. p. 340 (under Poa).

Spec. Char. Culms turfy, numerous, branched, 1-foot: leaves small, glabrous: rays of the ovate panicle, remote, alternate, somewhat diverging: spikelets linear, 30—40-flowered, acuminate, glabrous: lower spikelets deciduous: glumes yellow, obtuse.

Banks of the Ganges, not common.

(20) E. nigra. (*Nees.*)

Ident. Nees Ms.—Steudel l. c. p. 267.

Spec. Char.—Culm erect: leaves flat, linear, and with the sheaths glabrous: mouth of the sheaths naked or bearded: panicle racemosely decompound, spreading: rays divided from the base, flexuose, sub-capillary, smooth, lower ones almost opposite: axils sparingly bearded: spikelets long-pedicelled, 4—8-flowered, leaden brown: rhachilla waved: glumes lanceolate, acuminate: lower valve ovate, acutish, 3-nerved, nerves scarcely prominent, upper naked, shorter: caryopsis ovate, compressed and trigonous, truncated, crenulate-striated, channelled behind.

Peninsula.

(21) E. atropurpurea. (*Hochst.*)

Ident. Hochst. l. c., N. 938.—Steudel l. c. p. 267.

Spec. Char. Culm erect, compressed, simple, 1—2-feet: sheaths stiffly bearded, especially at the mouth: ligula very short, torn, ciliated: lower leaves flat, short, upper narrow, folded inwards, nervosely striated: panicle shining, expanded, rays solitary or twin, capillary, beset with a few thin hairs at the base, raylets alternate, here and there divided, forming 1-spiculate pedicels longer than the spikelet: spikelets lanceolate, darkish, loosely 5-flowered: glumes unequal, lanceolate, acuminate: lower valve ovate-lanceolate, nerveless, except the keel, very smooth.

Neilgherries.

(22) E. parviglumis. *(Hochst.)*

Ident. Hochst. l. c., N. 936.—Steudel l. c.

Spec. Char. Culm from the base or a little above it branched, somewhat compressed, geniculate, and with the elevated-striated sheaths glabrous, the latter sparingly hairy at the mouth: leaves flat, convolute, pale glaucous, bristly towards the apex, more or less with longish, spreading, adpressed hairs, at length glabrate: panicle ovate-oblong, loose, rays solitary, alternate, branched almost from the base, erect-spreading, more or less hairy in the axils, raylets divided, capillary, divisions forming pedicels equalling or exceeding the spikelets: spikelets linear, 8—10-flowered: glumes very unequal, lower minute: either valve somewhat truncately obtuse at the apex, bristly scabrous.

Neilgherries.

GENUS XXXV. UNIOLA.

Triandria Digynia. *Sex: Syst:*

Deriv. From *Unus* one and alone; the glumes are united.

Gen. Char. Juba, panicle or simple raceme: rays solitary: spikelets 3—20-flowered: glumes 3—5, seldom upper one 7-nerved: florets more or less distichously imbricated, lower ones 1—3, in many barren, glume-shaped, 1-valved, seldom dissimilar to the upper ones, much shorter: lower valve muticous or cuspidate, 7—11-nerved, upper a little shorter, folded: scales 2, somewhat truncated, naked, or connate with villi: caryopsis linear, elliptic, compressed.

(1) U. Indica. *(Spreng.)*

Ident. Spreng. Syst. I. 349.—Dalz. l. c. p. 298.

Syn. Poa unioloides, *Roxb. l. c. p.* 339.

Spec. Char. Culm decumbent at the base, branched, ascending,

1—2-feet, round, smooth: leaves glaucous, rather short: mouth of the sheaths bearded: panicle ovate-oblong, half the length of the plant: branches short, simple, horizontal, fascicled below, solitary above: spikelets long-pedicelled, 16—20-flowered, with a bluish-purple tinge, ovate.

Peninsula. Bengal.

GENUS XXXVI. DACTYLIS.

Triandria Digynia. *Sex: Syst:*

Deriv. From *Dactylon* a finger; the head is divided as to give the resemblance of fingers.

Gen. Char. Panicle glomerate, secund: spikelets 2—7-flowered: glumes 2, somewhat unequal-sided, keeled, mucronate or awned, somewhat one-sided at the apex, upper usually thinner, nerveless, concave: valves 2, herbaceous, lower one 5-nerved, keeled, mucronately awned, keel ciliated: upper one 2-keeled: stigmas plumose: scales 2, 2-cleft: caryopsis glabrous.

(1) D. lagopodioides. *(Linn.)*

Ident. Linn. Mant. 33.

Syn. Koeleria brevifolia, *Spreng.*—Poa brevifolia, *Kunth Enum. I.* 324.—D. brevifolia, *Koenig. Roxb. l. c. p.* 342.

Engrav. Burm. Ind. t. 12, fig. 1. (?)

Spec. Char. Culm ascending: branches simple, short: leaves short, lanceolate from a broad base, rigid, convolute and pungent at the apex: spike terminal, ovoid or sub-rotund, white, dense: spikelets about 4-flowered.

Common on salt ground near the sea.

GENUS XXXVII. ELYTHROPHORUS.

Monandria Digynia. *Sex: Syst:*

Deriv. From *Elytron* an envelope, and *Phoreo* I bear, alluding to the involucre.

Gen. Char. Panicle cylindric, glomerately spiked: involucre of the glomerules many-leaved: spikelets 3—7-flowered: flowers distichous, beardless: glumes 2, keeled, subulately awned at the apex, nearly equal, shorter than the spikelet: valves 2, lower keeled, 3-nerved, subulately awned at the apex, upper a half shorter,

2-keeled, keels winged, 3-lobed at the apex: stamens 1: styles 2, stigmas elongated, puberulous: caryopsis rather terete, elongated, glabrous.

(1) E. ARTICULATUS. *(Beauv.)*

Ident. Beauv. Agrost.—Steudel l. c. p. 301.

Syn. Echinalysium strictum, *Trin.*—Dactylis spicata, *Willd.*

Engrav. Beauv. t. 14, fig. 2.—Kunth Gram. II. t. 154.

SPEC. CHAR. Root fibrous: culms turfy, simple; leaves flat, elongated, exceeding the culm: panicle interrupted: involucre of the glomerules 3—7-leaved, leaves exceeding the glomerules.

Malabar. Coromandel.

GENUS XXXVIII. TRIPOGON.

Triandria Digynia. *Sex: Syst:*

Deriv. From *Treis* three, and *Pogon* a beard, alluding to the three bristles of the lower valves.

GEN. CHAR. Spikelets many-flowered, flowers imbricated on a slender axil at the slightly bearded nodes, perfect, 2-valved: glumes 2, shorter than the spikelet, lower one smaller, embracing, obliquely sharpened, somewhat præmorse on the other side, upper one 2-toothed, short-subulate between the teeth, awl equalling the teeth, springing from the united apex of the twin dorsal nerve: valves 2, lower ovate, incurved at the sides, bi-laciniate at the apex, 3-nerved, segments muticous, three straight bristles being interposed rising from the middle nerve and two lateral ones: upper oblong, more membranaceous, flat upwards, 2-cleft at the slightly obtuse apex, lower one convolute, somewhat 4-nerved: scales 2, coloured, conical, truncated, glabrous, narrow: filaments capillary: styles filiform, distant: stigmas loosely villous: caryopsis elongate-cylindric, slightly compressed, truncated and bi-denticulate.

(1) T. BROMOIDES. *(Roth.)*

Ident. Roth. Nov. sp. 79.—Steudel l. c. p. 301.

Syn. Festuca mysorensis, *Heyne.*—Avena mysorensis, *Spreng.*—T. lanatus, *Hochst. in Steudel l. c. var.*

SPEC. CHAR. Root fibrous, flexuose, yellowish, cæspitiferous: culms erect, simple, 1—foot, thin, glabrous: leaves linear, narrow, flat or convolute, and with the sheaths hairy: ligula membranaceous, very short, cut: spikes secund, rhachis angular, flexuose scabrous: spikelets alternate, oblong, sessile, 7—8-flowered, adpressed to the rhachis, afterwards spreading: glumes oblong, obtuse, 3-nerved, short-awned: florets imbricated, at length distichous: lower valve encircled at the base by a bundle of very short hairs.

Mysore. Neilgherries.

(2) T. FILIFORMIS. (*Nees.*)

Ident. Nees in litt. Steudel l. c.

SPEC. CHAR. Leaves filiform, loosely villous: spike lax, lower glume twice shorter, subulate-acuminate, broader side truncate and 2-toothed: lateral bristles of the valve much longer than the segments, twice shorter than the middle bristle.

Peninsula.

(3) T. GRIFFITHII. (*Wight & Arn.*)

Ident. Wight and Arn. ex Nees Ms.—Steudel l. c.

SPEC. CHAR. Culm low, slender: leaves narrow, pubescent: spike lax: lower glume twice shorter, obovate, obliquely emarginate and 2-lobed, lobes acute, muticous, longer one extrorsely 1—2-denticulate: lateral bristles much shorter than the middle one, the latter nearly equalling the valve.

Peninsula.

(4) T. UNIDENTATUS. (*Nees.*)

Ident. Nees in litt.—Steudel l. c.

SPEC. CHAR. Leaves convolute-setaceous, glabrous: spike straightish, lower glume twice shorter, acuminate, the other side coarsely 1-toothed: lateral bristles 3 times longer than the segments, twice shorter than the middle bristle.

Peninsula.

GENUS XXXIX. FESTUCA.

Triandria Digynia. *Sex: Syst:*

Deriv. From the Celtic word *Fest*, meaning food.

SPEC. CHAR. Panicle or raceme: spikelets at length flattened, 2—many-flowered: florets distichous: glumes 2, unequal, herbaceous, usually keeled: paleæ 2, herbaceous, lower one acute at the apex, mucronate or awned: upper 2-keeled: scales 2, glabrous, 2-cleft: stamens 2, seldom 1—2: styles short: stigmas plumose: caryopsis linear-oblong, flattened, adhering to the paleæ, or free.

(1) F. Indica. *(Retz.)*

Ident. Retz. Obs. iv. 21.

Syn. Digitaria Malabarica, *Roem. and Schult.*—Poa Malabarica, *Linn.*—Melica diandra, *Roxb.*

Engrav. Rheede Mal. xii. t. 45.

Spec. Char. Culm in moist places erect, in dry procumbent, azure green: panicle contracted, erect, half the part at the same time flowering and spreading, then contracted and the other part flowering: spikelets compressed, somewhat 6-flowered, sub-aristate.

Malabar. Coromandel mountains.

SECT. X. BAMBUSACEÆ.

Fruticose or arborescent: culms slender or thick, usually fistular, seldom solid, branched, thorny, or unarmed: leaves of the trunks withering, of the branches contracted at the base in the form of a petiole, broadish: sheaths distichous, close: panicle seldom much compound, usually more contracted and depauperate: spikelets many-flowered, seldom 1-flowered by abortion, lower florets often imperfect, 1-valved, resembling glumes: glumes 2, convex, many-nerved, chartaceo-herbaceous, often supported by bracteoles: fertile florets 2-valved, lower valve herbaceo-chartaceous, muticous or mucronate, many-nerved, upper one large, 2-nerved: scales 3, large, or none: stamens 6, seldom 3: styles usually joined together at the base, 2—3-cleft: caryopsis free, posticously furrowed.

GENUS XL. BAMBUSA.

Hexandria Triandria. *Sex: Syst:*

Deriv. From *Bambos*, an Indian term.

Gen. Char. Spikes panicled: spikelets many-flowered: flowers imbricate-distichous, some lower ones imperfect neuter 1-paleaceous, the rest with two paleæ, sometimes all hermaphrodite, sometimes one, the rest males: glumes 2, small, muticous, concave: paleæ sub-coriaceous, lower one concave sharp-mucronate at the apex, or subulate, upper one narrow, 2-keeled: stamens 6, seldom 3: ovary pubescent at the apex, sometimes glabrous: style terminal, very long, pubescent, 2—3-cleft at the apex: stigmas plumose: scales 3, entire, ciliated: caryopsis free, enclosed by the paleæ.

(1) B. vulgaris. *(Schrad.)*

Ident. Schrad. et Wendl. Coll. II. t. 47. Dalz. l. c. p. 329.

Engrav. Rupr. Bamb. t. 40, fig. 47.

Spec. Char. Culm unarmed, 20—50 feet: branches green, opaque, striated and furrowed, widely piped: sheaths above hirsute with dark-coloured hairs: leaves linear-lanceolate, acute, 6—10-inches long, 9—18 broad: spikelets oblong-lanceolate, acuminate, compressed, herbaceous, 6—8-flowered.

Western coast. One of the largest of the species.

(2) B. arundinacea. (*Willd.*)

Ident. Willd. sp. II. 245.—Roxb. l. c. p. 191.

Syn. Bambos arundinacea, *Retz.*—Arundo Bambos, *Linn.*—Nastus arundinaceus, *Smith in Rees Cycl.*

Engrav. Roxb. Cor. I. t. 79.—Rupr. Bamb. t. 13, fig. 50.

Spec. Char. Culm thorny: sheaths downy, bristly in the mouth: leaves lanceolate, rounded at the base, scabrous above and at the margins: spikes from all the nodes branched, compound and decompound, regularly clustered: spikelets sessile, oblong-lanceolate.

Mountainous districts.

(3) B. spinosa. (*Roxb.*)

Ident. Roxb. l. c. p. 198.

Syn. Arundo arbor, *Linn. flor. Zeyl. p.* 47.—Arund-arbor spinosa, *Rumph.*

Engrav. Rheede Mal. I. t. 16.

Spec. Char. Culm thorny: sheaths bristly at the mouth: floral leaves lanceolate, acuminated, attenuated at the base, smoothish: terminal spike large, leafy, expanded: branches lax, elongated, bent down or pendulous, simple or compound: spikelets erect, in two's or three's: outer valve very acute: style 2-cleft to the middle.

Bengal.

(4) B. stricta. (*Roxb.*)

Ident. Roxb. l. c. p. 193, and Cor. I. t. 80.

Syn. Dendrocalamus strictus, *Nees.*

Spec. Char. Culms straight, thorny, or unarmed: leaves short-petioled, lanceolate, rounded at the base: branches of the panicle simple, very long: clusters of spikelets very dense, oval, equidistant.

Coromandel and Western coasts. A small straight species and the kind used for boar-spears.

(5) B. ARUNDO. *(Klein.)*

Ident. Nees in Linn. ix. p. 471.

SPEC. CHAR. Culms thorny, 8—9-feet: mouths of the sheaths naked: floral leaves ovate-lanceolate, rounded at the base, shortly-petioled, smooth: spike terminal, ample, leafy, branches spreading, simple or compound: spikelets one inch long, erect, approximated in three's, upper ones alternate, 6—8-flowered.

Western Ghauts.

GENUS XLI. MELOCANNA.

Hexandria Trigynia. *Sex: Syst:*

Deriv. From *Melon* an apple; alluding to the fruit.

GEN. CHAR. Spike compound: spikelets attenuated, cylindric-oblong, fascicled, long-peduncled, peduncle jointed: bracts long-involucrate, 3—many-flowered, lower florets male or 1-valved neuter, upper floret 2-valved, hermaphrodite: ovary ovate: stigmas villous: pericarp very large, hard, fleshy, glabrous, point curved inwards.

(1) M. BAMBUSOIDES. *(Trin.)*

Ident. Trin. in Rupr. l. c. p. 64.

Syn. B. baccifera, *Roxb. l. c. p.* 197.

Engrav. Roxb. Cor. III. t. 243.

SPEC. CHAR. Culm unarmed, very lofty, 50—60-feet, erect, apex only branched: leaves bifarious, short-petioled, broadly ovate-lanceolate, glabrous: ovaries perceptibly canescent, exceeding the valves, conical, long-acuminate, when ripe transformed into apple-shaped fruit with a long incurved acumen: seed solitary, broad, ovate.

Chittagong mountains.

(2) M. RHEEDII. *(Rupr.)*

Ident. Rupr. l. c. 65.—Steudel l. c. p. 332.

Syn. Beesha Rheedii, *Kunth.*

Engrav. Rheede Mal. v. t. 60.

SPEC. CHAR. Fruticose, arborescent, 16-feet: leaves arundinaceous, lanceolate, glabrous: spikes cone-shaped at the nodes of the branchlets, acuminate: florets whitish, in the middle of which is a globular-oblong floret with a greenish style: fruit flat, oblong-rotund, acuminate, flesh dense, whitish within, insipid.

Peninsula. Travancore.

GENUS XLII. DENDROCALAMUS.

Hexandria Trigynia. *Sex: Syst:*

Deriv. From *Dendron* a tree, and *Calamos* a reed.

Gen. Char. Spikelets glomerately spiked, arranged in a compound spike, somewhat many-flowered: glumes shorter than the spikelets, muticous, lower one smaller: florets three, hermaphrodite, imbricated, 2-valved, inferior valve ventricose, subulate-mucronate, upper one narrower, obtuse, inflexed at the sides, 4-nerved, extreme or third floret either perfect or hermaphrodite-neuter: stamens 3: anthers 2-cleft at both ends, linear: ovary short: style long, villous, thickened at the base, compressed tetragonal: stigmas 2, villous, narrow.

(1) D. Balcooa. *(Nees.)*

Ident. Roxb. l. c. p. 196 (under Bambusa).

Spec. Char. Arboreous, unarmed: leaves bifarious, lanceolate, cordate at the base, margins slightly hispid: sheaths longer than the joints, ligula bearded: spikes verticelled, composed of numerous sessile sub-globular spikelets, 4—6-flowered.

Bengal.

(2) D. Tulda. *(Nees.)*

Ident. Roxb. l. c. p. 193 (under Bambusa).

Spec. Char. Arboreous, unarmed: leaves bifarious, sub-sessile, linear-lanceolate, pointed, cordate or rounded at the base, 6—12-inches long: sheaths longer than the joints, terminating in two lateral stipulary processes: spikelets lanceolate, sessile, 4—8-flowered.

Bengal.

GENUS XLIII. ARUNDINARIA.

Triandria Trigynia. *Sex: Syst:*

Gen. Char. Spikelets 2—many-flowered, spiked on a depauperated panicle, sometimes solitary, rhachilla jointed: glumes two, shorter than the florets, acute, muticous, many-nerved, lower smaller: florets alternate, somewhat distant, 2-valved, hermaphrodite, upper ones occasionally abortive: lower valve conformable to the glumes, upper one almost equal, compressed, 2-keeled, back narrow, channelled, sides flat, connivent: scales 3, conspicuous, membranaceous, ovate: stamens 3: anthers linear, deeply cleft at the base: ovary glabrous, styles 2—3, concrete at the base: stigmas plumose: caryopsis oblong, compressed, posticously deeply 1-furrowed, free.—Fruticose or arborescent grasses, branches fasciculately half-verticelled from the nodes: leaves with the petioles jointed at the base.

(1) A. HISPIDA. *(Steudel.)*

Ident. Steudel l. c. p. 335.—Herb. Hohenhack Ind. Or. 1282.

SPEC. CHAR. Branches somewhat verticelled, sheathed, leafy: sheaths hispid, scabrous, or glabrescent on the same branchlet, imbricated, usually bristly at the mouth: leaves sub-alternate, distichous, glaucescent, unequal, broad-lanceolate, acuminate, somewhat pointed: panicles many among the branches, very unequal, sessile and peduncled: spikelets 2—5-flowered: glumes twice shorter than the florets, acuminate or obtuse: valves hispidulous, obtuse, mucronulate.

Sispara forests, Neilgherries.

SECT. XI. ROTTBOELLIACEÆ.

Inflorescence spiked, rhachis in many jointed: spikelets 1—2-flowered, very rarely 3-flowered, placed in the hollow of the rhachis, solitary or twin, one pedicelled, often withering: one flower of either 2-flowered spikelet incomplete: glumes 1—2, or none, coriaceous: paleæ membranaceous, seldom awned: styles 1—2, very short or wanting.

GENUS XLIV. OROPETIUM.

Triandria Digynia. *Sex: Syst:*

GEN. CHAR. Spike compressed, not jointed, bifarious: spikelets compressed in the marginal hollows of the rhachis, flexuose, solitary, sessile, alternate, 1-flowered, rudiments of the upper flower hairy, minute: glumes 3, muticous, lower one minute, ovate, thinly membranaceous, upper lanceolate, slightly convex, coriaceous, longer than the flower: paleæ 2, muticous, nearly equal, lower one keeled and boat-shaped, upper 2-keeled: stigmas somewhat penicilliform: scales 2, sub-cuneate, glabrous.

(1) O. Thomæum. *(Trin.)*

Ident. Trin. fund. Agr. 98.

Syn. Nardus Thomæa, *Linn.*—Rottboellia Thomæa, *Willd.*—R. pilosa, *Willd.*

Engrav. Roxb. Cor. II. t. 132.

Spec. Char. Culms erect, compressed, 1-inch: leaves bifarious, numerous, somewhat setaceous: spikes terminal, solitary, subulate, distichous, compressed: flowers in the hollow of the rhachis all hermaphrodite.

Peninsula. Grows on old walls.

GENUS XLV. HEMARTHRIA.

Triandria Digynia. *Sex: Syst:*

Deriv. From *Hemi* half, and *Arthron* a joint.

Gen. Char. Spikes slightly compressed, half-jointed: spikelets in two rows, two in each joint, one sessile attached to the rhachis through the upper glume, the other pedicelled, pedicel closely connate with the rhachis: glumes free, both fertile, 2-flowered: flowers enclosed, hyaline, muticous, lower 1-paleaceous neuter, upper 2-paleaceous hermaphrodite: glumes 2, parallel to the rhachis, oblong, acute, unequal: styles terminal: stigmas plumose: scales 2, truncated, glabrous.

(1) H. Coromandeliana. *(Steudel.)*

Ident. Steudel l. c. p. 358.

Syn. Rottboellia compressa, *Roxb. l. c. p.* 354.

Engrav. Roxb. Cor. II. t. 156.

Spec. Char. Culms many, creeping, scandent, 5—10-feet, hard, glabrous, compressed: sheaths short: leaves numerous, bifarious, soft: spikes peduncled, terminal and axillary: peduncles jointed in the middle and there bracteated: flowers opposite, all hermaphrodite, 1-flowered: glumes nearly equal, longer than the joint, cartilaginous, obtuse: corolla 3-valved.

Borders of tanks in Bengal and Peninsula.

GENUS XLVI. VOSSIA.

Triandria Digynia. *Sex: Syst:*

Gen. Char. Spikes compressed, jointed: spikelets 2-flowered, immersed in the joints of the hollow rhachis: lower flower male, upper hermaphrodite: glumes 2, dissimilar, outer cartilaginous, flat, prolonged at the apex into a point, inner chartaceous, muticous, keeled and boat-shaped: scales 2, cuneate, dentate: ovary sessile: stigmas plumose.

(1) V. CUSPIDATA. *(Wall.)*

Ident. Wall. and Griff. in Journ. As. Soc. Beng. v. t. 23.—Steudel l. c. p. 359.

Syn. Ischœmum cuspidatum, *Roxb.*

SPEC. CHAR. Culms jointed, thick, floating in fresh waters, ascending: leaves linear, acute, glabrous, retrorsely hispid at the margin: spikes terminal, in threes: ligula undivided, densely ciliated.

Tanks in Bengal, flowering in October.

GENUS XLVII. OPHIURUS.

Triandria Digynia. *Sex: Syst:*

Deriv. From *Ophis* a serpent, and *Oura* a tail.

GEN. CHAR. Spikes solitary or many fascicled, alternate: joints of the loosening or continuous rhachis either alternately or flower-bearing on both sides: spikelets immersed in deeply excavated joints, solitary, 1—2-flowered: outer floret barren, upper fertile, either enclosed, muticous: glumes 2, lower 5—7-nerved, upper 2—3-nerved: scales 2, cuneate: stigmas plumose.

(1) O. CORYMBOSUS. *(Gœrtn.)*

Ident. Gœrtn. Carp. III. p. 4.—Steudel l. c. p. 359.

Syn. Rottboellia corymbosa, *Linn.—Roxb. l. c. p.* 355.—Œgilops exaltata, *Retz.*—R. punctata, *Retz.*

Engrav. Gœrtn. l. c. t. 181, fig. 4.—Roxb. Cor. II. t. 181.

SPEC. CHAR. Culms 3—5-feet, erect, round, rigid, leafy at the base: leaves narrow, ciliated at the base: spikes axillary, somewhat fascicled, filiform, the joints alternately flower-bearing: outer glume entire, smooth.

In pastures in Gujarat and the Deccan.

(2) O. PERFORATUS. *(Trin.)*

Ident. Trin. Act. Petr. 1833, p. 246.

Syn. Rottboellia perforata, *Roxb.*—Thyridostachyum perforatum, *Nees.*

Engrav. Roxb. Cor. II. t. 182.

Spec. Char. Culms simple, 3—5-feet: sheaths woolly at the mouth and above the base: leaves glabrous, hispid at the margin: spikes axillary, solitary: joints flower-bearing at both sides, dissepiment perforated: outer glume entire, smooth.

Bengal. Peninsula.

GENUS XLVIII. ROTTBOELLIA.

Triandria Digynia. *Sex: Syst:*

Deriv. In honour of C. F. Rottboel, a Danish Botanist.

Gen. Char. Spike terete, jointed: spikelets 2 in each joint, one sessile 2-flowered, immersed in the rhachis, the other pedicelled withering, pedicel sometimes closely adnate to the rhachis: flowers enclosed, lower 1—2-paleaceous male or neuter, membranaceous or hyaline, upper one membranaceous hermaphrodite: glumes 2, nearly equal in length, outer concave, coriaceous, inner keeled and boat-shaped, seldom wanting: scales 2, fleshy, obliquely truncated: stigmas plumose.

(1) R. exaltata. *(Linn.)*

Ident. Roxb. l. c. p. 354.—R. Br. prod. 206.

Syn. Stegosia Cochinchinensis, *Lour.*

Engrav. Roxb. Cor. II. t. 157.

Spec. Char. Leaves and sheaths strigosely hairy: spikes full of florets, beardless: glumes obtuse, outer hermaphrodite nerveless, and with the rhachis very scabrous, male nerved, slightly scabrous.

Peninsula.

(2) R. glabra. *(Roxb.)*

Ident. Roxb. l. c. p. 353.

Spec. Char. Culm creeping at the base, ascending, 1—3-feet, glabrous: leaves alternate, approximated, short, bifariously spreading, ensiform: spikes axillary, solitary or twin, subulate, trigonal, shortly pedicelled: flowers opposite, the length of the joints (nearly all) hermaphrodite: glumes cartilaginous, outer obliquely emarginate, inner acute: corolla 3-valved.

Bengal.

(3) R. Cymbachne. *(Willd.)*

Ident. Willd. Spec. I. 465.—Steudel l. c. p. 362.

Syn. Cymbachne ciliata, *Retz.*

Spec. Char. Culms slender, simple or branched, naked or 1-leaved: leaves radical, short, sparingly beset with long hairs and back and mouth of the sheath: spikes twin, dimidiate, linear: rhachis-flexuose, concave externally: glumes of the male floret adpressed to the rhachis, outer one linear, obtuse, ciliated at the back, inner half-ovate, compressed, coloured, winged at the back, wrapping the 2-valved corolla which is shorter than the calyx: female glume one, somewhat 2-cleft, ciliated at the margin: corolla none.

Bengal.

(4) R. lœvis. *(Retz.)*

Ident. Retz. obs. III. p. xi.

Syn. Mnesithea lœvis, *Kunth l. c. p.* 466.

Spec. Char. Culms ascending, covered upwards by the leafless sheaths: peduncles very long: leaves short, keeled, hairy at the mouths of the sheaths: spike simple, straight, jointed, with 2 lateral alternate spikelets at each joint: calyces ovate, smooth: outer glume cartilaginous, inner membranaceous.

Tranquebar.

GENUS XLIX. MANISURIS.

Triandria Digynia. *Sex: Syst:*

Deriv. From *Manis* a scaly lizard, and *Oura* a tail, alluding to the appearance of the spikes.

Gen. Char. Spikes either solitary at the apex of the branchlets or collected and alternate in the raylets, sheathed at the base: joints of the fragile rhachis short: spikelets imbricated, dissimilar, lower very shortly pedicelled, orbiculate or oblong, hermaphrodite: outer glume coriaceous, pelviform, nerveless, inner 3-nerved: perianth 2-valved, muticous, upper seated on a thick pedicel, ovate, acutish, male less than the glumes, 3—7-nerved: stigmas plumose: seed orbicular.

(1) M. granularis. *(Swartz.)*

Ident. Swartz flor. Ind. I. 186.—Dalz. l. c. p. 300.—Roxb. l. c. p. 352.

Syn. Peltophorus granularis, *Beauv.*—M. polystachya, *Beauv.*—Cenchrus granularis, *Linn.*

Engrav. Roxb. Cor. II. t. 118.—Beauv. flor. I. t. 14.

Spec. Char. Root fibrous: culm branched, erect, 6-inches to 1-foot, nodes hairy: sheaths somewhat inflated, papillose and hairy: leaves lanceolate, sub-cordate at the base, ciliated on the margin: spikes from the sheaths solitary or several together, unequally peduncled: glume of the fertile flower very hard, wrinkled and tubercled.

Very common on barren lands in the Peninsula.

(2) M. myurus. *(Linn.)*

Ident. Roxb. l. c. p. 351.

Syn. Peltophorus myurus, *Beauv.*

Engrav. Roxb. Cor. II. t. 117.—Beauv. Agrost. t. xx. fig. 11.

Spec. Char. Culm branched from the base, 1-foot and upwards: nodes hairy: sheaths and leaves hairy or glabrous, the latter linear-lanceolate: spikes scarcely exserted from the sheath, solitary: lower glume of the fertile spikelet oblong, flat, membranaceous at the margin.

Coromandel.

SECTION XII. ANDROPOGONEÆ.

Spikelets 2-flowered: lower flower always incomplete: valves more tender than the glumes, usually hyaline.

GENUS L. ANDROPOGON.

Triandria Digynia. *Sex: Syst:*

Deriv. From *Aner Andros* a man, and *Pogon* a beard, alluding to the tufts of hairs on the flowers.

Gen. Char. Spikes solitary or joined together, or digitate or arranged in a simple or compound panicle: spikelets lanceolate or obovate, twin, one pedicelled male or female or neuter or withering, the other sessile, 2-flowered, both florets or only one 2-valved: lower floret neuter or male, upper hermaphrodite or female: glumes 2, coriaceous, muticous, seldom awned: lower valves hyaline, lower muticous or awned: ovary glabrous: styles terminal, stigmas plumose: scales 2, truncated: caryopsis glabrous, wrapped round by the valves and glumes.

(1) A. PERTUSUS. *(Willd.)*

Ident. Roxb. l. c. p. 258.—Willd. sp. iv. 920.

Syn. Holcus pertusus, *Köen.*

Engrav. Beauv. Agr. t. 23, fig. 2.

SPEC. CHAR. Culm jointed, smooth, ascending, 1-foot: nodes glabrous or bearded: leaves linear, narrow, glabrous or pubescent: spikes 4—7, somewhat fascicled: joints and pedicel of the male spike slightly villous, uppermost hairs longer: awn five times longer than its own spikelet, the latter bearded below, ciliated above, foveolate in the middle.

Bengal. Peninsula.

(2) A. SERRATUS. *(Retz.)*

Ident. Retz. obs. v. 21.—Roxb. l. c. p. 253.

Syn. Lepeocercis serrata, *Trin. fund.*—A. caricosus, *Linn.*

Engrav. Trin. l. c. 208, t. 18.

SPEC. CHAR. Culm decumbent, much branched, 2-feet and upwards, filiform, bearded at the knees: sheaths glabrous: ligula very short, membranaceous, torn: leaves linear, scattered with piliferous glands towards the base: spike solitary, simple: joints and pedicel of the male spikelet bearded: outer glume of the lower spikelet obovate, obtuse, tridenticulate, 11—13-nerved, inner one narrower, of equal length, ovate-lanceolate, 3-nerved: valve very narrow, ending in a twisted geniculate awn.

Bengal and elsewhere, in pasture grounds.

(3) A. STRIATUS *(Klein.)*

Ident. Klein in Willd. spec. iv. 903.

Syn. A. nervosus, *Rottl. in Edin. N. P. Journ.* 1835, *p.* 185.

SPEC. CHAR. Root fibrous, woody: culms branched at the base, ascending: leaves striated, glabrous: sheaths bearded at the mouth: spike solitary, terminal: outer glume of the hermaphrodite floret 3—5-nerved, acuminate, ciliated at the margin, awn many times longer than the flower: outer glume of the male spikelet 5-nerved, cuspidate, ciliated at the margin, ending in a capillary awn.

Malabar.

(4 A. CONTORTUS. *(Linn.)*

Ident. Linn. sp. 1480.—Roxb. l. c. p. 253.

Syn. Heteropogon hirsutus, *Pers. syn.*—H. contortus, *Roem. and Schult.*—Stipa spicata, *Thunb. prod.* 19.

Engrav. Schrank. Handb. t. 342, fig. 2.

SPEC. CHAR. Culm erect, branched, 1—2-feet between, round and 2-edged: sheaths and nodes smooth: leaves flat, setaceous, acuminated, rough: spike solitary, terminal, cylindric, drooping: rhachis smooth below, where it is occupied by male and neuter flowers, above covered with short brown hairs: awns twisted together.

Peninsula. Western coast. Common.

(5) A. POLYSTACHYUS. *(Roxb.)*

Ident. Roxb. l. c. p. 265.—Dalz. l. c. p. 301.

Syn. Anthoxanthum avenaceum, *Roxb.*—Heteropogon polystachyum, *Schult. Mant. II.* 460.

SPEC. CHAR. Culms 4—5-feet, straight, branched: leaves ensiform, straight, acute, ciliated at the base: spikes simple, many together from the axils of the leaves, each elevated on a long-jointed sheathing peduncle, 1—2-inches long: lower part of the spike perfectly smooth, upper part of the rhachis clothed with stiff dark brown hair: awns twisted together.

Western sides of the Mahableshwur hills. Rather a rare grass.

(6) A. HOHENHACKERI. *(Hochst.)*

Ident. Hochst. in Herb. Hohenhack. No. 301.—Steudel l. c. p. 368.

SPEC. CHAR. Culm erect, simple or branched, somewhat compressed, glabrous: sheaths hairy at the mouth: leaves linear-lanceolate, hairy above: ligula short, ciliated: spike solitary, terminal, rhachis hairy: pedicel of the male floret glabrous: glumes hairy: awns very long, geniculated in the middle, hirsute.

Mangalore. Neilgherries.

(7) A. OLIGANTHUS. *(Hochst.)*

Ident. Hochst. l. c. N. 1288.—Steudel l. c.

SPEC. CHAR. Culms prostrate at the base, branched, rooting, ascending, leafy, glabrous, blackish at the nodes and there occasionally pubescent: leaves lanceolate, acute, keeled, and with the sheaths hairy: spikes long-pedicelled from the sheaths, solitary or twin, short, few or many-flowered: flowers tern from the silky hairy joints of the rhachis, outer ones on a short hairy pedicel reduced to glumes, truncated at the apex: middle floret sessile, perfect: lower valve quite glabrous, involving the upper one: awn twisted, geniculate.

Neilgherries.

(8) A. MONANDRUS. *(Roxb.)*

Ident. Roxb. l. c. p. 260.

SPEC. CHAR. Culm erect, filiform, branched: leaves narrow, hairy at the base: sheaths hairy at the mouth: spikes solitary, terminal and axillary, long-peduncled: rhachis jointed, flexuose, hairy: flowers hermaphrodite and female, latter pedicelled: outer glumes and outer valves of the corolla in both florets awned, hermaphrodite monandrous.

Mountainous districts.

(9) A. TENELLUS. *(Roxb.)*

Ident. Roxb. l. c. p. 254.—Dalz. l. c.

SPEC. CHAR. Culm 2—3-feet, decumbent, branched, very thin and delicate: nodes villous: leaves slender, slightly hairy at the base: spikes paired, erect, short-pedicelled, outside imbricated with two rows of sessile awned hermaphrodite flowers, inside with rows of pedicelled neuter awnless ones: rhachis jointed and hairy: outer glume oblong, striated, hairy, 3-toothed.

Near Surat. Bengal in hedges.

(10) A. BINATUS. *(Retz.)*

Ident. Retz. obs. v. 21.—Roxb. l. c. p. 255.

SPEC. CHAR. Culms filiform: peduncles 1—3, terminal and lateral, filiform: spikes twin, woolly: joints of the rhachis beset with yellow fascicled down: glumes striated, one larger acuminate, one smaller truncated, 2-toothed: outer valve awned, inner muticous.

Bengal.

(11) A. FILIFORMIS. *(Roxb.)*

Ident. Roxb. l. c. p. 256.

Syn. A. Roxburghianus, *Schult.*—Psilostachys filiformis, *Dalz. l. c. p.* 305.

SPEC. CHAR. Culms cæspitose, filiform, erect: leaves small, slender, glabrous: spikes 2-conjugate, terminal, filiform: all flowers sessile, hermaphrodite, diandrous, quite glabrous: corolla terminated by a long awn.

Pasture lands near Calcutta. Mahableshwur.

(12) A. tridentatus. *(Roxb.)*

Ident. Roxb. l. c. p. 257.

Spec. Char. Culms slender, erect: leaves small: spikes terminal, twin, hirsute: flowers geminate, one sessile, both hermaphrodite: glumes hirsute, outer ones cuneate, truncated, 3-toothed: corolla 4-valved, outer one 2-cleft, awned.

Coromandel.

(13) A. simillimus. *(Steudel.)*

Ident. Steudel l. c. p. 373.

Syn. Ischæmum scrobiculatum, *W. and A. ex Nees Mss.*

Spec. Char. Creeping: culms slender, elongated: leaves linear-lanceolate, pubescent, bearded at the base: spike 2-cleft: spikelets ovate: lower glume convex, sub-ventricose, very smooth at the base for a short way, striated towards the apex and surrounded with a marginal wing, apex obtuse, 2-cleft, all the margins hooded and bent inwards, upper one acuminate, bidenticulate, slightly bristly: bristle of the floret twice longer than the spikelet: rhachis on both sides flattened, broadish, alternately half-forked, twin-flowered: joints and pedicels grey-ciliated.

Peninsula.

(14) A. Arnottianus. *(Nees.)*

Ident. Nees Act. N. C. xvii. suppl. I. 195 (under Meoschium).—Steudel l. c. p. 375.

Spec. Char. Culm low, branched and with the leaves glabrous: leaves linear: sheaths ventricose, especially the upper ones and these furnished with a small leaf: spikes twin, short, rhachis and pedicels ciliated: lower glume of the ovate-oblong sessile spikelet transversely wrinkled from the base to the middle, cartilaginous, glabrous: pedicelled spikelet hemiologamous, muticous.

Peninsula.

(15) A. Tong Dong. *(Steud.)*

Ident. Steudel l. c. p. 375.

Syn. Moeschium Royleanum, *Nees Mss.*

SPEC. CHAR. Culm fasciculately branched at the apex: leaves lanceolate-linear, hairy: spikes twin, all the spikelets hemiologamous, lower one bristly, upper muticous: lower glume of both transversely wrinkled beyond the middle, cartilaginous.

Silhet.

(16) A. ARISTATUM. *(Roxb.)*

Ident. Roxb. l. c. p. 319 (under Ischæmum).

SPEC. CHAR. Culm decumbent at the base, rooting, branched, ascending, 1—2-feet: nodes woolly: leaves ensiform, hairy, cordate at the base, coloured at the edges, hispid: spikes secund: angles of the flexuose jointed rhachis and pedicels hairy: outer glume of the sessile floret membranaceous at the edge, 2-cleft and striated, inner boat-shaped, keeled, ciliated, somewhat awned: hermaphrodite florets of each flower awned.

Bengal. Peninsula. Not common. Chiefly found in newly formed pastures.

(17) A. ELATUS. *(Nees.)*

Ident. Nees Ms. in Steudel l. c. p. 376.

SPEC. CHAR. Culm branched at the base, strong: leaves lanceolate-linear, elongated, attenuated at both ends, hirsute: ligula ovate-oblong, stiff, 2-parted: spikes twin or single: lower glume of the sessile spikelet oblong, cartilaginous beyond the middle, hirsute at the back, strongly 3—4-nodulose on both sides towards the base: joints of the rhachis and pedicels ciliated.

Silhet.

(18) A. RUGOSUS. *(Gœrtn.)*

Ident. Gœrtn. in Steudel l. c. p. 376.

Syn. Ischœmum rugosum, *Salisb.* *Roxb. l. c. p.* 320.

Engrav. Gœrtn. Carp. III. t. 181.—Salisb. Ic. I. t. 1.

SPEC. CHAR. Culm simple, procumbent: nodes glabrous: leaves lanceolate-linear, very narrow: spikes twin: joints triquetrous, obsoletely hairy at the lateral angles, pedicel surrounded at the base with short hairs, hairy at the angle of the back: lower spikelet transversely wrinkled, awned, nodulose below or smooth, male muticous.

Bengal. Peninsula; growing among rice.

(19) A. SEMISAGITTATUS. *(Roxb.)*

Ident. Roxb. l. c. p. 320 (under Ischœmum).

Spec. Char. Culm decumbent at the base, rooting, branches erect, glabrous : leaves ovate-lanceolate, semi-sagittate with a cordate base : spikes sub-secund : spikelets twin, bearded at the base : outer glumes transversely wrinkled : hermaphrodite floret awned.

Bengal, in newly formed pastures.

(20) A. cordatifolius. *(Steud.)*

Ident. Steudel l. c. p. 376.

Syn. Ischœmum conjugatum, *Roxb. l. c. p* 321.

Spec. Char. Culm branched, creeping at the base, filiform: sheaths glabrous: leaves short, acute, broad-cordate at the base: spikes connate on a clavate peduncle : rhachis hairy, jointed, flowers in pairs 4—8 on a single spike, one sessile the other sub-sessile: glumes of either floret flat, woolly : sessile, floret awned.

Pasture lands near Calcutta.

(21) A. geniculatus. *(Roxb.)*

Ident. Roxb. l. c. p. 322 (under Ischæmum).

Spec. Char. Culms geniculate, creeping, rooting, smooth : leaves small, ensiform: spikes conjugate, closely approximated: rhachis jointed, flexuose, angles acute, hairy: outer glume of the sessile floret furnished at the apex on both sides with hard serrulated crests, inner one crested at the back below the apex : glumes of the pedicelled floret boat-shaped, mucronate or somewhat awned below the crested apex : outer paleæ of the fertile floret 2-cleft, awned.

Bengal.

(22) A. asthenos. *(Steud.)*

Ident. Steudel l. c. p. 377.

Syn. Ischæmum tenellum, *Roxb. l. c. p.* 323.

Spec. Char. Culm weak, branched at the base, creeping : branches erect, joints bearded : leaves linear, hairy at the base and at the mouths of the sheaths : outer glume of the sessile floret truncated, rest all cuspidate : hermaphrodite flower awned.

Bengal.

(23) A. Courtallensis. *(Steud.)*

Ident. Steudel l. c. p. 377.

Syn. Apocopis Wightii, *Nees Ms.*

Spec. Char. Spikes twin, secund-flowered or solitary in four rows : spikelets awned : lower glume obcordate.

Courtallum.

(24) A. mollicomus. *(Kunth.)*

Ident. Kunth Gram. I. t. 96.—Dalz. l. c. p. 301.—Steudel l. c. p. 379.

Spec. Char. Culm and branches grooved, apex and upper nodes villous: leaves linear, flat, roughish: sheaths keeled, smooth: spikes terminal, digitate, 2—4: spikelets in four rows, clothed with silky hairs: hermaphrodite florets long-awned, sterile ones pedicelled and mutic: rhachis and pedicels hairy on one side, awn rough, spirally twisted.

Near Surat.

(25) A. Bladhii. *(Retz.)*

Ident. Retz. obs. II. 27.—Roxb. l. c. p. 259.

Spec. Char. Culm erect, branched, nodes villous-bearded: ligula membranaceous, shortly hairy: leaves flat, sparingly hairy, especially at the mouths of the sheaths: spikes 3—8, collected together, fasciculately sub-alternate, lower ones short-peduncled: joints and pedicel of the neuter spikelet hairy at the margins, uppermost hairs longer: inner glume of the sessile spikelet elliptic, obtuse, slightly hirsute, upper 3-nerved, glabrous: awn 4 times longer than its own spikelet, scattered below with short, above with long hairs: lower spikelet similar to the upper.

Bengal, in hedges and road-sides.

(26) A. bifoveolatus. *(Steud.)*

Ident. Steudel l. c. p. 380.

Syn. A. scrobiculatus, *Nees Mss.* (not Delile).

Spec. Char. Culm branched, apex tapering, nodes bearded: spikes fascicled, rhachis ciliated, bearded below the spikelets, the latter coloured ciliolate, male coarsely 2—3-foveolate at the back.

Peninsula.

(27) A. lanceolatus. *(Roxb.)*

Ident. Roxb. l. c. p. 257.

Syn. Batratherum lanceolatum, *Nees in Ed. P. J.* 1835, *p.* 181.

Spec. Char.—Culms ascending from rooting joints: leaves lanceolate, cordate, stem-clasping, bristly-ciliate: spikes in twos or fours, peduncled: joints and pedicels somewhat woolly: flower sessile awned: outer glume sharply pectinate-serrulate, smooth at the back: beard of the joints of the rhachis long.

Coromandel.

(28) A. SCANDENS. *(Roxb.)*

Ident. Roxb. l. c. p. 258.—Dalz. l. c. p. 301.

SPEC. CHAR. Culms long, branched, creeping or climbing over bushes, long-rooted from the joints, smooth and deeply grooved on one side, flower-bearing extremities erect, 1—2-feet long: nodes woolly: leaves sometimes a little hairy above: spikes 3—6, terminal, short pedicelled, sub-panicled: flowers in approximate pairs, one hermaphrodite, sessile, the other male and pedicelled: glumes lanceolate, hairy.

Deccan, common. Bengal. Peninsula.

(29) A. INCURVATUS. *(Retz.)*

Ident. Retz. obs. v. 21.

SPEC. CHAR. Culms filiform, 2-feet, branched, leafy: leaves linear, radical ones many, culm ones few: spikes many on a long filiform, peduncle sub-digitate: flowers twin, hairy, bearded at the base, female pedicelled awned, male sessile, mutic: calyx in both 1-glumed, obtuse: awn long-twisted, geniculate.

Tranquebar.

(30) A. STRICTUS. *(Roxb.)*

Ident. Roxb. l. c. p. 260.

SPEC. CHAR. Culm straight, 1—2-feet, branched above, glabrous, nodes bearded: leaves slender, ciliated at the base: spikes fascicled on a long common peduncle, 3—6: rhachis hairy: glumes of both florets scrobiculate on both sides at the apex: awn long flexuose.

Mountainous localities.

(31) A. RUDIS. *(Nees.)*

Ident. Nees Ms. (under Batratherum).—Steudel l. c. p. 383.

SPEC. CHAR. Nodes bearded: leaves ovate-lanceolate, finely acuminated, above together with the sheaths ciliated, stiff, hirsute from tubercles: spikes 2—3, somewhat digitately packed together, peduncled, loosely few-flowered: rhachis pubescently scabrous, scattered towards the tops of the joints with a few bristles: glumes oblong-lanceolate, acutish, finely scabrous, lower one coarsely muricated towards the quadrifarious apex, upper one bristly ciliated before the apex, muticous.

Silhet.

(32) A. CONFERTIFLORUS. *(Steud.)*

Ident. Steudel l. c. p. 385.

SPEC. CHAR. Culm erect, firm, quite glabrous together with the nodes and sheaths: ligula ovate, exserted, torn and cleft at the apex: leaves narrow-lanceolate, long acuminate, denticulate-scabrous at the edges: panicle very long, branches leafy, divided: bracts lanceolate, spike-bearing: spikes binate, again bracteate: peduncles enclosed, short, glabrous: joints and pedicels densely hairy: glumes nerveless: awn thin, geniculate, the length of the florets.

Neilgherries.

(33) A. POLYNEUROS. *(Steud.)*

Ident. Steudel l. c.

SPEC. CHAR. Culm erect, straight, glabrous: ligula ovate, exserted, torn and cleft: leaves lanceolate, acuminately bristly, smooth at the edges, sub-glaucescent: panicle sometimes simple, sometimes more compound, many-flowered: primary bracts usually leafy-appendiculate at the apex, secondary ones mucronulate: peduncles enclosed: spikes 4—8-flowered: glumes oblong-ovate, many-nerved, nerves in the younger ones scarcely conspicuous: awn geniculate, thin, exserted portion the length of the florets.

Neilgherries.

(34) A. SCHÆNANTHUS. *(Roxb.)*

Ident. Roxb. l. c. p. 274.

Syn. Cymbopogon Schænanthus, *Spreng.*

Engrav. Rheede Mal. xii. t. 72.—Wall. pl. As. rar. III. t. 280.

SPEC. CHAR. Culm erect, 5—7-feet, simple, glabrous: leaves many, bifarious near the base, above few, soft, slightly scabrous at the margins: spikes of the leafy fascicular panicle many, axillary and terminal: spathe boat-shaped: spikelets twin on a common peduncle: rhachis jointed, waved, hairy: florets all muticous: male corolla 1-valved.

Malabar. Travancore. The well known Lemon-grass.

(35) A. HAMULATUS. *(Nees.)*

Ident. Nees Mss.—Steudel l. c. p. 385.

SPEC. CHAR. Culm branched, filled with pith, and with the nodes smooth: leaves linear, filiform, acuminate, scabrous at the margin, and with the sheaths glabrous: ligula round: spikes twin, short, few-flowered, fasciculately panicled, reflexed: branches of the panicle racemose, straight: peduncles twin, shorter than the bract: rhachis and pedicels white-hirsute: spikelets oblong-lanceolate, lower glume of the fertile one 4—6-nerved, marginate towards the apex: bristle flexuose, twice longer than the spikelet, segments of the valve linear.

Silhet.

(36) A. Iwarancusa. *(Roxb.)*

Ident. Roxb. l. c. 275.

Spec. Char. Root perennial, the fibres aromatic: culms erect, generally simple, 2—6-feet, smooth: leaves elongated, linear, margins hispid: panicle linear, intercepted, composed of numerous fasicles of slender, pedicelled, thin, 5-jointed spikes, each fascicle furnished with its own proper boat-shaped spathe and many chaffy bracts.

Kurrachee. Ahmedabad. Hurdwar.

(37) A. Martini. *(Roxb.)*

Ident. Roxb. l. c. p. 277.

Spec. Char. Root long, fibrous: culm erect, branched, 5—6-feet, glabrous: leaves elongated, very delicate, soft, glabrous, acuminate: ligula membranaceous: panicles linear, sub-secund: spikelets twin: rhachis jointed, woolly: corolla of the hermaphrodite floret 1-valved, awned, male muticous.

Central India, as far as Delhi. Between the Godavery and Nagpore.

(38) A. nardoides. *(Nees.)*

Ident. Nees flor. Afr. Austr. 116.—Dalz. l. c. p. 302.

Syn. A. calamus aromaticus, *Royle.*—A. pachnodes, *Trin.*

Spec. Char. Culm, erect, simple, tall, 6-feet, very smooth, filled with pith: ligula large, ovate: leaves from a broad amplexicaul base broadly linear, 1-foot, margins rough, sheaths smooth: spikes twin, few-flowered, between fasciculate and panicled, reflexed, forming a supra-decompound narrow elongated panicle: rhachis and pedicels silvery-strigose: spikelets smooth.

Khandeish.

(38) A. heteroclitus. *(Nees.)*

Ident. Nees l. c. p. I15.

Syn. Anthistiria hetroclita, *Roxb. l. c. p.* 249.

SPEC. CHAR. Culm slender, glabrous: leaves linear, acuminate, scabrous, hairy above from tubercles: ligula truncated: spikes racemosely compound, approximated at the tops of the branches, short-peduncled, fascicled, solitary or twin, 2—3-merous: common peduncle glabrous, very short, within the bract: bracts lanceolate-acuminate, coarsely tubercled and bristly at the sides: pedicels hairy: sessile floret linear, scabrous, bearded at the base and apex, five times shorter than the awn: neuter ones subulate, scabrous, scattered with bulbous bristlets.

Near Calcutta.

(39) A. PUNCTATUS. *(Roxb.)*

Ident. Roxb. l. c. p. 264.

Syn. A. perfossus, *Nees et Meyen.*

SPEC. CHAR. Culm decumbent at the base, then erect, simple, 2—4-feet, covered by the sheaths, filled with spongiose gluten: leaves large, long, copious, scattered with long hairs at the base: rays of the erect oblong panicle numerous, simple, erect, secund: outer glumes of the hermaphrodite and neuter calyx scrobiculate: awn long, flexuose.

Mountainous localities.

(40) A. PUMILUS. *(Roxb.)*

Ident. Roxb. l. c. p. 273.—Dalz. l. c. p. 302.

SPEC. CHAR. Culms branched, smooth, erect, 1-foot: leaves rather small, particularly the floral ones, which are almost reduced to sheaths: panicle composed of numerous axillary and terminal conjugate hirsute secund spikes, elevated on slender, joined peduncles, embraced by many delicate chaffy bracts at the base: flowers in pairs on the joints of the hairy rhachis, one sessile bi-sexual, the other peduncled and male: glumes of hermaphrodite flower cuspidate.

About Surat. Coromandel.

(41) A. CONTROVERSUS. *(Steud.)*

Ident. Steudel l. c. p. 391.

Syn. A. laxus, *Roxb. l. c. p.* 271.

SPEC. CHAR. Root somewhat woody: culm declinate at the base, rooting at the joints, rest erect, 1—15-feet, woody, glabrous: leaves scabrous at the margin: rays of the loose ovate, nodding panicle spreading, interstices woolly: raylets racemose, 4—6-spiked, pedicelled, rhachis jointed: flowers twin: awn twisted.

Hedges and banks of watercourses.

(42) A. PARVIFLORUS. *(Roxb.)*

Ident. Roxb. l. c. p. 274.

SPEC. CHAR. Culm much branched, filiform, ascending, 1—2-feet: leaves numerous, linear, small, slightly obtuse: panicle leafy, thin: spikes axillary, minute, peduncled, solitary, twin, or tern: rhachis jointed, waved: peduncles very slender, geniculate in the middle: common spathes leafy: either flower awned, pedicelled one rudimentary.

Circar mountains.

(43) A. MONTANUS. *(Roxb.)*

Ident. Roxb. l. c. p. 267.

SPEC. CHAR. Culm frutescent at the base, creeping, 3—4-feet: sheaths bearded at the throat: leaves slender, elongated, hairy at the base: rays of the sub-verticelled conical panicle branched, racemosely spiked: rhachis flexuose, hairy, flowers twin, hermaphrodite one awned, awn twisted, 2—3-times longer than the floret, neuter one muticous.

Mountainous localities.

(44) A. GLABER. *(Roxb.)*

Ident. Roxb. l. c. p. 267.—Dalz. l. c. p. 302.

SPEC. CHAR. Root perennial: culms sub-erect, much branched, smooth, 3—4-feet: leaves glossy, smooth: panicle ovate, verticelled, ramifications simple or 2—3-cleft: flowers paired, hermaphrodite one sessile and awned, male pedicelled, awnless: glumes smooth, purple: outer valve pitted on the back.

Deccan, common. Bengal.

(45) A. FASCICULARIS. *(Roxb.)*

Ident. Roxb. l. c. p. 265.

SPEC. CHAR. Culm geniculate, 4—5-feet, branched: sheaths hairy at the throat: leaves small, retrorsely scabrous: fascicles of the erect compound panicle remote, alternate, spiked from many racemes, filiform, often branched, secund: joints of the rhachis compressed, woolly: hermaphrodite floret woolly, awned, neuter muticous without a corolla.

Mountainous localities.

(46) A. MURICATUS. *(Retz.)*

Ident. Retz. obs. III. 95 and V. 20.—Roxb. l. c. p. 265.

Syn. Anatherum muricatum, *Beauv.*—Phalaris Zizania, *Linn.*—A. squarrosus, *Linn.*—Vetiveria odorata, *Virey.*

Engrav. Beauv. Agr. t. 22.

SPEC. CHAR. Culm erect, compressed, 5—6-feet: nodes smooth: leaves linear, narrow, sub-bifarious, rigid, elongated: panicle verticelled: branches numerous, simple, spreading: joints of the rhachis smooth: glumes minutely prickly on both sides, nearly equal, muricated.

Bengal. Peninsula. From the fragrant roots are made the "Khuskus" tatties.

(47) A. ACICULATUS. *(Retz.)*

Ident. Retz. l. c. v. 22.

Syn. Chrysopogon aciculatus, *Trin. fund. p.* 88.—Centrophorum chinense, *Trin. l. c. t.* 5.—Rhaphis trivialis, *Lour. Coch.* 676.

Engrav. Trin. Ic. I. t. 8, 9.—Rheede Mal. xii. t. 43.

SPEC. CHAR. Culms erect, rooting at the base, simple or branched, 1—2-feet: nodes, sheaths and leaves smooth, the last somewhat radical and abbreviated, lanceolate, margins rough and prickly: panicle terminal, linear-oblong, branches sub-verticelled, simple, hirsute towards the apex: glumes of the hermaphrodite floret almost equal, upper 2-cleft with the awn about twice the length of the floret.

Bengal. Peninsula. Travancore.

(48) A. VERTICILLATUS. *(Roxb.)*

Ident. Roxb. l. c. p. 263.—Dalz. l. c. p. 303.

SPEC. CHAR. Root woody, perennial: culms erect, simple, very leafy, round, smooth: margins of the leaves minutely spinous, hairy on the inside near the base: panicles erect, conical, lax, composed of many verticelled, simple, filiform, waved, drooping, 3-flowered branches: spikelets surrounded with much brown hair: inner glume of the hermaphrodite floret awned.

Mountainous localities.

(49) A. PETIOLATUS. *(Dalz.)*

Ident. Dalz. l. c. p. 303.

Syn. A. petiolaris, *Trin.* (under Spadiopogon).

Spec. Char. Culms erect, 3-feet, simple below, dichotomously branched above, semi-terete, smooth and shining: sheaths smooth, keeled, ciliated on the margin: leaves petioled, broad-lanceolate, very thin and tender, sparingly pilose on both sides, bristle-pointed: petiole 4-inches long, slender, grooved: inflorescence whitish, panicled: panicle branched below, above composed of simple alternate spikes 1-inch long: sessile spikelet with the glumes glabrous, the pedicelled one bearded at the base, and covered with long white hairs, all 7—9-nerved: paleæ of both spikelets awned, that of the pedicelled spikelet much larger.

Bombay. The existence of a distinct petiole in this species, so unusual in grasses, is a remarkable fact. (Dalzell.)

(50) A. Sprengelii. *(Kunth.)*

Ident. Kunth En. I. 508.

Syn. Pollinia fulva, *Spreng. pug. II.* 10.

Spec. Char. Culm 2-feet, glabrous: lower leaves flat, slightly obtuse, ciliated: sheaths pilose: rays of the spreading panicle verticelled, capillary: pedicels furnished with a very long tawny beard: outer sheaths of the florets awned, bearded, ciliate: awn of the hermaphrodite twisted, very long.

Bengal.

(51) A. increscens. *(Steud.)*

Ident. Steudel l. c. p. 396.

Spec. Char. Culm much branched, straight: leaves longer than the sheath, linear, acuminate, callosely denticulate: rays of the panicle 3—5-spiked, one spikelet fertile, bristled much longer than its own spikelet: upper glume of the fertile spikelet long-bristled, glabrous at the back: male spikelets acute: pedicels rusty hirsute from the base.

Courtallum.

(52) A. Peninsulæ. *(Steud.)*

Ident. Steudel l. c. p. 396.

Syn. Chrysopogon Arnottianus, *Nees.*

Spec. Char. Culm branched: leaves linear-elongated, sub-ciliate at the base: branches of the panicle 3-spiked: male glumes and upper valve of the fertile floret subulate-acuminate: lower glume of the fertile spikelet smooth at the side, ciliated above: bristle four times longer than its own spikelet, beard and ciliæ of the pedicels short, tawny.

Peninsula.

(53) A. NODULIBARBIS. *(Hochst.)*

Ident. Hochst. in Herb. Hohenhack. No. 934.—Steudel l. c. p. 396.

SPEC. CHAR. Culm almost entirely sheathed, 2-feet, glabrous: sheaths striated, mouth and margin hairy: leaves lanceolate-linear, striated, sparingly hairy at the margin and surfaces, upper ones much smaller: rays of the lax panicle sub-verticelled, filiform, simple or 2-cleft at the apex: flowers tern at the apex of the ray-lets, lateral ones twin, sterile, lanceolate, acuminate, 3—5-nerved, ciliated, pedicels and base of the fertile florets golden-hairy: glumes of the fertile floret nearly equal, muticous, back and margin bristly ciliated: awn twisted below the middle, tawny-hairy, geniculate above the middle, more than twice exceeding its own spikelet.

Neilgherries.

(54) A. BREVIARISTATUS. *(Steud.)*

Ident. Steudel l. c. p. 396.

Syn. A. aristulatus, *Hochst. l. c. No.* 1285.

SPEC. CHAR. Culm erect, sheathed, leafy, 1—2-feet: sheaths striated, glabrous: ligula densely pilose: leaves linear, keeled, flat or plaited, hairy: panicle rather lax, contracted, rays sub-verti-celled, unequal, raylets capillary, 3-flowered at the apex lateral ones twin, sterile, pedicelled, pedicels and base of the three florets golden-hairy, triandrous: outer glume of all florets slightly awned, awn of the fertile floret hairy, strong, somewhat twisted as far as the knee, bristly above.

Neilgherries.

(55) A. FULVUS. *(Spreng.)*

Ident. Spreng. pug. II. p. 8.—Steudel l. c. p. 398.

SPEC. CHAR. Culm 3-feet, glabrous: nodes woolly bearded: leaves pilose hirsute: ligula bearded: branches of the panicle capillary, naked, 3-flowered at the apex: pedicels and glumes villous: male florets twin, muticous, hermaphrodite one very long awned, awn twisted, hirsute.

Bengal.

(56) A. FLABELLIFORMIS. *(Roxb.)*

Ident. Roxb. in Spreng. pug. II. 9.—Steudel l. c. p. 399.

SPEC. CHAR. Culm much branched, glabrous, slender, 2-feet and upwards: knees bearded: leaves very numerous, rigid, somewhat 3-cornered, upper by degrees dilated from a very narrow base, coloured, scariose: spikes solitary, half-enclosed by the sheath of the leaves: rhachis and pedicels of the sterile floret hairy.

Bengal.

(57) A. MILIFORMIS. *(Schult.)*

Ident. Schult. Mant. II. 448.

Syn. A. miliaceus, *Roxb. l. c. p.* 272.

SPEC. CHAR. Culm branched, tall, 6—10-feet: leaves ensiform-lanceolate, soft, glabrous, minutely bristly at the margin: branches of the large, lax, erect panicle long, slender, verticelled, compound, expanded or nodding: calyx 2-glumed, oval, hairy: corolla 3-valved, in the hermaphrodite flower awned.

Lucknow.

(58) A. CONJUGATUM. *(Roxb.)*

Ident. Roxb. l. c. p. 255.

Syn. Saccharum conjugatum, *Spreng.*

SPEC. CHAR. Culm straight, much branched, filiform: spikes conjugate: either flower hermaphrodite, awned: outer calycine valves lanceolate, much ciliated.

Bengal.

(59) A. IMBERBIS. *(Retz.)*

Ident. Retz. obs. vi. 35.

Syn. Ischæmum aristatum, *Linn.* Meoschium aristatum, *Beauv. Agr. t.* 21, *fig.* 4.

SPEC. CHAR. Culms at the base resting on the ground and there rooting: nodes smooth: leaves cordate-lanceolate: peduncle long, naked: spikes twin, joints and pedicels quite smooth: lower spikelet bitorulose on both sides, upper neuter aud muticous.

Peninsula. Western coast.

(60) A. PILOSUS. *(Wight.)*

Ident. Wight in Madr. Journ. Sc. No. 7 (under Ischæmum).—Dalz. l. c. p. 305.

SPEC. CHAR. Diœcious: culms 4—5-feet, smooth: leaves glaucous, smooth: spikes terminal, fascicled, 3—4 together, white and hairy: sessile spikelet with the lower flower male, the upper female, pedicelled floret female, all bearded with long white hairs, upper valve of the female floret awned: glumes all minutely 2-cleft.

Deccan: common in black soil.

GENUS LI. ANTHISTIRIA.

Triandria Digynia. *Sex: Syst:*

GEN. CHAR. Panicle slightly sheathed, compound, seldom a simple raceme: spikelets properly seven, compound at the apex of the raylets, 4 sessile, verticelled, neuter or male, encircling the short-stalked hermaphrodite, to which are attached two, males or neuter, pedicelled: glumes many-nerved: hermaphrodite valve awned: scales truncated, somewhat fleshy: stamens 3, in many abortive: germen oblong: styles 2: stigmas penicilliform: caryopsis free, not furrowed, covered by the glumes and valves.

(1) A. CYMBARIA. *(Roxb.)*

Ident. Roxb. l. c. p. 251.—Dalz. l. c. p. 304.

Syn. Andropogon cymbarius, *Linn.* — Cymbropogon elegans, *Spreng.*

SPEC. CHAR. Cæspitose: culms many, erect, 3—6-feet, much branched, smooth and solid: joints smooth: leaves lanceolate, elongated, smooth, 1-foot long: panicle thyrsoid, linear, leafy, erect, composed of innumerable bracteated fascicles: bracts boat-shaped, ending in a long subulate point, sometimes coloured, generally fringed with many long rigid hairs: flowers 7 in each fascicle, 4 male surrounding the base of the common pedicel, sessile.

Coromandel mountains. Peninsula. Concans.

(2) A. CILIATA. *(Linn.)*

Ident. Linn. Suppl. 113.—Roxb. l. c. p. 247.

Engrav. Cav. Ic. t. 459.—Beauv. Agr. t. 23, fig. 7.

SPEC. CHAR. Annual: culms erect, 2-feet, slender, smooth, often coloured: leaves few, ensiform, very narrow, broader at the base, and there more ciliated, particularly the small floral leaves: panicles sometimes drooping: involucres longer than the flowers, smooth, cuspidate: hermaphrodite florets bearded at the base: glumes hard, obtuse, a little hairy, changing to dark brown: accessory florets six, all neuter.

Concans.

(3) A. CIMICINA. *(Edgew.)*

Ident. Edgeworth in As. Journ. 1852, p. 182.

SPEC. CHAR. Culms erect, surrounded by a pilose ring: sheaths acutely keeled, keel papillose, ligula hairy: leaves longish, acuminate, scabrous at the margin, entire towards the base, serrulate towards the apex: sheaths long-ciliated at the edges: panicles branched, leafy, more or less drooping, peduncles extra-axillary, surrounded with hyaline scales, racemose, papillose: involucre acute, cup-shaped: spikelets 7, 4 verticelled male pedicelled involucrate, one central and hermaphrodite pedicelled between two males, or four outer pedicels surrounded by white hairs: glumes two, acute, elliptic, outer one 5—7-nerved, inner 3-nerved: valves two linear, torn at the apex: outer glume ovate, acuminate, 2-toothed at the apex, lower one acute, inflexed at the edge, one valve linear prolonged into a long twisted geniculate awn, the other truncated embracing the ovary.

In moist places in central and northern provinces.

(4) A. WIGHTII. *(Nees.)*

Ident. Nees Mss.—Steudel l. c. p. 400.

Syn. A. Bladhii, *Wight. Heyne. Rottl. Royle.*—A. prostrata, Trin. (not And. prostratus, *Linn.*)—Cymbopogon glandulosus, *Spreng.*

SPEC. CHAR. Culm compressed, procumbent: leaves linear, short-aciculate, scabrous at the edges, glaucous, floral, sheaths bracteal and with the 6—9 male spikelets 5—7 nerved, glandularly tubercled and hirsute: fertile spikelet, slightly acute, 2-toothed, scabrous.

Peninsula. (?)

(5) A. LINNEANA. *(Steud.)*

Ident. Steudel l. c. p. 401.

Syn. Andropogon prostratus, *Linn.*—Anthistiria prostrata, *Roxb. l. c. p.* 250.

SPEC. CHAR. Culms many, much branched, geniculate, smooth, prostrate, rooting: flowers alternate, smooth, scabrous at the margin, scarcely longer than their own sheaths: sheaths compressed broader than the leaf: peduncles filiform umbellately 5-flowered from the ultimate wings of the leaves and tops of the branches, ecalyculate: a short beard instead of a calyx: hermaphrodite floret central, glume bivalved, oblong: awn twisted, longer: male florets two similar, muticous, seated at the base of the hermaphrodite, pedicelled, lateral ones four muticous, pedicelled.

Peninsula.

(6) A. POLYSTACHYA. *(Roxb.)*

Ident. Roxb. l. c. p. 248.

SPEC. CHAR. Culms erect or ascending, 1—2-feet: leaves sub-ciliated from an attenuated base: panicles slender, erect, branches few, alternate, axillary: spathes exceeding the flowers, sub-aristate, accessory florets 6, three valved males, outer glumes of the four sessile ones papillose, ciliated at the apex: hermaphrodite flowers bearded at the base: glumes hard, short-awned: awn of the 1-valved corolla long, thick, hairy.

Bengal.

(7) A. SCANDENS. *(Roxb.)*

Ident. Roxb. l. c. p. 248.

SPEC. CHAR. Culms branched, scandent, geniculate, rooting from the joints: leaves ensiform, floral ones ciliated at the base: panicles copious, rays with many raylets: peduncle within a spathe: spikelets incomplete, four lower ones sessile, bearing glandular hairs at the margin, two pedicelled: hermaphrodite one slightly hairy: awn long, straight, rusty.

Bengal.

(8) A. ARUNDINACEA. *(Roxb.)*

Ident. Roxb. l. c. p. 251.

Syn. Cymbopogon arundinaceus, *Schult.*

SPEC. CHAR. Culms erect, geniculate, glaucous, 6—12-feet: leaves slender, channelled at the base, hispid at the margin: panicle very long, branches numerous with many raylets: peduncle within a spathe, pubescent: spikelets incomplete, four lower ones sessile with 2 pedicelled, tawny villous: hermaphrodite one somewhat silky-pubescent.

Bengal. Peninsula.

GENUS LII. APLUDA.

Triandria Digynia. *Sex: Syst:*

Deriv. A term signifying Chaff, in allusion to the appearance of the involucres.

GEN. CHAR. Panicle compound, joint involucrated by a spathe at the apex of the raylets, 3-flowered: lower spikelet sessile, 2-flowered, two lateral ones pedicelled, one or both withering or reduced to abruptly acuminated glumes: florets of the lower spikelet bipaleaceous, lower male, upper hermaphrodite: glumes two muticous, lower lanceolate, 2-cleft at the apex, somewhat channelled, base dilated into a blister or short tube, to which is attached the upper one, keeled: paleæ shorter, lower hermaphrodite, 2-cleft, awned or muticous: stigmas plumose.

(1) A. ARISTATA. *(Linn.)*

Ident. Roxb. l. c. p. 324.

Syn. Andropogon glaucus, *Retz.*—A. communis, *Arn.*

SPEC. CHAR. Culm rooting at the base, ascending, branched, 2-feet: nodes and sheaths smooth: leaves lanceolate, acute at the base, revolute at the margin, attenuated into a short petiole: panicle contracted, involucre of the rays ovate: involucel lanceolate, 2-toothed: hermaphrodite flower ciliated at the back, awned.

Common in hedges. Bengal. Peninsula.

(2) A. GENICULATA. *(Roxb,)*

Ident. Roxb. l. c. p. 327.

SPEC. CHAR. Culms creeping, scandent, slender: nodes tumid: leaves linear-lanceolate, attenuated at both ends: ligula torn: branchlets of the terminal panicle numerous, slender: spathes cuspidate, fascicles 3-flowered, one flower composed of three sessile hermaphrodite ones and a male, remaining 2 pedicelled, one very small abortive, the other polygamous, all muticous.

Banks of the Ganges.

GENUS LIII. IMPERATA.

Diandria Digynia. *Sex: Syst:*

Deriv. Named after Ferrante Imperati, a Neapolitan botanist of the 16th century.

GEN. CHAR. Panicle contracted, spike-shaped, cylindric: spikelets twin, one sessile, the other pedicelled, all fertile, jointed at the base, 2-flowered: glumes 2, nearly equal, muticous, outwardly beset with very long silky hairs: lower flower 1-valved, upper hermaphrodite: valves 2, minute, muticous: stamens 2: styles 2, elongated: stigmas plumose.

(1) I. Kœnigii. *(Nees.)*

Ident. Nees flor. Afr. I. 89.

Syn. Saccharum Kœnigii, *Retz.*—S. Thunbergii, *Retz..*—S. cylindricum, *Roxb. l. c. p.* 234.

Spec. Char. Culm erect, simple: leaves linear, attenuately plaited at the base, short acuminated at the apex: sheaths densely hairy at the margins: panicle spiked, elongated, cylindric: pedicels scarcely dilated at the apex: glumes coloured, four times shorter than the involucrating hairs: styles a little longer than the glume.

Bengal. Peninsula. Much used for thatching houses.

GENUS LIV. AMBLYACHYRUM.

Diandria Digynia. *Sex: Syst:*

Gen. Char. Racemes twin, fasciculate-digitate: spikelets attached to the jointed rhachis, solitary, 1-flowered, cylindric: glumes 2, somewhat cohering into a tube, obtuse at the apex, ciliated and cleft: valves 2, lower 1-nerved, awned from the apex, upper nerveless: stigmas plumose: caryopsis oblong, glabrous, smooth.

(1) A. mangalorense. *(Hochst.)*

Ident. Hochst. in Steudel l. c. p. 413.

Spec. Char. Culm erect, thin, simple, or somewhat branched, half-a-foot, glabrous: sheaths and lanceolate leaves hairy from glands, the latter lanceolate, flat, straws very short: glumes tawny-hirsute: awn twice the length of the spikelets, somewhat geniculate, hirsute below.

Mangalore.

GENUS LV. SACCHARUM.

Triandria Digynia. *Sex: Syst:*

Deriv. From the Arabic *Sukkar*, from whence the English word Sugar.

Gen. Char. Spikes panicled, compound: spikelets more or less lanceolate, girt at the base with long wool, rest naked or villous, twin at the joint of each rhachis, one sessile, the other pedicelled: glumes acute, equal: florets two, lower one neuter 1-valved muticous, upper hermaphrodite 2-valved: valve either muticous or awned: stigmas plumose, often denticulate with simple hairs: scales 2, obsoletely 2—3-lobed at the apex, free: stamens 1—3: stigmas villous, thick, violet: caryopsis free.

(1) S. SPONTANEUM. *(Linn.)*

Ident. Roxb. flor. Ind. I. p. 235.

Syn. S. biflorum, *Forsk.*—Imperata spontanea, *Trin.*

SPEC. CHAR. Culm 1—12-feet, smooth, full of pith: leaves narrow-convolute, much acuminated to a very fine point; panicle elongated, close or spreading: branches half verticelled and spiked, joints and pedicels clothed with long white silky hairs: glumes acuminated, half the length of the hairs of the base, the upper one finely fringed: spikelets 1-flowered, twin, one sessile neuter, the other pedicelled and hermaphrodite: neuter spikelets without paleæ: paleæ of hermaphrodite flower fringed.

Banks of the Deccan rivers. Bengal. Peninsula.

(2) S. SARA. *(Roxb.)*

Ident. Roxb. l. c. p. 244.

SPEC. CHAR. Culm erect, 8—16-feet, often the thickness of a finger at the base: leaves flat, narrow, upper ones shorter, broader, attenuated from the base to the apex into a very thin stiff acumen, concave, all aculeated at the margin: sheaths fasciculately hairy at the throat: rays of the dense panicle alternate, upper ones sub-verticelled, triquetrous, ramifications decompound, bristles stiff, long, white, covered with the 2-valved calyx: flowers twin, one sessile, corolla 3-valved, fimbriate.

Near Calcutta.

(3) S. FUSCUM. *(Roxb.)*

Ident. Roxb. l. c. p. 236.

SPEC. CHAR. Culm erect, 5—8-feet, pilose at the apex: sheaths pilose at the margin: leaves sub-lanceolate, glabrous: rays of the erect linear panicle verticelled, compound: glumes ciliate at the margin: wool of the base short, spare: corollas 3-valved.

Bengal, in damp places.

(4) S. SEMIDECUMBENS. *(Roxb.)*

Ident. Roxb. l. c. p. 236.

SPEC. CHAR. Culm procumbent at the base, rooting, erect upwards, 8—16-feet, glutinous: leaves narrow, channelled, very acutely hispid at the margins: panicle ovate or oblong, erect, large: branches compressed, verticelled, compound: inner glume ciliated: corolla 1-valved.

Bengal, in damp places.

(5) S. PROCERUM. (*Roxb.*)

Ident. Roxb. l. c. p. 243.

SPEC. CHAR. Culm erect, 10—20-feet, thick: leaves sword-shaped, flat at the base, elongated into a thin point, white-ribbed, hispid at the margin: branches of the erect ovate panicle verticelled, compound and decompound: calyx purple: corolla of the pedicelled flower 3-valved.

Bengal.

(6) S. EXALTATUM. (*Roxb.*)

Ident. Roxb. l. c. p. 245.

SPEC. CHAR. Culm woody at the base, 10—16-feet: leaves flat, firm, attenuated from the middle to the apex, aculeolate at the margin: sheaths villous at the mouth: panicle linear, packed together: rays sub-verticelled, short, branched: rhachis tapering, striated: glumes acuminate, and with the pedicels covered with long yellowish-white hairs: corolla of the sessile floret 3-valved.

Circar valleys.

(7) S. MUNJA. (*Roxb.*)

Ident. Roxb. l. c. p. 246.

SPEC. CHAR. Culm straight, 8—10-feet, glabrous: leaves hispid, marginate, long, linear, white-nerved, channelled at the inner base: panicles large, oblong, spreading: branches verticelled and supra-decompound: all flowers hermaphrodite: corollas 2-valved.

Near Benares.

(8) S. CANALICULATUM. (*Roxb.*)

Ident. Roxb. l. c. p. 246.

SPEC. CHAR. Culm erect, 8—10-feet: leaves half-cylindric-subulate, deeply channelled, very long: panicle linear-oblong, nearly 2-feet, hairs long silvery, numerous: ramifications simple and verticelled: glumes thick at the base, callous, fimbriated at the margin: corolla 1-valved.

Bengal.

(9) S. PROPINQUUM. *(Steud.)*

Ident. Steudel l. c. p. 406.

SPEC. CHAR. Culm erect, 4-feet: leaves long-sheathed, very narrow, half-tapering-convolute, channelled, scabrous at the margin, nearly equalling the culm: top of the sheath enlarged, embracing the base of the panicle, terminating in a leaf equalling it: panicle spicately branched, narrow, rays solitary, twin or tern, few-flowered: florets alternately twin, one sessile, the other pedicelled, beset at the base with very thin silky hairs: glumes ovate-lanceolate, ventricosely gibbous at the base: valves very thin, almost equalling the glumes: anthers orange.

Coromandel.

(10) S. ARUNDINACEUM. *(Retz.)*

Ident. Retz. obs. iv. p. 14.

Syn. S. Benghalense, *Retz.*

SPEC. CHAR. Culm thick, 10-feet: leaves broad verticelled, somewhat adpressed: rays of the packed panicle verticelled, triangular, straight, stiffish, divided: calyces furnished with long hairs: corollas 2—3-valved, polygamous, point from the entire very short apex not exceeding the glumes.

Bengal.

ADDENDUM.

ORDER CYPERACEÆ.

Insert after GENUS ISOLEPIS *p.* 536.

GENUS ASCOLEPIS.

Gen. Char. Capitulum involucrated: scales everywhere imbricated from the pits of a hemispherical terete receptacle, of the same shape, all flower-bearing, convolute-concave at the base, terminating in a very long point: stamens three (?) (one *Rich.*) style 3-cleft, equal at the base: bristles or small scales none: achenium ovate-oblong, naked.

(1) A. tenuior. *(Steudel.)*

Ident. Steudel l. c. p. 105.

Spec. Char. Culm thin, erect, somewhat flaccid, weak, smooth: leaves very narrow from a loose dilated straight sheath, flattish or sub-convolute, shorter than the culm, slightly glabrous: leaflets of the somewhat 2-leaved involucre many times longer than the capitule, thin, recurved or straight: spikes of the capitule 1—3: receptacle terete, oblong, lowest scales oblong-ovate, upper ones narrower, all mucronate, squarrosely recurved, pale: achenium ovate-oblong, sub-truncate at the apex, smooth, naked.

Bengal.

INDEX OF TAMIL SYNONYMS.

INDEX OF MALYALUM SYNONYMS.

Malyalum	Botanical name
Acatsja-valli	Cassytha filiformis
Adaka	Areca catechu
Ainee-marum	Artocarpus hirsutus
Ailum-cheddie	Elettaria cardamomum
Akkrootee	Aleurites triloba
Alpam	Bragantia Wallichii
Amolago	Piper malamiri
Ampana	Borassus flabelliformis
Anantali-maravara	Cymbidium ovatum
Ana-parua	Pothos scandens
Ana-schorigenam	Urtica heterophylla
Angeli-maravara	Saccolabium guttatum
Arana-panna	Aspidium splendens
Araya-anjelee	Antiaris saccidora
Arealu	Urostigma religiosum
Atti-meer-alou	Ficus excelsa
Atti-alou	Ficus racemosa or glomerata
Auna-tippilie	Scindapsus officinalis
Ayence	Artocarpus hirsuta
Bala	Musa sapientum
Balari	Cyperus inundatus
Basaala-pou-maravara	Microstylis Rheedii
Basella	Basella cordifolia
Batti-schorigenam	Boehmeria interrupta
Beera-kuida	Hypolytrum giganteum
Beesha	Beesha Rheedii. Bambusa baccifera
Beetta-codie	Chavica betel
Bela-pola	Geodorum dilatatum
Beli-caraga	Panicum dactylon
Belluta-pota-tali	Crinum asiaticum. C. defixum
Belutta-adika-manyen	Celosia argentea
Belutta-modela-moucou	Polygonum rivulare
Bengieri	Sapium Indicum
Ben-pala	Euphorbia pallens
Biti-maram-maravara	Saccolabium præmorsum
Cadelari	Achyranthes aspera
Cadel-avenacu	Croton tiglium

Kansjiram-maravara	Cymbidium aloifolium
Kara-angolam	Aleurites triloba
Karimba	Saccharum officinarum
Karinpola	Caladium ovatum
Kastje-kelenga	Dioscorea alata
Kata-kelengu	Dioscorea aculeata
Kathou-theka-maravara	Eulophia virens
Kathou-inschi-kua	Curcuma Zedoaria
Katou-bala	Canna Indica
Katou-aloo	Ficus citrifolia
Katou-indel	Elate sylvestris
Katou-karua	Cinnamomum iners
Katou-kaida-maravara	Eulophia carinata
Katou-niruri	Phyllanthus vitis Idæa
Katou-patsjotti	Croton castanæfolium
Katou-ponnam-maravara	Liparis odorata
Katou-stjolam	Zizania terrestris
Katou-kapel	Sanseviera lanuginosa
Katou-katsjil	Dioscorea bulbifera
Katou-nuren-kelengu	Dioscorea pentaphylla
Katou-schena	Arum gracile
Katou-tsjurel	Calamus scipionum
Kirganeli	Phyllanthus niruri
Kodda-pail	Pistia stratiotes
Kodi-pullu	Andropogon Iwaruncusa
Kolli-tsjerou-mau-maravara	Cymbidium tenuifolium
Kol-pullu	Kyllingia umbellata
Kooa	Curcuma angustifolia
Kooghei	Do.
Kora	Cyperus hexastachyus
Kolsjiletti-pullu	Xyris Indica
Kudira-pullu	Crysopogon aciculatum
Kull-moollah	Bambusa arundinacea
Kunjaram	Strychnos nux vomica
Kuren-pullu	Panicum miliaceum
Mail-ombi	Antidesma sylvestris
Mala-inschi-kua	Alpinia allughas
Malan-kua	Kæmpferia rotunda
Mallam-toddali	Celtis orientalis
Manirouri	Phyllanthus turbinatus
Manja-kua	Kæmpferia pandurata
Manjella-kua	Curcuma longa
Mella-pana-kelangu	Curculigo orchioides
Mendoni	Methonica superba
Molago-codi	Piper nigrum
Mootamy	Eleusine coracana
Motta-pullu	Isolepis squarrosa
Mottenga	Kyllingia triceps
Mu-kelengu	Dioscorea sativa

Mulen-pullu	Cyperus diffusus
Mulenschena	Arum campanulatum
Naga-dante	Croton polyandrum
Nain-canna	Arundo-karka
Naru-kila	Phrynium capitatum
Nelam-pullu	Aneilema nudiflora
Nelenschena	Arum divaricatum
Neli-pouli	Phyllanthus longifolius
Nilika-maram	Emblica officinalis
Nir-cottam-pala	Euphorbia androsœmoides
Nir-poulla	Phyllanthus depressus
Nir-pulli	Cyanotis axillaris
Nir-tsjembu	Calla calyptrata
Niruri	Phyllanthus niruri
Nir-valli-pullu	Leersia aristata
Noeli-tali	Stilago bunias
Nooren-kelengu	Dioscorea pentaphylla
Ottel-ambel	Damasonium Indicum
Panambu-valli	Flagellaria Indica
Peecupameni	Tragia mercurialis
Pee-mottenga	Kyllingia monocephala
Pee-pounagam	Rottlera tinctoria
Perim-tsjurel	Calamus latifolius
Perin-kaida-tuddi	Pandanus *sp.*
Perin-nirusi	Melanthesa turbinata
Perin-teregam	Ficus *sp.*
Perin-vullie-kelenga	Dioscorea alata or sativa
Pilavoo	Artocarpus integrifolia
Podava-kelengu	Dioscorea hirsuta
Pongalam	Putranjiva Roxburghii
Ponnagam	Rottlera tinctoria
Ponampou-maravara	Liniodorum spathulatum
Pota-pullu	Cyperus rotundus
Ramacciam	Andropogon schænanthus
Schœdaveli	Asparagus sarmentosus
Schadida-calli	Euphorbia antiquorum
Schena	Amorphophallus campanulatus
Scherubala	Ærua lanata
Scheru-cadelari	Achyranthes prostrata
Scherunam-cottam	Bridelia scandens
Schorigenam	Tragia involucrata
Schovanna-modela-mucca	Polygonum glabrum

INDEX OF

BENGALEE & HINDOSTANEE SYNONYMS.

Name		Language	Botanical name
Ada ..	.. ..	B. H.	Zingiber officinalis
Aggur ..	.. ..	H.	Aquillaria Agallocha
Agooroo	.. ..	B.	Aquillaria Agallocha
Agya-ghas	.. ..	H.	Andropogon schœnanthus
Ak ..	.. ..	B.	Saccharum officinarum
Akasha-vullee	.. ..	B.	Cassytha filiformis
Akhroot	.. ..	B.	Aleurites triloba
Akeroot	.. ..	H.	Juglans regia
Akhoos ..	.. ..	B.	Rottlera dicocca
Akola ..	.. ..	H.	Aleurites triloba
Algooch	.. ..	B. H.	Cymbidium tesseloides
Aloo ..	.. ..	B.	Caladium sagittæfolium
Alu ..	.. ..	H.	Arum campanulatum
Alugnuta	.. ..	B. H.	Cymbidium tesseloides
Amaba-huldee	.. ..	B. H.	Curcuma reclinata
Amada ..	.. ..	H.	Curcuma amada
Amla ..	.. ..	B. H.	Emblica officinalis
Amlika	.. ..	H.	Do.
Ani-peepul	.. ..	B.	Urostigma religiosum
Anol ..	.. ..	B.	Arundo bifaria
Anola ..	.. ..	B. H.	Emblica officinalis
Anooli ..	.. ..	H.	Do.
Anvelcutti	.. ..	H.	Do.
Aomla ..	.. ..	H.	Do.
Aongra ..	.. ..	H.	Do.
Aranda ..	.. ..	H.	Ricinus communis
Arbi ..	.. ..	H.	Arum Colocasia
Arend ..	.. ..	H.	Ricinus communis
Arhukee	.. ..	H.	Cytisus Cajan
Arindi ..	.. ..	B.	Ricinus communis
Arjura ..	.. ..	B.	Phyllanthus tetrandrus
Arzan ..	.. ..	H.	Panicum pilosum or italicum
Ashoo-cuchoo	.. ..	B.	Colocasia antiquorum
Ashwertha	.. ..	B.	Urostigma religiosum
Bag-achera	.. ..	B.	Pisonia aculeata
Bag-barendee	.. ..	B.	Jatropha curcas
Bagha-nulla	.. ..	H.	Tradescantia axillaris
Baishee	.. ..	B.	Salix tetrandra & tetrasperma

Botvir	H.	Elœagnus angustifolius
Boyah	H.	Eleusine Coracana
Briktshee	H.	Butomus umbellatus
Buch	B. H.	Zingiber zerumbet
Bachnag	B.	Methonica superba
Budbuhari	B.	Limodorum bicolor
Bujur-buttoo	H.	Corypha umbraculifera
Buksa	B.	Rottböellia glabra
Bullum-doomoor	B.	Ficus scabrella
Buncampa	H.	Kœmpferia rotunda
Bun-chandur	B. H.	Flagellaria Indica
Bunda	H.	Cymbidium tesseloides
Bun-doomoor	B.	Ficus hirta
Bungali-elachee	B.	Amomum subulatum
Bun-huchoo	B.	Arum colocasia
Bun-huldee	B.	Curcuma aromatica
Bun-hoojlee	B.	Phyllanthus multiflorus
Bunnaranga	B. H.	Gelonium fasciculatum
Bun-nuti	B.	Amarantus fasciatus
Bun-palung	B.	Rumex Wallichianus
Bur	B.	Ficus Indica
Bura-beta	B. H.	Calamus fasciculatus
Bura-choocha	B. H.	Cyperus Iria
Bura--elachi	B.	Amomum dealbatum
Bura-gach	B.	Croton oblongfolium
Bura-goot-hoobhi	B.	Kyllingia umbellata
Bura-jal-garti	H.	Panicum setigerum
Bura-juvari	B. H.	Scirpus tetragonus
Bura-nir-bishee	H.	Scirpus glomeratus
Bura-panee-murich ..	B.	Polygonum pilosum
Bura-pini-nuti	B.	Poa Chinensis
Bura-shama	B.	Panicum hispidulum
Bura-sootee	B.	Rottboellia exaltata
Burethee	B.	Cyperus verticillatus
Burhul	B.	Artocarpus lachoocha
Buro-keruee	B.	Euphorbia hirta
Buroo	H.	Arundo Karka
Burook	H.	Asphodelus clavatus
Buro-yavanee	B.	Trichelostylis miliacea
Burrie-toovir	H.	Cytisus cajan
Burunda	B.	Panicum uliginosum
But	B.	Ficus Indica
Buthooa	B.	Chenopodium album
Buzur-bootoo	H.	Corypha umbraculifera. cas circinalis
Cachalu	H.	Arum colocasia
Cajur	H.	Phœnix dactylifera
Camul	H.	Rottleria tinctoria
Cangan-cangn	H.	Panicum Italicum

43

Canta-gurgur	B.	Coix barbata
Capoor-huldee	H.	Curcuma Zedoaria
Carbi	H.	Sorghum vulgare
Carchuramu	B.	Curcuma Zerumbet
Cariari	H.	Methonica superba
Cas	H.	Saccharum spontaneum
Caseru	H.	Cyperus tuberosus
Cathal	H.	Artocarpus integrifolia
Chaara	H.	Achyranthes lanata
Chagul-put-putee ..	H.	Euphorbia chamœsyce
Chakun-tuubnna	B.	Celtis orientalis
Chakweet	B.	Chenopodium viride
Chambuk	H.	Kœmpferia rotunda
Champa-nuttee	B.	Amaranthus polygamus
Chamash	H.	Arum sp.
Chandal	H.	Antiaris saccidora
Chandana	B. H.	Santalum album
Chaplash	H.	Artocarpus Chaplasha
Char-kucha	B.	Arum Colocasia, *var.*
Char-mughz	H.	Juglans regia
Chaulal	H.	Amaranthus polygamus
Chawl	H.	Oryza sativa
Chaga	H.	Achyranthes lanata
Chechka .. .	B. H.	Scirpus plantagineus
Cheecheerea	B.	Achyranthes lappacea
Cheeka	B. H.	Scirpus plantagineus
Cheekon	H.	Celtis orientalis
Cheeloo-nutteza	B.	Amarantus polygonoides
Cheena	B. H.	Panicum miliaceum
Cheena-ganzi	B.	Xyris Indica
Chelmeri	H.	Cicca disticha
Cheenee	H.	Saccharum officinarum
Chenna	B. H.	Panicum miliaceum
Cheramella	B.	Cicca disticha
Cher-kanta	B. H.	Chrysopogon aciculare
Chotogothoobee	B.	Cyperus dubius
Choto-jolgantee	B.	Panicum repens
Choto-pine-nutti	B.	Cynodon filiformis
Chichiria	B. H.	Achyranthes aspera
Chincha	B.	Ficus Chincha
Chinnie	H.	Acalypha betulina
Chiri-chira	H.	Milium sanguinale
Chirchera	H.	Achyranthes aspera
Chooa	B.	Celosia argentea
Chooka-palung	B.	Rumex vesicarius
Choolae	H.	Amarantus polygamus
Choonoha	B. H.	Cyperus compressus
Choon-khurkee	B.	Apluda aristata
Choopri-aloo	B. H.	Dioscorea globosa
Chooree	H.	Amarantus campestris

Chora-kanta	H.	Chrysopogon aciculare
Chota-kajoor	H.	Phœnix humilis
Chota-keroee	H.	Euphorbia chamœsyce
Chota-pendaloo	H.	Dioscorea aculeata
Chotee-elachee	H.	Elettaria cardamomum
Chotee-koomaree	H.	Smilax oxyphylla
Chowur	B.	Curcuma caulina
Chumalipatee	B. H.	Cyperus pangorei
Chumbuk	H.	Pancratium zeylanicum
Chumli-sag	H.	Amarantus polygamus
Chundra-moola	B.	Kæmpferia galanga
Chunder-moolee	B.	Urtica tuberosa
Cumul	H.	Rottlera tinctoria
Cungni	H.	Panicum Italicum
Cupala	H.	Rottlera tinctoria
Dab		Poa cynosuroides
Dabee-dobee	B.	Xyris Indica
Dabri	B.	Eragrostis cynosuroides
Dal-urur	H.	Cajanus Indicus
Damra-shama	B.	Oplismenus frumentaceus
Danga-ghechoo	B.	Ophioglossum cordifolium
Danga-gurgur	B.	Coix gigantea
Danta-rag	B.	Amarantus gangeticus
Darchini	B.	Cinnamomum iners
Debkhotee	H.	Celosia argentea
Dedhan	H.	Andropogon bicolor. A. saccharatum
Deepuk	B.	Celosia cristata
Dengooa	B. H.	Amarantus gangeticus
Dephal	B.	Artocarpus lachoocha
Detara	B.	Andropogon serratum
Deu-gullar	H.	Calamus extensus
Dhal	H.	Cytisus cajan
Dhan	B. H.	Oryga sativa
Dhooli-bansh	B.	Dendrocalamus balcooa
Doob	H.	Agrostis linearis. Cynodon dactylon
Doodhee	H.	Euphorbia tristis
Dooi-keesha	B.	Amomum sericeum
Doolaba-chumpa	B.	Hedychium coronarium
Doombur	H.	Ficus glomerata
Doorba	B.	Cynodon dactylon
Dora-biaroo	H.	Panicum verticillatum
Drob	H.	Polygonum aviculare
Duddhi	H.	Euphorbia hirta or thymifolia
Dul´	B.	Panicum stagninum
Dungura	B.	Ficus hirsuta
Duntee	B.	Croton polyandrum

Durma	B.	Amphidonax karka. Arundo Benghalensis
Duya-kuya	B.	Achyranthes lappacea
Erlachie	H.	Elettaria cardamomum
Ersha-mingula	B.	Methonica superba
Ehteera	B.	Ophioglossum cordifolium
Elwa	H.	Aloe perfoliata
Erundie	H.	Ricinus communis. Jatropha curcas
Esrabel	H.	Aristolochia Indica
Faltar	H.	Borassus flabelliformis (*fem.*)
Felfildraz	H.	Chavica Roxburghii
Felfil-gird	H.	Piper nigrum
Gab-nul	B.	Amphidonax Benghalensis
Gada-poorna	B.	Boerhaavia procumbens
Gagandhool	H.	Pandanus odoratissimus
Gaglee	H.	Arum maculatum
Gandar	H.	Andropogon muricatum
Gandbel	H.	Andropogon schænanthus
Gangatiah	H.	Achyranthes alternifolia
Gangbena	B.	Panicum strictum
Ganjh	H.	Anatherum muricatum
Ganna	H.	Saccharum officinarum
Geel-chumli	B.	Amarantus tenuifolius
Gewa	H.	Excœcaria agallocha
Ghanur	H.	Panicum dactylon
Ghechoo	H.	Aponogeton monostachyon
Gheekomar	H.	Aloe Indica
Gheentee-nutee	B.	Amarantus tenuiflorus
Ghetkol	B.	Typhonium orixense
Ghrito-koomaree	B. H.	Aloe perfoliata
Ghundo-bela	H.	Andropogon citratum
Ghun	B.	Cyperus rotundus
Glatchandul	B.	Methonica superba
Goyahya	B.	Andropogon punctatum
Gobura-dengooa	B.	Amarantus lividus
Goea	B.	Areca catechu
Gola-methee	B.	Cyperus seminudus
Gol-mirch	H.	Piper nigrum
Gol-mulunga	B.	Cyperus elatus
Gol-shingra	B.	Quercus serratus
Goolar	H.	Ficus racemosa
Gooli-kesh	H.	Amarantus cruentus
Gooree	B.	Eriocaulon quinquangulare
Goori	H.	Scirpus squarrosus
Goori-kuchoo	B.	Arum colocasia
Goori-schiora	B.	Ficus rubescens

Goorooma	B. H.	Apluda aristata
Goorooma	H.	Limodorum virens
Goothoobee	B.	Cyperus monocephalus
Gootia-shook-china ..	H.	Smilax lanceæfolia
Gooti-sheora	B.	Ficus heterophylla
Goruk-pluma	B.	Limodorum virens
Guana	B.	Nipa fruticans
Guara	B.	Elœagnus conferta
Gubna	B.	Nipa fruticans
Guj-pippul	B.	Scindapsus officinalis
Gundha-bena	B.	Andropogon schænanthus
Gundbel	H.	Do.
Gundha-goorana	B.	Andropogon glabrum
Gungatiga	B.	Achyranthes alternifolia
Gunna	H.	Saccharum officinarum
Guraniya-aloo	B. H.	Dioscorea rubella
Gurgur..	H.	Coix barbata
Guya-ushwuttha	B.	Ficus cordifolia
Guz-peepul	B.	Scindapsus officinalis
Hajur-muni	B.	Phyllanthus urinaria
Hakoee	B. H.	Croton polyandrum
Hakoon	H.	Croton Roxburghii
Halla	H.	Blyxa octandra
Hamkatajoli	B.	Phyllanthus reticulatus
Harchara	H.	Flagellaria Indica
Harfuroorie	H.	Cicca disticha
Hari	H.	Aristolochia Indica
Harpung	H.	Arum gracile
Harrialee	H.	Agrostis linearis
Heluncha	B. H.	Hingcha repens
Hema-champa	B.	Hedychium flavum
Hental	B.	Phœnix paludosa
Hijli-badam	H.	Aleurites triloba
Hirina	H.	Smilax glabra
Hogla	B.	Typha elephantina
Hooret	B.	Achyranthes centrostachys
Hoohooriya	B.	Achyranthes aspera
Hooroo	B.	Sapium Indicum
Huldee	B. H.	Curcuma longa
Huldee-moorga	B.	Celosia cristata
Humula	B.	Kæmpferia galanga
Huri	H.	Casuarina muricata
Hurida	B.	Curcuma longa
Huri phul	B.	Phyllanthus cheramela
Hurivilasinee	B.	Curcuma longa
Hurmur-gallar	H.	Calamus quinquenervius
Hurria-shook-china ..	B.	Smilax glabra
Ibharankusha	B. H.	Andropogon Iwarancusa

Ik	B. H.	Saccharum officinarum
Isarmel	B. H.	Aristolochia Indica
Ishurmool	B. H.	Do.
Isrievayl	H.	Do.
Jadwar..	H.	Curcuma Zedoaria
Jaggeri..	H.	Holcus saccharatus
Jalgantee	B.	Panicum helopus. P. hirsutus
Jalmootee	B.	Cyperus pygmœus
Jamalghota	H.	Croton tiglium
Janeka	B.	Rhopala robusta
Janewa..	H.	Agrostis linearis
Janghi	H.	Hydrilla verticillata
Jaree	H.	Holcus saccharatus
Jaroo	H.	Aristida setacea
Jarge	H.	Valisneria alternifolia
Jatadhari	H.	Celosia cristata
Jaundri	H.	Sorghum vulgare
Jeeapotra	H.	Putranjiva Roxburghii
Jeebun	B.	Sponia orientalis
Jeel-chumli	B.	Amarantus tenuifolius
Jeel-gurgur, or Kanch ..	B. H.	Coix lacryma
Jhaaji	B.	Chara involucrata
Jidoo-palung	B.	Salicornia Indica
Jol-palung	B.	Rumex acutus
Jondla	H.	Sorghum vulgare
Jooar-jooaree	H.	Holcus saccharatus
Joopi	B.	Scirpus anceps
Joopi-kunka	B. H.	Panicum tenellum
Jow	B.	Casuarina muricata
Jowera	H.	Rhopala robusta
Juguga-dumoor	B.	Ficus glomerata
Junar	H.	Andropogon bicolor
Junglee-adruk	H.	Zingiber capitatum
Junglai-huldee	B.	Curcuma Zedoaria
Junglai-kandi	H.	Dracontium polyphyllum
Junglai-piaz	H.	Erythronium Indicum
Junglai-kajoor	B.	Phœnix acaulis
Jutamasi	H.	Cyperus stoloniferus
Juvani	B.	Scirpus quinquangularis
Jyal	B.	Croton tiglium
Kach-kula	B. H.	Musa paradisiaca
Kagara..	H.	Saccharum spontaneum
Kajur	H.	Elate sylvestris
Kajooli..	B. H.	Saccharum officinarum
Kakhur	B. H.	Curcuma Zedoaria
Kakoon	H.	Panicum Italicum
Kaku-doomoor	B.	Ficus oppositifolia
Kala-deodhan	B.	Andropogon bicolor

Kala-huldee	B.	Curcuma cæsia
Kala-jooar	H.	Andropogon bicolor
Kala-kuchoo	B.	Arum colocasia
Kala-mirch	H.	Piper nigrum
Kamaloo	B. H.	Dioscorea alata
Kamhogla	B.	Typha elephantina
Kamrup	B.	Ficus benjamina
Kamud	H.	Rottlera tinctòria
Kanch-gurgur	B.	Coix lacryma
Kanchkoori	H.	Tragia cannabina
Kanchura	B.	Commelyna Benghalensis
Kanda	H.	Erythronium Indicum
Kanduli	B.	Commelyna nudiflora
Kangni	B. H.	Panicum Italicum
Kangoo-kungnee	B.	Do.
Kanjam-boora	H.	Kœmpferia angustifolia.
Kanka-juriya	H.	Milium filiforme
Kankhura	B.	Urtica tenacissima
Kanoor	B. H.	Crinum Zeylanicum
Kanooraka	H.	Commelyna Benghalensis
Karshera	B.	Do.
Kanta-kuchoo	B. H.	Pothos cæsia
Kantal	B.	Artocarpus integrifolia
Kanta-man	B.	Pothos heterophylla
Kanta-nuti	B.	Amarantus spinosus
Kapila	H.	Rottlera tinctoria
Karak-bet	B.	Calamus latifolius
Karbi	H.	Sorghum vulgare
Kariari	H.	Methonica superba
Kas	H.	Saccharum spontaneum
Kashiya	B.	Do.
Kashta	B.	Curcuma xanthorhiza
Kat-chandan	H.	Santalum album
Katch-kula	B. H.	Musa sapientum
Katee-rajgeree	H.	Amarantus spinosus
Kathœa-bun-jhoopie ..	B.	Dendrobium veratrifolium
Kathajorung	B.	Kœmpferia secunda
Kathlee	H.	Panicum frumentaceum
Krtheea-laffear	B.	Hedychium gracile
Kathea-tilook-seer ..	B.	Hedychium flavum
Kanto-aloo	B.	Dioscorea pentaphylla
Kayla	H.	Musa paradisiaca
Kea	B.	Pandanus odoratissimus
Kea-kanta	B.	Pandanus fetidus
Keco	B. H.	Costus speciosus
Keeramar	H.	Aristolochia bracteata
Keyjoor	H.	Phœnix dactylifera
Kendru	B.	Commelyna nudiflora
Keora	H.	Pandanus odoratissimus
Keshar	B.	Scirpus kysoor

Keshoor	B.	Rottlera tinctoria
Keshuree-melunga	B.	Fimbristylis schœnoides
Ketgi	H.	Pandanus odoratissimus
Khamach	H.	Carpopogon niveum
Khas-khas	H.	Anatherum muricatum
Khoodee-okra	B. H.	Croton plicatum
Khoodi-jam	B. H.	Antidesma paniculata
Khor or Khror	B.	Anatherum muricatum
Khoree	B.	Saccharum semidecumbens
Khugura	B.	Saccharum spontaneum
Khul	H.	Œrua lanata
Khuloa	H.	Saccharum officinarum
Khum-aloo	B.	Dioscorea alata
Khurma	H.	Phœnix dactylifera
Kiraneli	B.	Phyllanthus niruri
Koda	B.	Paspalum scrobiculatum
Kolshia	B.	Leersia aristata
Kolukung	B.	Piper nigrum
Kolunjan	B.	Alpinia galanga
Komaree	B.	Aloe litoralis
Konee	B. H.	Poa unioloides
Koobel	H.	Andropogon martini
Koodom-bet	B.	Calamus polygamus
Kooknora-neja	B.	Methonica superba
Kookoor aloo	B. H.	Dioscorea anguina
Kookoor-chita	B.	Tetranthera Roxburghii
Koomala-jundi	B.	Rottlera tinctoria
Koomurka	B. H.	Smilax ovalifolia
Koonk	B.	Phœnix acaulis
Koonkee	B.	Sorghum cernuum
Kooppie	H.	Acalypha Indica
Koosh	B. H.	Poa cynosuroides
Kooshiar	B.	Saccharum officinarum
Koost	B.	Costus speciosus
Kootha	B. H.	Poa cynosuroides
Kora	H.	Panicum Italicum
Koraloo	H.	Do.
Koratiya-juvani	B. H.	Scirpus complanatus
Korya-doombar	H.	Ficus oppositifolia
Korunkoosha	B.	Andropogon nardus
Kuchiree	B.	Arum fornicatum
Kuch-kuchiya	B.	Papyrus tegetiformis.
Kuchoo	B.	Colocasia antiquorum
Kuchoo-gundhubee	H.	Calla aromatica
Kudali	B.	Phrynium dichotomum. Musa sapientum
Kukto-pooin	B.	Basella cordifolia
Kula	B.	Musa sapientum
Kula-moocha	H.	Andropogon laxum
Kullooa	B.	Saccharum officinarum

Kulusnar	B. H.	Panicum paludosum
Kamula	B.	Kæmpferia galanga
Kunda	H.	Tacca pinnatifida
Kungoo	B. H.	Setaria Italica
Kunjan-boora	H.	Kæmpferia angustifolia
Kunka-nuti	B.	Amarantus atropurpureus
Kunkoora	B.	Urtica tenacissima
Kunoor	H.	Pavia Indica
Kunuk-jhinjhi	H.	Polygonum elegans
Kunwar	H.	Aloe Indica
Kupoor-kuchree	H.	Hedychium spicatum
Kuran-kusha	B. H.	Andropogon Iwarancusa
Kuratiya juvani	H.	Scirpus complanatus
Kurbi	H.	Sorghum vulgare
Kurboor	B.	Curcuma reclinata
Kurbuthwa	B.	Chenopodium gangeticum
Kurelli	B.	Commelyna benghalensis
Kurki	B.	Rotboellia perforata
Kurma	H.	Phœnix dactylifera
Kusha	H.	Poa cynosuroides
Kushneer	B.	Ficus elastica
Kutchoor	H.	Curcuma Zerumbet
Kuth-goolurea	H.	Ficus goolerea
Kutul-but	B.	Ficus laccifera
Kuya-duya	H.	Achyranthes lappacea
Kyeree	H.	Euphorbia chamæsyce, hirta or thymifolia
Lahara	H.	Holcus spicatus
Lalbichutee	H.	Urtica interrupta
Lal-betoo	B.	Chenopodium album
Lal-champa-nutee ..	B.	Amarantus polygamus
Lal-chirchiri	H.	Achyranthes aspera
Lal-guranya	B.	Dioscorea purpurea
Lal-moorga	B. H.	Celosia cristata
Lal-luta-kudum	H.	Urtica globulifera
Lal-serinchee	H.	Achyranthes ferruginea
Lal subjuya	H.	Canna Indica
Langool	B.	Methonica superba
Langul	B.	Commelyna salicifolia
Lanka-saj	B.	Euphorbia tirucalli
Lapta	H.	Panicum verticillatum
Loaree	B.	Phyllanthus longifolius
Loari	B.	Andropogon Bladhii
Lodh	B.	Phyllanthus longifolius
Louka	H.	Pontederia vaginalis
Lovari	H.	Andropogon scandens
Lupta	H.	Panicum semi-verticillatum
Luta-doomoor	B. H.	Ficus vagans
Luta-kudum	H.	Urtica naucleiflora

Luta-muhooriya	B.	Achyranthes alternifolia. Digera muricata
Lutco	B.	Pierardia sapida
Lutha	B.	Do.
Lutman	H.	Deeringia celosioides
Maad	B. H.	Eleusine coracana
Maat-tumbree	H.	Amarantus oleraceus
Machootie	H.	Polygonum aviculare
Madarpatee	B. H.	Phrynium dichotomum
Madoor-katee	B. H.	Cyperus tegetus
Madunirbisha	B. H.	Kæmpferia angustifolia
Mahaburee-butch ..	B. H.	Zingiber Zerumbet
Mainphul	H.	Aleurites triloba
Mairrua	H.	Cynosurus cristatus
Makura-jali	B. H.	Eleusine Egyptiaca
Malankura	B. H.	Eleusine Indica
Man-kuchoo	B. H.	Arum Indicum
Maoz-ka-jhar	B. H.	Musa sapientum
Mapoori-bet	B.	Calamus gracilis
Markea..	B.	Rottlera tetracocca
Marsa	H.	Amarantus oleraceus
Matunkuri	H.	Eleusine Indica
Melencha	B.	Ischœmum aristatum
Miarmee	B.	Limodorum candidum
Mirchia-gand	H.	Andropogon Iwarancusa
Moarba	B.	Sanseviera Roxburghiana
Mocha	H.	Musa sapientum
Mookta-juree	B.	Acalypha Indica
Mookta-patee	B.	Phrynium dichotomum
Moorgabie	H.	Sanseviera zeylanica
Moor-moori	H.	Scirpus squarrosus
Moostaka	H.	Cyperus rotundus
Mootha..	B. H.	Cyperus rotundus
Moothoo	B.	Cyperus hexastachyus
Morung-elachee	B. H.	Amomum aromaticum
Moti-munda	B.	Tacca lœvis
Moo-aloo	B. H.	Dioscorea aculeata
Muede-lukree	B.	Tetranthera apetala
Muhabaree-buch	B.	Zingiber Zerumbet
Mukoo	H.	Andropogon bicolor
Munga	B.	Sanseviera zeylanica
Munja	H.	Saccharum munja
Munrwee	H.	Cynosurus coracanus
Munta	B. H.	Ischœmum aristatum
Murha	B. H.	Eleusine coracana
Murta	H.	Sanseviera zeylanica
Myna	B.	Paspalum stoloniferum
Naee	B.	Arundo karka

Naga	B.	Cyperus tenuis
Nagla	H.	Eleusine coracana
Nagree	B.	Euphorbia antiquorum
Nagur-mootha	B.	Cyperus tenuis
Nal	H.	Arundo karka
Nana-wita	B.	Gnetum scandens
Nara-shij	B. H.	Euphorbia antiquorum
Nardul	H.	Panicum interruptum
Nareel	H.	Cocos nucifera
Narikel	B. H.	Do.
Narnul	B.	Amphidonax karka
Natchnee	H.	Eleusine coracana
Neela-kuntha	B.	Curcuma cœsia
Niah-mooslie	H.	Curculigo orchioides
Nigala	H.	Arundo karka
Nirabisi	H.	Curcuma Zedoaria
Nirbisee	B.	Kyllingia monocephala
Nooreea	H.	Achyranthes scandens
Nooka	B.	Pontedera vaginalis
Nubaree	B.	Cicca disticha
Nuckchilnie	H.	Trophis aspera. Epicarpurus orientalis
Nul	B.	Amphidonax karka
Nuree	B.	Cicca disticha
Oaloa	B.	Tetranthera fruticosa
Obujee	H.	Rumex obtusifolius
Ol	B. H.	Amorphophallus campanulatus
Oodbeg	B.	Areca catechu
Oogul	H.	Fagopyrum esculentum
Ooloo	B.	Saccharum cylindricum
Oombur	H.	Ficus glomerata
Orol	B.	Cajanus Indicus
Orook	B.	Laurus glaucescens
Osia	H.	Anatherum muricatum
Pahari-pipul	B.	Piper sylvaticum
Pakar	B.	Ficus venosa
Paluk	H.	Piper nigrum
Palung	H.	Beta benghalensis
Pana	B.	Pistia stratiotes
Panee-doorba	B.	Agrostis tenacissima
Panee-juma	B.	Salix tetrasperma
Panee-kuchura	B.	Commelyna salicifolia
Panee-kula	B.	Damasonium Indicum
Panee-merich	H.	Polygonum flaccidum
Panee-mulunga	B.	Cyperus distans
Pangla	H.	Pavia Indica
Panie-shira	B.	Hemarthria compressa

Name		
Pankooshee	B.	Phyllanthus multiflorus
Pan-kula	H.	Limodorum nutans
Pansheeroo	B. H.	Rottboellia compressa
Panshioolie	B.	Phyllanthus multiflorus
Papura	H.	Ulmus integrifolia
Paris-pipul	H.	Ficus lucida
Pata-khuree	B. H.	Saccharum fuscum
Pata-seyala	B.	Blyxa octandra
Patee	B. H.	Cyperus inundatus
Patee-patee	B.	Phrynium dichotomum
Paya-tullo	H.	Bambusa baccifera
Peea-bansh	B.	Dendrocalamus tulda
Peeplee	H.	Pothos peepla
Peepul	H.	Urostigma religiosum
Pengi-nachi	H.	Panicum glaucum
Petinar	B. H.	Panicum fluitans
Phunnus	H.	Artocarpus integrifolia
Pilchee	H.	Cytisus scoparius
Pilpil	B.	Piper nigrum
Pindalu	H.	Rottlera Indica
Pipeera-saree	H.	Urtica pentandra
Pitoli	B. H.	Trewia nudiflora
Pitras	B. H.	Curcuma longa
Poee	H.	Basella alba or rubra
Poog	B.	Artocarpus integrifolia
Poona-chumpa	B.	Alpinia nutans
Poonag	B.	Rottlera tinctoria
Poouka	B.	Amarantus polygamus
Poori	B.	Saccharum officinarum
Ptoon	H.	Euphorbia nivulia
Puloo	B.	Bambusa balcooa
Puluka	H.	Poa plumosa
Purjunee	B.	Curcuma xanthorhiza
Purkutta-doomoor ..	B.	Ficus fruticosa
Pusnee	B. H.	Oryza sativa
Putchuk	H.	Aucklandia costus
Putputi-chetchka ..	B. H.	Isolepis articulatus
Putteon	H.	Euphorbia nervifolia
Ruckta-bun-pooi	B.	Basella rubra
Ragee	H.	Eleusine coracana
Rakhal-susa	B.	Karivia umbellata
Ramanagee-kula	B.	Musa ornata
Rami	B.	Urtica tenacissima
Ram-jakiaha-kulla ..	B.	Musa sapientum
Ram-kula	B. H.	Do.
Rangantheya	B.	Amaranthus atropurpureus
Ranga-shak	B.	Amarantus gangeticus
Rangoowa	B.	Areca gracilis
Rawla	H.	Panicum Italicum

Rewund-chini	H.	Rumex tuberosus
Roosa	H.	Andropogon Iwarancusa
Rotaloo	H.	Dioscorea sativa
Rukta-sirinchee	B.	Achyranthes ferruginea
Rukto-guraniya-aloo	B.	Dioscorea purpurea
Run-chandur	B. H.	Flagellaria Indica
Rusna-jaji	B. H.	Valisneria alternifolia
Ruttee	H.	Hedychium spicatum
Sada-bori	H.	Asparagus racemosus
Sada-hazar-muni	B.	Phyllanthus niruri
Sada-kanoor	B.	Pancratium triflorum
Sada-nuteeya	B.	Amarantus oleraceus
Sadrus	H.	Cinnamomum nitidum
Salli-tunga	B. H.	Cyperus compressus
Salo-kuchoo	B.	Colocasia fornicata
Sanchi-bet	B.	Calamus rotang
Sanwar	H.	Panicum frumentaceum
Sar	H.	Saccharum sara
Sarkara	H.	Saccharum procerum
Sarkuchoo	B.	Colocasia nymphæfolia
Sarput	H.	Saccharum procerum
Satawree	H.	Asparagus sarmentosus
Sathi	B.	Curcuma zerumbet
Seyndie	H.	Elate sylvestris
Seeah-mooslie	H.	Curculigo orchioides
Seehund	H.	Euphorbia antiquorum
Seergoo-loolli	B.	Rottlera peltata
Seetal-patee	B. H.	Phrynium dichotomum
Senthi	H.	Saccharum sara
Seora	H.	Trophis aspera
Setaver	H.	Asparagus ascendens
Seyard	H.	Euphorbia antiquorum
Shalincha	B.	Achyranthes triandra
Shaloo	H.	Holcus saccharatus
Shama	B.	Panicum colonum. P. frumentaceum
Shara	B.	Trophis aspera
Shwet-kerua	B.	Euphorbia thymifolia
Sheyala	B.	Blyxa octandra
Shij	B. H.	Euphorbia nereeifolia
Shoochi-mookkee	B.	Sanseviera zeylanica
Shook-china	H.	Smilax glabra
Shoonti-ghas	B.	Pennisetum holcoides
Shoora-aloo	B. H.	Dioscorea nummularia
Shoosh-meer	H.	Amomum repens
Shoothee	B.	Curcuma zerumbet
Shootthugnee	B.	Boerhaavia diffusa
Shwet-panee-murich	B.	Polygonum lanatum
Shwet-surva-juya	B.	Canna Indica

Name		Botanical name
Shwet-busunda	B.	Acalypha Indica
Shwet-gothoobi	B.	Kyllingia monocephala
Shwet-moorga	B.	Celosia argentea
Shwet-poorna	B.	Boerhaavia erecta
Sidhoul	H.	Hedychium spicatum
Simar	H.	Blyxa octandra
Sirki	H.	Saccharum procerum
Souballi	H.	Croton plicatum
Soodoorshun	B.	Crinum defixum
Soontha	B. H.	Zingiber officinale
Soopara	H.	Areca catechu
Soorea	B.	Tetranthera quadrifolia
Sooshila	B.	Celosia cristata
Soosni-aloo	B. H.	Dioscorea fasciculata
Sooti-moolie	B.	Asparagus sarmentosus
Sora-aloo	B.	Dioscorea nummularia
Sottraj	H.	Tradescantia axillaris
Soubali	H.	Crozophora plicata
Sufed-mooslie	H.	Asparagus sarmentosus
Sufed-pooin	B.	Basella alba
Sun	H.	Bridelia spinosa
Sundel	H.	Santalum album
Sunderbuns	B.	Excæcaria agallocha
Sundhigool	B.	Laurus lanceolaria
Sun-goola	H.	Calamus erectus
Suphee	B.	Myrica integrifolia
Suran	H.	Arum campanulatum
Surasarum	H.	Melanthesa rhamnoides
Surson	H.	Do.
Suthri	H.	Dioscorea aculeata
Suttee	H.	Hedychium spicatum
Swatee	B.	Panicum holcoides
Takapana	B.	Pistia stratiotes
Tal	B. H.	Borassus flabelliformis
Tala-kuttee	H.	Burmannia disticha
Talee	B.	Corypha umbraculifera
Taliera	B. H.	Corypha taliera
Tal-loora	B.	Curculigo orchioides
Tal-moolie	B.	Do.
Tal-noor	B.	Do.
Talmuroo	B.	Fimbristylis royéniana
Tanajinya	B.	Poa punctata
Tar	B.	Alpinia allughas
Tar	B.	Curculigo orchioides
Teekor	H.	Curcuma angustifolia
Telungshora	B.	Limodorum longifolium
Teng	B.	Saccharum procerum
Thoor	H.	Cajanus Indicus
Thuhar	H.	Euphorbia nereifolia

Tidhara	H.	Euphorbia antiquorum
Tikhri	H.	Boerhaavia diffusa
Titur-kleoo	B.	Dendrobium clavatum
Toong	B.	Rottlera tinctoria
Toon-tooni-nuti	B.	Amarantus fasciatus
Toor	H.	Cajanus Indicus
Trinpali	H.	Manisuris granularis
Tukla	H.	Rottlera tinctoria
Tulda-bansh	B.	Dendrocalamus tulda
Uch	H.	Saccharum officinarum
Udambar	H.	Ficus glomerata
Udhie-charie	H.	Achyranthes aspera
Ud-i-hindi	H.	Aquilaria agallocha
Ud-i-samudri	H.	Do.
Udruck	H.	Zingiber officinale
Ugoor	B. H.	Aquilaria agallocha
Ukhrot	B.	Aleurites triloba. Juglans regia
Ulutchandul	B.	Methonica superba
Umbla-bela	B.	Arum bulbiferum
Unter-gunga	H.	Pistia stratiotes
Unul	B.	Amphidonax bifaria
Upang	B.	Achyranthes aspera
Urhur	H.	Cajanus flavus
Urkasi	H.	Tragia cordata
Uruee	H.	Caladium esculentum
Useer	H.	Anatherum muricatum
Wally-kola	B. H.	Musa sapientum
Zard-chob	H.	Curcuma longa
Zeminkand	H.	Arum campanulatum

INDEX OF TELUGU SYNONYMS.

Adavi-chama	Amorphophallus sylvaticus
Adavi-cheruku	Saccharum procerum
Adavi-godhumulu	Coix barbata
Adavi-kanda	Arum lyratum
Adavi-kikkasi-gaddi	Amphidonax bifaria
Adavi-mamena	Boerhaavia erecta
Adavi-nabhi	Gloriosa superba
Adavi-pippali	Chavica sylvatica
Addi-vitella-guddaloo	Scilla Indica. Erythronium Indicum
Adivi-carmida	Jatropha curcas
Adivi-cunda-gudda	Dracontium polyphyllum
Agaru	Aquilaria Agallocha
Agni-kashtamu	Aquilaria Agallocha
Agni-sikha	Gloriosa superba
Akaso-tamara	Pistia stratiotes
Akoo-jemmoodoo	Euphorbia nivulia
Alla-batsalla	Basella alba
Allam	Zingiber officinalis
Allike	Scirpus dubius
Allu	Paspalum scrobiculatum
Allu-bach-chali	Basella alba
Allu-bassalla	Do.
Amada-kada	Cyanotis axillaris
Amadum	Ricinus communis
Amala-kamu	Emblica officinalis
Amudapu-chettu	Ricinus communis
Ananti-chettu	Musa paradisiaca
Antara-valli-tige	Cassytha filiformis
Antarei-tamara	Pistia stratiotes
Arelli, or Aretti	Musa sapientum
Arike	Paspalum scrobiculatum
Arikota	Poivrea Roxburghii
Aru-chungali	Andropogon montanum
Aruga	Paspalum scrobiculatum
Arukanla-kachoram	Curcuma amada
Aru-kanapula-kranuga	Saccharum officinarum
Asakalu	Paspalum sp.
Asseriki	Emblica officinalis.
Asualayana-daibha-gaddi	Poa cynosurioides

Aswaththamu .. .. Urostigma religiosum
Ataka-mamidi .. .. Boerhaavia erecta, procumbens, or diffusa
Ataka-marmailli .. .. Boerhaavia procumbens
Atti-chettu .. .. .. Ficus glomerata
Attika-namedie-varysoo .. Boerhaavia tuberosa
Avuru-gaddi .. .. Andropogon muricatum

Bachchali-kura .. .. Basella cordifolia
Badiki .. .. .. Sapium cordifolium
Balloerakashie-gudda .. Arum macrorhizon
Balrakis .. .. .. Arum fornicatum
Barom-hiss .. .. .. Saccharum cylindricum
Barranki-chettu .. .. Ficus asperrima
Beeum ... . Oryza sativa
Bellum .. .. .. Saccharum officinarum
Betamu .. .. .. Calamus rotang
Betta-pundoo .. .. Calamus viminalis
Bhadra-tunga-gaddi .. .. Cyperus hexastachyus
Bharjapatri-chettu .. .. Betula bhojpatra
Bholum .. .. .. Aloe perfoliata
Bhooma-katchkay .. .. Zingiber roseum
Bhu-strunam .. .. Andropogon schænanthus
Bhutala-bairi .. .. Croton oblongifolium
Bidura-nana-bizam .. .. Euphorbia thymifolia
Billa-juvvi .. .. .. Ficus nitida
Billappa .. .. .. Scirpus globosus
Billoo-gaddi .. .. .. Saccharum spontaneum
Boda-mamidi .. .. Ficus oppositifolia
Bodda-chettu .. .. Ficus glomerata
Boddi-chettu .. .. Macaranga Roxburghii
Boma-mari .. .. .. Ficus asperrima
Bomma-jemoodoo .. .. Euphorbia antiquorum
Bomma kachchika .. .. Costus speciosus
Bongu-veduru .. .. Bambusa arundinacea
Bonta-ariti-chettu .. .. Musa Paradisiaca
Bonta-chamalu .. .. Oplismenus frumentaceous
Bonta-chemoodoo .. .. Euphorbia antiquorum
Bonta-shama .. .. Panicum frumentaceum
Booda-tunga.. .. .. Scirpus maximus
Bramha-nedi .. .. Ficus oppositifolia
Brooma-nadi .. .. Ficus glomerata
Burong .. .. .. Ficus heterophylla
Buroni-chettu .. .. Ficus rubescens

Camunchie-poorie .. .. Andropogon schænanthus
Candaloo .. .. .. Cajanus Indicus
Canipoo-taja.. .. .. Roxburghia gloriosoides
Carjoora-pandoo .. .. Phœnix dactylifera
Carpoo-wolandoo .. .. Cajanus Indicus

Castoorie-passapoo .. .. Curcuma Zedoaria
Cattimandoo .. .. .. Euphorbia Cattimandoo
Chaga .. .. .. Sanseveria Zeylanica
Chakra-kelei .. .. Musa Paradisaica
Chakravarti-kara .. .. Chenopodium album
Challa .. .. .. Asparagus racemosus
Challag-hedaloo .. .. Asparagus sarmentosus
Challa-munta .. .. Fluggea leucopyrus
Chama .. .. .. Colocasia antiquorum
Chama-gudda .. .. Caladium esculentum
Chama-kada .. .. .. Sanseviera Zeylanica
Chama-koora .. .. Caladium esculentum
Chamalu .. .. .. Oplismenus frumentaceus
Chamee .. .. .. Prosopis spicigera
Chanchali-kura .. .. Digera muricata. Achyranthes alternifolia
Chandanum .. .. .. Santalum album
Changa-gudda .. .. Sanseviera Zeylanica
Changala .. .. .. Costus Arabicus
Changali-gaddi .. .. Panicum commutatum
Chata-kanda .. .. .. Colocasia nymphæfolia
Chedu-baddu-dumpa .. .. Dioscorea pulchella
Cheempirie-kutta .. .. Aristida setacea
Cheepa-bora-gaddi .. .. Panicum corymbosum
Chega .. .. .. Sanseviera Roxburghiana
Chemudu .. .. .. Euphorbia tirucalli
Chendurapu .. .. .. Rottlera tinctoria
Cheneehala-koora .. .. Achyranthes polygonoides
Cheni .. .. .. Oryza sativa
Cherukoo-bodi .. .. Saccharum officinarum
Chiklenta .. .. .. Panicum verticillatum
Chikala-kara .. .. Amarantus fasciatus
Chitta-eita .. .. .. Phœnix farinifera
China-dala-gondi .. .. Tragia cannabina
Chinikala-bunda .. .. Aloe litoralis
Chinnie-aku .. .. .. Acalypha betulina
Chippa-gaddi .. .. Andropogon schænanthus
Chipara-gaddi .. .. Aristida setacea
Chirakura .. .. .. Amarantus polygonoides
Chiri-nana-pala .. .. Euphorbia sp.
Chirugu-chettu .. .. Caryota urens
Chiruta-ita .. .. .. Phœnix farinifera
Chittamudopu-chettu .. .. Ricinus communis
Chitti-duru .. .. .. Vanda Roxburghii
Chola .. .. .. Eleusine coracana
Chukkali-chettu .. .. Epicarpurus orientalis
Chunchoo-gaddi .. .. Dioscorea pentaphylla
Chunda .. .. .. Tacca pinnatifida
Commoolekka .. .. Croton lacciferum
Condapanna .. .. .. Corypha umbraculifera

Telugu	Botanical name
Conda-pashpoo	Globba bulbifera
Conda-vetto	Rottlera dioica
Cooroo-vayroo	Anatherum muricatum
Corah	Panicum Italicum
Cunda-gudda	Tacca pinnatifida
Cunthaloo	Cajanus Indicus
Cushelli	Anthericum tuberosum
Dagla-kura	Amarantus polygamus
Darbha, or Dubha	Poa cynosuroides
Dava-dari	Phyllanthus turbinatus
Dayla-hura	Amarantus polygamus
Desavali-pendalam	Dioscorea purpurea
Devata-dhamjamu	Sorghum saccharatum
Doggali-kara	Amarantus polygamus
Doola-ghonda	Tragia involucrata
Doola-ghooila	Aristolochia Indica
Doolia-ghunda	Tragia cannabina
Droom-brasticum	Alpinia galanga
Doosa	Panicum fluitans
Dumparashtrakam	Globba orixensis
Eddi	Heteropogon contortus
Eddu-mutte-dumpa	Pouzolzia tuberosa
Eddu-toka-dumpa	Dioscorea glabra
Eeinta	Elate sylvestris
Eesara	Aristolochia Indica
Elaki-chettu	Elettaria cardamomum
Elika-tunga-gaddi	Sporobolus coromandelianus
Elika-bora-gaddi	Fuirena ciliaris
Embudu-chettu	Pisonia villosa
Emmeuta	Ficus nitida
Emmoduga	Do.
Enuga	Carpopogon monospermum
Enuga-junum	Typha elephantina
Erandamu	Ricinus communis
Erra-bondola-kobbari-chettu	Cocos nucifera
Erra-dogali-kura	Amarantus polygamus
Erra-jilama-vadlu	Oryza sativa
Erra-juvvi	Ficus nitida
Erra-kala-bunda	Aristolochia Indica
Erra-kodi-juttu-tola-kura	Celosia cristata
Erra-mudapu-chettu	Ricinus communis
Erra-mulu-goranta	Amarantus spinosus
Erra-purugudu	Phyllanthus reticulatus
Erra-usirika	Phyllanthus urinaria
Eti-malle	Polygonum tomentosum
Gadda-kanda	Colocasia esculenta
Gadda-nelli	Sponia Wightii. Celtis orientalis

Gaddi-janumu .. .. Sorghum cernuum
Gadida-guda-para .. .. Aristolochia bracteata
Gadi-janoo .. .. .. Andropogon laxum
Gadimi-donda-pendalam .. Dioscorea alata
Godha-poorna .. .. Boerhaavia procumbens
Gaggera-chettu .. .. Pandanus odoratissimus
Gaja-pippali .. .. .. Scindapsus officinalis
Gantelu .. .. .. Penicillaria spicata
Garike .. .. .. Cynodon dactylon
Gedangi-mogali .. .. Pandanus odoratissimus
Gelleba-tunga .. .. Cyperus tenuiflorus
Gericha .. .. .. Cynodon dactylon
Gerike-kassoovoo .. .. Agrostis linearis
Ghella-gaddi .. .. Coix barbata
Ghendum .. .. .. Santalum album
Gheœdoo-tunga .. .. Cyperus seminudus
Gidda-jonna .. .. .. Sorghum vulgare
Giruka-tati-chettu .. .. Phœnix paludosa
Gojjangi .. .. .. Pandanus odoratissimus
Golagàndi .. .. .. Cyanotis axillaris
Golimidi .. .. .. Coix barbata
Gorapa .. .. .. Scirpus tridentatus
Goru-chuttu-gadda .. .. Eulophia virens
Gotti-gadda .. .. .. Spathium chinense
Goirla .. .. .. Aristolochia Indica
Gujju-kanne-komali .. .. Boerhaavia stellata
Gujju-narikedam .. .. Cocos nucifera
Guna-pendalam .. .. Dioscorea globosa
Gunda-tunga-gaddi .. .. Scirpus kysoor
Gundra .. .. .. Panicum uliginosum
Gurrapu-saka-tunga .. . Scirpus maritimus
Guruga .. .. .. Celosia argentea
Guvi-manu .. .. .. Ficus virens

Hazar-munee .. .. Phyllanthus urinaria
Hemanto .. .. .. Ficus nitida
Hintalamu .. .. .. Phœnix paludosa

Ijadi-gadda .. .. .. Roxburghia gloriosoides
Ilakura .. .. .. Salsola Indica
Isapaboragaddi .. .. Panicum corymbosum
Iswara-chettu . .. .. Aristolochia Indica
Ita-chettu .. .. .. Elate sylvestris

Jala-tunga .. .. .. Cyperus procerus
Jammi-chettu .. .. Prosopis spicigera
Jammu-gaddi .. .. Typha elephantina
Janapalaseru .. .. Antidesma pubescens
Janapalseru .. .. .. Antidesma paniculata
Jegura .. .. .. Cluytia patula

Jemudu .. .. .. Euphorbia tirucalli
Jiguru-chettu .. .. Caryota urens
Jongra .. .. .. Curcuma montana
Jonnalu .. .. .. Sorghum vulgare
Juttamansi .. .. .. Cyperus stoloniferus
Juvi .. .. .. Ficus tsiela

Kachoram .. .. .. Kœmpferia galanga
Kadapara .. .. .. Aristolochia bracteata
Kadishen .. .. .. Cluytia collina
Kaidaryamu .. .. .. Myrica sapida
Kakamuste .. .. .. Sponia Wightii
Kaki-medi .. .. .. Ficus oppositifolia
Kaki-veduru .. .. Saccharum spontaneum
Kala-banda .. .. .. Aloe vulgaris
Kala-juvi .. .. .. Ficus tomentosa
Kall-alun .. .. .. Ficus religiosa
Kalla-ravi .. .. .. Do.
Kamachie-kussoo .. .. Andropogon citratum
Kamanchie-gaddi .. .. Andropogon schœnanthus
Kamma-regu .. .. Artocarpus lachoocha
Kammeraku .. .. .. Chavica betel
Kampalam .. .. .. Zingiber sp.
Kanapa-chettu-badanike .. Vanda Roxburghii
Kanapa-tige .. .. .. Roxburghia gloriosides
Kandaloo .. .. .. Cajanus Indicus
Kandari-chettu .. .. Crinum sp.
Kandu-rellu-gaddi .. .. Saccharum fuscum
Kandy .. .. .. Cytisus cajan
Kanki-putri .. .. .. Pisonia villosa
Kanne-komali .. .. Boerhaavia stellata
Kantoo-kelangoo .. .. Dioscorea aculeata
Kanupula-cheruku .. .. Saccharum officinarum
Karakar-booda .. .. Ficus asperrima
Karasa .. .. .. Ficus ampelos
Karata-lamu .. .. .. Borassus flabelliformis
Kar-pooshpa .. .. .. Zingiber cassamunar
Karra-tunga .. .. .. Mariscus dilutus
Kar-sodi .. .. .. Eleusine Indica
Karu-ellamu .. .. .. Zingiber cassumunar
Karu-amudam-dumpa .. .. Jatropha tuberosa
Karu-bachchali .. .. Basella alba
Karu-chodi .. .. .. Eleusine coracana
Karu-guggilam .. .. Gelonium lanceolatum
Karu-indu .. .. .. Pisonia aculeata
Karu-japhara .. .. Rottlera laccifera
Karu-pashpu .. .. Curcuma montana
Karu-pendalam .. .. Dioscorea nummularia
Karu-uda-gaddi .. .. Panicum mucronatum
Kasatunga .. .. .. Fimbristylis bispicata

Kassavoo .. .. .. Andropogon muricatum
Kasturi-pasupu .. .. Curcuma Zedoaria
Kati-amadam-chettu .. .. Jatropha glandulifera
Katle-chettu .. .. .. Chrysopogon acicularis
Kaya-pendalam .. .. Dioscorea crispata
Kaza-godda .. .. .. Urginea coromandeliana
Keechlie .. .. .. Curcuma zerumbet
Kerdrajuree .. .. .. Putranjiva Roxburghii
Kesara-chettu .. .. Crinum defixum
Ketaki .. .. .. Pandanus odoratissimus
Khajurapoo-chettoo .. .. Phœnix dactylifera
Khooshi-tunga .. .. Scirpus bispicatus
Khrishna-tamara .. .. Canna Indica
Kichakai .. .. .. Bambusa arundinacea
Kichlie-gudda .. .. Curcuma zerumbet
Kikkassa-gaddi .. .. Amphidonax karka
Kiloo .. .. .. Salicornia brachiata
Kimda-tunga .. .. Schænus articulatus
Kiraruga .. .. .. Paspalum scrobiculatum
Kistapa-tamara .. .. Smilax ovalifolia
Kivia-pippala .. .. Salicornia Indica
Kobbari-chettu .. .. Cocos nucifera
Koda-pana .. .. .. Corypha umbraculifera
Kodi-juttu-tota-kura .. .. Celosia cristata
Kolilakshamu .. .. Coix barbata
Kola-poka .. .. .. Areca catechu
Kola-tunga-muste .. .. Cyperus pertenuis
Komaretti .. .. .. Musa paradisiaca
Konda-amada-kada .. .. Tradescantia panicularis
Konda-amadum .. .. Croton Roxburghii
Konda-dantena .. .. Smilax ovalifolia
Konda-gurava-tige .. .. Do.
Konda-jophara .. .. Rottlera dicocca
Konda jeri .. .. .. Andropogon fascicularis
Konda-jilugu .. .. .. Caryota urens
Konda-jonna .. .. Sorghum vulgare
Konda-juvvi .. .. .. Ficus tuberculata
Konda-kalava .. .. Kæmpferia rotunda
Konda-kandaloo .. .. Cytisus cajan
Konda-kanamu .. .. Saccharum exaltatum
Konda-kasina .. .. Rottlera dicocca
Konda-malle .. .. Polygonum barbatum
Konda-marri .. .. Ficus tomentosa
Konda-pasupu .. .. Globba bulbifera
Konda-poka .. .. .. Areca catechu
Konda-rakis .. .. .. Arum montanum
Konda-ravi .. .. .. Ficus vagans
Konda-saka-tunga .. .. Scleria lithosperma
Konda-tamara .. .. Smilax ovalifolia
Konda-veltu .. .. .. Rottlera dicocca

Konki .. .. .. Pisonia villosa
Kora-maddi .. .. .. Bridelia retusa
Koroman .. .. .. Bridelia spinosa or crenulata
Korasana-chettu .. .. Ficus Dæmonum
Korimidi .. .. .. Coix barbata
Korallu .. .. .. Setaria Italica
Koshtamu .. .. .. Costus speciosus
Kottika .. .. .. Spathium Chinense
Koyalu .. .. .. Salicornia brachiata
Koyya-pippali .. .. Salicornia Indica
Koyya-tola-kura .. .. Amarantus tristis
Krishna-ajaru .. .. Aquilaria Agallocha
Khrisna-chandanum .. .. Santalum album
Khristna-tamara .. .. Canna Indica
Kuchehela .. .. .. Anthericum tuberosum
Kuchoora .. .. .. Curcuma Zerumbet
Kudra-juree .. .. .. Putranjiva Roxburghii
Kummara-baddu .. .. Smilas ovalifolium. Dioscorea aculeata

Kunda-amadi-kada .. .. Tradescantia paniculata
Kunda-amadoo .. .. Croton polyandrum
Kunda-jeri .. .. .. Andropogon fasciculatus
Kunda-kanumoo .. .. Saccharum exaltatum
Kunda-mallier .. .. Polygonum barbatum
Kunda-punookoo .. .. Rottboellia exaltata
Kunkuma-puvvu .. .. Rottlera tinctoria
Kuppanti-chettu .. .. Acalypha Indica
Kura-pasupa .. .. Zingiber Cassumanar
Kuroor-soloo .. .. Eleusine Indica
Kurra-tunga .. .. Cyperus spinulosus
Kursee .. .. .. Cluytia collina
Kusa-darbha-gaddi .. .. Poa cynosuroides
Kushee-tanga .. .. Scirpus bispicatus
Kussavoo .. .. .. Anatherum muricatum

Lakshminarayana .. .. Crinum asiaticum
Lakuchamu .. .. .. Artocarpus lachoocha
Lamajjakanu .. .. Anatherum muricatum
Lavu-cheruku .. .. Saccharum officinarum
Linga-miriyam .. .. Crozophora plicata
Lottipitta .. .. .. Isolepis articulata

Madana-ganti .. .. Alternanthera sessilis
Maddee-rooba-chettu .. .. Eleusine stricta
Madinika .. .. .. Boerhaavia stellata
Mahaputra-juvi .. .. Putranjiva Roxburghii
Maitantos .. .. .. Amphidonax karka
Malaka-kaya-pendalam .. Dioscorea bulbifera
Mamidi-allam .. .. Curcuma amada
Manchi-kanda .. .. Arum amorphophallus

Vishama-kondanaru .. .. Sanseviera Roxburghii
Visha-mungali .. .. Crinum Asiaticum
Vodala .. .. .. Poivrea Roxburghii
Vidavali .. .. .. Andropogon muricatum
Vodisa .. .. .. Cluytia collina
Vuda-goddi .. .. .. Panicum flavidum
Vuda-tallam.. .. .. Poa bifaria
Vudata-tota-gaddi .. .. Eleusine coracana

Wodesha .. .. .. Cluytia collina

Yarala .. .. .. Putranjiva Roxburghii
Yavalu .. .. .. Hordeum hexastachyum

INDEX OF NAMES.